Oracle® WebDB Bible

Oracle® WebDB Bible

Rick Greenwald and Jim Milbery

IDG Books Worldwide, Inc.
An International Data Group Company

Foster City, CA ✦ Chicago, IL ✦ Indianapolis, IN ✦ New York, NY

Oracle® WebDB Bible

Published by
IDG Books Worldwide, Inc.
An International Data Group Company
919 E. Hillsdale Blvd., Suite 400
Foster City, CA 94404
www.idgbooks.com (IDG Books Worldwide Web site)

ISBN: 0-7645-3326-6

Printed in the United States of America

10 9 8 7 6 5 4 3 2 1

1B/RQ/QZ/ZZ/FC

Distributed in the United States by IDG Books Worldwide, Inc.

Distributed by CDG Books Canada Inc. for Canada; by Transworld Publishers Limited in the United Kingdom; by IDG Norge Books for Norway; by IDG Sweden Books for Sweden; by IDGBA Ltd. for Australia; by IDGBA (NZ) Ltd. for New Zealand; by TransQuest Publishers Pte Ltd. for Singapore, Malaysia, Thailand, Indonesia, and Hong Kong; by Gotop Information Inc. for Taiwan; by ICG Muse, Inc. for Japan; by Norma Comunicaciones S.A. for Colombia; by Intersoft for South Africa; by Le Monde en Tique for France; by International Thomson Publishing for Germany, Austria and Switzerland; by Distribuidora Cuspide for Argentina; by Livraria Cultura for Brazil; by Ediciones ZETA S.C.R. Ltda. for Peru; by WS Computer Publishing Corporation, Inc., for the Philippines; by Contemporanea de Ediciones for Venezuela; by Express Computer Distributors for the Caribbean and West Indies; by Micronesia Media Distributor, Inc. for Micronesia; by Grupo Editorial Norma S.A. for Guatemala; by Chips Computadoras S.A. de C.V. for Mexico; by Editorial Norma de Panama S.A. for Panama; by American Bookshops for Finland. Authorized Sales Agent: Anthony Rudkin Associates for the Middle East and North Africa.

For general information on IDG Books Worldwide's books in the U.S., please call our Consumer Customer Service department at 800-762-2974. For reseller information, including discounts and premium sales, please call our Reseller Customer Service department at 800-434-3422.

For information on where to purchase IDG Books Worldwide's books outside the U.S., please contact our International Sales department at 317-596-5530 or fax 317-596-5692.

For consumer information on foreign language translations, please contact our Customer Service department at 800-434-3422, fax 317-596-5692, or e-mail rights@idgbooks.com.

For information on licensing foreign or domestic rights, please phone +1-650-655-3109.

For sales inquiries and special prices for bulk quantities, please contact our Sales department at 650-655-3200 or write to the address above.

For information on using IDG Books Worldwide's books in the classroom or for ordering examination copies, please contact our Educational Sales department at 800-434-2086 or fax 317-596-5499.

For press review copies, author interviews, or other publicity information, please contact our Public Relations department at 650-655-3000 or fax 650-655-3299.

For authorization to photocopy items for corporate, personal, or educational use, please contact Copyright Clearance Center, 222 Rosewood Drive, Danvers, MA 01923, or fax 978-750-4470.

Library of Congress Cataloging-in-Publication Data

Greenwald, Rick.
Oracle WebDB bible / Rick Greenwald, Jim Milberry.
p. cm.
1. Oracle (Computer file) 2. Relational databases. 3. Web servers. I. Milberry, Jim. II. Title.
QA76.9.D3G7284 1999
005.7'13769- -dc21 99-35434
CIP

ABOUT IDG BOOKS WORLDWIDE

Welcome to the world of IDG Books Worldwide.

IDG Books Worldwide, Inc., is a subsidiary of International Data Group, the world's largest publisher of computer-related information and the leading global provider of information services on information technology. IDG was founded more than 30 years ago by Patrick J. McGovern and now employs more than 9,000 people worldwide. IDG publishes more than 290 computer publications in over 75 countries. More than 90 million people read one or more IDG publications each month.

Launched in 1990, IDG Books Worldwide is today the #1 publisher of best-selling computer books in the United States. We are proud to have received eight awards from the Computer Press Association in recognition of editorial excellence and three from Computer Currents' First Annual Readers' Choice Awards. Our best-selling *...For Dummies®* series has more than 50 million copies in print with translations in 31 languages. IDG Books Worldwide, through a joint venture with IDG's Hi-Tech Beijing, became the first U.S. publisher to publish a computer book in the People's Republic of China. In record time, IDG Books Worldwide has become the first choice for millions of readers around the world who want to learn how to better manage their businesses.

Our mission is simple: Every one of our books is designed to bring extra value and skill-building instructions to the reader. Our books are written by experts who understand and care about our readers. The knowledge base of our editorial staff comes from years of experience in publishing, education, and journalism — experience we use to produce books to carry us into the new millennium. In short, we care about books, so we attract the best people. We devote special attention to details such as audience, interior design, use of icons, and illustrations. And because we use an efficient process of authoring, editing, and desktop publishing our books electronically, we can spend more time ensuring superior content and less time on the technicalities of making books.

You can count on our commitment to deliver high-quality books at competitive prices on topics you want to read about. At IDG Books Worldwide, we continue in the IDG tradition of delivering quality for more than 30 years. You'll find no better book on a subject than one from IDG Books Worldwide.

John Kilcullen
Chairman and CEO
IDG Books Worldwide, Inc.

Steven Berkowitz
President and Publisher
IDG Books Worldwide, Inc.

Eighth Annual Computer Press Awards 1992

Ninth Annual Computer Press Awards 1993

X
WINNER

Tenth Annual Computer Press Awards 1994

Eleventh Annual Computer Press Awards 1995

IDG is the world's leading IT media, research and exposition company. Founded in 1964, IDG had 1997 revenues of $2.05 billion and has more than 9,000 employees worldwide. IDG offers the widest range of media options that reach IT buyers in 75 countries representing 95% of worldwide IT spending. IDG's diverse product and services portfolio spans six key areas including print publishing, online publishing, expositions and conferences, market research, education and training, and global marketing services. More than 90 million people read one or more of IDG's 290 magazines and newspapers, including IDG's leading global brands — Computerworld, PC World, Network World, Macworld and the Channel World family of publications. IDG Books Worldwide is one of the fastest-growing computer book publishers in the world, with more than 700 titles in 36 languages. The "...For Dummies®" series alone has more than 50 million copies in print. IDG offers online users the largest network of technology-specific Web sites around the world through IDG.net (http://www.idg.net), which comprises more than 225 targeted Web sites in 55 countries worldwide. International Data Corporation (IDC) is the world's largest provider of information technology data, analysis and consulting, with research centers in over 41 countries and more than 400 research analysts worldwide. IDG World Expo is a leading producer of more than 168 globally branded conferences and expositions in 35 countries including E3 (Electronic Entertainment Expo), Macworld Expo, ComNet, Windows World Expo, ICE (Internet Commerce Expo), Agenda, DEMO, and Spotlight. IDG's training subsidiary, ExecuTrain, is the world's largest computer training company, with more than 230 locations worldwide and 785 training courses. IDG Marketing Services helps industry-leading IT companies build international brand recognition by developing global integrated marketing programs via IDG's print, online and exposition products worldwide. Further information about the company can be found at www.idg.com.

1/24/99

Credits

Acquisitions Editor
John Osborn

Development Editor
Elyn Wollensky

Technical Editor
Todd E. Vender

Copy Editors
Nicole LeClerc
Mildred Sanchez

Production
York Graphic Services

Proofreading and Indexing
York Production Services

Cover Design
Murder By Design

About the Authors

Rick Greenwald has been active in the field of data processing for over 15 years, including stints with Data General, Cognos, Gupta, and Oracle Corporation. He is the author of five other books on technology and dozens of articles and analyst pieces.

Jim Milbery has been involved in the software business for over 16 years and has worked for a variety of high-tech companies including Digital Equipment Corporation, Ingres, Uniface, and Revere. He is currently a partner with the technology consulting firm Kuromaku Partners LLC, where he provides strategic consulting to a diverse group of clients. Jim lives in Easton, Pennsylvania with his lovely wife, Renate, and two spoiled cats.

Jim Milbery — This book is dedicated to my father, Ken Milbery. Here's to you Dad, no son loves his father more than I love you.

Rick Greenwald — For the two women in my life: LuAnn and Elinor Greenwald.

Preface

How This Book Is Organized

The first part of this book provides an overall introduction to the basic architecture and design of Oracle WebDB. WebDB is a byproduct of the Internet revolution and enhancements to the Oracle database. Developers who are familiar with Oracle and PL/SQL will be familiar with the overall architecture of WebDB from their experiences with database programming. In order to support the capabilities of the Internet, WebDB extends Oracle's computing architecture in several new directions. The first chapter of the book introduces you to the basic components of WebDB and explains how these features fit into the overall architecture. Once you understand the basic moving parts of WebDB, the next task is to install and configure WebDB. Chapter 2 explains the various configuration and installation options for WebDB. Although Oracle makes the actual installation process quick and easy, there are a number of post-installation configuration settings that you will need to make in order to maximize the capabilities of WebDB. The last chapter in Part I takes you through the user interface features of the WebDB development environment. WebDB uses the browser as the interface for both development and deployment of applications, and the user interface is pure HTML. Chapter 3 walks you through the user interface techniques Oracle added to make the browser a powerful environment for developing applications.

Part II describes the various builder wizards in detail. The core functionality of WebDB is driven by a set of component builders that walk you through the process of creating components such as reports, forms, charts, calendars, and hierarchies.

WebDB builds on your preexisting Oracle databases, and the starting point for most WebDB applications is an investigation of these databases. Chapter 4 shows you how to browse your databases through the WebDB interface, and also acts as an introduction to the WebDB environment. The next logical step is to build some custom reports against this data, and Chapter 5 introduces you to the Report Builder Wizard. In Chapter 5, you will also learn how to use the Query Wizard to create reports by "pointing and clicking." WebDB reports can also be built from handcrafted SQL queries, and the second portion of this chapter shows you how to make use of your SQL expertise. WebDB embraces some advanced reporting concepts, and Chapter 6 shows you how to enhance your reports with variables and how to join multiple tables inside a single report. In Chapter 7, we show you how to build simple, single-table forms that accept parameters and display and update data. WebDB's form capabilities are powerful enough to handle master-detail forms and forms that are based on Oracle stored procedures. Chapter 8 explains the intricacies of working with these advanced concepts.

When it comes to displaying data, the age-old adage "A picture is worth a thousand words" is often correct. The designers of WebDB clearly understood this concept when they designed the Chart Builder Wizard.

Chapter 9 explains how to use the Chart Wizard to create colorful charts and graphs from the data in your database. You will learn how to build simple charts and how to shape your data to fit into the charting concept. In addition to the charting object, WebDB also offers specialized tools for creating calendars and hierarchies. Time-sensitive data, such as events or even shipping information, can be displayed as calendars.

Chapter 10 walks you through the process of extracting date information from your data and plotting data items as calendar entries. In some cases, you may have nested relationships in your data. For example, in an inventory system, parts are often composed of other parts. WebDB provides the Hierarchy Wizard to help you build interactive reports that plot your data as a series of nested reports.

Chapter 11 shows you to how identify and display hierarchical data in your database with the WebDB Hierarchy Wizard. WebDB provides a level of insulation between the developer and the underlying HTML code. However, there may be cases in which you want to "roll your own" HTML code and WebDB provides the Dynamic Pages Wizard to address this need.

Chapter 12 describes the Dynamic Pages Wizard and provides additional details on mixing SQL code with HTML tags.

The third part of the book marks the transition from building component objects to creating multiuse components and complete Web sites. WebDB provides a number of tools for building component objects in the Shared Component Library that can be used by the core WebDB wizards. The first chapter in this section, Chapter 13, describes the capabilities of the List-of-Values wizard. Lists of values provide the combo boxes, radio buttons, and check boxes that are used to make selections and enter values into fields. Once you have added lists of values to your reports and forms, you can combine the resulting objects into Web applications using the Menu Builder. Chapter 14 takes you through the process of building menus with WebDB and linking menu choices to your reports, forms, calendars, charts, and hierarchies. Although you may have large groups of developers building these objects, you can enforce a consistent look and feel for your components by using WebDB's template capabilities. Chapter 15 examines building and deploying color schemes, fonts, images, and templates to your preexisting reports and forms. You can create consistent headers and footers for your Web pages and apply a standard set of colors to your applications with templates. WebDB enables you to create applications that both read and write data in your databases, and it becomes important that you adequately protect the integrity of your database. Chapter 16 shows you how to use the JavaScript language to create data validation routines that can be used in your WebDB forms to provide data integrity at the browser level. As your applications begin to grow in size and complexity, you can ensure that your users are able to navigate effectively through your applications with links. Web users are accustomed to clicking through links to locate related data items, and WebDB provides a powerful Link Wizard to design similar connections inside WebDB components. In Chapter 17, you will learn how to design links and embed them inside of your forms, reports, charts, calendars, and hierarchies. The final chapter in Part III introduces you to the Site Builder tool within WebDB. Through Site Builder, you can design complete Web sites for organizing and deploying your component objects. Site Builder provides a framework for collaborative Web applications.

The fourth section of this book covers the details of managing and securing your WebDB applications. Chapter 19 looks at the various administration tools that you can use to locate components, manage version control, and move objects between systems. Experienced Oracle database administrators and project managers will see how to effectively manage and control the WebDB development environment through the security tools and procedures as they apply to WebDB. Chapter 20 provides a basic primer on Oracle database security and walks you through the process of applying this knowledge to the WebDB environment. After you deploy your WebDB applications, your database administrators can monitor the performance and usage of these applications through WebDB's monitoring tools. Chapter 21 describes the various tools that WebDB provides for locating performance bottlenecks and monitoring end-user activity.

The last section of the book covers some advanced WebDB topics. WebDB is a powerful tool, but the development and deployment environments are tightly intertwined, making it difficult to move your applications into production. In Chapter 22, we show you the various deployment architectures you can use with WebDB and how to move your applications from development into production. Chapter 23 extends the deployment discussion to include Site Builder and explains how to add content to your Site Builder sites. You will learn how to create privileged end-user accounts that your power users can use to assist you in the process of maintaining your Web site. Both Site Builder and WebDB itself can leverage your existing investments in web PL/SQL programming with the Oracle Web Toolkit. Chapter 24 shows you how to add custom PL/SQL procedures to your WebDB applications and gain access to the complete functionality of the Oracle database.

What's on the CD-ROM

The CD-ROM attached to the back cover of this book provides a trial copy of WebDB along with the various sample component objects and images referenced in the examples. Appendix A provides a complete list of the contents of the CD-ROM, and you will find a README.TXT file on the CD that explains any late-breaking changes to the content on the CD-ROM.

Contacting the Author(s)

Jim Milbery can be reached at Kuromaku Partners (http://www.kuromaku.com), located in Easton, Pennsylvania, or through his e-mail address at jmilbery@kuromaku.com.

Rick Greenwald can be reached at greenie@interacess.com.

Acknowledgments

The authors would like to thank all the people at Oracle who helped them in the creation of this book, including Rob Giljum and the entire development team. In particular, we would like to thank Steven Leung and Akila Kumar, who helped us throughout the writing and production process. Most importantly, we would like to bow in reverence in the general direction of the inestimable Todd Vendor, who provided timely advice and insight into the WebDB development process.

Contents at a Glance

Contents

Introduction

PART I

✦ ✦ ✦ ✦

In This Part

✦ ✦ ✦ ✦

CHAPTER 1

Introducing WebDB

In This Chapter

Why WebDB?

The Evolution of Internet Computing

WebDB and Internet Computing

The Components and Architecture of WebDB

The Architecture of a WebDB Application

Welcome to *Oracle WebDB Bible.* As the name implies, this book is intended to give you everything you need to go out and build complete application systems and Web sites with Oracle's WebDB product. This chapter serves as an introduction to WebDB — both the product itself and the needs the product was designed to address.

Why WebDB?

Normally, a book like this would not begin with such an open question. By the time that most computer books are published, the products and technical areas they address have firmly established themselves, so a question such as this would not be necessary.

But WebDB is a different type of product. It comes from one of the leading established technology companies in the world, Oracle Corporation, yet it delivers a solution for a new type of development and deployment environment. It is a brand new product, yet it is built on a technical foundation that has been around for years. It combines the robustness and depth that have long been associated with Oracle, but delivers it in a dramatically easy-to-use package that has not been typical of Oracle's products.

WebDB also displays characteristics of both a mature product and an early release of a product. Part of this is historical. The main portions of the WebDB product have been available as shareware within the Oracle community for over a year under the names WebView and, more recently, Site Builder. Experienced Oracle field personnel created WebView and Site Builder in order to address the real needs of Oracle users. This developmental history is responsible for WebDB's rich functionality. At the same time, there are still techniques you can use to extend the reach of WebDB solutions as users discover the intricacies of the new product.

In fact, WebDB is ideal for addressing the needs of a new type of computing, which we call *Internet computing*. You probably are already engaged in some form of Internet computing, but for the purpose of understanding WebDB better, we explore the concepts behind Internet computing in more detail in the next section.

The Evolution of Internet Computing

The first thing to understand about Internet computing is that it is, for the most part, really nothing new. Internet computing can be seen as a part of the general evolutionary path of information systems.

For the first several decades, information systems all conformed to a fairly simple model. The computing power was kept in a centralized location, and users accessed that computing power through the use of character-based terminals, as seen in Figure 1-1.

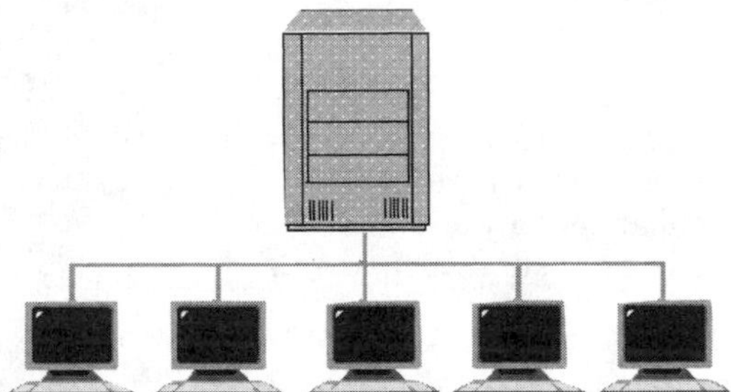

Figure 1-1: Traditional computing model

These terminals were thought of as dumb in that they did nothing more than provide a way for humans to interact with computers. The terminals eventually evolved some basic functionality, but, by and large, they existed for the single purpose of converting human input into a form that computers could understand.

The centralized computing power was kept segregated from the users inside special environments, and the people responsible for maintaining these centralized machines, the MIS staff, were all-powerful.

But as the need for information systems grew, it became impossible for the MIS staff to keep up with the demand for these systems. At the same time, information systems were becoming so widespread that they were being limited by the inability of the average person to use them.

These intersecting factors provided the impetus for the client/server revolution. Although client/server computing, as implemented in the architecture shown in Figure 1-2, is normally associated with personal computers, we believe the true driving force behind the success of client server computing is due to its foundation: the graphical user interface, or GUI. The primary difference between a GUI and a character-based terminal is that with a graphical interface, the computer responds to the user, while with a traditional dumb terminal, the user must learn how to respond to the computer. This fundamental shift in the way that humans and computers interacted was also made possible by the use of personal computers as the primary human interface. PCs had the processing power to be able to handle the increased requirements of responding to graphical interaction.

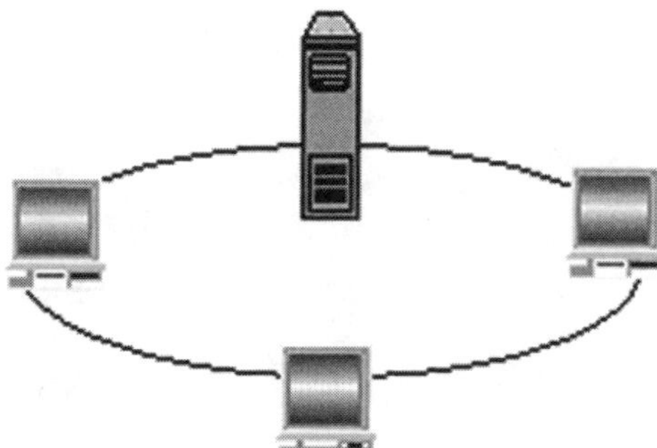

Figure 1-2: Client/server computing model

All of this was well and good, but, as is often the case, the pendulum swung too far in the direction of this decentralized approach. Client/server systems are inherently more costly to deploy and maintain because they are decentralized systems. It is more complex to manage hundreds of computers than it is to manage a single centralized computer resource. As client/server systems spread like wildfire, the cost of managing them has risen to unacceptable levels.

Enter Internet computing. Internet computing, as shown in the architecture in Figure 1-3, provides the best of both worlds — the rich user interface and interaction of client/server computing coupled with the centralized management of traditional computer systems. The main difference between Internet computing and client/server computing is in the nature of the communication between the client and the server. In client/server computing, a persistent connection is maintained between the client and the server. In Internet computing, there is no persistent connection between the client and the server. Internet computing is called *stateless* computing, because the state of the interaction between the client and the server is abandoned as the connection is terminated after each communication.

You can think of the difference between stateless and *stateful* computing as the difference between a letter and a telephone call. In a telephone call, once you establish a connection with another party, you do not have to worry about where they are located again during the conversation. In a letter, each interchange has to include address information.

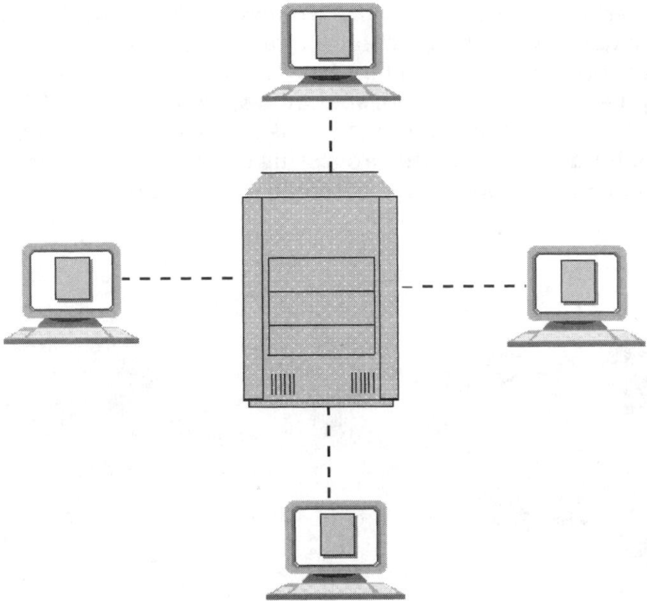

Figure 1-3: Internet computing model

What does this mean in terms of the applications that are suitable for Internet computing? Basically, it means that applications that require a great deal of coordination between the client and the server are not good candidates for Internet computing. These types of applications, usually referred to as *online transaction processing* applications, or OLTP, handle a high volume of transactions from many users.

For more detail on appropriate application types, please see the "Stateless versus Stateful" sidebar.

Stateless versus Stateful

The explanation in the main body of the text may seem a bit too simplistic for some of you. You want to know exactly what impact the stateless nature of Internet computing can have on your applications and their design.

The best way to illustrate the difference between stateless and stateful applications is to discuss two applications—one that would not be appropriate for Internet computing and one that would.

An online stock trading system can serve as an example of an inappropriate application for Internet computing. A user could place an order for a stock at market price. Before actually executing the trade, the system would seek a confirmation from the user of the actual price of the trade. Once the confirmation is received, the trade is executed.

In the stock market, prices fluctuate on a second-by-second basis. When the server application sends a confirmation request back to the client, it must have a way of reserving the request for the trade until the confirmation is received. In other words, the state of transaction must be preserved until the confirmation is received, which would require a lot of coding and probably some less-than-optimal design.

Note that the problem with this application comes from the interaction of a relatively slow user process—the confirmation of the order—with the rapidly changing prices in the stock market. There is nothing in this application that could not be accomplished with Internet computing if this requirement were lifted. And in fact, stock trading systems have become one of the primary examples of electronic commerce over the Internet. You can't get the same absolute confirmation of a purchase price or activity that you could if you were talking to a broker over the telephone, but the difference is not severe enough to prevent people from using this much more convenient system.

An order entry system could be an appropriate Internet application. Orders can easily be submitted through an Internet computing application. The difference between an order entry system and an online stock trading system is that the interaction between the user and the system data does not have to occur in real time. An order is submitted and the confirmation is sent back to the user. The worst-case scenario is that a product may not be in stock when the user places the order, but this is easily handled by indicating that an item is on back order.

What types of applications are appropriate for Internet computing? Fortunately, most applications do not have the same needs as OLTP applications, and Internet computing can handle them. The ideal Internet computing application makes a lot of information available to users and accepts a smaller amount of data back from the user. Internet computing applications can be extremely flexible in the amount and type of data they publish to a user. All in all, Internet computing can handle the vast majority of information systems.

And, best of all, Internet computing is browser-based. The only software needed to act as a client in an Internet computing system is a browser. This feature alone can significantly lower the cost of implementing and maintaining the system—it is a thing of beauty.

If Internet computing is the platform you are planning to use to deploy your application system, WebDB is the tool you should use to create it.

WebDB and Internet Computing

WebDB is a tool designed to create Internet computing application systems. WebDB not only creates information systems that run in the Internet computing environment, but the product itself is an Internet computing application. This means that all the advantages of Internet computing apply to the actual process of building applications with WebDB as well as to the applications created with WebDB.

In this chapter, we use the term *WebDB site* somewhat interchangeably with the term *WebDB application system.* In fact, a WebDB application system is very much like a normal Web site. For WebDB, a site is a collection of a variety of brower-based information, from standard static HTML pages to data-driven dynamically constructed pages to interactive forms to any datatype supported by a browser, including graphics and sound. WebDB gives users and developers the ability to freely add new information to a site, such as breaking news related to the site.

The congruence between a Web site and a WebDB application system makes WebDB the most appropriate tool for creating Internet computing applications.

The Architecture of a WebDB Site

We are almost ready to introduce you to the components of WebDB, but before we get to that introduction, we must explain how a WebDB site is implemented.

There are three basic pieces to a WebDB system, with each of them serving a specific function. Not surprisingly, these are the same pieces that were described as the components of Internet computing.

The following three pieces make up a WebDB system:

✦ Client — The function of the client component is to act as the user interface to information stored in a WebDB site. The use of the browser as the client environment means that all WebDB content will take the form of an HTML page. The page could be static or dynamically generated. It could include different media types, including graphics. It could act as a way to collect information from the user, through the use of a form. But at its core, it is still an HTML page, nothing more or less. This concept will help you to understand the framework of a WebDB information system.

For development with WebDB, the only browsers that have been tested are Netscape Navigator version 4.0.7 or later and Microsoft's Internet Explorer version 4.1 and later.

✦ Communications — The WebDB client uses HTTP to communicate with the server. This typically means that TCP/IP is the underlying communications protocol between the client and the server machines. Note that the communications protocol is **not** an Oracle communications protocol, so SQL*NET or Net8 are not required for WebDB clients.

The server machine that contains the listener must have one of these protocols installed to interact with an Oracle database.

The function of the communications component is to pass requests for pages to the server component and to receive the HTML pages that are returned from the server.

✦ Server software — WebDB needs two different types of server software: a listener that picks up the HTTP requests from the client, and an Oracle server capable of executing the WebDB application code.

WebDB Components

WebDB has a number of different components that help you to create, deploy and maintain a WebDB application system. These components are organized around five basic functions, which are the five choices from the top level WebDB menu:

✦ ***Browsing*** application components and data in the Oracle database used for WebDB

✦ ***Building*** WebDB components, database objects

✦ ***Administration*** of WebDB components and configuration parameters

✦ ***Monitoring*** the operation of your WebDB system

✦ *Working* with WebDB **sites**

When you first enter WebDB, you choose one of these areas before moving on to working on your own WebDB components. The top-level menu is accessible from any location within the WebDB environment, so it acts as a basic context switcher for the development environment.

The remainder of this section describes the options available for the first four top-level menu. The Site Builder Component is described in more detail later in the book.

Browsing

As explained above, the WebDB environment is, in effect, hosted by an Oracle database. All the information used by WebDB and WebDB applications is contained within the Oracle database, with the exception of some of the images used for the HTML pages created by WebDB. The data used as the source of information for dynamically built WebDB content is typically kept in the Oracle database. The code that makes up both the WebDB product itself and the components built with WebDB are all contained in PL/SQL packages, which are typically executed by the Oracle database.

The Browse functionality of WebDB gives you the ability to examine the different types of objects and data in the Oracle database that act as the host for WebDB. You can use different options in the Browse section of WebDB to examine the WebDB components stored in the database, as well as standard database objects, such as tables, indexes and a variety of other more specific database objects. The browsing capabilities in WebDB can also be used by regular end users to access their own data in the Oracle database, because all data access through WebDB is controlled by standard database security.

Building

The Build functionality of WebDB is where your development effort normally starts. This area gives you the ability to build the WebDB user interface components.

You will no doubt spend most of your time building user interface components in WebDB. There are four basic types of user interface objects, each of which uses one or more wizards.

Read-only builders

Because Internet computing is based around publishing information, WebDB provides several different builders that enable you to create read-only HTML pages.

Table 1-1
Read-Only Component Builders

Button	*Name*	*Description*
	Reports	The Report Builder in WebDB leads you through the process of creating reports. A report is a dynamic HTML page created from a query on data in the Oracle database. The Report Builder can create HTML-based reports, ASCII preformatted data, and Excel spreadsheets directly from database data. You can create reports that accept parameters to produce dynamic reports based on selection criteria. When you create a report with parameters, WebDB automatically creates a parameter entry form for you. There are also a number of default parameters that can be applied to every report, either by you or by your users, to control things like sort order.

Button	Name	Description
	Charts	Sometimes information can be more clearly understood if it is presented in the graphical format of a chart. WebDB's Chart Builder makes it easy to create charts based on data in the Oracle database. The Chart Builder is not intended to replace sophisticated data analysis tools, but rather to provide a quick and easy graphical display of results for database data. WebDB's chart building capability is used throughout the system by WebDB itself. All of the graphs that are provided by the monitoring tools are built with chart component.
	Calendars	WebDB's Calendar Builder is used for information that can be categorized by a calendar date. The Calendar Builder automatically creates a calendar graphic and inserts the relevant data into the appropriate place in the calendar.

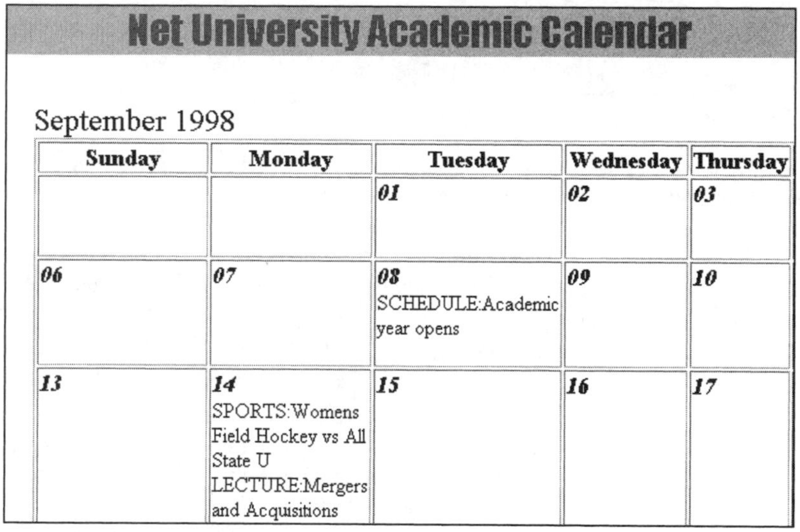

Net University Academic Calendar

September 1998

Sunday	Monday	Tuesday	Wednesday	Thursday
		01	02	03
06	07	08 SCHEDULE:Academic year opens	09	10
13	14 SPORTS:Womens Field Hockey vs All State U LECTURE:Mergers and Acquisitions	15	16	17

Figure 1-4: A calendar created with the calendar builder

Read-write builders

The basic method for capturing information from a user in the world of Internet computing is the use of a form.

Table 1-2
Read-Write Component Builders

Button	Name	Description
	Forms	WebDB's Form Builder can create forms based on tables, views, and stored procedures. You can create simple single-table forms, query-by-example forms, and even master-detail forms. WebDB's Form Builder enables you to add client-side validations and lists of values, which can be represented in a variety of ways, such as a list box or series of radio buttons in the form.

HTML builders

Because WebDB applications exist in the context of HTML pages, WebDB gives you two different builders that help you to work directly with HTML pages and frames.

Table 1-3
HTML Component Builders

Button	Name	Description
	Dynamic Pages, HTML with SQL	The Report Builder described in Table 1-1 helps you create standard reports based on the data in the Oracle database. You can also create HTML pages that are more free-form and do not necessarily adhere to the more rigid structure of a report but still blend dynamic data from the Oracle database with standard HTML elements. These dynamic HTML pages are stored in the Oracle database, just like other WebDB components.
	Frame Drivers	One of the standard elements of HTML pages is the use of frames. WebDB includes frame drivers that help you construct frames for your WebDB site and also provide built-in frame management. The frame drivers automatically trigger an action in one frame from a selection in the other frame.

Organization builders

There are two basic ways to organize your WebDB site: through the use of menus on the HTML pages of your application or by using hierarchies to build linkages that are based on the relationships inherent in the data you are using to build your pages.

Table 1-4 **Organization Builders**		
Button	***Name***	***Description***
	Menus	WebDB's Menu Builder helps you construct menus and hierarchies of menus that can access the objects you build with WebDB's other tools. Menus can also be used to create navigation paths for users. WebDB's menus can link to its own components as well as to any other Web object that can be reached via a URL.
	Hierarchies	The WebDB Hierarchy Builder automatically navigates through nested relationships in your database (like the classic employee/manager hierarchy). The Hierarchy Builder makes it easy to create complex linked applications by joining different WebDB components based on data values.

You can also include normal HTML links to any URL as part of most of the user interface components in a WebDB application, or a Link component, which is one of the shared components in the Shared Component Library.

You can access the user interface builders from a shortcuts menu bar that is at the bottom of almost all of the tools in WebDB, as shown in Figure 1-5.

Figure 1-5: The shortcuts bar

When you build a site, you use a different set of tools to set up complete Web sites and to define site-wide configuration parameters, such as the background images for the site and the particulars of the appearance of all of the pages in the site. When you define a WebDB site, you also automatically include some features that are part of the standard WebDB functionality set, such as giving users the ability to add news items to the site, either directly or with administrator approval. We describe the tools you use to implement these activities in the following sections.

Administering

Oracle has been in the business of providing enterprise strength products for over a decade. WebDB not only gives developers an environment to create application systems, but also provides equally powerful tools to help administer the resulting applications.

Table 1-5
Administrative Tools

Button	*Name*	*Description*
	Manage Users and Privileges	All WebDB applications exist within a security matrix. When a user accesses a WebDB application, they log in with a user name and password. WebDB administrators can limit access to different WebDB components and data based on the identity of a user. WebDB provides tools that enable an administrator to create security roles, which can designate security for multiple users and reduce the burden of assigning and maintaining security.
	Component Finder	As you build more and more WebDB applications, you will find that your Oracle database contains hundreds of components. The Component Finder can search for components across component types and creators, making it easy to find that certain piece whose name just happens to have slipped your mind. The Component Finder can be used from many different WebDB builders.
	Utilities	The WebDB utilities provide the capability to move content between applications and sites. A site administrator can quickly export both content and data, which can be copied onto a second system. Content can also be automatically replicated using the Oracle database's built-in replication facilities. WebDB even provides a utility for creating your own component builders if you need to create similar components repeatedly.
	Shared Component Library	One of the most powerful features of WebDB is the capability to build components that can be reused by multiple applications or application components. These components can be logical entities, such as lists of values or JavaScript programs, multimedia objects such as image files, or links that provide navigation between different WebDB components. The Shared Component Library provides a powerful productivity boost for developers by enabling them to create these components once and then reuse them throughout their WebDB site. The Shared Component Library not only reduces development time by enabling object reuse, but, more importantly, WebDB developers can reduce maintenance by only having a single copy of these reused components.

Monitoring

In order to ensure that your WebDB system is running optimally, WebDB provides a set of monitoring tools that enable you to check on a variety of system usage statistics.

Table 1-6
Monitoring Tools

Button	*Name*	*Description*
	Monitor Activity	WebDB's monitoring tools provide the site administrator with the ability to track the usage of the individual content and manage performance. WebDB automatically keeps track of content usage and performance statistics. The site administrator can use the monitors to view system usage, to set logging options, and to monitor the performance of a WebDB site in real time.

In addition to the monitoring tools that are a part of the main menu structure of WebDB, the Site Builder portion of WebDB can compile site-based statistics that are not part of the general monitoring capabilities of WebDB.

How a WebDB Application Is Structured

We have introduced you to the basic types of components you can create with WebDB. The final step in this introduction is to help you to understand how these components can be combined into a WebDB site.

All WebDB sites start with a single home page. The home page for a WebDB site, like all other components in the WebDB site, is accessed through a *Universal Resource Locator,* or *URL.* Any URL can be used to access information in a WebDB site.

A simple WebDB site could consist of nothing more than a home page, but most WebDB sites use the home page as a starting point for the remainder of the information in the site. The home page could lead to different sections of information in the site, and each section could contain many different types of WebDB components. Figure 1-6 illustrates a typical WebDB site.

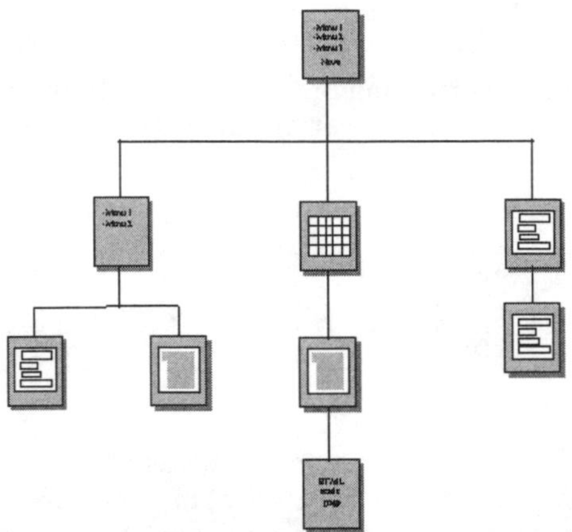

Figure 1-6: The structure of a WebDB site

All links between components are implemented with standard HTML link syntax. The links could come from a menu that you build with the menu builder component, through link objects created as shared components, or through links created through the Hierarchy Builder. These links could be static, in the sense that they always link to the same content, or they could be used to pass information through parameters to the server that would dynamically generate different pages.

There are a few minor limitations on the types of information that can be put on the home page or other pages, and there are certainly some good design practices you should use in creating your WebDB application. We discuss both of these topics later in the book.

Creating WebDB Application Systems

At this point, you might be feeling a little worried about the potential complexity of the task ahead of you. All these different components to keep track of and we haven't even touched on the code you have to write to create these components.

Fear not. WebDB, with its emphasis on centralized storage and management of components, makes it easy to track the different pieces of a WebDB application. And don't worry about learning code—there normally isn't any.

As you will see in the remainder of this book, WebDB is a *declarative* development environment. This means that instead of writing lots of procedural code, you merely have to supply a set of values that describe the functionality of your WebDB component. Each WebDB builder has a wizard that prompts you for the appropriate parameters and can supply online help about the parameters. After you supply these parameters, WebDB generates the underlying PL/SQL code that actually builds the HTML pages of your application.

There is no need to know much about PL/SQL to create applications with WebDB. If you want to change an application, you merely edit the values you originally supplied to the wizards.

You can, however, use JavaScript on the client or PL/SQL procedures on the server to extend the functionality inherent in your WebDB application system. Because of this, you can do almost anything you want with WebDB, within the confines of the limitations of the static nature of HTML.

In certain sections of this book, we tell you a little more about the underlying code that WebDB generates and how to extend it, if necessary. But aside from the special cases used in these chapters, you will not write logical code to create the application system used in this book.

Wrapping Up

This chapter has given you a basic understanding of WebDB, the computing needs it satisfies, and the basic structure of WebDB and WebDB components. This chapter has only provided the briefest of introductions to WebDB. Onward into WebDB—biblically speaking.

✦ ✦ ✦

Installing WebDB

In This Chapter

Although you are probably chomping at the bit to start to use WebDB, you still have to install it. This brief chapter walks you through the installation process for the WebDB product itself, including setting up the WebDB listener and configuring data access to WebDB.

In addition to setting up the basic product environment, you also have to set up the sample database that you will be using throughout the book. This database is based on the information needs of a university. We explain the structure of the database and give you complete instructions on installing it.

Installing WebDB

A copy of WebDB is included on the CD-ROM that accompanies this book. The installation instructions that follow walk you through the process of installing this copy of WebDB. If you are installing WebDB from a different source, please refer to the product documentation for installation instructions.

The product installation described in this chapter is for the NT version of WebDB, because that is what is included with this book. In addition, Appendix A describes the entire installation process for WebDB, the sample database, and the components that you will build throughout this book.

Which Version of WebDB?

The version of WebDB that is included with this book is the first release of Version 2 of WebDB. By the time this book is released, there will no doubt be a maintenance version available. Some of the examples in this book will not run exactly as described with the software that comes with this book — such is the problem with the time-consuming production process for the book and the more rapid nature of software releases. We strongly recommend that you go to the Oracle Technology Network at `http://technet.oracle.com` to download the most current version of WebDB and follow the installation instructions included with that version.

Even if you install WebDB from another source, you have to finish the setup process detailed in the following sections of this chapter to load the sample data and create the sample users.

If you have a copy of SQL*Plus on a client machine, you can copy the files onto the client machine and proceed from there. We suggest you follow this approach so that there is a copy of SQL*Plus available for the installation process.

The basic procedure calls for you to run the setup.exe program to install WebDB. There is a file on the CD-ROM called WebDB.txt that gives you the appropriate directions for finding the setup.exe program.

1. Run the setup.exe file. This brings up the initial screen shown in Figure 2-1.

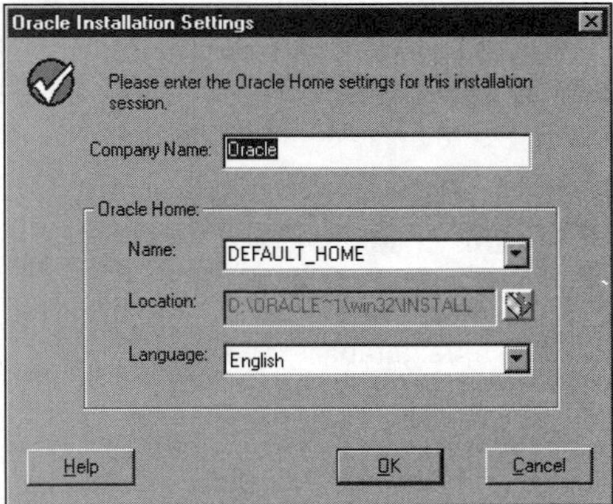

Figure 2-1: The first screen of the WebDB installation process

2. Enter your company name, or any other name that you wish to use to identify yourself, in the top field and select the appropriate location for the target instance of Oracle. If you are not sure of which instance to select, check with your database administrator or use the DEFAULT_HOME default selection.
3. Click the OK push button.
4. On the next page of the installer, leave the radio button labeled Typical Install selected and click the OK push button.

The Typical Installation Process

All information stored in an Oracle database is stored in a *tablespace.* A tablespace is nothing more than one or more physical files that hold data. The Typical Install for WebDB seeks out an appropriate tablespace by starting with the name TOOLS, followed by USER, USER_DATA, USR, and others. Typically, one of these tablespaces is available for the installation process.

The tablespace must have at least 30MB available in order to load WebDB. If you are unsure if the target tablespace has enough space, check with your database administrator.

You can create your own tablespace for WebDB, but if you do, you have to use the custom installation option. Because the Typical Install does so much for you, such as handling a preexisting installation of a listener, we recommend going with the Typical Install if at all possible.

5. On the next page of the installer, as shown in Figure 2-2, enter the password for the SYS user on the target Oracle database. You should also enter the hostname for your server and a port number for the WebDB listener. If your hostname is identified by a DNS name, you should have the complete DNS name listed, such as `www.mycompany.com`.

We recommend using the port number of 4000, which is unlikely to interfere with any other ports that have already been defined.

At this point in the installation process, you may see a warning dialog box that tells you that a copy of the PL/SQL Web Toolkit Packages was found on your server. These packages are a standard set of PL/SQL procedures that are used to create HTML. The packages come with a number of different Oracle products, including the Oracle Application Server (OAS), so they may already exist as part of your Oracle environment. We recommend replacing them with the new version of the packages that comes with WebDB — but you should check with your DBA to make sure this will not affect other applications running on the server.

If, by the time you install WebDB, there are newer versions of the OAS packages, you can leave them as is.

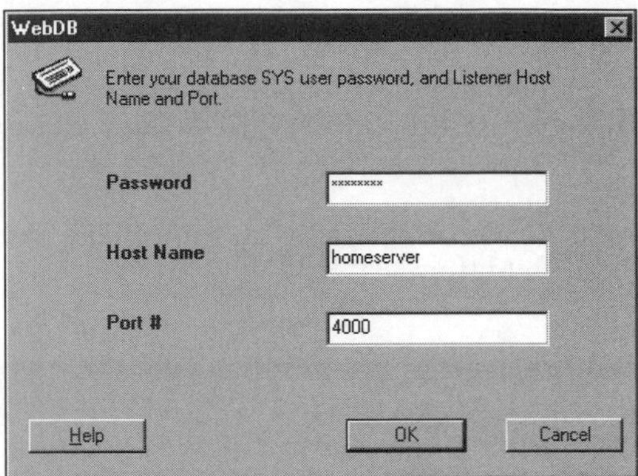

Figure 2-2: The installation process – logging in and selecting a server and port

6. On the next page of the installer, as shown in Figure 2-3, select the version of the Oracle database that will run WebDB and click the OK push button.

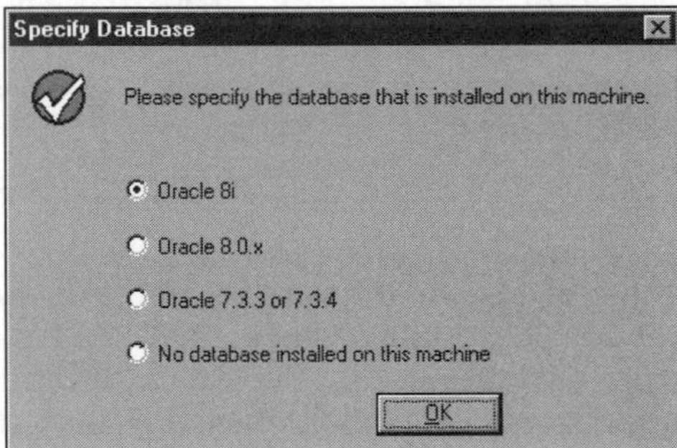

Figure 2-3: The installation process – selecting a version of Oracle

The installation process automatically creates a user named WEBDB and installs all the WebDB packages under that user name. If you already have a user named WEBDB on the target server, you are asked if you want to rename the existing WEBDB user or stop the installation process. We refer to the owner of the WEBDB packages as WEBDB throughout the rest of the book, so we recommend you use that user name to avoid confusion.

Once you have gone through these screens, the WebDB installation process gives you one final chance to stop the installation process.

7. Begin the installation by clicking the OK push button in the confirmation box.

Once you choose to begin the installation of the WebDB packages, the installation process takes over. At one point during the installation, the installer brings up SQL*Plus and uses it to load the appropriate packages for the product.

The installation of the WebDB packages takes a while—usually over half an hour. When it is done, you see a dialog box that asks if you want to install a beta version of the WebDB languages file, which helps you run the WebDB product in other languages. You can install this if you like, but this is the last you hear about it—at least in this version of this book!

When the installation is complete, you see a success dialog box, as shown in Figure 2-4, that recaps the location of WebDB, the user name, and password, and tells you how to modify the listener settings.

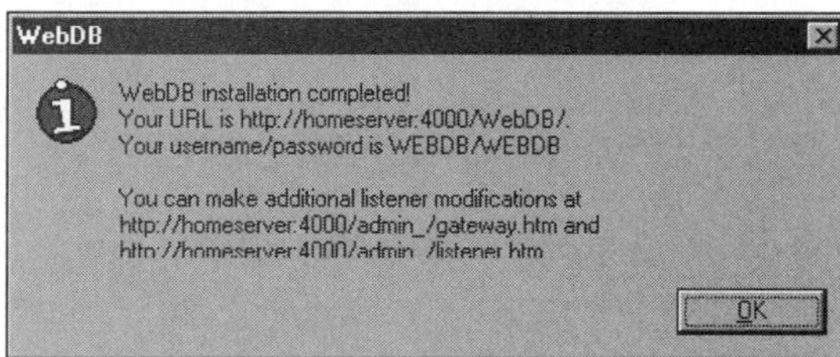

Figure 2-4: The completion of the installation process

The installation process for WebDB creates a Data Access Definition that automatically logs a developer on to WebDB with the user name that you installed WebDB under, which should be WEBDB for the purposes of this book.

As part of the installation process, WebDB automatically installs its own lightweight Web listener, which accepts requests that come into the server over the port specified for the listener. We recommend using this listener for your development environment because it is already installed.

Note

WebDB comes with its own lightweight Web listener, but you can use it with any standard Web server, including Microsoft's IIS, Oracle's Application Server, or Netscape's Enterprise Server, through the use of a CGI interface. Please refer to the WebDB documentation for more information on using WebDB with one of these listeners.

Structure of the Sample Database

All the modules you will create in this book are based on a mythical university called Net University.

All the scripts you need to load the data structures and data into your Oracle database are included in a self-extracting ZIP file called netuniversity.exe. This file also includes some documentation on the structure of the database, which is explained in this section.

Copy the file called netuniversity.exe from the Data directory on the CD-ROM that accompanies this book to its own directory on your hard drive. Run the file to extract the scripts and documentation.

Because these files are used by SQL*Plus, you may want to install them on the machine with your Oracle database because it will probably have SQL*Plus installed.

There are 16 tables in the sample data. The tables, columns, and their relationships are shown in an Adobe Acrobat file called College.pdf. Eight of the tables are interrelated in one data complex, four in another, and three in another, with the relationships between the tables in each complex defined through a series of primary and foreign keys.

The core of the schema is the UGRADS table, which contains information about the individual students enrolled at Net University, known to its students and alumni as good old NetU. The basic table layout for the UGRADS table complex is shown in Figure 2-5.

The UGRADS table is connected to the two tables used to enforce referential integrity and for descriptive values. The first is the STATES table, which translates state codes into state names. The second is the CLASSES table, which translates a code for the year that represents the specific class, such as the class of 1999, to a more descriptive name, such as Freshmen or Alumni.

Each student can have a major, so the UGRADS table is linked to the MAJORS table. The MAJORS table is in turn linked to a table named MAJOR_REQS, which describes the required courses for the major.

Each student can take classes at NetU, so the UGRADS table is linked to a TRANSCRIPT table that registers the courses that the student has taken. Because each course has a result, the TRANSCRIPT table is linked to a GRADES table. The COURSE_CATALOG table serves as a master reference for all courses, so both the TRANSCRIPT and MAJOR_REQS tables use it to verify that a course exists and to get additional information about the course.

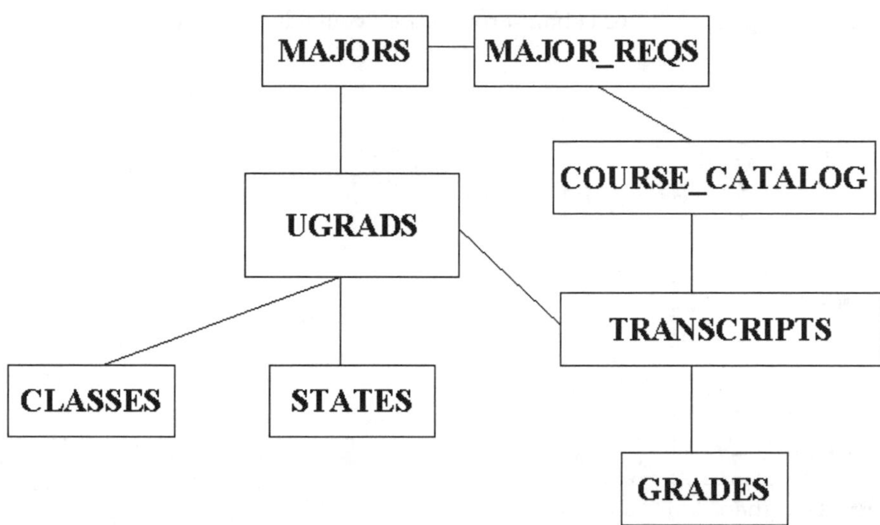

Figure 2-5: The UGRADS table complex

There is a complex of tables called ALUMNI, PLEDGES, DONATIONS, and RESTRICT_CODES used to track alumni donations to Net University's various fund-raising drives. This complex is shown in Figure 2-6.

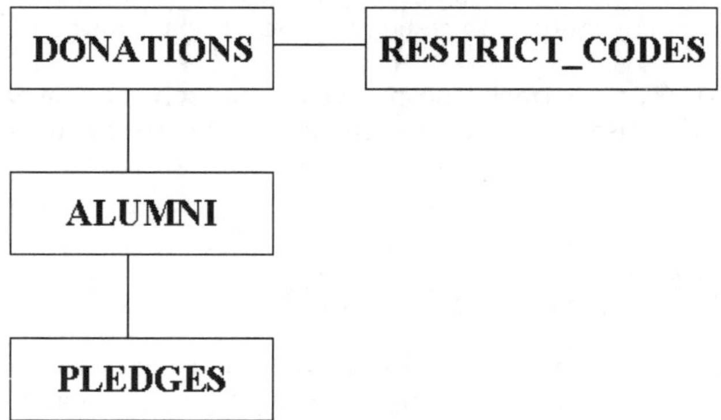

Figure 2-6: The DONATIONS table complex

These tables are included to provide some large tables full of numeric information, which are very useful for creating charts. If you examine the columns in the ALUMNI table, you can see that it is quite similar to the UGRADS table. There is also a stored procedure you will use that automatically adds a row to either the UGRADS table or the ALUMNI table from the same WebDB form component.

The last complex of tables is built around the events at NetU and shown in Figure 2-7.

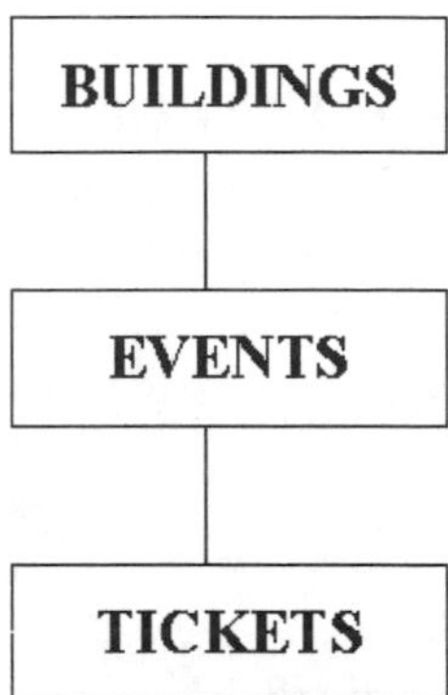

Figure 2-7: The EVENTS table complex

The EVENTS table is linked to two other tables in the schema. The first is the BUILDINGS table, which contains maps of the campus that provide detailed information for event locations, and the second is the TICKETS table, which tracks the tickets purchased for an event through a WebDB interface. These three tables are not directly related to the other tables in the schema, but they are included so that the examples in this book can work with date-type data and so that you can create a cool ticket-vending application with some additional PL/SQL procedures.

Finally, the REVISION_HISTORY table tracks the changes to this schema as it was developed. You do not need to use it in the rest of the book — it is strictly present for documentation.

Installing the NETU Sample Data

We have included a script that automatically loads all the sample data into your Oracle database. All you need is your trusty companion, SQL*Plus. The authors of this book, being longtime Oracle users, tend to rely on SQL*Plus. Although it has a somewhat ugly character interface, it gets the job done.

Because the installation script calls a lot of other scripts, and because you can have those scripts anywhere that you want, you have to change the working directory of SQL*Plus to the directory that contains the installation script.

1. Open the property sheet for SQL*Plus. If you are using SQL*Plus for Windows, you should change the directory listed in the Start in: text box to the directory you specified for the files from netuniversity.exe in the previous section. For other versions of SQL*Plus, you should make sure that the files are in your current working directory.

If you had stored the decompressed files in a directory called C:\NETU, the property sheet for SQL*Plus would look like Figure 2-8. It is a good practice to create a separate tablespace for an application.

You can create a tablespace through Oracle Enterprise Manager, or through the trusted Oracle text-based tool, SQL*Plus.

2. Start up SQL*Plus from a machine that has access to your target Oracle database.

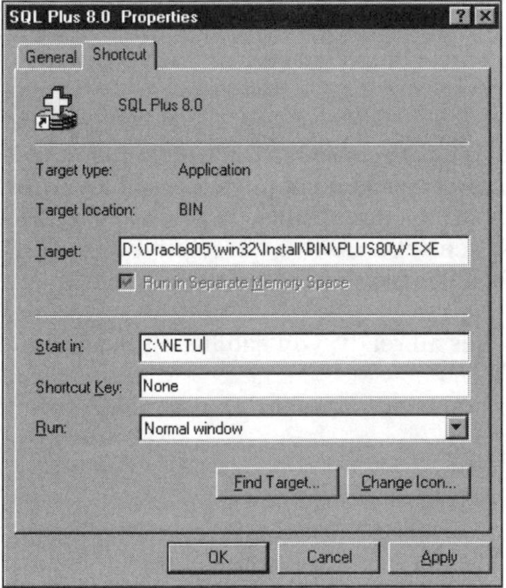

Figure 2-8: The property sheet for SQL*Plus

3. Log on with the user name and password of a user that has DBA privileges, or at least CREATE_TABLESPACE privileges.

If you do not have access to a user with DBA privileges, you can ask your support group to create the tablespace for you. If you are not the normal DBA of the target database, make sure you check with the normal DBA before creating these tablespaces.

4. When SQL*Plus starts, enter the following code at the prompt:

```
CREATE TABLESPACE NETU_SPACE
       DATAFILE 'filename' SIZE 30M
       DEFAULT STORAGE (
              INITIAL 100K
              NEXT 100K
              MINEXTENTS 2
              MAXEXTENTS 50);
```

Replace *filename* with the complete pathname of the actual physical file for the tablespace.

You can simply hit the Enter key while entering a command in SQL*Plus to go to the next line. A command is not executed until you enter that all-important semi-colon (;) at the end of the line.

The SIZE keyword indicates the overall size of the tablespace you are creating. The rest of the keywords shape the way that the Oracle database initially allocates disk space for the tablespace and how it grabs more disk space when needed. If you would like more information on creating tablespaces, please refer to the Oracle documentation.

You also need to specify a *temporary tablespace* for the user schema you are about to create. A temporary tablespace, as the name implies, is used for transitory data, such as the tables used internally for sorting results. Most Oracle databases already have a temporary tablespace set up with a descriptive name like TEMPORARY_DATA, which you can use for temporary table space.

Now that you have your tablespaces all ready, you can install the NETU data.

5. Start SQL*Plus with a user name and password that has DBA privileges.
6. Enter the following line of code:

```
@netu_install netu tablespace temp_tablespace;
```

Here, `tablespace` and `temp_tablespace` are the name of the tablespace you created earlier in this section and the name of the temporary tablespace for your Oracle database.

The second parameter for the `netinstall` procedure is the name of the schema that will hold the NetU data. This has to be a user name that does not currently exist. The user is created with a password that is the same as the user name. You do not have to use NETU as the user name, but we refer to the NETU user for the rest of the book, so it makes sense to use that name for the sake of conformance.

This script only creates a user and adds the data to that user's schema. You could, theoretically, have any user build the WebDB components that access that data. But

WebDB modules are created as PL/SQL procedures. You cannot assign data access privileges to a procedure — you can only assign those to the schema that owns the procedure. Because all of the data the sample application uses resides in the NETU schema, it makes a lot of sense to build the components in that schema also.

7. When the script completes, enter the following:

```
exit
```

Then hit Enter to leave SQL*Plus.

Tip

For this same reason, it also makes sense to have all the modules for a single WebDB application system in a single schema. You could conceivably have more than one application in the same schema, but because you can have a whole lot of modules in each application, it makes good sense to have a different schema for each WebDB application system you create.

We have found that the best practice to use is to build the WebDB components in one schema, but to have another user build the components. For this application, you build the components in the NETU schema that was just created, but you use the WEBDB user to build the components.

1. Open a browser and enter the URL for WebDB. Log on as user WEBDB. The default password for the created WEBDB user is also WEBDB.
2. Click the Administer menu choice from the main WebDB page and then select User Manager from the Administer page.
3. Scroll to the bottom of the page and find the NETU user that you just created. Click the name NETU, which takes you directly to the User Manager page shown in Figure 2-9.

The only change you have to make to the NETU user is to enable the schema for building components.

4. Check the check box labeled Component Building Schema in the middle of the User Manager page.
5. Click the push button labeled Apply in the upper-right corner of the panel to add this internal permission to the NETU user.

Now that you have enabled the NETU schema to accept components, you have to create a new user and give it the ability to build components in that schema.

6. Return to the main Administer page and click the User Manager choice.
7. In the top panel of the page, enter the information for a new user named NETUDEV. Give the user a password, confirm the password, and select the WebDB Developer check box at the bottom of the panel.

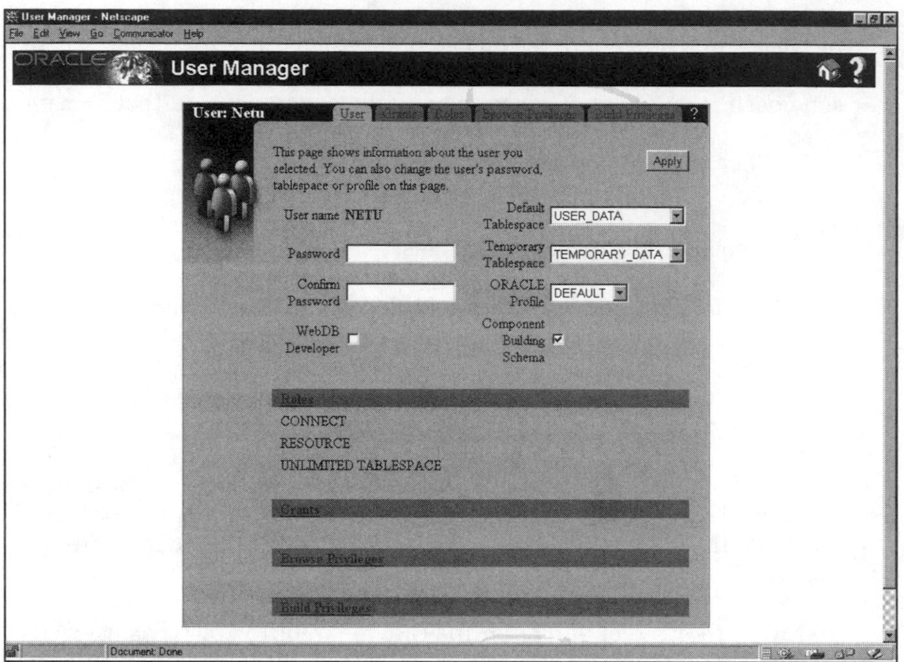

Figure 2-9: The User Manager page

8. Select the tablespace and temporary tablespace you created earlier in this chapter.
9. Click the Create push button.

Once you click the Create push button, WebDB goes out and creates the Oracle user and schema for you and takes you to the User Manager page for the new NETUDEV user. You have to make a few changes in the privileges for this new user.

It is good practice to store a complete WebDB application system in a single schema. Because you may give this schema data access permissions beyond what you would normally allow a user, it also makes sense to use a different user name to actually build the components in that schema. With this arrangement, you can keep the security issues for the home schema separate from any user considerations.

10. Scroll to the bottom of the page and click the Build Privileges hotlink to bring up the Build Privileges page, as shown in Figure 2-10.

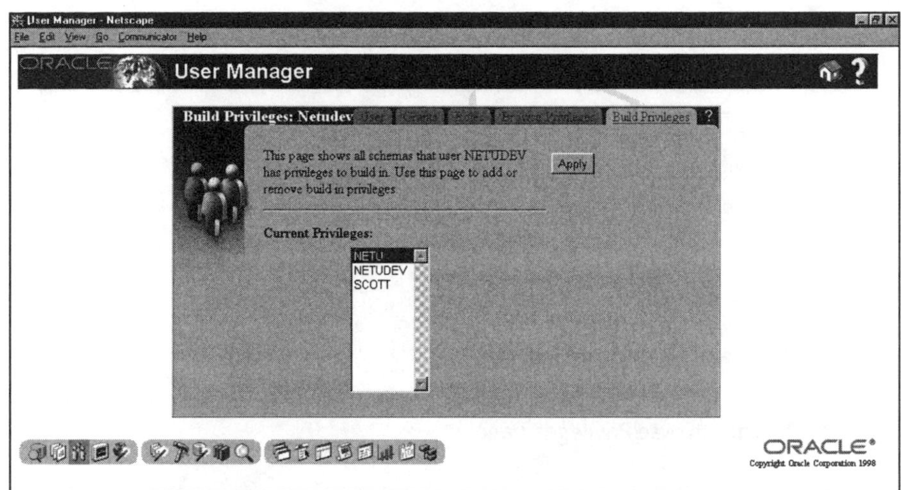

Figure 2-10: The Build Privileges page

You can see that, by default, the new user has been given build privileges for its own NETUDEV schema. You should take that away, but give the NETUDEV the ability to create components in the NETU schema.

11. Select the NETU schema in the list box at the bottom of the panel and click the Apply push button.

When you click the Apply push button, the user is given the ability to build in all the schemas listed in the list box at the bottom of the panel. The list box that shows the schemas is actually a multiselect box, so you could grant build privileges for more than one schema at the same time. Because you selected the NETU schema, which automatically deselected all the other schemas, the build privilege for the NETUDEV schema was taken away by WebDB.

12. Click the User tab to return to the main panel for the NETU user. If you scroll to the bottom of the page, you should see the NETU schema listed under Browse Privileges and Build Privileges.

When you explicitly grant the build privilege for a schema, the browse privilege is also granted to the user, which gives this user the right to browse database objects in the named schema. The designers of WebDB figured that this would be a good default, because you would probably want a developer to also to be able to check the data in a schema. If you don't want to allow browse privileges, turn the option off by clicking the Browse Privileges hotlink (as shown in Figure 2-11), unchecking the check box in the column labeled Browse In for the schema, and clicking the Apply push button.

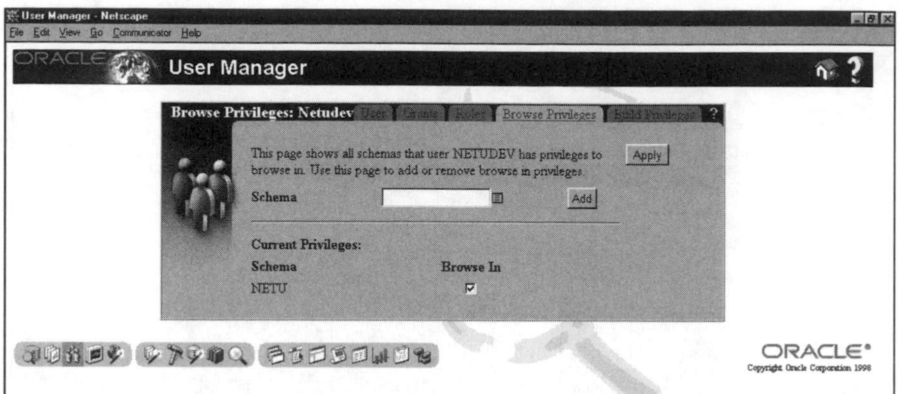

Figure 2-11: The Browse Privileges page

You have successfully created the user to build the example applications in this book. The default installation causes WebDB to prompt you for a user name and password every time you bring it up. You should always log in as the new NETUDEV user, unless the instructions in this book explicitly tell you otherwise.

As long as you are logged on as the WEBDB user, you can set up a virtual directory so that WebDB can find the images for the sample application.

13. Return to the Administer main page in WebDB.
14. Click the Listener Settings menu choice.
15. When you get to the Oracle WebDB PL/SQL Gateway page, click on the Change Listener Settings menu choice.
16. Scroll down the page until you reach the section titled Directory Mappings, as shown in Figure 2-12.
17. For the Physical Directory, enter the directory **WebDB20** under the directory you put the decompressed files in when you installed the NETU scripts as shown in Figure 2-12.
18. For the Virtual Directory, you *must* enter **/NETU/** for the examples to work properly.
19. Click the Apply push button to put your changes into effect.

The new NETUDEV user does not have the database privileges necessary to use every available menu choice in WebDB. For instance, if you go to the Administer page, you only see a single menu choice. In order to get access to the other menu choices, a user would have to have DBA privileges on the target database. Being a DBA is a very powerful situation, and one that your own database administrators may not be likely to grant to a mere WebDB developer. For this reason, whenever

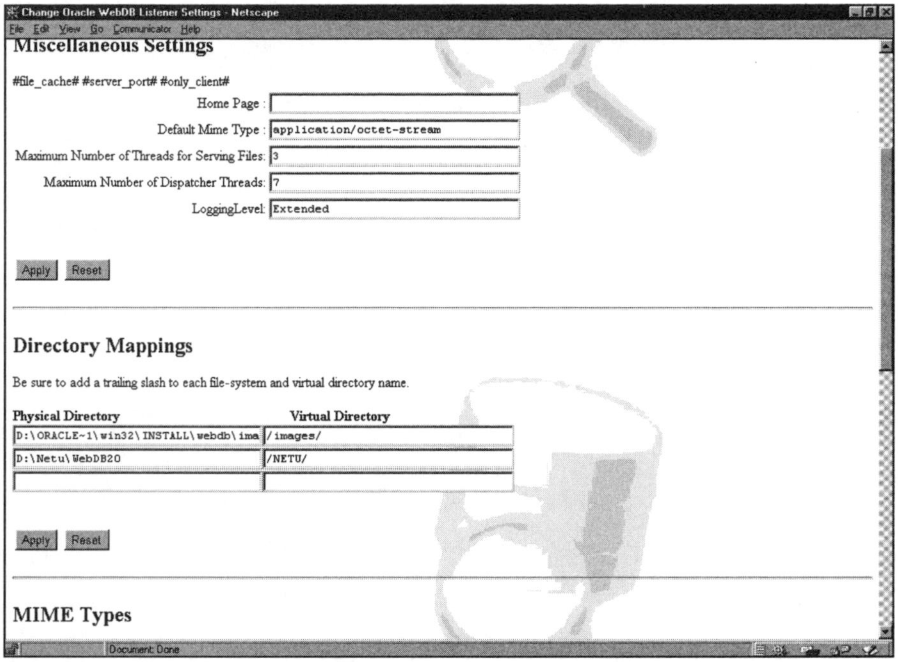

Figure 2-12: Setting up a virtual directory

we come to a section in the book that requires the use of this advanced privilege, we specifically instruct you to log on as a different user, such as WEBDB.

Later in this book, you will explore the Site Builder capabilities of WebDB. Because you have to be a DBA to use Site Builder, we suggest that you grant DBA privileges to the NETUDEV user for those sections of the book.

Your development environment for the rest of this book is now set up properly. You are ready to move on.

Wrapping Up

This chapter walked you through the installation of WebDB and the sample database you will use for the rest of this book. You are ready to start getting familiar with the WebDB development environment.

✦ ✦ ✦

The WebDB Environment

✦ ✦ ✦ ✦

In This Chapter

Introducing the WebDB Development Environment

Navigation Options

Standard Header Bar

Shortcuts Bar

Other Navigation Options

The WebDB Component Finder

✦ ✦ ✦ ✦

Now that you have installed WebDB, you are ready to start exploring the WebDB development environment. This chapter introduces you to all the basics you need to start using WebDB. Most of the chapter deals with the different ways you can navigate to different WebDB component builders and other modules. Finally, you will learn how to use the WebDB Component Finder to retrieve components from the WebDB repository, which can be seen as a prototype for all types of searches in WebDB.

Introducing the WebDB Development Environment

You have installed WebDB, and you've brought up several WebDB HTML page. Before you go any farther into the product, it's worth taking a few minutes to look at the browser environment that WebDB lives in.

As we have mentioned before, WebDB lives utterly and completely in a browser. WebDB has been tested, with Microsoft's Internet Explorer 4.0.1 with Service Pack 1 installed, as shown in Figure 3-1, and with Netscape Navigator 4.0.7, as shown in Figure 3-2. The startup page in each of these popular browsers is shown below.

We do not have a particular preference as to which browser you use, but we both use Netscape Navigator as our primary browser. Because of this, all upcoming screen shots in the book use Navigator as the browser environment. However, as you can see from the previous illustrations, there is very little difference in the appearance of WebDB between the two browsers.

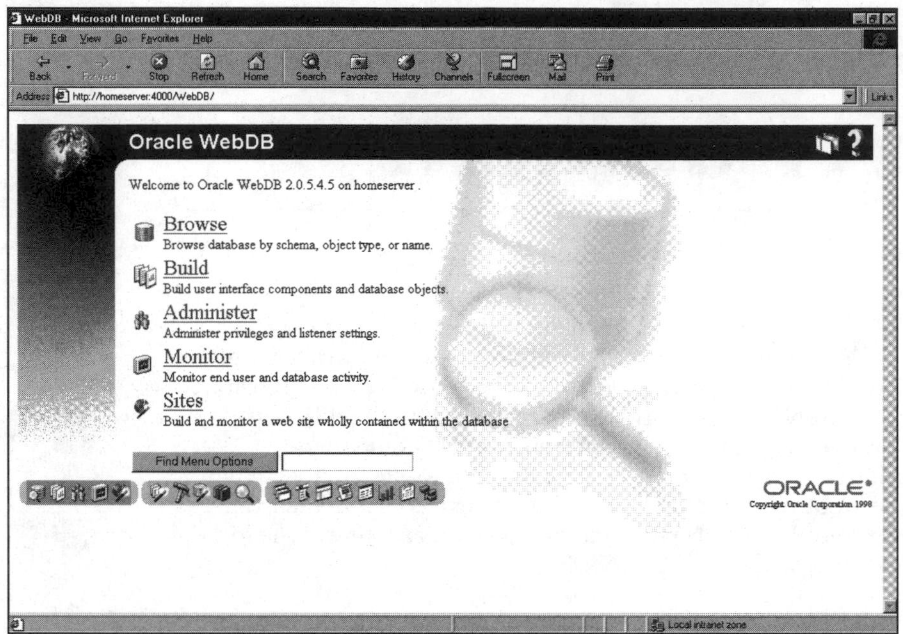

Figure 3-1: WebDB running inside Microsoft Internet Explorer

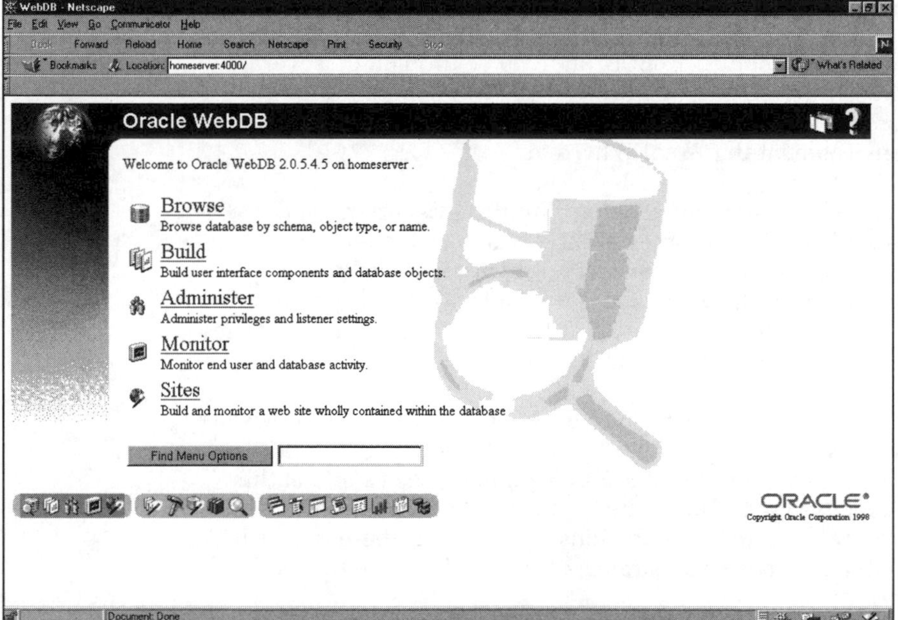

Figure 3-2: WebDB running inside Netscape Navigator

You can change the look of the WebDB environment through the standard settings on your browser. Most of the text displayed in WebDB is standard HTML text, and most browsers give you the ability to change the color and font of displayed HTML text.

All the standard browser features work while you are using WebDB. This means that you can use the navigation features of the browser, such as bookmarks or a favorites list and the Forward and Back buttons of the browser. You should be aware of the fact that each of the pages used in the WebDB environment is custom generated when the URL for that page is requested. Some pages, such as the starting page shown previously, will always look the same for a specific user, but other pages will display different types and amounts of information based on the information that is sent to WebDB along with the URL. Because of this, you should try and stick to using the internal navigation options of WebDB when you are moving around in the WebDB environment.

There are times when you can use the Forward and Back browser buttons to circumvent the WebDB menuing system to your advantage. For example, if you have forgotten a particular item, you can navigate back with your browser to find the item and its value and then use the Forward button to return to the proper WebDB panel. We recommend that you become familiar with the development environment navigate in this manner, as it can lead to problems if used improperly. You will sometimes have to use the navigation buttons of your browser to move back into the WebDB environment after you have run a WebDB component.

The WebDB home page has two features that are standard on all WebDB pages: the standard header bar and the shortcuts bar at the bottom of the page. In addition to these standard features, the WebDB home page has a couple of special features that make it easier for you to navigate through the WebDB environment. We look at the standard header bar and the shortcuts bar in the next sections, and then cover the special features of the home page.

The Standard Header Bar

Every page in WebDB has the same look and feel. The top of every main page in WebDB features the standard header bar, shown in Figure 3-3, which also extends down the left-hand side of the page on some screens.

Figure 3-3: Standard header bar

The standard header bar does more than just provide a nice graphic for WebDB. There are three hot spots in the standard header bar that give you access to basic information about the WebDB environment.

The three hot spots in the standard header bar are as follows:

- ✦ The Help icon, which takes you to the help system
- ✦ The Connection Information icon, which gives you valuable identification information
- ✦ The Home/Frames icon, which performs one of two functions, depending on your location in WebDB

The Help icon

On the right-hand side of the standard header bar, you see a yellow question mark, which is the Help icon. When you click the Help icon, WebDB checks to see if you have a browser window open with WebDB help displayed. If you do, WebDB displays a help page for WebDB. If there is no help window open, WebDB opens one and displays the help page.

When you use the Help icon to get to help from the standard header bar, WebDB help is shown in a framed window as illustrated in Figure 3-4, with a table of contents frame on the left and a frame to display the help text on the right. As with all framed browser pages, you can adjust the width of either window by simply dragging the frame between the windows with the primary mouse key held down.

The Contents frame has the look of a tabbed dialog box with three different tabs. Of course, it is not a true tabbed dialog box because it is rendered with HTML, but it is designed to look like the familiar Windows help system. The leftmost tab in the Contents frame displays a navigational menu for the help system. If a page icon

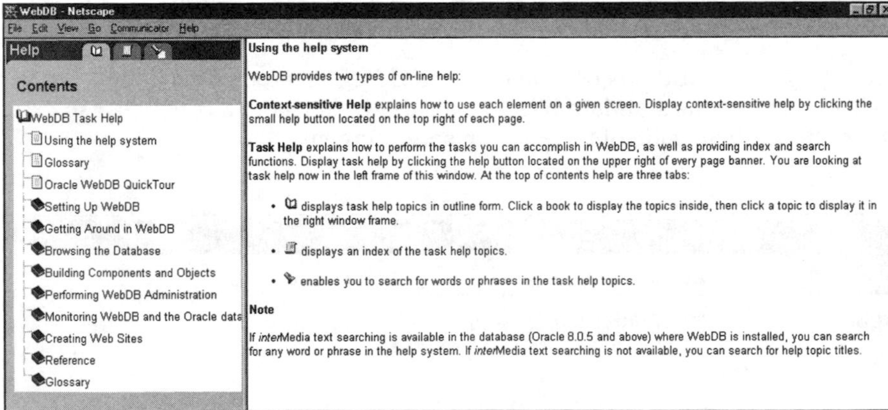

Figure 3-4: WebDB help window frame

appears before an entry, it indicates that the entry points to an HTML page in the help system. If a book icon appears before an entry, it indicates that the entry is a menu item, which contains additional menu items and page pointers, but does not point to a page itself. Because the Contents frame is an HTML document, each change in the layout of the frame requires a new static HTML page, which causes the frame to be repainted each time a new HTML page is requested by clicking one of the book icons.

The middle tab in the help Contents frame displays index entries for the help system. These index entries are brief text descriptions of the available help pages. Clicking one of the descriptions brings up the associated help text in the right-hand help frame.

The rightmost tab in the help contents frame displays a search system for help. The search system, which is shown in Figure 3-5, contains a data entry field you can use to enter any text you would like to find in the help system. After you enter a text string in the data entry field, click the Find button to populate the Contents frame with a list box with text descriptions of all the help system pages that contain the selected word. Simply click one of the descriptions to bring up the associated help text.

There is another type of help available in WebDB. Whenever you are on a page that has some data entry fields, a small version of the yellow question mark icon appears in the header for the portion of the page that has the data entry fields. This Help icon also brings up online help, but it brings up specific help for the page you are currently working on rather than the framed help window. You can always get to this general help because the standard header bar appears on every page. However, there may be times when you don't need the complete set of navigational options, so you would choose the more localized data entry help.

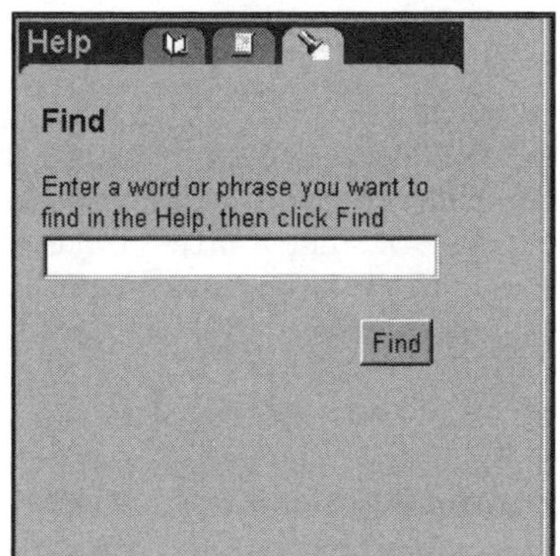

Figure 3-5: Searching for keywords

The Connection Information icon

The Connection Information icon somewhat hidden from view. That big picture of the world is a hot spot that brings up the Connection Information page, shown in Figure 3-6, when you click on it.

When you are developing applications with WebDB, you are always connected to an Oracle database. The Connection Information page displays everything you need to know about who you are and what you can do with WebDB.

There are two tables in the Connection Information page. The top table reports on the environment of your connection with three columns — the name of the particular environment attribute, the value for the attribute, and a hot link that enables you to change the value for the attribute, if applicable. Most of the data contained in the table is strictly informational, in the sense that you cannot change it. Some of the information in this table may not be very meaningful to you, such as the server name, if you are working on a single-server Oracle system. However, keep in mind that WebDB can be used as well in a massive enterprise system with dozens of different servers as it can with a single server, so the ability to confirm which server you are working on could potentially save you some very unpleasant surprises.

The two environmental attributes you can change are your user name and your password. At this point, we have not yet introduced the concept of different WebDB users, but we cover that topic later in this chapter.You will learn more about how different WebDB users interact with WebDB throughout this book.

The lower table in the Connection Information page lists the security roles that have been granted to the current WebDB user. You will learn more about security later in the book.

The Home/Frames icon

The Home/Frames icon, referred to from now on as the Home icon, has a dual role as the name implies. The Home icon is just to the left of the Help icon. If you are on any page other than the WebDB home page, the icon looks like a little house and clicking it takes you back to the home page. Because the home page of WebDB is like the central switching station for the product, you may find yourself frequently returning to this page.

If you are already on the home page, the Home icon changes its appearance to represent a couple of overlapping pages. This icon enables you to see the WebDB home page as a two-frame page, with a Contents frame on the left and the standard page on the right, as shown in Figure 3-7.

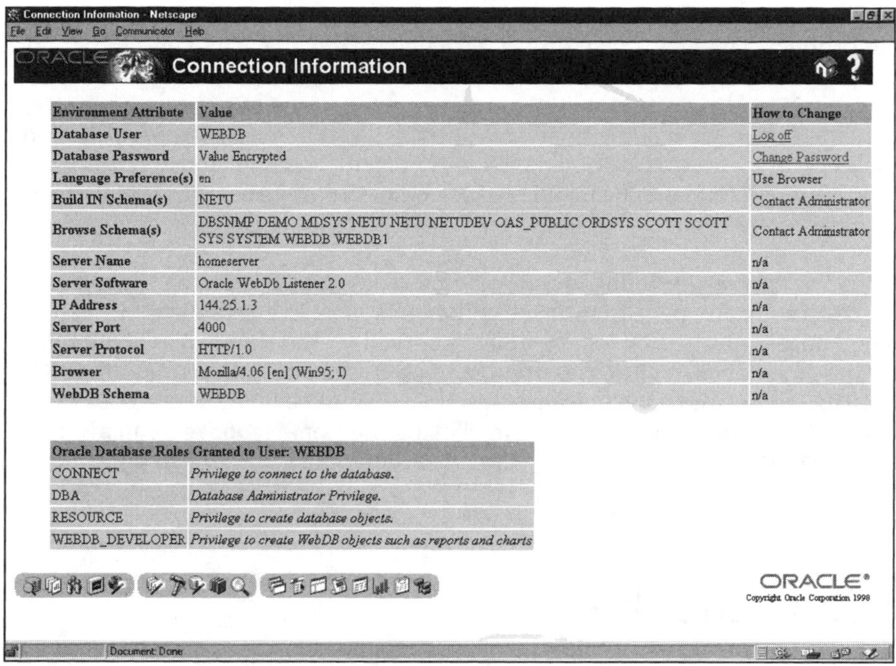

Figure 3-6: Connection Information page

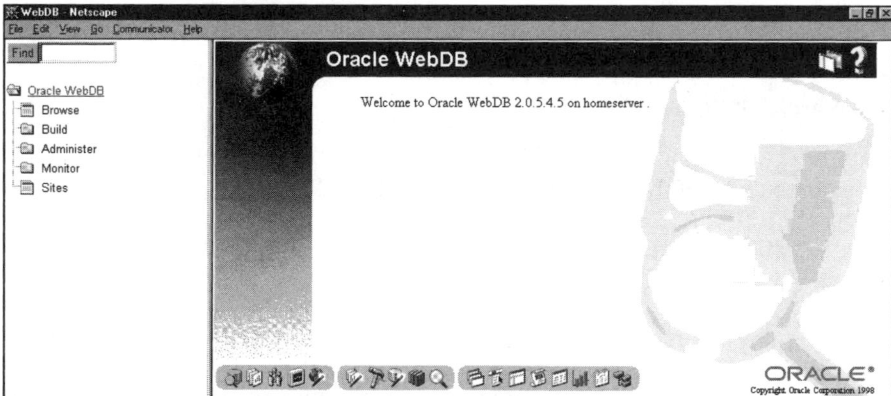

Figure 3-7: Frames view of WebDB home page

The Contents page of the framed version of WebDB also includes a Find box. The Find box enables you to search quickly through the text of the menu choices to find a particular word or phrase. The results of the search are displayed in the right frame with hot links to the menu choices that match the search criteria.

As you will quickly discover in using WebDB, there are a lot of different modules to the product. The menu structure is designed to add an easy-to-understand flow to the product. But once you get familiar with WebDB, you may find it cumbersome to click continually through multiple levels of menu pages to get where you want to go. The framed view of the home page enables you to locate the WebDB module you wish to work with quickly and navigate there with a single mouse click. WebDB is smart enough to leave the menu choices off of the WebDB pages if you are working with the menu frame.

If you want to return to the unframed version of WebDB, you can simply use the Home icon on any page to return to the home page. Every time you return to the home page with the Home icon, you are served up the Home page in its unframed format. You can also click the topmost entry in the navigation tree, titled "Oracle WebDB," to return to the unframed version of WebDB. If you want to keep using the navigational frame, just refrain from clicking the Home icon. You can always reduce the size of the left-hand frame by dragging the frame separator to give more space to the main frame.

The Shortcuts Bar

The easier it is to navigate through WebDB, the easier it is to develop WebDB application systems. The shortcuts bar provides a way to get to the most commonly used modules in WebDB from any page in the WebDB environment.

Figure 3-8: Shortcuts bar

The shortcuts bar (shown in Figure 3-8) consists of three groups of related icons:

- ✦ The standard header choices
- ✦ The Build menu choices
- ✦ The user interface component builders

Each one of the sections of the shortcuts bar is composed of a series of icons. Each icon displays a tips-style help text box that describes the icon if you leave the mouse over it for a few seconds, as long as the browser you are using supports pop-up tool tips. When you are on any of the pages that the icons in the shortcuts bar link to, the corresponding icon is highlighted by changing the background color of the icon from light gray to dark gray.

Standard header choices

The standard header choice section of the shortcuts bar gives you hot links that replicate the standard header choices displayed on the home page of WebDB. The links in this section of the shortcuts bar give you access to the main menu pages that enable you to do the following:

✦ Browse the WebDB database

✦ Build user interface components

✦ Administer users, security, and your WebDB server activity

✦ Monitor user and database activity

✦ Build and monitor WebDB sites

Build menu choices

The second segment in the shortcuts bar gives you easy access to the menu choices in the main Build Menu page. The links in this section of the shortcuts bar give you access to the following:

✦ The menu page for building user interface components

✦ The menu page for utilities that help you manage your components

This menu choice only operates if you are logged in as a user with DBA privileges.

✦ The wizard that walks you through the creation of various database objects

✦ The menu page for creating and managing shared components

✦ The Component Finder, which we look at in more detail later in this chapter

You will probably spend the majority of your time building the components you will use in your WebDB applications. This section of the shortcuts bar was included to make it easy for you to get to the main pages for managing WebDB components.

Component builders

The final segment in the shortcuts bar gives you easy access to the various wizards that help you build components. These wizards are also accessible through the User Interface Components menu. The links in this section of the shortcuts bar give you access to the wizards that walk you through the creation of the following items:

✦ Forms

✦ Menus

- Frame drivers
- Dynamically constructed HTML pages
- Reports
- Charts
- Calendars
- Hierarchies

Other Navigational Aids

One of the most common sources of frustration in a user interface is the inability to get where you want to go. The standard header bar and the shortcuts bar are meant to make it easy for you to get to the places you frequently want to go, and to provide this functionality in exactly the same way on every page in the WebDB environment. But your navigation choices may change depending on where you are in the WebDB environment.

Every WebDB page that is not part of a wizard has a text-based listing of navigation links at the bottom of the page. This text-based listing starts with the title "Back:" and consists of a listing of the main menu pages in WebDB, with the parent menu for the page listed first, the parent of that page listed next, and so on. This means that the last link in the list is always "Oracle WebDB," because it points to the home page for WebDB. For instance, if you are on the first page of the Form Building section of WebDB, the text links section looks like the following:

```
Back: User Interface Components, Build, Oracle WebDB
```

The User Interface Components menu page directly preceded this page, and the Build Menu page directly preceded the User Interface Components menu page.

Pages that are part of a WebDB wizard do not have these text links at the bottom of the page, for the simple reason that you shouldn't go anywhere when you are in the middle of using a wizard. You will learn a little more about wizards in the next section.

The other key navigational aid is the Find text box and push button. The Find functionality is located at the bottom of the WebDB home page and at the top of the left-hand frame in the framed version of WebDB. When you enter text into the text box and click the Find push button, WebDB returns a listing of menu choices that contain the entered text. The Find functionality returns not only menu choices that contain the text, but also menu choices whose description contains the text. This can be extremely useful, because there may be times when you know what you want to do but are unsure of the name of the WebDB part that enables you to do it.

As an example, say you wanted to edit one of your components. Enter the word **edit** into the Find text box and click the Find push button. WebDB is not able to find any menu choice that included the text in the title, but it returns the menu choice that contained the text in its descriptions, as shown in Figure 3-9.

The Find Components menu choice, which was returned from this search, is the first step toward editing a component. You will learn more about this component finder later in this chapter.

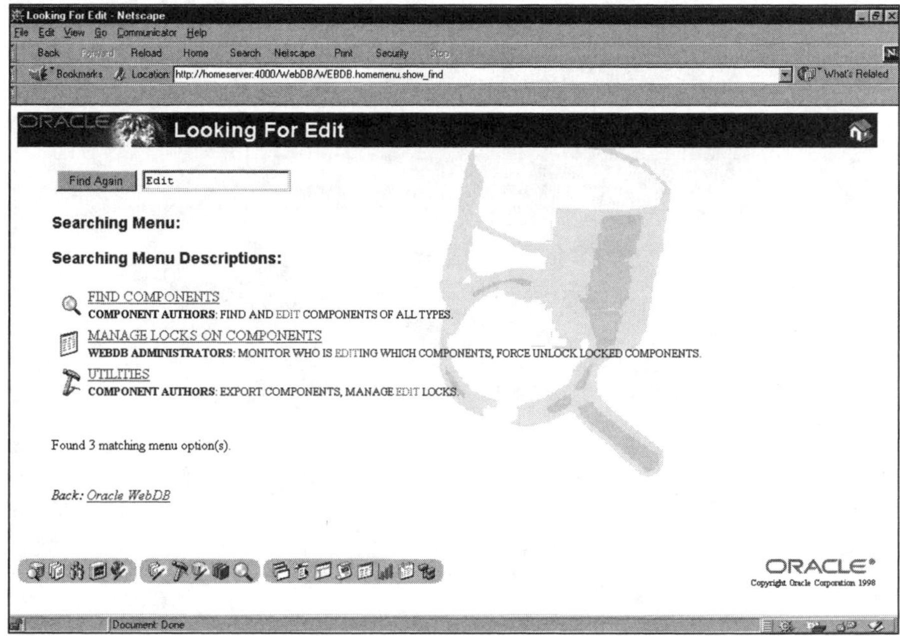

Figure 3-9: Find menu options results

A Few Words About Wizards

In the previous section, you read about a WebDB wizard. Most WebDB components are built using wizards. You are probably familiar with wizards from other software products. A wizard is a series of forms that prompt you for information that it uses to create something for you. In many other products, wizards are used to gather information and generate code for you, which you subsequently have to understand and maintain. WebDB's wizards do generate code under the covers, but you never have to see the code it generates.

WebDB is what is called a *declarative* development environment. This means that the process of development is no more than the process of declaring the values for a series of parameters. You don't have to write code. Even more importantly, you don't have to debug and maintain code. If you want to change the way a WebDB component operates, simply change the declared parameters.

The wizard is not necessarily the first page that displays from a particular menu choice, but you can always tell when you are in a wizard by a few common user interface conventions, as displayed in Figure 3-10.

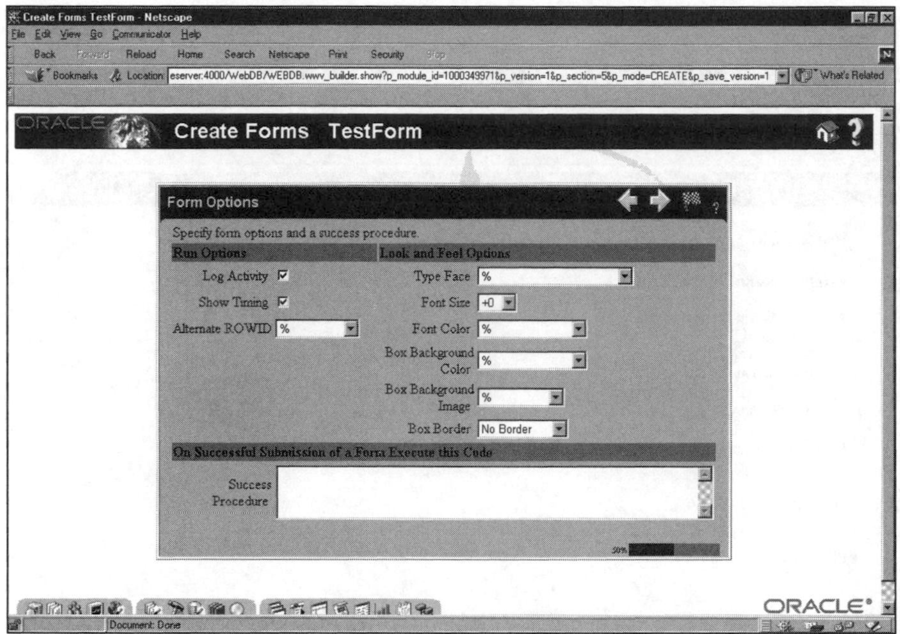

Figure 3-10: A wizard panel

Each page in a wizard contains a panel, which has a border on the top and left sides with the same color scheme as the standard header for WebDB. In the upper-right corner of the panel is a small Help icon. When you click this Help icon, it brings up a help page that corresponds to the current wizard page. As noted above, this appears in a slightly different form than the more general and navigable help that comes up when you click the Help icon in the standard header bar.

To the left of the Help icon are one or two arrows. These arrows walk you through the wizard. The right-pointing arrow takes you to the next page of the wizard, while the left-pointing arrow takes you to the previous page of the wizard. There is only a right-pointing arrow on the first page of each wizard, because there is nowhere to go back to from the first page. Correspondingly, the last page of each wizard only contains a left-pointing arrow.

At the top far right of most of the wizard panels is an icon that looks like a checkered flag. When you click this icon, WebDB automatically accepts all of the default choices for the remaining panels and builds the component.

In the lower-right corner of the wizard panel is a small progress bar. This bar indicates how far you have come in the process the wizard is guiding you through. The bar is a fairly rough estimate, because it counts each page in the wizard equally, when some wizard pages contain a single entry and others contain many entries.

Most pages in a wizard also contain a brief text description of the purpose of the entries for that page located below the wizard panel. This description is not present on some wizard pages that contain lots of entries in the interest of conserving screen real estate.

The last page in every wizard has a graphic of a checkered flag, a message telling you that you have completed the wizard, and a single push button labeled "OK." The end result of a wizard is to generate a component using the information you have supplied to the wizard. The component is only generated after you click the OK push button on the final screen, although the entries you have made in the wizard's pages are preserved as you enter them and move through the pages of the wizard.

All the parameters on all the forms have default values, and any parameters that can only accept a particular of values have value lists associated with them.

The designers of WebDB have tried to present the various pages in the wizards that prompt you for information in a logical order. For instance, the wizard for creating a form component prompts you for a schema and name for the form; the name of the table or view the form is based on; the formatting and validation of the columns on the form; basic options for the display and running of the form; the buttons that will be displayed on the form; the descriptive text that will be displayed on the form; and any additional procedural code you would like to add to the form. Keep in mind, though, that the component is only created once you have successfully navigated through the entire wizard and clicked the OK push button or clicked on the Finish Flag. Until that time, all the information you have entered for the component is held in a waiting area in the Oracle database. It is best if you do not use any of the navigation options in the browser itself to leave a wizard until you have completed the process of creating the component. If you leave a wizard before you have completed going through all the steps of the wizard, WebDB simply does not save any values for the parameters on the untouched pages of the wizard. This could result in errors when you return to re-edit the component. If you really have to leave a wizard before you complete all the pages in the wizard, you should use the checkered flag icon to accept the default values for the pages in the wizard you have not completed.

You will spend a lot more time with the wizards in the rest of this book, but you know enough about their general structure for now.

Component Finder

WebDB is a very powerful tool. You can create all sorts of components and weave them together into a robust application system. Keeping track of all of these components doesn't sound that hard when you are developing your first few smaller systems. But as you use WebDB to design and implement more and more complex sites, it becomes more and more difficult to remember all the components in your site. And when you start to work with multiple developers and weave components together into application systems, tracking the components could become a nightmare. Not for WebDB — it stores the components securely in the Oracle database — but for you, the poor human developer.

The WebDB Component Finder is designed to help you locate and use components. It can be used as a virtual gateway to all the other modules in WebDB, because once you locate a component you can quickly open it in the appropriate development module.

It helps to have a guide, so we will give you an introduction to the Component Finder and also present a typical WebDB user interface right now.

1. If you are still logged on as the NETUDEV user, log off using the choice in the Connection Information page and call the URL to enter WebDB again, logging on as user WEBDB.
2. Return to the WebDB home page. Click the Build menu choice.
3. Click the Find Components menu choice.

This brings up the Component Finder page, as shown in Figure 3-11.

The Component Finder page gives you the ability to enter criteria to be used when searching for different components. Table 3-1 shows the six basic types of criteria.

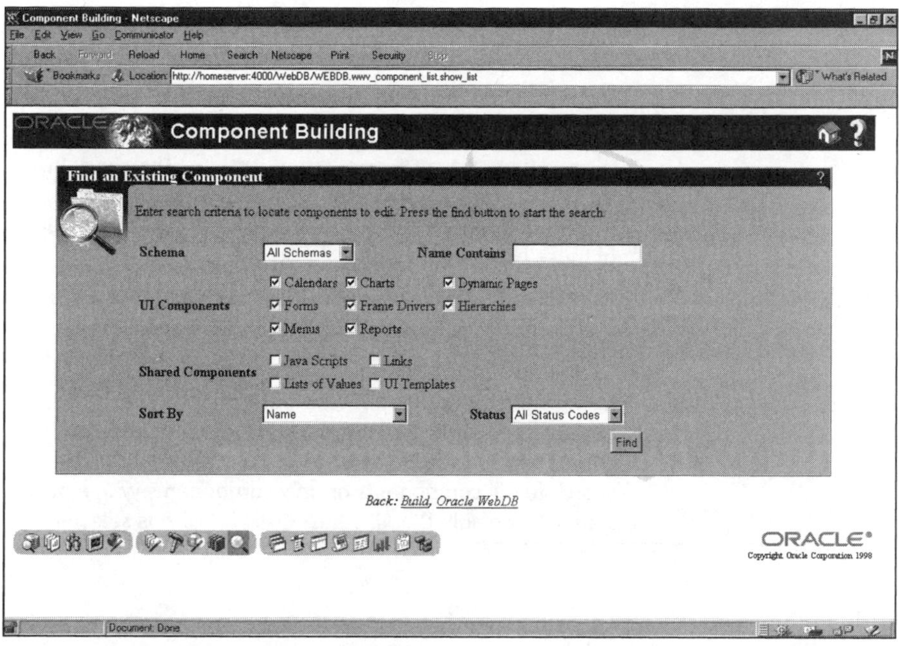

Figure 3-11: The Component Finder page

Table 3-1 Component Finder Selection Criteria	
Name	***Description***
Schema	Each component in WebDB is stored as part of a schema. Typically, each WebDB application system is stored under a single schema. You can look for a component in one schema or all schemas. The choices for schema are presented in a combo box that lists all schemas that the current user has security access to. By default, the All Schemas choice is selected.
Name Contains	This data field enables you to enter text included in the name of the components that are returned from the search. It makes a lot of sense to have a naming convention for your components in the name of the component itself, both for documentation purposes and to be able to use this search feature effectively.
UI Components	The UI Components section of the Component Finder main page has a series of check boxes for the eight different types of user interface components. You can check any number of these boxes. By default, all the boxes are checked.

continued

Table 3-1 *(continued)*

Name	*Description*
Shared Components	Shared components are components that can be used across many different WebDB application systems. The check boxes for these four types of shared components work the same way as the check boxes for the UI components, except that by default all of these check boxes are unchecked.
Sort By	The Sort By combo box enables you to specify the single value to use to sort the returned components. By default, the Name value is selected.
Status	Each user interface WebDB component has a status code. Whenever you edit a component, the previous copy of the component is saved in an archive. The Status combo box lets you search for all components or only components with a particular status. By default, the All Status Codes choice is selected.

At this point, you just want to see how the Component Finder works, so you don't have to change any of the default criteria in the page.

4. Click the Find push button at the bottom of the page.

The page returned to you initially looks familiar. The top of the page is simply a repeat of the criteria selection page of the Component Finder. Scroll down past that information and you see a listing of components as shown in Figure 3-12.

Each component is listed on its own line at the bottom of the page. Each component listing includes an icon and text string that identify the type of component, the schema the component resides in, the component name, the time the component was created and the last time the component was modified, the name of the user who created and modified the component, and the current status of the component.

The name of the component may also include a little yellow icon with the word NEW in it. This icon indicates that the component was created within the last seven days. Typically, it does not take very long to create a WebDB component, so this icon is a quick way to locate the components still under development.

The name of the component is actually a hot link to the appropriate editor for that component type.

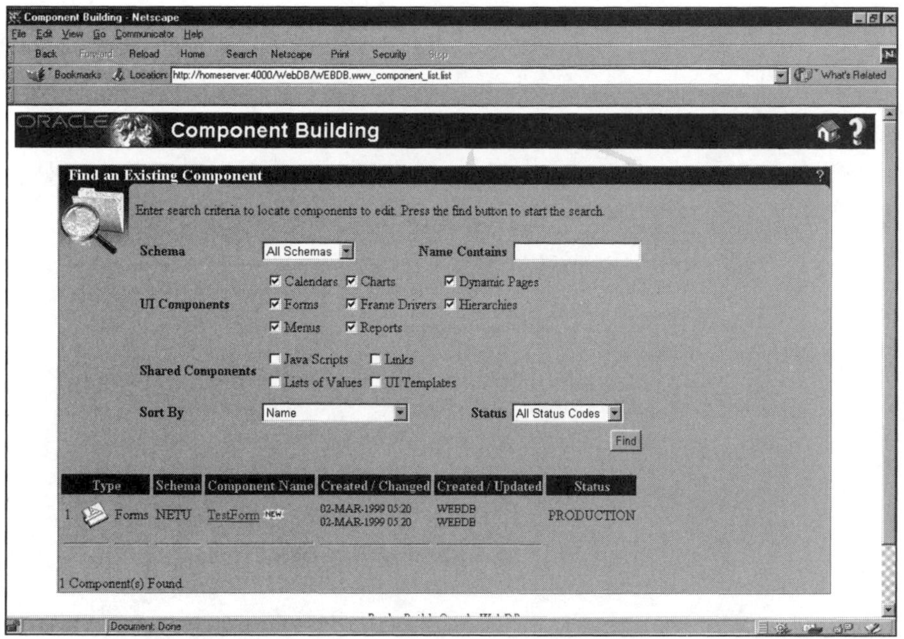

Figure 3-12: Components returned in the Component Finder

5. Click the name for one of the components returned in the Component Finder.

You can see that the Component Finder is not only a quick and easy way to locate particular components, but it can also act as kind of switchboard for editing components. Rather than having to go back to the main Build page, you can select the menu choice for the type of the component. By either searching for the component or selecting the component from the list of recently created components, you can use the Component Finder to quickly jump into an editing session for any type of component.

You will probably find yourself using the Component Finder as one of your main navigational aids during the development of complex WebDB application systems.

Wrapping Up

In this chapter, you got your feet wet in learning the basics of WebDB operation. You are now ready to start creating WebDB applications systems — and this task will take you through the rest of this book.

✦ ✦ ✦

P A R T

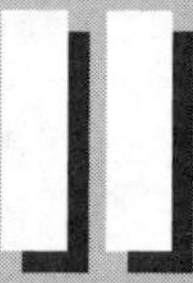

Building WebDB Components

✦ ✦ ✦ ✦

In This Part

✦ ✦ ✦ ✦

Browsing the Database

✦ ✦ ✦ ✦

In This Chapter

Basic Database Object Definitions

Selecting Database Objects

Querying Data

Querying and Updating Data

Inserting Data

Interacting with Other Database Objects

✦ ✦ ✦ ✦

WebDB, as you have already been told repeatedly, is built on an Oracle database. The Oracle database provides a number of things to your WebDB application—a secure storage mechanism, an engine that you can use to implement your application logic, and a way to help implement security. But, for most of you, your Oracle database's primary purpose is to store your organization's data. You have probably been using your Oracle database for this purpose long before you even thought of getting involved with WebDB.

This chapter covers using WebDB to interact with the data in your database. In a way, this is an overly simplistic statement. After all, almost everything you build with WebDB is used to interact with your data in one way or another. This chapter focuses on using the simple data object browser that is a part of WebDB, and subsequent chapters cover building components that interact with your data in more specific and customizable ways.

Basic Database Object Definitions

Before you jump right into interacting with your data through the WebDB browser, you might want to get a basic understanding of the different types of data objects that can be stored in an Oracle database that the WebDB data browser can be used with. If you are already familiar with standard relational database object types, you can skip this section.

The Oracle database can store a wide variety of database objects. All of these objects can be accessed with WebDB. The following table gives you a brief description of the most important database objects that you encounter when you create applications with WebDB.

Table 4-1
Database Objects

Object	*Purpose*
Table	A table is the basic unit of storage for data in a relational database. A table contains *columns,* which hold the individual pieces of data. A table is made up of *rows,* which represent the complete set of columns for the table. If you are familiar with file-based database systems, the equivalent entities for a table, column, and row are a file, field, and record.
View	A view, as the name implies, is another way to look at the data in a table. A view can represent a subset of the columns in a table or a combination of columns from one or more tables. A view is also sometimes used to enforce security on the data in the underlying table by limiting the rows a particular user can see. A view is the product of an SQL statement, and, as such, does not directly store data. Instead, it gives access to the data in the underlying tables the view is based upon.
Index	An index is a database object that is related to a particular table. An index is made up of one or more columns in a table, and is used to give faster access to rows in the table. Indexes can also improve performance by returning rows from the database sorted by the values in the index.
Procedure	A procedure is a piece of logic that is stored and executed in an Oracle database. Traditionally, Oracle procedures have been written in a language called PL/SQL. With Oracle8*i*, procedures can be written in either PL/SQL or Java. A procedure is a set of logical steps that can be called up and that return one or more values. All of the functionality you use in your WebDB modules is implemented with Oracle procedures; although, because WebDB is a declarative environment, you do not have to write any PL/SQL or Java code.
Trigger	A trigger is a specific piece of logic that is called when a particular database event occurs. Triggers are attached to tables, and you can specify that a trigger be executed when a database event such as adding or deleting a row in a table takes place. Triggers use the same syntax as procedures to implement their logic.
Sequence	A sequence is a special type of database object that has only one purpose: it supplies the next number in a sequence of numbers. Sequences are often used to assign unique identifiers to rows in a database table.

Many other database objects can be contained in an Oracle database, such as snapshots, packages, clusters, and functions. If you are new to Oracle, you will probably not have to deal with these types of database objects as you create WebDB application systems. If you are familiar with Oracle and its database objects, you no doubt already understand what these objects are, so no more explanation is necessary here.

The rest of this chapter concentrates on explaining how WebDB enables you to interact with the main types of database objects listed above.

Browsing Database Objects

You can browse objects in the Oracle database that acts as the repository for your WebDB development environment. You can access this part of WebDB by selecting the Browse menu choice on the main WebDB menu.

In the following sections, you will learn about the pages in the Browse area of WebDB that you will use to select a list of objects to browse.

As any of you who have Oracle databases in production know, an Oracle database can contain hundreds, if not thousands, of objects. When you first enter the Browse area of WebDB, you are presented with a series of pages that help you limit the number of objects you can browse.

Selecting database objects

The first page you encounter in the Browse area of WebDB prompts you for some basic selection criteria for the objects you may want to browse.

1. Start up WebDB and log on as the NETUDEV user.
2. Click the Browse menu choice on the WebDB home page.

This first page (see Figure 4-1), which is called Find Database Objects, gives you three ways to limit the objects that are in the list of objects returned to you. The first selection criterion is based on the name of the schema for an object. As you may know, all objects in an Oracle database exist in a schema. The schema is the name of the owner of the object.

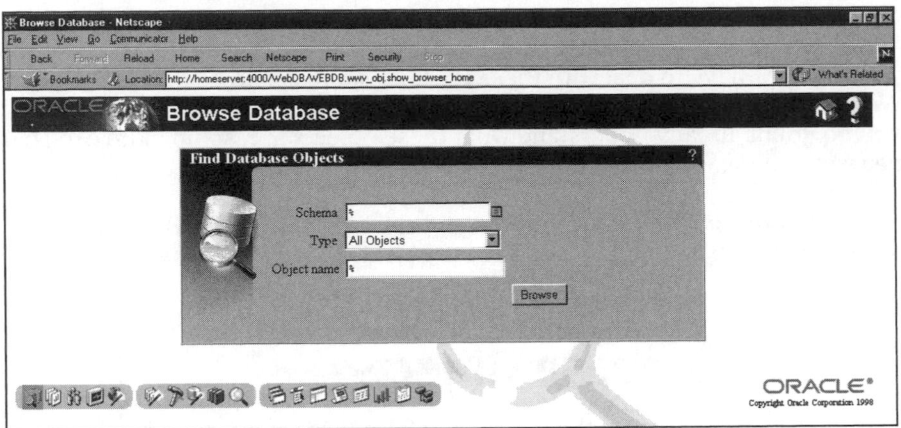

Figure 4-1: Selecting objects to browse

Notice that the data entry field for the name of the schema has what looks like a little page to the right of the field. You will see this icon throughout the WebDB environment, always to the right of a data entry field. When you click this symbol, it brings up another browser window that enables you to search through the existing values to select a value for the field. This symbol represents what WebDB calls a PopUp list-of-values. You can use this type of lookup in your own WebDB applications, and you will learn how to create and use them in Chapter 13.

3. Click the page icon to the right of the Schema data entry field.

When you click the list icon next to the data entry field for the schema, you get a search dialog window that enables you to select a schema name from the list of existing schemas, as shown in Figure 4-2. You can use this window to select the schema name that contains all the data for the sample application you will build for the examples in this book.

4. Enter the first few letters of the name you selected for the user who owns the data for the sample application followed by the percent (%) sign, and click the Find push button.

The "%" sign that you used in the Find box is the standard Oracle wild card. This symbol represents any number of characters in a selection criterion. The wild card symbol, by itself, is the default entry for many selection conditions in WebDB. Using a wild card, by itself, as a selection condition has the effect of having no selection conditions, because it instructs WebDB to select all values.

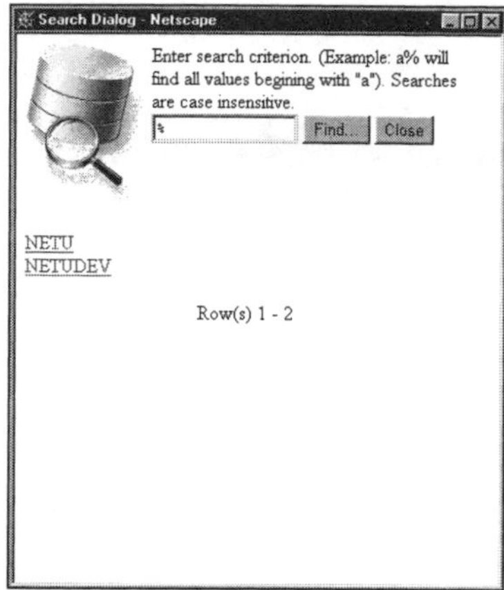

Figure 4-2: Selecting a value for a schema name

You can use a wild card at the beginning, in the middle, or at the end of a sequence of characters, but using the wild card at the beginning of a string of characters can result in poor performance.

The search of schema names returns all names that match the selection criteria you entered in the Find field. Each of the returned names is a hotlink. When you click the hotlink, the value for the link is inserted into the schema field and the Search dialog box is closed.

5. Click the user name for the NETU user in the Search box.

The second selection criterion is a combo box that lists all the different types of database objects that can be found in an Oracle database, as well as the default choice of choosing all database objects. You can either choose to select all database objects or only one type of object. If you select more than one type of object, WebDB organizes all the database objects in a way that makes it easy to deal with them. WebDB also gives you the option to choose two groups of related database objects — Tables and Views; or Packages, Procedures and Functions.

The final selection criterion enables you to specify all or part of the name of a database object. If you use a naming convention for your objects (which is highly recommended), selecting objects based on a part of their name can help you limit the returned objects to those associated with a single project or part of a single project.

6. Click the Browse push button on the Find Database Objects page.

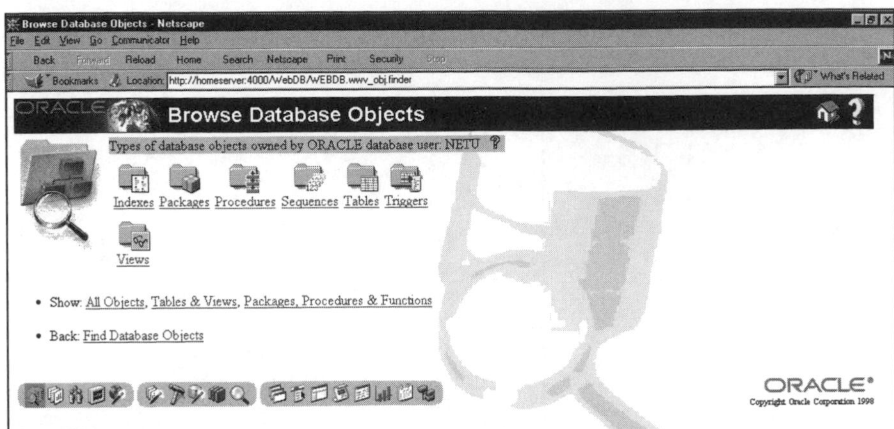

Figure 4-3: The top-level list of database objects

The top-level list of database objects is shown in Figure 4-3. When you ask WebDB to select all database objects for you to browse, your results screen includes two ways to select the type of object you want to browse. The top portion of the page has an icon for each different type of database object, with the name of the object underneath the icon. Both the object and the icon act as hotlinks to a list of the corresponding type of object. Underneath the icons, you can see the text-based set of hotlinks for some of the groups of objects. The text-based set of hotlinks also includes a choice for All Objects.

The rest of the browsing sequence for database objects is different for each type of object. Because you have the most options for your actions when you are browsing the data in a table, we discuss browsing all of the other types of database objects before moving on to browsing the data in a table.

Browsing an index

The WebDB browsing capability helps you discover more about the composition and configuration of the indexes in your Oracle database.

7. Click the icon for Indexes on the Browse Database Objects results page.

If there are any newly created objects, the New icon is displayed beside them. This icon can help you rapidly spot those database objects you have recently created, which can be very handy during the development process.

8. Click the icon for the CLASSES_PK index.

It is a good practice to use a naming convention for your indexes – such as adding the suffix PK onto indexes – that serve as the primary key of a table. We used Oracle's Database Designer to create the NetU data model, and this tool can help you to set database standards such as naming conventions for indexes and keys.

The beginning of the page that is returned for browsing an index list is shown in Figure 4-4. This page lists all of the information about the index that is in the data dictionary. This includes the name of the owner of the index, the table the index is associated with, and the characteristics of the index, such as the type of index and the way it is populated within the database.

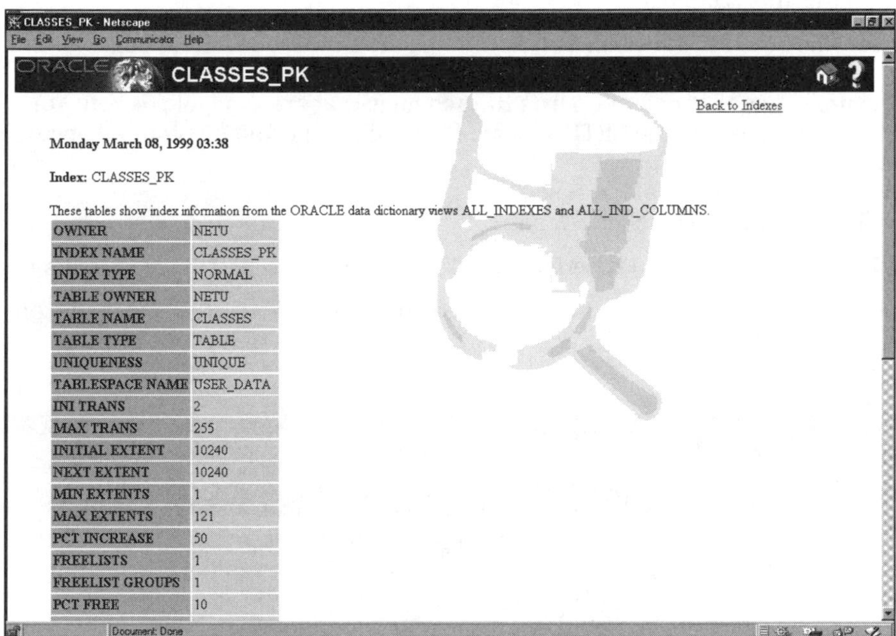

Figure 4-4: Browsing an index

Below the listing of all the standard characteristics for the index is an icon that links to the data dictionary comments about the index. The data dictionary comments are basic descriptions of the columns shown in the upper part of the page that act as a kind of help system for the columns.

At the very bottom of the page is a list of the columns that make up the index, and a link that enables you to get the same data dictionary help for these columns that was available for the columns in the previous index description.

You don't have the ability to change values in an index through the Browse area in WebDB, because index values are part of the contents of their associated row. If you want to change an index value, you can do so by browsing the contents of the row, which we explain later in this chapter.

Browsing a procedure

Procedures have very different characteristics than indexes or tables, so the browsing method for procedures is different from that of other database objects.

9. Return to the main Browse page in WebDB by clicking the highlighted icon in the shortcuts bar.
10. Click the Browse push button on the Find Database Objects page.

The next page that comes up lists the schemas that are available to you. You only have access to the NETU schema for which you explicitly granted access to your user.

11. Click the NETU schema icon.
12. Click the icon for Procedures on the Browse Database Objects results page.
13. Click the icon for the New Class Year procedure. The page returned from this action is shown in Figure 4-5.

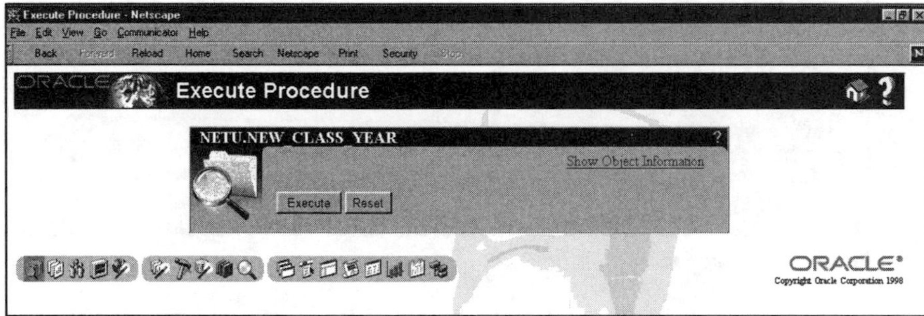

Figure 4-5: Browsing a procedure

If you want to see more information about the procedure, such as the code that the procedure executes, you can click the Show Object Information link in the upper-right side of the panel.

14. When you browse a procedure with WebDB, you are given the ability to execute the procedure in the database, so click the Execute push button for the procedure you selected.

When you execute a simple procedure such as New Class Year, all WebDB returns is an icon that indicates whether the procedure executed successfully (as shown in Figure 4-6) or unsuccessfully.

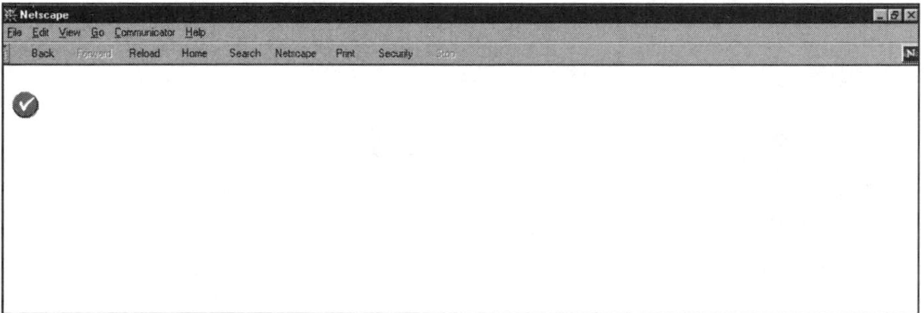

Figure 4-6: The result of a simple procedure

A procedure can accept input and deliver results. If you execute a procedure that requires input parameters, WebDB prompts you for the values for the parameters when you select the procedure. If a procedure returns data results, WebDB presents those results to you after the procedure has completed.

Browsing a trigger

As described previously, triggers are a way of automatically executing database logic in response to database events. Browsing a trigger gives you the relevant information about a trigger that is similar to the information you get about an index.

15. Use the Back push button in your browser to return to the previous page, and then return to the main Browse page and click through to the listing of database objects.

16. Click the icon for Triggers on the Browse Database Objects results page.

17. Click the icon for the CREATE_EVENT_ID trigger.

As with the information for an index, the information returned when browsing a trigger describes the trigger and the way the trigger works, as shown in Figure 4-7. You can see when the trigger is fired and the text of the body of the trigger, which is the PL/SQL code that implements the logic of the trigger.

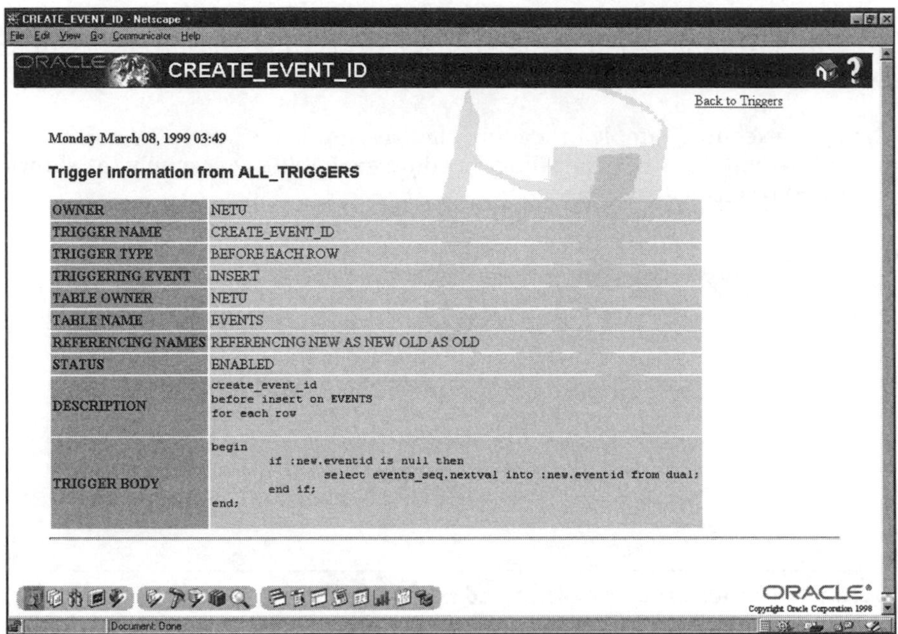

Figure 4-7: Browsing trigger information

Browsing a table or view

Tables and views are the most important objects in your database. After all, they are the objects that hold and display your data, which is the primary purpose of a database. All of the other database objects revolve around the data in the tables. Consequently, the WebDB browsing interface for these objects offers you the most flexibility and a lot of options for interaction.

Many of the options available to you in browsing your database tables are also available in other parts of WebDB.

Although you can select either tables or views through the selection criteria for browsing database objects, they interact somewhat differently with the data. The Oracle database, like most databases, only allows you to insert data with certain types of views — those that are directly based on a single table. Because WebDB is designed for end users who may not understand this limitation, you are not given the ability to update or insert data through a view with the Browse interface.

18. Return to the main Browse page and click through to the listing of database objects.

19. Click the text-based hotlink titled Tables & Views at the bottom of the search results returned in the Browse Database Objects area of WebDB.

20. Click the icon for the Events table.

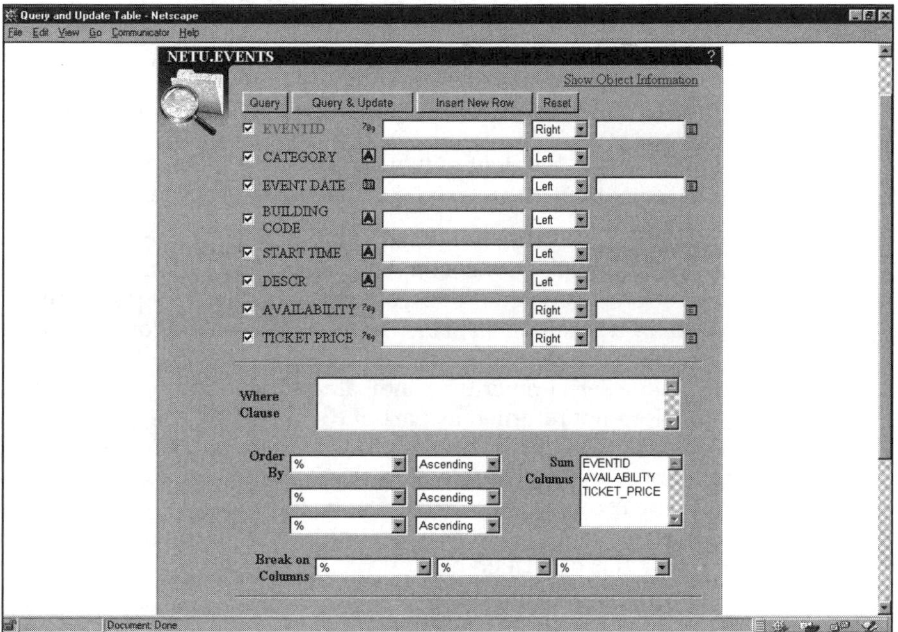

Figure 4-8: Browsing a table — query and insert page

The page that is initially returned when you select a table to browse is used to enter selection criteria for the data that will be returned from the table, as shown in Figure 4-8. It can also be used to insert data into the table, as you will see later.

The basic areas of the query and insert page are as follows:

✦ **Column Information** — The selection page includes a line for each column in the table. The line for each column includes the name of the column, an icon to the right of the column name that indicates the datatype of the column, such as a character, a number or a date, and a check box to the left of the column name. If the check box is checked, it indicates that the corresponding column is returned for browsing as part of the results for the query on the table. By default, all of the check boxes are initially checked. If the name of the column is in bold red text, it means that the column is part of the primary key of the table.

After the data entry box for a column, there is a combo box that enables you to specify how you want the data returned from the query aligned. The data returned from your query is displayed in an HTML table object, and you have the option of aligning a column's data to the right, left, or center within the column. If a column in the database table is a character or date column, the default alignment for the data is left-justified. All other column types have a default alignment of right-justified.

If a column in the database table does not contain character data, you see another text entry box to the right of the alignment combo box. This final text box enables you to specify the formatting for the column data. This text box has a Find icon to the right of it, which you can use to retrieve all the valid types of formatting for the particular column datatype.

✦ **Column Selection Criteria**—Each column line also includes a text entry field to the right of the datatype icon. You can add selection criteria in these fields. The selection criteria could be a specific value that you want all returned data to match, or a relational expression, such as > or < followed by a value. You can use the "%" wild card as part of the selection criteria for character fields. You can have selection criteria indicated for columns that are not checked, and therefore not returned as part of the results of the query. You can only have a single selection criterion for each column using the fields on the column lines. If you have selection criteria indicated for more than one column, the returned rows must match all criteria. If you want to use more complex selection criteria, you can enter them in the data field for the WHERE clause, which is described next.

✦ **WHERE Clause**—The WHERE clause is a standard part of the SQL language. The WHERE clause is used to implement selection criteria in an SQL statement. You can enter any valid WHERE clause in the Where Clause text field with either the keyword WHERE that you would with a normal SQL statement included or without the WHERE keyword. A WHERE clause can include any combination of logical criteria, including multiple specifications joined together by the keywords AND and OR. You can enclose sets of conditions within parentheses to specify that they should be evaluated before the entire clause is evaluated. If you are using string values in the WHERE clause, you have to enclose them in single quotes. If you specify an invalid WHERE clause in the Where Clause field, WebDB returns an error when you attempt to browse the data. The WHERE clause can be implemented in a sophisticated manner that is beyond the scope of this small introduction—if you are familiar with SQL, you already know that. If you want more information on the various ways you can use the WHERE clause, please refer to the standard Oracle SQL documentation.

✦ **Order By**—There are three combo boxes that enable you to specify the columns WebDB uses to order the rows returned from your query. Each combo box contains a list of all of the columns in the table. You can specify that each ordering column is used to sort the data in either Ascending order, which is the default, or Descending order. If you specify more than one column for ordering the data, the column specified in the topmost Order By box is the primary sort column, the next column is the secondary sort column, and so on. In other words, if you specified that you wanted the rows returned in the EVENTS table ordered by CATEGORY and then LOCATION, the rows would be returned sorted by CATEGORY, with the rows within each CATEGORY group sorted by LOCATION. Just as with selection criteria, you can sort the rows returned from the database based on the value of a column that is not included in the display of the query.

✦ **Sum Columns**— The Sum Columns list box gives you the ability to specify that WebDB should calculate and display the sum of a numeric column in the table. The Sum Columns list box lists all the numeric columns in the table. You can select any of the columns by clicking them. By default, WebDB sums the values for the column at the end of the query. If you want to sum intermediate values, you can specify the column containing those values as one of the Break on Columns described next. You can select one or more columns to sum.

✦ **Break on Columns**— The Break on Columns section of the selection criteria page has three combo boxes that list the columns in the table or view that you are querying. When you specify a column as a break column, WebDB does two things. First, WebDB only shows the value for the column the first time it displays. The rest of the rows that have the value have a blank space, which can make the results of the browse easier to read. Second, if you have selected any of the columns in the Sum Columns list box, the value for that sum is displayed in the blank line and then reset to 0. If you select a column for a break, the data returned is automatically sorted on the break column.

✦ **Output Format**— You can choose to have the output from your browsing of the table displayed three ways: as HTML-based text; as straight, unformatted ASCII text within a single HTML table column; or in Microsoft Excel data format, which makes it easy to transfer data taken from your Oracle database to personal productivity tools. If you choose to save the data in Excel format, you are prompted for a filename that is used to store the data.

✦ **Maximum Rows**— The field that enables you to specify the maximum number of rows returned from a query is near the very bottom of the selection criteria page, but it can have a dramatic effect on the return of rows from the query. The maximum number of rows returned indicates the maximum number of rows returned from a query on a single page, not the total maximum number of rows returned. If there are additional rows in a table that match the selection criteria, the page has, by default, a push button at the bottom of the page that enables you to retrieve the next set of rows. The value for the maximum number of rows directly affects the overall size of the page, which correspondingly affects the amount of time it takes to retrieve the rows over your network. The default value for this field is 20. If you have large rows of data, a slow connection to the database server, or a combination of these factors, you get a better response time by limiting the number of rows returned on each results page.

✦ **Show Null As**—You can use this data field to enter a value that is displayed in place of null values in the database. The default value for this field is (null).

✦ **Query Options**—The Query Options box gives you several different choices for the way that you want the data returned from the query to appear. You can choose one or more options in the list box with the standard key combinations for your platform—holding down the Ctrl key while you click an option in the Windows environment, for instance.

Table 4-2
Query Options Values

Query Option	*Meaning*
Show SQL	If you choose this option, WebDB shows you the SQL statement it constructs to get your data before it retrieves the data. If you are familiar with the SQL language, you can check it with this option to make sure you have made the right choices on the query selection page. If you are not familiar with SQL, you might be able to learn about the language by examining the SQL that results from the choices you have made. This Query Option is not selected by default.
Display Results in Tables With Borders	This option causes the data to be returned with borders surrounding the table. This Query Option is not selected by default.
Show Total Row Count	Selecting this option causes WebDB to display the total number of rows at the end of the returned data.
Count Rows Only	This option also shows you the total number of rows returned, but selecting this option suppresses the display of the actual data. A single line of data is returned that gives you the total number of rows that would have been returned. If you are familiar with SQL, this option is the equivalent of asking for a COUNT(*) in an SQL statement.

continued

Query Option	Meaning
Show Paging Buttons	By default, WebDB returns data a page at a time and displays one or two push buttons at the bottom of the page that enable you to move to the next or previous set of rows, as appropriate. If this option is not selected, WebDB does not display these paging push buttons at the bottom of the page. Instead, WebDB returns the number of rows specified in the Maximum Rows field. If this option is not selected, it can reduce the amount of data that is sent from the database server, but it can also give a misleading impression of the amount of data that satisfies the selection criteria. You do not know whether the amount of data returned is the complete set of data or just the maximum number of rows. In addition, you can avoid much of the overhead of additional data by simply choosing not to request additional pages of data. Because of this, the Show Paging Buttons option is chosen by default.
Show HR between rows	This option inserts a horizontal rule (HR) between each row returned. This can be useful if your rows contain a lot of data and stretch over several rows in the browser.
Replace ASCII new lines with HTML breaks	This option replaces the ASCII new line characters with the character when a new row of data begins.

Before moving on to actually retrieving data from the database, you should note the link in the upper-right corner of the panel labeled Show Object Information. If you click this link, it gives you a concise summary of the information in the data dictionary about this table, as shown in Figure 4-9.

This information includes listings and links for any indexes, constraints, and triggers that are associated with the table. You can click any of these links to get more information about the particular associated object.

Once you have entered the selection criteria for retrieving data from a table, you can click the Query push button to return data from the database.

21. Select the CATEGORY table as a break column.

22. Click the Query push button.

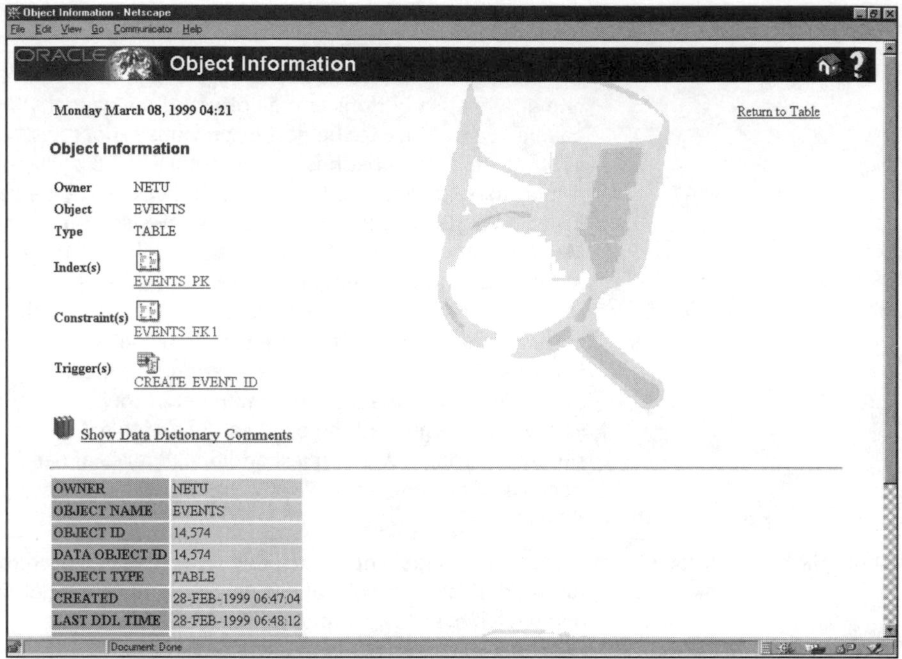

Figure 4-9: Object information about a table

The data that is returned from a data query with a break specified for the CATEGORY is shown in Figure 4-10.

There are three other push buttons at the top of the query and update table. The Reset push button, which is displayed at the top of the page at the far right, resets the default values in the query criteria page to null values.

The other two push buttons, Query & Update and Insert New Row, are used for writing data to a database table, and are discussed in the next section.

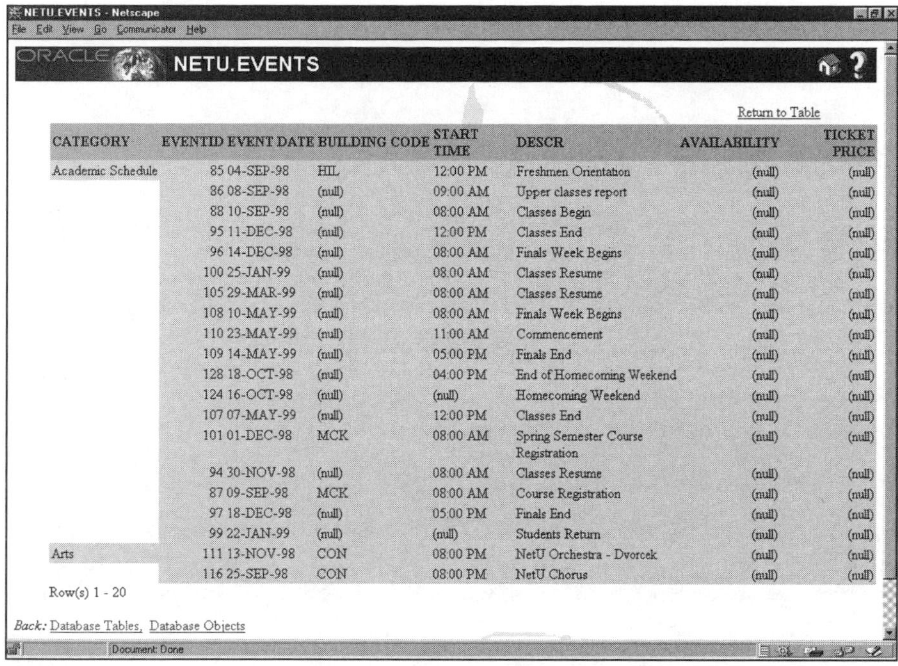
NETU.EVENTS

Return to Table

CATEGORY	EVENTID	EVENT DATE	BUILDING CODE	START TIME	DESCR	AVAILABILITY	TICKET PRICE
Academic Schedule	85	04-SEP-98	HIL	12:00 PM	Freshmen Orientation	(null)	(null)
	86	08-SEP-98	(null)	09:00 AM	Upper classes report	(null)	(null)
	88	10-SEP-98	(null)	08:00 AM	Classes Begin	(null)	(null)
	95	11-DEC-98	(null)	12:00 PM	Classes End	(null)	(null)
	96	14-DEC-98	(null)	08:00 AM	Finals Week Begins	(null)	(null)
	100	25-JAN-99	(null)	08:00 AM	Classes Resume	(null)	(null)
	105	29-MAR-99	(null)	08:00 AM	Classes Resume	(null)	(null)
	108	10-MAY-99	(null)	08:00 AM	Finals Week Begins	(null)	(null)
	110	23-MAY-99	(null)	11:00 AM	Commencement	(null)	(null)
	109	14-MAY-99	(null)	05:00 PM	Finals End	(null)	(null)
	128	18-OCT-98	(null)	04:00 PM	End of Homecoming Weekend	(null)	(null)
	124	16-OCT-98	(null)	(null)	Homecoming Weekend	(null)	(null)
	107	07-MAY-99	(null)	12:00 PM	Classes End	(null)	(null)
	101	01-DEC-98	MCK	08:00 AM	Spring Semester Course Registration	(null)	(null)
	94	30-NOV-98	(null)	08:00 AM	Classes Resume	(null)	(null)
	87	09-SEP-98	MCK	08:00 AM	Course Registration	(null)	(null)
	97	18-DEC-98	(null)	05:00 PM	Finals End	(null)	(null)
	99	22-JAN-99	(null)	(null)	Students Return	(null)	(null)
Arts	111	13-NOV-98	CON	08:00 PM	NetU Orchestra - Dvorcek	(null)	(null)
	116	25-SEP-98	CON	08:00 PM	NetU Chorus	(null)	(null)

Row(s) 1 - 20

Back: Database Tables, Database Objects

Figure 4-10: Data returned from the EVENTS table for browsing

Interacting with Data

As you have probably already noticed, the browsing interface for tables can also be used to update data in a table or to insert new data in a table. WebDB uses two slightly different approaches for updating and inserting data.

Updating data

The selection criteria page has four push buttons at the top and bottom of the page — one for simply querying and returning data, one for querying data for update, one for inserting data, and one to reset the form.

23. Return to the Query and Update table from the query results page by clicking the Back push button of your browser.

If you use the Back push button on your browser to return to the selection page, your selection criteria are still on the page. If you use the hotlink labeled Return to Table, you will return to the default selection page.

24. Click the Query & Update push button at the top of the page.

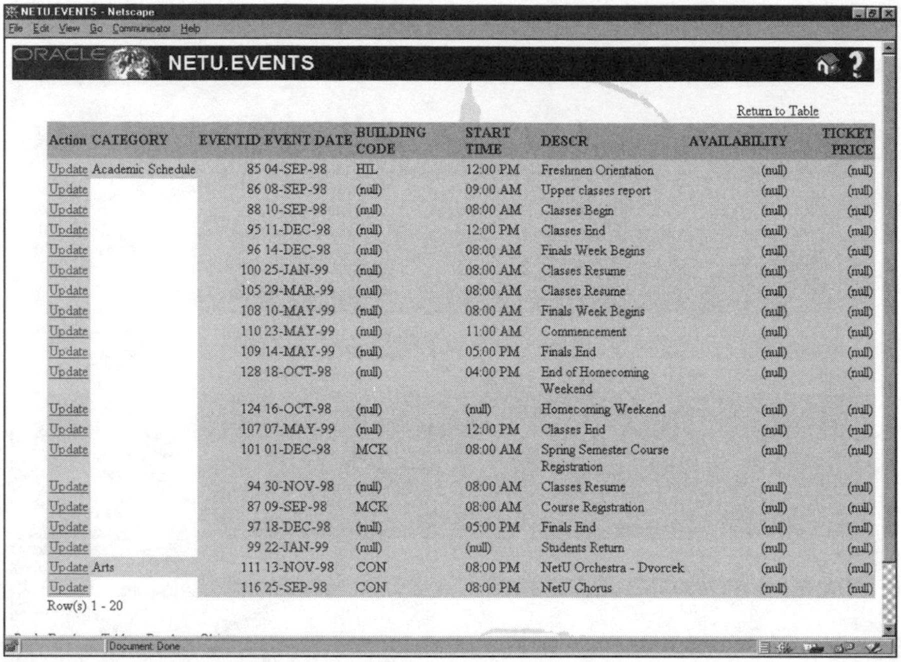
NETU.EVENTS - Netscape
File Edit View Go Communicator Help
ORACLE
NETU.EVENTS
Return to Table
Action CATEGORY EVENTID EVENT DATE BUILDING CODE START TIME DESCR AVAILABILITY TICKET PRICE
Update Academic Schedule 85 04-SEP-98 HIL 12:00 PM Freshmen Orientation (null) (null)
Update 86 08-SEP-98 (null) 09:00 AM Upper classes report (null) (null)
Update 88 10-SEP-98 (null) 08:00 AM Classes Begin (null) (null)
Update 95 11-DEC-98 (null) 12:00 PM Classes End (null) (null)
Update 96 14-DEC-98 (null) 08:00 AM Finals Week Begins (null) (null)
Update 100 25-JAN-99 (null) 08:00 AM Classes Resume (null) (null)
Update 105 29-MAR-99 (null) 08:00 AM Classes Resume (null) (null)
Update 108 10-MAY-99 (null) 08:00 AM Finals Week Begins (null) (null)
Update 110 23-MAY-99 (null) 11:00 AM Commencement (null) (null)
Update 109 14-MAY-99 (null) 05:00 PM Finals End (null) (null)
Update 128 18-OCT-98 (null) 04:00 PM End of Homecoming Weekend (null) (null)
Update 124 16-OCT-98 (null) (null) Homecoming Weekend (null) (null)
Update 107 07-MAY-99 (null) 12:00 PM Classes End (null) (null)
Update 101 01-DEC-98 MCK 08:00 AM Spring Semester Course Registration (null) (null)
Update 94 30-NOV-98 (null) 08:00 AM Classes Resume (null) (null)
Update 87 09-SEP-98 MCK 08:00 AM Course Registration (null) (null)
Update 97 18-DEC-98 (null) 05:00 PM Finals End (null) (null)
Update 99 22-JAN-99 (null) (null) Students Return (null) (null)
Update Arts 111 13-NOV-98 CON 08:00 PM NetU Orchestra - Dvorcek (null) (null)
Update 116 25-SEP-98 CON 08:00 PM NetU Chorus (null) (null)
Row(s) 1 - 20
Document: Done

Figure 4-11: Data returned for update

When you return data for updating, it looks very similar to the data returned from a normal query, as shown in Figure 4-11.

Using the selection criteria page to retrieve data that you can update is no different from using the selection criteria page to retrieve data that is only for reading. You can specify all the same selection and formatting options as you would to simply query the data. The data is returned in an almost identical format to the data returned for browsing, except that each row has a column at the beginning of the row with a hotlink on the Update label. When you click this hotlink, you are taken to a new page, as shown in Figure 4-12.

The update page has a data entry field for each column that was displayed in the returned data. Each field is filled with the values for the row you chose to update. You can change any of the values on this page.

Once you have modified the data on this page, you can click the Update push button to send your changes to the database and return to the previous browsing window. If you want to roll back the changes you have made on this page, you can click the Reset push button, which returns the data values that were present when you first came to this page, and then click the Update push button.

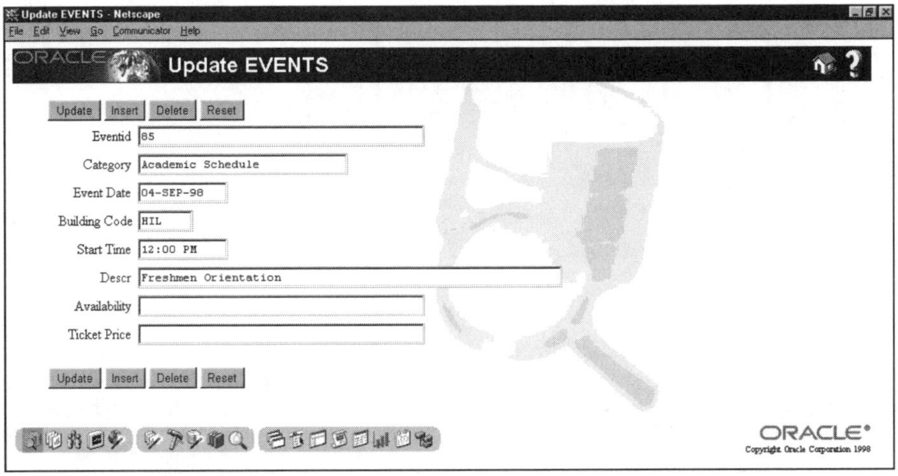

Figure 4-12: Updating data

You can also use the Update functionality to delete rows from the database. You query the data for update and click the Update hotlink to select the row. Once the update page comes up, click the Delete push button to delete the data from the database.

If you want to cancel a pending database change, you can simply use the Back button on your browser to return to the previous page. WebDB doesn't take any action until you click the appropriate push button on the Update page, so any changes you made in that page are lost when you return to the previous page.

Inserting data

To insert a new row of data into a database table, you use the same page that you use for specifying query conditions. Instead of entering selection criteria, you enter the values that you want to insert into the database and click the Insert New Row push button.

If you insert data into a table by clicking the Insert New Row push button, you get a result page back from WebDB similar to the page shown in Figure 4-13.

If you have inserted data that is appropriate for the columns and the table, you get a success message page as shown in Figure 4-13. But sometimes it doesn't quite work out that way.

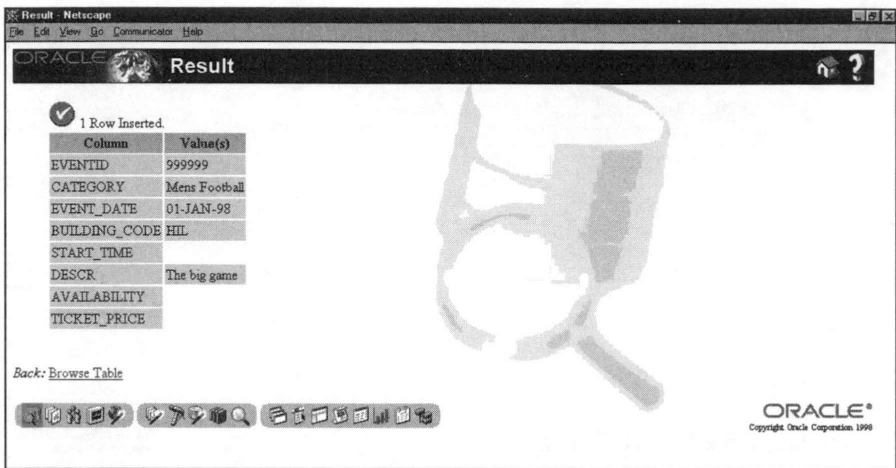

Column	Value(s)
EVENTID	999999
CATEGORY	Mens Football
EVENT_DATE	01-JAN-98
BUILDING_CODE	HIL
START_TIME	
DESCR	The big game
AVAILABILITY	
TICKET_PRICE	

Figure 4-13: The results of a successful insert

Issues with writing data

WebDB does give you an easy way to insert and update data in the database through the Browse interface; however, WebDB is not smart enough to make sure that the data you are entering is valid data. When you define a database table, you usually specify some sort of integrity rules for the data. These rules can require that a value for a particular column must already exist in a different column in a different table.

For instance, the CATEGORY column in the EVENTS table can only have certain values that already exist in the CATEGORIES table. The page that you can use to insert or update data in the Browse section of WebDB does not perform any checks to make sure that your data adheres to the integrity rules for the data in the database. The Oracle database checks these rules before it makes any changes to the data, and the database returns an error to you if the new values for the data violate any of these rules, as shown in Figure 4-14.

The Browse interface to your data is very useful, but it is not designed to replace a custom application system you might use WebDB to build. Just as the browsing capability of WebDB does not replace the report components, the same capability does not replace the need to create customized forms for entering data. If you want to allow end users to modify data in the database, you should design a form for them to use that enforces all the integrity constraints in the form to avoid this type of error message. Later in this book, you will learn how to create user interface objects based on lists of values to specifically avoid this type of database integrity error.

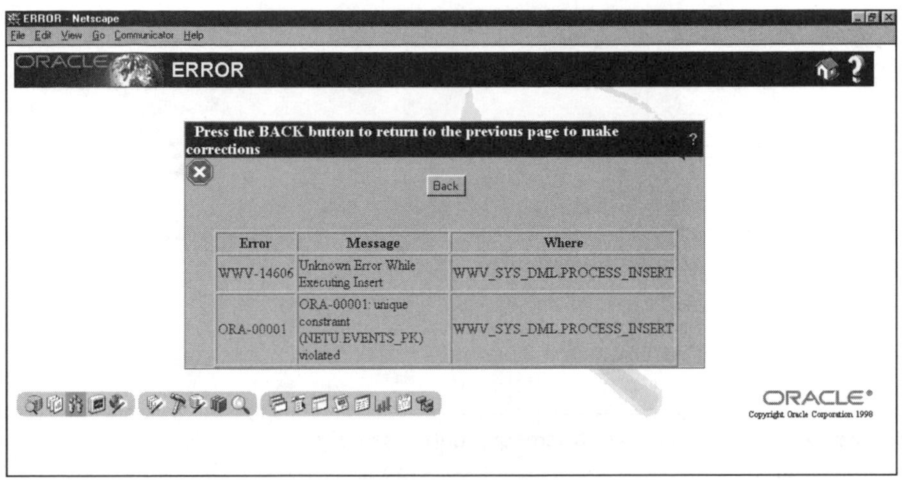

Figure 4-14: An error returned from the Oracle database because of integrity rules

Creating Database Objects

This chapter has covered browsing different database objects. One thing you cannot do through the WebDB browsing interface is create new database objects.

You can create database objects with WebDB through the Build interface. WebDB provides you with somewhat less power when you create database objects than it does for creating other components, but you can still use this functionality to add objects to your database.

Because the script you used to load the sample data into your database created all the necessary database objects for you, you do not need to actually create any database objects for this book. As a result, this section only discusses the typical pages used to create database objects.

The area of WebDB that is used to create database objects is found off the main Build menu, under the menu choice for Database Objects. You can also get there through the shortcuts toolbar.

The main page for building database objects is shown in Figure 4-15. This page gives you graphical menu choices for creating different types of database objects — functions, indexes, packages, procedures, sequences, synonyms, tables, triggers, and views.

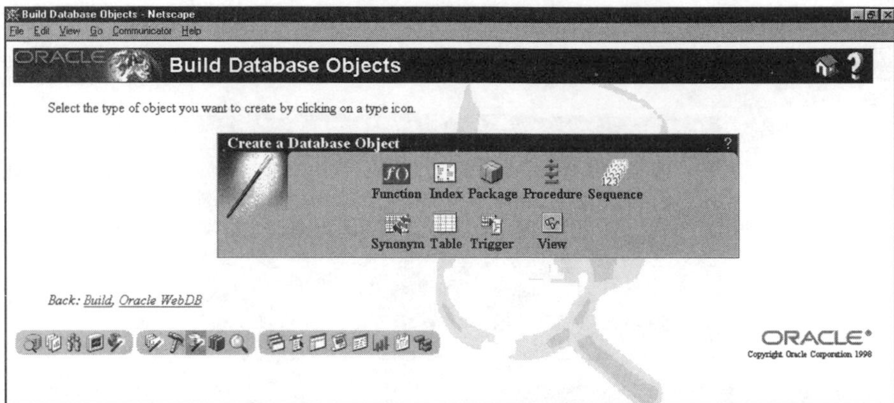

Figure 4-15: The main page for creating database objects

If you click an icon to create one of the database objects, you are taken to a wizard that walks you through the process of creating the specified type of database object. Because all of these creation wizards are fairly similar, you can get an idea of the range of wizards by examining two of the more commonly used wizards.

Creating a table

You can start by exploring the wizard for creating database tables. Because you do not need to perform any actions in this section, there aren't any specific instructions, but you can follow along with the explanation by clicking the Table icon on the main Build Database Objects page.

The first page, as shown in Figure 4-16, is the same for all of the database object creation wizards — in fact, it is the first page for all WebDB wizards, as you will see throughout this book. You must select a schema from a list of schemas that are available to you, and then you must enter a name for the table that the wizard will create. Each table must have a unique name within its own schema. If you enter a name for an object that already exists in the schema, WebDB notifies you of this conflict with an error message as soon as you leave the first page. You must return to the page and give the table a different name.

All the different types of database objects have a slightly different set of pages for most of the rest of the wizard operations. The purpose of all but the final page in the wizards is to prompt you for the information needed to create the database object. For a database table, the next page in the wizard (shown in Figure 4-17) enables you to enter the columns that make up the table. The page has spaces to enter information about six columns in the table. If you need to define a table that has more than six columns, you can click the Add More push button at the bottom of the panel.

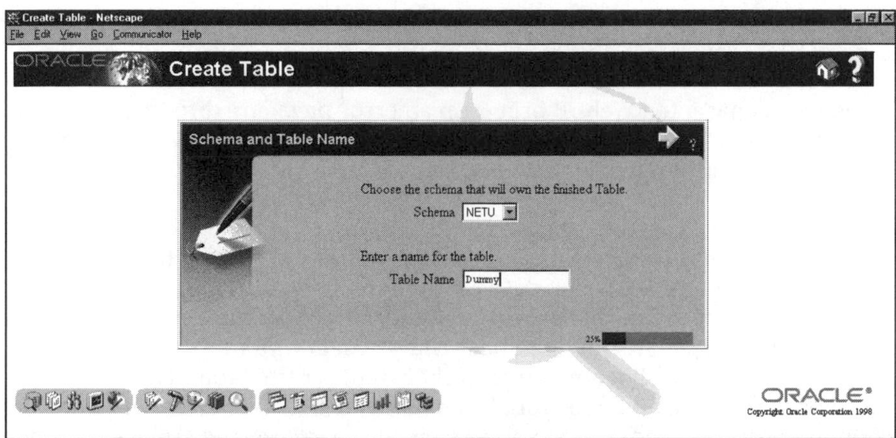

Figure 4-16: The first page of the table creation wizard

For each column, you have to enter a column name, a datatype for the column, a length for the column, and, if the column is a numeric column, a precision for the column. Each column has check boxes that enable you to specify whether null values are allowed for the column or not, and whether the column is a primary key for the table.

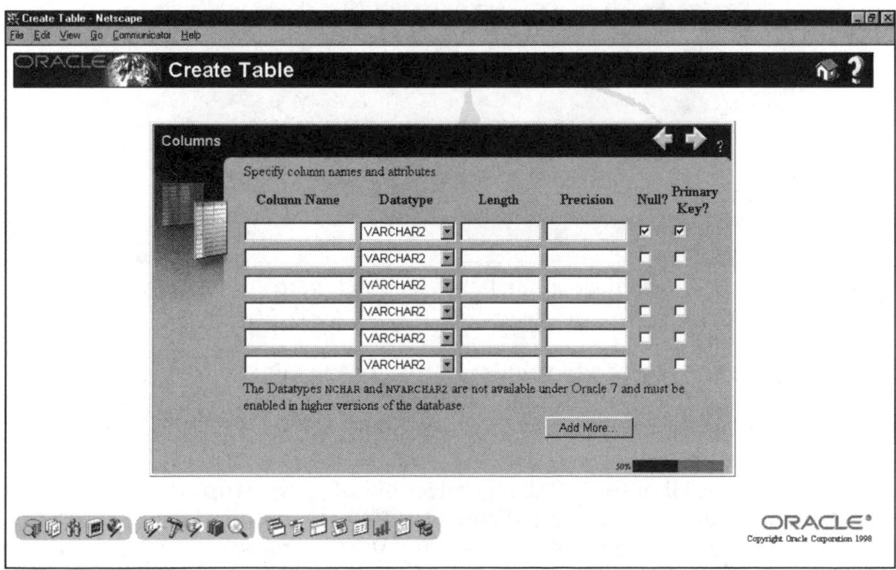

Figure 4-17: The Columns page in the table creation wizard

When you try to move to the next page in the table creation wizard, WebDB does some rudimentary error checking for the values you entered for the columns. For instance, if you entered a value for the Precision data field for a column that you defined as a character, WebDB brings up an error page and directs you back to the previous page of the table creation wizard. Similarly, WebDB gives you an error if you assign a length to a column defined as an INTEGER.

The next page of the table creation wizard, as shown in Figure 4-18, prompts you for information about how the data in the table will be stored. You have to specify the tablespace for the table, which defaults to the tablespace specified for the schema that owns the table. You can also specify information about the extents for the table. An *extent* is an area of disk space that is used for a table. The initial extent is the amount of space allocated for the first extent for the table. The next extent is the amount of space allocated for all subsequent extents needed for the table. The minimum and maximum extent values specify the fewest and greatest number of extents that can be used for a table. All values for all the extent fields use an integer followed by either the letter *K* for kilobytes or the letter *M* for megabytes.

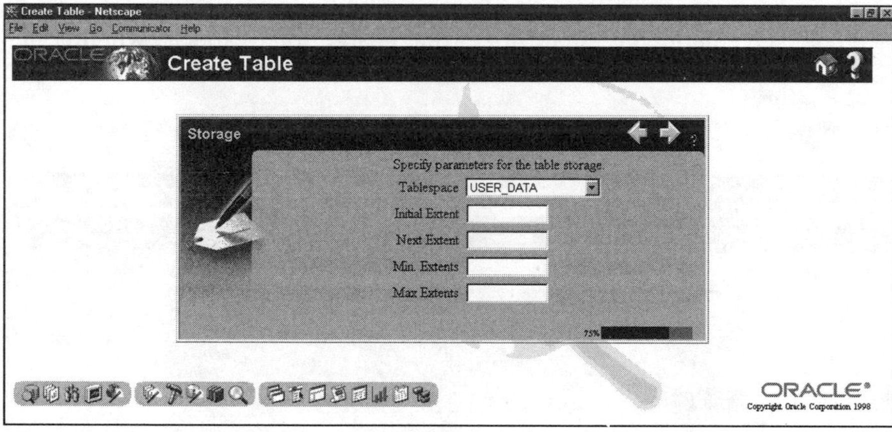

Figure 4-18: The Storage page in the table creation wizard

You don't have to specify any values on the storage panel of the table creation wizard, because the extent information is optional and the tablespace has a default value.

The final page for all of the database object creation wizards is the same for all WebDB components, as shown in Figure 4-19. When you click the OK push button, WebDB creates a table in the database using the parameters you designated in the wizard and returns you to the main page for building database objects.

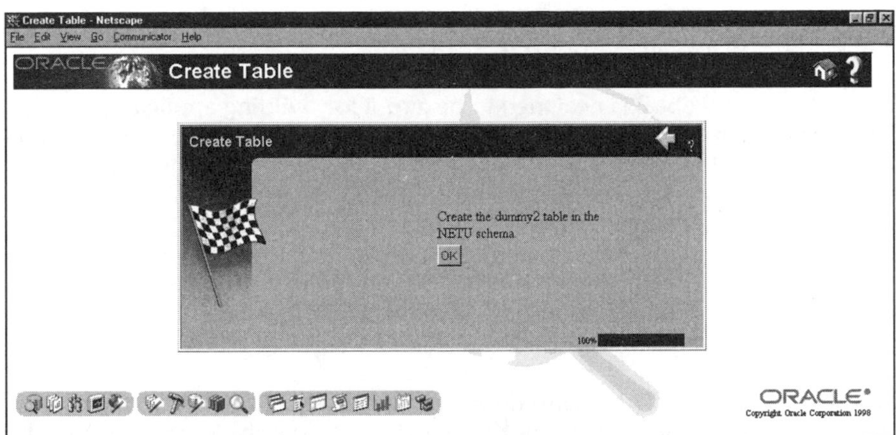

Figure 4-19: The final page of the table creation wizard

Some of the other database object creation wizards are not quite so wizard-like. The view creation wizard, for example, simply prompts you for the name of the view and then gives you a text area where you can add the SQL necessary to create the view. If you enter an SQL statement that does not properly execute, WebDB sends you an error page after you click the OK push button at the end of the wizard, as shown in Figure 4-20.

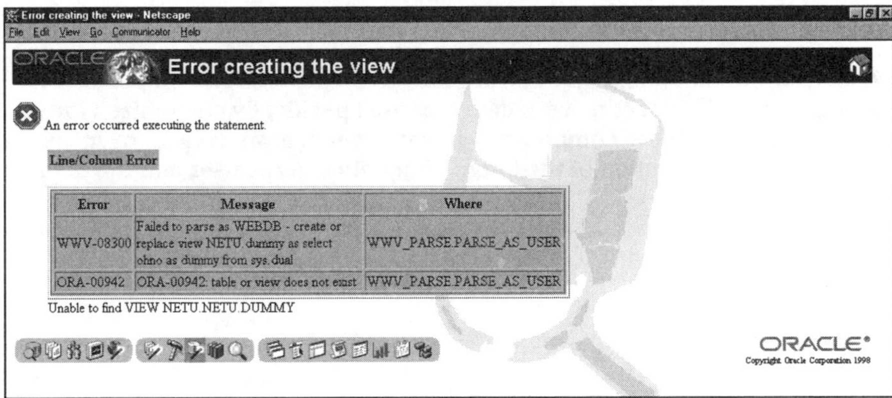

Figure 4-20: The results of an SQL error in creating a view

Although it has some useful features, the database object builder is more like a utility than a true WebDB builder. It's nice to be able to create a table by just entering some parameters, but it is not that much more difficult to enter the SQL statement, especially if you are already familiar with SQL. Why would you use the database object builder in WebDB instead of a different Oracle utility, such as the Oracle Enterprise Manager or even SQL*Plus?

Remember that WebDB is designed to be a tool for building applications, not databases. There are many wonderful utilities and products out there to help you to design and build your database. And, as an Oracle user, you probably already realize that spending time designing and implementing your database objects provides a solid foundation for any subsequent use of the database in applications. But there may be times when you are using WebDB and want to quickly add a database object without leaving the WebDB environment. There may be other times when you cannot get to another utility or tool from the machine that you are running but you can use WebDB because it only requires a browser environment.

WebDB's database object wizard does give you one small advantage: It correctly creates a database object without the need for SQL syntax. Most of us have had the frustrating experience of starting one of these statements with the word "craete," which doesn't work so well.

Wrapping Up

The browsing capability in WebDB is an extremely powerful part of WebDB. In fact, you may choose to use WebDB as one of your options for administering data and database objects because it is so easy to use. But the capabilities delivered by the Browse functionality of WebDB are too generalized to be of use in creating WebDB application systems.

In the next few chapters, you will learn how to create WebDB components for reading data and interacting with data that are specifically customized for your application tasks. These components give you much more control over the appearance and operation of the interaction between the user and the data.

✦ ✦ ✦

Building WebDB Reports

In This Chapter

Building a Simple Report Component

Editing a Report Component

Running a Report

Using a computer is, at its most basic level, a matter of working with data. Most data is read much more often than it is written. Reporting is the process of reading data and presenting it in a meaningful and understandable format, so building a report is a good place to start learning about WebDB components.

Because many of you have probably come to WebDB in part to make data from your Oracle database widely available over the Internet or an intranet, you will be creating and using a lot of reports with WebDB.

Building a Basic Report

You can jump right into building your first report component with WebDB. You can build a report component either by using the Query Wizard or by writing an SQL statement that supplies data to the report. The first page of the Report Builder Wizard is the same for both methods, and is followed by two slightly different sets of pages, and then concluded with the same set of pages for both methods.

Defining a report

You use the first page of the Report Builder Wizard to identify the report you are building.

1. Log into WebDB as the NETUDEV user.
2. Click the Build menu choice on the WebDB home page.
3. Click the User Interface Components menu choice on the main Build page.

4. Click the Reports menu choice on the main User Interface Components page.

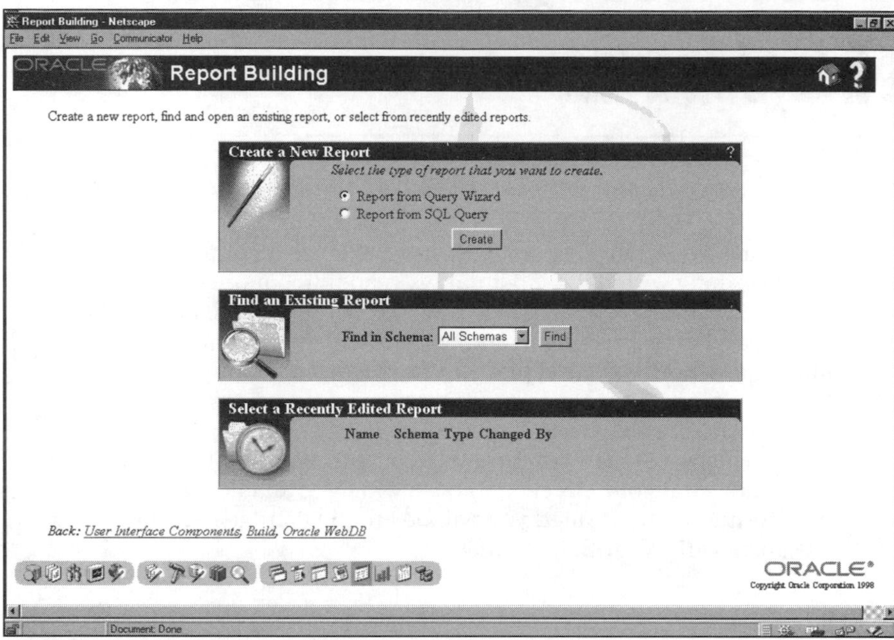

Figure 5-1: The first page of the Report Builder Wizard

You have arrived at the main page for creating report components, which is illustrated in Figure 5-1. You could have also gotten to this page by clicking the Reports icon in the shortcuts bar located at the bottom of most pages in WebDB. You can see that the Reports icon in the shortcuts tool bar is highlighted when you are in the report building section of WebDB, which provides an easy way to return to the beginning of the report building process.

The first page of the Report Builder Wizard has a similar look and feel to the first page of all of the other component creation wizards in WebDB. At the top of the page, there is a panel with two basic options for defining how you want to create a report:

✦ With the Query Wizard, which walks you through a series of pages that help you define the data you want in the report

✦ By creating your own SQL statement

Both of these choices deliver the same result — they enable you to define the data for the report. You will learn more about these two options later in this chapter.

The middle panel in the first page of the Report Builder enables you to search for a particular report by searching either all schemas for which you have security access or by selecting a particular schema to search. The results of the search are returned on a page similar to the one displayed in Figure 5-2, with a summary of the search criteria at the top of the page and a brief description of each report below. You can call up any of the returned reports for editing by clicking the Component Name, which acts as a hotlink that takes you to the editing area for reports.

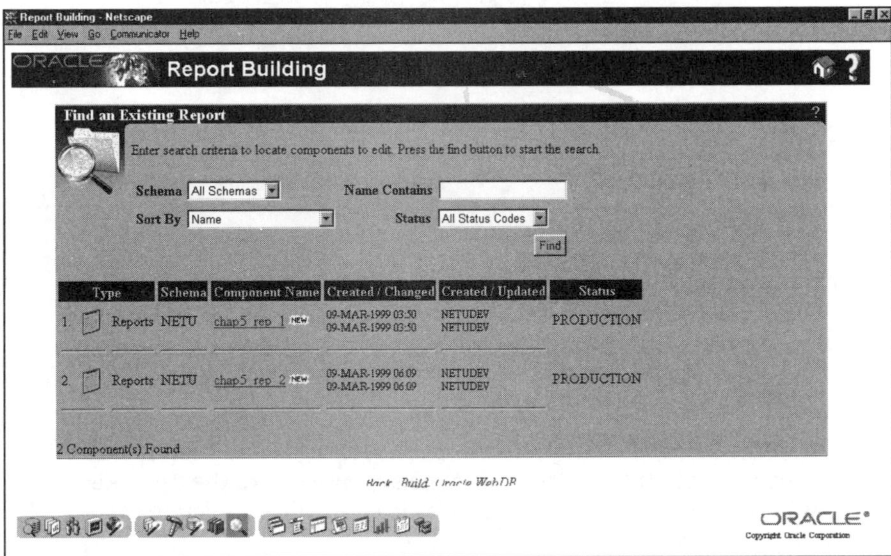

Figure 5-2: Sample screen returned by searching for a report by schema

At the bottom of the first page of the Report Builder Wizard is a panel containing a list of the most recently created WebDB report components. If you want to quickly return to some of your most recently created reports, you can simply click the report name at the bottom of the first Report Builder Wizard page to bring up the report component and edit it. You will use this interface later in this chapter to work on a report you create in this section.

Use the Query Wizard initially to define the data for your first simple report. You can then take a look at the same process of defining data with an SQL query later in this section.

5. Click the radio button that selects the Query Wizard for defining data in the top panel of the main Report Building page.

6. Click the Create push button to bring up the page shown in Figure 5-3.

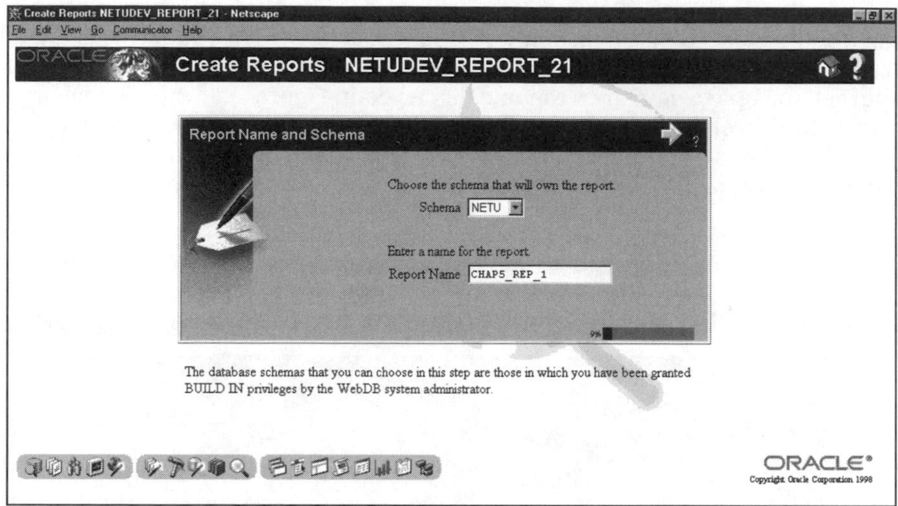

Figure 5-3: The first page of the Report Builder Wizard

You have arrived at the first page of the Report Builder Wizard. There are two data fields on this page. The top field asks you for the name of the schema that will hold the report you are creating. As with all other parts of WebDB, the schema combo box lists all the schemas that you have Build Privileges for. Keep in mind that the schema you select in this combo box is the schema where the report is stored, not necessarily where the data the report uses is kept. You will define the actual report data in the next few pages.

The second data field asks for a name for the report, which is actually the name of the procedure stored in the WebDB repository that creates the report at run time. You can enter any report name that is unique in its own schema. Of course, you should use some naming convention for all of your WebDB components to make it easier to find them later in the development process. Because the purpose of this report is to be a part of the example application system you are building for this book, we have chosen the chapter number followed by a descriptive identifier followed by a number as our naming convention.

7. Select the NETU schema in the top combo box in the first Report Builder Wizard page and enter the name **ch5_rep_1** as the name of the report.

8. Click the Next arrow on the Report Name and Schema page, which is the yellow arrow pointing to the right at the top of the panel.

The first page of the Report Builder Wizard is the same whether you are defining the data with the Query Wizard or creating your own SQL statement. The next few pages in the Report Builder Wizard are different, depending on whether you are using the Query Wizard or entering an SQL query by hand. The next two sections discuss each of the two methods that define the data used in a simple report, and then the chapter continues with the pages in the Report Builder Wizard that are common to both approaches.

The Query Wizard

The Query Wizard is the part of the Report Builder Wizard that walks you through the definition of the columns you use as the basis for your report, and also enables you to indicate selection criteria to be passed to the report.

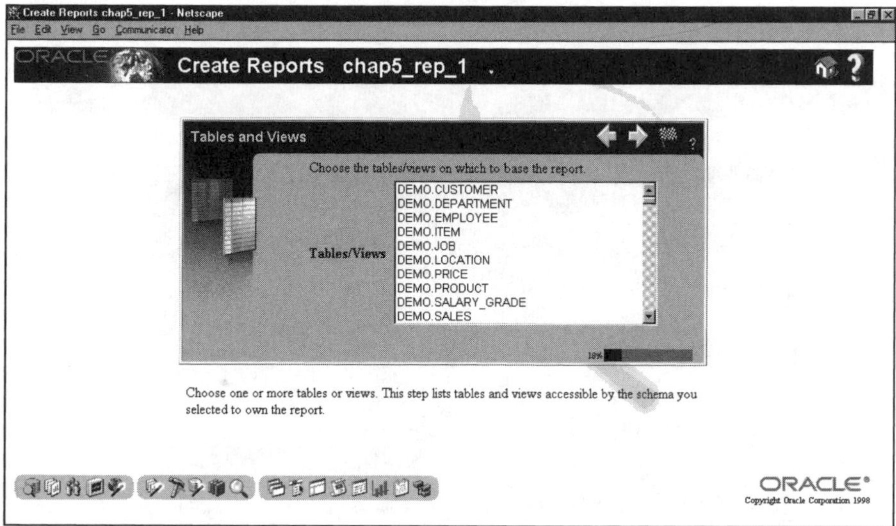

Figure 5-4: The second page of the Report Builder Wizard with the Query Wizard

The second page of the Report Builder Wizard with the Query Wizard is shown in Figure 5-4. This page has a simple list box with all the tables and views that you can access. Each table is displayed with the schema name for the table preceding the table name, separated by a period. For reporting, there is no difference between using a view or a table, as you are only reading the data.

Because you can use one or more tables or views in a report, you can select more than one table or view in the list box in this page of the Query Wizard portion of the Report Builder Wizard. You can use the standard methods of selecting multiple files, such as clicking individual files while holding down the Ctrl key, or selecting a range of tables by clicking the top and bottom entries in the range while holding down the Shift key. To select a range of tables, you can also click a table and drag the mouse over the desired range.

Note The previous description applies to using WebDB on a PC. On a Mac, the keystrokes are slightly different to conform to the Mac standard.

There is a lot to learn about in the Report Builder Wizard, so you should select a single table from the NETU sample data for this first report.

9. Select the NETU.UGRADS table and click the Next arrow.

The next page of the Query Wizard, shown in Figure 5-5, enables you to select the columns that appear in the report from the tables or views you have selected.

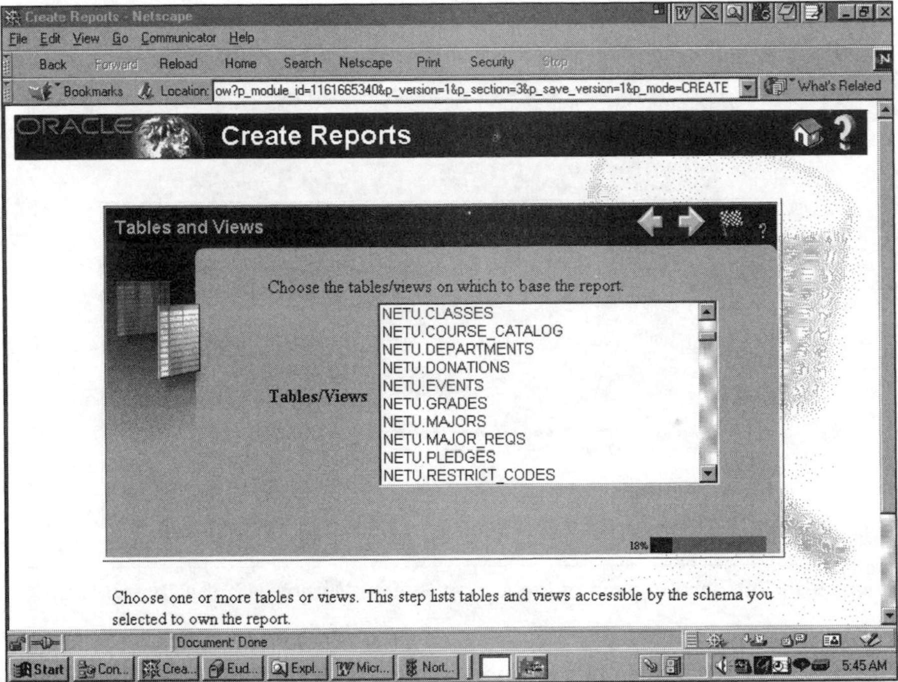

Figure 5-5: Selecting columns in the Query Wizard

This page has the familiar look and feel of a pick list in the client/server environment. You can select one or more columns in the left-hand list box and move them to the right-hand list box with the right-arrow push button between the two list boxes. You can move selected columns from the right-hand list box to the left by following the same procedure and clicking the left-arrow push button. There are also two additional push buttons that enable you to move all the columns from one list box to the other. The columns are added to the Selected Columns list box in the order that they are moved to this list box. You do not have to select a column to use it for a selection or join condition.

Your report is built to display the columns in the order that they were moved to the Selected Columns list box, so you have to make sure your selections in are displayed in the right order to guarantee the correct formatting and functionality in your finished report. You can move individual columns up and down in the Selected Columns list box by using the up- and down-arrow push buttons to the right of the list box.

10. Select the column UGRADS.MAJOR in the left-hand list box and move it to the right-hand list box by clicking on the right arrow push button between the list boxes.

11. Follow the same instructions to move the UGRADS.CLASSYR, UGRADS.LASTNAME, UGRADS.FIRSTNAME, and UGRADS.PHONE columns to the Selected Columns list box.

You have to move the MAJOR and CLASSYR columns individually, but you could select the LASTNAME, FIRSTNAME, and PHONE columns at the same time and move them all over with a single click on the right-arrow push button. You could also move all these columns to the Selected Columns list box together, and then move the MAJOR and CLASSYR columns to the top of the column list.

12. Click the Next arrow on the Table/View Columns page.

The next page that comes up as part of the Query Wizard section of the Report Builder Wizard enables you to define conditions used to limit the data shown in the report. Because we cover adding conditions later in this chapter, you can simply go past this page.

13. Click the Next arrow on the Column Conditions page.

The next page of the Query Wizard portion of the Report Builder Wizard, as shown in Figure 5-6, enables you to specify the formatting for the columns you selected on the previous page.

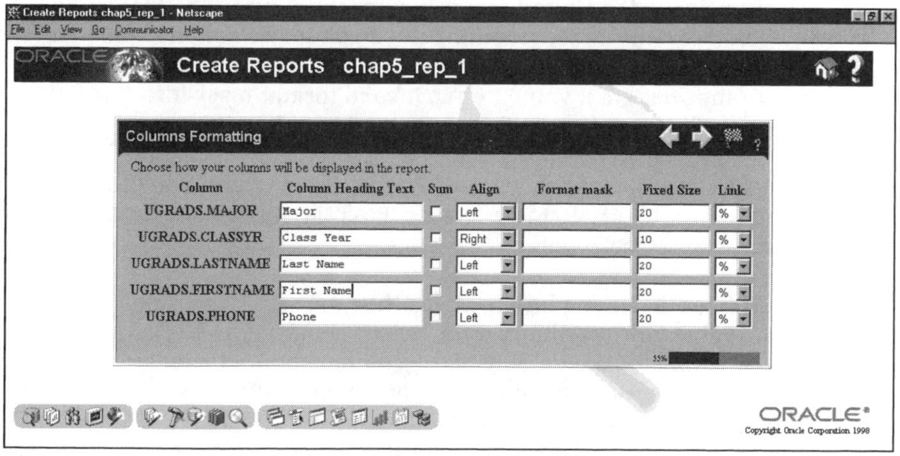

Figure 5-6: Formatting columns in the Query Wizard

There is a formatting line on this page for each column you have selected for the report. For each column, you can specify the text that appears in the column heading, which, by default, is the name of the column with the first letter capitalized.

14. Change the Column Heading Text for the CLASSYR column to **Class Year**, the LASTNAME column to **Last Name**, and the FIRSTNAME column to **First Name**.

Each formatting line contains a check box that you can select to indicate that the column can potentially be summed in the report. If you just check the Sum box, your report will have sums at the end of each page for the page and for the total report up to that time. If you want to sum a value after a particular value in a column in the report changes, you have to order the report according to that column and break the report on the column. You will learn how to do this later in this chapter.

Be aware that you can check the Sum box for any column in your report, including character and date columns. It doesn't make sense to be able to sum any values that are not numbers, so you should not check the Sum box for any nonnumeric columns.

The next field in the column line is a combo box where you can specify how the value of the column is formatted—left, right, or centered. The default value for the alignment is left-justified for character and date values and right-justified for numeric values. The column headings and any summed values are also aligned based on the value specified in this combo box.

The next field in each column line enables you to format the value in the column line. You can use standard Oracle formatting for numeric or date values. Basically, this means you can specify the separators and the decimal symbol for a number and the display format for a date. If you have a column that you wanted to display as a monetary value in the United States, you would type **$999,999,999.99** into the formatting field, with the 9s representing the digits in the column value and the dollar sign, the commas, and the decimal point added for clarity. Leading zeros are automatically suppressed. If you enter an invalid format mask into this field, the resulting report has the value displayed as a string of # signs.

What types of formatting can you use? Any format mask that you can use with the Oracle function TO_CHAR, to be specific. Basically, this means currency symbols, commas, and decimal points.

The next field in each column line contains the number of characters that are used to display the value for the column if the report is output as ASCII, or preformatted, text. The fixed length for the display of the column should be long enough to contain the largest possible value for the column and any formatting characters you have added to the column. The default values for the data in your report are pretty simple: 10 for numeric values, 20 for dates, and 20 for character values. You will probably have to adjust these values, but only if you plan on using preformatted ASCII text as the output format for your report. The value for this column is ignored for HTML or Excel formats.

The final field in each column formatting line enables you to specify a link for the column. Links are one of the primary ways that you can build complete application systems with WebDB. You will learn more about links in Chapter 17 of this book.

15. Click the Next arrow on the Columns Formatting page.

The rest of the pages for the Report Builder Wizard are the same whether you use the Query Wizard or an SQL statement to specify data for the report. Before moving on to those pages, you should learn how to specify data with an SQL statement, and why you might want to take that approach on occasion.

Specifying data with SQL

On the first page of the Report Builder Wizard, your first choice is to use the Query Wizard, as described previously, and your second choice is to base your report on an SQL statement. The two methods of defining report data end up in the same place, but it is worth understanding both methods, regardless of which one you choose to use for a particular report.

Because you can only define one report at a time, if you have been using the Query Wizard up to this point, you have to finish out the report before you can begin creating a report with an SQL query. If you plan to use the Query Wizard mainly with WebDB and you are following along with the instructions for the book, just read through this section. You will be able to pick up with the process for the remainder of the pages of the Report Builder Wizard with your original report.

1. If you want to finish the previous report, click the checkered flag at the top of the page.
2. Return to the main Report Building page by selecting the Reports icon from the shortcuts bar.
3. Select the Report from SQL Query option and click the Create push button.
4. Select the NETU schema to own the report and give the report the name of **ch5_rep_2**. Click the Next arrow.

The first page in the Report Builder Wizard for describing the data source for a report with an SQL query is shown in Figure 5-7.

The only field in this page is a large scrollable text field where you can enter your SQL query. The text window has a default SQL statement, which you have to remove.

5. Select the entire SQL query in the text window and delete it.

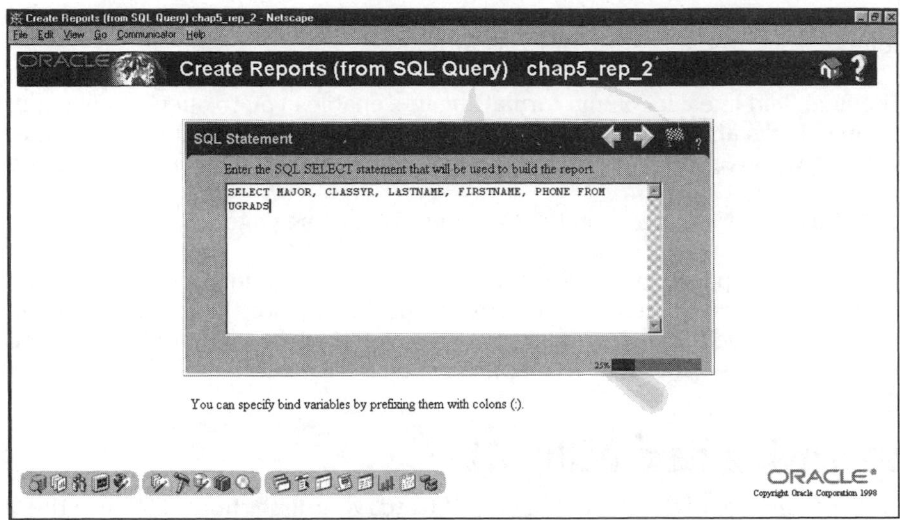

Figure 5-7: Specifying an SQL query in the Report Builder Wizard

6. Enter the following query into the text window in the SQL Statement page of the Report Builder Wizard:

   ```
   SELECT MAJOR, CLASSYR, LASTNAME, FIRSTNAME, PHONE FROM UGRADS
   ```

   The SQL statement you have just entered gives you the same data for your report that the steps you took in the Query Wizard did.

7. Click the Next arrow on the SQL Statement page.

Figure 5-8 shows the next page that comes up in the Report Builder Wizard. It looks a lot like the page you can use to specify the formatting options for individual columns in the Query Wizard, with one small difference.

If you are using WebDB with a version of Oracle prior to Version 8, there is another difference. For pre-Oracle8 use, the column names are shown as C_001, C_002, and so on. This is because the standard return values from a query in versions of Oracle prior to Version 8 only gave these default column names – in Version 8 and later, the return values specify the actual names of the columns.

There is no option to provide a link for a column on the Columns Formatting page when you are creating your own SQL statement. You can still include a link for a report that you base on an SQL query, but you have to specify the syntax for the link as part of your SQL statement. As mentioned previously, you will learn a lot more about links later in this book.

In order to provide nicer headings for the report and to match up with the data that was specified with the Query Wizard, you should change the Column Heading Text for some of the fields.

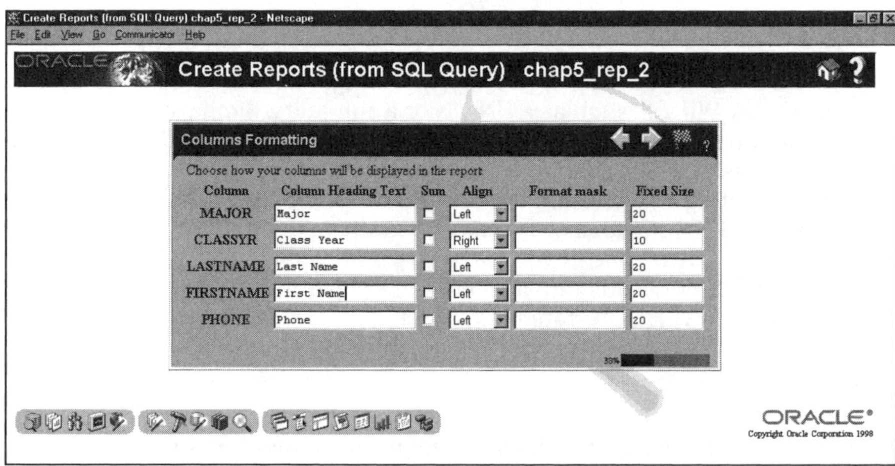

Figure 5-8: Column formatting with an SQL query

8. Change the Column Heading Text for the CLASSYR column to **Class Year**, the LASTNAME column to **Last Name**, and the FIRSTNAME column to **First Name**.
9. Click the Next arrow on the Columns Formatting page.

Before moving on to the rest of the Report Builder Wizard, it makes sense to review why you would want to use an SQL query instead of the Query Wizard to specify the data in your report. There are three basic reasons for this choice:

✦ You are already familiar with SQL. If you are experienced with SQL, you very well may find the process of entering an SQL query faster and more straightforward than using the Query Wizard. There is the possibility that you might make a mistake when entering your SQL query. However, the SQL statement is submitted to the Oracle database as soon as you attempt to move to the next page in the wizard and any errors are returned to you at that point.

The error-handling capability of WebDB for SQL statements is not the best. The errors you receive back are often less than helpful in pointing to the part of the SQL statement that may be at fault. The authors of this book have found that it makes sense to use a tool like SQL*Plus to refine your SQL statement and then cut and paste the statement into WebDB.

✦ You already have reports that are based on existing SQL statements. You can directly lift SQL statements from existing reports and paste them into the SQL statement text window. Reusing existing SQL statements ensures the use of a correct SQL statement and makes using your own SQL statement faster than trying to re-create the statement with the Query Wizard.

✦ You want to specify data in a way that goes beyond the capabilities of the Query Wizard. This can cover a lot of ground. You may want to use a SQL construct that you cannot implement through the easy graphical interface of the Query Wizard, such as a UNION or a subquery. Similarly, you may want to add some parameters to your report that the Query Wizard does not allow, such as using comparison operators (BETWEEN, for example), or implementing a compound condition. You might also want to use some of the power of SQL functions or formatting to shape the data before it goes to the report. As an example, if you wanted to combine the data in the LASTNAME and FIRSTNAME fields into a single value separated by a comma, you could use the following SQL statement:

```
SELECT MAJOR, CLASSYR, (LASTNAME || ', ' || FIRSTNAME) Name,
PHONE FROM UGRADS
```

The bottom line on using an SQL statement as the foundation for your reports is that you can use any valid SQL statement to define the data for the report. We believe that it is always better to be able to use a product to accomplish your specific task, and the ability to write your own SQL statements gives you a lot of flexibility. You will use your own SQL statements later in this book to create reports that deliver information outside the realm of the Query Wizard.

The rest of the Report Builder Wizard is the same for both methods of defining data.

Shaping your report

The rest of the pages in the Report Builder Wizard shape the report that is based on the data you just specified. The remaining steps for creating your first full report are the same, regardless of whether you used the Query Wizard or not, so you can continue building either ch5_rep1 or ch5_rep2 for the rest of this section.

The next page of the Report Builder Wizard, shown in Figure 5-9, contains a lot of display options for your report.

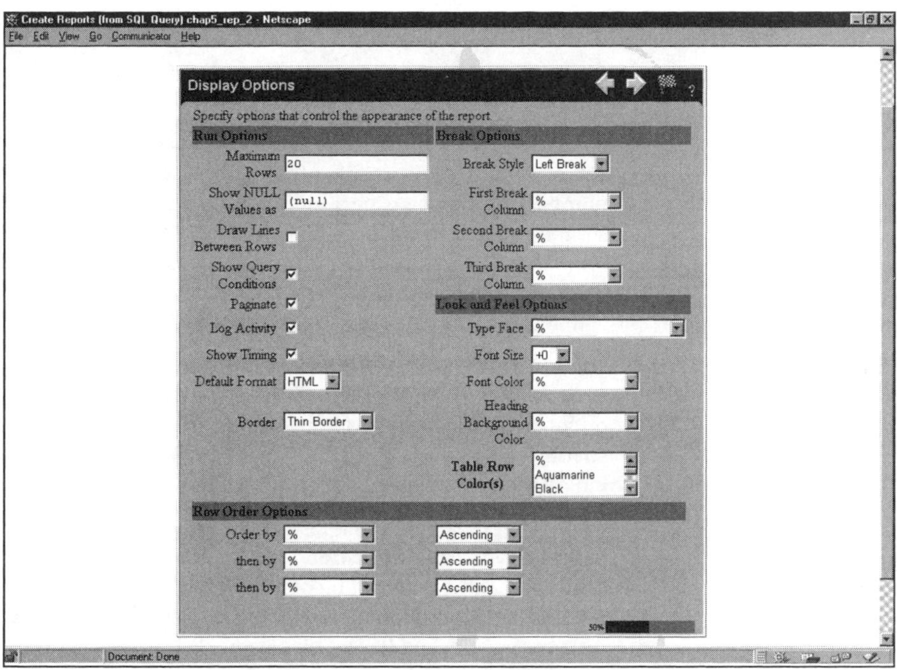

Figure 5-9: Display options in the Report Builder Wizard

Table 5-1 **Display Options**	
Options	***Effect***
Maximum Rows	The Maximum Rows option enables you to specify how many rows are returned on each page of your report. The more rows that are returned per page, the more data per page, and the longer the page takes to be sent back to the client browser from the server. If there are more rows in your report than can fit on a single page, a Next push button appears at the bottom of the page. If the user has moved to a page beyond the first page of the report, a Previous push button also appears at the bottom of the page. There is always a status line at the bottom of the page that indicates which set of rows are displayed on the page.

Continued

Table 5-1 (continued)

Options	*Effect*
	If you want to have the entire report delivered as a single page, set the Maximum Rows value to a number at least equal to the number of rows you expect to be returned from the query and set the Paginate check box to unchecked. This is especially important if you plan to direct the output to an Excel file and want to make sure that all the data is included in the spreadsheet. The default value for Maximum Rows is 20.
Show NULL Values as	You can specify what value you want in your report when the underlying data contains a null value. The default value for this option is (null). Because a null value is different from a series of spaces for a character field, you might want to have some way of indicating nulls with this option. If you want to suppress the display of any value for NULLs in the database, you can enter ** **, which is HTML-speak for a blank. The authors do not recommend this approach, because WebDB automatically suppresses the display of repeating values for a break field, and having blanks for NULLs might cause some confusion.
Draw Lines Between Rows	This check box causes a horizontal line to be inserted between each row in the report. By default, this option is unchecked.
Show Query Conditions	This check box indicates whether you want to display the query conditions for a report at the bottom of the report page.
Paginate	The Paginate option determines whether the push buttons for paging through reports are included at the bottom of the report page. By default, this option is checked. If you uncheck this option, it means that the report only returns the first page of the report. This can be handy if you are sorting the report in a certain order and only want to see the top values for the report. But it can also be very dangerous in that it could give an inaccurate view of the data, because there is no indication on the first report page as to the existence of additional rows for the report.
Log Activity	WebDB gives you the option of logging all WebDB activity for later review. By default, this option is checked.
Show Timing	Your report can show the amount of time the server took to assemble the page returned to the browser if this option is checked. By default, this option is checked.

Options	Effect
Default format	WebDB gives you three different options for formatting your overall report. The first option, which is selected by default, is HTML. HTML format means that your report is formatted using standard HTML proportional fonts in an HTML table. This is the option with the most formatting flexibility, so you will use it frequently. The second option is Excel format. This option outputs the data from the report as an Excel-compatible file. This option is ideal if you are extracting data from your Oracle database for use in a spreadsheet or other data format that can import Excel files. The third option is ASCII text. ASCII formatting means that the report is presented in a fixed-width standard ASCII format. In HTML terms, this means the report is presented between <PRE>, or preformatted, tags. You may want to use this option if the eventual purpose of the report is to take the straight text and put it into another text document that does not support HTML.

Table 5-2
Break Options

Options	Effect
Break Style	This option only has one choice: Left Break.
Break Columns	There are three combo boxes for break columns. The first combo box you select is the primary break column, the second is the next break column, and the third is the final break column. Selecting a column for a break column does not necessarily cause the rows in the report to be sorted on that column value—it only suppresses the display of repeating values for the row. In other words, if you specified MAJOR as the first break column and CLASSYR as the second break column, and specified these as the first and second Order By column, your report would look like Figure 5-10.

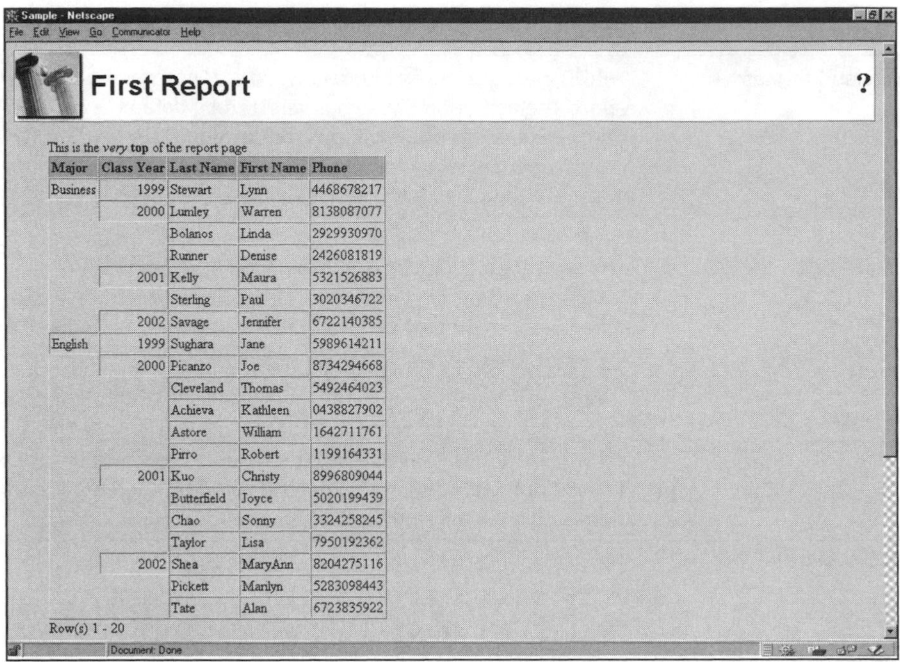

First Report

This is the *very* **top** of the report page

Major	Class Year	Last Name	First Name	Phone
Business	1999	Stewart	Lynn	4468678217
	2000	Lumley	Warren	8138087077
		Bolanos	Linda	2929930970
		Runner	Denise	2426081819
	2001	Kelly	Maura	5321526883
		Sterling	Paul	3020346722
	2002	Savage	Jennifer	6722140385
English	1999	Sughara	Jane	5989614211
	2000	Picanzo	Joe	8734294668
		Cleveland	Thomas	5492464023
		Achieva	Kathleen	0438827902
		Astore	William	1642711761
		Pirro	Robert	1199164331
	2001	Kuo	Christy	8996809044
		Butterfield	Joyce	5020199439
		Chao	Sonny	3324258245
		Taylor	Lisa	7950192362
	2002	Shea	MaryAnn	8204275116
		Pickett	Marilyn	5283098443
		Tate	Alan	6723835922

Row(s) 1 - 20

Figure 5-10: Break groups in a report

Table 5-3
Look and Feel Options

Options	*Effect*
Type Face	HTML gives you the option of using different typefaces, and this combo box gives you a choice of the potential typefaces for your browser. If a user accesses your report with a browser that does not support the typeface you have chosen, the report is displayed in a default font. You can also define *font families* that indicate the replacement font for an unavailable font. Fonts are detailed in depth in Chapter 15. The default for this option, the "%" wild card, also causes the report to be displayed in the default font for the browser.

Options	*Effect*
Font Size	There are eight values for this option — +1 through +4; –1 through –3; and 0, the default choice. Any value other than the default causes the font to be either larger or smaller than the default font. The font size controls the size of the font in the body of the report, but does not affect the size of the heading of the report.
Font Color	This combo box enables you to select the color for the report font from a list of font colors that are available on your browser. The default value, the "%" wild card, causes the font to use the default color for the template or browser you use for the report. Templates are explained in Chapter 15.
Heading Background Color	This combo box enables you to select the color for the background of the heading of the report. The default value, the "%" wild card, causes the heading to use the default color for the template or browser you use for the report.
Table Row Color	All the data in a WebDB report is returned in an HTML table if you choose HTML as the display option. As the name implies, this combo box enables you to choose the background color for the report table from a list of colors. The default value for this choice, the "%" wild card, means that there is no color specified for the table background and the table defaults to the color of the background page. You could also select more than one color in this box either to emulate the old green-page reports of yore or just to annoy your users. Keep in mind that this background color is only for the cells of the table, so selecting a color here that contrasts with the default background color for the template you choose in a subsequent page could result in a truly ugly report.

In fact, the overall effect of the look and feel options can be to produce a report that is jarring and unattractive, as illustrated intentionally in Figure 5-11.

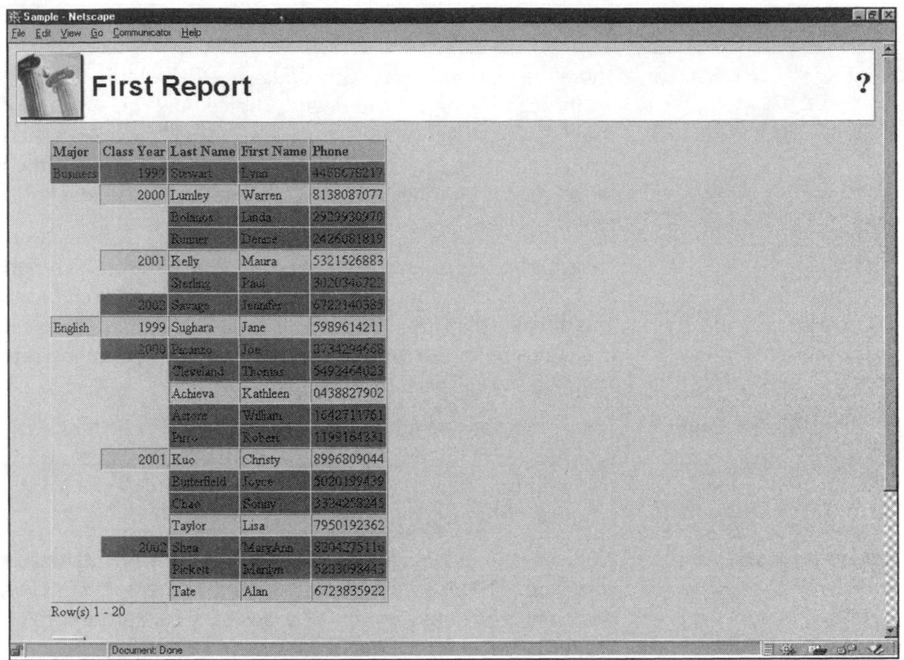

Figure 5-11: A truly ugly report

The Row Order Options section of the Display Options page consists of three lines of two combo boxes. The first combo box enables you to select the column value to use for the top-level sort of your report from a list of columns in your report. The default value for the first combo box is the "%" wild card, which means that the report is not sorted. The second combo box enables you to choose to sort the rows in either ascending order, which is the default, or descending order. This first line of the Row Order Options section is where you choose the primary sorting column — the column that is used to sort the report into major groupings.

The second line in the Row Order Options section of this page has the same fields as the first line in the section. The difference between the two lines is that the choices you make in this section are used to implement the secondary sort order — the way that the rows are sorted within the primary sort groups defined by the previous line's entries.

The final line in the Row Order Options section of this page also has the same fields as the first two lines. This final line is used to implement the third sort order — the way the rows are sorted within the secondary groups defined by the previous line's entries.

You do not have to enter a value for any of the lines in the Row Order Options section. WebDB uses the first sort specification it finds as the primary sorting order, so if you enter a value for the second line in the Row Order Options section and not the first, the values entered in the second line become the primary sort options.

10. Click the Next arrow to move to the next page in the Report Builder Wizard.

The next page in the Report Builder Wizard enables you to set options for the parameters and the buttons displayed for a report, as shown in Figure 5-12.

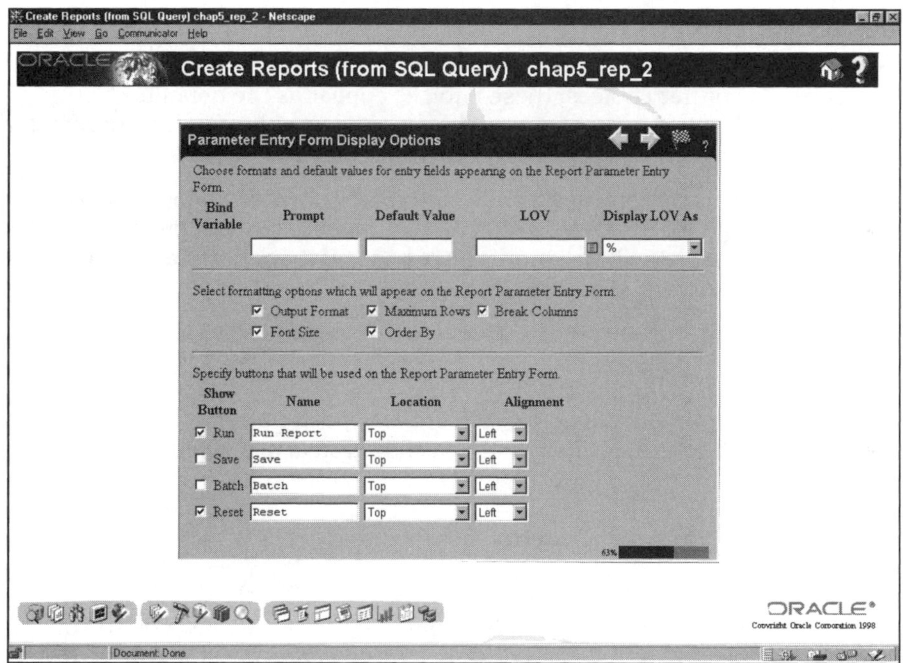

Figure 5-12: The Parameter Entry Form Display Options page in the Report Builder Wizard

The top portion of Parameter Entry Form Display Options page, henceforth called the Parameter page, gives you the ability to specify information about any parameters that you have selected for this report. Because you have not selected any parameters, there are no bind variables displayed in this section of the page.

The next portion of the page gives you the ability to specify which formatting options are displayed on the parameter form for the page. If you enable the display of an option on the parameter form, you give any user who can get to the parameter form the ability to change that option from the value you have specified.

By default, all of the formatting options — Output Format, Maximum Rows, Break Columns, Font Size, and Order By — are checked for display in the parameter form. When the display option is shown on the parameter form, the value you have selected for it is shown as the default value.

As you will see shortly, any WebDB report can be run directly or through a parameter form. The parameter form, by default, has two push buttons at the top of the page: the Run push button and the Reset push button. The final section of this page of the Report Builder Wizard gives you the ability to specify which of the four push buttons is included on the page. The four push button options are as follows:

- **Run** — This button causes the procedure that causes the report to be run and the results of the procedure to be returned to the browser.
- **Save** — This button saves the options chosen in parameters. Once a user has saved his or her choices, these choices appear as the defaults every subsequent time he or she runs the report. The ability to save parameter choices on a user-by-user basis is a nice feature of WebDB.
- **Batch** — This button submits the report job to a batch queue. There is a single batch queue for each WebDB server. Once a report is submitted in batch, the user can check the batch status page to see if the report has been executed and, if it has completed, to view the report.
- **Reset** — This button resets the choices in the parameter form to the default choices.

You can specify four attributes for each of these push buttons. The first attribute is a check box that indicates whether the push button is displayed on the Parameter page.

The second attribute for each button is a field that accepts the name that appears on the push button.

The third attribute for each button is a combo box that enables you to specify the location of the push button. Each push button can appear at the top of the parameter form, the bottom of the parameter form, or the top and bottom of the parameter form. If a push button is not shown by checking the Show Button check box at the far right, the functionality offered by that push button is not available to the user of the report.

The fourth attribute for each button is a field that enables you to indicate whether the push button is aligned to the left or right of the page. WebDB always determines the position of the push buttons by going through a simple process. WebDB goes through the push button list from the top to the bottom to form push button groups based on location, and then positions each group justified either to the left or to the right. For example, if you select the Run and Batch push buttons to be at the top of the page and the Save and Reset push buttons to be at the bottom of the page, your default parameter form looks like Figure 5-13.

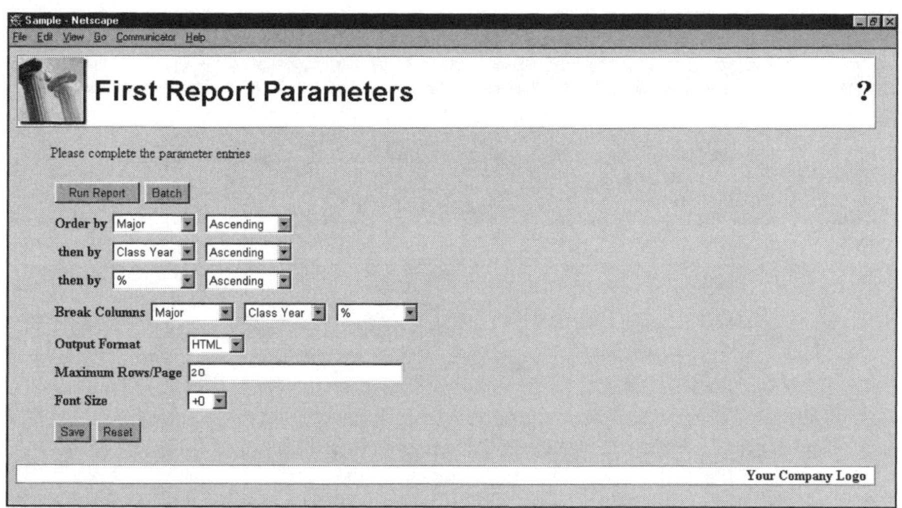

Figure 5-13: Alignment of push buttons on the parameter form for a report

11. Select all of the push buttons for display on the report.
12. Click the Next arrow on the Parameter page.

The next page in the Report Builder Wizard, as shown in Figure 5-14, gives you a lot of control in shaping the overall appearance of your report.

The first field on this page is one of the most powerful choices you can make in the Report Builder Wizard. WebDB supports an object known as a *template.* A template provides the default layout for all of the entities in a WebDB application system — reports, forms, charts, calendars, and all the other WebDB objects.

WebDB comes with a number of default templates. The template you choose gives a standardized look and feel to your report, the parameter form for your report, and the help pages for the report and the parameter forms.

In Chapter 15, you will learn how to create your own templates, but right now you can see the power of templates by selecting one of them for your report.

13. Click the drop-down arrow for the Template combo box and select PUBLIC.TEMPLATE_6.
14. Click the Preview Template push button to see the basic template design.

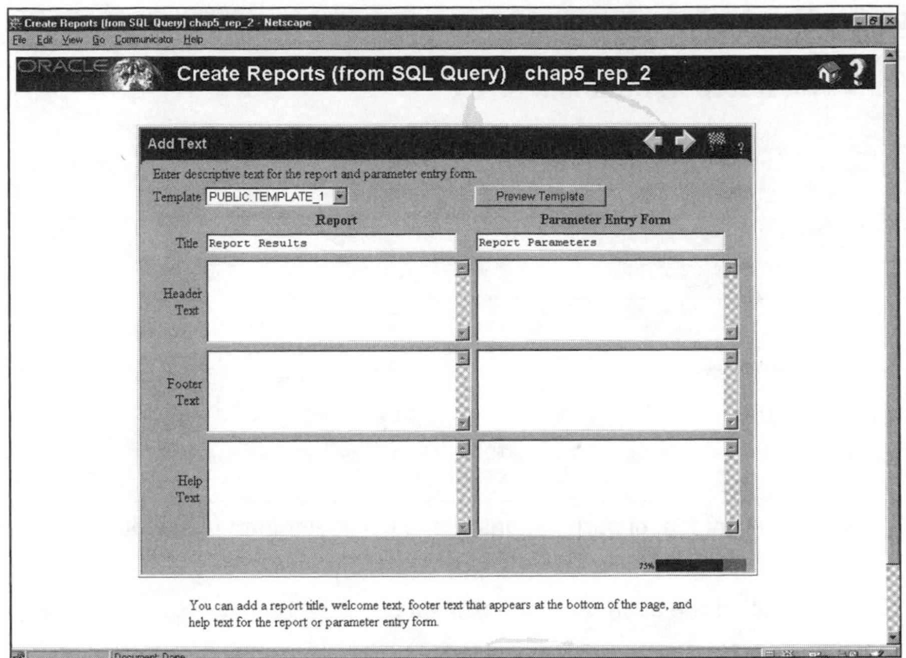

Figure 5-14: The Add Text page of the Report Builder Wizard

When you choose to preview a template, WebDB opens a little window in your browser to show you the template. If you return to the browser, select another template, and click the Preview push button, the newly selected template appears in the template window. Figure 5-15 shows the template design for PUBLIC.TEMPLATE_6.

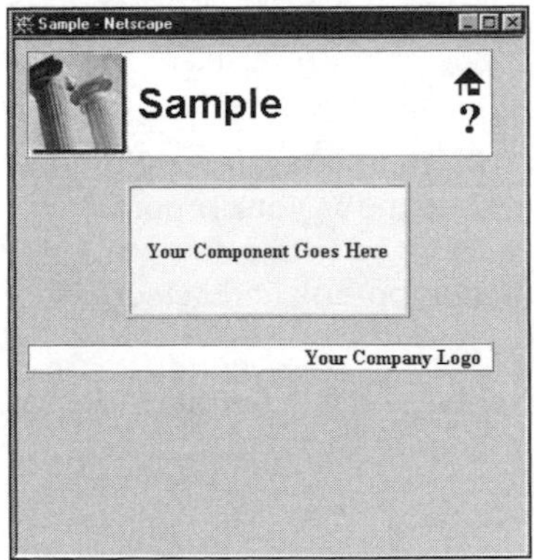

Figure 5-15: Previewing a template

If you look at the template for PUBLIC.TEMPLATE_6, you can see that it is more than just another pretty face. The public template enables you to specify a company name or graphic. More importantly, the template has two hotlinks on it. One link looks like a little house, which always takes the user back to a home page you specify, and the other link looks like a question mark, which brings up a help page for the associated page, whether it is a report page or a parameter form.

The rest of the fields on the Add Text page help you shape your report by adding text to the report. You can add the following four types of text:

Title	Displayed at the top of the first page of the report and the parameter and help pages, and is also used as the identifying title in the title bar of the browser
Header Text	Displayed at the top of each report page or parameter form, just below the title on the first page of the report
Footer Text	Displayed at the bottom of every page of the report or the parameter form
Help Text	Displayed in a separate page for the report and parameter forms

You can specify this text separately for either the report pages or the parameter forms. WebDB treats this text as straight HTML, so you can include HTML formatting tags in the text you enter for any of these areas.

15. Enter **First Report** and **First Report Parameters** into the Title fields for the report and the parameter entry form, respectively.
16. Enter **This is the <I>very</I> <B>top</B> of the report page** for the Header Text for the report.
17. Enter **Please complete the parameter entries** for the Header Text for the parameter entry form.
18. Enter **<CENTER>You can save your choices as defaults by clicking on the
<B><I>Save</I></B>
 push button.</CENTER>** as the Footer Text for the parameter entry form.
19. Enter **There is no help for this basic report.** as the Help Text for the report.
20. Click the Next arrow on the Add Text page.

The next page of the Report Builder Wizard gives you the opportunity to add PL/SQL code that executes before or after the display of the page or the header for the page. For now, you can just move past it.

21. Click the Next arrow on the Advanced PL/SQL code page.

At last! You have arrived at the final page in the Report Builder Wizard, as shown in Figure 5-16.

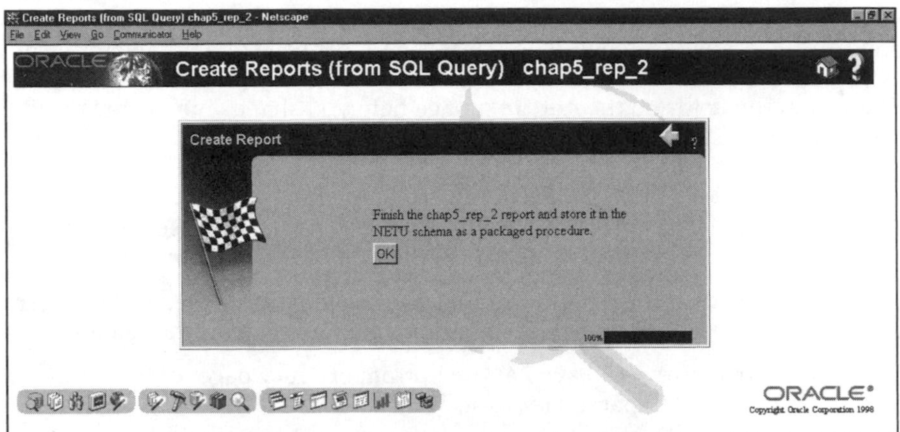

Figure 5-16: The last page of the Report Builder Wizard

You can see this is the last page by the triumphant image of the checkered flag at the left of the panel. However, don't treat this page as simply a formality. This page is where WebDB makes all the magic happen.

Up until this point, you have been giving values for the parameters that WebDB uses for your report. These parameters have been stored in WebDB's internal data tables. But these parameters are not used in the actual production of your report. WebDB uses the parameters you have entered to create a PL/SQL procedure. When your application system calls this WebDB report, it is actually calling the PL/SQL procedure that runs and creates the report as output.

WebDB creates this all-important procedure when you click the OK push button on the final page of the Report Builder Wizard.

22. Click on the OK push button on the Create Report page.

You did it! You created your first report. The next section helps you explore some of the functionality of this rather simple report.

Don't use the Back button in the browser to return to a page in the Report Builder Wizard once you have finished generating the report. If you move to a previous page in a wizard once you have completed the component, you generally get a WebDB error. If you want to modify something in a component after you have created it, find the component with the Component Finder and then select the Edit link.

Running Your Report

So far, all you have is a procedure that supposedly produces a report for you. You are probably dying to see the results of your work.

Once you have successfully created the procedure for your report, WebDB immediately does two things for you. One of these things is internal — the status for the report changes from EDIT to PRODUCTION. When a component has a status of PRODUCTION, the values of the parameters that control the generation of the procedure that run a component have not changed since the procedure was generated. In other words, the component has not been changed since the procedure for the component was generated. If you were to leave a creation wizard before reaching the final page and clicking the OK push button, the component would have a status of EDIT. The same status would be set if you were to leave an editing session without clicking the Finish push button, which you will learn about shortly.

The other thing that WebDB does for you is to bring up a page that enables you to run and manage your report object, as shown in Figure 5-17.

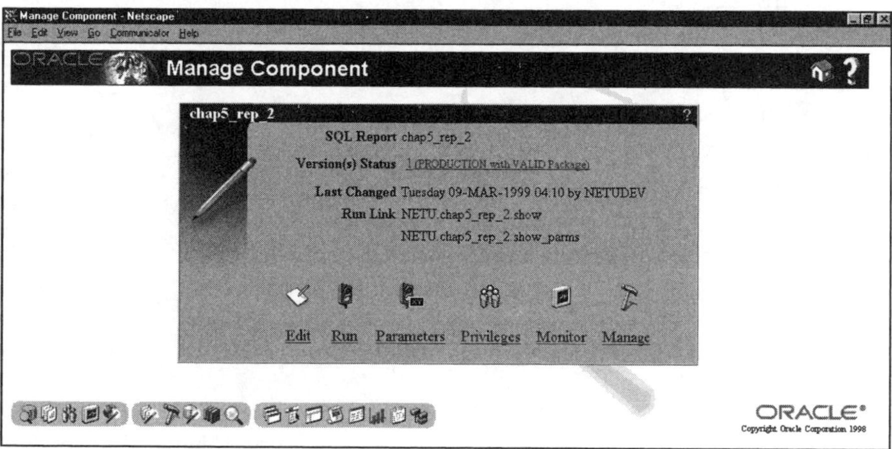

Figure 5-17: Managing your report

There is some basic information about the component at the top of the panel and in the six linked options at the bottom of the panel. The information about the component includes the name of the component, a list of all of the versions of the component, the time the component was last changed, and the existing ways to call the component.

Each time you edit and regenerate a component, WebDB saves the previous version of the component and the values for its parameters in an archive version. The archived versions of a component are numbered in increments of 1 (starting with 1), and given the status of ARCHIVE. You will learn more about WebDB's version control in Chapter 19. You will also learn more about the procedures listed in the Run Link portion of the panel later in this section.

The links at the bottom of the page should all be enabled. This is the standard situation for a component that has been successfully created. If you had left the Report Builder Wizard before you had generated the procedure for the report, the Run and Parameter links would not be enabled on this page.

But enough about this page for now. You probably just want to run your report.

23. Click the Run link at the bottom of the panel.

The first page of your first report should look like Figure 5-18.

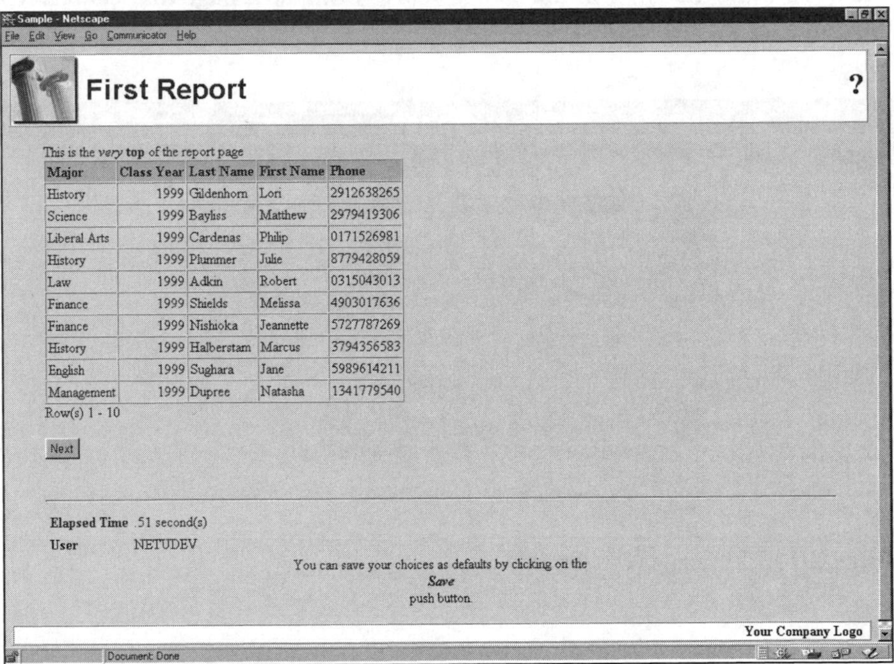

Sample - Netscape
File Edit View Go Communicator Help
First Report
?
This is the *very* **top** of the report page

Major	Class Year	Last Name	First Name	Phone
History	1999	Gildenhorn	Lori	2912638265
Science	1999	Bayliss	Matthew	2979419306
Liberal Arts	1999	Cardenas	Philip	0171526981
History	1999	Plummer	Julie	8779428059
Law	1999	Adkin	Robert	0315043013
Finance	1999	Shields	Melissa	4903017636
Finance	1999	Nishioka	Jeannette	5727787269
History	1999	Halberstam	Marcus	3794356583
English	1999	Sughara	Jane	5989614211
Management	1999	Dupree	Natasha	1341779540

Row(s) 1 - 10
Next
Elapsed Time .51 second(s)
User NETUDEV
You can save your choices as defaults by clicking on the
Save
push button.
Your Company Logo
Document: Done

Figure 5-18: The first page of your first report

The report shown in Figure 5-18 only has ten rows on the page so you can see the headers and footers clearly.

There are a few things you may immediately notice about this report. First, the design template you specified for the report gives it a nice look and feel, regardless of the fact that the data in the report could be arranged in a more meaningful fashion. Second, the report title and heading you specified appear in their appropriate places.

At the bottom of the report page, notice the line of text that indicates which rows of the report are displayed on the page — in this case, the first ten rows of data. Below this line of text is the Next push button, which you will use shortly to go to the next page of the report.

Also, note the indication of how much time elapsed between the request for the report page and its delivery, the name of the user who requested the report, and the time the report was executed.

Before leaving this page, you might want to check out the help page for the report.

24. Click the Help icon in the top-right corner of the report page.

The help page that appears looks like Figure 5-19.

Figure 5-19: Your first help page

The help page has the same look and feel as your report, thanks to the uniform use of the template by WebDB.

You may notice that there is no icon to return you to the home page — no little picture of the house you saw when you previewed the template. The reason for this is that you have not specified a home page for the template. It would not really make sense to have the Home icon when you are running the report from the development environment anyway, because you don't want to return to the home page for WebDB.

If you want to return to the Manage Component page of WebDB, you have to use the Back push button of your browser to return past the first page of the report. Before going back to the Manage Component page of WebDB, check out the rest of the report.

25. Click the Back push button of the browser to return to the first report page.
26. Click the Next push button at the bottom of the report page until you reach the end of the report.

Notice that each page of the report can have a different elapsed time, and that the text describing the rows in the report changes for each page. You can also see that the intermediate pages of the report have both a Next and Previous push button and that the last page of the report only has a Previous push button, as you would expect.

27. Click the Back push button for the browser to return to the first page of the report.
28. Click the Back push button of the browser to return to the Manage Component page of WebDB.

Why did you use the Back push button for the browser rather than the Previous push button in the report page? Keep in mind that clicking the Previous push button for the report page sends a request to the WebDB report component to generate an HTML page with the previous set of rows. This is different than returning to the previously viewed page in the browser. If you were to use the Previous push button to return to the first page of the report, clicking the Back push button in your browser would take you back to the last page shown in the browser—which would be the second page of the report. Because you want to get back to the Manage Component page, you have to get back to the page that was viewed right after that page: the first page of the report the first time you called it. In short, navigation with the browser is between static pages, while navigation with the push buttons in your report causes new pages to be created.

Now that you have completed that exciting run through your first report, you can take a look at running the same report with the built-in parameter form generated by WebDB.

29. Click the Parameters link for your first report at the bottom of the Manage Component page.

The page that appears in your browser should look like Figure 5-20.

Where did this page come from? You didn't request any parameters for this report, right?

But you did accept the defaults for Parameter Form page of the Report Builder Wizard. These default choices caused the appearance of the parameters you see in a page that has been formatted with the same design template specified for the report.

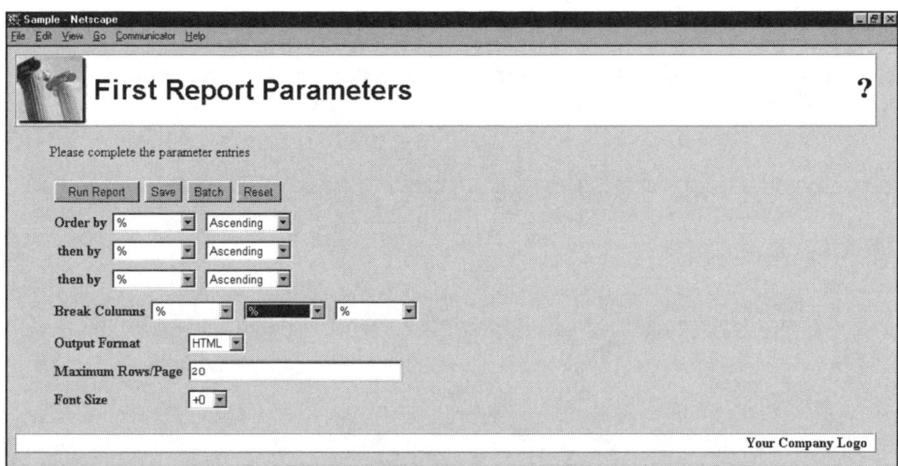

Figure 5-20: The parameter form for your first report

The parameter form has the title and header text you entered in the appropriate page of the Report Builder Wizard, as well as the formatted footer text you added on the same page of the Report Builder Wizard. If you were to click the Help icon, you would see that a default Help page would be returned, because you did not specify any help text for the Report Parameters page.

The Report Parameters page gives the user the ability to apply three levels of sorting on the report; to specify the report format for the report; to limit the number of rows that are displayed on any one page of the report; to indicate if there are any break groups in the report; and to change the font size for the report. The default values for all of these options are the same as the default values for the options in the Report Builder Wizard. In fact, the choices the user makes for these options shape and change the report in exactly the same way that the choices would work if you made them as part of the development process.

The best way to understand how these parameters work is to try them out.

30. Change the first Order by combo box to Major and the second Order by combo box to Class Year.

Notice that the names displayed in the Order by combo boxes are the headings you gave for the columns rather than the column names. Because the people who use this report may be totally unaware of the structure of the underlying data, but are no doubt familiar with the report headings, using these report headings for the Order by combo boxes is more user friendly.

31. Change the first two Order by combo boxes and the first two Break Columns combo boxes to Major and Class Year. Change the Maximum Rows/Page to 10.

32. Click the Run Report push button at the top of the Report Parameters page.

The report that comes back to your browser looks like the page shown in Figure 5-21.

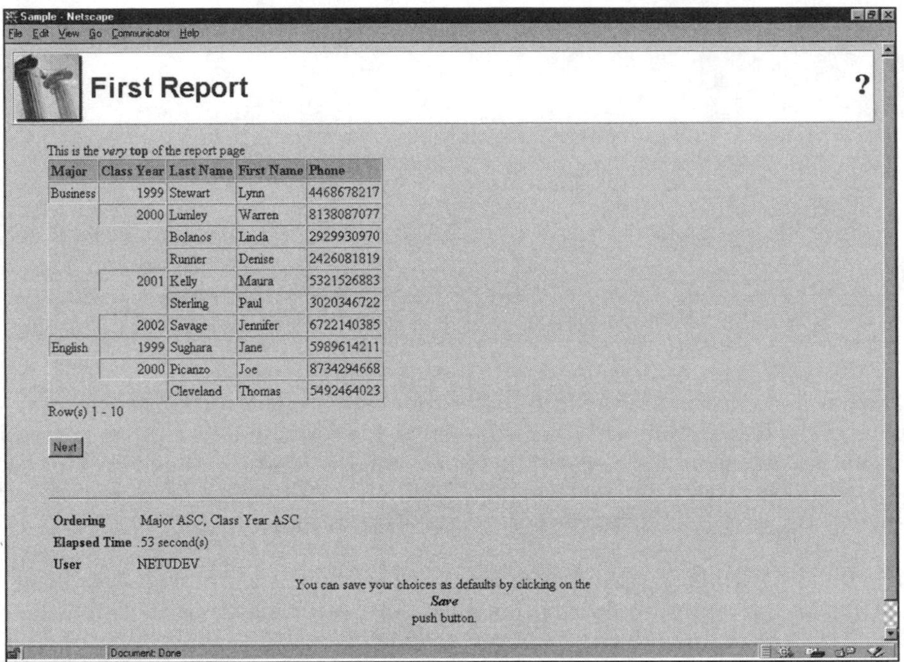

Figure 5-21: Your first report, conditioned by parameters

This report looks much better. The data is sorted in a more meaningful order, and the break groups suppressed the repetition of redundant data, which gives the entire report a cleaner look. This is probably the way you wanted the report to look all along. You will edit the report later in this chapter to make this the standard look for the report, but you have one more thing to discover about using the parameter form before you move on.

33. Use the Back push button in the browser to return to the parameter form for the report.

34. Click the Reset push button at the top of the report page.

You can see that the Reset push button resets the values for the parameter entry fields to their default values. You can use the Save push button in the report parameter form to establish your own default values.

35. Change the value for the first two Order by combo boxes to Major and Class Year and the values for the first two Break Columns combo boxes to Major and Class Year.
36. Click the Save push button at the top of the page.
37. Change the value for the first Order by combo box and the Break Columns combo box to something else.
38. Click the Reset push button at the top of the page.

Using the Save push button causes the current values for the parameters to be saved as your individual preferences. Each different WebDB user can save his or her own parameter defaults in the same way, which makes WebDB applications flexible and easy to use.

There seem to be a lot of parameter options available to the user in a default WebDB report. Do you really want to give the user this much control over the report in a production application system?

Well, probably not. The developers of WebDB wanted to make the product as flexible as possible, so they did give a lot of leeway to people using WebDB to create application systems. In most systems, though, you want to eliminate the display of some of the parameters through modifying the Parameter Options, as you will do later in this chapter when you edit the report.

At this point, you have been calling your report from within the WebDB development environment. You can call your report directly, which means that the default values for the parameters are used, or you can use the parameter form to call your report. You do this by specifying two different URLs that call two different procedures in the report package that was generated — one that calls the report (the "show" procedure), and one that calls the "show_params" procedure.

1. Enter the following text into the navigation window of your browser:

   `http://`*`servername:port`*`/WebDB/netu.ch5_rep_2.show`

In this URL, *servername* and *port* are replaced with the appropriate values for your site and *netu* represents the name of the schema you stored the report in. The name that you were supposed to give to the current report is ch5_rep_1 or ch5_rep_2, depending on which report you actually completed. If you gave it a different name, substitute that name in the URL.

You should see the same report in your browser that appeared when you clicked the Run link in the Manage Component page of WebDB. WebDB addresses all components with the same form of URL: the server for WebDB, followed by the virtual directory for the WebDB components, followed by a three-part locator made up of the schema name, module (or, more technically, package) name, and the procedure name you use to call the component.

To show you how to use different procedures to call the same basic WebDB component, you can try a couple more URLs in your browser.

2. Enter the following text into the navigation window of your browser:

   http://*servername*:*port*/WebDB/netu.ch5_rep_2.show_parms

In this URL, *servername* and *port* are replaced with the appropriate values for your site and *netu* represents the name of the schema you stored the report in. The name that you were supposed to give to the current report is ch5_rep_1 or ch5_rep_2, depending on which report you actually completed. If you gave it a different name, substitute that name in the URL.

This URL should bring up the parameter entry page in the browser.

3. Enter the following text into the navigation window of your browser:

   http://*servername*:*port*/WebDB/netu.ch5_rep_2.help

In this URL, *servername* and *port* are replaced with the appropriate values for your site and *netu* represents the name of the schema you stored the report in. The name that you were supposed to give to the current report is ch5_rep_1 or ch5_rep_2, depending on which report you actually completed. If you gave it a different name, substitute that name in the URL.

This URL should bring up the customized help page for the report you just created. There will probably not be very many times when you want to directly access the help page from a WebDB application, but seeing the results of this URL reinforces the way that WebDB components are stored and recalled.

You've seen a lot of functionality already in your WebDB reports. The next step is to understand how you can modify existing reports to make some of the functionality you added as a user a part of the default operation of the report.

Editing Your Report

Most people do not create perfect components with WebDB (or any development tool or language) on the first try, if for no other reason than the process of development should be an iterative process where end users continually supply feedback. In the case of your current report, you have already seen that adding some sorting instructions and making the report break on some columns can improve the appearance and usefulness of your basic report. You can make these features part of the standard report by editing the parameters you entered as part of the report building process.

First, you have to get back into WebDB.

1. Re-enter the WebDB development environment by using the Back push button in your browser or by entering WebDB through the home page.
2. Click the Reports icon in the shortcuts bar.

You have returned to the main Report page. This time, instead of building a report from scratch, go back to the report you already created and modify the way it operates.

3. Scroll to the bottom of the main Report page and select the ch5_rep_2 (or ch5_rep_1) report you just created.
4. Click the Edit link in the Manage Component panel.

This report should be at the top of the panel titled Select a Recently Edited Report. The main edit page for reports, as shown in Figure 5-22, appears in your browser.

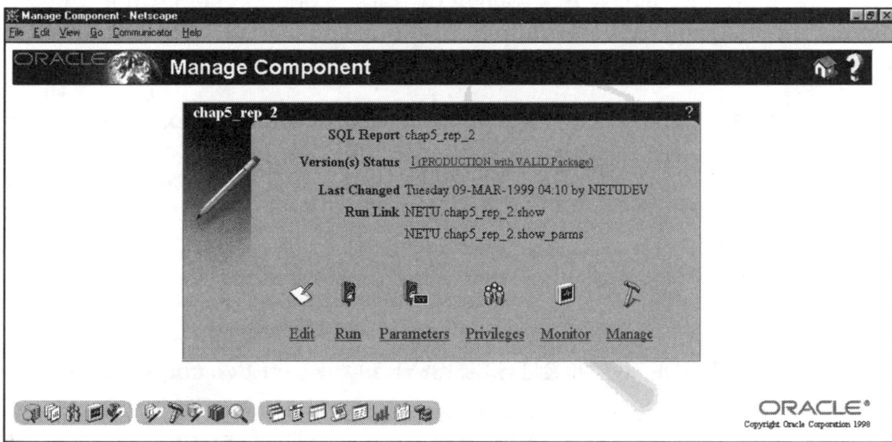

Figure 5-22: The edit page for reports

The edit page for WebDB report components has the familiar look of a tabbed dialog box. Of course, it is not really a tabbed dialog box, because it only uses HTML for display. However, it operates in the same way. The "tabs" in the top part of the panel enable you to bring up different pages that pretty much correspond to the pages of the Report Builder Wizard. The tabs control the following, in order from right to left:

 SQL statement (if the report was created with a SQL statement)

Column formatting

Display options

Parameter entry form display options

Add text

Advanced PL/SQL coding

The only tab not represented in the list is the Join Conditions tab, which is shown if the report has more than one table and was created with the Query Wizard. A *join condition* is a particular type of selection criterion that specifies how two different tables used in the same query are joined together.

When you hold your mouse over one of the tabs, a floating help window helps you identify the meaning of the tab, although after a short while you will be able to quickly understand the icons on each tab.

When you click any one of the tabs, WebDB serves up the appropriate page for editing the parameter values associated with that tab. To familiarize yourself with the editing process, you can start by adding the sorting and break options to the report that worked so well in the previous section.

5. Click the Display Options tab in the Edit Reports window, which is the third tab from the left.
6. Scroll down the page to get to the Break Options section. Select UGRADS.MAJOR and UGRADS.CLASSYR in the first two combo boxes.
7. Go to the first line of the Row Order Options area of the page. Select UGRADS.MAJOR from the first combo box and UGRADS.CLASSYR from the second combo box.

Because you are now in the development environment for WebDB, you can see the actual table and column name in the Row Order Options area. WebDB figures that if you are developing the reports, you are more interested in the underlying column identifier and less likely to become confused by it, as opposed to an end user who probably knows columns by their heading in the report.

You have made your changes. Your final step in the editing process is to regenerate the package for the report.

8. Click the Finish push button at the top of the Edit Reports window.

If you are near the server machine, you can probably hear the disk spinning after you click the Finish push button, as WebDB creates a new PL/SQL package to generate your report based on the new set of parameters. Even if you are not near the server, you can see that this step takes a moment or two.

If you were to click the Cancel push button, a new package would not be created, and all the values for the parameters used to create the package would revert back to the values they had before you began to edit the component.

When the generation of the report is completed, you are returned to the Manage Component page for the report. But this time the page looks a little different, as shown in Figure 5-23.

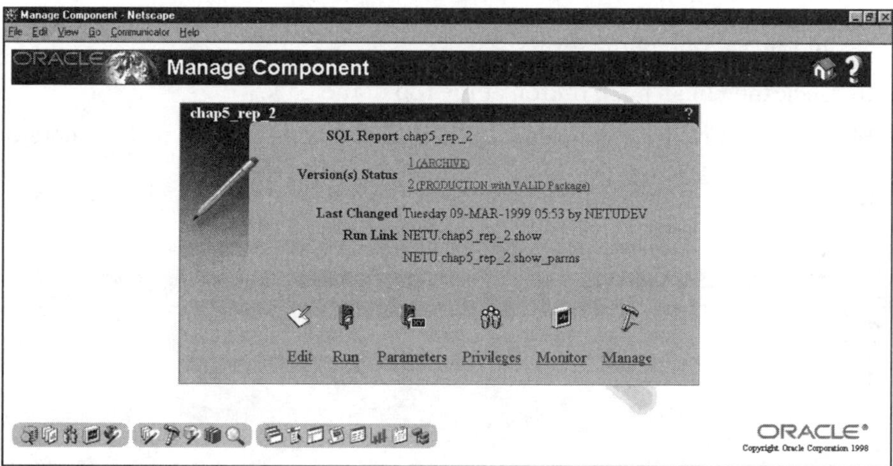

Figure 5-23: The Manage Component page for an edited component

When you look at the second part of the panel labeled Version(s) Status, you can see that you have more than one version listed. If you have only edited the report once, you should see a version numbered 1 with a status of ARCHIVE, and a version numbered 2 with a status of PRODUCTION with VALID Package. When you generated the new version of the report, WebDB automatically saved the previous versions of the report for you. By default, when you click any of the links at the bottom of the page, the information for the most recent version of the component appears. You can click a previous version to access it if you need to. You can only have one version of a component with a PRODUCTION status.

The best way to see the changes that you have made at work is to run the report.

9. Click the Run link at the bottom of the page.

Voila! You can see the report properly sorted, with the appropriate break points. Because you called the report directly, the personal preferences you saved with the parameter form earlier are not enforced, so you know that the changes you made to the report parameters have had desired effect.

But this does bring up another issue. What if you like the current display of the report so much that you want to prevent a user from changing the sort order or the break options, but you still want to give them the other parameter form options? You can edit the report again to take these options off the report parameter form.

10. Return to the Manage Component page for the current report and click the Edit link.
11. Click the Button Options link in the Edit Reports page.
12. Click the Order by and Break Columns check boxes to deselect them in the middle section of the form.
13. Click the Finish push button at the top of the page.
14. When you return to the Manage Component page, select the Parameters link.

The new version of the Report Parameters page should look like Figure 5-24.

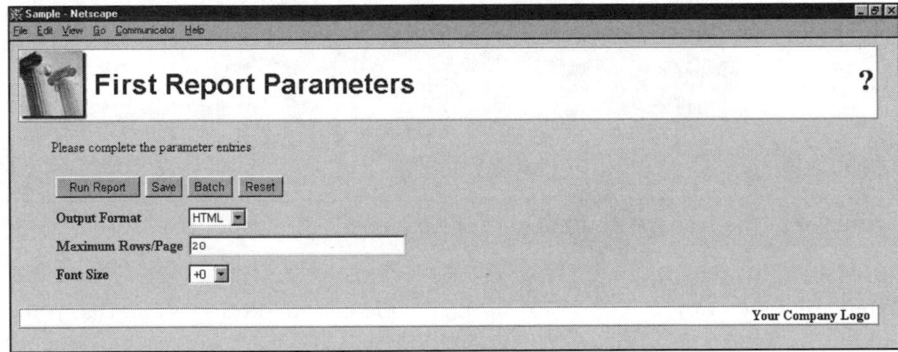

Figure 5-24: The new version of the Report Parameters page

The new version of the Report Parameters page still enables users to select the output format, the maximum number of rows per page, and the font size for the report, but they can no longer adjust the sorting order of the report or how the breaks are applied to the report.

By giving you the ability to only allow the user modify some of the run-time characteristics of a report, WebDB enables you to decide how much flexibility an individual report can have. No flexibility, when you call the report with the default procedure and the report uses only the choices you have made in the development process; a lot of flexibility, when you use the default parameter form; or some flexibility, when you limit the parameter form.

You may have noticed the other links at the bottom of the Manage Component page, which has acted as a mini–home page for editing your reports. These three links — Privileges, Monitor, and Manage — are common for all components, and they will be explored in depth in Chapter 19.

There is quite a bit more to learn about using and shaping WebDB reports, but you are no doubt ready for a break. The next chapter continues to explore options for building reports. Some options that we look at include adding your own parameters for specifying selection criteria at run time; creating reports with multiple tables; leveraging the power of SQL to create reports outside the realm of default WebDB functionality; using PL/SQL code to extend the power of your reports; and using WebDB's built-in batch report facility.

Wrapping Up

Reporting on data contained in your Oracle database is one of the main purposes of WebDB. You can create reports with the easy-to-use Query Wizard or specify the data yourself in an SQL statement. With either method, WebDB gives you a great deal of control over the functionality in your report.

When WebDB creates the package for your report, it creates not only the procedure for showing your report, but also procedures that enable you to present end users with a parameter form they can use to shape the report to their own preferences. End users can even store their own preferences, which act as the default choices for the parameters the next time they run the report.

WebDB gives you the ability to edit the parameters that control the generation of the report package and automatically keeps earlier versions of the report for you.

The next chapter explores some of the more advanced features for creating reports with WebDB.

✦ ✦ ✦

Advanced Reporting Techniques

✦ ✦ ✦ ✦

In This Chapter

✦ ✦ ✦ ✦

In the previous chapter, you learned the basics of reporting on data with WebDB. The reports you can create with the techniques you already know will answer many of your informational needs, especially when you consider that you can create and run these reports from any browser.

This chapter takes you further into the power of WebDB reporting. You will learn how to limit the data in a report through the use of parameters and combine data from multiple tables in your report. You will get a glimpse of how you can use your own SQL statements to go beyond the limitations of the WebDB Report Builder Wizard. And you will find some pointers to other areas in this book that can give you even more information on using WebDB reports.

Adding Parameters to Your Report

You have probably already noticed that WebDB's Report Builder gives you the ability to add parameters to your reports. These parameters are added to the parameter page that is automatically generated for you by WebDB as part of the report package.

One of the chief uses for parameters is to enable your users to specify selection criteria at run time for a report. You can create a single report component that can be used for a wide variety of different information, depending on the values of the criteria.

For instance, the report you created in the last chapter displayed data in a meaningful way, but perhaps it displayed too much data. Maybe a typical user of this report is not interested in all the students in all the majors, but only in all the students in one particular major.

1. Go to the main page for reports in WebDB by selecting Build from the main WebDB menu, then User Interface Components, and then Reports.
2. Scroll to the bottom of the page and select the report chp5_rep_1 from the list of recent reports.

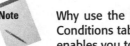

If you did the work in the last chapter, the report named chp5_rep_1 was completed with default values after specifying the query in the Query Wizard. If you did not do the examples in the last chapter, you can import the example with the script names chp5_rep_1.sql from the CD-ROM that accompanies this book or from the directory where you loaded the examples for this book. For details of how to import a WebDB module, please refer to Appendix A.

3. Click the Edit link at the bottom of the Manage Component page.
4. Click the Parameter Entry Form Display Options tab of the Edit Reports panel.

Why use the Parameter Entry Form Display Options tab instead of the Column Conditions tab? This tab sets up a parameter for a user, while Column Conditions enables you to specify conditions that are not available to the user.

You see a page that looks like Figure 6-1.

Because you are in the WebDB development environment, you are presented with a list of table and column names, as WebDB assumes you understand the underlying data structures for the report. You do not have to specify anything else for the parameter, because the user is given a choice of 11 selection conditions on the parameter page at run time.

5. Go to the Column Name combo box on the first line of the Parameters page and select the UGRADS.MAJOR column.
6. You should change the prompt for the condition. Enter **Major:** in the Prompt field for the new condition.

The data entry fields for LOV and Display LOV are used for list of values objects, which are covered in Chapter 13. You can leave them blank for now.

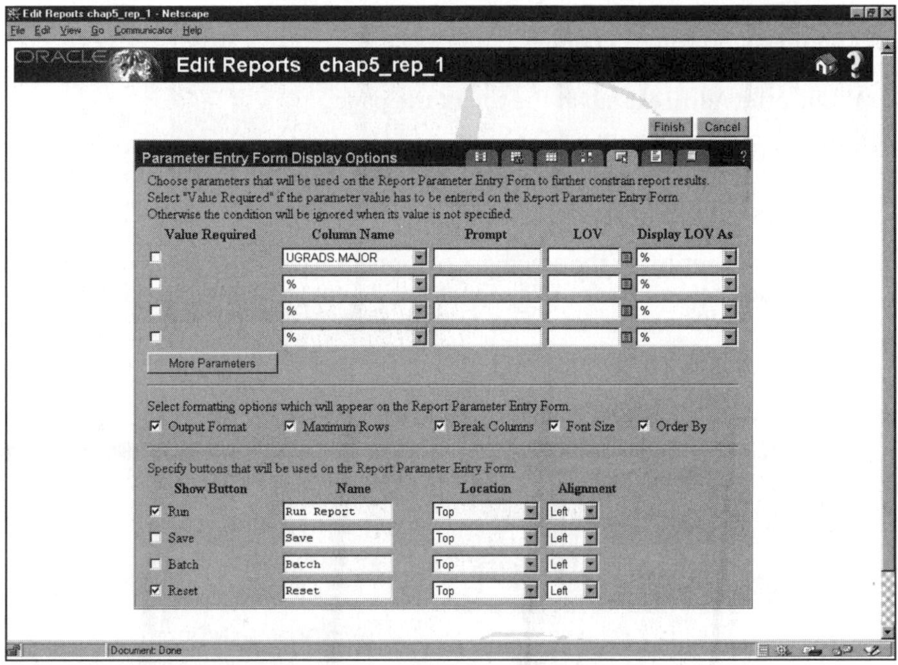

Figure 6-1: Editing report parameters

You also should not select the check box labeled Value Required on the far left-hand side of the column conditions line. When you check this choice, you force the user to select a condition before running the report. This option is useful if you are using a condition to prevent the return of large amounts of data in a report. Because you are just trying to give the user some options with this parameter, you should leave it unchecked.

Before you leave this page of the form, you should prevent the user from setting the Break Columns or Order By columns on the parameter page.

7. Uncheck the check boxes for Break Columns and Order By in the middle section of the Parameter Entry Form Display Options page.

8. You now want to set up the ordering and break groups for the report in your definition. Click the Display Options tab at the top of the page.

9. Change the first two column lines in the Row Order Options section to UGRADS.MAJORS and UGRADS.CLASSYR respectively.

10. Change the first two column lines in the Break Options section to UGRADS.MAJORS and UGRADS.CLASSYR, respectively.

Finally, you should assign it the same template so that it looks like the other reports and modules you will be creating.

11. Click the Add Text tab at the top of the page.
12. Select PUBLIC.TEMPLATE_6 as the template for the report. You could, of course, enter the titles, headings, and help from the previous report example.
13. Click the Finish push button.
14. When you return to the Manage Component page, click the Parameter link. The parameter page for this report now features a prompt and data field for the MAJORS column, as shown in Figure 6-2.
15. Click the Run Report push button without entering a value in the Major field.

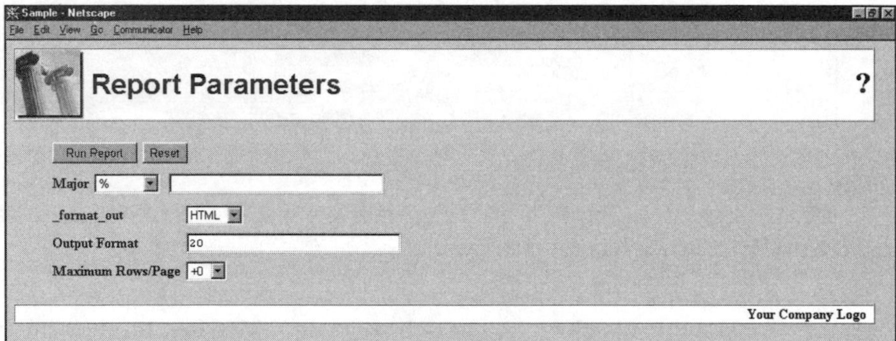

Figure 6-2: The Report Parameters page with a prompt for MAJORS

If a user does not enter a value for a selection criterion, the WebDB report package understands it to mean that the selection criterion should not be applied to the report.

16. Return to the parameter page by clicking the Back push button in your browser.
17. Select the "=" condition, enter **Business** into the Major field, and click the Run Report push button.

The report returned this time only shows you the information for business majors, as shown in Figure 6-3.

18. Return to the parameter page by clicking the Back push button in your browser.
19. Enter **B%** into the Major field and click the Run Report push button.

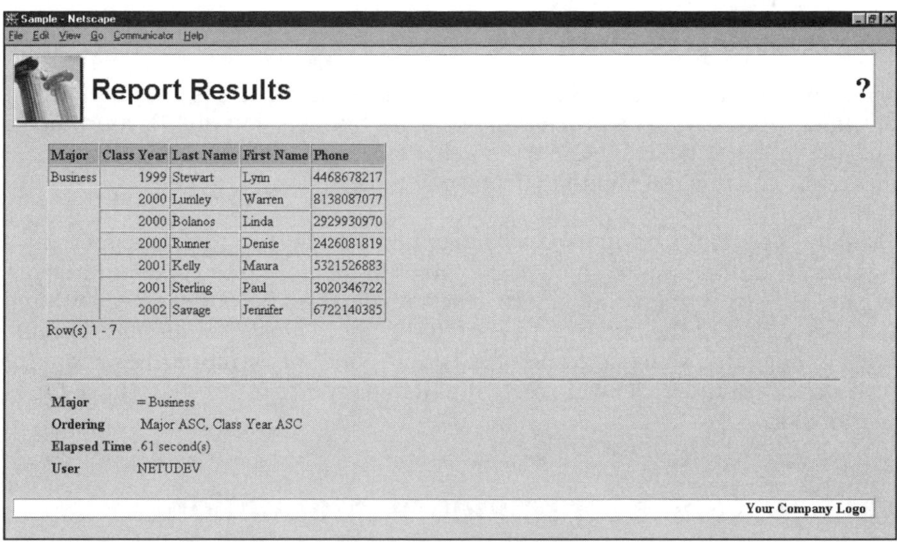

Major	Class Year	Last Name	First Name	Phone
Business	1999	Stewart	Lynn	4468678217
	2000	Lumley	Warren	8138087077
	2000	Bolanos	Linda	2929930970
	2000	Runner	Denise	2426081819
	2001	Kelly	Maura	5321526883
	2001	Sterling	Paul	3020346722
	2002	Savage	Jennifer	6722140385

Figure 6-3: Limiting the report with a parameter value

You can see that the report does not contain any data. If you are familiar with the concept of wild cards, you may be confused. After all, doesn't the "%" wild card mean that entering a value such as **B%** should at least return the business majors? However, remember that you entered the "=" sign as the relational operator for this condition.

20. Return to the parameter page by clicking the Back push button in your browser.
21. Change the value in the Conditions field to **like** and click the Run Report push button.

This time, you can see that the wild card worked the way you wanted.

You can enable your users to select criteria, but you cannot guarantee that the selection criteria makes sense — at least not with the default parameter page. You will learn later that you can use JavaScript to validate entries on a form, and you can create your own form with validation and link the form to a report. But the automatic generation of a parameter form certainly gives you a great deal of flexibility with very little work, and you can always include instructions on using the parameters in the header, footer, or help text for the form.

The next step toward enlarging the scope of your WebDB reports is to learn how to create reports that use data from more than one table.

Using Multiple Tables in a Report

One of the great benefits of a relational database like Oracle is the ability to *normalize* your data. The process of normalization lets you divide your data up into multiple tables and simply join the smaller tables together when you need information that is not included in any one table.

The database that is being used for the application in this book has gone through a process of normalization. Some of the tables in the database act as reference tables to a main table, which supply more descriptive names for codes used within the database. Some of the tables in the database have a *master-detail relationship* — a row in one table shares a common attribute with one or more rows in another table. In this section, you will create multitable reports for both of these types of relationships.

Multiple tables for reference information

It is easier to start by recreating your first report with another table that acts as a reference to a code in the UGRADS table. You have to create a new report from scratch because WebDB does not enable you to add another table to an existing report.

1. Return to WebDB development environment by using the Back button on the browser.
2. Return to the main Report page by clicking the Reports icon in the shortcuts bar.
3. Select the Report from Query Wizard radio button in the top panel and click the Create push button.
4. Select NETU as the schema name for the report and enter **ch6_rep_1** as the Report Name.
5. Click the Next arrow on the Report Name and Schema page.
6. Select both the NETU.UGRADS table and the NETU.CLASSES table, using the method supported by your client, such as clicking each of them while holding down the Ctrl key for a Windows client.
7. Click the Next arrow on the Tables and Views page.

When the Tables and Views page first appears, the SCOTT.DEPT and SCOTT.EMP tables are preselected. Select the first table without holding down the multiple selection key to automatically deselect these SCOTT tables.

Because you have selected two tables for this report, the next page in the Query Wizard looks like Figure 6-4.

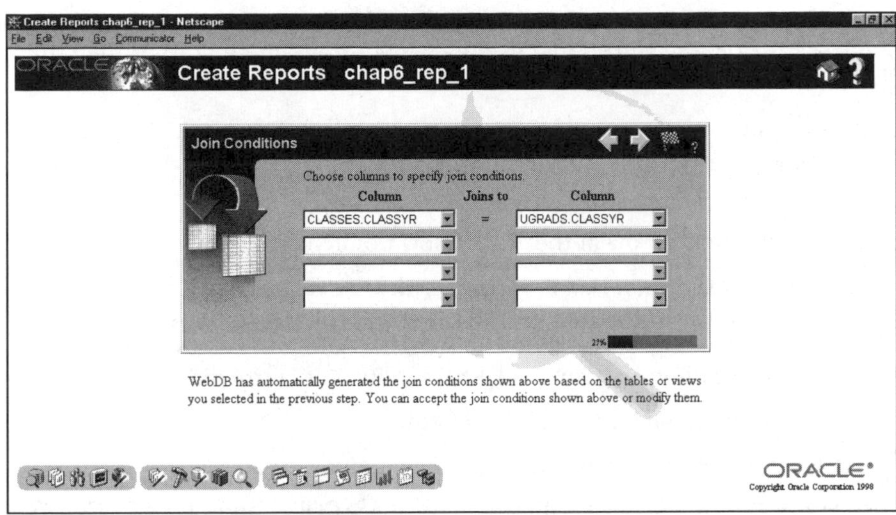

Figure 6-4: The Join Conditions page in the Query Wizard

The Join Conditions page has a simple purpose: It enables you to indicate the columns in the two different tables that act as a link between rows in the two tables. WebDB looks through the two tables to see if there is a relationship between the two tables, such as a *primary key–foreign key relationship,* or two columns that have the same name in both tables.

A primary key–foreign key relationship is a common way to associate two tables in a relational database. The value for the foreign key in one table refers to the value for the primary key in another table. This type of relationship is also used to enforce data integrity in the database. If anyone tries to enter a value into the CLASSYR column in the UGRADS table that does not already exist in one of the rows of the CLASSES table's CLASSYR column, the change is rejected by the database. You will learn more about enforcing data integrity in Chapters 13 and 16.

You can see that WebDB has discovered that the CLASSYR column in the UGRADS table is related to the CLASSYR column in the CLASSES table. This is the appropriate relationship to join these two tables, so you can simply accept the join condition.

8. Click the Next arrow on the Join Conditions page.

You are basically trying to reproduce the report that you created in the previous chapter, so you should add similar selection parameters on the next page of the Report Builder Wizard.

9. Click on the Next arrow in the Column Conditions page.

Because the whole purpose of this report is to display the easier-to-understand CLASSCODE column, you should use that as your parameter, rather than the CLASSYR column.

10. Select the UGRADS.MAJOR, CLASSES.CLASSCODE, CLASSES.CLASSYR, UGRADS.LASTNAME, UGRADS.FIRSTNAME, and UGRADS.PHONE columns in that order.
11. Click the Next arrow in the Table/View Columns page.
12. Change the Column Heading Text for the CLASSCODE column to **Class**. Change the Column Heading Text for the CLASSYR column to **Class Year**. Change the Column Heading Text for the LASTNAME column to **Last Name**. Change the Column Heading Text for the FIRSTNAME column to **First Name**.
13. Change the Align for CLASSYR to Center.
14. Click the Next arrow on the Table/View Columns page.
15. Select the UGRADS.MAJOR, CLASSES.CLASSCODE, and CLASSES.CLASSYR entries in the Break Options combo boxes.
16. Select the UGRADS.MAJOR column in the first line of the Row Order Options area of the Display Options page. Select the CLASSES.CLASSYR column and the Sort Order of Descending in the second line of the Row Order Options area.
17. Click the Next arrow on the Display Options page.

Why did you select the CLASSYR column and not the CLASSCODE column for sorting? You have to use the CLASSYR for sorting the report, because you want to show the class of 1999, then the class of 2000, and so on. If you were to select the CLASSCODE column for sorting, the entries would be sorted in alphabetical order, such as Freshman, Junior, Senior, and Sophomore.

Notice that the columns you selected for breaks are different from the columns you selected for sorting. There is nothing wrong with this. A break column controls how the WebDB report suppresses redundant data and creates totals, while the order by columns control the order that the rows of data in the report are sorted. In this case, you didn't have to explicitly sort on the CLASSYR column, because the CLASSYR and CLASSCODE columns are always linked. You want to break on the three columns named in the Break Options section because you want to suppress the display of both the redundant CLASSCODE and CLASSYR values.

In order to give your user the ability to limit the rows retrieved, you should add some parameters.

18. Select UGRADS.MAJOR in the first line of the Parameter Entry Form Display Options page. Set the prompt to **Major**. Check the Value Required check box.
19. Select the CLASSES.CLASSCODE in the second line of the page. Set the prompt to **Class**.

You can accept the default button choices for the report and move on to define some header and footer text for your report.

20. Click the Next arrow on the Parameter Entry Form Display Options page.
21. Select PUBLIC_TEMPLATE_6 as the template for the new report.
22. Enter **The <b>Major</b> parameter is required. The <b>Class</b> parameter accepts the name of the class, such as <I>Freshman</I>, <I>Sophomore</I>, <I>Junior</I> or <I>Senior</I>.** for the Parameter Entry Form's Header Text.
23. Click the Next arrow on the Add Text page.
24. Click the Next arrow on the Add Advanced PL/SQL code page.
25. Click the OK push button on the last page of the Report Builder Wizard.

You're ready to try out your new report. Because you have already seen how parameters work in your previous report, you can just run this report directly.

26. Click the Run link at the bottom of the Manage Component page.

Oops! Trying to run the report directly brings up an error page, as shown in Figure 6-5.

Remember — you indicated that the Major parameter required a value. This time, call the parameter entry form.

27. Return to the Manage Component page by clicking the Back push button on the error page.

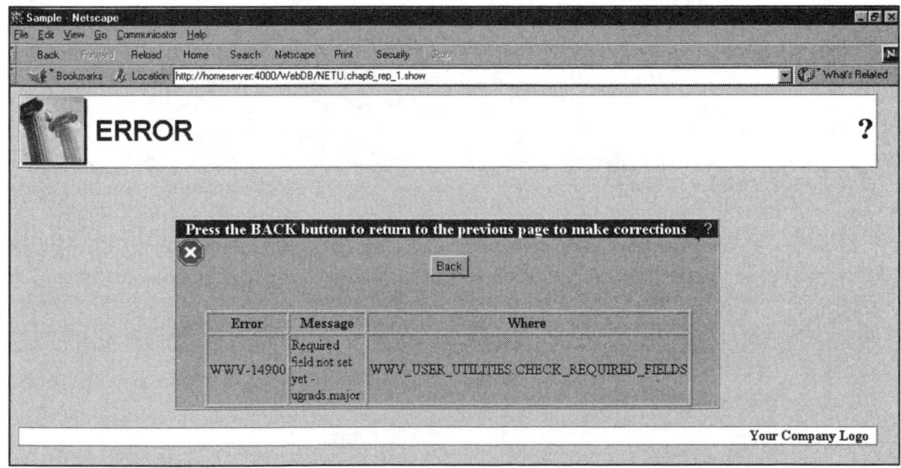

Figure 6-5: An error resulting from a missing required parameter

28. Click the Run link at the bottom of the Manage Component page. The parameter page should look like Figure 6-6.

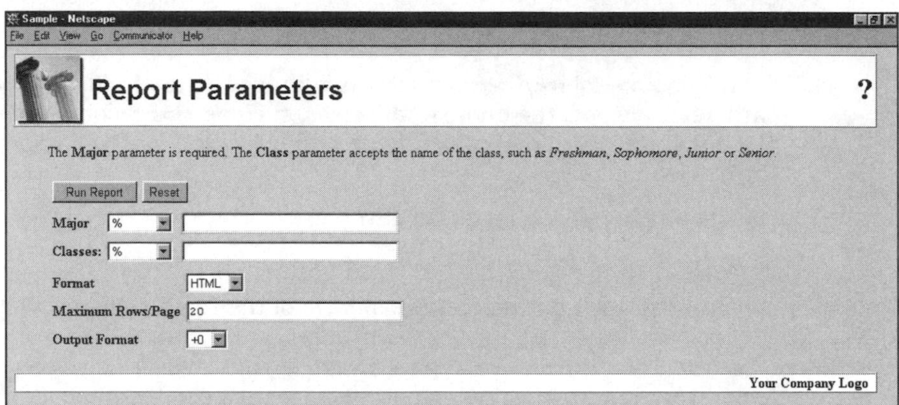

Figure 6-6: The parameter form for your report

29. Select "=" for the condition and enter **Business** for the value for the Major parameter.

30. Click the Run Report push button.

The report that appears should look like the report shown in Figure 6-7.

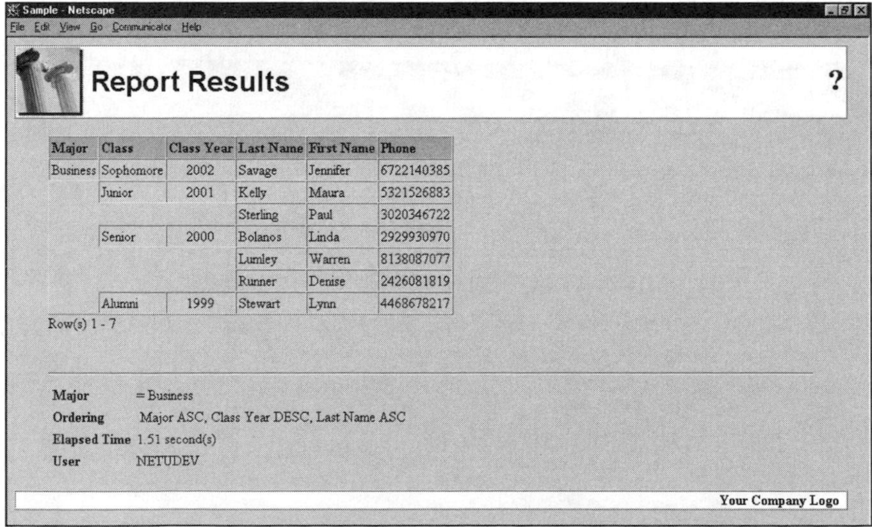

Figure 6-7: Your second report with data from UGRADS and CLASSES

You can see that everything worked as planned — the data is correctly sorted and the redundant values for MAJOR have been properly suppressed.

Multiple tables for master-detail relationships

One of the classic uses for linked tables in a relational database is to establish a master-detail relationship. In the Net University sample database you can see a master-detail relationship between the UGRADS table, which contains information about individual students, and the TRANSCRIPT table, which holds data about the courses each student has taken. These two tables can be linked together through the value in the ID column, which is used to uniquely identify a student.

1. Return to the WebDB environment by using the Back push button in the browser.
2. Return to the main Report page in WebDB by clicking the Reports icon in the shortcuts bar.
3. Select the Report from Query Wizard radio button and click the Create push button.
4. Select the NETU schema from Schema combo box and give the new report the name of **ch6_rep_2.**
5. Click the Next arrow on the Report Name and Schema page.
6. Select the NETU.COURSE_CATALOG table, the NETU.TRANSCRIPT table, and the NETU.UGRADS table on the Tables and Views page and click the Next arrow.

You will want to establish a master-detail relationship between the UGRADS table and the TRANSCRIPT table and a referential relationship between the TRANSCRIPT table and the COURSE_CATALOG table. Once again, WebDB has found the correct columns to use for the table joins — CAT_NUM and ID.

7. Accept the default join conditions by clicking the Next arrow on the Join Conditions page.
8. Select the UGRADS.LASTNAME, UGRADS.FIRSTNAME, TRANSCRIPT.YEAR, TRANSCRIPT.SEMESTER, and the COURSE_CATALOG.COURSE_NAME columns, in that order.
9. Click the Next arrow on the Table/View Columns page.
10. Click the Next arrow on the Column Conditions page.

You gathered information from all of the three tables as you needed it in your report. Notice that you did not need to include the ID column for your link in the report. The ID column is not really meaningful information in this database; instead, it is just used as a unique identifier to establish relationships between tables.

11. Change the Column Heading Text for the LASTNAME column to **Last Name** and the Column Heading Text for the FIRSTNAME column to **First Name.**
12. Click the Next arrow on the Columns Formatting page.
13. Select the UGRADS.LASTNAME, UGRADS.FIRSTNAME, and TRANSCRIPT.YEAR columns in the Break Options section of the page and select UGRADS.LASTNAME, TRANSCRIPT.YEAR, and TRANSCRIPT.SEMESTER as the Row Order Options.

You are hoping to be able to use a trick by breaking on the UGRADS.FIRSTNAME column but not sorting on it. This works as long as there are no two people with the same last name, which happens to be true in the sample database. However, in the real world, you would not depend on this likelihood and you would correspondingly lose the ability to sort on the SEMESTER column in a report based on the Query Wizard. When you enter your own SQL statements, you can, of course, increase the number of columns you use for sorting.

14. You should select the PUBLIC.TEMPLATE_6 template on the Add Text page to keep a consistent look and feel on your reports. You can set the remainder of the Display Options and the choices on the other pages any way that you like.
15. Continue to click the Next arrow until you can set the template name to PUBLIC.TEMPLATE_6 on the Add Text page. Once you have set this, you can click the checkered flag icon to finish the report. Click the Run link at the bottom of the Manage Component page to run the report.

The report should look like Figure 6-8.

You may not be exceptionally pleased with this particular report. There seems to be a whole lot of data. Keep in mind that you are looking at the course transcripts for all the students at the very popular Net University. You will use a report like this report later to report on a single student, so the amount of data should be more manageable. Also, notice that the report did not take an exceptionally long time to produce. This is, in part, because WebDB is only sending back the first 20 rows of the report, rather than the complete report.

The next section will help you to see how you can get around the limitations imposed by the Query Wizard by using your own SQL statements as the basis for a report.

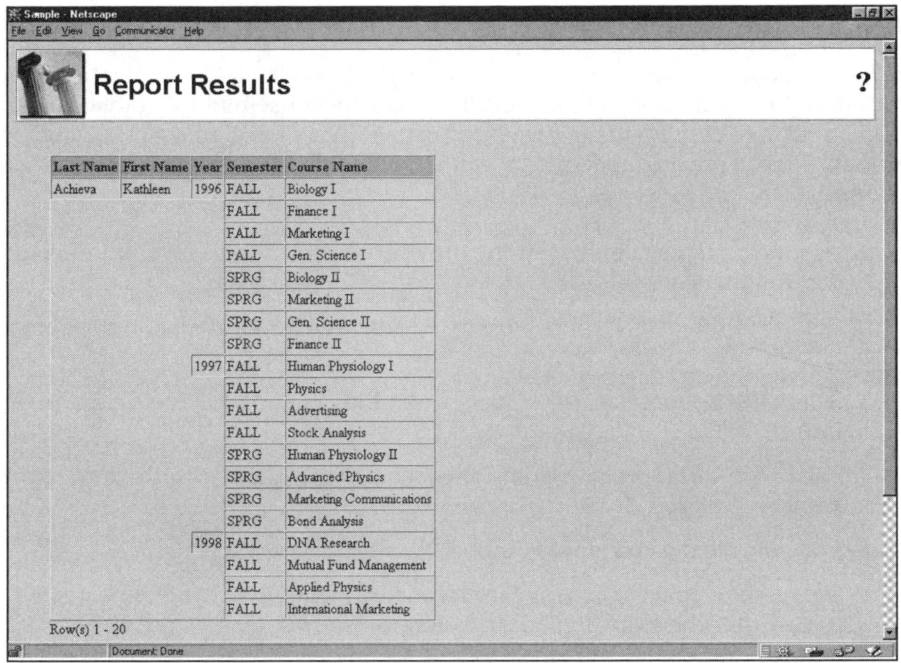
Report Results

Last Name	First Name	Year	Semester	Course Name
Achieva	Kathleen	1996	FALL	Biology I
			FALL	Finance I
			FALL	Marketing I
			FALL	Gen. Science I
			SPRG	Biology II
			SPRG	Marketing II
			SPRG	Gen. Science II
			SPRG	Finance II
		1997	FALL	Human Physiology I
			FALL	Physics
			FALL	Advertising
			FALL	Stock Analysis
			SPRG	Human Physiology II
			SPRG	Advanced Physics
			SPRG	Marketing Communications
			SPRG	Bond Analysis
		1998	FALL	DNA Research
			FALL	Mutual Fund Management
			FALL	Applied Physics
			FALL	International Marketing

Row(s) 1 - 20

Figure 6-8: Multiple table master-detail report

Using SQL as the Basis for Reports

You have seen how to create more robust reports by combining information from multiple tables, but at the same time you have run into some of the limitations imposed by WebDB's Query Wizard. The last report you created would have looked much better if you could have also sorted on the name of the course, so that someone viewing the data could find a particular course in a student's transcript quickly.

These limitations are primarily the result of using the Query Wizard. When the designers of WebDB created the product, they had to make some hard choices: Should they make an easy-to-use, point-and-click interface, or should they give users all the functionality of SQL?

By giving you the option of entering your own SQL, WebDB lets you surmount the limitations imposed by the design compromises that were necessary to keep the product usable. If you are familiar with SQL, you easily understand all of the statements that are used in the rest of this section. If you are not familiar with SQL, you still might want to read through this section to get some idea of how you can extend the functionality of WebDB reports by entering your own query strings.

Using SQL for formatting and sorting

The first report you will create using SQL as the basis for retrieving data will be a recast of the report you just finished. The report will use multiple tables, but also take advantage of the built-in formatting capabilities of SQL to make the data more readable in the finished report. You will also use SQL to implement your own sort conditions.

1. Use the Back push button of the browser to return to the WebDB development environment.
2. Return to the main Report page by clicking the Reports icon in the shortcuts bar.
3. Select the Report from SQL Query radio button and click the Create push button.
4. Select the NETU schema from Schema combo box and give the new report the name of **ch6_rep_3**.
5. Click the Next arrow on the Report Name and Schema page.
6. Delete the default SQL query from the text window on the SQL Statement page. Enter the following query exactly as shown:

```
SELECT UGRADS.LASTNAME ||', '|| UGRADS.FIRSTNAME As Name,
TRANSCRIPT.YEAR,
TRANSCRIPT.SEMESTER, COURSE_CATALOG.COURSE_NAME
FROM UGRADS, TRANSCRIPT, COURSE_CATALOG
WHERE UGRADS.ID = TRANSCRIPT.ID AND TRANSCRIPT.CATNUM =
COURSE_CATALOG.CATNUM AND UGRADS.ID = :ID
ORDER BY UGRADS.ID, TRANSCRIPT.YEAR, TRANSCRIPT.SEMESTER,
COURSE_CATALOG.COURSE_NAME
```

If you aren't the greatest typist in the world, you share something in common with the authors of this book. We have included the previous SQL statement in the ch6_sql1.txt file in the Chapter 6 directory under the Examples directory on the CD-ROM accompanying this book.

This looks like a somewhat complex SQL statement, but you can examine the different clauses in the statement section by section to understand it fully.

The first section is the list of columns that are selected for the report—the same functionality provided by the Table/View Columns page in the Query Wizard. In the previous SQL statement, we have qualified the names of each of the columns with the name of the table the column is a part of, although this is not strictly necessary for all of the columns. The only columns that require this sort of qualification are the ID columns in the UGRADS and TRANSCRIPT tables and the CATNUM columns in the TRANSCRIPT and COURSE_CATALOG tables, because all columns must be qualified if their name is not unique within the tables in the query. However, adding the table name to a column name is always a good practice for documentation purposes.

There is only one new thing in this section of the query. The first value selected is a concatenation of the value of the LASTNAME column, a comma and space enclosed within single quote marks, and the FIRSTNAME column, all joined using the Oracle SQL concatenation character, "||." This manipulation presents the student names in a more legible manner.

You must include a name for any concatenated or calculated column for the SQL statement to operate properly in WebDB.

The second section of SQL statement is a simple listing of the three tables that take part in this query: the UGRADS table, the TRANSCRIPT table, and the COURSE_CATALOG table.

The third section of the SQL query is the WHERE clause. The WHERE clause in this SQL statement actually serves three purposes. First, it lists the join conditions for the three tables. Second, it indicates that the results returned from this query are limited by a value for the ID column. Third, the colon that appears before the text :ID on the right-hand side of the equal sign indicates that the value for the ID column is supplied by what is called a *bind variable.* A bind variable in an SQL statement is a variable supplied when the query is run and bound into the actual SQL statement. This is exactly what a parameter specified in the WebDB Report Builder does, and you will see that WebDB understands this SQL syntax.

Finally, the SQL statement ends with an ORDER BY clause that specifies the sort order for the query. You can see that there are four sorting columns in the ORDER BY clause, which is no problem at all for the Oracle database executing this statement. The limitation on row ordering in WebDB is strictly a result of the user interface design of the Report Builder Wizard.

If you are entering the text of an SQL statement directly into the Report Builder Wizard, you may make a mistake (or two or three) when entering the text of the statement. Although WebDB catches any SQL errors when you try to move to the next page in the Report Builder Wizard or finish editing the report component, you may not find these errors to be as helpful as you would like in debugging the statement. We have found it useful to create and test our SQL statements in a standard utility such as SQL*Plus, and then cut and paste the statements into WebDB.

You have done all the really hard work for this report already, so you can move to the next page in the Report Builder Wizard.

7. Click the Next arrow on the SQL Statement page.

8. Click the Next arrow on the Columns Formatting page to accept the default values for the column names.
9. Select the columns NAME, YEAR, and SEMESTER, in that order, for the Break Options.
10. Click on the Next arrow on the Display Options page.

On the next page of the Report Builder Wizard, you can see that WebDB has recognized the bind variable and created a parameter for it.

11. Change the Prompt for the parameter to **ID:**.
12. Deselect the Break Control and the Order By check boxes in the middle of the page.

You do not have to specify any row ordering information on the Display Options page, because you have already taken care of the ordering of the data with the ORDER BY clause in your SQL statement. You do, however, have to tell WebDB to make a break group for each of the three columns in order to properly suppress the redundant data in the report.

13. Click the Next arrow on the Parameter Entry From Display Options page.
14. Select the PUBLIC.TEMPLATE_6 template from the Template combo box. Click the checkered flag to complete the report.

Of course, if you were designing this report for a production system, you would take the time to enter headers, footers, and help text for the report and its associated parameter page.

15. Click the Parameter link at the bottom of the Manage Component page to run the report.
16. Enter **1010** for the ID parameter on the report parameter page and click the Run Report push button.

The report should look like Figure 6-9.

By specifying your own SQL statement as the source for the data used by WebDB for a report, you can take advantage of the greater flexibility in sorting the rows of the report. In the next section, you will learn how you can also use the aggregate functions in SQL to extend your reports.

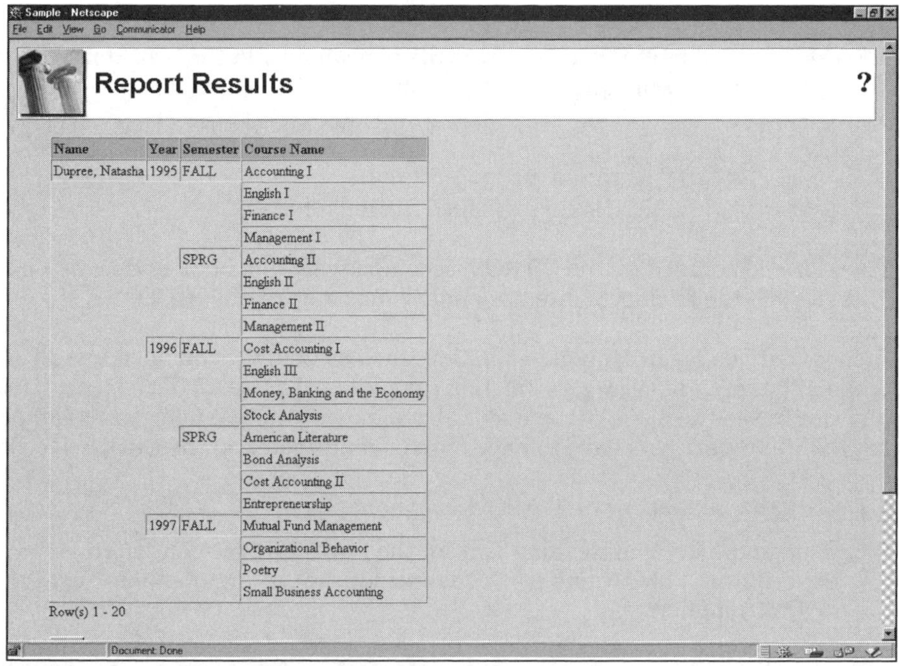

Name	Year	Semester	Course Name
Dupree, Natasha	1995	FALL	Accounting I
			English I
			Finance I
			Management I
		SPRG	Accounting II
			English II
			Finance II
			Management II
	1996	FALL	Cost Accounting I
			English III
			Money, Banking and the Economy
			Stock Analysis
		SPRG	American Literature
			Bond Analysis
			Cost Accounting II
			Entrepreneurship
	1997	FALL	Mutual Fund Management
			Organizational Behavior
			Poetry
			Small Business Accounting

Figure 6-9: An advanced report based on an SQL query

Using SQL for additional aggregate functions

An *aggregate function* is a function that acts on groups, or aggregations, of rows. In WebDB, the only aggregate function that you can use through the standard Report Builder interface is SUM, which adds together a group of numeric values.

There are other aggregate functions that you may want to use in your report. For instance, you might want to know how many students are in each different major at Net University. You can use the aggregate function COUNT to deliver this information.

1. Use the Back push button in the browser to return to the WebDB development environment.
2. Return to the main Report page.
3. Select the Report from SQL Query radio button and click the Create push button.
4. Select the NETU schema from Schema combo box and give the new report the name of **ch6_rep_4**.

5. Click the Next arrow on the Report Name and Schema page.
6. Delete the default SQL query from the text window in the SQL Statement page. Enter the following query exactly as shown:

```
SELECT MAJORS.MAJOR, MAJORS.MAJOR_DESC, COUNT(*) AS Students
FROM UGRADS, MAJORS
WHERE UGRADS.MAJOR = MAJORS.MAJOR
GROUP BY MAJORS.MAJOR, MAJORS.MAJOR_DESC
```

This query is included on the CD-ROM accompanying this book under the Chapter 6 directory in the Examples directory under the name of ch6_sql2.txt.

When you are using an aggregate function, such as COUNT, you must use all columns that are not aggregate functions as part of the GROUP BY clause. Because you want to see the name of the major and some descriptive information about the major in the report, you have to have both columns listed in the GROUP BY clause.

7. Click the Next arrow on the SQL Statement page.
8. Change the Column Heading Text for the MAJOR_DESC column to **Description.** Enter **Number of Students** for the Column Heading Text for the COUNT function.

All the functionality you need is encapsulated in the SQL statement you have just defined as the source of your report. You don't have to specify a row order, or a break clause. In fact, specifying these to WebDB would probably cause unpredictable results in your report.

9. Click the Next arrow on each page until you reach the Text Options page. Set the Template for the report to PUBLIC.TEMPLATE_6.
10. Click the checkered flag to finish and generate your report.
11. On the Manage Component page that appears after the report has been successfully generated, click the Run link.

The report that comes back should look like the report in Figure 6-10.

The last example in this section uses another aggregate function, AVG, to calculate the grade point average for each student, sorted by their major.

1. Use the Back push button in your browser to return to the WebDB development environment.
2. Return to the main Report page by clicking the Reports icon in the shortcuts bar.
3. Select the Report from SQL Query radio button and click the Create push button.

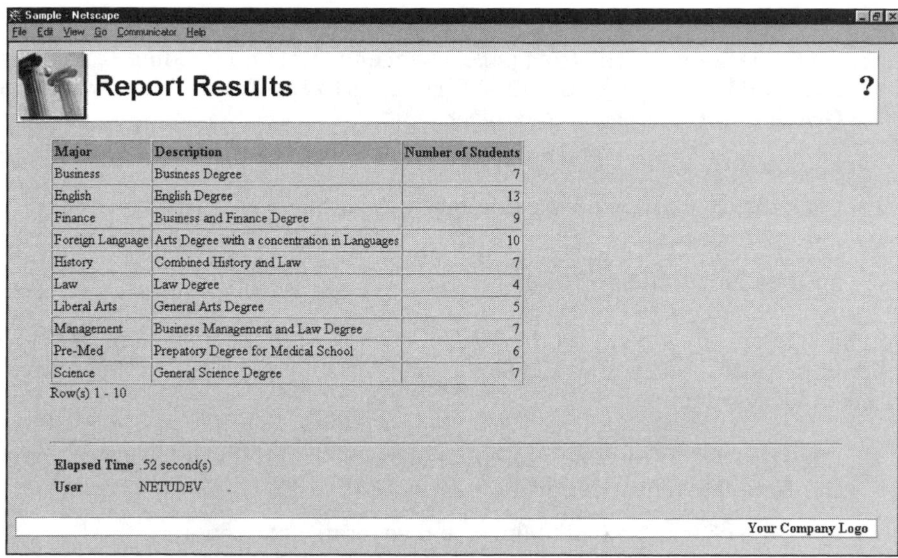

Major	Description	Number of Students
Business	Business Degree	7
English	English Degree	13
Finance	Business and Finance Degree	9
Foreign Language	Arts Degree with a concentration in Languages	10
History	Combined History and Law	7
Law	Law Degree	4
Liberal Arts	General Arts Degree	5
Management	Business Management and Law Degree	7
Pre-Med	Prepatory Degree for Medical School	6
Science	General Science Degree	7

Figure 6-10: Using the COUNT aggregate function in a report

4. Select the NETU schema from Schema combo box and give the new report the name of **ch6_rep_5**.
5. Click the Next arrow on the Report Name and Schema page.
6. Delete the default SQL query from the text window in the SQL statement page. Enter the following query exactly as shown:

```
SELECT UGRADS.MAJOR, UGRADS.LASTNAME, UGRADS.FIRSTNAME,
AVG(GRADES.NUMERIC_GRADE) AS Average
FROM UGRADS, TRANSCRIPT, GRADES
WHERE UGRADS.ID = TRANSCRIPT.ID AND TRANSCRIPT.GRADE =
GRADES.LETTER_GRADE
GROUP BY UGRADS.MAJOR, UGRADS.LASTNAME, UGRADS.FIRSTNAME
```

You can find this query on the CD-ROM accompanying this book in the ch6_sql3.txt file in the Examples directory under the Chapter 6 directory.

You need to use the GRADES table to get the numeric value for the letter grade that is listed in the TRANSCRIPT table. The AVG function automatically takes the sum of the values in the NUMERIC_GRADE column and divides it by the count of rows in the particular break group.

Once again, because you are using an aggregate function, you have to specify all the nonaggregate function columns in the GROUP BY clause.

7. Click the Next arrow on the SQL Statement page.
8. On the Columns Formatting page, change the Column Heading Text for the LASTNAME, FIRSTNAME, and AVG columns to **Last Name**, **First Name**, and **Grade Point Average** respectively.
9. Enter a format mask of **9.99** for the AVG column.
10. Click the Next arrow on the Columns Formatting page.
11. Select the MAJOR choice for the first combo box in the Break Options section on the Display Options page.

You have to specify a break on the MAJOR column because there is more than one student per major and you would like to suppress the display of the repetitive value of the MAJOR column.

12. Click the Next arrows on each page until you reach the Text Options page. Set the Template for the report to PUBLIC.TEMPLATE_6.
13. Click the checkered flag to finish and generate your report.
14. On the Manage Component page that appears after the report has been successfully generated, click the Run link.

The report you get back from WebDB should look like Figure 6-11.

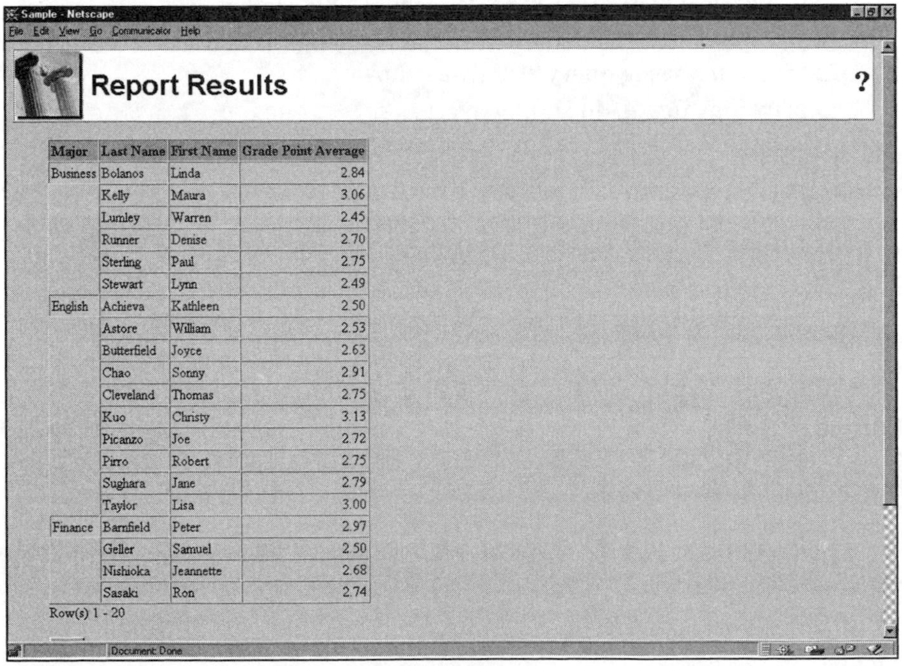

Sample - Netscape

Report Results

Major	Last Name	First Name	Grade Point Average
Business	Bolanos	Linda	2.84
	Kelly	Maura	3.06
	Lumley	Warren	2.45
	Runner	Denise	2.70
	Sterling	Paul	2.75
	Stewart	Lynn	2.49
English	Achieva	Kathleen	2.50
	Astore	William	2.53
	Butterfield	Joyce	2.63
	Chao	Sonny	2.91
	Cleveland	Thomas	2.75
	Kuo	Christy	3.13
	Picanzo	Joe	2.72
	Pirro	Robert	2.75
	Sughara	Jane	2.79
	Taylor	Lisa	3.00
Finance	Barnfield	Peter	2.97
	Geller	Samuel	2.50
	Nishioka	Jeannette	2.68
	Sasaki	Ron	2.74

Row(s) 1 - 20

Document: Done

Figure 6-11: Using the AVG function in a report

Although the wizard used with the Report Builder imposes some limits on the data that can be retrieved, you can use standard SQL to get around many of these limitations.

Later in this book, you will learn how to link these individual reports together to give a more complete picture of the data. You could call the report that provides a count of the students in each major and create a link from the field containing the major to the report that lists the students for each major and their grade point average. You could link from the student field in this report to a detailed listing of each student's classes and their grades in the classes, which would be a modified version of the report you created at the start of this section.

We have included linked versions of these reports in the sample code that comes with this book. You will find a script to install these linked versions in the directory for this chapter under the name linkrep.sql. The linked reports will all start with the characters ch6_rep_link.

More Information on Reporting

In the past two chapters, you learned a lot about using WebDB to create reports. Hopefully, what you discovered will address most of your reporting needs.

Two more topics covered later in this book will help you extend the capabilities of your reports even more. The first topic is the use of PL/SQL to implement logic at specific places in your reports. You have already seen the page in the Report Builder Wizard that gives you the ability to add PL/SQL code to your report. Chapter 24 covers using PL/SQL with WebDB components. The use of PL/SQL is a vast topic, and there are many excellent books on the subject, so the Chapter 24 is not a complete tutorial on PL/SQL. The chapter will help you to understand how PL/SQL interacts with WebDB components, which should be enough to guide an experienced PL/SQL developer in using the language with WebDB.

There is also a terrific feature of WebDB called *batch reporting*. You have also seen evidence of this feature already — the Batch push button that can be displayed on the report parameter page. When you click that push button, your report is sent to a queue to await execution. Using batch reports can help improve the throughput of your WebDB applications by using the Oracle database's internal queuing technology. The capability of the batch functionality of WebDB is covered in Appendix B of this book.

Wrapping Up

You can extend the functionality of the basic WebDB report in a variety of ways: using parameters to shape the selection of data for the report; creating reports with data from many different tables in your database; and using SQL to specify the data sources of your reports.

Reporting is a read-only process. Data comes to you, but you can't insert or update data in the database. The next two chapters introduce you to creating forms that can interact with the data in the database.

✦ ✦ ✦

CHAPTER 7

Building WebDB Forms

✦ ✦ ✦ ✦

In This Chapter

✦ ✦ ✦ ✦

Forms are the basic building blocks of interactive applications. Most of your application systems require you to create a significant number of forms. This chapter is your introduction to building forms with WebDB.

As you can imagine, WebDB gives you a lot of flexibility in creating forms to match your specific needs — far too much flexibility and power to cover in a single chapter. By the end of this chapter, you will be able to create a wide variety of basic forms. The next chapter will extend your form-building ability to cover more complex forms, such as master-detail forms, and actions that require the integration of other WebDB components.

What Is a Form in WebDB?

We all know what a form is. In a physical sense, a form is a preformatted piece of paper with headings to identify the information that is required on the form and blank spaces where you can enter that information.

The physical form translates into an electronic form pretty directly. The headings on an electronic form are static labels, while the blanks on the form are typically text fields where users can enter data. In the graphical world that WebDB lives in, user input can also be presented as a series of choices such as radio buttons or check boxes, or a list of values to choose from, such as a list box or a combo box.

But you have already created WebDB components that had these types of objects. The parameter forms that were automatically generated for the reports you designed in the previous two chapters had objects for user input. They were even called parameter forms.

But the key difference in WebDB between a form and a report centers on the way that these two different components interact with the Oracle database. A report *reads* data from the Oracle database. The user input that is accepted in parameter form is simply used to configure the data and the report that is returned to the user.

With all the different types of forms you can create with WebDB, the user has the ability to write data back to the Oracle database. This has a dramatic impact on the way you design and implement WebDB forms. The most important asset of any information system is its data. The value of the system lies in its capability to store and return large amounts of data. With a report, the user is *never* allowed to add new data to the database, so this important asset is always safe. You still may need to add security to reports because you are concerned about unauthorized people reading your data, but no one is able to damage the integrity, or correctness, of your data through a report.

A form, however, is different. Users can write data to the database and, if you are not careful, they can write logically incorrect data to the database compromising the value of the data and any and all decisions that are based on it. Because of this, you have to think about ways to protect the integrity of your data as you create WebDB forms.

Furthermore, most forms have a single primary purpose: entering data into the database. Consequently, the way you design your forms is somewhat different from the way you might design your reports. When a user is working in a form, they are typically dealing with a single row at a time. This is in direct contrast to reports, which almost always involve many rows of data for a single report or page in a report.

In the end, it is easy to determine when you want to create a WebDB form as opposed to a WebDB report. If the user has to write data to the database, a form is the appropriate component.

What Types of Forms Does WebDB Support?

WebDB lets you build four different types of forms. These types of forms are the following, in order of increasing complexity:

- **Query-by-Example (QBE) forms.** A QBE form is a quick and easy way of gathering selection criteria for a subsequent query. A QBE form enables the user to enter values or conditions for one or more columns in a table that are used to limit the data returned.
- **Forms based on tables or views.** The table- or view-based form is the most common type of form. These types of forms are based on a single table or view, and can be used to insert or update data in the corresponding table or view.

✦ **Forms based on stored procedures.** An Oracle stored procedure can accept any number of parameters. These parameters act like the columns in a normal Oracle table. When you create a form based on a stored procedure, the process of writing data sends the values entered to the parameters of the stored procedure, just as it would send the values to the columns of the underlying table. You may sometimes create a stored procedure to handle more sophisticated processing logic, and WebDB enables you to easily integrate that logic into WebDB components.

✦ **Master-detail forms.** Master-detail forms enable you to enter the values for a master row and more than one associated detail rows. Master and detail rows are normally linked by a common column or key relationship. WebDB's master-detail forms automatically handle all the integrity issues that come when you are writing to more than one table.

A form based on a view can only update the view if the view is updateable in the underlying Oracle database. Please see the Oracle documentation for further details on determining whether a view is updateable. Be aware that in order to update a table or view with a PL/SQL procedure, the owner of the procedure must have direct security access to the tables in the view, and that WebDB forms, like all other WebDB components, are actually created from a PL/SQL procedure. The direct owner of the PL/SQL package that generates a WebDB component is the owner of the schema of the component, which is what a PL/SQL package is stored in. This owner must have explicit write access to the underlying tables the view is based on—security access granted to the owning schema as part of a role is not sufficient to allow write access. The owner of the schema that stores the procedure for a WebDB form must be explicitly granted write access to all tables and views the form interacts with.

The QBE form is the easiest type of form to use to begin understanding WebDB forms, because it gives you the least number of options. Your excursion into the land of forms starts with a simple QBE form.

Creating a QBE Form

The first form component you will create with WebDB is a simple Query-by-Example form. In order to understand, with the least confusion, the different options available to you when creating forms, you should start by creating a form for a table that has a limited number of columns. For your first form component, you will create a QBE form based on the COURSES table in the WebDB sample database.

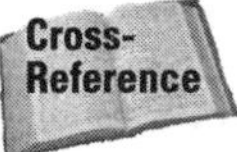

For a description of the WebDB sample database, which is based on a university scenario, please refer to Chapter 2.

You start to build your component on the WebDB home page.

1. Click the Build menu choice on the WebDB home page.
2. Click the User Interface Components menu choice on the main Build page.
3. Click the Forms menu choice on the main User Interface Components page. You have arrived on the main Form Building page, as shown in Figure 7-1.

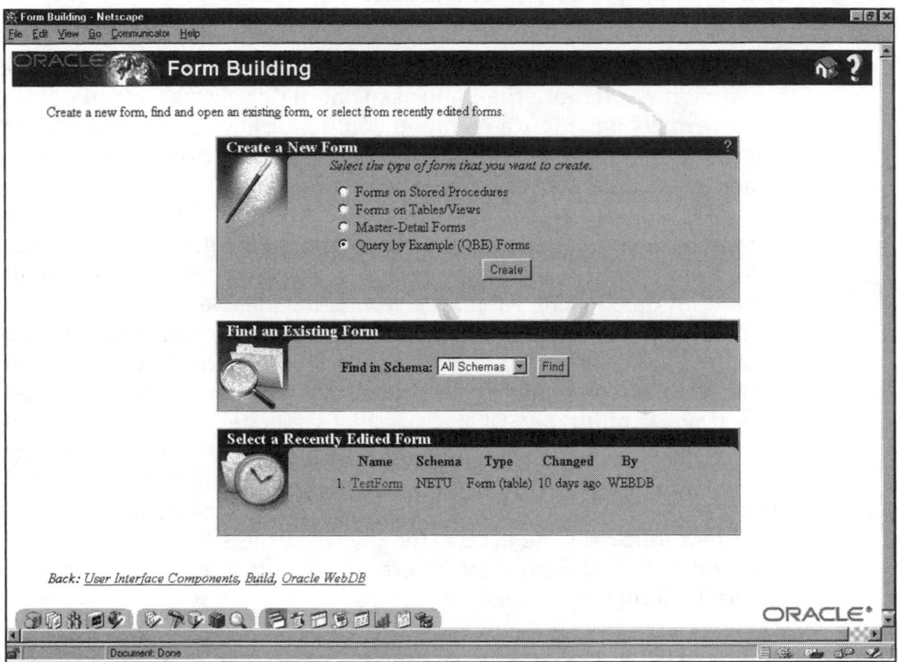

Figure 7-1: The main Form Building page

You could have also arrived at this page by clicking the Forms icon in the right-hand group of icons on the shortcuts bar.

Like the main Report Building page, this page has three panels:

- ✦ The top panel — which you use when creating a new form component. You select which type of form component you want to build and click the Create push button to enter the Form Builder Wizard.
- ✦ The middle panel — which you can use to search any one schema or all schemas for existing form components.
- ✦ The bottom panel — which lists the forms you have worked on most recently and provides links to begin immediately editing the component.

As mentioned previously, this first form is a QBE-type form component. To begin:

4. Select the Query by Example (QBE) Form radio button and click the Create push button. The first page of the Form Builder Wizard for QBE forms looks like Figure 7-2.

If you have been reading this book in order, you can see that the first page of the QBE Form Builder Wizard looks a lot like the first page of the Report Builder Wizard. You select a schema that stores the form component package and give the component a name.

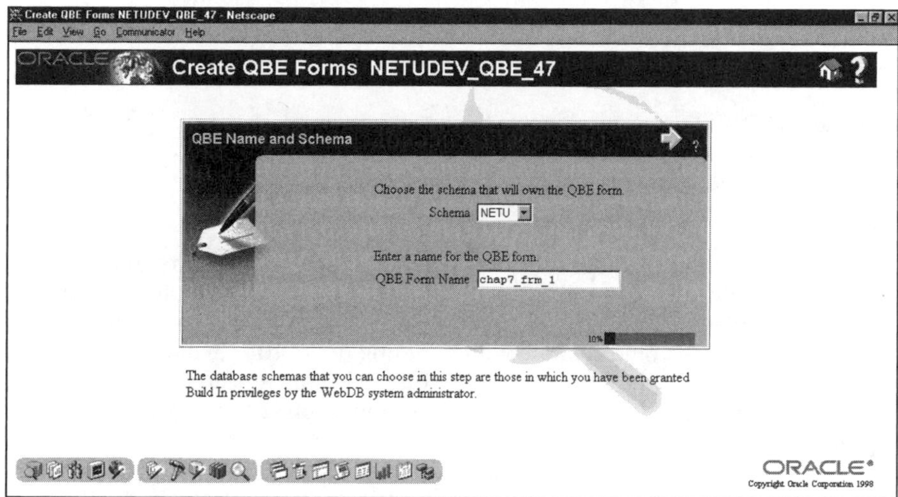

Figure 7-2: The first page of the Form Builder Wizard

5. Leave the NETU entry selected in the Schema combo box and name the form **ch7_frm_1**.
6. Click the Next arrow on the QBE Name and Schema page.

The next page in the Form Builder Wizard, as shown in Figure 7-3, asks you to select a single table or view that will be the basis of the form. The default value for the Table/View combo box is the SCOTT.EMP table, if you have a standard installation of Oracle.

7. Select the NETU.MAJORS entry in the Table/View combo box.
8. Click the Next arrow on the Table or View page of the Form Builder Wizard.

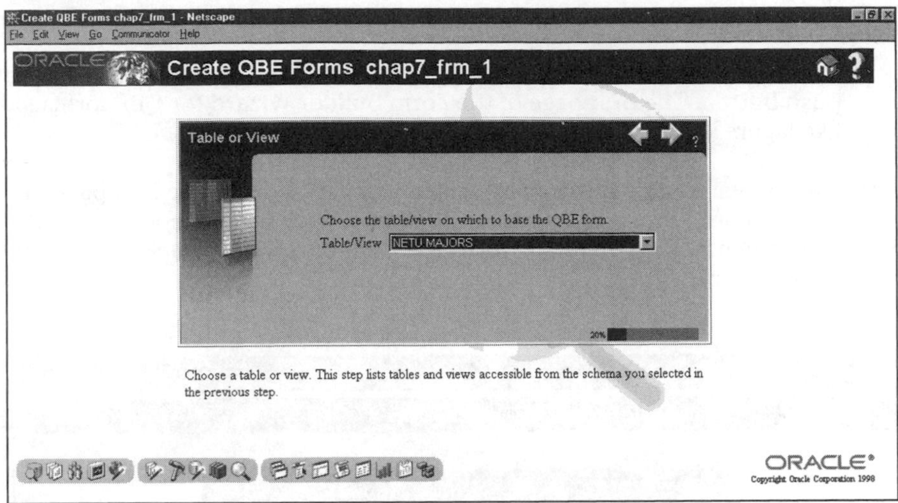

Figure 7-3: The Table or View page in the Form Builder Wizard

The next page of the QBE Form Builder Wizard displays a list box that enables you to select the columns that will appear in the QBE form. By default, all of the columns are selected. If you want to eliminate some columns from the form that are generated, click the column name while holding down the Ctrl key to deselect the column while leaving the other columns selected. This method works for a PC; if you are not using a PC, use whatever key combination is appropriate for your platform.

For your first QBE form, you might as well leave all the columns in the form.

9. Click the Next arrow on the Table/View Columns page to accept the default selection of all the columns in the MAJORS table.

The next page in the QBE Form Builder Wizard, shown in Figure 7-4, also looks familiar. The formatting options on the page are also available on the Columns Formatting page for reports. The reason for this is very simple. Once users enter their selection criteria into a QBE form, they click a push button in the form to run a report, just as they would for a parameter form for a report.

10. Change the Column Heading Text for the MAJOR_DESC column to **Major Description**.
11. Click the Next arrow on the QBE Results Page Formatting page.
12. Click the Next arrow on the Link Display Options page.

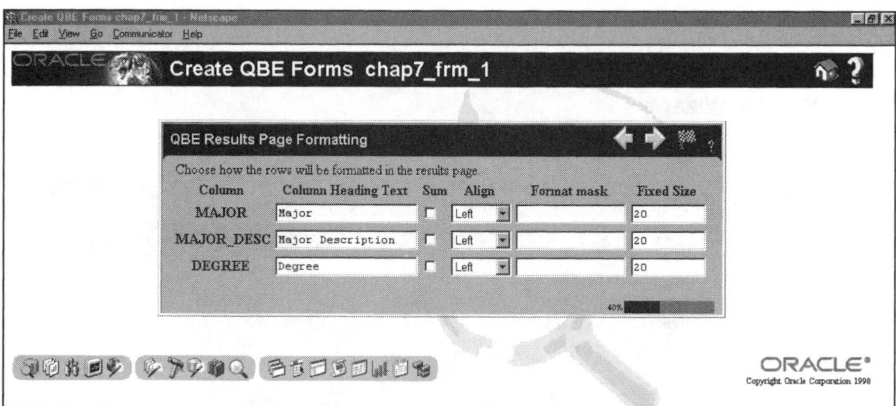

Figure 7-4: The column formatting page in the QBE Form Builder Wizard

You may have noticed that there was no place on the QBE Results Page Formatting page to enter a link for any of the columns on the results page. With a QBE form, you can only have a single link in the results, and you specify that link on the next page of the Form Builder Wizard for QBE forms, as shown in Figure 7-5.

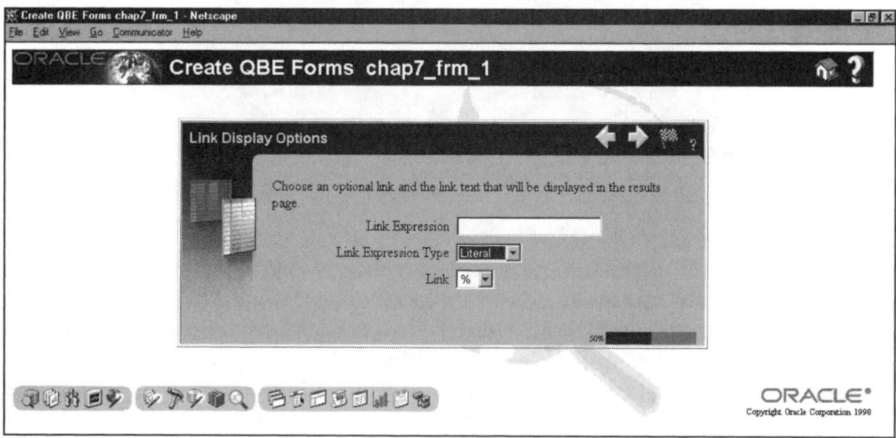

Figure 7-5: Specifying links for a QBE form's results pages

Chapter 17 concentrates on creating and using links, so you don't have to specify anything on this page of the QBE Form Builder Wizard. You should notice, however, that you can specify a label for the link with Link Expression, that is associated with the link in the results returned from the QBE form's query. In a report, a link operates off a specific value in a specific column.

The next page in the QBE Form Builder Wizard is the Display Options page, which is shown in Figure 7-6. This page should look very familiar if you have already created a report — it has all the same display options as the corresponding page in the Report Builder Wizard.

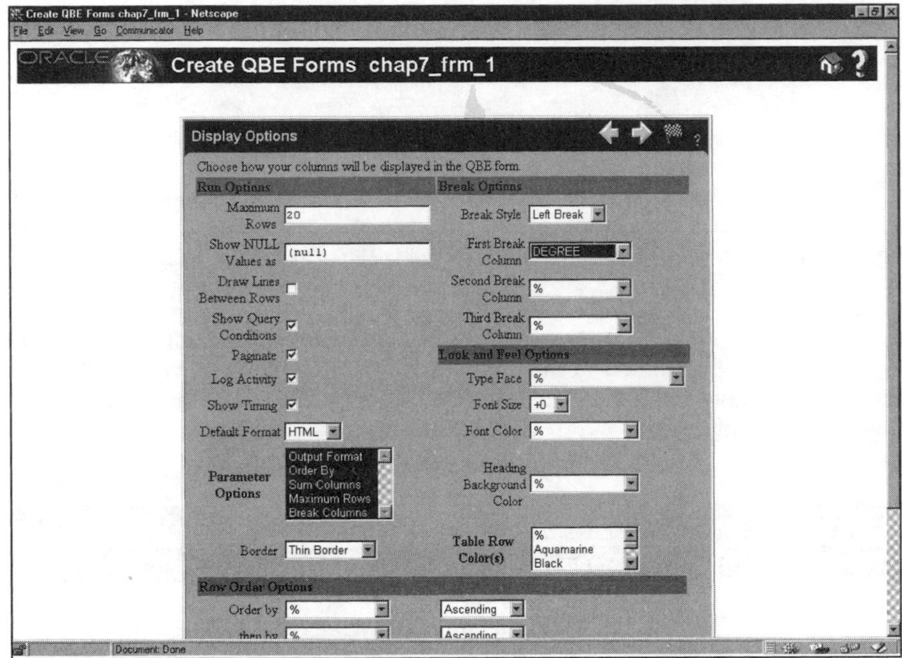

Figure 7-6: The Display Options page in the QBE Form Builder Wizard

The only significant difference between the report's Display Options page and the QBE form's Display Options page is the Parameter Options list box. The Parameter Options list box in the QBE Form Builder Wizard contains the same entries that are handled by check boxes in the Report Builder Wizard, except that this list box includes an option that enables a user to specify which columns they would like to sum at run time (Sum Columns), and it doesn't include a parameter for the font size.

Because a QBE form is both more basic and more flexible than a standard report, it makes sense to enable a user to dynamically select the columns they want summed at run time.

13. Select the DEGREE entry in the First Break Column combo box in the Break Options area of the Display Options page.
14. Click the Next arrow on the Display Options page.

You may also notice that you do not have the option to show the SQL generated by the QBE form. Because the QBE form can also be used to insert data into a table or view, the lack of this choice makes sense for the QBE form.

Once again, the next page in the QBE Form Builder Wizard (shown in Figure 7-7), looks very familiar. The Button Options page lets you specify which of the five standard push buttons you want to be included on the QBE page. The four push buttons titled Query, Save, Batch, and Reset perform the same functions as their counterparts in the Report Builder Wizard and are described in detail in the first report builder section. The only difference is that the first push button for a report is labeled Run Report by default, while the corresponding push button in the QBE form is labeled Query. The extra push button for a QBE form is the Insert push button. And herein lies the rub — the main difference between a QBE form and a parameter form for a report is that a user can insert data with the first page in a QBE form component.

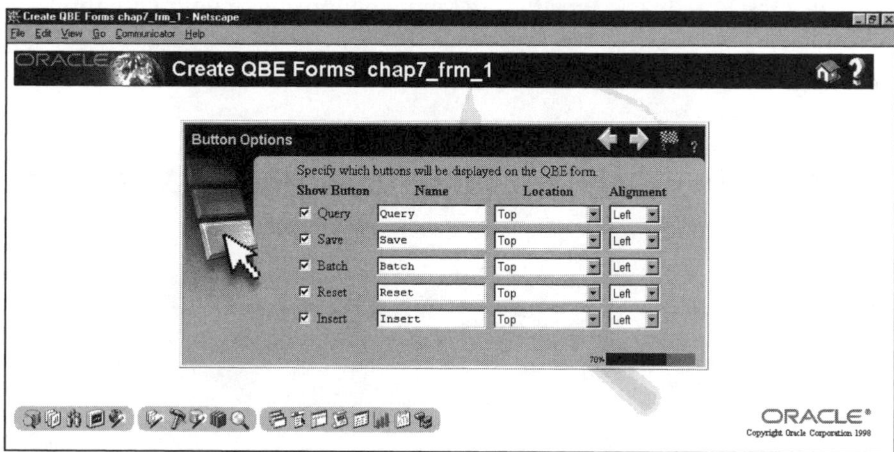

Figure 7-7: The Button Options page in the QBE Form Builder Wizard

15. Click the Next arrow on the Button Options page.

The next two pages in the QBE Form Builder Wizard enable you to choose the template and specify header, footer, and help text for the QBE parameter form and the QBE results form just like the corresponding form for the Report Builder Wizard. There is only one small difference. In the Report Builder Wizard, the header, footer, and help text fields for the report are listed on the left side of the page and the same fields for the parameter form are on the right side of the page. In the QBE Form Builder Wizard, the initial QBE form is listed on the left, while the results, which correspond to the body of the report, are on the right.

Because the next two pages in the Form Builder Wizard are virtually identical to the same pages in the Report Builder Wizard, they are not shown or described in this chapter.

16. Select the PUBLIC.TEMPLATE_6 choice in the Template combo box.
17. Click the Next arrow on the Text Options page.
18. Click the Next arrow on the Add Advanced PL/SQL code page.
19. Click the OK push button on the Create QBE Form page.

Once WebDB has completed generating the package for your QBE form, you are presented with the same Manage Component page that you received after generating a report component. You can use the links at the bottom of the page in the same way that you use the links at the bottom of the Manage Component page for a report.

20. Click the Run link on the Manage Component page for your QBE form.

The page returned to your browser looks exactly like a report, as shown in Figure 7-8.

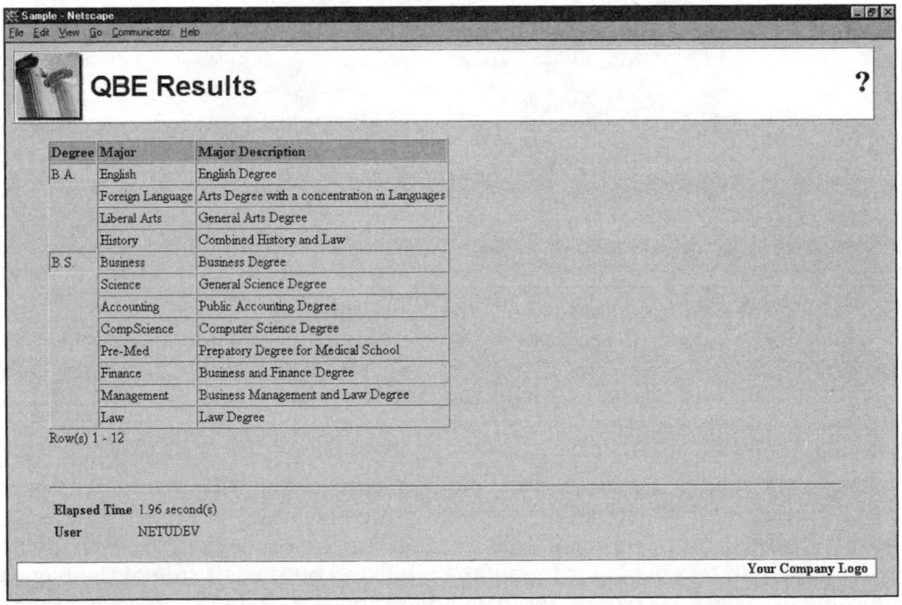

Sample - Netscape

File Edit View Go Communicator Help

QBE Results ?

Degree	Major	Major Description
B.A.	English	English Degree
	Foreign Language	Arts Degree with a concentration in Languages
	Liberal Arts	General Arts Degree
	History	Combined History and Law
B.S.	Business	Business Degree
	Science	General Science Degree
	Accounting	Public Accounting Degree
	CompScience	Computer Science Degree
	Pre-Med	Prepatory Degree for Medical School
	Finance	Business and Finance Degree
	Management	Business Management and Law Degree
	Law	Law Degree

Row(s) 1 - 12

Elapsed Time 1.96 second(s)
User NETUDEV

Your Company Logo

Figure 7-8: The results of your first QBE form

The parameter page for a QBE form, however, looks a little bit different than the parameter page for a report.

1. Use the Back push button of your browser to return to the Manage Component page inside of the WebDB development environment.
2. Click the Parameters link at the bottom of the page.

The QBE Parameters page is shown in Figure 7-9. This parameter page, which, in reality, is the main product of the QBE form building process, looks quite different from the parameter page for a report.

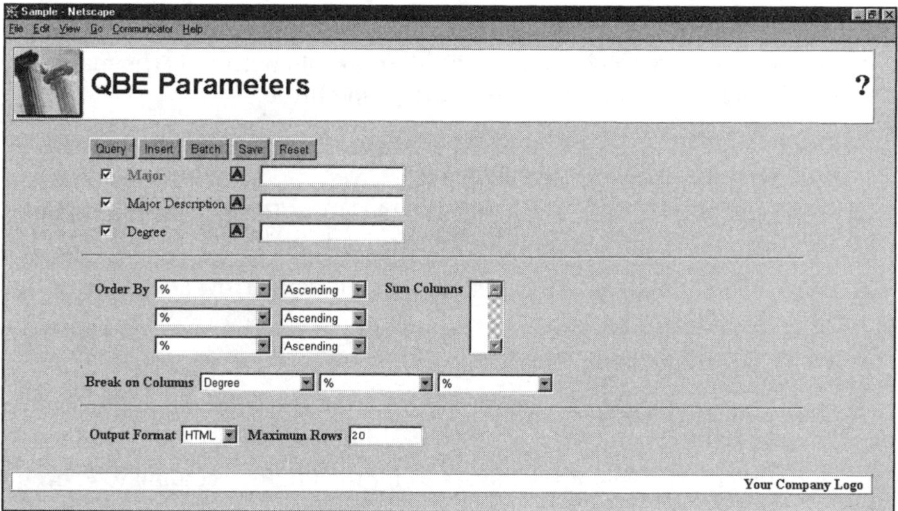

Figure 7-9: The QBE Parameters page

First off, you can see all the columns in the table listed in rows at the top of the page. The fields for these columns have some different attributes than those for standard parameters on a report parameter page. The first object in a row is a little check box that indicates if you want the column displayed in the results — just like the check box in the Browse database interface. The check box is followed by the name you indicated for the column heading for the column. Then there is an icon that looks like a big letter *A* between the label for the field and field. This icon indicates that these fields accept alphanumeric values. In addition, one of the field labels is red. This is an indication that this column does not accept null values, so the user must enter a value for the field.

At the bottom of the page, you can see another difference between this QBE form and a report parameter form. The first difference is that there is a very thin list box on the right of the Order By fields labeled Sum Columns. This list box has no entries for this form. The entries in the Sum Columns box list the columns that a user could specify should have totals in the returned results. Only numeric columns can have totals, and, because there are no numeric columns in the MAJORS table, no entries are listed and the Sum Columns list box is sized accordingly. Of course, you could suppress the display of this section of the QBE form by deselecting the Sum Columns entry in the Parameter Options list box in the QBE builder.

In order to see how the Sum Columns option on the QBE form works, you can quickly build another QBE form.

3. Use the Back push button of your browser to return to the Manage Component page inside of the WebDB development environment.
4. Return to the main Form Building page by clicking the Forms icon in the right-hand section of the shortcuts bar at the bottom of the page.
5. Select the Query by Example (QBE) Forms radio button on the main page of the Form Builder and click the Create push button.
6. Enter **ch7_frm_2** into the QBE Form Name field and click the Next arrow at the top of the Form Name and Schema page.
7. Select the NETU.COURSE_CATALOG table in the Table/View combo box. Click the Next arrow at the top of the Table or View page.
8. Leave all the columns selected and click the Next arrow at the top of the Table/View Columns page.
9. To change the Column Headings:
    a. Change the Column Heading text for the CATNUM column to **Catalog Number**.
    b. Change the Column Heading text for the PREREQ column to **Prerequisite**.
    c. Change the Column Heading text for the COURSE_DESC column to **Course Description**.

You can already tell that there is a numeric column in the COURSE_CATALOG table, because the CREDITS column is right-justified with a fixed size of 10 by default.

10. Click the Next arrow at the top of the QBE Results Page Formatting page.
11. Click the Next arrow at the top of the Link Display Options page.
12. Click the Next arrow at the top of the Display Options page.
13. Click the Next arrow at the top of the Button Options page.
14. Select the PUBLIC.TEMPLATE_6 choice from the Template combo box at the top of the Text Options page. Click the checkered flag to complete the QBE form.

You may have found it a bit tiresome to click through all the pages in the QBE Form Builder Wizard when you were only accepting the default choices. You could have accomplished the same thing by giving your QBE form a name and clicking the checkered flag icon at the top of any of the pages. This icon accepts all the default choices for all of the pages and generates the report. You could then go back to the QBE form component and edit those few places where you wanted to change the default values.

15. To see the sum option at work, click the Parameters link at the bottom of the Manage Component page.

You can see that this QBE form is a bit more crowded than your first QBE form. There are more fields for entry, and more of them are required. In order to see how the sum option works, you have to make a couple of choices in the form.

16. Select the Credits choice in the Sum Columns list box. Select the Prerequisite choice in the first Break on Columns combo box.

If you don't specify a break column, you only get a sum for each page. If you select a break column, you get a sum for each break group and each page.

On the last QBE form, you didn't even use the selection criteria that were presented on the form. These criteria fields work a little bit differently than those on the parameter page of a report.

17. Enter **SCI%** into the field labeled Catalog Number.
18. Enter **>= 4** into the field labeled Credits.

These selection criteria include wild cards and relational operators. Unlike a report, the QBE fields can accept either standard values or a combination of standard values, wild cards, and relational expressions. Of course, you can specify any single relational operator in the parameter form for a report, but you would have to remember to use the "like" condition properly for the comparison.

19. Click the Query push button in the QBE form.

The results returned to the browser look like the results in Figure 7-10. You can see that the QBE results have been properly grouped, and that a sum has been computed for each group, as well as for the page and the total report.

You can also see that WebDB has laid out the results in an HTML table, so columns with long values, such as the Course Description, automatically wrap in place.

Up to this point, you have simply been using the QBE form as a parameter form. You still have not attempted to use the form to write data back to the database, which you will attempt now.

20. Use the Back push button of the browser to return to the main QBE form.
21. Click the Reset push button to clear the data entry fields.
22. Enter **SCI1000** as the Catalog Number, **Test course** as the Course Description, and **5** as the Credits.

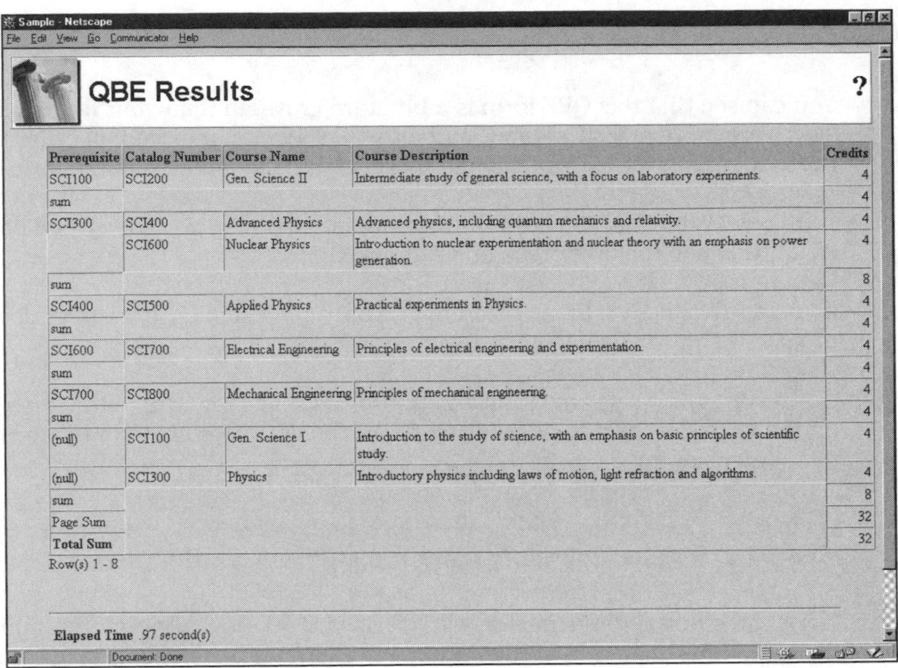

Prerequisite	Catalog Number	Course Name	Course Description	Credits
SCI100	SCI200	Gen. Science II	Intermediate study of general science, with a focus on laboratory experiments.	4
sum				4
SCI300	SCI400	Advanced Physics	Advanced physics, including quantum mechanics and relativity.	4
	SCI600	Nuclear Physics	Introduction to nuclear experimentation and nuclear theory with an emphasis on power generation.	4
sum				8
SCI400	SCI500	Applied Physics	Practical experiments in Physics.	4
sum				4
SCI600	SCI700	Electrical Engineering	Principles of electrical engineering and experimentation.	4
sum				4
SCI700	SCI800	Mechanical Engineering	Principles of mechanical engineering.	4
sum				4
(null)	SCI100	Gen. Science I	Introduction to the study of science, with an emphasis on basic principles of scientific study.	4
(null)	SCI300	Physics	Introductory physics including laws of motion, light refraction and algorithms.	4
sum				8
Page Sum				32
Total Sum				32

Row(s) 1 - 8

Elapsed Time .97 second(s)

Document: Done

Figure 7-10: Results from a QBE form with a sum

You can easily see that all three of these fields are required—their labels are in red.

23. Click the Insert push button on the QBE form. You get a success notification from WebDB, which looks like the page shown in Figure 7-11.

Column	Value(s)
CATNUM	SCI1000
PREREQ	
COURSE_NAME	
COURSE_DESC	Test course
CREDITS	5

Figure 7-11: Successfully inserting a row from a QBE form

24. Use the Back push button of the browser to return to the main QBE form.
25. Click the Reset push button to clear the data entry fields.
26. Enter **SCI%** into the field labeled Catalog Number.
27. Click the Query push button in the main QBE form.

You can see that the row of data you entered is now in the database, because it is returned as part of your report. As mentioned previously, this ability to write data to the database is the main difference between using a QBE form and using a report parameter form. But what happens when a user tries to insert invalid data into the database?

28. Use the Back push button of the browser to return to the main QBE form.
29. Click the Reset push button to clear the data entry fields.
30. Enter **SCI1001** as the Catalog Number and **Test course II** as the Course Description.
31. Click the Insert push button.

Welcome to the world of data integrity! You have received your first error page from a WebDB form. The error message delivered by WebDB, as shown in Figure 7-12, is not the most easily decipherable message in the world, especially for an end user. But the important part of the error returned is that the Oracle database guarded the integrity of the data being inserted into the database. The database knew not to allow null values for the CREDITS column, so it rejected the row you just tried to insert.

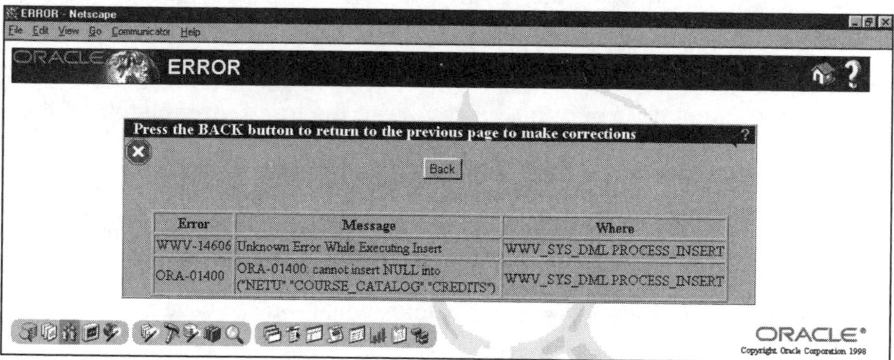

Figure 7-12: An INSERT error from a QBE form

This should not have come as a surprise to the user, at least not to a user who understood that the red color of the label for the Credit field meant that the field required an entry. Of course, not every user is so well informed, so you will see later in the book how to prevent those types of errors from occurring.

Null data is not the only problem that can occur when trying to insert or update data. To see another type of integrity violation at work, you can try to insert a row using the QBE form for the MAJORS table you created earlier in this section.

32. Use the Back push button of the browser to return to the Manage Component page of the WebDB environment.
33. Click the Forms icon in the shortcuts bar to return to the main Form Building page.
34. Scroll to the bottom of the page and click the form labeled ch7_frm_1 to bring up the QBE form for the MAJORS table.
35. Click the Parameters link at the bottom of the Manage Component page to run the QBE form.
36. Enter **Baseball** into the field labeled Major, **America's Pastime** into the field labeled Major Description, and **B.H.** (for Bachelor's Hobby) into the field labeled Degree.
37. Click the Insert push button.

Where did this other error come from? The DEGREE column in the database is limited to only allowing the values of B.A. or B.S., the only two degrees that are allowed at Net University.

There is nothing you can add in a simple QBE form to avoid these errors. You will see in the rest of this chapter and this book how to avoid these errors with other types of forms and shared objects in WebDB.

QBE Form or Report Component?

It looks like the QBE form is a lot like using a report with parameters. A user can insert data with a QBE form, but a developer could always keep the Insert push button off the QBE form to safeguard the data. When should you use each type of object?

The main differences between the QBE form and the parameter form are as follows:

✦ You can allow a user to dynamically specify a column that can be summed with a QBE form, while you can't with a parameter-driven report.

✦ You can only have a single link in a QBE form, while you can have many different links in a report.

✦ You can use SQL to shape the data in a report, which you cannot do with a QBE form.

What choice should you make? The functionality differences are not that significant, because most reports do not require more than one link and the other types of functionality can be implemented in either solution. If you really want to give your users unlimited selection capabilities, the QBE form is probably a better idea, because your users to have access to many different combinations of fields and the QBE form saves on screen real estate and makes the results easier to obtain. If your users require this type of functionality, they will probably not mind that some of the labels on the QBE form are red while others are not.

Whatever you do, you should probably pick one of the two forms of report interaction and stick to it to avoid confusion.

QBE forms, as you have seen, are as much like WebDB reports as they are like traditional form components. The next section leads you through the creation of a form based on a table. This gives you a lot more flexibility in determining how the user interacts with the form while writing data to the database.

Creating a Form Based on a Table

If you are developing a WebDB application whose primary purpose is to enter data in the database, you will create a lot of form components that are based on tables or views.

This version of WebDB that is available at the time of this writing only includes the ability to create a structured layout for forms. The next incremental version of WebDB, Version 2.1, which may be available by the time you read this, will also allow you to lay out forms in an unstructured manner, similar to creating a user template.

1. Return to the main Form Building page in the WebDB environment.
2. Select the Forms on Table/Views radio button in the top panel of the page and click the Create push button.

The first part of the table-based Form Builder

The first page of the Form Builder Wizard for a form based on a table or view looks just like the first page of the Form Builder Wizard for a QBE form — or for a report, for that matter.

3. Accept the default Schema of NETU and enter **ch7_frm_3** as the Form Name.
4. Click the Next arrow on the Form Name and Schema page.

The second page of the Form Builder Wizard for a form based on a table or view also looks just like the corresponding page for a QBE form. To help illustrate the difference between this type of form and a QBE form, you should create your new form based on the same table as one of the QBE forms you created.

5. Select the NETU.MAJORS table in the Tables/Views combo box.
6. Click the Next arrow on the Tables or Views page.

The next page of the Form Builder is the most important and complicated page in the entire process of creating a form.

Column formatting and validation

The next page of the Form Builder Wizard for a table-based form is different from any page you have seen before, as shown in Figure 7-13.

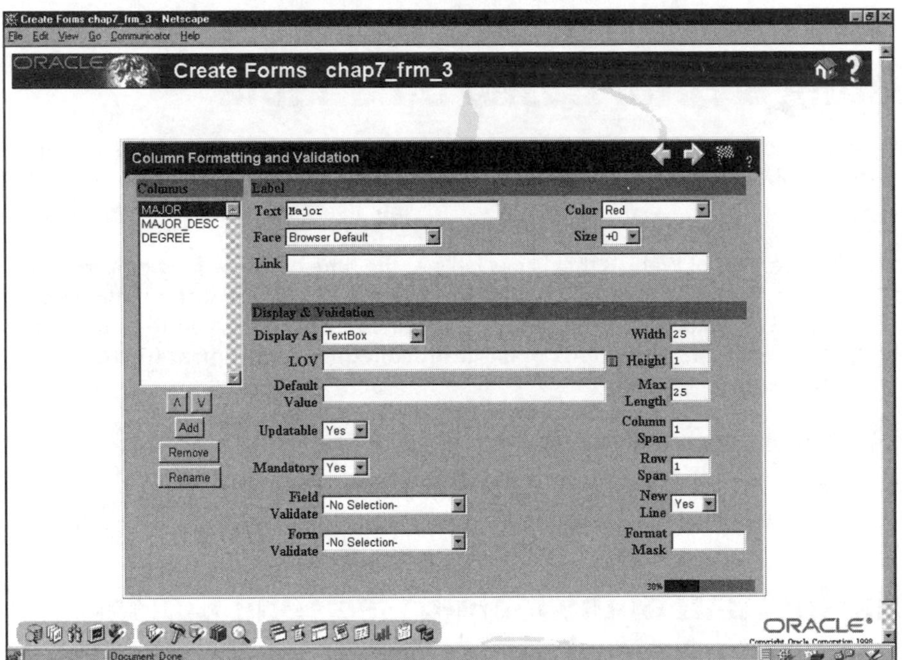

Figure 7-13: Column Formatting and Validation page for a table-based form

This page lets you format the columns that appear on the page as well as some validation for each of the columns.

The Columns list box

The first thing to notice is the Columns list box to the left of the page. The Columns list box contains all the columns in the table the form is based on. The order that the columns appear in the list box specifies the order that the labels and fields for the columns appear on the generated form. By default, the columns appear in the Columns list box in the order they appear in the table. You can use the up- and down-arrow buttons just below the list box to move a column up or down within the Columns list box to adjust the order of the elements in the generated form.

There are three push buttons below the up- and down-arrow push buttons. If you select a column in the list box and click the Remove push button, the selected column is removed from the list after you confirm the deletion by clicking an OK push button in a dialog box. If you select a column and click the Rename push button, you can give the column a different name.

The name of a column is used by WebDB to create the SQL statements that insert and update data in the database. Because of this, you should never change the name of a column in the database except for one situation. If the name of a column in the database has changed and you want to bring a form that includes that column's name into conformation with the database, you can change the name of the column to correct it without having to recreate the entire form from scratch.

You can also add a new column to the Columns list by clicking the Add push button. Adding an entry to the Columns list adds a label and field to the form that are generated from your specifications. Because a column can be used for formatting the WebDB form — as described in the following sections on the Horizontal Rule object and in the discussion of Row Span and Column Span — there may be a need to add a false column to the list. For example, if you wanted to have a horizontal rule between the label and column for the MAJOR_DESC column and the DEGREE column, you could add an entry to the Columns list box, move that column between the two other columns, and format that column as a horizontal rule.

You can use this functionality in the form you are building.

7. Click the Add push button below the Columns list box. Enter the name **Rule** for the object and click the OK push button.
8. When you return to the Columns list, use the up- and down-arrow push buttons to position the Rule column between the MAJOR_DESC and the MAJOR columns.
9. Set the Display As combo box for the Rule column to Horizontal Rule.

When you select a column from the Columns list box, all of the entries you make on the rest of the page apply to that column and that column only. This may take some getting used to at first, and you may find yourself changing values of the wrong column. It will save you some trouble if you train yourself to start every change in the Column Formatting and Validation page by selecting the column you wish to change.

The Label area

There are two basic areas on the rest of the page that you can use to shape how the entries for a column appear and operate. At the top of the page, you can specify how the label for a column is displayed. The fields for the text of the label, the color of the label, the typeface (or face) for the label, and the size of the label should be self-explanatory. The default choice for a typeface is Browser Default, which causes the label to use the font the user has set as a default for their browser. Any other font choice overrides whatever the user has set for their browser.

There is a combo box that you can click to bring up a list of valid colors for your label. By default, if a column in the database is required, the label for that column is shown in red. Remember that each of the formats you specify in these fields applies only to the label for the column in the generated form — not the data entry object for the column.

You should change some of the standard settings for the form you are building.

10. Click the MAJOR_DESC column in the Columns list box. Change the Text for the label to **Major Description**.

The last field in the upper section of the Column Formatting and Validation page can accept the name of a link. Links are a type of WebDB object that can be used to connect two different WebDB components. You will learn more about links in Chapter 17.

Data entry and validation

On the left-hand side of the bottom portion of the page, you can specify what type of object you want for data entry and some basic validation rules for the object. The first field in this section of the page is a combo box that contains all the various types of HTML objects that are available to you for each of your columns.

You should be aware that the body of every WebDB form is formatted within an HTML table object, with one column of the table for the label for a column, and a second column in the table for a data entry object for the column. For more detail about the layout of the actual table for the form, please see the next section on row span and column span.

Table 7-1
HTML Objects Available for Forms

Object	*Description*
Blank	This choice causes a blank space to be inserted into the two columns in the form table created for the form by WebDB. The Blank option prevents either the label or the data from being present in the table if it is applied to a field based on a database column.
CheckBox	The CheckBox HTML object creates one or more check boxes for data entry in the form table. This option is only valid if you specify a List-of-Values object for the column, or for a column that can only accept two values. It only makes sense to use a CheckBox object if you only have two possible values for a column.
ComboBox	The ComboBox HTML object creates a combo box that contains all of the valid values for an object in the table form. This option is only valid if you specify a List-of-Values object for the column.
Hidden	This option suppresses the display of the data for a column in the table, but the data is still present in the appropriate column in the table. You might want to use this option if you don't want the data to be seen in the browser but you do want it to be used as part of a logical routine that was a part of the page
Horizontal Rule	This option replaces the label portion of a column with a Horizontal Rule HTML object. When you use this option, the Width value in the Column Formatting and Validation page is used to indicate the width of the horizontal rule, and the Height value is used to indicate the thickness of the rule. Keep in mind that, by default, the horizontal rule only occupies the column of the form table for the label, not for the data entry object. If you want a horizontal rule that crosses the entire browser page, you have to increase the column span, as described in the next section.
Image	An Image HTML object is necessary if the column contains image data. An Image object cannot be edited. You might also want to use an Image object if you are going to use images to improve the appearance of your form.
Label Only	This choice causes a blank space to be inserted into the column in the form table reserved for the data entry object. The Label Only option prevents the data from being present in the table.

Continued

Table 7-1 *(continued)*

Object	***Description***
MultiSelect	The MultiSelect HTML object is a list box that contains all the values from the List-of-Values object indicated for the column. As the name implies, a user can select one or more values from the MultiSelect object, so the source of the column has to have some means of interpreting the multiple choices for insertion and updating. If you want to limit a user to a single value in a list, you should use the Popup object.
Password	A Password object is just like a text box object, except that all characters are shown as asterisks when retrieved or entered.
Popup	The Popup option puts a little pop-up icon to the right of a text entry box. If the user clicks the icon, WebDB brings up the standard Find dialog box so the user can search a large group of possible values and select one for the value of the text box. A Popup object, because it includes a text object, also enables a user to directly enter a value into the text box, so you may have to add some additional validation logic for the column. This option is only valid if you specify a List-of-Values object for the column.
RadioGroup	The RadioGroup HTML object creates a group of radio buttons for the acceptable values for the column. If a default value is specified for the column, the radio button for that choice is selected by default. This option is only valid if you specify a List-of-Values object for the column.
TextArea	The TextArea HTML object is a text entry box. The Height value lower on the page determines the number of rows in the box, while the Width value determines the width of the box. The Text Area box automatically performs word wrap.
TextBox	The TextBox is the default HTML object for data entry. If you specify a Max Length value that is greater than the Width value, the data in the TextBox scrolls as a user enters or scrolls through it.

Although the information in a hidden field is not visible on the page in the browser, the data is a part of the ACSII HTML code returned to the browser. If a user chooses to view the source code of the page, they are able to see the data.

The rest of the columns below the Display As combo box all have to do with the validation of the value for the column. An LOV is a List-of-Values object. An LOV is used to limit the values that a user can enter for a particular column. Chapter 13 covers LOVs in detail, and you will see one in action later in this chapter.

The Default Value for a column is displayed in the data entry object for the column whenever there is no other value present, such as when you are inserting a row into the database. If you are inserting a row into the database and click the Reset button, the value for the data entry object is reset to the Default Value.

To see this in action, set a default value for the DEGREE field.

11. Select the DEGREE column in the Columns list. Enter **B.S.** in the Default Value field.

The Updateable combo box contains two values: Yes and No. As the name implies, the value for the Updateable combo box specifies whether a user is allowed to update an existing value for a column. Choosing No for the Updateable parameter causes the value for the column to be displayed as a text label. If a column is not updateable, there is no data entry object displayed for the column, so even if a user is adding a new row to the table, they are not able to add a value for the column.

The Mandatory combo box also contains Yes and No values. If you select Yes for the Mandatory parameter, a user is not able to write data to the database if the column does not contain a value. By default, all columns in the database that are specified as NOT NULL have the value for the Mandatory parameter set to Yes, as well as having the label for the column displayed in red.

The last two combo boxes on the left-hand side of the Column Formatting and Validation page enable you to specify a JavaScript validation routine for the column. The two combo boxes display all of the JavaScript routines that you can access. You will learn about creating shared JavaScript routines later in the book, but it is important to understand the difference between the Field Validate option and the Form Validate option.

As the name implies, the Field Validate function is fired every time a user leaves the corresponding field. The Form Validate function is fired every time a user clicks one of the push buttons in the form. This timing difference leads to two big differences in the way each of these validation methods works. The Field Validate function gives immediate feedback to the user. If a field is required, for instance, as soon as they leave the required field, you can bring up a little dialog box to tell them that the field requires a value. However, you can *never be sure* that a Field Validate function will be fired because a user may never enter, and therefore never leave, a field.

Note

You may be saying to yourself, "Yes, but what if it's the first field on the page?" You would be right in believing that the cursor is automatically placed in the first field on a page—as long as it's the first field on the page. If someone comes along later and changes the position of the column on the page, you are back to the situation where the Field Validate function may not fire.

Because of this, you should carefully consider whether you want a JavaScript function to run for immediate feedback as a Field Validate function, or for guaranteed execution at a later time as a Form Validate function, or even in both places. If you have specified form validation functions for more than one column in the form, the functions execute in the order the columns appear on the page.

Form layout

On the right-hand side of the bottom portion of the page are a series of fields that let you control how you want the objects for a column arranged in the form page. To understand how the entries for these fields shape the appearance of your form, you should understand the way WebDB uses HTML objects to create its forms.

All of the labels and fields in a WebDB form are laid out in an HTML table object, as mentioned earlier in this chapter. Each column in the Columns list box requires two columns in the HTML form table: one for the label, and one for the data entry object.

An HTML table object is a very flexible object. Each row in the table can have any number of columns. In addition, the columns in a table are dynamically formatted to accept the widest entry in the column. So, if you have a table form where every column is on its own line, the width of the table column for the labels of the columns would be the width of the largest label specified.

With this in mind, you can start to understand how the values for the parameters on the right side of the Column Formatting and Validation page for a form affect the appearance of the generated form.

The Width value determines the width of the data entry object for the column. The Height value determines the height of the data entry object for the column. The only type of HTML object that can have a height of more than one is the TextArea, as described in Table 7-1, although the thickness of a horizontal rule is affected by the Height value.

The Max Length parameter specifies the maximum length of the data within the data entry object. If the Max Length is longer than the width, the data in the object scrolls as the user enters data wider than the width or moves their cursor through the value in the object. If you specify a Max Length that is shorter than the width of the object, the generated form does not allow any characters greater that the Max Length to be entered into the object. The Max Length only applies to TextBox, TextArea, and Popup objects.

Column span means that an object can span more than one column. To appreciate this, refer to the drawing in Figure 7-14.

Figure 7-14 shows a standard form where each column has a label and a text box that are approximately the same size. The label and the text box are each in their own column in the table object for the page. We have included lines in this figure to show you where the columns in the table object are actually located.

In Figure 7-15, you can see that the labels and the text boxes for the last two fields have been placed on the same line.

Label	Column1
Label	Column2
Label	Column3
Label	Column4

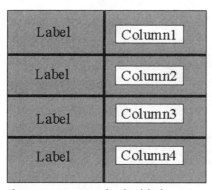

Figure 7-14: Standard table layout of a form

Label	Column1	Label	Column2
Label	Column3		
Label	Column4		
Label	Column5		

Figure 7-15: Table layout of a form with two columns on the same line

You can get this type of arrangement by selecting No in the New Line combo box for Column2.

In Figure 7-16, you have the same arrangement as in Figure 7-15, but this time you enlarged the size of the text box for Column1 in the first line, adding a new line after Column1 and setting the New Line for Column3 to No.

You can see that this new arrangement has caused the third label and text box to be pushed all the way over to the right where they start after the end of the text box for the Column1 on the first line.

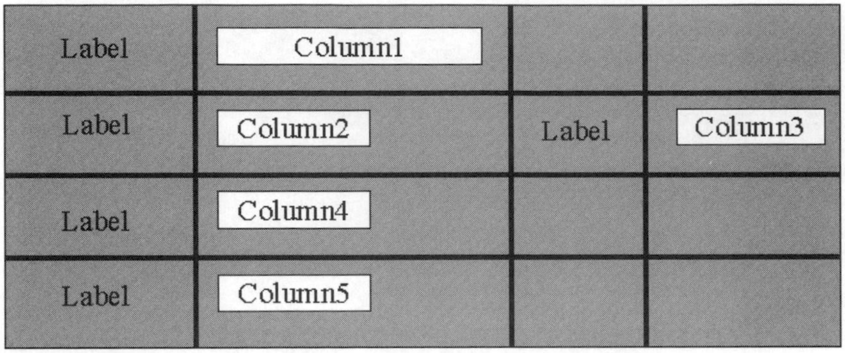

Label	Column1		
Label	Column2	Label	Column3
Label	Column4		
Label	Column5		

Figure 7-16: Table layout of a form with a very wide column

The reason for this is simple. By enlarging the size of the text box for Column1, you also caused the size of the second column in the table to increase to accommodate the column. The simple way around this problem is to change the Column Span value for Column1 to 3, which lets the text box for Column1 span more than one columns in the table, resulting in the form shown in Figure 7-17.

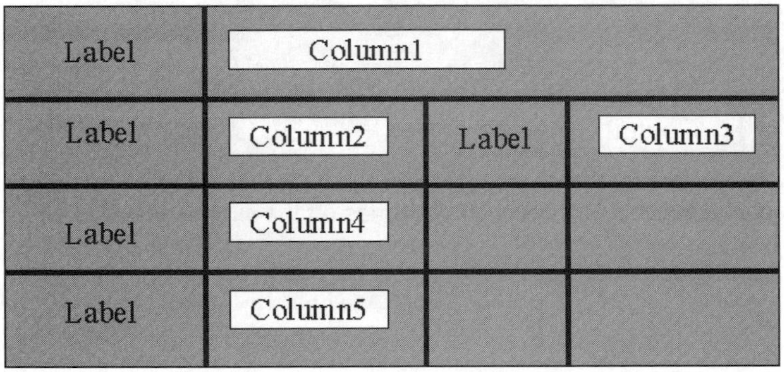

Label	Column1		
Label	Column2	Label	Column3
Label	Column4		
Label	Column5		

Figure 7-17: Table layout of a form with a very wide column spanning multiple columns

A similar situation applies to the Row Span entry. If you indicate that a data entry object for a column takes up two rows, the next two rows are aligned to the right of the data entry object for that column. Figure 7-18 shows the result of specifying a Row Span of 2 for Column1 with the same widths that were used in Figure 7-16 where all the columns had an equal width. The labels and fields for Column2 and Column3 are both situated to the right of the label and field for Column1, because Column1 was specified as spanning two rows. Column2 was on the same row as the beginning of Column1 because there was no new line selected for it. Column3 is in the second row, but just beneath Column2 because Column1 spans two rows.

Label	Column1	Label	Column2
		Label	Column3
Label	Column4		
Label	Column5		

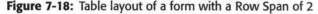

Figure 7-18: Table layout of a form with a Row Span of 2

Keep in mind that the only data entry object that can actually be bigger than a single row is the text area object. No matter what you set for the height for a text box, for instance, it still only takes up a single row in the table that formats the data entry area of your form.

You can learn how these layout options work in your form by modifying the Rule column you added to the form.

12. Select the Rule column in the Columns list. Set the Width of the column to 400, the Height of the column to 3, and the Column Span of the column to 2.

The New Line combo box contains Yes and No values. If you select the No value, the label and data entry columns in the form table are put in the same row of the form table as the previous columns. By default, the New Line setting is set to Yes. And, as you would imagine, the New Line setting has no affect on the first column in a form, since there is no preceding column.

Finally, there is a field at the very lower-right corner of the Column Formatting and Validation page where you can enter a format mask for dates and numbers.

For more information on format masks, please refer to the section on format masks in Chapter 5.

13. Click the Next arrow on the Column Formatting and Validation page.

We've covered a lot in this section, and you have learned a great deal of the details of how WebDB forms are built and displayed. The rest of the Form Builder Wizard is a comparative snap.

Form options

The Form Options page, as shown in Figure 7-19, contains a number of parameters that apply to the operation of the complete form, rather than the individual columns as on the previous page in the Form Builder Wizard for table-based forms.

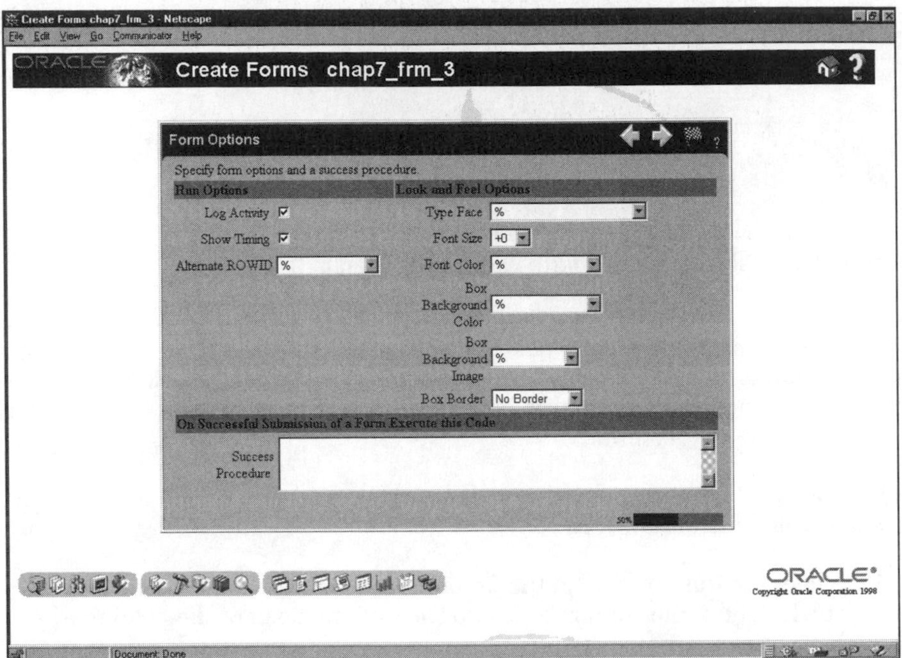

Figure 7-19: The Form Options page in the table-based Form Builder Wizard

There are three main areas on the Form Options page. The left-hand side of the page contains parameters that affect the operation of the form at run time. The Log Activity check box enables you to indicate that you want all activity for this form logged in the database. The logging activity does consume some resources, but it probably won't be noticeable in terms of run-time performance. Because each log entry does take up a row in a table in the database, it makes sense to turn this option off unless you want to specifically monitor the activity of this form for a particular reason. The default value for the Log Activity check box is checked.

The Show Timing check box, if checked, adds a little line to the bottom of the form that shows the amount of time it took for the form to be created and sent to the user. Because this information is probably pretty meaningless to the average user, you should probably turn it off for most of your forms. The default value for the Log Activity check box is checked.

The Alternate ROWID combo box enables you to select one of the columns in your table and use it to uniquely identify a row in a table. The reason this combo box is labeled Alternate is because the ROWID is an internal value maintained by the Oracle database to uniquely identify every row in every table. The ROWID is used by WebDB in its own operations and is discussed in detail in the next chapter in the section on updating data. The default value for the Alternate ROWID combo box is the "%" wild card, which tells WebDB that there is no Alternate ROWID for the form.

The second area on the Form Options page is to the right of the page and shapes the look and feel of the generated form page. The Type Face, Font Size, and Font Color values are used for all columns on the page that have not had these values specified on the Column Formatting and Validation page. These values only affect the general text areas of the form, such as the header, footer, and help text, and override any default values specified for these attributes in the template used for the form. The default values for these parameters are "%," which tells WebDB to use any existing values for the Type Face and Font Color, or "+0," which provides the default text size for all of the text in the form.

All data entered into a data entry field uses the same default font, regardless of what you have specified for the Type Face or Font Color in this page of the Form Builder Wizard.

The last three parameters in the look and feel section of this page refer to the capability to include the form table inside of a box. If you want to have a box around the form table that contains the labels and data entry objects, you have to specify a border for the box in the Box Border combo box. You have two choices for the formatting of the border: thick or thin. The default value for the Box Border parameter is No Border.

If you have specified a border for the form, you can also specify the background color for the area inside of the border in the Box Background Color combo box. Some templates have a box and box color as part of their overall look and feel, but any values you select for the form on this page override the template selections.

The final field in this section of the page is the Box Background Image. You can specify an image that makes up the background of the form page, but this image must already have been imported into the WebDB system.

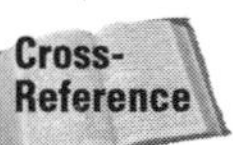

You will learn more about importing images in Chapter 15.

To see how this works, you can add a box to your form.

14. Select the Thin Border entry in the Box Border combo box.

15. Select Blue, Light as the Box Background Color.

The bottom section of this page gives you the opportunity to add some procedural logic that is executed when the form you are creating is successfully submitted. A form is submitted when a user clicks either the Insert, Update, or Delete push button on the form. The form is successfully submitted if the database accepts the data action submitted by the form. The time when the database successfully accepts the data is a different time than the form validation functions mentioned previously. All of the validations on the Column Formatting and Validation page are executed in the browser before the form is sent to the server. The server executes the Success Procedure you enter here once the data has been successfully submitted. Because of this, the Success Procedure must be coded in PL/SQL, which is understood by the Oracle server, rather than in JavaScript, which the browser understands.

One of the typical uses of a Success Procedure is to return a page to the browser indicating the success of the action and possibly some data that was affected by the action.

You can accept the rest of the defaults for this page.

16. Click the Next arrow on the Form Options page.

Button options

The Button Options page, as shown in Figure 7-20, looks very familiar if you have already built a report component.

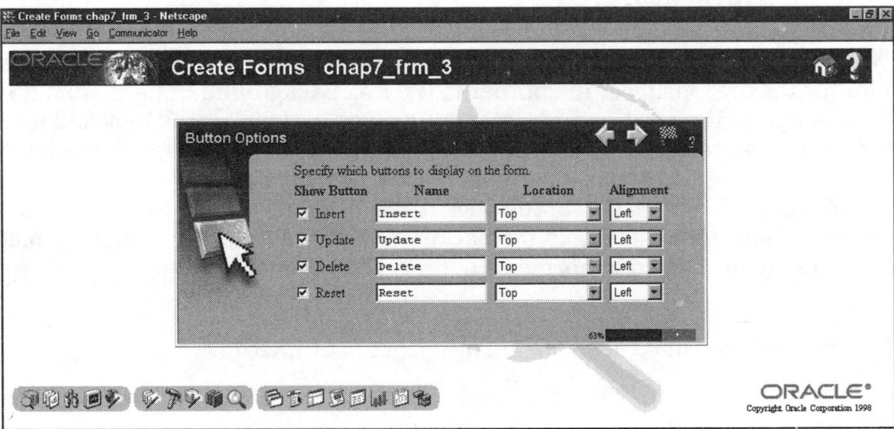

Figure 7-20: The Button Options page for a table-based form

Each button has a Name, a Location, and an Alignment, as well as a check box to indicate whether the button is shown on the page. All of these are described in the section on button options in Chapter 5.

The buttons for a form are, naturally, different from the buttons on a report. Instead of having buttons to run a report, save the report parameters, or execute the report in batch, you have the choice of including buttons for inserting data, updating data, or deleting data.

You never see all of these push buttons on the same form page. The forms WebDB builds are smart enough to know whether you have retrieved a row to update or delete, or whether you are using the form to insert a new row. The form returned to a user has either the Insert push button or the Update and Delete push buttons. The next chapter covers using forms for updating and deleting data in detail.

The Reset push button for a form has two different functions, depending on the perceived actions for the form. If a form is being used for inserting data, clicking the Reset push button resets the values in the form to their default settings. If the form is being used for updating data, clicking the Reset push button returns the values in the form to the values that were originally returned from the database.

You can accept all of the default choices on this page.

17. Click the Next arrow on the Button Options page.

The rest of the Form Builder

The last three pages of the Form Builder Wizard also look familiar to you if you have already created a report component.

The next page of the Form Builder Wizard is the Text Options page. You can specify header, footer, and help text in the main text entry areas for this page, and you can select a template in the combo box at the top of the page. Because the corresponding page was already described in Chapter 5, you can simply select a template so that your form has the same look and feel as the previously created forms and reports and move on.

18. Select the PUBLIC.TEMPLATE_6 template in the Template combo box.
19. Click the Next arrow on the Text Options page.

The next page of the Form Builder Wizard enables you to enter PL/SQL code to extend the functionality of your form. In reality, the PL/SQL code you add to the form is integrated in with the PL/SQL package used by WebDB to create and process the run-time version of the form. There is a whole chapter devoted to the use of PL/SQL procedures later in the book where you can learn much more about integrating PL/SQL code into your WebDB components.

A form can run PL/SQL code at the times a report can—before displaying the page and header, and after displaying the footer and the page—as well as before and after processing the form.

20. Click the Next arrow on the Advanced PL/SQL code page.

The final page of the Form Builder Wizard, like the final page of all the user interface component wizards, features a checkered flag and an OK push button. Clicking the OK push button tells WebDB to generate the PL/SQL package for your form component.

21. Click the OK push button on the Create Form page.

As with the forms you created earlier in the chapter, WebDB takes you to the Manage Component page for the form once you have successfully created it.

Run Form

You are ready to start to use your first table-based form.

22. Click the Run push button on the Manage Component page.

And here is your form, as shown in Figure 7-21.

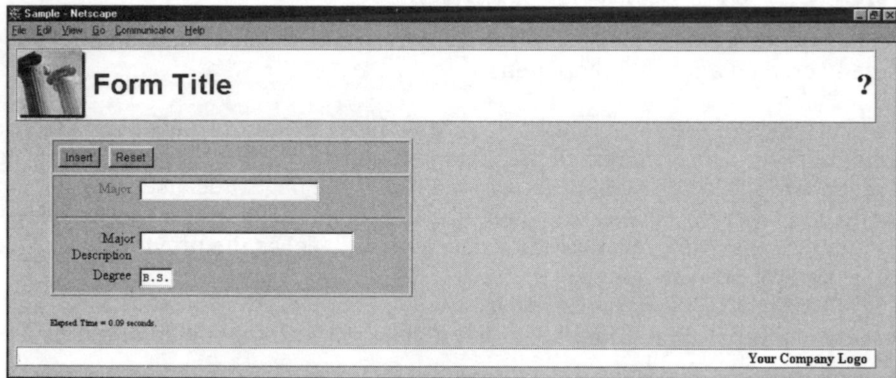

Figure 7-21: Your table-based form running

You might as well jump right into adding data to the database. But in order to see how the form can help to prevent data entry errors, you should first try to do something you don't want your users to do and see how your WebDB component automatically prevents this type of mistake.

23. Enter **The newest major at Net University — nothingness**. into the Major Description text field. Notice how the data scrolls through the text field.
24. Enter **B.N.** (for Bachelor of Nothing) into the Degree field.
25. Click the Insert push button.

The good news is that your form caught the error in your entry, as shown in Figure 7-22 — you are required to have a value in the Major field. WebDB caught the error because the field on the form associated with the MAJORS column is automatically designated as a Mandatory field, because the MAJORS column in the database was designated as NOT NULL.

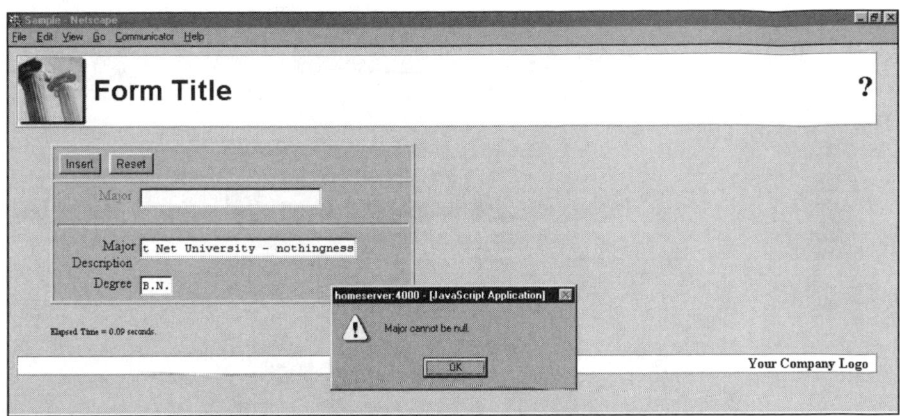

Figure 7-22: An error in your form

You can also see that the error box that popped up, as shown in Figure 7-22, was generated with JavaScript. It was generated from within the browser, before your data ever went out to the server. If the Major field was not designated as Mandatory, and you tried to insert this row into the MAJORS table, the Oracle server would have returned an error to the WebDB application. But the error would have been too cryptic for the average user, and you still would have sent the data to the server and received a message back from the server with the error. Catching the error in JavaScript code in the browser is easier for the user and more efficient.

You can fix up your data and try to reinsert the row.

26. Enter **Baseball** into the Major field. Change the entry in the Major Description to read **The newest major at Net University — baseball**.
27. Enter **B.B.** (for Bachelor of Baseball) into the Degree field.
28. Click the Insert push button.

Now you can see the type of error that is returned from the database when you violate an integrity rule when writing data. The page shown in Figure 7-23 is unattractive and not very informative for most users. In fact, even a developer like you might not easily understand just what went wrong.

You could go back to browse the MAJORS table and click through to discover exactly what the NETU.AVCON_MAJOR_DEGREE_000 constraint is all about, but this option is not available to your end users. To save you the trouble, we can tell you that the DEGREE column in the MAJORS table can only have a value of B.S. or B.A. — Net University is not avant-garde enough to understand the need for a Bachelor of Baseball diploma.

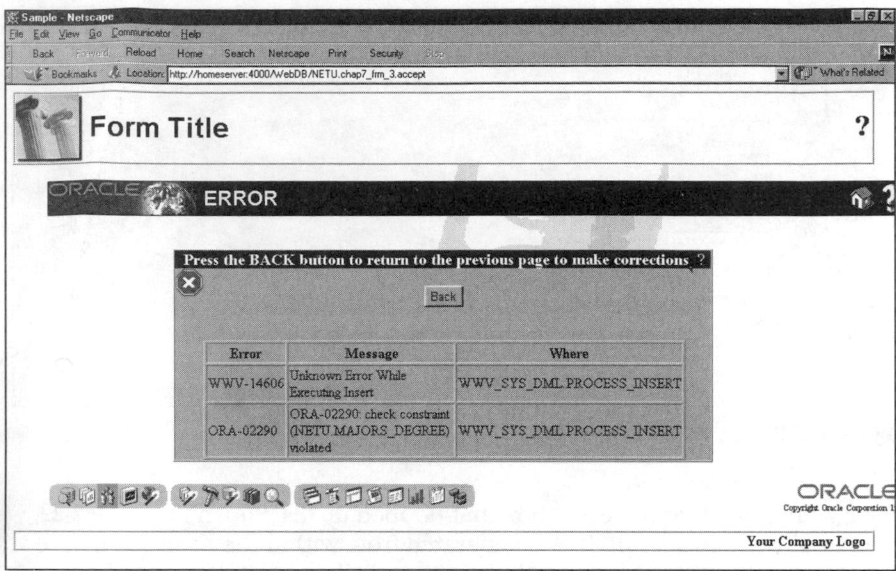

Figure 7-23: An error returned from the database following an invalid attempt to write data

The best way to handle an error like this is to prevent it from ever happening, which you can easily do by editing your form.

Edit Form

You can edit a form by changing the same parameters in the same pages that were used by the Form Builder Wizard.

1. Click the Back push button in your browser to return to the Manage Component page within the WebDB environment.
2. Click the Edit link at the bottom of the page.

The Edit Forms page, as shown in Figure 7-24, has the look of a tabbed page, just as the Edit Reports page did. The tabs at the top of the panel act as links to the different pages of the Form Builder.

Your task is to prevent the user from entering invalid data for DEGREE column in the MAJORS table in the database. Because there are a limited number of valid values allowed for the DEGREE column, it makes sense to use a List-of-Values object to present the valid choices to the user.

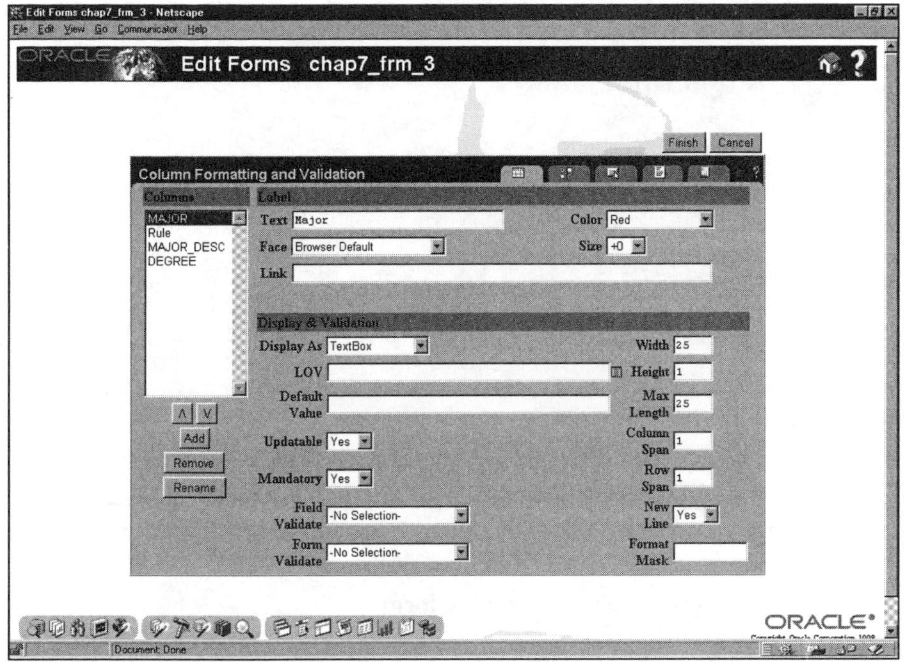

Figure 7-24: The Edit Forms page

3. Select the DEGREE column in the Columns list box.
4. Enter **NETU. DEGREELOV** into the LOV text box in the Display & Validation section of the Column Formatting and Validation page.
5. Select the Radio Group choice in the Display As text box.
6. Click the Finish push button. You have used an LOV that was automatically installed as part of the sample application.

Please see Appendix A for more details on how to import shared objects such as List-of-Values objects into your WebDB environment. The file with the DEGREELOV is called DEGREELOV.SQL and is in the Chapter 7 directory of the Examples directory on the accompanying CD-ROM.

Once you choose an LOV object for a Column, you can format the LOV object as a RadioGroup, a CheckBox, a ComboBox, a MultiSelect, or a Popup. Because there are only two valid choices for the Degree column, and because these choices are not likely to change in the near future, the RadioGroup is probably the best way to display the list of values.

7. Click the Run link at the bottom of the Manage Component page to run your form again to see the results of your changes. The newly modified form looks like Figure 7-25.

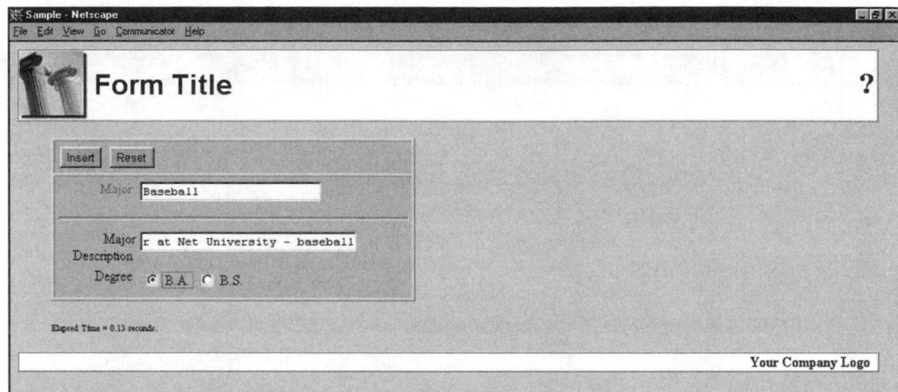

Figure 7-25: Your form with a radio button group

8. Now enter **Baseball** into the Major field and **The newest major at Net University — baseball**. into the Major Description field. Select the B.A. radio button.
9. Click the Insert push button on the form.

Once the record is properly inserted into the database, by default you get a page listing your success, as shown in Figure 7-26.

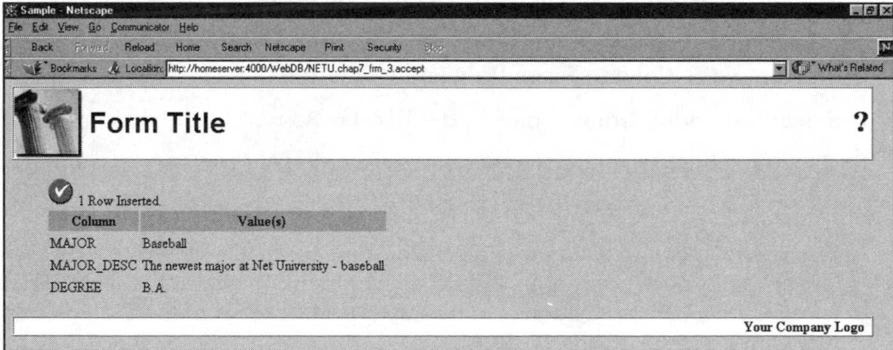

Figure 7-26: Success inserting a row with a table-based form

You could create your own success page by adding PL/SQL or HTML code to the Success Procedure in the Form Builder.

Wrapping Up

So far, so good.

You have created a QBE form that you can use to specify selection criteria, shape the results, and even insert data into a database table. You have created a form based on a table that you can use to enter data into your database. You even learned some basic methods you can use to preserve the integrity of your data and prevent user entry errors.

In the next chapter, you will learn how to create a form based on an Oracle stored procedure, which will give you the ability to take advantage of the sort of sophisticated interaction with the database you can build into stored procedures. You will learn how to create a form that is based on a master-detail relationship between two tables. And you may have been wondering how to use a form to update or delete existing data. You will see how to use the forms you have already created to achieve that goal.

✦ ✦ ✦

CHAPTER 8

Building Forms — Part II

✦ ✦ ✦ ✦

In This Chapter

Creating a Form Based on a Stored Procedure

Updating and Deleting Data with Your Form

Master-Detail Forms

✦ ✦ ✦ ✦

In the last chapter, you learned how to create basic forms. The forms you created gave you the ability to write data to your Oracle database, and they were certainly easy to build. This chapter introduces you to the two other types of forms you can build — forms based on stored procedures and master-detail forms — and helps you understand how to use the forms you have created to update or delete existing data in your database.

Forms Based on Stored Procedures

If you are new to the Oracle database, or to relational databases in general, it is probably worth spending a little time discussing the purpose and structure of stored procedures before moving on to building forms based on these stored procedures.

Defining stored procedures

Structured Query Language (SQL) was popularized in the 1970s and added an important dimension to the world of data processing. SQL gives developers a more-or-less standard language and interface to use to interact with data in a wide variety of relational databases. Oracle rose to prominence as the leading relational database in the world, in part because of its adherence to the SQL standard.

Note

We assume that you have a basic working knowledge of SQL throughout this book, as you have already seen in the chapters on reporting. Although you do not need to understand SQL to use WebDB, you can broaden the range and functionality of WebDB with timely use of SQL, so we recommend that you learn the basics of the language to complement your knowledge of WebDB.

SQL combines simplicity and power, but it mainly revolves around the actions needed to read and write data. There are times when a developer or a database administrator would like to supplement SQL with their own unique, procedural logic. Stored procedures get their name from two simple facets of their existence: they can be used to create virtually any type of logical procedure, and they are stored and executed in the database. Stored procedures were the precursor to today's server-based applications, such as those you are building with WebDB.

The Oracle database uses a procedural language called PL/SQL for its own stored procedures. If you want to understand the capabilities of PL/SQL, all you have to do is to look at WebDB itself. All the WebDB components you create are actually groups of PL/SQL stored procedures, called *packages,* that are generated by WebDB and stored and executed in the Oracle database. In fact, WebDB itself is written as a collection of PL/SQL procedures, and when you install WebDB, you are actually installing those PL/SQL procedures.

WebDB and stored procedures

Many of you are probably already experienced Oracle users and pretty familiar with PL/SQL. If you have been using Oracle for a while, you probably have existing PL/SQL routines that you use to interact with the data in your Oracle database. WebDB enables you to create forms easily that are based on your PL/SQL procedures.

Stored procedures can include parameters that are passed to the procedure as part of the procedure call. WebDB treats these parameters just like it treats the columns in a table. When you select a stored procedure as the foundation for a form, WebDB queries the stored procedure to discover the number and type of parameters the procedure expects to receive, just as it does for a table or view.

At this time, the forms you build with WebDB can only send data to a PL/SQL procedure. Some PL/SQL procedures create their own internal cursors that can be used to scroll through a set of data in the same way that you would use a standard SQL cursor to scroll through the result set from an SQL query. You cannot take advantage of this capability of stored procedures with the first release of WebDB.

You can use a PL/SQL function, which returns a single result, as a part of a standard SQL statement in WebDB.

The sample stored procedure

The sample NETU database includes a stored procedure that you can be use to insert data into the database based on a simple logical criterion.

The NETU database is used for more than just tracking students and their courses. The database also includes information about NetU alumni and their contributions to their alma mater. An alumnus can either send in a check as a donation, or send in a pledge for a donation and follow it with a check later.

The only difference between these two actions is whether or not a check is included. If a check is present, the contribution is a donation; if there is no check, the contribution is a pledge.

The stored procedure `netu_add_donation` accepts the data about the donation and automatically inserts it into the appropriate table, depending on the presence or absence of a check number.

The `netu_add_donation` stored procedure is as follows:

```
procedure netu_add_donation (p_id number, p_fund
varchar2, p_restriction varchar2,
        p_amount number, p_gift_date date, p_checkno number)
    as
    begin
       if p_checkno is null then
    -
    - No check, this must be a pledge
    -
         insert into pledges (donation_no, id, fund,
            pledge_amount, pledge_date, pledge_no)
         values (null, p_id, p_fund, p_amount, p_gift_date,
            pledges_seq.nextval);
       else
    -
    - Check number means that this is a donation receipt
    -
      insert into donations (donation_no, id, fund,
        restriction, amount, gift_date, check_number)
      values (donations_seq.nextval, p_id, p_fund,
        p_restriction, p_amount, p_gift_date, p_checkno);
       end if;
    end netu_add_donation;
```

Building a form based on a stored procedure

Building a form based on a stored procedure is very much like building a form based on a table or view.

1. Go to the main Form Building page in WebDB by clicking the Forms icon in the shortcuts bar. You should be logged onto WebDB as the NETUDEV user.
2. Select the Forms on Stored Procedures choice in the Create a New Form panel and click the Create push button.

The first page of this wizard looks just like the first page of the other component builder wizards. You are prompted for a storage location for the form you are building and the name of the form.

3. Select the NETU schema in the Schema combo box and enter **ch8_frm_1** as the Name of the form.
4. Click the Next arrow on the Form name and Schema page.

The next page in the wizard prompts you to select an existing PL/SQL procedure for the form. When you drop down the list in the combo box, you may see a whole lot of stored procedures listed, as shown in Figure 8-1.

Where did the procedures come from? They were created for you by WebDB, just as you created the sample reports and forms in earlier chapters. All the procedures created by WebDB are used to accept parameters and then return an HTML page the browser, so they would not really be suitable as the basis for a form you would build with this wizard.

5. Select the netu.netpackage.netu_add_donation procedure in the Procedure combo box.
6. Click the Next arrow on the Create Forms (Procedures) page.

The extended name for the procedure includes the name of the owner schema (netu), followed by a period and the name of the package (netpackage) that contains the procedure, followed by a period and the name of the procedure.

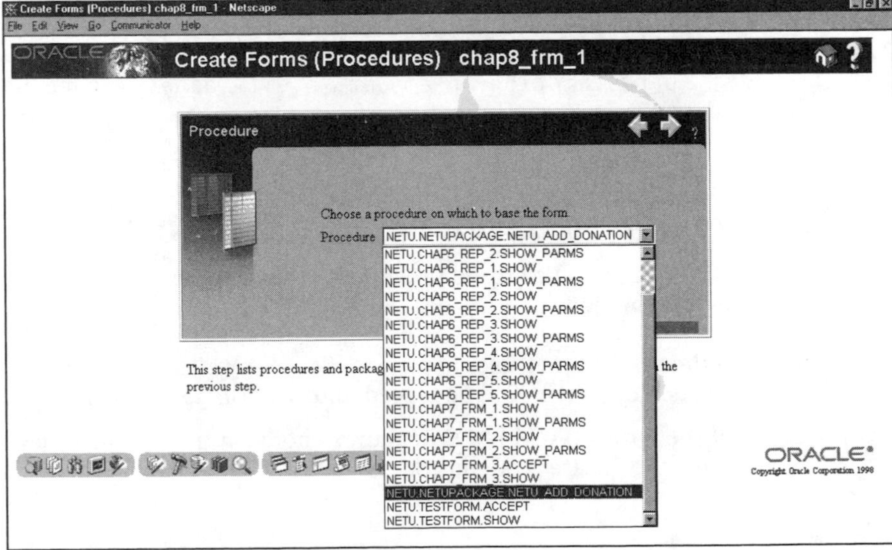

Figure 8-1: Existing stored procedures

The next page in the Form Builder Wizard for procedures looks very familiar. In fact, aside from a different title at the top of the panel, this page is identical to the corresponding page for formatting columns in the other form builder wizards.

There are only four differences:

- ✦ The first difference is that all the names of the parameters begin with the characters "P_". The "P," as you could probably guess, stands for "Parameter," and giving the parameters for a stored procedure names that begin with "P_" is a standard practice for Oracle stored procedures. You will probably want to change the labels for the parameters in your form.
- ✦ The second difference is that all the parameters have a width of 30 and a maximum length of 2000. WebDB assigns all parameters these same values, so you will probably have to change these values too.
- ✦ The third difference is that all the labels for these parameters have a Color of Aquamarine by default.
- ✦ The last difference is that all the parameters are marked as Mandatory.

This is a good guess by WebDB, because most stored procedures are expecting to receive values for all their parameters.

7. Select the P_ID column in the Columns list box. Change the Text in the Label section to **Alumni ID**. Change the Max Length and the Width to 6 and the color to Red.

The P_ID parameter must have a value that already exists as the ID of a person in the ALUMNI table. That makes the P_ID field ideal for using a list-of-values pop up. In following the WebDB standard, you will set the color for all the mandatory fields to Red.

8. Set the Display As combo box to Popup and enter **NETU.ALUMNILOV** for the LOV field.
9. Select the P_FUND column in the Columns list box. Change the Text in the Label section to **Fund**. Set the Color in the Label section to Black. Change the Display As to Radio Group. Set the LOV to NETU.FUNDLOV and the Default Value to Annual Fund.

If you have not loaded the samples for the book, you have to load the list of values for the FUND types by importing the fundlov.sql script, the list of values for the ALMUNI by importing the alumnilov.sql script, and the list of values for the RESTRICTION by importing the restrictlov.sql script. Please see Appendix A for instructions on how to import objects.

Because there are only two valid values for the FUND parameter, it makes sense to use a simple list of values that are displayed as a group of radio buttons. You will learn much more about lists of values later in Chapter 13.

Since you have indicated a default value for the radio group, a value will always be selected for this parameter, so you no longer have to have the name of the parameter in red.

10. Select the P_RESTRICTION column in the Columns list box. Change the Text in the Label section to **Donation Restriction** and the Color to Red. Set Display As to Popup. Set the LOV to NETU.RESTRICTLOV and the Default Value to **Unrestricted**. Set the New Line to No.
11. Select the P_AMOUNT column in the Columns list box. Change the Text in the Label section to **Amount** and the Color to Red. Change the Max Length and Width to 15. Set the Format Mask to **$999,999,999.99**, because the fund-raisers at NetU are very hopeful that one of their alumni will hit the big time.
12. Select the P_GIFT_DATE column in the Columns list box. Change the Text in the Label section to **Gift Date** and the Color to Red. Change the Max Length and Width to **10**.

The Oracle database only accepts date values in the format of DD-MON-YYYY—two numbers for the day, three letters for the month, and four numbers for the year. You should note this format limitation in the help for this form.

13. Select the P_CHECK_NUMBER column in the Columns list box. Change the Text in the Label section to **Check Number**. Change the Color to Black, because this field is not mandatory. Change the Mandatory combo box value to No. Change the Max Length and Width to 10. Set the Default Value as null.

If there is no check number, the stored procedure knows to enter the data as a pledge rather than a donation. Unfortunately, if the user does not enter a value for the check number, WebDB does not include the P_CHECK_NUMBER parameter in the call to the stored procedure and the procedure does not execute properly. In order to avoid this, a missing check number must be listed as the value null, which sends the parameter with a null value to the procedure. Of course, you might want to create a JavaScript validation, which you will learn about in Chapter 16, to check for a numeric value or the text of null.

14. Click the Next arrow on the Argument Formatting and Validation page.

The Display Options page also looks very familiar, except that there is no combo box for an Alternate ROWID. As you will see in the next section, the Alternate ROWID is only meaningful when a form is going to be used to update data. Because you cannot update data in the traditional sense through a stored procedure, there is no need to specify an Alternate ROWID.

15. Click the Next arrow on the Display Options page.

The push buttons displayed on the Button Options page, as shown in Figure 8-2, are more like the push buttons for a report than for the forms you have been working on.

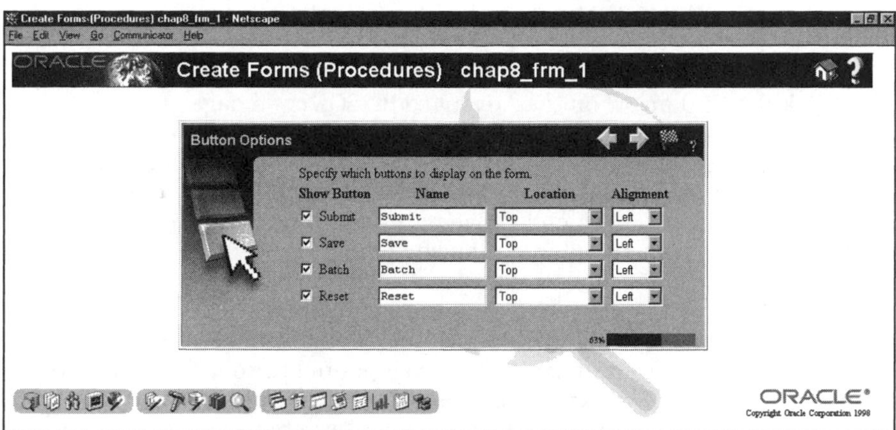

Figure 8-2: Button options for a form based on a stored procedure

The first push button is labeled Submit. When you are using a stored procedure, you simply submit the procedure, and then it executes. Although this particular stored procedure is used to insert data into the database, many other stored procedures do not perform this type of operation, and WebDB has no way of knowing the eventual result of the procedure. It would probably be best to make the name on this particular push button more meaningful.

16. Change the Name of the Submit push button to **Insert**.

The next two push buttons are straight from the report component — Save and Batch. These two push buttons perform the same functions for a stored procedure that they do for a report, saving the individual user's preferences and submitting the execution of the stored procedure to a batch queue. Because a stored procedure cannot be used to update and delete data in the same way that a form based on a table can, you can understand why these push button options are not present. The reason for the Save and Batch push buttons is that stored procedures are often used to perform database-related tasks, such as performing database-wide calculations and writing the results to summary tables. These types of stored procedures are run repeatedly and the user may want to reduce their impact on the performance of the overall database system.

17. Click the Next arrow on the Button Options page.

The final three pages are identical to the final three pages of the other form components. You can specify text options that enable you to add text to the header and footer of the page displayed to users, associate help text with the page, and give the page a standard look and feel with a template. To make this component look like the other components you have created, you should assign a template.

18. Select the PUBLIC.TEMPLATE_6 choice from the Template combo box.
19. Click the Next arrow on the Text Options page.
20. Click the Next arrow on the Advanced PL/SQL code page.

You might wonder why the Advanced PL/SQL code page exists for a form based on a stored procedure. After all, why would you add more PL/SQL code to a stored procedure written in PL/SQL code? The purpose of this page is to enable you to add PL/SQL code that executes at some specific points in the creation of the *page* that is presented to the user as the interface for this component.

If you have been using Oracle for a while, you probably have some stored procedures that you want to use in your WebDB application. These stored procedures were not necessarily designed with an appropriate user interface, so the need to add customized logic to surround a form based on a stored procedure is the same as the corresponding need for other components.

21. Click the OK push button on the last page of the Form Builder Wizard.

Time to see the form at work.

22. Select the Run link at the bottom of the Manage Component page for the form you have just created. The form looks like Figure 8-3.

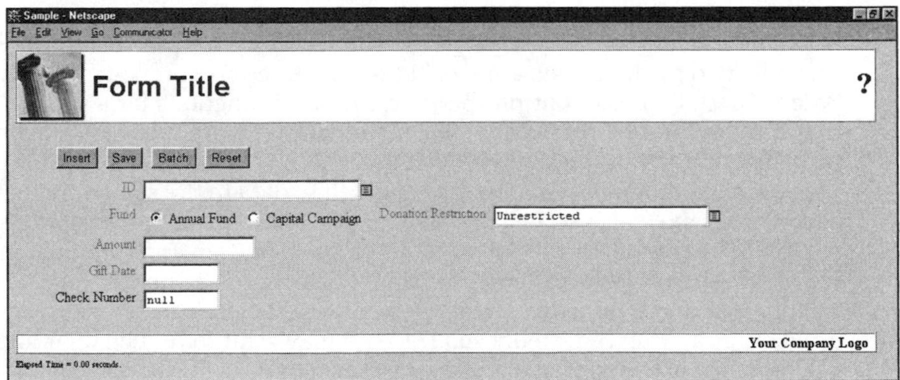

Figure 8-3: The form based on a stored procedure

23. Enter your own information into the fields on the page. Click the Insert push button.

You can see that you get a default success page after the stored procedure has successfully completed. The default success page for a stored procedure is probably even a little more meaningless than the default success page for a normal form, because a stored procedure is generally designed to hide the complexity of its operation from the user of the procedure. This form would be an excellent candidate for a customized success procedure, which you will learn more about in Chapter 24 on PL/SQL coding in WebDB.

You have just entered a pledge to contribute to NetU, but perhaps you want to either change the amount of that pledge or remove it entirely. You want to go back to the database and change or delete this errant row, but the forms you have created so far do not appear to allow you to delete, or for that matter update, data. You specified that the appropriate Update and Delete push buttons should be on the form, but they have not yet made an appearance. In the next section, you will learn why that is so and how to correct this apparent mistake in the component generated by WebDB.

Updating and Deleting Data

So, how come there are no Update or Delete push buttons? WebDB obviously knows about these activities, or it wouldn't have given you the option to have those push buttons on your forms. You selected the push button to appear on the form, but they haven't shown up yet. Where have these push buttons gone?

In fact, the forms you created are working perfectly, and WebDB is ahead of you in this particular situation. To understand what is going on, you just have to think about the requirements for writing data to the database.

If you are going to insert a new row into the database, you should be presented with a more or less blank form. You enter all of the data into the form, and then you insert the row into the database. This is what you have been doing with your forms up to this point.

If you want to update or delete data from the database, the first step in the process is to retrieve the row you want to operate on. If you call a form in a way that specifies a row for retrieval, WebDB gives you the form with the push buttons for Update and Delete, but not for Insert. If you call a form without any specifications for a row, WebDB knows that you can only insert a new row into the database.

When you click the Run link at the bottom of the Manage Component page for a form, you are calling the SHOW procedure for the form without any parameters, which results in an insert-only page being returned to you in the browser.

WebDB uses the concept of a ROWID to retrieve a specific row from the database. As mentioned in the previous chapter, the ROWID is an internal, invisible column maintained by the Oracle database that can uniquely identify any row in any table in the database. The ROWID provides a powerful function to Oracle. Unfortunately, the value for the ROWID is not related in any way to the data in the row, which makes it meaningless to those of us who are using the database.

Remember the Alternative ROWID? You can specify a column in a database table as an Alternative ROWID. When you identify a column in the table as an Alternative ROWID, WebDB uses this column in place of the standard ROWID for identifying a particular row in the table.

This description should make it obvious that the perfect candidate for an Alternative ROWID is the primary key of the table—at least when the primary key of the table consists of a single column. The primary key should be a value that uniquely identifies each row in a table and, in fact, you will probably find yourself using the primary key for the Alternative ROWID in most of your WebDB forms.

In order to see how this works, you have to create a simple link object. WebDB links are a nontrivial topic. Links, as their name implies, are the building blocks for the structure of large portions of your WebDB application system. Chapter 17 examines links in detail. For now, you will just build a simple link to help you understand and test the ways your form can be used to insert and update data in your Oracle database.

1. Return to the WebDB development environment by using the Back push button in the browser.
2. Go to the Shared Components main page by clicking the Shared Components icon in the shortcuts bar.
3. Click the Links menu choice on the Shared Components page.

The Manage Links page, shown in Figure 8-4, has the same three panels that appear on the main pages for the other components.

The biggest difference is in the options that are presented in the list of recently edited links, which you will use later in this section.

For now, you should begin the process of creating a new link.

4. Click the Create push button in the top panel of the Manage Links page.

The process of creating a link begins, in the same way as most other WebDB components, with a page that prompts you for the schema to store the link component in and a name for the link.

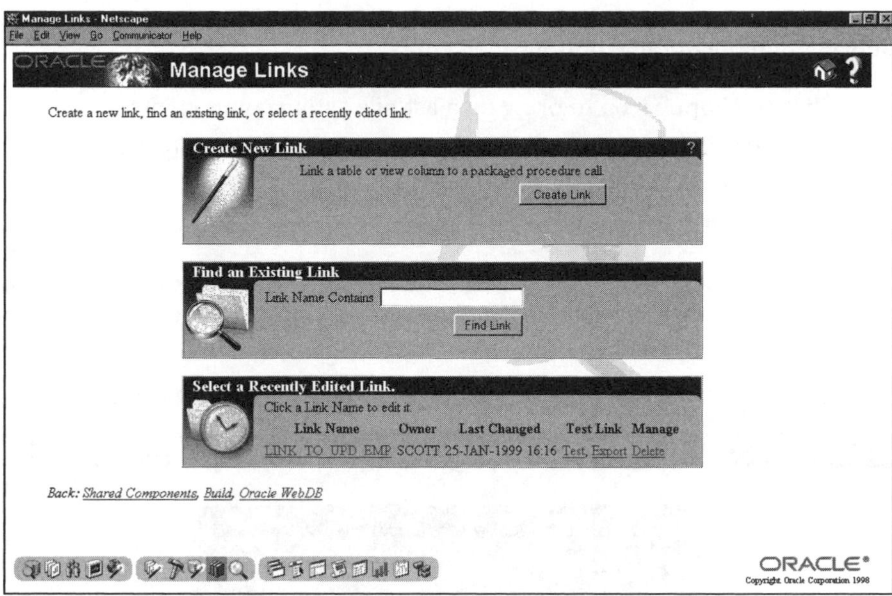

Figure 8-4: The main page for creating and managing WebDB links

5. Enter **ch8_lnk_1** for the name of the link and click the Next arrow on the Link Name page. The next page in the Link Wizard, as shown in Figure 8-5, enables you to specify the target, or destination, for the link.

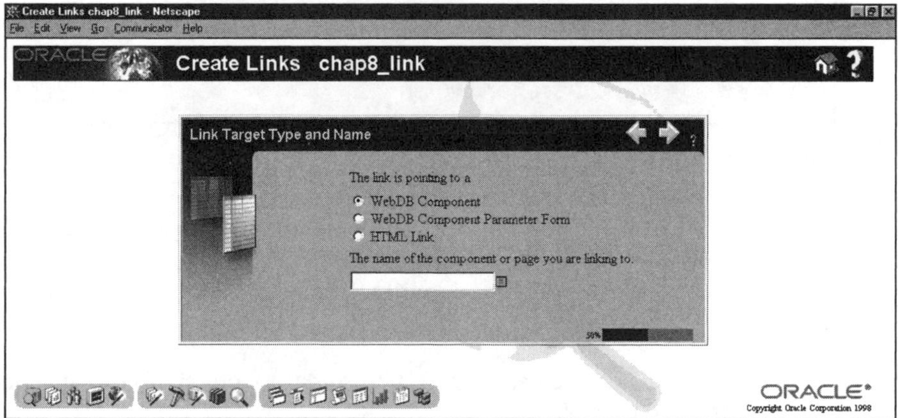

Figure 8-5: The second page of the Link Wizard

You want to link to the form you created in the last chapter, so you should leave the WebDB Component radio button selected.

6. Click the Popup icon to bring up a list of existing components.
7. Select the NETU.ch8_frm_3 component. You may have to go to the next page of components to find it.
8. Click the Next arrow on the Link Target Type and Name page.

On the second page of the Link Wizard, you indicated the target of the link. On this page, which is shown in Figure 8-6, you will specify how the target will be called.

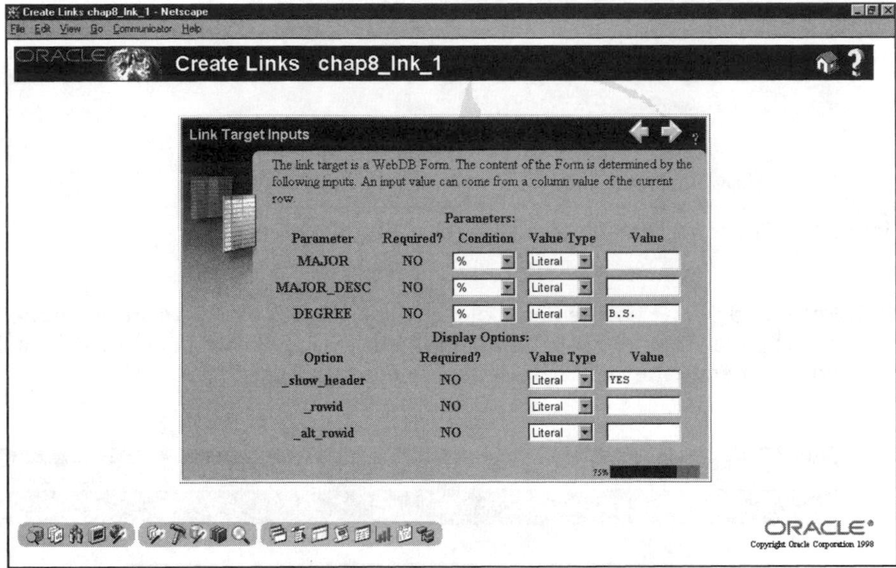

Figure 8-6: The third page of the Link Wizard

The top portion of this page enables you to identify which values will pass to the target component. All the parameters of the target form are listed because you could use any of them to help to identify the specific instances of data in the target form.

Chapter 17 is devoted entirely to links, so don't worry if this explanation is a little sketchy at this point.

9. For the MAJOR parameter, set the Condition to =, the Value Type to Column, and the Value to **MAJOR**.

These settings indicate that the calling component passes the value for the MAJOR column when it calls the target form.

The lower portion of the page enables you to set the other parameters associated with the component. All of these parameters are generated by WebDB for controlling the operation of the component, and they all begin with the underscore character to ensure that they don't conflict with the names of any existing parameters in PL/SQL procedures. The only parameters you have to deal with for this simple link are the _rowid and the _alt_rowid parameters.

10. Set the _rowid and the _alt_rowid parameters to **MAJOR**.
11. Set the Value Type for the _rowid parameter to Column.

By setting these two parameters, you are telling WebDB that the value for the _rowid parameter comes from the value for the MAJOR column, and that the value used to uniquely identify a row, the _alt_rowid parameter, is the MAJOR column in the target component.

12. Click the Next arrow on the Link Target Inputs page.
13. Click the OK push button on the last page of the Link Wizard.

You have created the sample link. So far, so good. Now you have to build a report to use the link.

14. Go to the Report Building page by clicking the Reports icon in the shortcut bar.
15. Select the Report from Query Wizard radio button in the top panel and click the Create push button.
16. Leave the schema name as NETU and name the report **ch8_rep_1**. Click the Next arrow on the first page of the wizard.
17. Select the NETU.MAJORS table and click the Next arrow on the Tables and Views page.
18. Select all the columns in the table for the report by clicking the >> push button. Click the Next arrow on the Table/View Columns page.
19. Click the Next arrow on the Column Conditions page. You have arrived at the page where you will put your link to work.
20. For the MAJOR column, select ch8_lnk_1 as the Link.
21. Click the Next arrow on the Column Formatting page.
22. Click the Next arrow on the Display Options page.
23. Click the Next arrow on the Parameter Entry Form Display Options page.
24. Select the PUBLIC.TEMPLATE_6 template for this report and click the checkered flag icon to finish the report.

All that is left now is to make sure the link works and to see if it really does let you update and delete rows.

25. Select the Run menu choice from the Manage Component page. The report should look like Figure 8-7. You can see that the values for the Major column are shown like hotlinks on a standard HTML page.

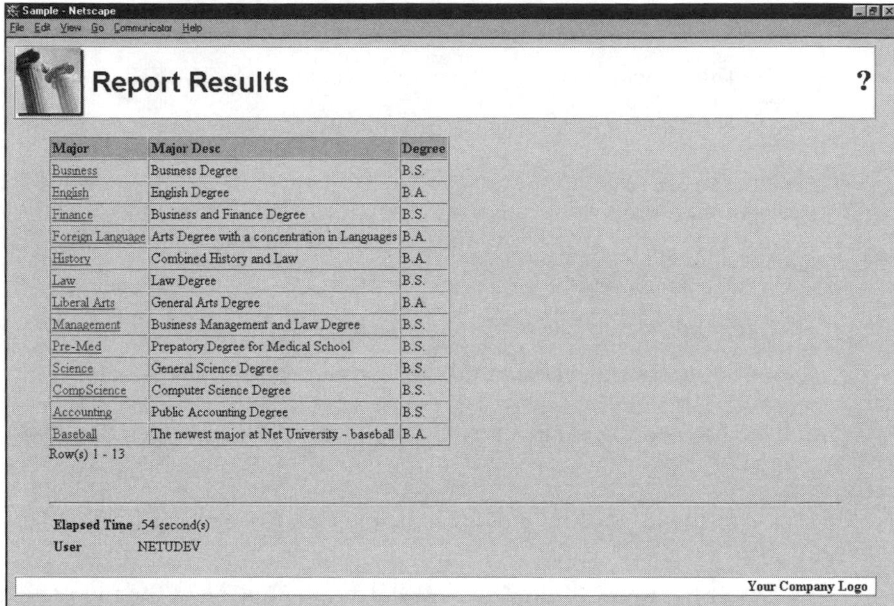

Major	Major Desc	Degree
Business	Business Degree	B.S.
English	English Degree	B.A.
Finance	Business and Finance Degree	B.S.
Foreign Language	Arts Degree with a concentration in Languages	B.A.
History	Combined History and Law	B.A.
Law	Law Degree	B.S.
Liberal Arts	General Arts Degree	B.A.
Management	Business Management and Law Degree	B.S.
Pre-Med	Prepatory Degree for Medical School	B.S.
Science	General Science Degree	B.S.
CompScience	Computer Science Degree	B.S.
Accounting	Public Accounting Degree	B.S.
Baseball	The newest major at Net University - baseball	B.A.

Row(s) 1 - 13

Elapsed Time .54 second(s)
User NETUDEV

Your Company Logo

Figure 8-7: A report with links

26. Click the link for the Baseball major you entered in the last chapter.

Voilá! There is your form, as shown in Figure 8-8, with the Update and Delete push buttons added just as you'd hoped they would be.

WebDB recognized that the form was called with a value for the _rowid parameter — this caused the Update and Delete push buttons to appear. The value for the _alt_rowid parameter tells WebDB to use the value passed for the ROWID parameter to equal a value in the MAJOR column of the destination table.

Because you entered a fictitious major in the previous chapter, you can delete it in this form. If you have linked to the major that you entered in the previous chapter, click the Delete push button.

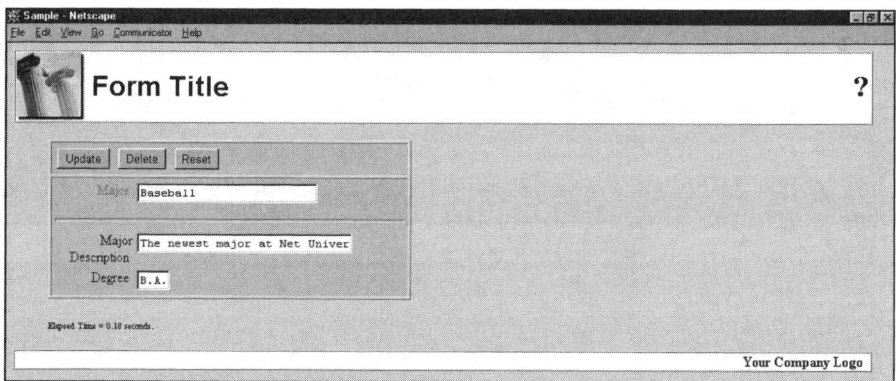

Figure 8-8: A form called with a ROWID

Once you take an action with the Delete push button, WebDB returns a success page to assure you that your database interaction successfully completed.

In the past two chapters, you have learned everything necessary to start building all the forms you need in your WebDB application system, one table at a time. There is one type of form that is based on two tables that is so common in applications that WebDB enables you to create the form directly in a single pass through a WebDB wizard. The last section in this chapter shows you how to create one of these master-detail forms.

Master-Detail Forms

Up until this point, you have been dealing with individual forms based on individual tables or stored procedures. Many of the forms you create in any application system are based on individual tables in the database. Due to the connectionless nature of the HTTP communications between a browser and a server, this makes a lot of sense. You want to deal with tables as atomic units for updating and inserting data. If two tables are somehow related, you can simply build separate forms for each table and implement the relationship by building a WebDB link.

But WebDB gives you the ability to build forms based on two tables that are part of one of the most common types of relationships, the *master-detail relationship.* In a master-detail relationship, a single row from the master table is related to one or more rows in a detail table and linked by a common value that exists in both tables.

Master-Detail Relationships and Arrays

One of the significant ways that relational databases changed the design of databases was to introduce the concept of related multiple tables that reduce the storage of redundant data. Master-detail relationships are the result of this advance. Rather than store, for instance, lots of student information with each record in a student transcript, the rows in the TRANSCRIPT table contain a value in their ID column that matches the value in the ID column of the UGRADS table. The ID column in the UGRADS table is the primary key of the table, and the primary key of the TRANSCIPT table points back to the primary key of its master table.

If you have been used to designing a nonrelational system, you may have used an array to implement the same type of relationship. A master-detail relationship has several advantages over an array. For instance, the rows in both the UGRADS table and the TRANSCRIPT table are smaller than a single row containing all of the data would be, which makes retrieval faster if someone just wants to see the student information or calculate on values in the TRANSCRIPT. More importantly, a master-detail relationship is dynamic. A student can take a single class or a thousand classes and the relationship doesn't change. With an array, you have to predefine the maximum number of details that can be assigned to a single master.

Relational databases are designed to join related tables very rapidly, so there is no real performance penalty to using master-detail relationships between tables rather than an array. In fact, the rules for good relational database design forbid the use of arrays.

You will see that creating a master-detail form results in building a complex of forms: one for querying and inserting the master table; one for returning results from a query of the master table; and a final form for editing and inserting detail tables. The good news is that you can use the Form Builder Wizard to go through a single process that creates all these forms and their associated functionality in one fell swoop.

Building a master-detail form

There are a number of master-detail relationships in the NETU sample database. But, as with previous examples, you build a master-detail form based on two of the smaller tables in the database. This way, you can focus on the process of building the form, rather than on tracking and formatting a table with a lot of different columns.

Beginning the building process

You start out building a master-detail form in the same way that you began to build the other form components.

1. Return to the main Forms page. Select the Master-Detail Forms radio button from the radio button group in the top panel and click the Create push button.

As with the other component builders, the first page of the Master-Detail Form Builder Wizard requires you to indicate which schema in the database will own the resulting form. You also must give the form a name.

2. Select the NETU schema from the Schema combo box and name the form **ch8_frm_2**. Click the Next arrow on the Master Detail Form Name and Schema page.

The next page of the wizard prompts you for the master and detail tables that will be used in the form, as shown in Figure 8-9.

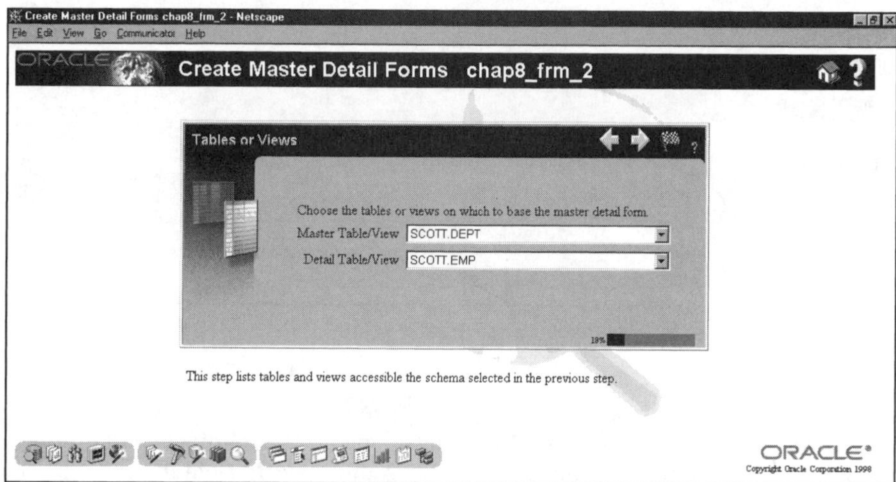

Figure 8-9: Specifying master and detail tables for a master-detail form

3. Select the NETU.MAJORS table in the Master Table/View combo box and the NETU.MAJOR_REQS table in the Detail Table/View combo box. Click the Next arrow on the Tables or Views page.

The next page of the Master-Detail Form Builder Wizard is used to specify the join between the master and detail tables. WebDB uses some intelligence in proposing candidates for the link, including checking if there is a foreign key relationship between the two tables or, failing that, if there are matching column names in the two tables.

4. Accept the proposed join condition between the MAJOR column in both tables by clicking the Next arrow on the Join Conditions page.

Formatting options

The next page of the Master-Detail Form Builder Wizard, shown in Figure 8-10, is a little different from other pages you have encountered in other flavors of the Form Builder Wizard.

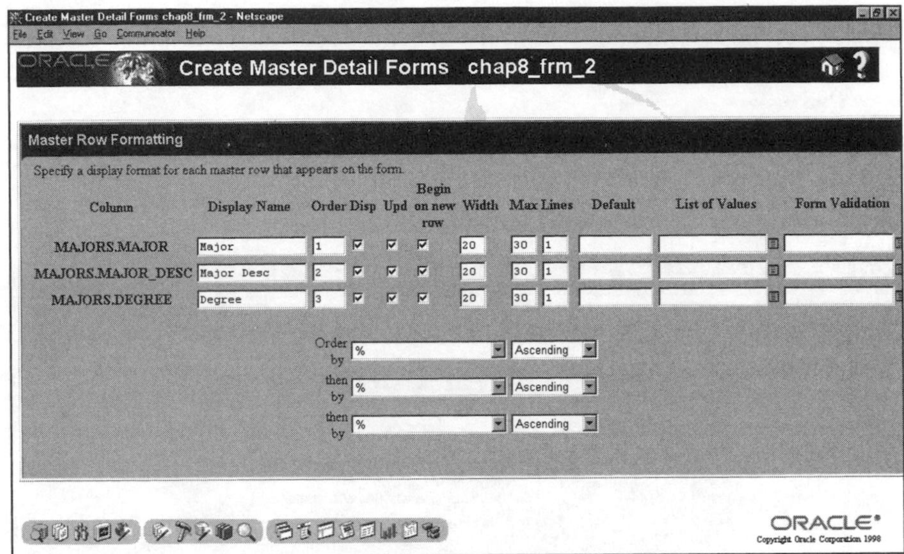

Figure 8-10: Formatting columns in the master table

You have seen most of the choices on this page before in the Column Formatting page of the other form builders, although the formatting choices are laid out in rows and columns in this page. The Display Name, Width, Default, and List of Values columns work in exactly the same way as they do in the other builders. The Max column has the same function as the Max Length text box in the other form builders, and the Begin on new row check box has the same function as the New Row check box.

There is also an entry field for Form Validation, although the field validation choice seems to be missing. The form-level validation is used because multiple rows are always displayed in the form that is used to insert new master rows.

The field-level validation is not all that's missing. You don't seem to have a lot of the other choices available to you when building a normal, standalone form, such as a choice of the type of data entry object that each column has. In this respect, the master-detail form is somewhat limited. There is a specific format that the forms you create with the Master-Detail Form Builder take. The rows in the master table are at the top of the form, laid out in a series of rows, and the detail rows (if present on the form) appear below the master row, and are also laid out as a series of rows. The only real formatting option that you have for the data entry objects in your master-detail form is to indicate whether the data entry object is a simple text box or a text area. You can indicate that a data entry object is a text area by specifying a number greater than 1 in the Lines text box. You can also set the order that the columns appear on the form by adjusting the values in the Order column for each column.

At this point, you may be bridling against this limitation, but when you see the functionality that is automatically built into your master-detail forms, you will be considerably happier.

You can always build your own master-detail forms with two form components linked together if you choose to reject the default layout and operation of the automatic master-detail forms.

There are two more ways you can shape the appearance and functionality of the fields for the master table in your master-detail form. Notice that there are two check boxes for each column: Disp, which stands for Display, and Upd, which stands for update. If you want the value for a column in the master table to show up on the page when the user is simply displaying the values for the table, you should leave the Disp check box checked. If you want to give the user the ability to update the value for a column in the master table, you should leave the Upd check box checked.

There are plenty of times when you want to give the user the ability to retrieve and view both the master and detail rows for a table, but prevent them from changing the values in the master rows. In the case of the MAJORS and MAJOR_REQS table, you might want to give the person using the form the ability to add requirements for a major, but not to change the values listed for the name, description, or degree for an existing major.

Finally, you have the ability to specify the order in which the rows in the master table are displayed on the forms with the series of combo boxes at the bottom of the form. These combo boxes provide the same interface and functionality that the Row Order combo boxes provide in the report builders.

5. Change the Display Name for the MAJORS.MAJOR_DESC column to **Major Description**.
6. Uncheck the Upd check boxes for all of the columns in the master table.
7. Change the Width and Max values for the MAJORS.MAJOR_DESC column to 40 and 50 respectively.
8. Change the Width and Max values for the MAJORS.DEGREE column to 4.
9. Click the Popup icon to the right of the List of Values text field for the MAJORS.DEGREE column. Find NETU.DEGREELOV in the Find box and click it to select it for the list of values.
10. Select the MAJORS.DEGREE choice in the Order by combo box and the MAJORS.MAJOR choice in the then by combo box.

Note: If you have not already loaded the preexisting LOV objects into the WebDB database, you should import the object called courselov.sql into your database. (If you did not load the degreelov.sql LOV in the previous chapter, you should import that object also.) You should also load the course_exists.sql validation routine, which you will use later in this chapter. For information on how to import objects, please refer to Appendix A.

11. Click the Next arrow on the Master Row Formatting page.

The next page of the Master-Detail Form Builder Wizard, as shown in Figure 8-11, gives you most of the same formatting options for the rows in the detail table that the previous page gave you for the rows in the master table.

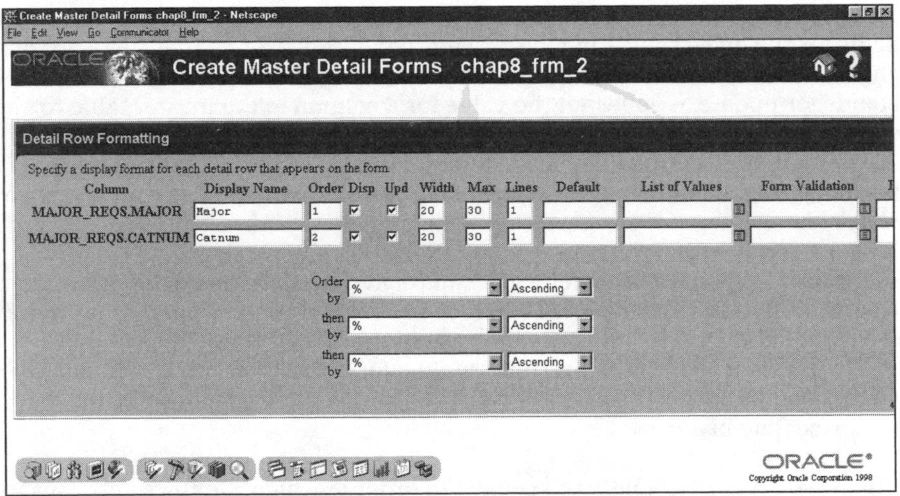

Figure 8-11: Formatting columns in the detail table

The only real difference between formatting the detail table and the master table is that you do not have the option to specify that a column begin on a new row in the detail rows section of the form. Some of the forms of the master-detail form that generated from your parameters will only have a single master row on the form. Because of this, you have the luxury of reserving additional page real estate by spreading the columns for the master table over several lines on the page. You will always see more than one detail row in all of the form varieties that are in your finished component, so the detail rows must always appear on a single line in the page.

12. Change the Display Name for the MAJOR_REQS.CATNUM column to **Catalog Number**.

13. For the MAJOR_REQS.CATNUM column, find the NETU.COURSELOV List of Values object using the Popup for the List of Values text box and select it as the List of Values.
14. Click the Next arrow on the Detail Row Formatting page.

The column named CATNUM in the MAJOR_REQS table is not the most descriptive column. It is used to enter the catalog code for the prerequisite courses for a particular major. However, when a user is adding new rows to the detail table, they are able to identify the courses by more than just the catalog number by using the NETU.COURSELOV LOV object. An LOV object in a detail table is always displayed as a combo box, so the end user of this form is able to select the more descriptive course name shown, and the catalog number is inserted into the data entry field for the CATNUM column.

Display options

The next page of the Master-Detail Form Builder Wizard is shown in Figure 8-12. It is titled Display Options, and it is similar to the other Display Options pages for the other types of forms.

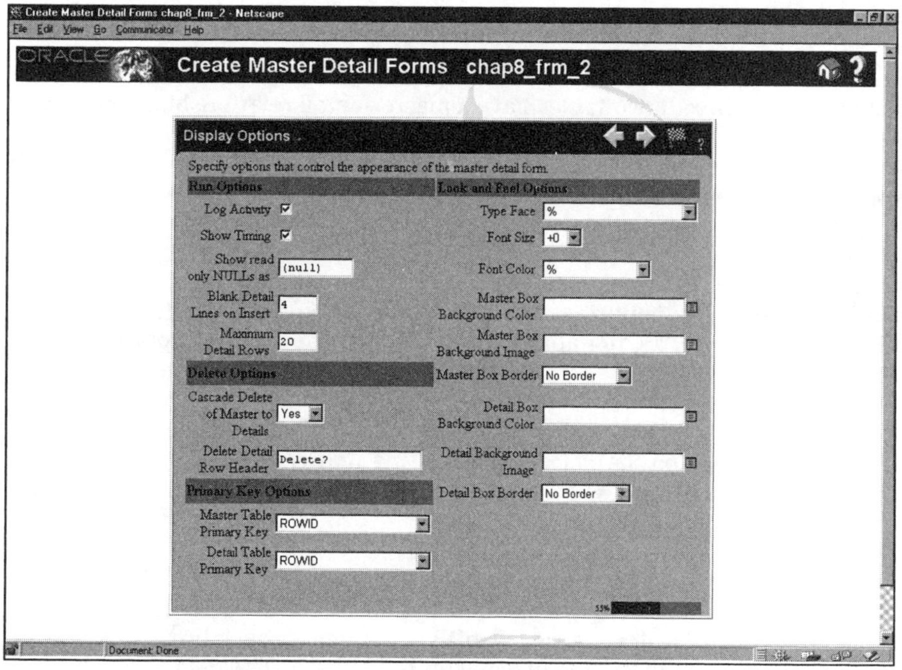

Figure 8-12: Display Options for a master-detail form

There are some new options shown in each of the four sections of the page. The Run Options section in the upper-right corner of the page has an entry box where you can specify how you want NULL values displayed in the read-only versions of the master-detail form. This option is familiar to you if you have already built a few reports. It appears here because some of the ways that master-detail forms are displayed are more like reports than the forms you have already built.

There are two additional choices in this section. The Blank Detail Lines on Insert text box enables you to specify how many blank lines you would like displayed at the bottom of each version of the master-detail form that allows the user to add new rows to the detail table. The number you enter for this option, in effect, determines how many new detail rows the user can add with a single page.

The Maximum Detail Rows parameter controls how many rows are shown on read-only detail pages, just like the Maximum Rows parameter controls the number of rows shown on a single page in a report. If there are more detail rows than the specified number in this parameter, a Next push button appears at the bottom of the page.

The section of the Display Options page located below the Run Options section on the left-hand side of the page is titled Delete Options. There are two fields in this section that control how detail rows are deleted.

The first item in the Delete Options section is the Cascade Delete of Master to Details combo box. If two tables have a master-detail relationship, you have to determine what to do with the detail rows that are associated with a particular master row if the master is deleted. WebDB gives you two choices. The first is that you can delete all associated detail rows when the master row is deleted, which is implemented by leaving the default value of Yes in the combo box. The other choice is that you can leave the orphaned detail rows in the database when the master row is deleted, which is implemented by changing the value of the combo box to No. This is obviously an important decision, so you should check with your database administrator if you are not absolutely certain which action is appropriate for your detail table.

This type of cascading deletion of detail rows is often automatically implemented with a trigger on the delete action for the master table. If this is true for your database, you should select No for this field, because you do not want to duplicate the actions of the trigger.

The other field in the Delete Options section, labeled Delete Detail Row Header, enables you to indicate the column heading for the delete option for rows in the detail table. As you will soon see, WebDB generates a check box for each row displayed in the detail section of a master detail form. The default heading for this column of check boxes is Delete. You have the option of changing this heading and, for this master-detail form, you will.

15. Change the Delete Detail Row Header to **Delete?**.

The last section on the left-hand side of the Display Options page is titled Primary Key Options. Because a form can retrieve rows of data and then update or delete them, WebDB must have a way of uniquely identifying each row in the table. WebDB uses a primary key to identify the rows in a table. By default, WebDB uses the ROWID column, which is an internal column that uniquely identifies every row in the database. The ROWID value is used internally by WebDB and it does not appear on any page in the form. You can, if you wish, specify a different primary key that will be used by WebDB for this purpose for either the master or detail tables, but generally there is no need to do this.

Note

The primary key option is only used internally by WebDB. As a result, it is different than the ROWID and ALT_ROWID parameters that you used for a normal form, which are used to determine if a form is being called for inserting new data or updating existing data. These different modes of data interaction are automatically handled by the different versions of the master-detail form.

The final difference between the Display Options for a master-detail form and the Display Options for other types of forms is minor. On the right-hand side of the page under the Look and Feel section, you have the option of specifying a box border, color, and background image for a box for the master or detail portions of the resulting forms.

16. Click the Next arrow on the Display Options page.

Button Options page

The Button Options page for a master-detail form, as shown in Figure 8-13, is also different from the Button Options page for a normal form.

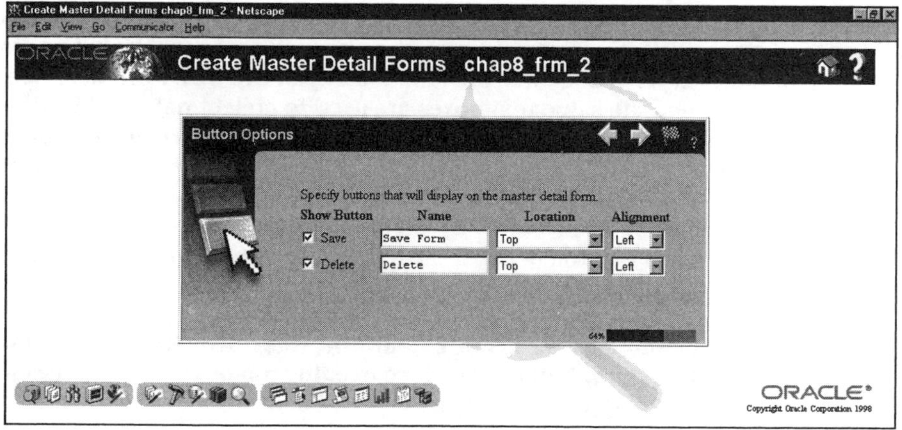

Figure 8-13: Button Options page for a master-detail form

There are only two button options for the form: Save Form and Delete. These are the only two options that affect both the master and detail rows in the form. The Save Form push button causes the form to save all the changes in the master and the detail form. The Delete push button deletes the row in the master table and potentially deletes all the associated rows in the detail table, depending on the option you selected for the cascade delete in the Display Options page.

If a user wants to insert or delete individual rows in the detail table, he or she does this by entering data into a row or checking a Delete check box for the row. These changes are implemented when the user clicks the Save Form push button.

If a user wants to insert a new row into the master table, he or she can use the Master Row Finder form, which is described on the next page of the Form Builder Wizard.

17. Click the Next arrow on the Button Options page.

Master Row Finder

Typically, working with master-detail tables involves two steps. First, a user has to specify which master row they want to work with, and then he or she can retrieve the detail rows associated with that master row to continue his or her work.

The Master Row Finder page in the wizard, as shown in Figure 8-14, is the first page that is used as part of a master-detail complex of forms.

As you can see, the Master Row Finder is a standalone form, with its own header, footer, and help text specified in the text areas at the bottom of the page.

The Master Row Finder implements two types of actions through two push buttons on the page. The first push button is the Add button. As the name implies, this button is used to add a new master row when the user clicks it. The second push button is called the Query button, and it is used to retrieve rows from the master table based on the selection criteria entered in the text boxes for the master table. This functionality is very much like the functionality of the QBE form described in the previous chapter. The same text boxes are used to collect data that is inserted into a new row of the master table or to indicate selection criteria for retrieving data from the master table. The only difference is which push button the user selects.

This page also enables you to specify if the parameter options for ordering the rows and limiting the maximum number of rows show on the Master Row Finder page.

18. Enter **You can enter a new major by entering data and clicking the <I>Add New</I> push button. You can retrieve existing majors by entering selection criteria and clicking on the <I>Query</I> push button.** for the Header Text.

19. Click the Next arrow on the Master Row Finder page.

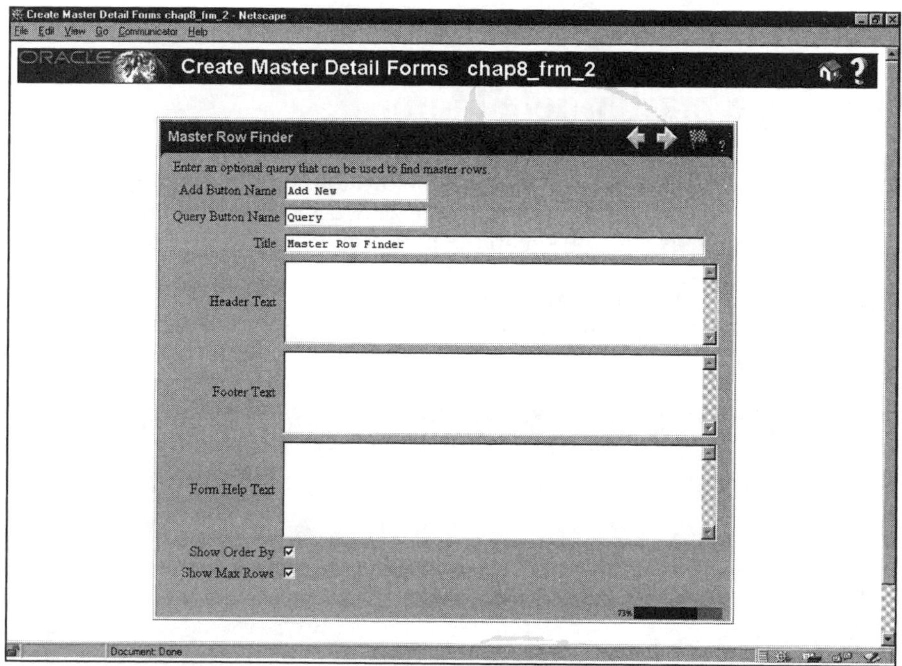

Figure 8-14: The Master Row Finder page in the Master-Detail Form Builder Wizard

Finishing the master-detail form

The last three pages of the Master-Detail Form Builder Wizard bring us back to familiar territory. The next page in the wizard prompts you for the text options for the two other forms generated as part of the master-detail form. The first is the Master Row Finder Results page, which is returned after you submit the Master Row Finder page you have just finished specifying, and the second is the Master Detail page, which is the main master-detail form.

All you really have to do in this form is select the same template you used with your other components to ensure that this master-detail form complex has the same look and feel as the rest of your application.

20. Select the PUBLIC.TEMPLATE_6 template in the Templates combo box.
21. Click the Next arrow on the Text Options page.
22. Click the Next arrow on the Advanced PL/SQL code page.

You have reached the final page of the Master-Detail Form Builder Wizard. The only thing left to do in the development process is generate the form.

23. Click the OK push button on the Create Master Detail Form page.

Your form is ready to run.

Running a master-detail form

As with other components, you have two choices of how to run your master-detail form. You could run the basic master-detail form directly by clicking the Run link at the bottom of the Manage Component page. However, this would not lead to a very satisfactory result, as you will see in the next step.

24. Click the Run link at the bottom of the Manage Component page for your master-detail form. You will see the form that appears in Figure 8-15.

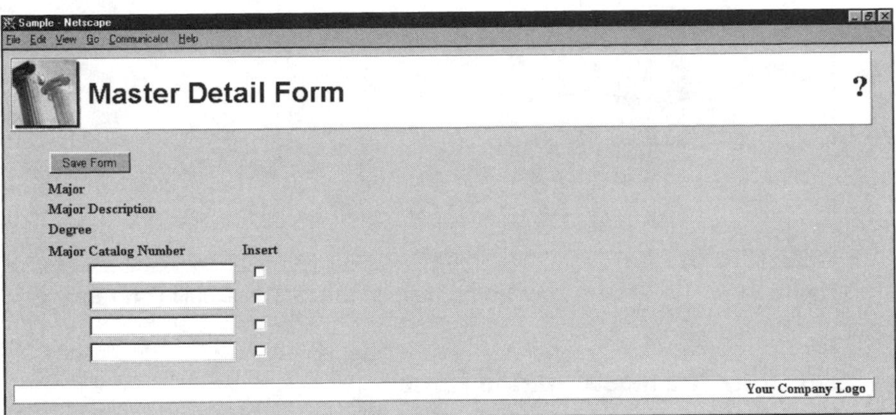

Figure 8-15: Running the master-detail form directly

As you can see, the form looks a bit, well, naked. There are no values for the master row. This is because the main master-detail form expects to be called from a parameter page that supplies all the information needed about the master row.

You can also see that the Delete? push button is missing, which is another symptom of the form being called without displaying any rows from the master table.

25. Return to the WebDB environment by clicking the Back push button of your browser.
26. Click the Parameters link. The page that comes up in the browser looks like a QBE form, as shown in Figure 8-16.

This form can be used to select a master row from the MAJORS table by clicking the Query push button, with or without selection criteria entered into the data fields for the columns in the table. You could also use this form to insert a new major into the MAJORS table.

Sample - Netscape
File Edit View Go Communicator Help
Master Row Finder
?
You can enter a new major by entering data and clicking on the Add New push button. You can retrieve existing majors by entering selection criteria and clicking on the Query push button.
Query
Add New
MAJOR
MAJOR DESC
DEGREE
B.A.
Order By
DEGREE
Ascending
MAJOR
Ascending
%
Ascending
Maximum Rows
20
Your Company Logo

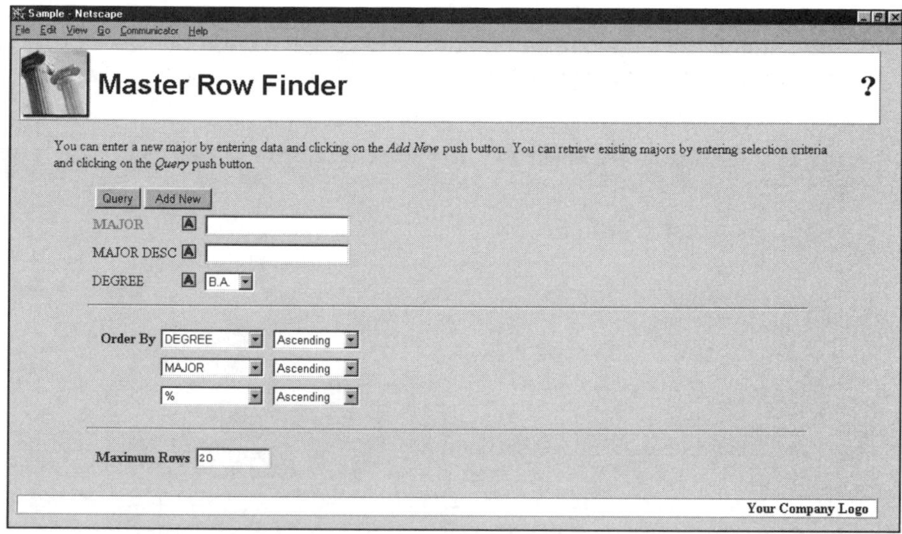

Figure 8-16: The master-detail parameter form

27. You do not want to insert any new rows — you just want to retrieve some master rows as a starting point to adding detail rows. Click the Query push button in the master parameter form.

The form that appears after you click the Query push button is the show_masters form, as shown in Figure 8-17. As the name implies, the main purpose of this form is to show the master rows in a master-detail relationship. The first column of the show_masters form is labeled Action, and it contains a single action link that is labeled Edit. If you click the link, it takes you to the main detail form.

28. Click the Edit link to the left of the History row.

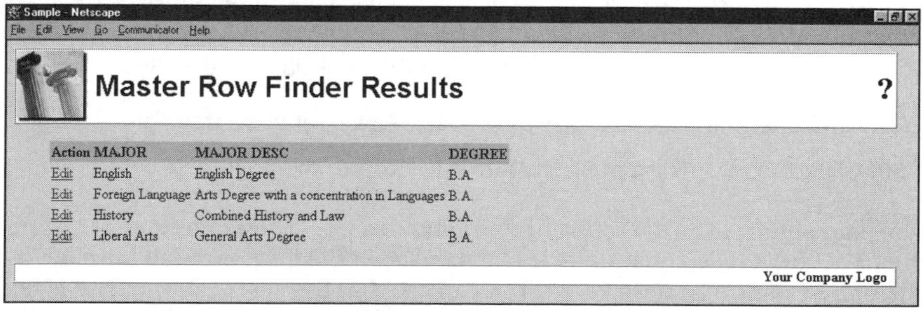

Sample - Netscape
File Edit View Go Communicator Help
Master Row Finder Results
?
Action MAJOR MAJOR DESC DEGREE
Edit English English Degree B.A.
Edit Foreign Language Arts Degree with a concentration in Languages B.A.
Edit History Combined History and Law B.A.
Edit Liberal Arts General Arts Degree B.A.
Your Company Logo

Figure 8-17: The show_masters form

You have finally arrived at your destination — the main form that enables you to enter detail rows that are automatically associated with the master row you selected, as shown in Figure 8-18.

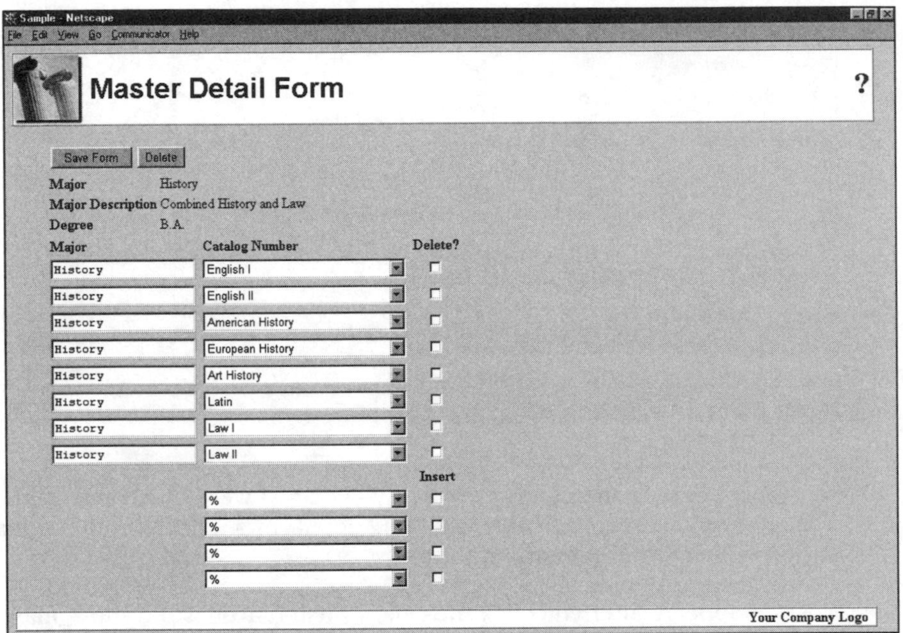

Figure 8-18: The main detail form

You can see the values for the master row displayed at the top of the form, the existing detail rows listed below the master (each with its own Delete? check box), and four rows at the bottom of the page that you can use to insert new detail rows. Notice that the text boxes for the value of the MAJOR column are not listed next to the rows for inserting detail rows. This is because all new detail rows are automatically assigned the value for the MAJOR column of the master table. You can update the value of the MAJOR column for existing detail rows.

29. Click the Delete? check box next to the Law I detail course.

30. Click the Save Form push button at the top of the page.

The page returned as the result of this action has a success message at the top of the page and a recapitulation of the main page of the master-detail form, with the currently valid detail rows listed. You can see that the Law I prerequisite is no longer present. You should add it back to the detail table to see how to use the form to add new rows.

31. Click the combo box in the first insert row at the bottom of the page and select the Law I entry.

32. Click the Insert check box to the right of the row you just used to specify another prerequisite.

33. Click the Save Form push button at the top of the page.

When your page returns, you can again see the success message at the top of the page, and the Law I prerequisite has been added to the detail table.

Your main detail form works well, but not flawlessly. You can see a potential problem by trying to add a duplicate row to the detail table, which is not allowed by the underlying database table.

34. Click the combo box in the first insert row at the bottom of the page and select the Law II entry.

35. Click the Insert check box to the right of the row you just used to specify another prerequisite.

36. Click the Save Form push button at the top of the page.

The page returned to you this time is not quite so happy, as shown in Figure 8-19. Remember that you did not specify any type of validation for the detail form, so you can go back to the form and add a validation routine to the form, which prevents this type of problem in the future.

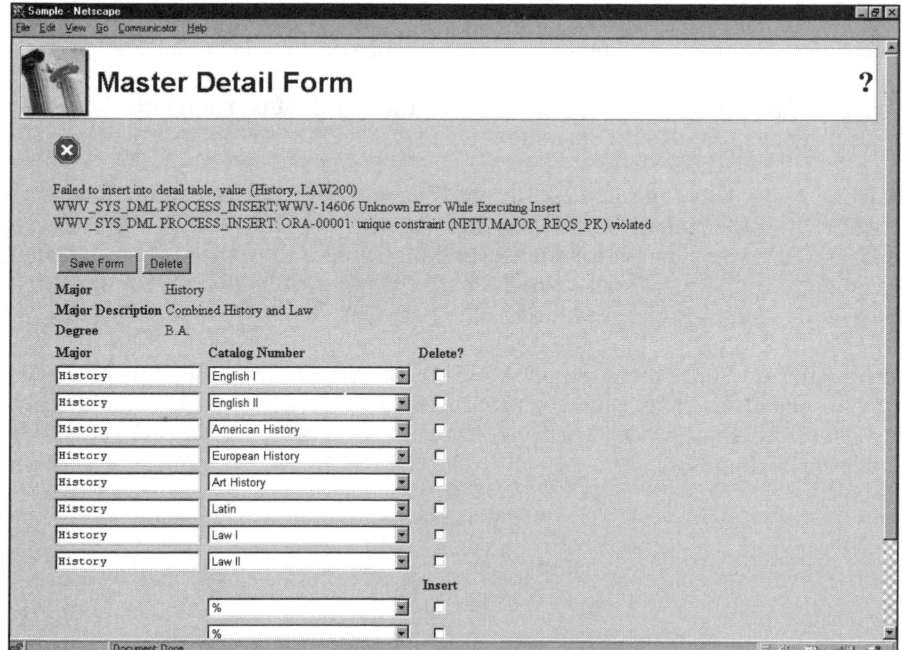

Figure 8-19: An unsuccessful insert into the detail table

37. Return to the WebDB environment by clicking the Back push button of your browser.
38. Click the Edit link. Click the Detail Row Formatting tab.
39. For the MAJOR_REQS.CATNUM column, find the NETU.COURSE_EXISTS validation routine and select it as the Form Validation.

Note

The JavaScript for this validation routine was not included with the code for this book as the file javascript.sql. You can go to the Web site for the book, www.webdb-bible.com., to get the script.

40. Click the Finish push button to regenerate the form component.
41. Click the Parameters link at the bottom of the Manage Component page for the form.

You should try to insert a duplicate row again to see if the validation routine works.

42. Click the Query push button in the master parameter form.
43. Click the Edit link to the left of the History row.
44. Click the combo box in the first insert row at the bottom of the page and select the Law II entry.
45. Click the Insert check box to the right of the row you just used to specify another prerequisite.
46. Click the Save Form push button at the top of the page.

This time, your result is much better, even though the insertion fails. You see an error message just like the one shown in Figure 8-20.

The end result was the same as the last time you tried to insert a duplicate row into the MAJOR_REQS table, but at least this time the user was able to receive an error message that was much more helpful and instructive than the last time. The error was caught in the browser as a result of the JavaScript validation routine, rather than being caught in the server after the data was sent.

Although the release included on the CD-ROM that accompanies this book may not fully support form-level validation routines, the current version, available through the Oracle Technology Network site, `http://technet.oracle.com`, should fully support this functionality.

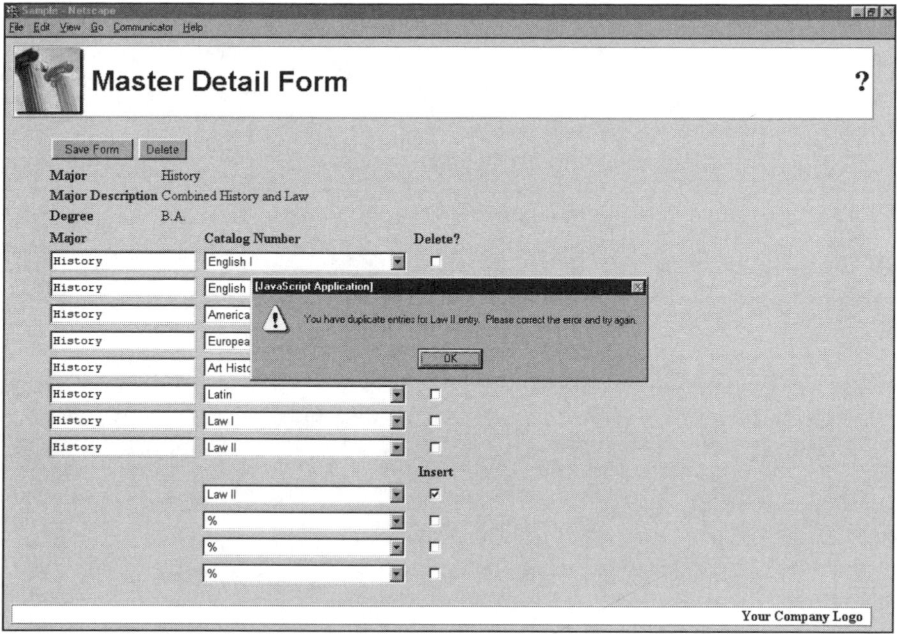

Figure 8-20: Catching the error message

Wrapping Up

In this chapter, you completed examining some of the more complex features in WebDB form components, including building forms based on stored procedures and creating master-detail form components through a single process. In addition, we revealed to you the secrets of using a form component for updating and deleting data.

This is far from the end of using forms in your WebDB application system. You will use other forms as you learn about the rest of the functionality in WebDB. And, as we stated back at the beginning of the previous chapter, you will build many forms as you create your applications with WebDB. However, in order to cover the breadth of the features delivered with WebDB, we have to move on to building other components.

✦ ✦ ✦

Building Charts

Since the dawn of flow charts, people have found it easier to comprehend large amounts of information when it is presented in a graphical format. Computers, which are used for storing and processing larger amounts of data than a normal person can easily absorb, can create reports based on summaries of this data. However, the most convenient way to quickly spot trends and to understand the big picture is through a chart.

WebDB charts, like all other WebDB components, have their strengths and weaknesses. Although you may not find the broadest range of options and flexibility, WebDB charts are certainly quick and easy to build. And, like all other WebDB components, they offer a significant amount of user interaction and they are available to anyone who has access to a browser.

In This Chapter

Building Charts with the Query Wizard

Building Charts Based on an SQL Statement

Creating Charts with the Query Wizard

A chart is essentially a type of report. Both the chart and the report have a single purpose: to present data to the user to read. Because of this, you will find that pages of the Chart Builder Wizard most closely resemble those of the Report Builder Wizard. However, because a chart is a very particular type of report, the process of building it is a bit more concise than the process of creating a general report.

Beginning the process

You start the process of building a chart component in much the same way that you start the process of building other components.

1. Enter the WebDB development environment as the NETUDEV developer.

If you have not yet loaded the sample NETU database, please refer to Chapter 2 for instructions on how to install the sample data and create the necessary users.

2. Go to the main Chart Building page, either by navigating through the Build ➪ User Interface Components ➪ Charts pages or by going directly to the page by clicking the Chart icon in the shortcuts bar.

The first page of the Chart Building area of WebDB looks exactly like the first page of the Report Builder Wizard, as shown in Figure 9-1.

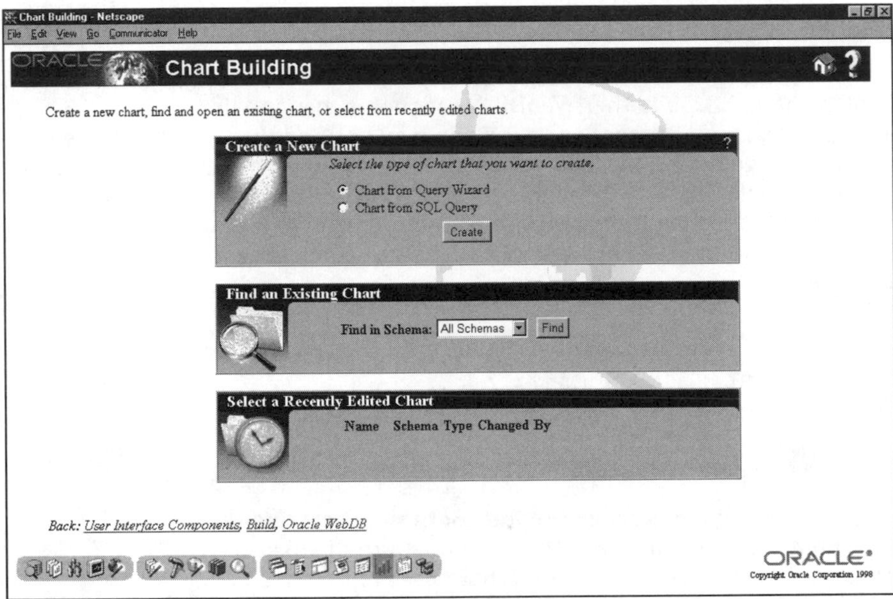

Figure 9-1: The main page of the Chart Builder Wizard

There are three panels on the page. The top panel enables you to create a chart based on either rows and columns that you specify through a Query Wizard or with your own SQL statement.

The second panel gives you a way to search through any of the schemas you have access to for a chart component, while the third panel enables you to quickly select any of the most recent chart components you have worked on. The last two panels take you to the Manage Component page for the component, from which you can run, edit, or manage the component.

Because you have not built a chart component yet, start with one of the flavors of the Chart Builder Wizard.

3. Select the radio button for the Chart from Query Wizard and click the Create push button.

The second page of the Chart Builder Wizard looks exactly like the second page of the other wizards you have encountered so far. You have to indicate where the component you build will reside in the database and give the component a unique name.

4. Select the NETU choice from the Schema combo box.
5. Enter **ch9_cht_1** as the name of the component.
6. Click the Next arrow on the Chart Name and Schema page.

The next page of the Chart Builder Wizard prompts you to identify the name of the table or view that you want to base the chart on. In the sample database included with this book, there is a table, DONATIONS, that is ideal for chart building. The DONATIONS table contains a record of donations made by all the alumni to the two basic charitable funds. You can sort the data in this table based on the identity of the alumni, the fund the donation was intended for, or any restrictions on the use of the funds. Because there are a lot of rows in the table, and because contribution levels are exactly the sort of thing that administrators at old Net University want to see quickly summarized, use the DONATIONS table as the main source table for all the charts you build in this chapter.

7. Select the NETU.DONATIONS table in the Tables/Views combo box.
8. Click the Next arrow on the Tables or Views page.

Describing the chart

The next page of the Chart Builder Wizard, shown in Figure 9-2, is the most important page in the wizard.

This page is where you specify the data that will be used to create the chart. In some ways, this is the cleanest high-level page in any of the wizards in WebDB. By selecting and entering values in just a few fields, you tell WebDB about the relationships that it will use to build the resulting chart.

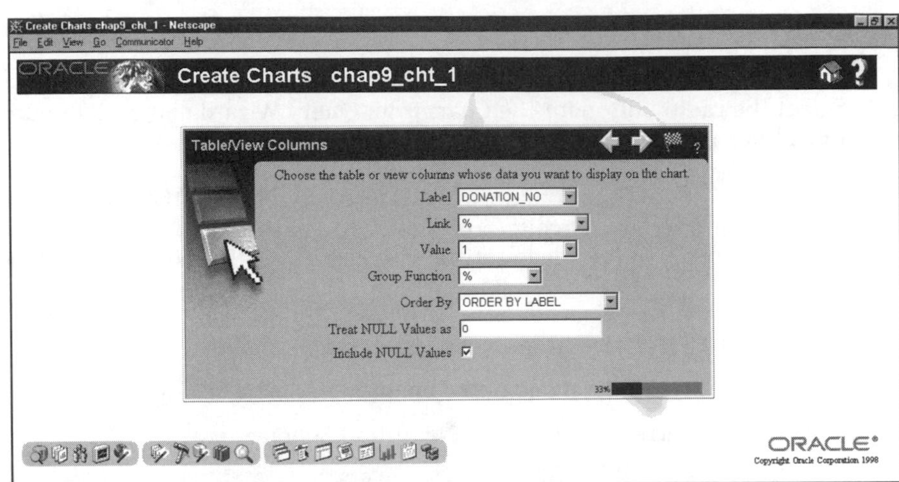

Figure 9-2: The Table/View Columns formatting page in the Chart Builder Wizard

Table 9-1 describes the seven data entry elements listed on this page and the way to use them.

Table 9-1
Data Entry Elements for Formatting Chart Columns

Element	*Usage*
Label	The Label combo box gives you a choice of the columns in the table you have selected. The column you indicate in this combo box is used as the grouping value for the resultant chart component. The Group Function is applied to all the rows on the basis of the value of the Label column. For instance, if you choose FUND as the Label, the values in the chart are presented based on the different values for the FUND column. The column chosen as the label also, as the name implies, provides a value for the label in the chart.
Link	As with all WebDB components, you can associate a Link object with the chart. The Link object must be previously defined as a shared component, and the combo box displays all the Link objects that the owning schema has access to. Links are commonly used with chart components, because a chart typically gives a high-level view of the data and users frequently want to drill down for a more detailed report based on the different categories presented in the chart.

Element	*Usage*
Value	The Value field is where you specify the column that provides the values that are used as the basis for the chart. You can see that this is a combo box that brings up a list of the numeric columns in the selected table. The default value for the Value field is 1. Use this default value if you are planning on selecting a Group Function that is not dependent on the values in a table row—such as the Count function. In fact, assigning a Value of 1 and doing a Sum function gives the same results as doing a Count on the group.
Group Function	The Group Function combo box lists the functions you can use to summarize the data in each of the groups of the chart. There are seven aggregate functions available to you: **AVG** gives you the average for each group in the chart. **COUNT** gives you a count of the number of rows for each group in the chart. **MAX** gives you the maximum value for any single row for each group in the chart. **MIN** gives you the minimum value for any single row for each group in the chart. **STDDEV** gives you the standard deviation from the norm for each group in the chart. **SUM**, the most commonly used group function, gives you a sum of the values for the column listed as the Value column for each group in the chart. **VARIANCE** is mainly used for computing standard deviations. There is more documentation on this function in the standard Oracle documentation, but if you don't know what a standard deviation is, you probably will never use this function. The default value for the Group Function combo box is the "%" wild card. If you select the wild card, there is no group function applied to the groupings in the chart. You may want to use this function if the chart data is already in the summarized format you want, but you want to present it in a graphical manner.
Order By	The Order By combo box gives you a limited number of choices as to how you want to order the data presented in your chart. Remember that you really only have two values in your chart: the label and the value based on each group in the chart. Because of this, your only choices for the Order By combo box are ORDER BY LABEL, ORDER BY LABEL DESC, ORDER BY VALUE, and ORDER BY VALUE DESC. The DESC stands for descending, while the other selections are in ascending order.

Continued

Table 9-1 *(continued)*

Element	*Usage*
Treat NULL Values as	A NULL value indicates the absence of a value. Therefore, you have to tell your chart component what value to use for NULLs that it finds in the data. Typically, this value is 0, which is the default.
Include NULL Values	There may be times when you do not want to include NULL values in the calculations used for each group. If you know that some of the rows in the target table have NULL values, you might want to exclude them from some types of aggregate calculations for a more accurate view of the data. For example, if you were using your chart to display the average donation, you might want to eliminate the rows with NULL values from the aggregate function, because they would bring the value of the average down. The default for this check box is checked, which keeps rows with NULL values for the column selected as the Value included in the calculations for the chart.

Your first chart component is pretty straightforward. You simply want to see the total amount of donations for each of the two alumni funds.

9. Select FUND in the Label combo box.
10. Select the AMOUNT column from the Value combo box.
11. Select SUM as the Group Function.
12. Click the Next arrow on the Table/View Columns page.

The next page of the Chart Builder Wizard enables you to specify selection criteria columns for your chart. Although you can only use two columns in your chart—one for the grouping and one for the value—you can include any number of columns as part of the selection criteria used to shape the data for the chart. You don't need any selection criteria for this simple chart.

13. Click the Next arrow on the Column Conditions page.

Display options

The next page of the Chart Builder Wizard, as shown in Figure 9-3, is similar to the page you can use to indicate display options for reports and other WebDB components.

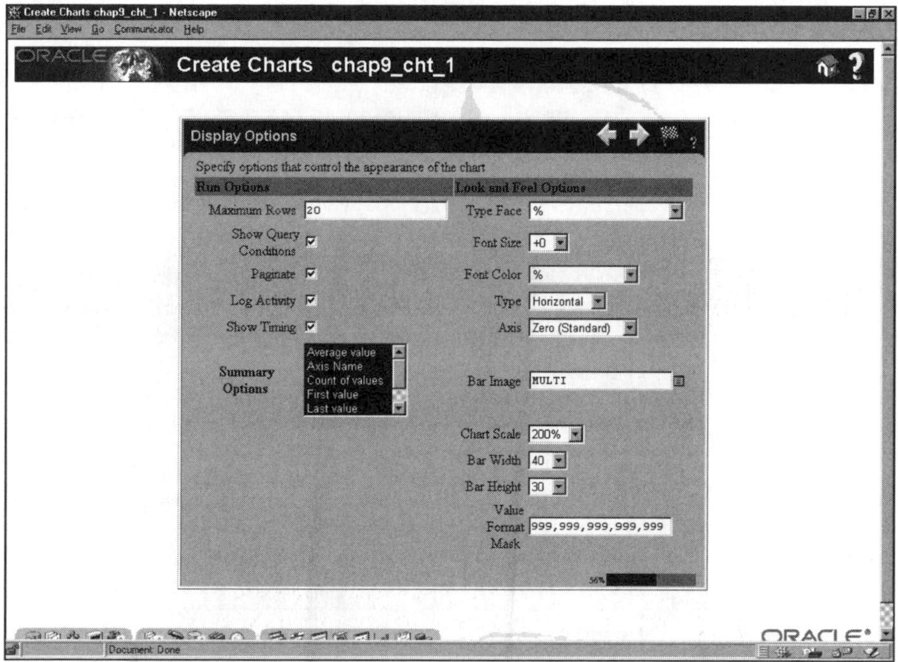

Figure 9-3: Display Options for a chart

Many of the selections available to you are exactly the same as the selections that were described when reports were first discussed in Chapter 5. The Maximum Rows, Paginate, Log Activity, and Show Timing elements in the Run Options section of the page perform the same functions as they do for a report. The Type Face, Font Size, and Font Color elements in the Look and Feel Options section of the page also perform the same functions as their counterparts in the report. For more information on any of these options, please refer to Chapter 5.

Table 9-2 describes the rest of the elements on the page.

Table 9-2
Display Options Unique to Charts

Display Options Run Options	***Usage***
Summary Options	The Summary Options list box contains a list of information that may be displayed at the bottom of each page of the chart. By selecting a summary option in this multiselect list box, you cause the summary information to be selected by default. If the chart is run directly by calling the RUN procedure, only those summary options you have selected are displayed. If a user accesses the chart through the parameter form, the summary options you choose are selected by default in the Summary Options list box presented on the parameter form. Most of the summary options are aggregate functions. These functions include Average Value, Count of Values, Maximum Value, and Sum of Values, which are user-friendly names for the same aggregate functions available in the Chart Builder Wizard. The other summary options—Axis Name, First Value, and Last Value—simply display some of the information available in the chart in the summary at the bottom of the page. If you select a summary option, the aggregate calculation is derived from all of the information shown on the page. For instance, if you select First Value, the summary displays the first value for the page, not for the overall chart.
Look and Feel Options	***Usage***
Type	There are only two Types available to you for your charts: a horizontal bar chart (the default) or a vertical bar chart.
Axis	The Axis combo box enables you to specify where you want to place the main perpendicular axis of the chart. The default value of Zero (Standard) uses zero as the left axis in a horizontal chart and as the bottom axis in a vertical chart. The Average Value choice uses the average value as the center axis for the chart. Those bars in the chart with smaller values appear to the left of the axis in a horizontal chart and below the axis in a vertical chart. The First Value and Last Value choices use the first and last values on the page respectively as the axis, and the values for each bar are grouped around them as they are for the Average Value axis. The Minimum Value and Maximum Value choices cause a similar effect, although these axes are always to one side of the chart because they represent the extremes of the values presented in the chart.

Display Options Run Options	*Usage*
	The value for the axis can be listed as one of the summary options at the bottom of the chart page. If you are using any axis other than the default zero-based axis, you should include the value for the axis.
Bar Image	The Bar Image text box enables you to specify the basic image you use for the bars in your chart. There is a pop-up icon to the right of the text field that enables you to select the bar image from a list of the available bar styles. There are seven different color choices and a Multiple colors choice listed in the pop-up list. If you choose any of the single color choices, your chart appears as a series of bars in that color. If you choose the Multiple colors option, your chart appears in a number of different colors.
Chart Scale	The Chart Scale combo box enables you to choose a scale percentage for the chart. The percentage relates to the overall size of the page, but all you really need to know is the bigger the percentage, the larger the chart appears in relation to the page.
Bar Width	The Bar Width combo box enables you to select the size (in pixels) of each bar on the page of a *vertical* chart.
Bar Height	The Bar Height combo box enables you to select the size (in pixels) of each bar on the page of a *horizontal* chart.
Value Format Mask	The Value Format Mask enables you to specify the formatting for the display of values for the bars in the chart.

You can leave all the display options with their default values for your first chart. In some of the charts you will create later, you will want to shape the options.

14. Click the Next arrow on the Display Options page.

Finishing the chart

The rest of the pages in the Chart Builder Wizard are very similar or exactly the same as the corresponding pages in the Report Builder Wizard.

If you are unfamiliar with these pages and their implications, refer to Chapter 5, where they are explained in detail.

The Parameter Entry Form Display Options page is very similar to the same page for a report. The only difference is in the center section of the page, where the Parameter Entry Form options are slightly different.

As with a report component, the Parameter Options list box is a multiselect list box that enables you to specify which parameter options elements are exposed to the user in the parameter form for the report. The Include NULLs, Maximum Rows/Page, and Type options perform the same functions as their counterparts on the Display Options and Table/View Columns pages. These parameters display the default values you select for them in the Chart Builder Wizard, but the user can override your defaults if the parameters are displayed. The Axis option displays the value used for the axis at the bottom of the page. The Summary parameter option, if selected, gives the user a iist box with all of the summary options that were discussed in the previous section.

The button options are the same as the button options for report components, so you can just accept the defaults.

15. Click the Next arrow on the Parameter Entry Form Display Options page.

You have to assign the same template to your chart as you have to all the other components you have created.

16. Select the PUBLIC.TEMPLATE_6 choice in the Template combo box.
17. Add the following text to the Header Text area: **<center><b>Total Revenue By Fund</b></center>**.

You can use standard HTML tags in your header, footer, and help texts. You do not need to add any extended PL/SQL procedures to your chart, so you can proceed to the end of the wizard and create the chart package.

18. Click the checkered flag icon on the Text Options page to complete the generation of the chart module.

Running your chart

You can see the results of your work by running your chart. Because you want to see how the parameters affect the latest generation of the chart, you should start the chart from the parameter form page, even though you are going to accept all the default values for the parameters.

1. Click the Parameters link at the bottom of the Component Manager page.

Figure 9-4 shows the parameter page for a chart.

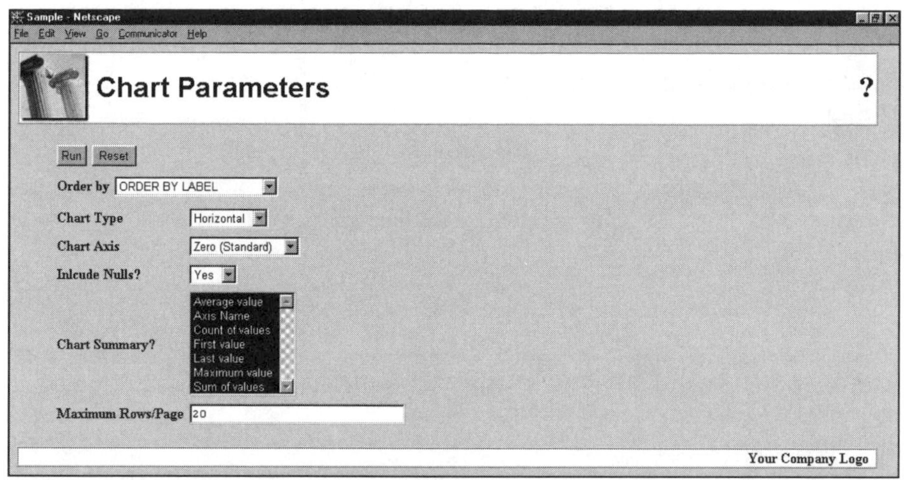

Figure 9-4: The parameter page for a chart

You can see the familiar push buttons at the top of the page, and the familiar text field for the Maximum Rows/Page. The Order by combo box looks familiar, but, as in the builder, there are only four options available. The Chart Type, Chart Axis, and Include Nulls? combo boxes contain the same choices and defaults that you specified in the Chart Builder Wizard. The Chart Summary is a list box with all the options selected. To see their effect on the chart, you should leave them all selected at this time, but a user could change the selected entries using the standard key combinations for a multiple select list box.

As with a report, you could have included the Save push button and the Batch push button on the page for a user, although they are not shown by default.

2. Click the Run push button.

Your first chart appears, as shown in Figure 9-5.

Not the most exciting chart, but it does get across some valuable information. You can see at a glance that the Annual Fund has received more revenue than the Capital Campaign, although not that much more in relative terms. You can also see that all of the summary information for the chart page is included at the bottom of the page. The information includes the average value for the two bars in the chart, the fact that the Axis of the chart is at 0, the number of entries in the chart by the label of Count, the first and last values displayed on the chart, the minimum and maximum values for the chart page, and the sum of all the values displayed on the chart page.

3. Move the cursor over one of the bars in the chart. If your browser supports the display of tips, you can see the label and value for the bar displayed.

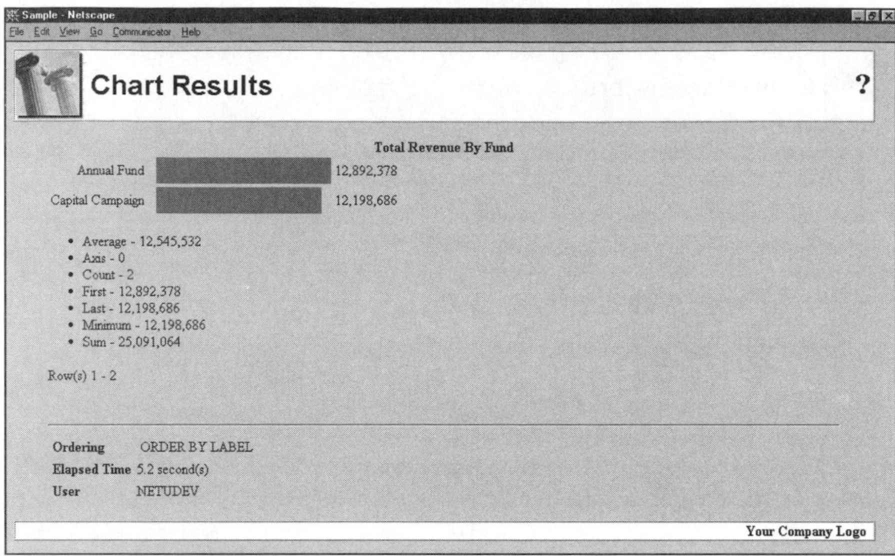

Figure 9-5: Your first chart

Of course, for this particular chart, the Axis, Count, First, Last, Maximum, and Minimum values are pretty meaningless, so the chart would probably be more to the point if you eliminated these lines from the chart page.

4. Return to the parameter page for the chart by clicking the Back push button in your browser.
5. Click the Average Value choice in the Chart Summary list box. Notice that all the other choices are deselected when you select another choice.
6. Hold down the Ctrl key (for Windows) and click the Sum of Values choice in the Chart Summary list box.
7. Click the Run Chart push button on the parameter page for the chart.

The new version of this chart page is much less cluttered with useless information. You have gotten pretty much all you can get out of this simple but useful chart. Your next basic chart will present even more information in a simple-to-understand format.

Creating a more complex chart

Now that you are familiar with the basics of creating a chart, you can create a chart that displays many more values. You can also limit the parameters that are available to a user at run time to suit the needs of the chart.

1. Return to the main Chart Building page by returning to the WebDB environment and clicking the Chart icon in the shortcuts bar.
2. Select the Chart from Query Wizard radio button in the top panel and click the Create push button.
3. Select the NETU schema and enter **ch9_cht_2** for the Chart Name.
4. Click the Next arrow on the Chart Name and Schema page.
5. Select the NETU.DONATIONS table and click the Next arrow on the Tables or Views page.

The next page, the Table/View Columns page, is where the main attributes of the chart are specified, so you will do most of your work here.

6. Select RESTRICTION as the Label, AMOUNT as the Value, and SUM as the Group Function.
7. Deselect the Include NULL Values by clicking the check box.

Because you are expecting the average donation to be a standard summary value, you don't want to include nulls in the calculation.

8. Click the Next arrow on the Table/View Columns page.
9. Click the Next arrow on the Column Conditions page.
10. In the Display Options page, hold down the Ctrl key (for Windows) and deselect the First value and Last value entries in the Summary Options list box.

This particular chart is going to display the total contributions for each type of restriction. Because of this, the first and last values on a page are not meaningful, so you have deselected them as default options. These summary options still appear in the Summary list box on the parameter form, so a user could still ask for them, but for the sake of convenience and reducing confusion, it makes sense to have them not selected by default.

11. Change the Value Format Mask to **$999,999,999,999.99.**
12. Click the Next arrow on the Display Options page.
13. Deselect the Include Nulls choice in the center of the Parameter Entry Form Display Options page.

As mentioned previously, to avoid confusion over the average contribution you don't want the null values to be included in the chart. This chart is being designed for use by your fund-raising staff, who are not that technically savvy. Also, you don't want to give them the ability to include null values in the chart, because they don't really understand the concept of nulls and averages. By removing the parameter from the parameter form, you can avoid the run-time errors and the confusion this might cause.

14. Click the Next arrow on the Parameter Entry Form Display Options page.
15. Select the PUBLIC.TEMPLATE_6 template.
16. Change the Title for the Chart to **Funds by Restrictions** and the Title for the Parameter Entry form to **Funds by Restrictions chart parameters.**
17. Enter **This chart displays contributions made to all funds by fund restriction.** as the Header Text.
18. Click the checkered flag on the Text Options page to build the chart component.

This chart is a little bit more complex, because it displays many more values than your first chart.

19. Click the Parameter link at the bottom of the Manage Component page.

You can see that this parameter page is just a little bit different from your previous parameter page. The Include Nulls check box is gone, and the First value and Last value choices in the Chart Summary list box are not selected. Because you are going to run the report with the standard, zero-based axis, you do not need to see the meaningless information about the basis for the axis in the chart.

20. Deselect the Axis choice in the Chart Summary list box.
21. Click the Run Chart push button.

Figure 9-6 shows the generated chart.

When you look at the chart a little more closely, you can see that the values in the RESTRICTION column are not that useful. These values are codes, rather than understandable names and, because this chart might be used by people who are not intimately familiar with the meaning of these codes, it would be nice to show more descriptive names. There are more descriptive names available for the restriction codes, but they are in a separate table. In order to use them, you have to create your own SQL statement, as the Query Wizard only allows you to use a single table in your chart. You will learn how to do this in the next section.

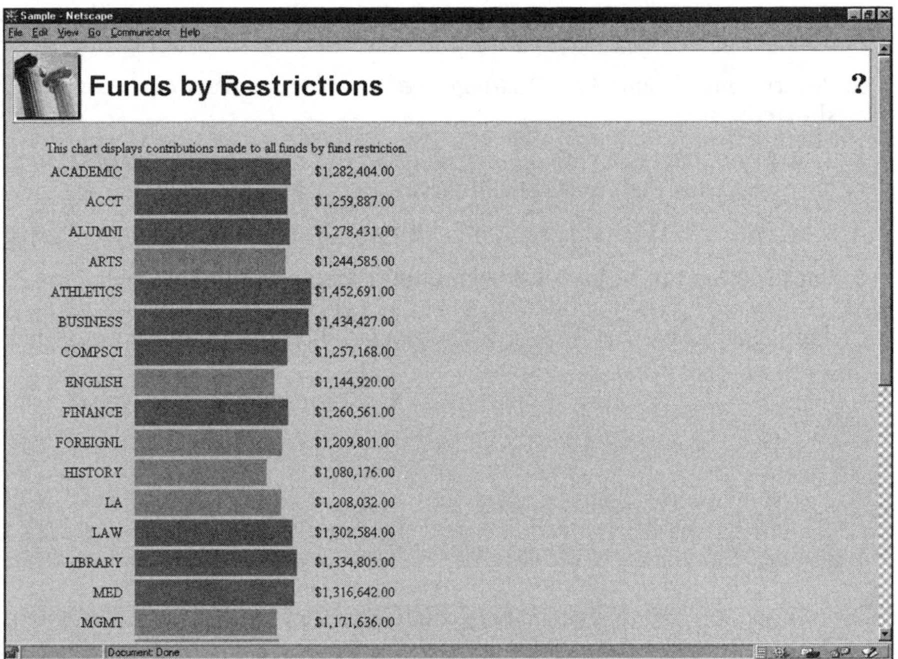

Figure 9-6: Your second chart

Creating Charts Based on an SQL Statement

The Query Wizard that comes as part of the Chart Builder Wizard makes it easy to quickly build basic charts. But, you may find yourself trying to access data that is outside the capabilities of the Query Wizard. You have already experienced one of those situations in the last chart you created to show the donations for a fund based on restrictions placed on the donations, but the only descriptive information available for a restriction was a cryptic code. Having a code for a restriction makes a lot of sense for a normalized database structure, but it is less clear for those end users reading charts based on a single table.

By using the ability to describe the data source for a chart with your own SQL statement, you can easily surmount this difficulty and still provide run-time flexibility to the user through the use of chart parameters.

Charts based on multiple tables

The first chart you base on an SQL statement is essentially an enhancement of the chart you made in the previous section.

1. Return to the WebDB environment by clicking the Back push button in your browser.
2. Return to the main Chart Building page by selecting the Chart icon in the shortcuts bar.
3. Select the Chart from SQL Query radio button in the top panel of the main page and click the Create push button.
4. Select the NETU schema and enter **ch9_cht_3** as the Name of the chart.
5. Click the Next push button on the Chart Name and Schema page.

The next page of the Chart Builder Wizard looks a little bit different from what you might have expected.

```
select
    null      the_link,
    ENAME     the_name,
    SAL       the_data
from SCOTT.EMP
order by SAL desc
```

There is a text area there that enables you to specify your own SQL statement, but the sample SQL statement is not what you may have expected. There are only three columns in the statement, and each column has an alias listed for it.

To understand this statement, it is important to understand that WebDB is more than just a way of passing data from a database to a browser. The SQL statements that you specify, either with the assistance of the Query Wizard or by entering your own statement, act as a conduit to get a resultant set of data back from the database. WebDB then uses this data to construct the HTML pages that you and your users see on the browser.

Any SQL statement you use as the basis for a chart must have three and only three columns in the SELECT statement. The first column, which has the alias of `the_link`, is the internal name for any link which is associated with the chart. You will learn more about links in Chapter 17 of this book. If there is no link for a chart, this column should be given the value of null, which means there is no value for the column.

The second column, which has the alias of `the_name`, represents the same column you selected as the label in the Query Wizard. This is the value that is used for the names of the bars in the chart and is also used to group the data in the chart.

The final column, which has the alias of `the_data`, is the same column you specified for the value in the Query Wizard. This column supplies the value that is used to calculate the bars in the resultant chart.

You can't change the basic way a chart is constructed by WebDB by changing the number of columns. In fact, if you include more columns in the SQL statement that is used for a chart, you get an error when you try to move to the next page in the wizard. You can supplement the way the data is sorted and grouped and the number of tables involved in the chart, as the SQL statement you enter shows.

6. Enter the following text into the text area on this page:

```
SELECT NULL the_link,
       RESTRICT_NAME the_name,
       SUM(AMOUNT) the_data
FROM DONATIONS, RESTRICT_CODES
WHERE DONATIONS.RESTRICTION = RESTRICT_CODES.RESTRICT_CODE
GROUP BY FUND, RESTRICT_NAME
```

As with the SQL statements in earlier chapters, this statement is included in the Chapter 9 Examples directory on the accompanying CD-ROM under the name ch9_sql1.txt.

With this SQL statement, you add a second table to the chart and use a descriptive name for the chart. You can also see that you have added a `group by` clause to the statement that groups the donations by fund and then by the name for a restriction. This grouping has the effect of creating two bars for each restriction category—one for each different fund.

In order to see this at work, you should quickly finish the definition of the chart.

7. Click the Next arrow on the SQL Query page.

The next page is the Display Options page. Because you did not indicate any parameters in the SQL statement you entered, WebDB is smart enough to know you don't need the parameter definition page.

8. Change the Value Format Mask to **$999,999,999,999.99.**
9. Click the Next arrow on the Display Options page.
10. Click the Next arrow on the Parameter Entry Form Display Options page.
11. Select PUBLIC.TEMPLATE_6 in the Template combo box and give the chart and its parameter form an appropriate title and header. Click the checkered flag to generate the chart component.
12. Click the Parameters link at the bottom of the Component Manager page.
13. Click the Run Chart push button.

Your new chart is shown in Figure 9-7.

You can immediately see that the names of the restrictions used as labels in this chart add to the clearness of the chart.

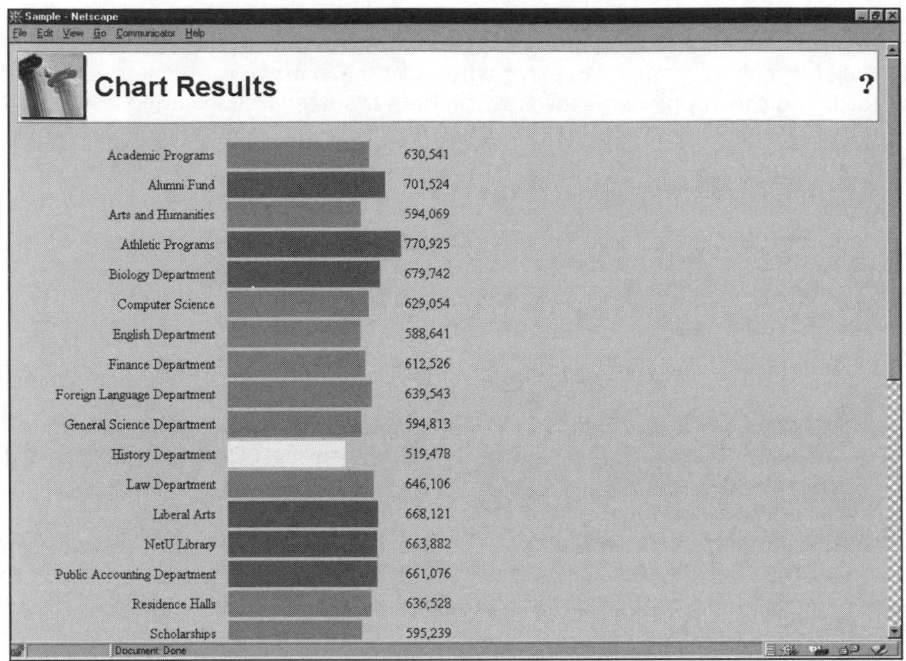

Figure 9-7: Your first chart from an SQL query

However, there is a little problem with this chart. If you scroll to the bottom of the page, you can see that there are more bars for this chart.

1. Click the Next push button at the bottom of the first chart page.

The second page of the chart looks suspiciously like the first page. The reason for this is that you specified that the donations were to be first grouped by fund and then by restriction. This means that all the bars on the first page of the chart represent contributions to the Annual Fund, and all the bars on the second page of the chart represent contributions to the Capital Campaign.

Trickery?

You may be wondering, "Why don't they just leave the report as it is, since each page of the report displays the fund totals for exactly one fund?" Because the maximum number of rows for a page and the actual number of fund restrictions are the same, you could just take the user parameter for the maximum number of rows off the parameter form.

This is a bad idea for two reasons. The first reason is that there is always a chance that the number of fund restrictions could change, which would require you to change this chart and other components that depend on there being a specific number of fund restrictions. Building a data dependency like that into an application is always an invitation for increased maintenance overhead.

The second reason is practical. Users cannot easily tell which page of the chart applies to which fund. You could add some header text that would explain this, or some PL/SQL code to somehow indicate the particular fund for the page, but it is probably easier just to give users an option as to which fund they want to see.

Because browsers only display a single page at a time, you may have to change your design philosophy a little bit to accommodate, and take advantage of, this fact. If users want to see a chart for each of the two different funds, all they have to do is to run one chart, use the Back push button to return to the parameter form, and then run the other chart. They can use the list of recently visited pages to quickly flip back and forth between the two charts.

But there is no way for users to know this, so you should go back and modify the basis of the chart.

2. Use the Back push button on your browser to return to the WebDB environment.
3. Click the Edit link for the ch9_cht_3 report.
4. Change the text of the SQL query to read as follows:

```
SELECT NULL the_link,
RESTRICT_NAME the_name,
SUM(AMOUNT) the_data
FROM DONATIONS, RESTRICT_CODES
WHERE DONATIONS.RESTRICTION = RESTRICT_CODES.RESTRICT_CODE
AND FUND = :fund
GROUP BY FUND, RESTRICT_NAME
```

   by adding the line AND FUND = :fund.

5. Click the Parameter Entry Form Display Options tab, which is the third tab from the left.

You can see that the bind variable you indicated in your SQL statement by preceding it with a colon (:) is recognized by WebDB as a parameter.

6. Click the Finish push button to generate the new chart.
7. Click the Parameters link at the bottom of the Manage Component page.
8. Enter **Capital Campaign** into the Fund text field.
9. Click the Run Chart push button.

This time, you can see that the chart only returns 20 bars. The value you entered in the Fund text field is listed at the bottom of the chart, so this chart is more easily understood by a nontechnical user.

It would be a good idea to put some text into the chart header that pointed the user to the Fund identifier at the bottom of the chart, because he or she may not be able to see the identifier when the top of the chart is in the browser.

But there is still a problem with this iteration of the chart. A user would have to know the exact name of a particular fund in order to select it. Because there are only a limited number of funds, you should be able to provide a list of values for the parameter form and you should clean up the parameter form by eliminating the parameters that you wouldn't want a user to change.

10. Use the Back push button on your browser to return to the WebDB environment.
11. Click the Edit link for the ch9_cht_3 report.
12. Go to the Parameter Entry Form Display Options tab and enter **NETU.FUNDLOV** for the LOV, **Capital Campaign** for the Default, and **Radio group** as the LOV type.

If you haven't loaded the sample application, you have to explicitly import this LOV by importing the fundlov.sql file that came with the samples on the CD-ROM accompanying this book. For information on importing files, please refer to Appendix A.

13. Click the Display Options tab.
14. Deselect the Count of values, First value, and Last value entries from the Summary Options list box.
15. Click the Paginate, Log Activity, and Show Timing check boxes to deselect them.
16. Go to the Parameter Entry Form Display Options tab. Deselect the Maximum Rows/Page and Summary entries from the Parameter Option list box.

By eliminating the Summary list box from the parameter form, you are ensuring that only those summaries that you selected are shown at the bottom of the chart.

17. Click the Finish push button.
18. Click the Parameters link in the Component Manager page to see the new parameter form.

You can see the effect that your parameter changes had on the new look of the parameter form in Figure 9-8. The form looks cleaner and the values for the fund parameter are clearly indicated.

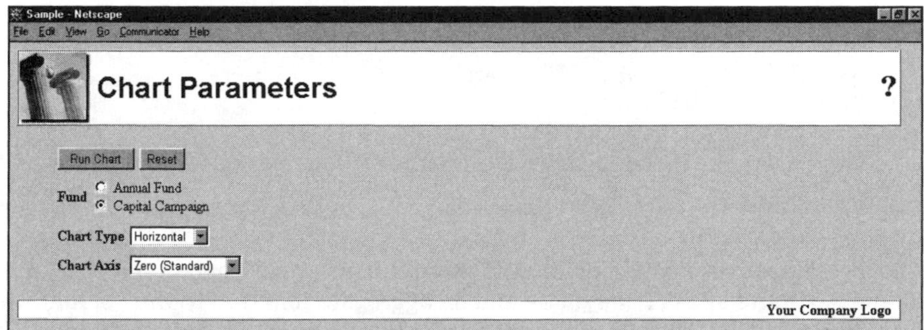

Figure 9-8: The new look of the parameter form for your first SQL-based chart

19. Select one of the values in the Fund radio group and click the Run Chart push button.

You can see that there are no push buttons at the bottom of the form, because, by deselecting the Paginate check box in the Display Options page, you forced the entire chart to be on a single page.

The new version of the chart is delivering just the right amount of information in an easy-to-comprehend manner, even for users who are not familiar with the structure of the underlying data. For your last chart, you will use an SQL statement to help you create values that are not in the underlying data.

Formatting values and limiting rows

Of course, the SQL language offers you some formatting options you can leverage when you are using an SQL query as the basis of your chart.

For this last chart, you will use formatting options and shape the way users can interact with the parameters of the chart to deliver some nice capabilities to your chart.

1. Return to the WebDB environment and click the Chart icon in the shortcuts bar.
2. Select the Chart from SQL Query radio button and click the Create push button.
3. Select the NETU schema and give the chart the name of **ch9_cht_4**. Click the Next arrow on the Chart Name and Schema page.

4. Enter the following code into the text area in the SQL Query page:

```
SELECT
       NULL the_link,
       LASTNAME || ', ' || FIRSTNAME the_name,
       SUM(AMOUNT) the_data
FROM DONATIONS, ALUMNI
WHERE DONATIONS.ID = ALUMNI.ID
GROUP BY LASTNAME, FIRSTNAME
ORDER BY 3 DESC
```

This query is included with the examples for the book under the name chap9_sql2.txt.

This query assigns a concatenation of two columns and a character string to the column with the alias of `the_name` and an aggregate function to the column with an alias of `the_data`. Because of the aggregate function, you have to include a GROUP BY clause in the SQL statement listing all the columns that are not the subject of an aggregate function. The GROUP BY clause for this statement has to include the LASTNAME and FIRSTNAME columns.

The order by clause in this SQL statement indicates that you want the rows to return to a descending order from the top value in the third column in the statement, the value returned from the SUM function on the AMOUNT column.

5. Click the Next arrow on the SQL Query page.
6. Deselect the Paginate, Log Activity, and Show Timing check boxes.
7. Deselect the Axis Name, Maximum value, and Sum of values choices in the Summary Options list box.

The intended purpose of this chart is to show either the top contributors or the lowest contributors, depending on how the chart is sorted. Because you have turned pagination off, all the entries in the chart are displayed, so having the maximum value displayed as a default is a bit redundant. This bar chart always uses a zero-based axis, so there is no sense having the axis name selected as a default. Finally, because this chart is almost always a partial listing of the alumni who have made donations, the sum of the values displayed on the page is probably not very meaningful.

8. Enter **$999,999,999,999.99** as the Value Format Mask.
9. Click the Next arrow on the Display Options page.

10. Deselect the show Axis check box in the middle of the page.
11. Click the Next arrow on the Parameter Form Display Options page.
12. Select the PUBLIC.TEMPLATE_6 choice in the Template combo box.
13. Add the following text as the Header Text for the Parameter Entry Form:

```
This chart can be used to show you the highest contributors
to all alumni funds.
<P>
You should specify the number of contributors you want to see
in the chart in the text field labeled <b>Maximum rows</b>.
You must specify a number in this field to avoid receiving an
extremely long chart.
<p>
```

This simple text, complete with HTML formatting for highlights, helps a user understand how to use the default capabilities of WebDB charts to produce the type of information he or she is interested in seeing.

As long as you are adding text, you might as well give the chart and the parameter form titles.

14. Add an appropriate title for the chart and parameter entry form.
15. Click the checkered flag on the Text Options page to generate the chart.

You are getting to be an old pro at this, so you might as well jump in and see the chart you just created.

16. Click the Parameters link on the Manage Component page.
17. Click the Run Chart push button on the parameter form.

The chart that is returned to you should look like the one shown in Figure 9-9.

There they are, the top alumni contributors to old Net U. With the simple extensions available in standard SQL, you were able to create a fairly useful chart with WebDB.

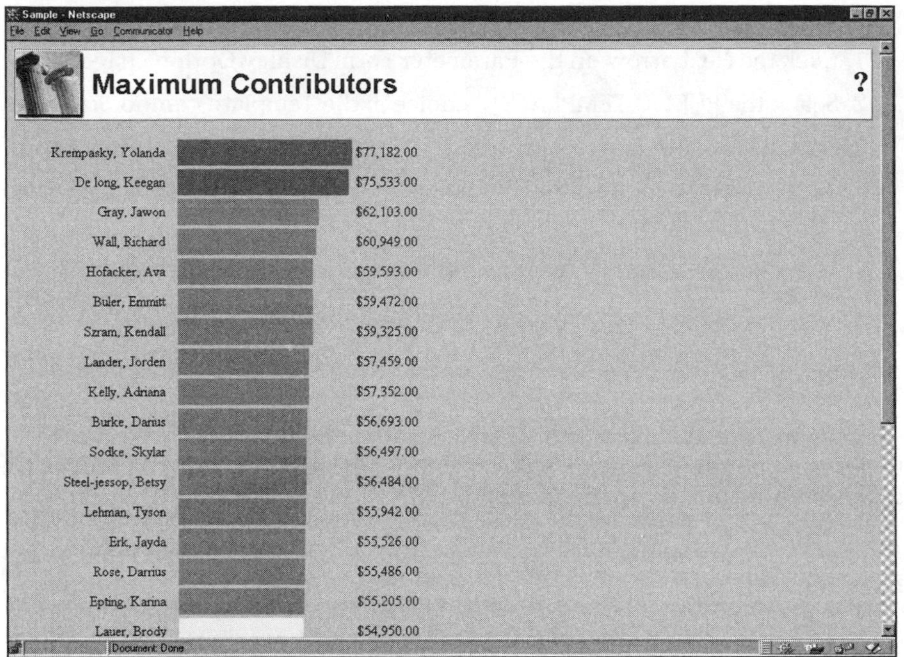

Figure 9-9: Top contributors chart

Wrapping Up

Charts have long been one of the most popular ways of displaying data, because they can transmit an overview of the general meaning of large amounts of data in a visual way. Although WebDB's charts do not necessarily provide you with all the functionality of some mature graphics products, they are fairly easy to create and, like all WebDB components, they run in a simple browser environment.

✦ ✦ ✦

Building WebDB Calendars

In This Chapter

Working with Oracle Date Fields

Building Simple Calendars

Advanced Calendar Formatting and Date Manipulation

Linking Calendars to other WebDB Components

In previous chapters you worked with forms, reports, and charts to create structured content from data in your database. WebDB's forms and reports enable you to build output formats that match the row- and column-style displays found in typical enterprise reports and Web pages. As you saw in Chapter 9, the Chart Wizard offers you a different view of your data by formatting the output according to numeric values stored within your database. The Calendar Wizard is designed to give you the same type of display freedom for your date fields that the Chart Wizard provides for your numeric fields.

Most databases are filled with date fields, and dates are an important component for many different types of records. For example, inventory systems make extensive use of date fields to value inventory items, control shipping, and determine product reorder points. Although you can display dates as standard text fields on reports and forms, there is an advantage to working with your date data in a different manner. You can often get a much clearer picture of your data when you visualize it in a new fashion — just as you did with a chart based on numeric data. The perfect way in which to visualize your date-based data is with a calendar. After all, if you are trying to visualize reorder points for an inventory, laying them out on a calendar can help you to get a clearer view of the big picture.

WebDB's Calendar Wizard is all about formatting your database data using date fields and a calendar display format. In this chapter, you will work with date-based fields to create sophisticated calendar views.

Understanding Oracle Dates

Almost every database that you work with includes some date fields. For example, even the simplest employee table has a field to store the date of birth. After all, how can the company know when it is time for you to retire if they are not keeping track of your birthday?

All time-sensitive information must be stored in a date/time field somewhere within the data. You can store date and time values in string fields, but you lose access to certain automatic date-handling features of the database if you do so. The Oracle database offers a special DATE datatype, which has its own unique data storage properties and features. No matter which date format you use, Oracle always stores the data in a special internal format that includes the month, day, and year along with the hour, minute, and second. Despite the fact that the datatype is called *date,* the field can actually be used to store time data as well.

Date arithmetic

The Oracle database recognizes the date format for a given field and understands that the functions you use on the field should use date arithmetic. For example, if you create a numeric database column and add one to it, Oracle performs an arithmetic *add* operation on the data. If you create the same field as a date field and add one, then Oracle increments the field by a single day, as shown in Listing 10-1.

Listing 10-1: Standard date arithmetic

```
create table test_date(mydate date)
/
insert into test_date values ('01-sep-1998')
/
commit
/
update test_date set mydate = mydate + 1
/
select * from test_date
```

The final SELECT statement in this code returns a value of 02-sep-1998.

Standard mathematical functions can be applied to dates, and Oracle automatically handles the conversion for you. The base of any arithmetic operation on dates is *days.* When you add an integer increment to a date, Oracle assumes that the integer refers to the number of days, and when you subtract dates from each other, Oracle returns the result as an integer of a number of days. In addition to the basic mathematical operations, Oracle offers a number of date-specific mathematical functions, as shown in Table 10-1.

Table 10-1
Oracle Date Functions

Date Function	*Description*	*Example*
Add_months(date,count)	Adds a specified number of months to a given date value.	`add_months(to_date('01-sep-1998'), 5) = '01-feb-1999'`
Greatest(date1, date2,...)	Selects the most recent date from a list of dates in a single row.	`greatest(to_date('01-sep-1997'), to_date('01-sep-1998')) = '01-sep-98'`
Max(date_field)	Selects the most recent date from a specified date field for a set of records.	`select max(mydate) from mytable`
Least(date1, date2,...)	Selects the oldest date from a list of dates in a single row.	`least(to_date('01-sep-1997'), to_date('01-sep-1998')) = '01-sep-1997'`
Min(date_field)	Selects the oldest date from a specified date field for a set of records.	`select min(mydate) from mytable`
Last_day(date)	Selects the last day of the month for the month value of the specified date.	`select last_day(to_date('01-sep-1998')) = '30-sep-1998'`
Months_between(date2,date1)	Calculates the difference, in months, between two dates. The result can be a floating point value or an integer depending on whether the comparison starts on the same day of the month.	`months_between('01-nov-1999', '01-sep-1998') = 14`

Continued

Table 10-1 (continued)

Date Function	***Description***	***Example***
New_time(date, current_time_zone, new_time_zone)	Calculates the specified date and time for the `new_time_zone` given the `current_time_zone` value.	`select newtime(mydate,'EST', 'PST') = converts mydate from eastern standard time to pacific standard time.`
Next_day(date,'day')	Calculates the date of the next specified day following a given date.	`select next_day('01-sep-1998', 'FRI') = '04-sep-1998'.` (The first Friday after the September 1 date.)
Round(date) Round(date,format)	Rounds the date to the closest day based upon the time value entered. If the time associated with the date is before 12 noon, the day remains the same. If the time is after 12 noon, the date rounds up to the next day.	`select round(mydate) from mytable`
Trunc(date) Trunc(date,format)	Sets the time of a specified date field to 12 a.m., in effect, truncating the time value from the date.	`select trunc(mydate) from mytable`

Note: In Table 10-1, a string value was converted to a date value with the `to_date` function before the date arithmetic could be performed.

Date formatting

The Oracle database provides an additional set of features for converting between character fields and date fields. Because Oracle stores dates internally in a specialized format, you cannot simply enter dates as strings and have them behave as dates. WebDB automatically formats date fields for you in forms, reports, charts, and calendars, but you need to convert dates explicitly from strings when you handcraft SQL queries inside the Calendar Builder. Oracle supports two basic data-conversion routines for dates: TO_CHAR and TO_DATE. The first function converts date fields to strings and the second function converts strings to date fields. Both functions accept a format parameter as follows:

```
to_char(date, format_string)
to_date(string, format_string)
```

The format string is an optional character string that defines a format to be used when the string or date is converted. WebDB uses this same format string for all of the date format masks in the other wizards. If you have formatted date fields using masks in any of the other content wizards, then you already know to use the format string with TO_CHAR and TO_DATE. Table 10-2 provides a list of some of the format strings available for dates and times.

Table 10-2
Selected Date and Time Format Mask Elements

Format Element	*Description*
DD	Day displayed as a number
DY	Day displayed as a three-letter abbreviation (MON)
DAY	Day displayed as a complete name (MONDAY)
MM	Month displayed as a number (9)
MON	Month displayed as a three-letter abbreviation (SEP)
MONTH	Month displayed as a fully-spelled string (SEPTEMBER)
YY	Year displayed as a two-digit number (98)
YYYY	Year displayed as a four-digit number (1998)
RRYY	Year displayed as a four digit number relative to the current century (98 = 1998, 01 = 2001)
YEAR	Year displayed as a text string (NINETEEN-NINETY-EIGHT)
HH	Hour displayed in a two-digit format (08:)
HH24	Hour displayed in a 24-hour format (20:)
MI	Minutes display of time (:56)

Continued

Table 10-2 *(continued)*

Format Element	***Description***
SS	Seconds display of time (:43)
AM	Displays a.m. or p.m. along with string as indicated (08:00 AM)

Within a date string, Oracle disregards any character other than the standard date format characters in the formatting of the output. If you include additional characters, Oracle simply includes them in the display. This is a useful feature that enables you to include punctuation (; - / : > =) within a format string.

The TO_CHAR function is used to format dates as strings for display purposes and the TO_DATE function is used to translate strings into dates using a specified format. The TO_DATE function is primarily used for inputting dates into the database from a SQL statement. WebDB automatically formats dates for you, so you do not normally need to use the TO_DATE function from within WebDB. The TO_CHAR function handles the conversion of a date to a specific display format. You will find more uses for this function within WebDB, especially when you are working with dynamic pages and calendars. The format string is easy to create and use, as shown in Listing 10-2.

Listing 10-2: Sample format query for TO_CHAR

```
select to_char(event_date, 'DAY – Month dd, yyyy')
as EventDate from events

EVENTDATE
----------------
SATURDAY  – November  21, 1998
MONDAY    – November  23, 1998
TUESDAY   – December  01, 1998
SATURDAY  – December  05, 1998
MONDAY    – December  07, 1998
THURSDAY  – December  10, 1998
SATURDAY  – December  12, 1998
FRIDAY    – November  20, 1998
```

You can test out the preceding query on the EVENTS table using SQL*Plus.

Notice that Oracle replicates the spaces and "- -" character exactly as you entered them into the format mask. You can use this identical mask within WebDB to format any date field. In fact, WebDB actually executes a TO_CHAR function for dates wherever you see a format mask for a date field.

Oracle automatically converts date expressions in WHERE clauses when the format is the standard DD-MON-YYYY format. If you use any other format in your query, you have to convert the string to a date using TO_DATE.

Building a Simple Calendar

The Calendar Wizard behaves much like any other WebDB content creation wizard. It appears as part of the Build menu and on the WebDB menu bar.

1. Select the Calendar menu choice from the WebDB menu bar and click the Create button in the top panel of the main Calendar page.
2. Set the Schema of your new calendar as NETU.
3. Name the calendar **netu_cal_events** and click the Next arrow on the Calendar Name and Schema page.

The initial content panel of the Calendar Wizard is less structured than in some of the other builders, such as the form or report builder wizards. The Calendar Wizard works off a standard SQL query as shown in Figure 10-1.

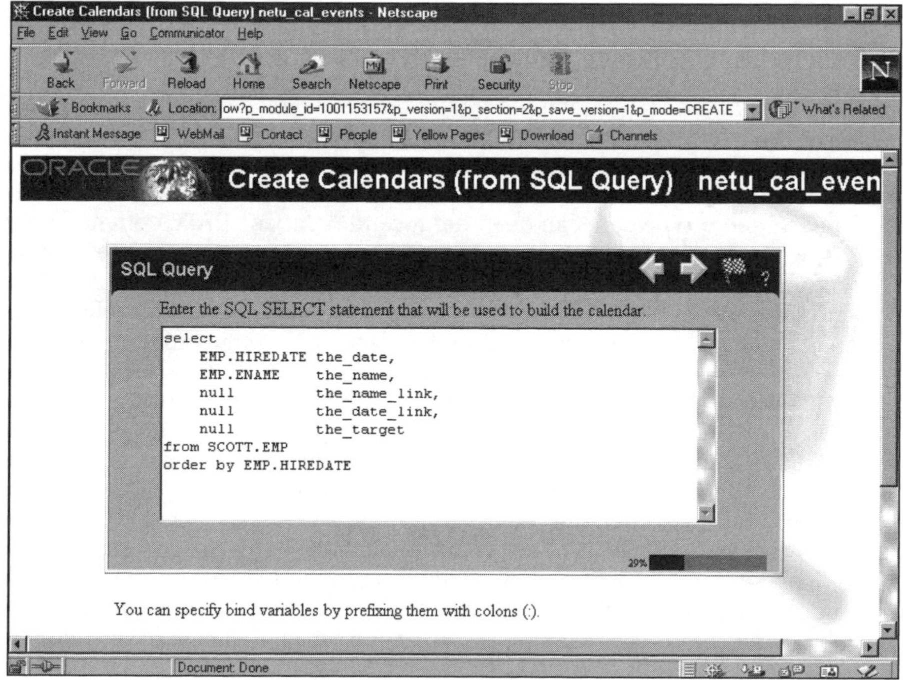

Figure 10-1: Building a calendar from an SQL query

Calendar query format

The key to building a calendar is the formatting of the SQL query, which is similar to the type of formatting used for a chart query. The query text is composed of the following nine basic sections:

- SELECT
- date
- name
- name link
- date link
- target frame
- FROM clause
- WHERE clause
- ORDER BY clause

The first part of the query is the SELECT keyword. In effect, you are entering a normal SQL SELECT statement, so the keyword SELECT is a requirement. In the end, the query that you enter here could just as well be entered into SQL*Plus as a simple select statement. The difference is how WebDB *interprets* the SELECT statement that you enter in the edit box, as shown in Figure 10-1.

The date field is the first item in the body of the SQL statement. The date field is the data item that the Calendar Wizard uses to generate the calendar display format. You will have an opportunity to determine the actual display of the calendar later on, but the data in this field is what determines how the data is deployed to the resulting calendar. The date can be either a valid database DATE column, a derived date using the TO_DATE function, or an arithmetic operation on a date field. The date is the value that appears in the day box on the calendar. You are going to build a calendar on the EVENTS table in the NETU schema. The EVENTS table contains information on the various events that take place at NetU, including sporting events, social events, and the academic calendar. The EVENT_DATE is the date field in the EVENTS table that you will use for the date field in the query.

The Calendar Wizard creates the calendar display and the date field determines *where* on the display that a particular record appears. The name is the data object that appears on the face of the calendar in the box supplied by the date, along with the date field. In the EVENTS table example, the CATEGORY field is a good choice for the name column. WebDB enables any expression that resolves down to a string to be used as the name field. You are free to use concatenation characters and string functions to create a complex string value for the name field.

The name link is a WebDB link to another WebDB component that is attached to the name field. The calendar display is an active object as opposed to a static report. If you include a name link, then WebDB attaches the link to the display of the name on the calendar. The end user is able to select the link on the face of the calendar and WebDB navigates to that component at run time. While dates and names are required to build calendars, links are optional. If you do not want to specify a name link, you must *pass* the NULL value as a placeholder for the name link.

The date link is the second link from the calendar to a second WebDB component. While the name link connects from the *value* in the calendar to an object, the date link connects from the *date* itself. While you might use the name link to show details for a particular entry on a calendar, you can use the date link to show additional details for *all* entries on a particular day. The date link is also optional. If you do not want to specify a date link, you must pass the NULL value as a placeholder. Typically, you use the date link to connect to a second component object that provides information that is specific to the particular date. For example, you might link a report that lists all of the pay dates from any single pay date on a calendar.

The target frame is the URL of a frame in which you want the optional link objects to be displayed. When you are viewing a calendar, it is often convenient to be able to see the big picture alongside the details. You can use a frame to display the details of either of the link fields next to the calendar. This can simplify the navigation of your calendar for the end user. Target frames are also optional, and you must *pass* a NULL placeholder if you choose not to use a frame.

The FROM clause is part of a standard SQL query. It is used to specify the table from which you are extracting the date and name fields. You can use a public synonym for your table name, or you can specify the table name preceded by the Oracle USERID of the owner of the table. The default behavior for the Calendar Wizard is to select data from a single table, but you are free to make use of multiple tables in the name and link fields to create a table join. If you join tables, you must specify the tables in the FROM clause.

The next section of the query is the WHERE clause, which is not shown by default in the Calendar Wizard. As with any SQL select statement, you are free to add a condition to the query using a WHERE clause. In the EVENTS table example, you may want to build a calendar based on a specific category of events. You could add a WHERE clause to restrict the calendar to build a football schedule by adding the following text to the query:

```
where category = 'Mens Football'
```

Alternatively, you can make your calendar a more general-purpose object by using a BIND variable within the WHERE clause. WebDB prompts for a value for the BIND variable when you run the parameterized version of the calendar. BIND variables are specified by using a colon (:) and a variable name to the right of the operator in the WHERE clause as follows:

```
where category = :enter_a_category
```

Although WebDB does not display a WHERE clause in the default display, you can add one as necessary.

The last item in the query is the ORDER BY clause, which determines the sort order of the calendar. You should always sort the calendar by the date field in order to present the calendar in a logical format. However, you may want to add the name field to the ORDER BY clause if you are likely to have many entries for a given date.

You will find it easier to build calendars incrementally. Initially, you should work to get the date and name portions of the query set before you attempt to add links or frames.

4. Enter the following query to build a simple calendar on the EVENTS table, substituting the USERID of your sample account for `netu` if you used a different name:

   ```
   select event_date, category, null, null, null from
   netu.events order by event_date
   ```

5. Click the Next arrow on the SQL Query page.

WebDB is particular about how you format the SQL statement in the query panel. Do not enter manual carriage returns within the field, but allow WebDB to word wrap the text that you enter into the field. If you format the query yourself and you include carriage returns, the calendar may not select any data when you run it.

Formatting the display

The Display Options panel is the next step in the Calendar Wizard. As with the other content builders, the Display Options panel is divided into two portions as shown in Figure 10-2. The left-hand side of the panel controls the Run Options for the calendar, and the right-hand portion of the panel controls how the calendar is displayed.

The Run Options group is composed of the following items:

- Maximum Months
- Show Monday-Friday Only
- Page Width
- Show Query Conditions
- Paginate
- Log Activity
- Show Timing

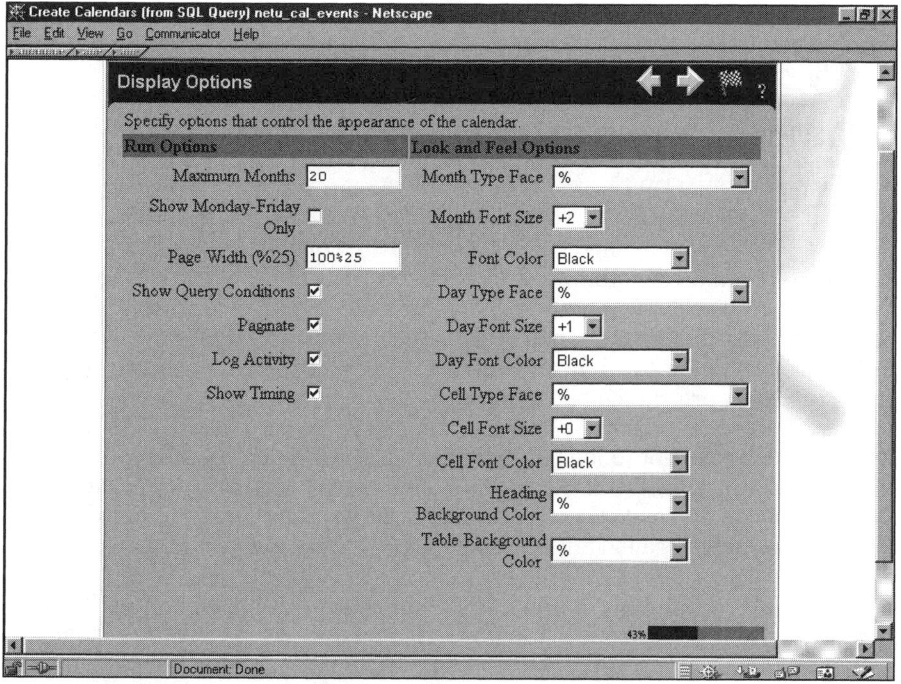

Figure 10-2: Display Options page

The first three options are unique to the Calendar Wizard. Maximum Months is used to specify the maximum number of months you wish to display for your calendar. You can specify a value as large as 1,000,000 for the number of months, and you must be sure to specify a large enough value to cover the range of the data in your calendar. WebDB stops outputting data once it hits the maximum number of months. If you have specified an ORDER BY clause, WebDB completes the sort before it cuts off the display so that you can be sure that the months displayed on the calendar match the earliest months in your query.

The Show Monday-Friday Only option is used to limit your calendar to a classic, business week calendar. If you select this option, WebDB does not display entries for Saturday and Sunday and it eliminates any data in the calendar that falls on a Saturday or a Sunday from the calendar display.

Calendars can eat up screen real estate if you have lots of data appearing on each date entry. WebDB provides you with the Page Width parameter to help you squeeze more data into a smaller area. You can enter a smaller value for the Page Width to reduce the size of the calendar relative to the Web page. The value you enter is an integer between 1 and 100, although WebDB does enable you to enter values that are greater than 100. Entering a value larger than 100 causes WebDB to default to its normal calendar size.

Enabling the Show Query Conditions check box causes WebDB to display the parameters that were used to create the calendar as well as the time at which the calendar was created at the bottom of the calendar display.

The Paginate check box determines whether or not WebDB builds push buttons into the output of the calendar for navigating between pages. If you choose not to use pagination, WebDB creates the calendar as one long HTML page.

Choose the Log Activity check box if you want WebDB to log usage of the calendar into the performance monitor log. You should elect to monitor your calendar object if you want to track how often the calendar is used, or if your users have been reporting performance problems. If you are dynamically calculating lots of the information in the body of the calendar, then you will want to monitor the calendar to be sure it is performing fast enough.

Even if you choose not to log the calendar's activity, you can choose the Show Timing option to have WebDB calculate basic timing information on the output of the calendar itself. WebDB calculates the timing as the difference between the time the component was called and the time the HTML is sent on to the browser.

The Look and Feel Options for the calendar object are similar to those that are provided for in the form and report builder wizards, except that you have control over the typeface, font, and color of different logical sections of the calendar. The options that you set here control the look and feel of the calendar as opposed to the data in the calendar, and each setting specifies a font, a font size, or a color value. Table 10-3 lists the various options and their associated values.

Table 10-3
Look and Feel Display Options

Option	*Description*
Month Type Face	Font name to be used to render the name of the month and the year at the top of each block of cells.
Month Font Size	The Month Font Size is a relative setting used to determine the size of the font in which the month is displayed. The base font size is the font of the text that is displayed in each cell. The default value of +2 renders the month name in a font size that is two sizes larger than the text in the cells.
Font Color	The Font Color is the WebDB color setting that is used to color the month name.

Option	Description
Day Type Face	Each calendar is displayed as a series of months followed by a table of the day names and day numbers for each of the days in the given month. The Day Type Face is the font name used to render the day of the week and the day number.
Day Font Size	Size of the font used to render the day of the week and day number, relative to the size of the text in the cells. The default value is one size larger than the text of the cells and one size smaller than the month and year.
Day Font Color	Color of the font used to render the day of the week and the day number.
Cell Type Face	The cell of the calendar maps to the name value that you specified in the SQL query. The cell value contains the data elements that appear on the face of the calendar, and the Cell Type Face is the font that is used to render the text.
Cell Font Size	The Cell Font Size setting determines the font size relative to the default text font size that is set by your browser. Selecting a larger value causes the body of your calendar to use more real estate. You may choose to use a smaller setting if the text data on your calendar is overly dense.
Cell Font Color	The Cell Font Color sets the color of the text that is displayed inside each box on your calendar. Cell font colors are determined by the color settings in the Shared Component Library.
Heading Background Color	The Heading Background Color sets the color that shows behind the days of the week on the calendar pages at the *top* of each calendar block. The color you select here displays on top of the template and background color that you set for the calendar.
Table Background Color	Sets the background color for the individual cells. As with the Heading Background Color, this color is used in addition to any background colors and images that you use.

6. To continue, accept the default options for your calendar and click the Next arrow.

Specifying Parameter Entry Form Display Options for the calendar

The next panel in the Calendar Wizard should be very familiar to you as it appears in all of the other content wizards in some fashion or another. The Parameter Entry Form Display Options panel enables you to choose the type and location of the run-time push buttons for the parameter form, as well as the parameters for the calendar, as shown in Figure 10-3.

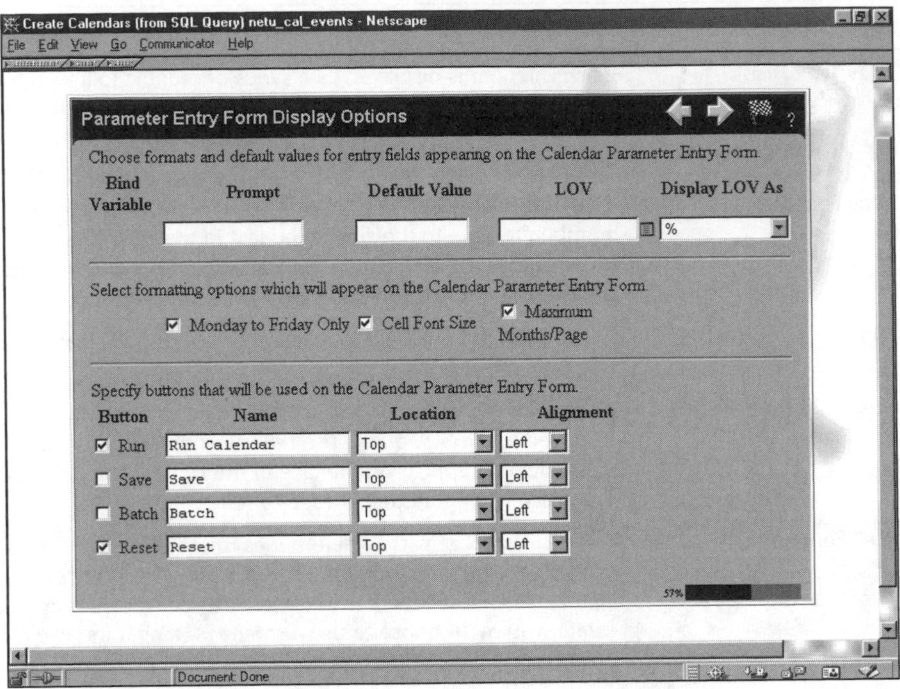

Figure 10-3: Parameter Entry Form Display Options for the calendar object

The top portion of the form enables you to specify values for any parameters that you included as part of the query definition. You can specify values for BIND variables or connect BIND variables to lists of values just as with reports or forms. Because you have yet to specify any parameters for the netu_cal_events calendar, this top panel appears empty.

The Calendar Wizard permits you to enable your end users to control three display options for the calendar: Monday-Friday Only, Cell Font Size, and Maximum Months/Page. The default setting for these three values enables the end user to control these settings from the parameter form. The Monday-Friday Only and the Cell Font Size settings were displayed and discussed on the preceding panel, but the Maximum Months/Page check box is a new parameter. This setting enables the end user to control the number of months that are shown on a single HTML page. In cases where your calendar accesses a large range of dates, this capability can make the resulting calendar easier to display by limiting the amount of data shown on any single page.

There are four button choices just like the choices for reports and calendars:

✦ **Run** — This button causes the procedure that produces the report to be run and the results of the procedure to be returned to the browser.

✦ **Save** — This button saves the options chosen in parameters. Once a user saves his or her choices, these choices appear as the defaults every subsequent time he or she runs the report.

✦ **Batch** — This button submits the report job to a batch queue. There is a single batch queue for each WebDB server. Once a report is submitted in batch, the user can check the batch status page to see if the report has been executed and, if it has completed, to view the report.

✦ **Reset** — This button resets the choices in the parameter page to the default choices.

You can specify three attributes for each of these push buttons. The first field for each push button accepts the name, which appears on the push button.

The second field for each push button is a combo box that enables you to specify the location of the push button. Each push button can appear at the top of the parameter page, the bottom of the parameter page, or at the top and bottom of the parameter page. Deselecting the check box to the right of any of the options disables that option altogether at run time. If a push button is not shown, the functionality offered by that push button is not available to the user of the report.

The final field for each push button enables you to indicate whether the push button is aligned to the left or right of the page. WebDB always determines the position of the push buttons by going through a simple process. WebDB goes through the push button list from the top to the bottom to form push button groups, based on location, and then positions each group justified either to the left or to the right.

7. To continue, click the Next arrow on the Button Options page.

Text options

The next panel in the Calendar Wizard is the Text Options panel. This panel enables you to add HTML and text to the body of your calendar as shown in Figure 10-4.

This page is exactly like the Text Options page for the other components. The first field on this page enables you to specify a template, which you can use to give a standard look and feel to all of your WebDB components.

Later in this book, you will learn how to create your own templates, but right now you can see the power of templates by selecting one of them for your report.

8. Click the drop-down arrow for the Template combo box and select PUBLIC.TEMPLATE_6.

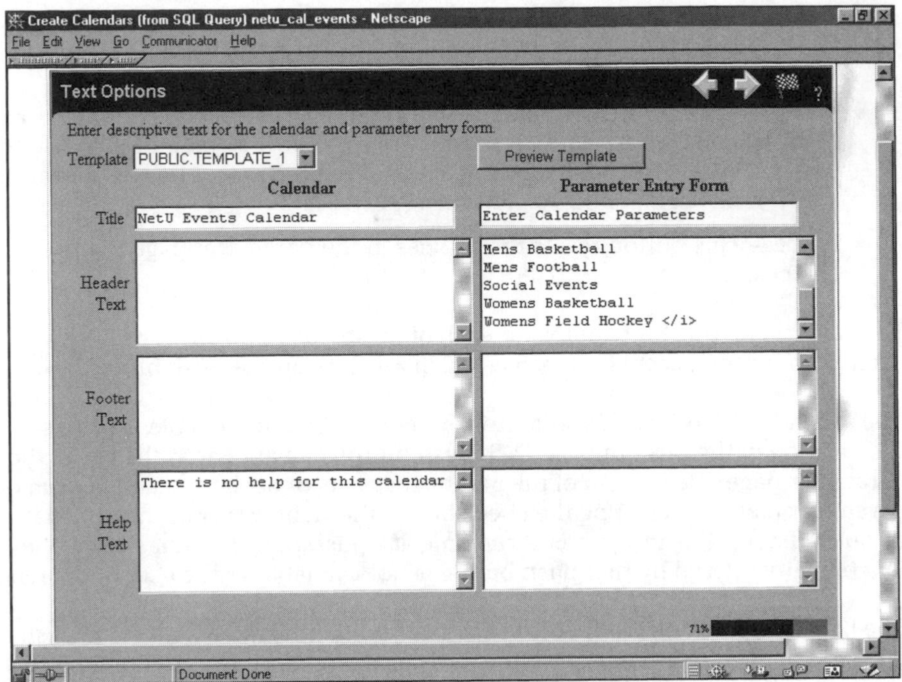

Figure 10-4: Text Options panel in the Calendar Wizard

9. Click the Preview Template push button to see the basic template design.

When you choose to preview a template, WebDB opens a little window in your browser to show you the template. If you return to the browser, select another template, and click the Preview push button, the newly selected template appears in the template window. Figure 10-5 shows the template design for PUBLIC.TEMPLATE_6.

The rest of the fields on the Add Text page help you shape your report by adding text to the report. You can add four types of text:

Title	Displayed at the top of the first page of the report and the parameter and help pages
Header Text	Displayed at the top of each report page or parameter page, just below the title on the first page of the report
Footer Text	Displayed at the bottom of every page of the report or the parameter page
Help Text	Displayed in a separate page for the report and parameter pages

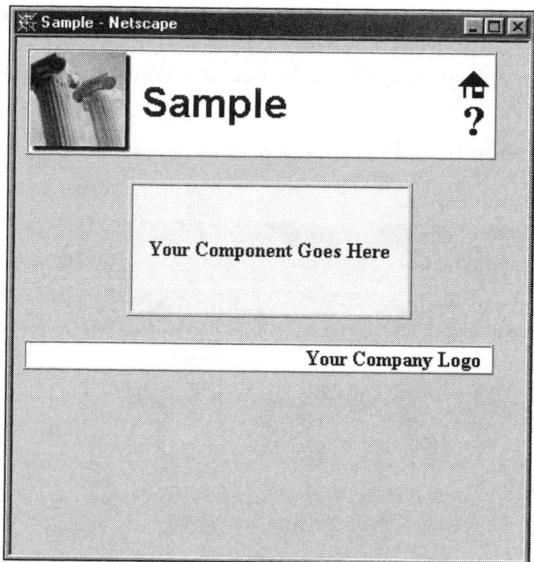

Figure 10-5: Previewing a template

You can specify this text separately for either the report pages or the parameter pages. WebDB treats this text as straight HTML, so you can include HTML formatting tags in the text you enter for any of these areas.

10. Enter **NetU Events Calendar** and **Enter Calendar Parameters** into the Title fields for the report and the parameter entry form, respectively.
11. Enter the following block of text and HTML tags into the Header Text for the parameter entry column:

```
<b>Categories:</b>
<i>Academic Schedule
Arts
Holiday
Lectures
Mens Basketball
Mens Football
Social Events
Womens Basketball
Womens Field Hockey </i>
```

12. Enter **There is no help for this calendar** as the Help Text for the calendar.
13. Reselect the PUBLIC.TEMPLATE_1 template for the calendar.
14. Click the Next arrow on the Text Options page.

    The next page of the Calendar Builder Wizard gives you the opportunity to add PL/SQL code that executes before or after the display of the page or the header for the page. You will learn more about using this page in Chapter 24, which covers advanced PL/SQL programming with WebDB. The Advanced PL/SQL panels give you the opportunity to select additional information from the database and format the data during the run of your calendar. For now, you can just move past it.

15. Click the Next arrow on the Advanced PL/SQL code page.

Figure 10-6: The last page of the Calendar Wizard

As with the other wizards, you can see that this is the last page by the triumphant image of the checkered flag at the left of the panel. As with WebDB's other content creation wizards, this is the point where WebDB uses the parameters that you have entered to generate the PL/SQL package that implements the calendar.

Up until this point, you have been giving values for the parameters that WebDB uses for your calendar. These parameters have been stored in WebDB's internal data tables. But these parameters are not used in the actual production of your calendar. WebDB uses the parameters you have entered to create a PL/SQL procedure. When your application system calls this WebDB calendar, it is actually calling the PL/SQL procedure that runs and creates the calendar as output.

16. WebDB creates the package when you click the OK push button on the final page of the Calendar Builder Wizard.

You have created your first WebDB calendar component. The next section helps you explore some of the functionality of this simple calendar.

Running the Calendar

Once you have successfully created the procedure for your calendar, WebDB immediately does the same two things that it does when you create any form, report, chart, dynamic page, hierarchy, or calendar.

First, it changes the status of the calendar from EDIT to PRODUCTION. When a component has a status of PRODUCTION, the values of the parameters that control the generation of the procedure that run a component have not changed since the procedure was last generated. In other words, the component has not been modified since the procedure for the component was generated. If you leave a creation wizard before reaching the final page and clicking the OK push button, the component has a status of EDIT. The second thing that WebDB does for you is to bring up a page that enables you to run and manage your calendar object, as shown in Figure 10-7.

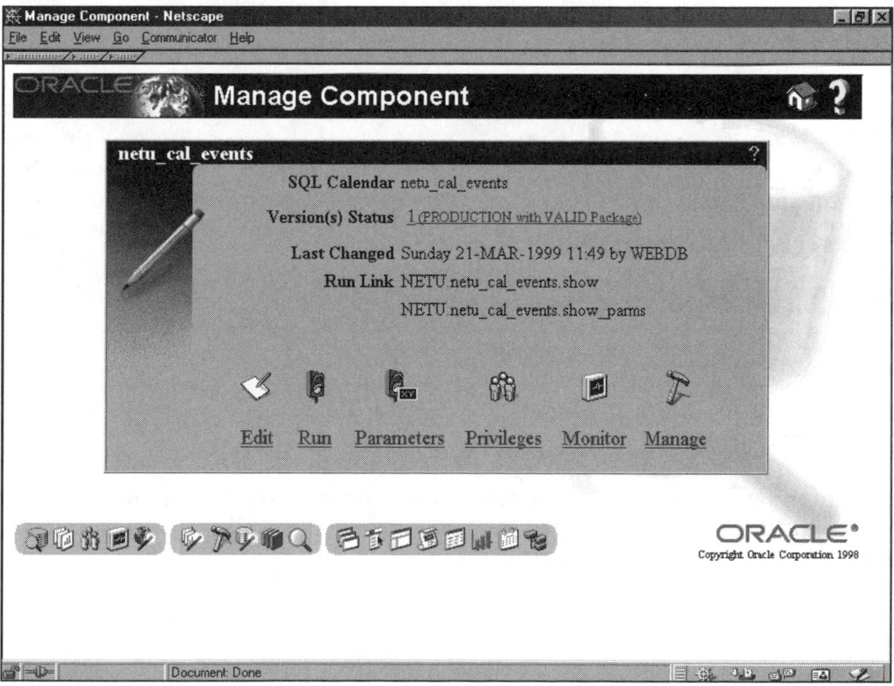

Figure 10-7: Managing a calendar component

There is some basic information about the component at the top of the panel and six linked options in the bottom part of the panel. The information about the component includes the name of the component, all of the versions of the component, the time the component was last changed, and the existing ways to call the component. You should be familiar with this panel from the other major content wizards, as the Manage Component page is used for all of the major components. Shared components such as menus, links, templates, colors, lists of values, fonts, and JavaScripts have a different Manage Component page because these objects behave differently.

Each time you edit and regenerate a component, WebDB saves the previous version of the component and the values for its parameters in an archive version. The archived versions of a component are numbered, starting with 1 in increments of 1, and given the status of ARCHIVE. You will learn more about WebDB's version control in a later chapter. You will also learn more about the procedures listed in the Run Link portion of the panel later in this section.

The links at the bottom of the page should all be enabled. This is the standard situation for a component that has been successfully created. If you had left the Calendar Builder Wizard before you had generated the procedure for the report, the Run and Parameter links would not be enabled on this page.

1. Select the Run Link to execute your new calendar.

You created the calendar with the default option of using a single HTML output page, the top of which is shown in Figure 10-8.

You can see the various components of the calendar in the figure. The title bar is in the same format as the title bar in any other WebDB component. If you click the question mark icon in the header, WebDB navigates over to the help text that you defined on the Text Options panel. The color scheme and font for the title in the heading are determined by the template that you chose for the calendar.

The body of the page is composed of a series of month-sized blocks with dates, days of the week, and data. At the top of each block is a title composed of the month name and the year. The interval size for the calendar object is months, and that is the smallest unit of output that the Calendar Wizard uses to format data. Even if the EVENTS table has only a single record in it, the calendar still shows a minimum of one month. It works much the same way that your wall calendar at home works. Even if you write in only one box of your wall calendar, the calendar itself still shows one whole month at a time.

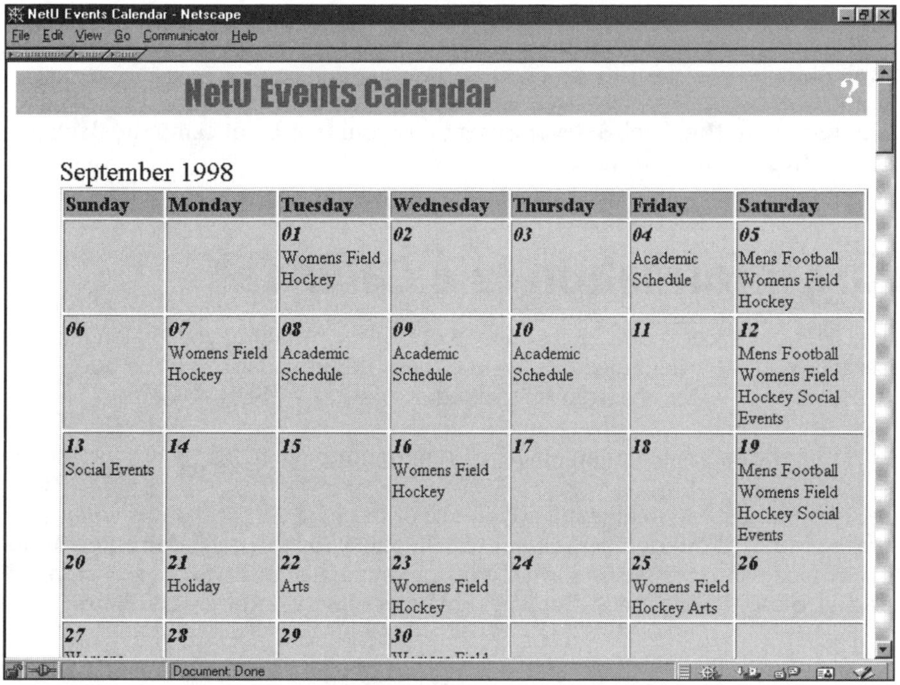

Figure 10-8: Top portion of the calendar page

WebDB calculates the first month of the calendar by sorting the data on the date that you defined in the SQL query. If you chose to sort the calendar on the name field, then the calendar is created in the order of the name field. In this case, you almost always get a complete month for each record, because there has to be a calendar object for each sort group in the returned data. Normally you sort your data on the date field in order to maximize the value of the calendar display. If you need to sort the data according to the name field, then you might be better off using a report or form to show the data.

One alternative to sorting the data on the name field is to link the calendar to another content object that displays the detail data in a different way. If you look at the calendar in Figure 10-8, you can see that the first entry is on September 1, 1998. The entry for that date is "Womens Field Hockey." There is no indication of who the Lady TabbyCats are playing, what time the game starts, or even where the game is being played. All of this information is stored in the EVENTS table, but it hasn't been made available to the calendar. If you scroll down through the calendar output, you find that the data gets even more difficult to dissect when there are multiple events on the same date. On September 4, 1998 there is an entry for the "Academic Schedule," but we have no idea what the details of this item are.

The solution to the problem is to add some new functionality to the calendar that displays additional information and provides some links from the calendar to other detail objects.

2. Return to the WebDB development environment by clicking the Back push button in your browser.

Adding Information to a Calendar

The Calendar Wizard provides you with options for making your calendar more useful. You have two choices: You can either add information to the body of the calendar, or you can link from the calendar to other WebDB objects.

1. Use the Edit link on the Manage Component page to edit your calendar object.

WebDB enables you to take full advantage of the PL/SQL extensions when you create your SQL queries. Although the SQL query for the calendar object requires that you use a very specific format, you can make use of PL/SQL extensions within the SQL query itself. The SQL query for the events calendar is as follows:

```
select event_date, category ,null,null,null
from netu.events order by event_date
```

WebDB uses the `event_date` field to create the date stream, and the category field is displayed within the cells on the calendar as you saw in the example run. In and of itself the category field does not offer enough information about the particular event. You can augment the category field with more information by concatenating any other character field to the category string. The key to string concatenation is the double-bar character. Table 10-4 shows you a list of possible combinations for the EVENTS calendar.

Table 10-4
String Concatenation

Concatenation String	*Description*
`Category || ':'|| descr`	Combines the category field with the ' : ' character followed by the description of the event.
`to_char(eventid)|| '-' || category || '@' || start_time`	The eventid field value is converted to a string followed by a dash ' - ', the category of the event, an at sign '@', and the start time of the event, which is already a string.
`Upper(category) || '-' || descr`	Converts category field to uppercase characters followed by a dash ' - ' and the description.

You are free to use any combination of functions and concatenation characters as long as the result is a single character string. The other requirement that you must follow is to name the resulting string using the AS clause as shown in the following snippet of code:

```
category||'-'|| descr as name
```

WebDB attempts to build a label for the string that you create and it greatly simplifies the process if you use the AS clause. It is possible that the string you create does not require the AS clause, but it is safer to get in the habit of specifying it whenever you use string concatenation. WebDB enforces a limit of 32 characters on the name that it can derive for your concatenated column. If you do not provide a name, or the string is longer than 32 characters, you get a parsing error within the wizard.

2. Edit the calendar and change the SQL statement to the following value:

```
select event_date, upper(category)||'-'||descr as
name,null,null,null from netu.events order by event_date
```

3. Use the Finish button to save the changes and then rerun the calendar.

The resulting calendar looks like the one shown in Figure 10-9.

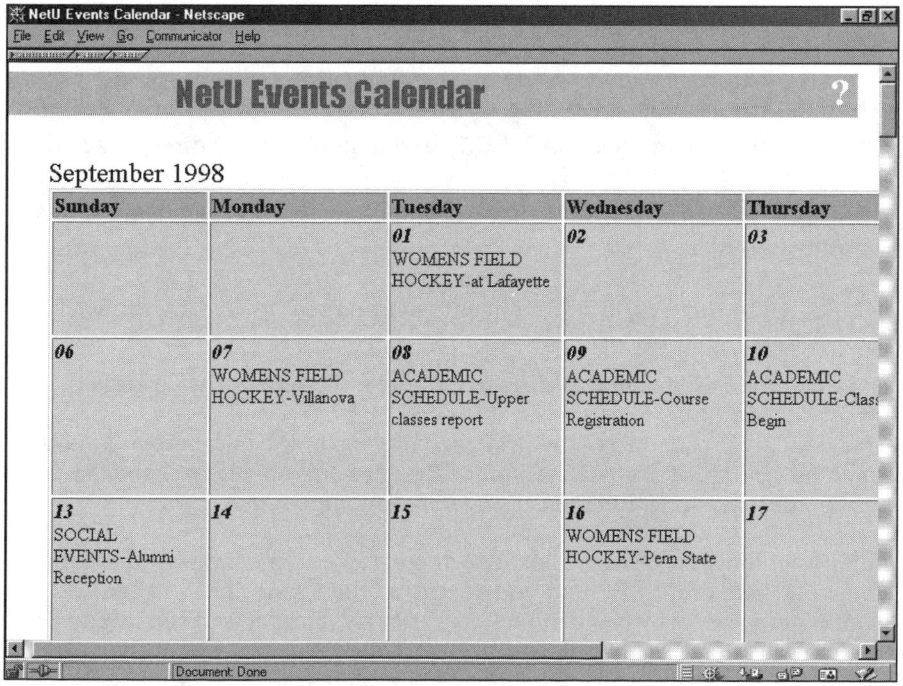

Figure 10-9: Calendar output using concatenated strings

The calendar now shows the category of the event followed by the description of the event. Each cell is easier to read, but the calendar itself is very unbalanced because some months have lots of events with lengthy descriptions, while other months appear narrow. Using records with uneven field lengths has this effect on the calendar. In cases where you need to provide lengthy descriptions that are uneven in length, you have two choices:

✦ Use the Display Options panel to force each month onto its own page. This has the effect of separating the displays for each month.

✦ Truncate the string to a consistent length that matches the shortest record length. You can use the MIN and LENGTH functions to determine the length of the shortest string.

A better choice might be to remove the details from the cells of the calendar and link to them using a second component.

Linking from the Calendar Cells

Rather than adding extra information to the body of the calendar, you can use the link fields within the SQL query to connect from the calendar cells to any other WebDB component. You will learn about WebDB links in detail in Part III of this book, but you can work with them in the calendar without understanding all the ins and outs.

1. Import the following two reports: ch10_rep_events and ch10_rep_schedule.
2. Copy the map images (MAP_*.GIF) to the /netu/ virtual directory path.

If you are unfamiliar with how to import WebDB components, please see Appendix A.

3. Return to the WebDB development environment by clicking the Back push button in your browser.
4. Click the Edit link in the Manage Component page for the calendar.

So far you have made use of the first two columns in the SQL statement, but the remaining columns have been left null. The third and fourth columns can be used to link the information within the cell to another component.

The third column is the name link, which creates a connection between the text of the display field and a URL that you specify as the name_link. You can add a second link, the date_link, which is connected to the day number and can link to a second component. WebDB enables you to use any valid link for either of the link columns. Normally you use the name_link to connect to data that is relevant to the cell data, and you use the date_link to connect to data that is relevant to the date itself.

You can also specify a frame URL as the fifth column, in which case WebDB displays the two links that you specified for the name and the date inside of a frame when the user uses either of the links. You need to be familiar with using WebDB's frame links in order to use them with the calendar object. Frames are an advanced topic that we examine in greater detail in the third part of this book. For the time being, you can leave the frame link null, but keep in mind that it is an option for displaying your calendar.

The form of the link text that you use for the name_link and the date_link is a specialized string based upon the standard procedure calling syntax of WebDB. Once again, you will have an easier time working with a link text if you have some experience with WebDB's Link Wizard. However, you do not need to use the Link Wizard to create links within the Calendar Wizard. The key to creating link text is to remember that each WebDB component is a self-contained PL/SQL procedure of its own. You can use the procedure name as the URL link from the calendar, and you can use the link to pass parameters.

Note Most of the other WebDB builders provide you with a structured field display panel that you can use to directly link from a field to an object. The calendar object does not provide this field option window, and your only recourse is to build the link directly in the SQL query. You are better off working with links and menus in detail before you attempt to make extensive use of links with the calendar object.

The link text itself is a stored procedure call that includes a parameter to be passed as shown in the following code snippet:

```
select event_date, category,
'NETU.ch10_rep_schedule.show?p_arg_names=my_date&p_arg_values='
||event_date as name_link, null, null as frame from netu.events
order by event_date
```

The key piece of information is highlighted in bold text in the code snippet, and it represents a call to a WebDB stored procedure. Every stored procedure call that you make using a manual link is composed of the following three parts:

- ✦ Package name
- ✦ Procedure parameter
- ✦ Parameter value

The package name is a concatenation of the Oracle USERID that owns the WebDB object, the name of the object, and the procedure name. In almost every case, the procedure name is a fixed value called ".show". The SHOW procedure is what WebDB uses to run a procedure that it creates, and you can find additional information about this all-important procedure in Chapter 17. The procedure name is followed by a question mark.

The second part of the procedure is a series of calls to the P_ARG_NAMES and P_ARG_VALUES array values. Once again, this will be clearer once you have completed the chapter on links, but for the time being all you need to understand is that this a parameter that is passed to the procedure. The last portion of the stored procedure call is the database value that you are passing as a parameter to the link.

In effect, you are creating a call to another WebDB component and passing a value to that component. The goal of doing all of this work is to link the text of the calendar to another detail object. In the spirit of the NetU example, you are going to provide detailed information about individual calendar entries by using two additional components.

The real value of the calendar object is twofold. First, you can use the calendar as a tool for getting a visual image of the big picture. In our example, the NetU calendar shows what the academic year looks like in terms of events. Second, the calendar serves as a menu for navigating to other content, which is the real value of a calendar. If you think about the calendar that you hang on your refrigerator as an example, you can see that it serves much the same purpose. While you use the calendar to make notes of key events, you probably do not write all the details about each event on the calendar page itself. For example, you probably write down the directions and the location of a certain event on another piece of paper, which you take with you as a reference. The calendar is used to remind you of the event and the date; it is not necessarily the storage space for *all* the relevant information.

The WebDB calendar works much the same way. Currently, the NetU calendar shows a minimal amount of information about individual events on the face of the calendar. You can use a second report or form to provide details on the event.

5. Edit the calendar object and change the SQL query to the following text:

```
select event_date, category,
'NETU.ch10_rep_schedule.show?p_arg_names=my_date&p_arg_values
='||event_date as name_link, null, null as frame from
netu.events order by event_date
```

6. Save the changes by clicking the Finish button.

As we mentioned earlier, be careful when you are entering text into the SQL Query text box. You *cannot* enter your own carriage returns — instead, let WebDB wrap the text automatically for you. If you insert manual carriage returns, WebDB generates errors when it attempts to parse the SQL query text.

When you rerun the calendar, the output should look similar to Figure 10-10.

Notice that the category text is now underlined within the cells. WebDB has linked the text to another component, and the browser acknowledges that a link exists by underlining the text.

1. Click either link for Saturday, September 5, 1998 to see output as shown in Figure 10-11.

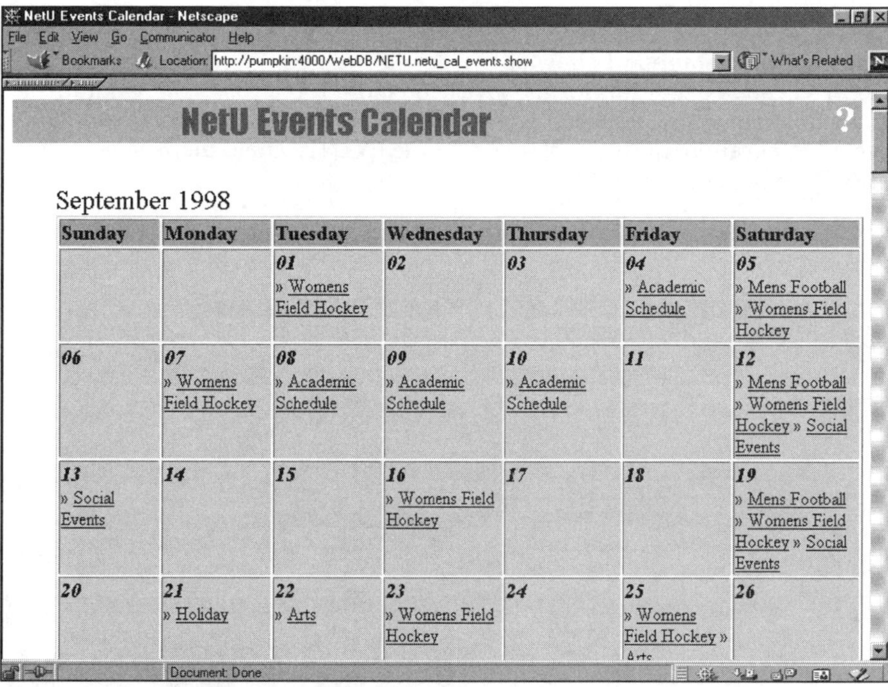

Figure 10-10: Calendar object with links

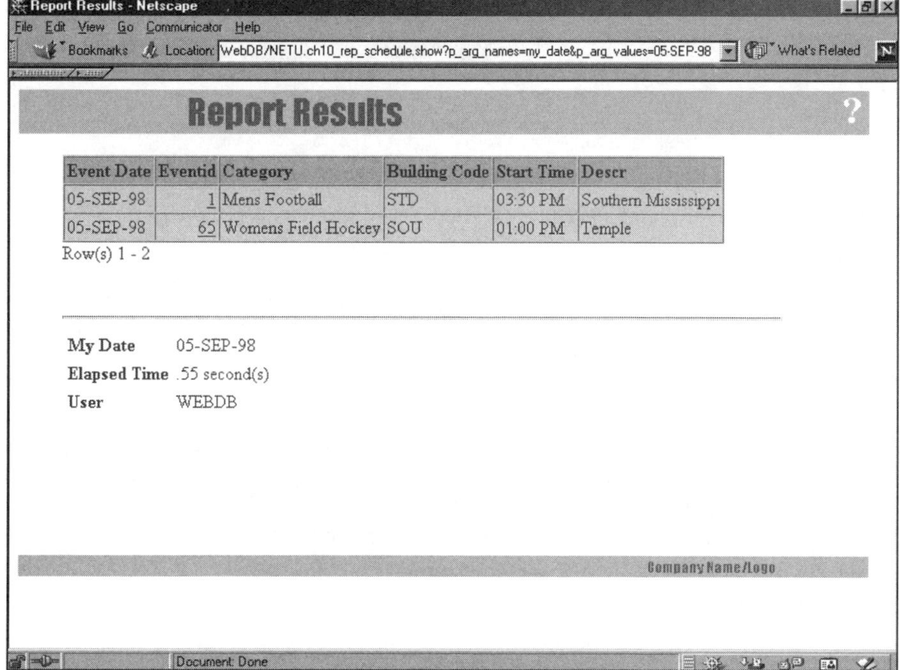

Figure 10-11: Link from the calendar to a report

The report object accepts a date parameter that is passed from the calendar, which in turn generates a report showing the details for all of the events for the selected date. You can see that this format gives you more room to display additional detailed information about the events. WebDB does not limit you to just this one level of integration, however. Notice that the EVENTID field displays as a link as well.

2. Click the link for EVENTID 1 to see the data shown in Figure 10-12.

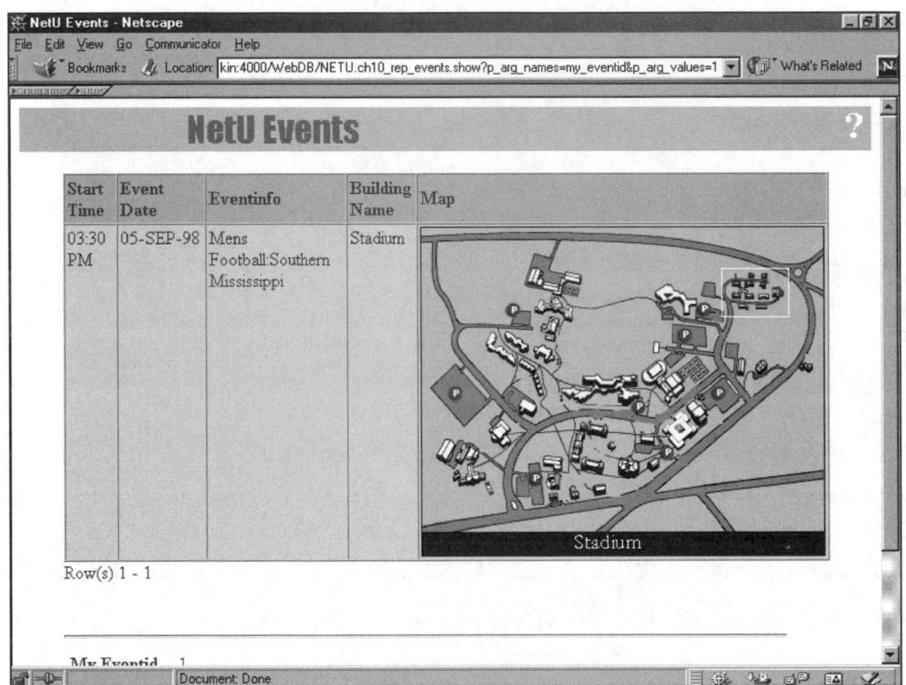

Figure 10-12: Nested links from the calendar

The EVENTID link connects from the day's schedule of events to a more detailed display of the selected event. The details include a map of the NetU campus with the location of the football stadium highlighted with a large white square.

If you navigate around through the various events, you find that some events do not have detailed records. This is because certain events are taking place off-campus and there is not a location record for the join operation. WebDB does not allow the use of the UNION operator in conjunction with parameters, which is the cause of the problem. If you find that your applications are joining to optional data, you are better off using VIEWS, which can be based upon the UNION clause.

This concept of nested linking is one of the keys of WebDB. End users have become accustomed to making use of the drill-through concept when they use Web applications, and WebDB has been designed to leverage this phenomenon. While you could load up the calendar with lots of detailed data, it is better to use the calendar as a navigation tool.

WebDB provides two opportunities for linking content on the body of a calendar. If you look back at Figure 10-10, you notice that the name link is connected to the text inside the cell. If you had used the link with the date link instead of the name link, the day number within the cell would be connected to the linked report. You are actually permitted to use both links on the face of the calendar at the same time. WebDB provides the date link as a link to other date-specific information and the name link as a link to content details. For example, you might create a report that details all the events that occur on a particular date in every month, such as payroll dates. You could connect this report to the date link and a second report detailing the current date to the name link. One link drills across the data and the other link drills into the data.

There is one additional piece of functionality you can add to this calendar that gives the user the ability to specify exactly what data they want in their calendar through the use of a parameter prompt.

Adding Parameters

Calendar objects support the use of parameter values and BIND variables just like any other WebDB object.

1. Return to the WebDB development environment by clicking the Back push button in your browser.
2. Click the Edit link on the Manage Component page for the calendar object and navigate to the SQL Query page.
3. Change the text of the SQL query to the following:

   ```
   select event_date, category,
   'NETU.ch10_rep_schedule.show?p_arg_names=my_date&p_arg_values
   ='||event_date as name_link, null, null as frame from
   netu.events where category like :my_category order by
   event_date
   ```

   The additional text of the query is shown in the code snippet in bold text. Calendars use BIND variables to supply parameters just like forms, reports, charts, and hierarchies. You can add a complete WHERE clause to the SQL query, which builds the calendar, and you can add parameters to the WHERE clause as shown in the previous code snippet. In the case of the calendar, you are adding a prompt that enables the user to select categories of events such as "Women's Basketball" or "Social Events."

4. Navigate to the Parameter Entry Form Display Options tab.

Once you add a BIND variable to the calendar, WebDB adds the entry to the list of parameters for the calendar as shown in Figure 10-13.

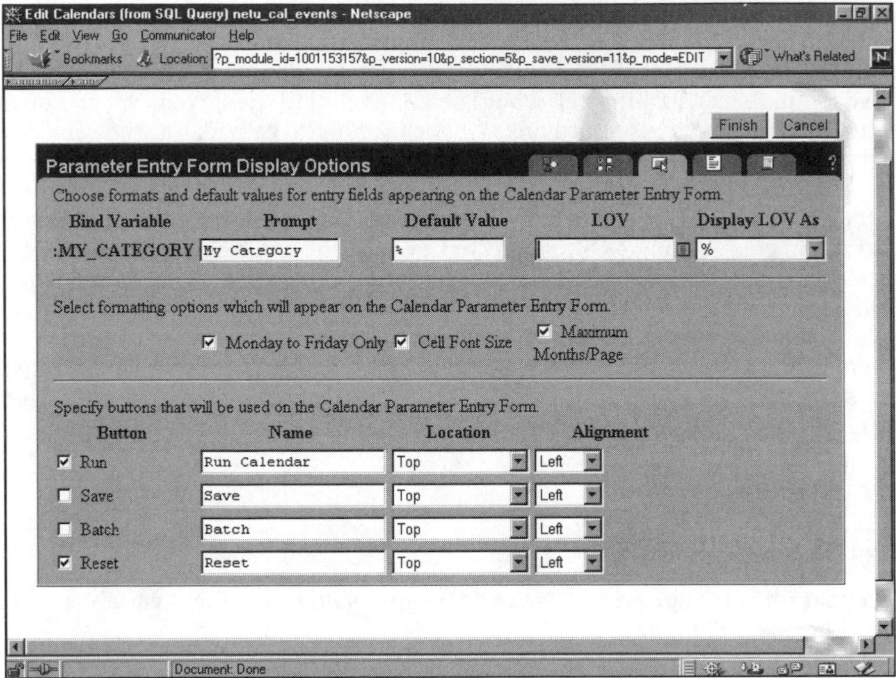

Figure 10-13: Calendar parameters

You can provide a default value for the parameter as shown in Figure 10-13, or you can also use a List-of-Values object just like with any of the other content wizards. You will learn more about using LOV objects in Chapter 17, and you can leave the LOV fields blank for the time being.

5. Enter the percent character (%) in the Value field. This causes the calendar to select all of the events if the parameter form is not used.

6. Save the changes and then use the Parameters link from the Manage Component page to run the calendar.

7. Enter the value **%Mens Football%** as the My Category value and change the Monday-Friday Only value to No as shown in Figure 10-14.

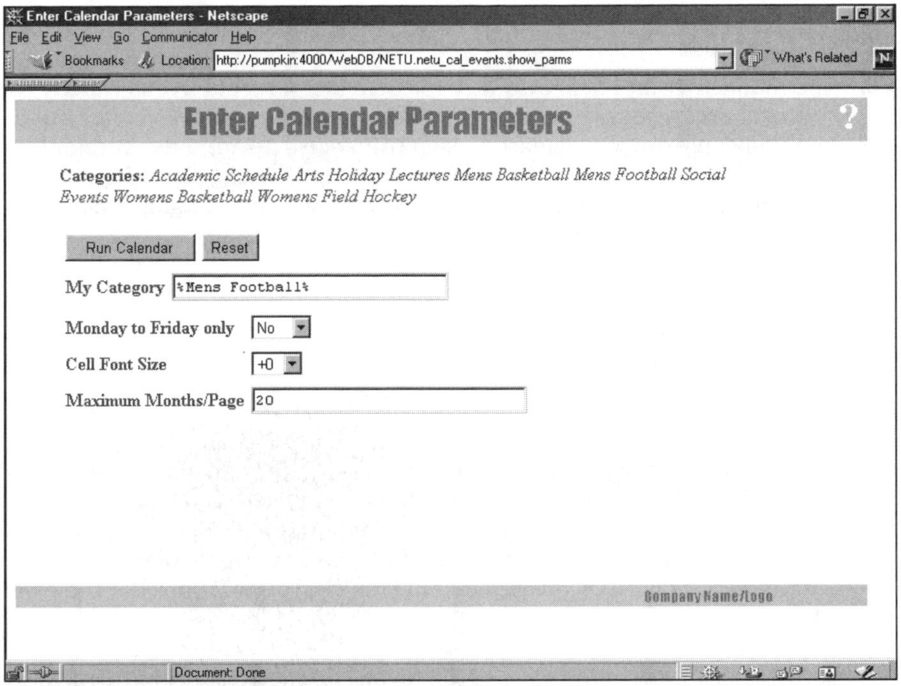

Figure 10-14: Parameter page for calendar object

Earlier in this chapter, you added some text to the parameter form. You can see the results of your handiwork in Figure 10-14. At the top of the page is a list of categories that the user can reference when he or she makes a selection for the My Category field. As you saw in previous chapters, you can attach a drop-down list box of values to the My Category field, and you will learn how to build your own list of values in the third section of this book. However, adding the list to the body of the form as text is a viable alternative, especially if you want to add detailed descriptions of the choices on the parameters page itself.

When you test the calendar using the Run Calendar button, you notice two interesting things about the calendar. First, the default behavior is to run the query for Monday-Friday Only unless you have changed the default on the parameter form. Second, when you choose a link on the face of the calendar, you still see a list of all of the events for the chosen day, not just the events that match your My Category parameter. The parameter is only used by the calendar to select data, and the link within the cell uses the *date* rather than the *category* to formulate its query. This is something to keep in mind when you plan out the drills for your application.

1. Test the parameter version of the calendar using an entry for the My Category parameter.
2. Return to the WebDB development environment by clicking the Back push button in your browser.

Managing Calendar Objects

The Manage Component interface for Calendar Objects works exactly the same as the form and report versions. WebDB automatically tracks versions of calendars and you can export calendars, assign privileges, delete older versions, and monitor the use of calendars. WebDB uses the same underlying panel for implementing the management interface. You can find more details about using advanced management techniques for components in Chapter 19.

Wrapping Up

WebDB's Calendar Wizard offers you an innovative tool for displaying date-sensitive data in an intuitive format. Calendars can be used as an alternative menu structure for navigating from dates to detailed content. They can also be used to give end users a better view as to how their data is organized by date. The Calendar Wizard offers a set of options that match the other content builders, but it requires more detailed coding than you may be used to. Once you have become familiar with creating your own SQL queries within WebDB, you will find that the calendar is easier to use.

Many of the advanced linking options you can include within calendars require some familiarity with the workings of the Link Wizard. The authors recommend that you stick to building simple calendars without links until you have completed Chapter 17. You have plenty of things to work on in the meantime, and you may want to concentrate on mastering date conversions and formatting with PL/SQL functions before moving on to links later in this book.

✦ ✦ ✦

Working with Hierarchies

✦ ✦ ✦ ✦

In This Chapter

✦ ✦ ✦ ✦

In the last three chapters, you learned how to create specific WebDB components for specific tasks. A master-detail form is used to link together two tables with a specific type of relationship, a chart is used primarily to display summary information, and a calendar is used to create HTML pages that revolve around dates. Each of the wizards you used is very powerful, enabling you to create a complex function that was automatically generated for you. In addition, each of these complex objects required a certain type of data relationship to exist in the data used for the object.

The hierarchy is another one of these types of complex WebDB objects. You can only use it for one specific type of data relationship. But the data relationship that a hierarchy is based on is quite common, and the WebDB component that is created to deal with a hierarchy is quite cool.

What Is a Hierarchy?

In the dictionary, a hierarchy is defined as "an order of persons or things ranked in grades." This definition also applies to the hierarchy object in WebDB. The essence of a hierarchy is the concept that a group of data is ranked, with each rank linked in some fashion to a lower rank.

The other key feature of a WebDB hierarchy component is the *recursive* nature of the relationships between the ranks. A recursive relationship is a relationship that is implemented between two instances of the same type of object. In practical terms, this means that a WebDB hierarchy is based on a relationship between two different columns in the same table.

The classic example of a hierarchical relationship is a parts explosion, as shown in Figure 11-1. A parts explosion enables you to see a master component at the top of the hierarchy, the components that make up the master component on the next level, the components that make up those child components on the next level, and so forth.

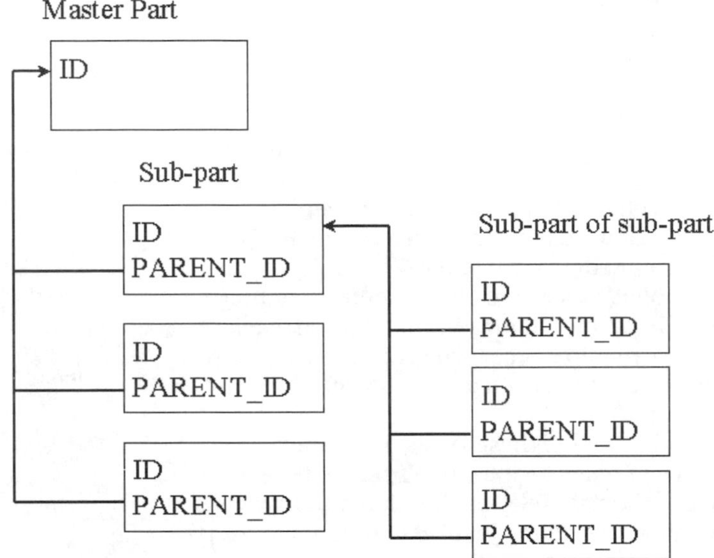

Figure 11-1: A parts explosion diagram

The parts explosion in Figure 11-1 is based on an ID column and a PARENT_ID column. If a part is part of a larger component, the PARENT_ID column contains a valid ID number for the parent part.

A similar situation exists in the infamous organizational chart. The relationship between the levels of the hierarchy is implemented through the use of an ID number for an employee and a MANAGER column that contains the ID value of an employee's manager. The hierarchy you build from the sample Net University data in this chapter is very similar to a classic organizational chart.

There is one more important attribute of a WebDB hierarchy component. As you have already seen from building a master-detail form in Chapter 8, it is fairly easy to design and implement a master-detail relationship. This type of relationship is called a *one-to-many* relationship because one master row relates to one or more detail rows.

It is much more difficult to implement a *many-to-many* relationship — so difficult, in fact, that most systems try and break down a many-to-many relationship to a collection of one-to-many relationships. WebDB hierarchies are implemented as a series of one-to-many relationships. This means that, in effect, a WebDB hierarchy looks like a pyramid, with one piece (a master piece) of data at the top of the hierarchy and multiple levels of details below. WebDB does provide a lot of really nice functionality within the pyramid of a hierarchy, which you will see throughout the rest of this chapter.

Building a Simple Hierarchy

The WebDB wizard for building a hierarchy is similar in many ways to the wizard you used for building a chart object. Like a chart, a hierarchy component provides some very powerful functionality within a fairly specific environment. And, like the Chart Builder Wizard, you do not need to enter very many parameters into the pages of the Hierarchy Wizard to create a complete WebDB hierarchy object.

1. Log on to WebDB as user NETUDEV, go to the main page for User Interface Objects, which is located on the main page for building objects. Select the Hierarchies menu choice.

The first page of the Hierarchy Builder Wizard is exactly like the first page of the other user interface wizards. You are prompted for a schema to store the resulting object in and a name for the object. As with the other builders, the combo box for the schema name only contains those schemas that your user name has access to, and, like other builders, the name you give to the object must be unique within the schema in which it resides.

Because there is only one way to create a hierarchy, the top panel of the main page contains a single push button.

2. Click the Create push button in the top panel on the main Hierarchy Building page.
3. Select the NETU schema (or the schema name for your user name if you did not create a NETU user when you installed the sample data), and name the object **ch11_hie_1**.
4. Click the Next arrow on the Hierarchy Name and Schema page.

The next page prompts you for the name of the table that contains the columns needed to implement the recursive, hierarchical relationship. The combo box for the table and view names contains the names of all the tables that you can access, but, of course, there are a limited number of tables that contain columns that can be used to build a hierarchy.

5. Select the NETU.UGRADS table in the Tables/Views combo box and click the Next arrow on the Tables or Views page.

You have now reached the page where all the magic happens, as shown in Figure 11-2.

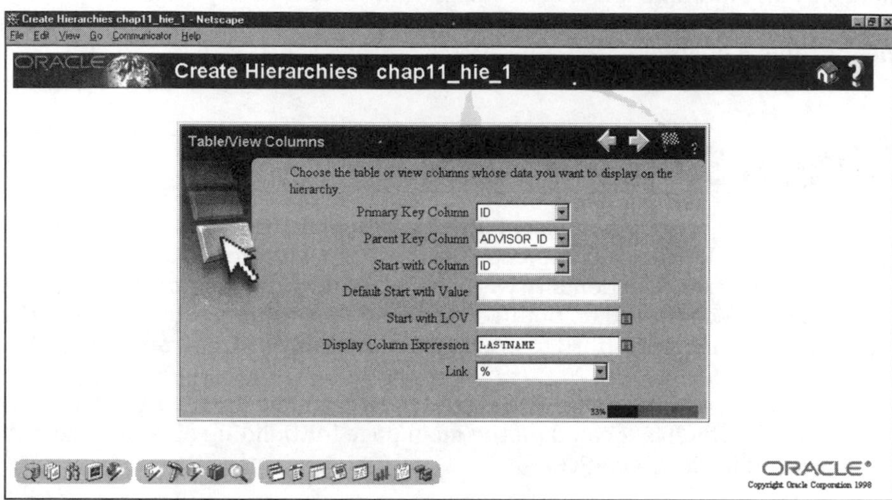

Figure 11-2: The Table/View Columns page

With just a few entries, you will now define the relationships and data that form the content of the resulting hierarchy.

6. Select ADVISOR_ID from the Parent Key Column combo box.
7. Leave the Primary Key Column as ID, the default.

The two columns listed in the Primary Key Column and the Parent Key Column combo boxes define the relationship that the hierarchy is built on. The value in the Parent Key Column should match a value that is in the Primary Key Column of another row of the same table. In the case of the UGRADS table, each student may have an advisor, whose ID is the value in the ADVISOR_ID column of their row in the table.

The Start with Column combo box is used to indicate the column that begins building the hierarchy. WebDB starts to build a hierarchy by looking in the ID column for a value indicated as the Start with Value. Then WebDB looks in the Parent Key Column for a matching value, and finally looks into the Primary Key Column for another matching value for the child. As you will see shortly, WebDB hierarchies can contain multiple levels of parents and children. The last piece of information you need to specify is the data that you want displayed in the hierarchy.

8. Enter **LASTNAME** into the Display Column Expression field.
9. Click the Next push button on the Table/View Columns page.

You do not need to have any conditions in your hierarchy, so you can skip by the Column Conditions page.

10. Click the Next arrow on the Column Conditions page.

The next page is the Display Options page shown in Figure 11-3. This page looks familiar, but there are some new option choices available.

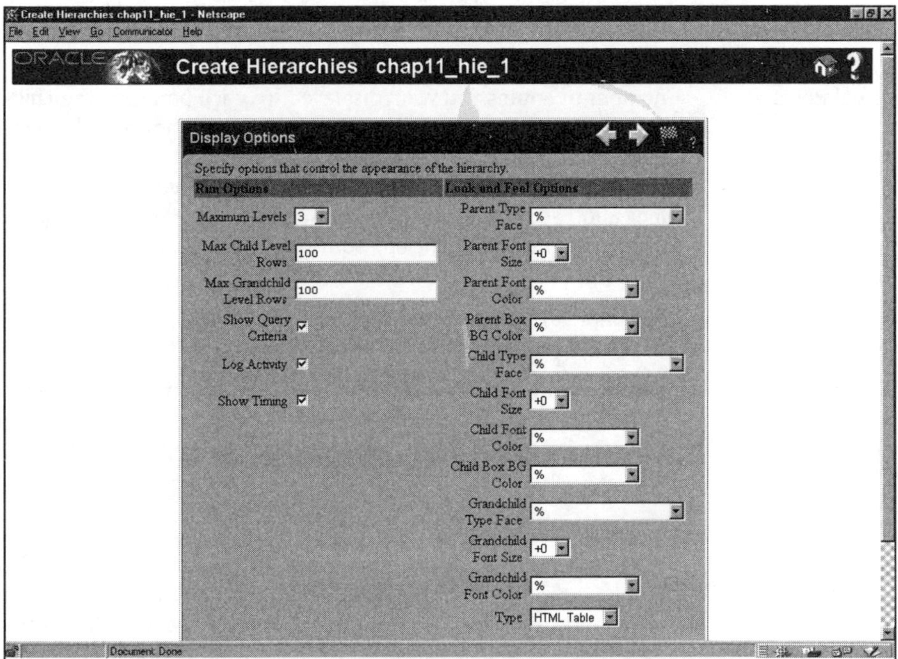

Figure 11-3: The Display Options page for a hierarchy

The Log Activity and Show Timing check boxes and the Type combo box serve the same function that they do for a report. Table 11-1 describes the new choices for the Display Options page for hierarchies.

Table 11-1 **Display Options for a WebDB Hierarchy**	
Option	***Description***
Maximum Levels	The Max Levels combo box enables you to specify how many levels in the hierarchy are displayed on a single page of the hierarchy. You can indicate that you want either two levels, which includes the parent and child levels, or three levels, the default, which also includes the grandchild level. Keep in mind that the maximum levels you specify in this combo box limits the number of levels displayed *on a single page,* not in the overall hierarchy. You will see this at work in the next section.
Max Child Level Rows	The Max Child Level Rows field enables you to specify the maximum number of entries you want displayed for each parent at the child level. Because the child level rows are displayed horizontally across the page, there may be times when you want to limit the number of child rows for formatting reasons. However, WebDB gives the user no indication as to whether there are additional child rows for a particular parent, so you should include some type of explanation for the user if you intend to limit the number of child rows. The default value for this field is 100.
Max Grandchild Level Rows	The Max Grandchild Level Rows field enables you to specify the maximum number of entries you want displayed for each parent at the grandchild level. Because the grandchild level rows are displayed vertically below the child row that is their parent, there is less of a reason to limit the number of grandchild rows. The default value for this field is 100.
. . . Type Face, Font Size, Font Color	The Look and Feel section of the Display Options page has combo boxes for the Type Face, Font Size, and Font Color for the parent, child, and grandchild levels of the hierarchy. You can indicate that each of these three potential levels in the hierarchy has a different typeface, size, or color. The Font Size combo box contains integers from –3 to +4, with a default of 0. These numbers indicate the relative sizing for each level in the hierarchy. The Type Face combo box contains a list of all possible typefaces, and the Font Color combo box contains a list of all possible font colors for a page. For more information on how to use fonts and colors, please refer to Chapter 15.
. . . Box BG Color	The parent and child levels in a hierarchy, by default, are specified in an HTML frame. This graphical device helps improve the readability of the hierarchy. You can specify a background color for the parent and child boxes with the respective combo boxes.

Now that we've reviewed the basic and new choices available on the Display Options page, it is time to begin creating the format for our hierarchy.

11. Select the Times New Roman, Times entry for the Parent Type Face combo box.
12. Select +3 for the Parent Font Size, Blue for the Parent Font Color, and Yellow for the Parent Box BG Color.

By selecting a different typeface, font size, and background color for the parent row in the hierarchy, you give the chart a theoretically more pleasing appearance.

13. Select Helvetica for the Child Type Face and +1 for the Child Font Size.
14. Select Courier for the Grandchild Type Face.
15. Click the Next arrow on the Display Options page.

The next page is the Parameter Entry Form Display Options page, which also looks very familiar. Here you can indicate parameters that the end user is offered to limit the retrieval of data for the hierarchy, you can limit the options that are shown on the parameter page, and you can set the push buttons that appear on the page.

The parameter options for hierarchies enables you to specify which parameters appear on the standard parameter form for the object. The Maximum Level, Max Child Level Rows, and Max Grandchild Level Rows choices enable the user of a hierarchy to specify the values for the three Display Options listed previously. The Start with Value choice enables the user to enter the base value for the hierarchy, which you specify on the Table/View Columns page in the builder. The Hierarchy Style combo box enables the user to indicate the type of output for the hierarchy.

All these parameters use the default values you have entered for them in the builder. A user can change the default values by using the Save push button on the hierarchy parameter entry page.

The button options look very much like the button options for a report that were described in detail in Chapter 5. The only real difference is that you don't have a Batch push button option for a hierarchy. Once you see how a hierarchy works, this makes perfect sense. A user can, and inevitably does, directly interact with a WebDB hierarchy component, so it doesn't make sense to submit a hierarchy as a batch job.

16. Click the Next push button on the Parameter Entry Form Display Options page.
17. Select PUBLIC.TEMPLATE_6 in the Template combo box.
18. Enter **Advisors and their students** as the Title for the Hierarchy.
19. Enter the following text into the Header Text for the Hierarchy:

```
This report shows the students that each advisor is
responsible for.
```

20. Click the checkered flag to generate the hierarchy component.

WebDB now generates the PL/SQL package that creates the component at run time and takes you to the Manage Component page for the recently created object.

You have built your first hierarchy. The next section shows you how to not only run a WebDB hierarchy component, but, more importantly, how you can interact with this highly responsive component.

Navigating Through a Hierarchy

Many of the other components you have created so far have a passive life in the run-time environment. For instance, when you run a report you have the option of shaping the data the report retrieves and the way the report is formatted through a parameter page, but the data returned from the report is totally static. In contrast, a hierarchy component provides much more interaction with the user, so you should spend more time than usual looking at the way the hierarchy operates at run time.

You start a hierarchy component in the same way that you start any other WebDB component from the WebDB development environment.

21. Click the Parameters link on the Manage Component page for your hierarchy component. You see the standard Hierarchy Parameters page, as shown in Figure 11-4.

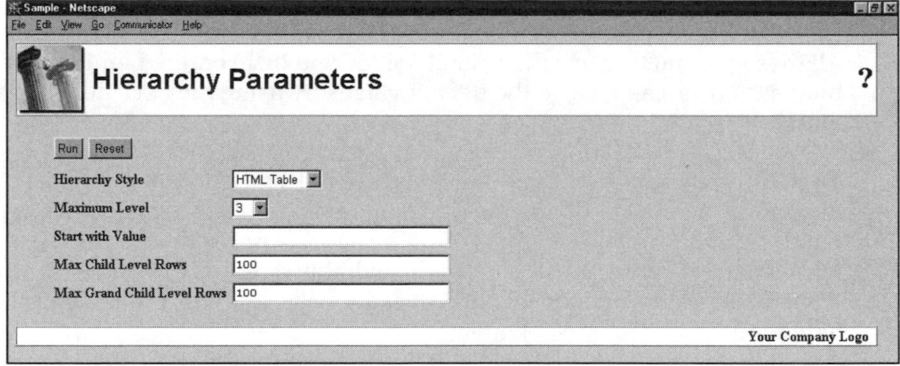

Figure 11-4: The standard Hierarchy Parameters page

22. Click the Run push button at the top of the page.

You may be a bit surprised at the result of your action. The page the WebDB hierarchy component returns contains the following message:

```
No data found, this data does not exist or you do not have
privilege to view it.
```

What happened? As we mentioned earlier in the chapter, a hierarchy has a starting point — the top of the pyramid of the hierarchy. A hierarchy *must* have a value for the Start with Value parameter, and because you did not indicate one as a default, the user must enter a value in order to produce a valid hierarchy.

23. Use the Back push button in the browser to return to the Hierarchy Parameters page.
24. Enter **1001** in the Start with Value text box.
25. Select 2 from the Maximum Level combo box.
26. Click the Run push button at the top of the page.

Now that's more like it. This time, the WebDB component returns a valid hierarchy description, as shown in Figure 11-5.

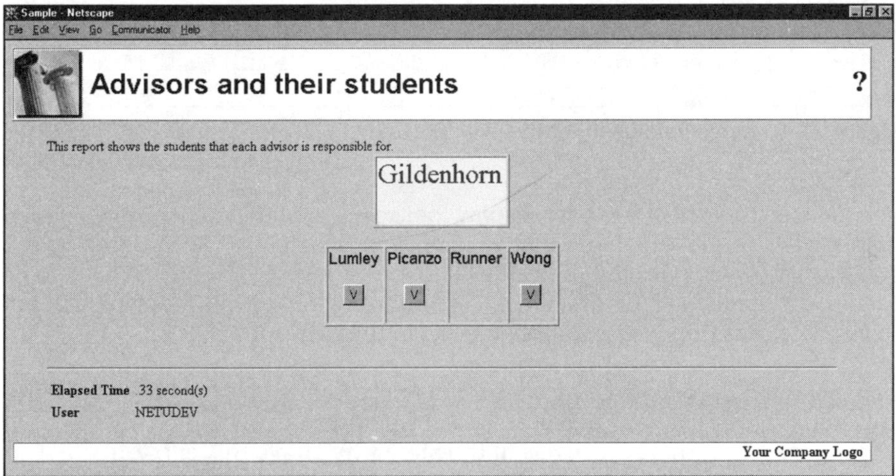

Figure 11-5: A valid two-level hierarchy

You can see that there are two levels displayed in the hierarchy. The top-level value, which is the employee with the ID that you entered into the Start with Value text field, is centered in the page and enclosed in a frame. The entries in the next level of the hierarchy are also enclosed in their own frames. Three of the values have push buttons with downward-pointing arrows on them, which indicates that the entry shown in this hierarchy can be a parent to other values in the hierarchy.

To graphically see what this means, you can use the push buttons on the page.

27. Click the down push button under the Lumley entry at the bottom level of the hierarchy.

Figure 11-6 shows the page that appears as a result of this action.

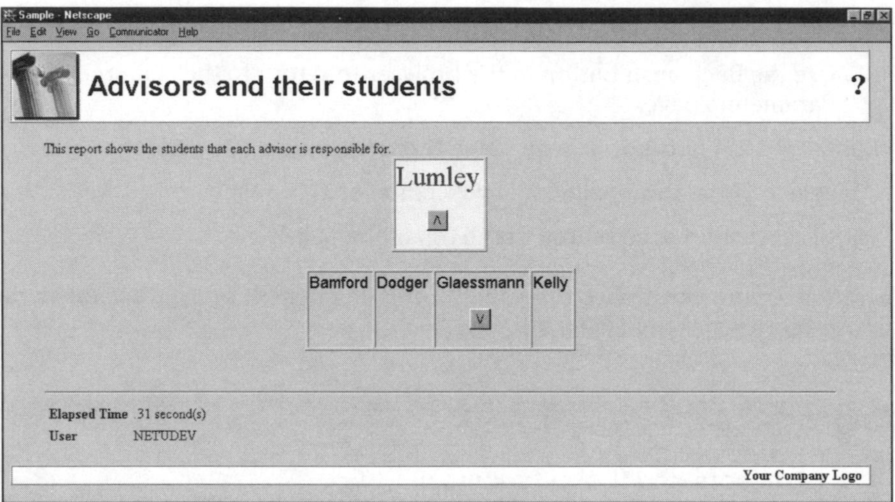

Figure 11-6: Moving down in a two-level hierarchy

You can see that this hierarchy display looks very much like the previous hierarchy display. The top-level value, which is Lumley in this display, is centered on the page and has its own frame, and the values in the next level in the hierarchy also have their own frames. The Glaessman entry on the right even has a down push button to indicate that there are additional levels in the hierarchy below.

The one big difference is the push button in the Lumley entry at the top of the hierarchy. This push button has an upward-pointing arrow, which means, as you might guess, that there are levels in the hierarchy above this entry. In other words, Lumley is not only at the top of this hierarchy display, but is also a child in another hierarchy display.

28. Click the up arrow at the top of the hierarchy.

The page that is returned as a result of this action is the same page that was initially displayed in the hierarchy. The displays you have been looking at contain only two levels in the hierarchy. The three-level hierarchical display is formatted a little bit differently than the two-level hierarchy display.

29. Use the Back push button in the browser to return to the Hierarchy Parameters page.

30. Select 3 in the Maximum Level combo box. Leave the value 1001 in the Start with Value text box.

31. Click the Run push button at the top of the page.

This time, the hierarchy display returned looks like Figure 11-7.

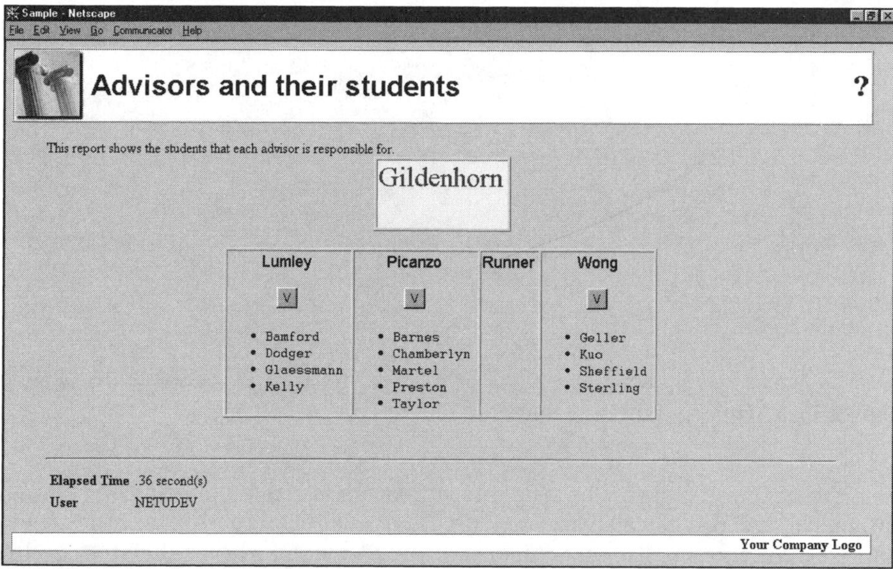

Figure 11-7: A three-level hierarchy

The same information is displayed in the three-level hierarchy as in the two-level hierarchy: the single parent, the framed displays, and the down push buttons. This hierarchy display also contains a third level in the hierarchy—the values preceded by a dot. In the last display, you knew that there were at least three levels of hierarchy by the existence of down push buttons in three of the four child entries; you just didn't know the values of that third level in the hierarchy. In this display, you can see the last names of the students whose advisor is advised by a student named Gildenhorn.

Let's see what happens when you try to drill down on the entries under Lumley as you did with the two-level display.

32. Click the down arrow under the Lumley entry in the child level of the hierarchy.

Figure 11-8 displays the result.

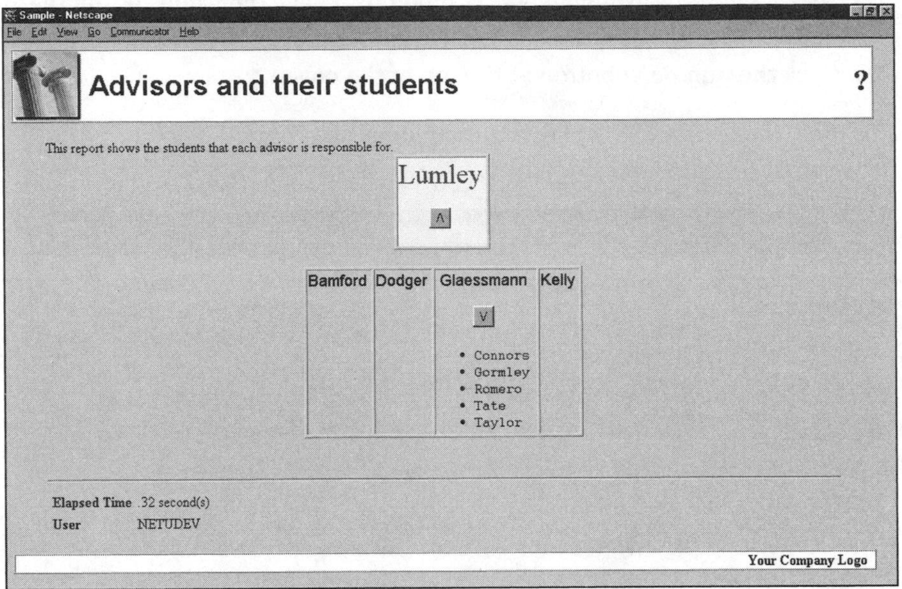

Figure 11-8: Drilling down in a three-level hierarchy

As expected, you can see the students whose advisor is Lumley in the child level of the hierarchy. You can also see, as with the two-level hierarchy, that the student named Glaessman is also an advisor to other students, who are listed in bulleted display in the same frame.

33. Click the down arrow under the Glaessman entry in the child row of the hierarchy.

Once again, you may be surprised by the display, as shown in Figure 11-9.

This display only has two levels. But remember, the parameter you changed was called Maximum Level. This means that the WebDB hierarchy component shows up to three levels, if there are three levels present. All the down arrow for Glaessman indicated was that Glaessman was a parent in the same hierarchical relationship that produced the display. WebDB has no way of knowing that the children in that relationship were already displayed in the three-level hierarchy.

Before leaving this chapter, you should spend some time making the hierarchy component display more useful information.

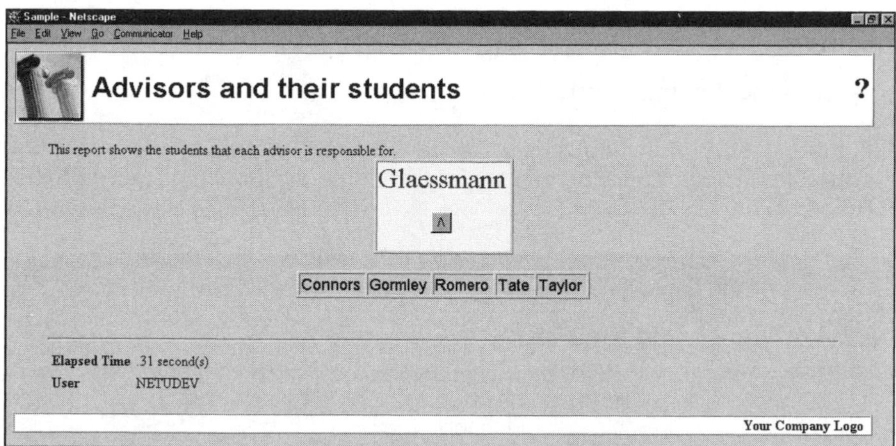

Figure 11-9: The bottom level of a three-level hierarchy display

Enhancing Your Hierarchy

You have probably already spotted some ways that you could improve the hierarchy you just created. One way is to help prevent user errors by giving the all-important Start with Value parameter a default value, so at least a user accepting the defaults would not run into the same problem that you did the first time you ran the hierarchy.

1. Use the Back push button in the browser to return to the Manage Component page in the WebDB development environment.
2. Click the Edit link.
3. The Table/View Columns tab, which is the first tab on the left, is displayed by default. Enter **1001** in the Default Start with Value text field.

This page enables you to increase the amount of information delivered. As you can tell by the label, the Display Column Expression can accept more than just a simple column name, even though the pop-up list only gives you a choice of individual columns. Be careful to enter the concatenation character, which is two vertical bars, and the single quotes properly. WebDB accepts the expression you enter into this field without any error checking, so if you make a mistake, you will only find out once you run the hierarchy.

4. Change the Display Column Expression to **LASTNAME || ', ' || FIRSTNAME.**
5. Click the Finish push button.
6. Click the Parameters link on the Manage Component page for the hierarchy component.

7. Check that the parameters page looks the same, except that the Start with Value now has a default of 1001. If it doesn't, begin again.
8. Click the Run push button at the top of the page.

This time, the hierarchy looks better, because each student and advisor is readily identifiable through their first and their last names, as shown in Figure 11-10.

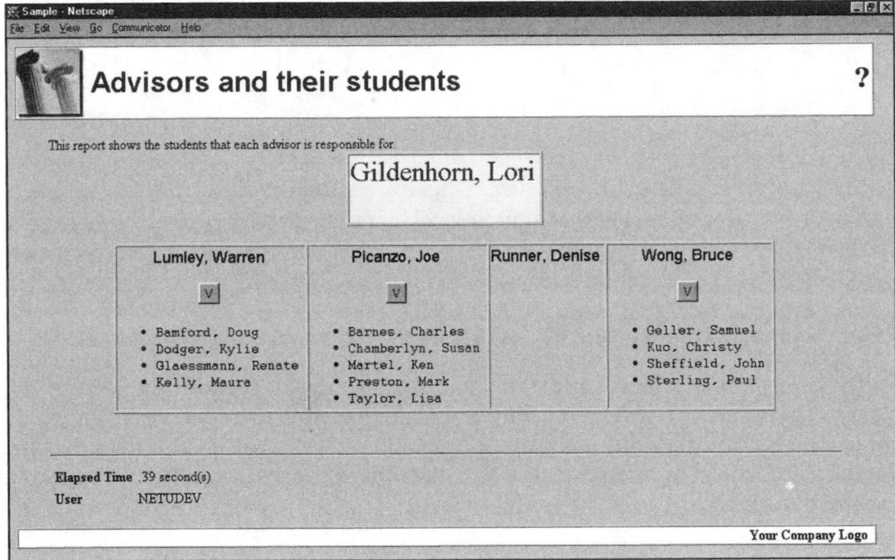

Figure 11-10: Second version of the hierarchy

By changing the Display Column Expression, you changed the way the data is displayed for all levels of the hierarchy.

There is one more modification that might improve the ease of use for the existing hierarchy. There is a kind of disconnect between the parameter page and the display pages for the hierarchy. The display pages use an easily understood expression to list the advisors and their students, while the parameter page currently requires a more difficult to remember and understand ID number for the starting point for the hierarchy. You can fix this situation by using a list of values for the starting value.

9. Use the Back push button in the browser to return to the Manage Component page in the WebDB development environment.
10. Click the Edit link and then click the Table/View Columns tab.
11. Click the pop-up icon to the right of the Start with LOV list box. Click the ADVISORLOV choice.

If the ADVISORLOV choice does not show up in the pop-up list, you have to load the advisorlov.sql script from the samples included on the CD-ROM for this book, as well as the studentlov.sql script which you will use shortly. Please refer to Appendix A for instructions on how to import objects by loading SQL scripts.

12. Click the Finish push button.
13. Click the Parameters link at the bottom of the Manage Component page.

You can immediately see the difference on the parameters page, as shown in Figure 11-11.

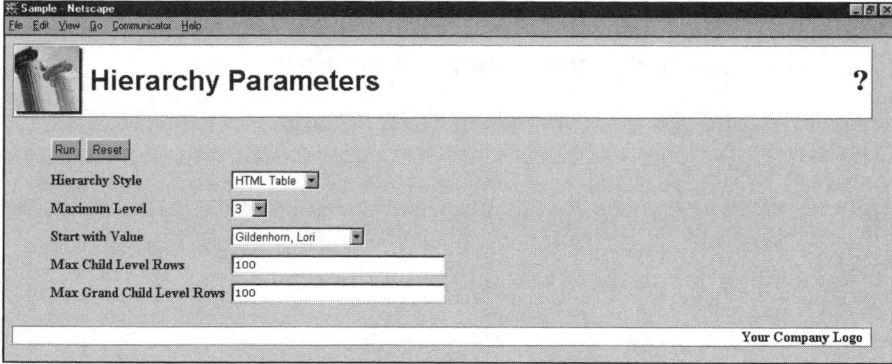

Figure 11-11: The Hierarchy Parameters page with a list of values

You can see that the text box for Start with Value has been replaced with a combo box, which is the only way that a list of values object for the Start with Value parameter is displayed on a parameter page. Notice that the value you entered in the development environment for the Default Start with Value is still having an effect — the advisor with the number you entered for that value (1001) is still the default choice in the list of values (Gildenhorn, Lori).

14. Click the Run push button at the top of the page to explore the hierarchy.

As you look around the hierarchy, you can see that it still operates just like the previous version of the hierarchy. The ADVISORLOV is a list of values that only displays those students who are at the top level of advisors: seniors who are advisors to underclass students, but who have no advisors themselves.

This limits the display of the hierarchy to the same format every time. The pyramid of the hierarchy always begins at the top level. However, it is not necessary to always start at the top with a hierarchy. You can change the list of values for the Start with Value for this hierarchy to see this principle at work.

15. Use the Back push button in the browser to return to the Manage Component page in the WebDB development environment.
16. Click the Edit link.
17. Change the Start with LOV entry to STUDENTLOV.
18. Click the Finish push button.
19. Click the Parameter push button.
20. Select the Lumley, Warren entry from the Start with Value combo box.

Because this list of values has a lot of values, you can quickly get to the approximate location for Lumley, Warren by entering the letter **l** in the combo box. This scrolls the display to the people whose last names start with an "l."

21. Click the Run push button at the top of the page.

The hierarchy looks a little bit different this time, as shown in Figure 11-12.

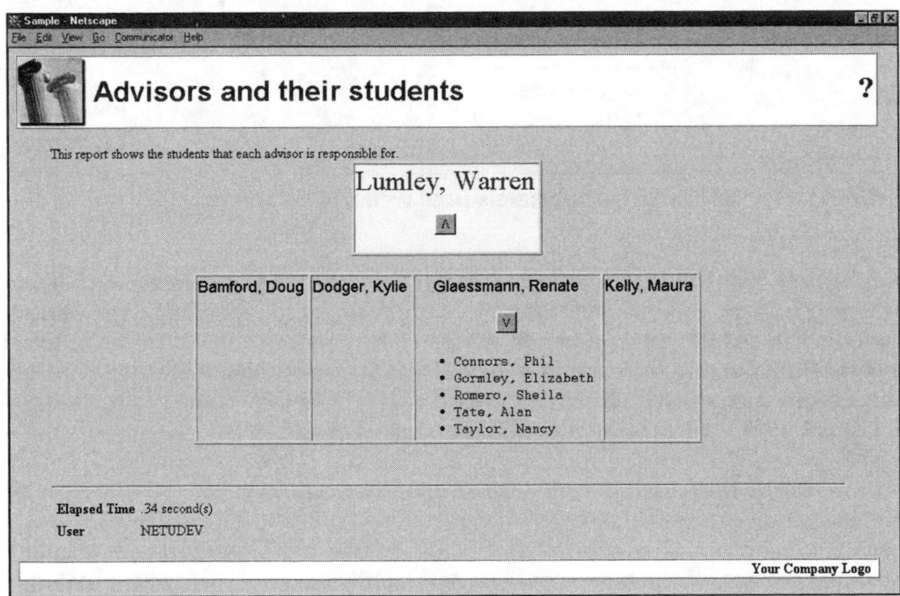

Figure 11-12: Starting a hierarchy in the middle

The hierarchy still works in the same way, but instead of starting at the top of the hierarchy, you have chosen a starting value that is in the middle of a hierarchy.

You can use this final version of the hierarchy in different ways than the previous version of the hierarchy because it applies to any student, rather than just looking at advisors from the top down. This illustrates the last point you should take away from this chapter. A WebDB hierarchy component is a way to display a specific type of data relationship through the use of a particular type of display. But that is the only limitation on this component. You can start a hierarchy anywhere that you want, and the WebDB component builds the appropriate levels for you, both above and below the selected starting value.

Wrapping Up

The hierarchy object is useful and unique. In some ways, it represents the peak of built-in functionality provided by WebDB. With just a few simple parameters, WebDB creates a powerful interactive component that can be used to view a specific type of data-based relationship. Although the use of the component is limited to a specific type of data relationship, the component provides a great deal of functionality that can be used to explore this common relationship.

✦ ✦ ✦

Working with HTML

CHAPTER 12

✦ ✦ ✦ ✦

In This Chapter

Dynamic Pages

Adding Your Own HTML Code

Using Multiple SQL Statements

Using WebDB Frames

Integrating Frames and Other Components

✦ ✦ ✦ ✦

In previous chapters, you have had the chance to work with WebDB's wizards to produce structured components. Although the eventual output of these components is HTML code, you do not need to concern yourself with the details of writing the HTML code itself, because the WebDB components generate the HTML for you. There are opportunities for entering a certain amount of handcrafted HTML code directly, such as when you add text to the headers and footers of pages. However, there may be times when you wish to have a finer grain of control over the HTML that is used to render a page. WebDB provides two additional components that are less structured and offer you more input opportunity than the content creation wizards.

The first of these components is the Dynamic Pages Wizard, which enables you to create your own SQL code directly and then mix this code with your own HTML. Dynamic pages enable you to build pages by using multiple SQL statements and blocks of PL/SQL code. You can also add extra HTML text alongside this code and create very complex HTML pages that rival handcrafted code.

The Frame Driver Wizard helps you link the SQL code that you write into other components, such as forms and reports, into an HTML framed page. These two wizards provide you with a finer grain of control over generated HTML code than is possible with the component builders you have used thus far.

Dynamic Pages

WebDB's Dynamic Pages Wizard is the most free-form tool that you will work with inside of the WebDB environment.

Part of the power of WebDB is that much of the low-level HTML coding is automatically handled for you. The downside of this approach is that you are required to live within the confines of the HTML code that WebDB knows how to generate. While there are certain exceptions to this rule, such as the ability to place custom HTML in headers and footers, you are still basically working within the confines of the WebDB structure. With the Dynamic Pages Wizard, you are free to build your own HTML code and WebDB manages this code for you. This enables you to closely mimic some of your existing static HTML code and enhance it with dynamic data. The price of this freedom is productivity, because the Dynamic Pages Wizard requires you to take complete control of the HTML code, while the other wizards take care of most of the detail work for you. Yet, conceptually the Dynamic Pages Wizard is simple, in that it enables you to mix SQL statements and handcrafted HTML code together in one manageable component.

1. Navigate to the WebDB menu bar and select the Dynamic Pages menu choice to display the initial page of the wizard as shown in Figure 12-1.

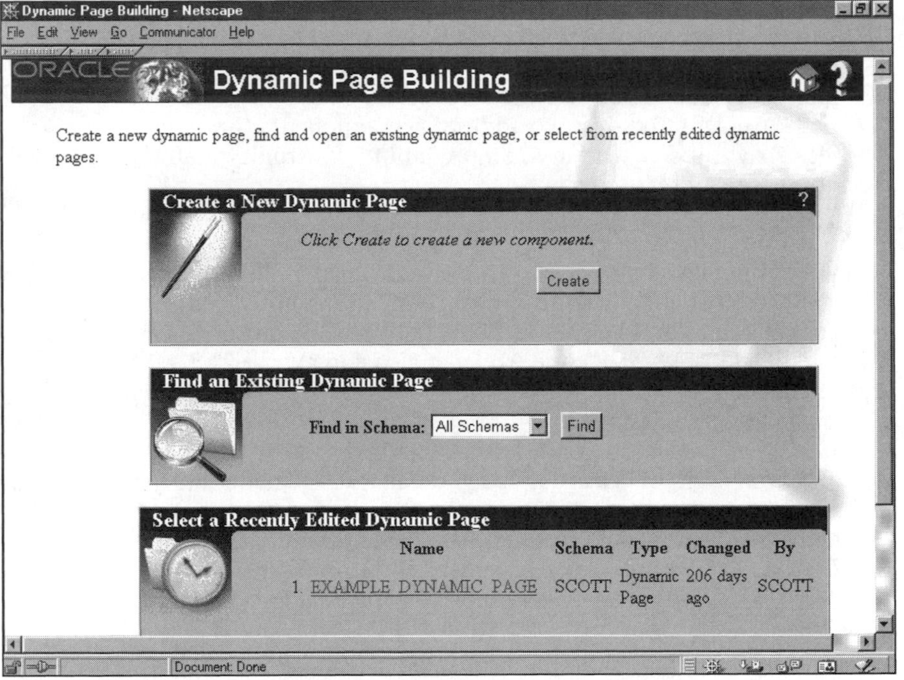

Figure 12-1: Dynamic Page Building panel

The initial page of the dynamic page builder looks the same as any of the other component wizards. The primary page is composed of three separate panels: a top panel for creating new dynamic pages, a middle panel for locating and editing existing pages, and a bottom panel that lists the most recently edited pages.

2. Select the Create button in the top panel to begin building a sample dynamic page.

   The next page in the Dynamic Pages Wizard also looks familiar. This page enables you to set the owner for the page you wish to create and to provide a meaningful name for the component. As with similar pages in other wizards, the Schema field is implemented as a drop-down list box containing only the Oracle USERIDs that you have been given permission to build in. WebDB automatically generates a unique component name for you, but as with the other component builders, we recommend that you use a more structured naming convention.

3. Select the Net University USERID for the Schema.
4. Enter a Dynamic Page Name for your sample page as shown in Figure 12-2.
5. Click the Next arrow to continue.

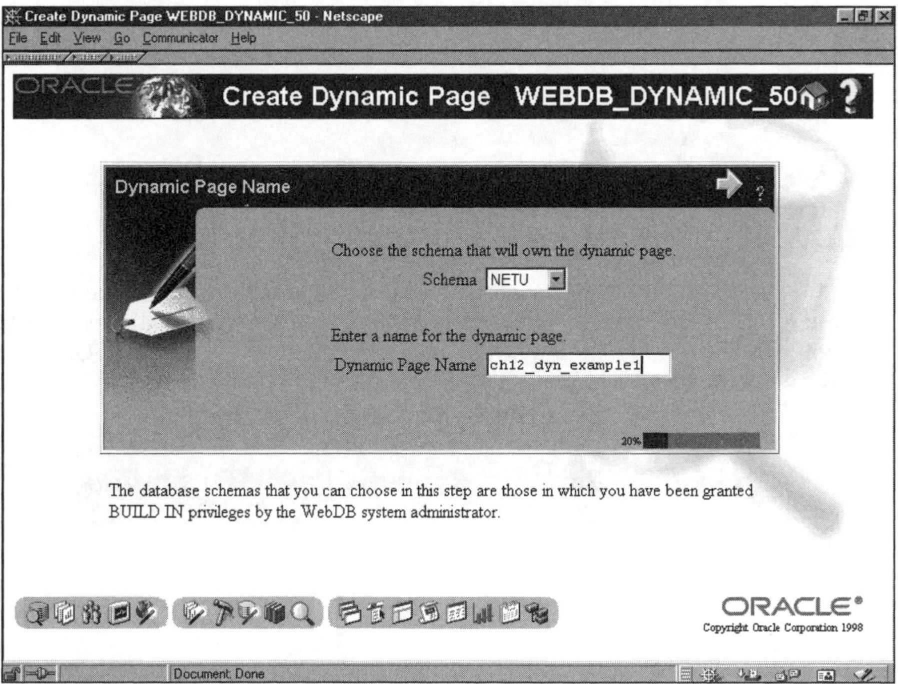

Figure 12-2: Dynamic Page Name panel

The key panel in the Dynamic Pages Wizard is the Dynamic Page Content panel shown in Figure 12-3.

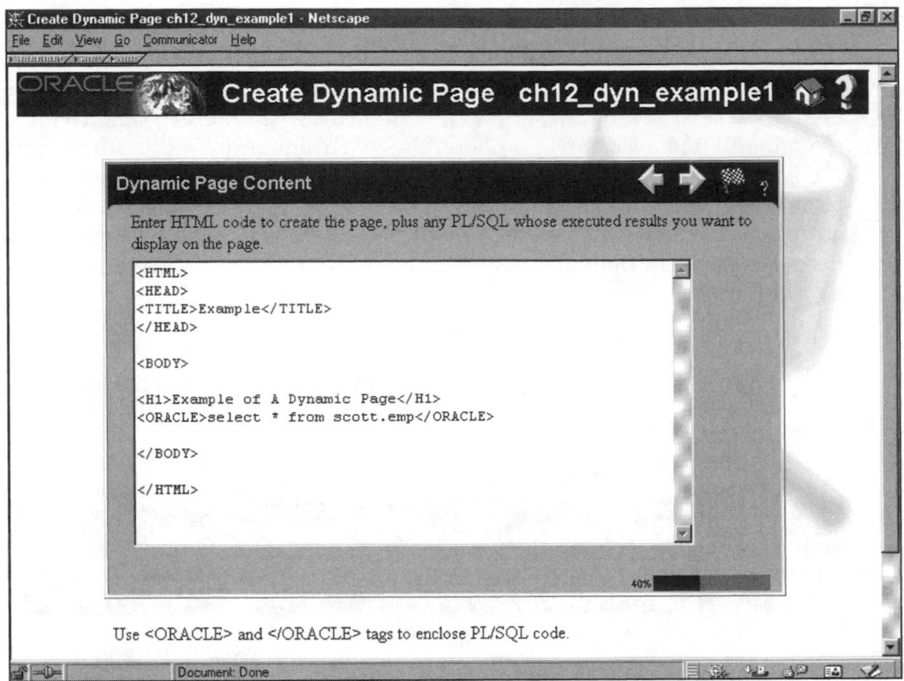

Figure 12-3: Dynamic Page Content panel

The complete functionality of the Dynamic Pages Wizard is contained in this single page. The page itself is nothing more than a single large HTML text box in which you can enter code. Initially this text box is filled with a sample SQL statement as shown in Listing 12-1.

Listing 12-1: **Standard Dynamic Page SQL statement**

```
<HTML>
<HEAD>
<TITLE>Example</TITLE>
</HEAD>
<BODY>
<H1>Example of A Dynamic Page</H1>
<ORACLE>select * from scott.emp</ORACLE>

</BODY>
</HTML>
```

The key to using the Dynamic Pages Wizard is understanding the format of the code that you enter into this single text area. Although the text area is essentially a free-form field, WebDB attempts to derive the format of the page by looking at the structure of the code you enter into this field.

There are essentially two types of code you can enter into this field. First, you can enter any block of text such as the phrase **Example of A Dynamic Page**, as shown in Listing 12-1. WebDB renders this text as entered into the text area in accordance with the normal processing rules of HTML. You can enhance any block of text by enclosing it within a pair of HTML tags. The HTML tags provide WebDB with the necessary clues as to how to format the text that you enter. Actually, WebDB itself does not do anything with either the text you enter or the tags other than passing the results on to the browser. In the preceding example listing, both of the text strings — `Example` and `Example of A Dynamic Page` — are surrounded by HTML tags to indicate that the first string is a title and the second string is a heading. You are free to use any HTML tag set that the browser can handle. In addition to enhancing and adding text strings, you are free to load images and links in the text areas as long as they are enclosed by the appropriate HTML tags. WebDB does not attempt to validate the HTML code you enter into this panel; it only passes it along to the browser at run time.

The remaining type of code that you can enter into this field are Oracle SQL statements enclosed within the Oracle-specific HTML tags <ORACLE> and </ORACLE>. Unlike the standard HTML tags, WebDB *will* search for these tags and then format the remainder of the Dynamic Pages Wizard using them.

WebDB fills the text area with a sample block of text that includes both types of code by default. You are free to modify this code and add or remove any of the elements as necessary to build the page layout that you desire. The Dynamic Pages Wizard features only a small number of panels and it is easy to use a build, test, and modify metaphor when designing your pages.

6. Edit the text between the <ORACLE> </ORACLE> tags to use the following SQL query:

   ```
   select sysdate from dual
   ```

7. Click the Next arrow to continue.

WebDB processes the text that is entered into the form and searches for the <ORACLE> tags. WebDB isolates the SQL code you enter between the tags and then builds you a panel that enables you to further customize the code as shown in Figure 12-4.

Initially, you may find that this particular panel is not overly useful, as its sole function is to isolate the SQL code and provide you with an opportunity to modify the code. The power of this panel only becomes obvious when you build *multiple* SQL statements into the same panel. For the time being, you can ignore this panel.

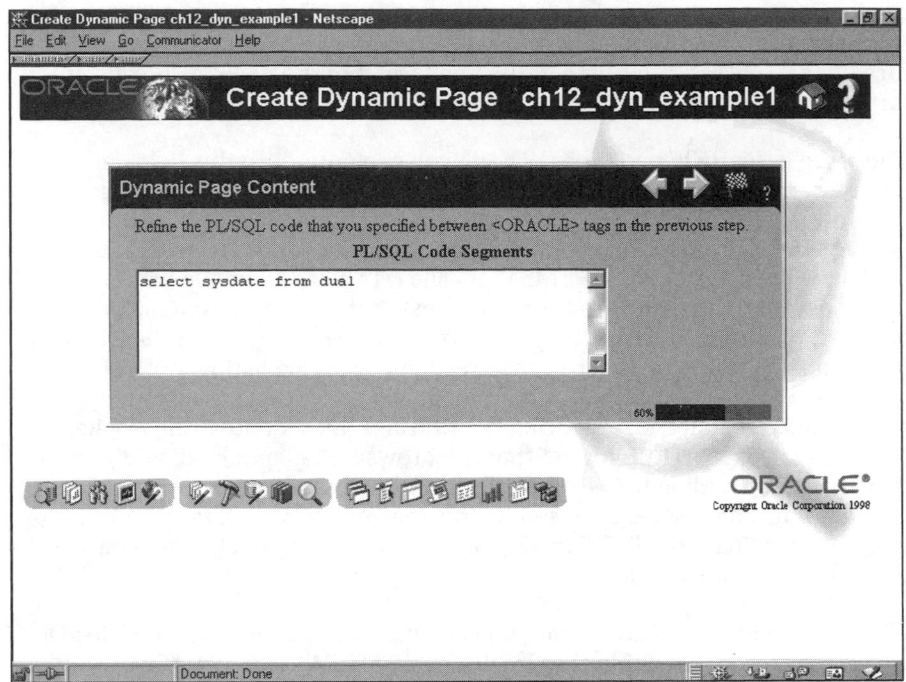

Figure 12-4: Dynamic Page Content panel

WebDB skips over the familiar text pages and PL/SQL code pages that you have become accustomed to in the other builder wizards, because you are in total control of the generated HTML page contents. The only remaining item for you to decide is whether or not WebDB should log the activity of the component, as shown in Figure 12-5.

8. Press the Next arrow to continue.

You will sometimes use dynamic pages as informal objects and you may choose not to log activity on these pages as you would some of the other components that you build.

If the dynamic page is being used to select data from the database and you plan on deploying it to users, we recommend that you select the logging option. Doing so ensures that you are tracking the performance of the dynamic page in the context of your application. WebDB does not paginate dynamic pages as it does other components, and you may find that the performance of dynamic pages appears to lag behind those of other objects because of this fact.

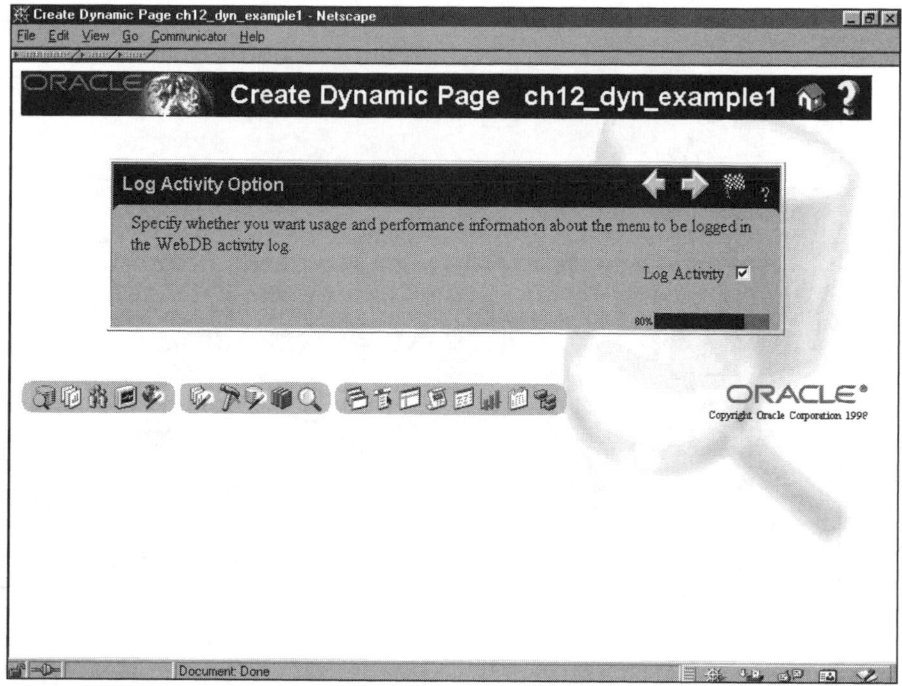

Figure 12-5: Log Activity Option panel

9. Select the logging option and click the Next arrow to continue.

   The last panel in the wizard is the confirmation page that includes the familiar OK button, which stores the component and creates the procedure. Even though dynamic pages are essentially HTML pages, WebDB still builds a database procedure to implement the routine just like any of the other component builders.

10. Select the OK button to create the dynamic page and continue as shown in Figure 12-6.

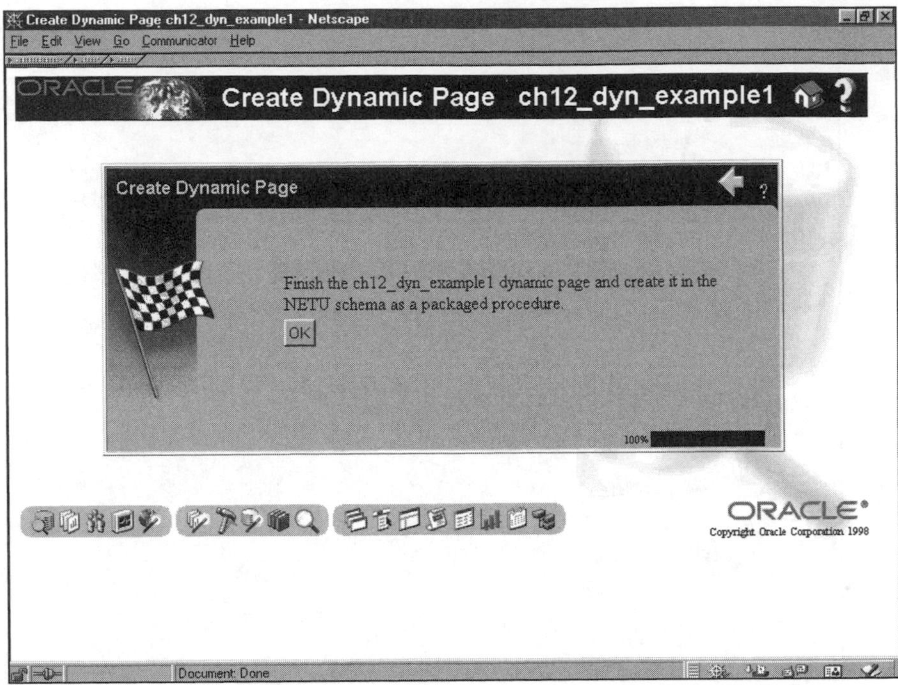

Figure 12-6: Create Dynamic Page panel

11. WebDB returns control to the Manage Component menu. Select the Run link to test out the new page.

The resulting HTML page is relatively simple, as you can see from Figure 12-7.

You will remember from the HTML code that there are only three objects in the source code: a page title, a heading, and the Oracle SQL code. During the wizard process you were not given the opportunity to set many of the formatting and processing options that you may have used within the other wizards, and this is reflected in the output of the page. For example, the page in Figure 12-7 does not make use of any templates and there are no provisions for setting the color scheme of the page, such as foreground or background colors. WebDB offers the dynamic page builder as a way for you to roll your own HTML, and therefore it does not provide many of the features you have relied upon in the other wizards.

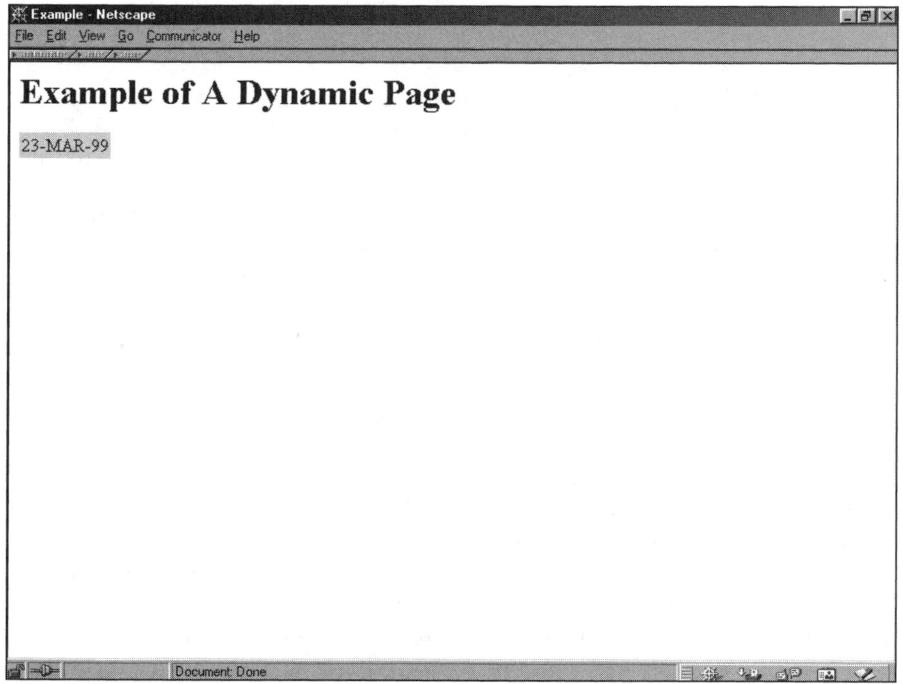

Figure 12-7: Example dynamic page

As you will learn shortly, you are still able to control many of these settings. The real difference is that you are required to enter the code by hand. The designers of WebDB purposefully left out the advanced settings pages in the Dynamic Pages Wizard so as not to interfere with the custom HTML that you might enter into your dynamic HTML pages. For example, if you were to provide a background color setting on your page in your own HTML code, as well as setting it on a display options panel, WebDB would not be sure of which setting to use. In order to avoid any such confusion, the templates and display options panels simply do not exist in the Dynamic Pages Wizard.

You can still perform all of the formatting functions, however, by editing your own HTML directly inside of the page itself. For example, the background color for your page can be set by using the BG HTML parameter in the <BODY> tag.

Adding additional HTML code to the page

The Dynamic Pages Wizard is designed to provide flexibility for the HTML gurus within your organization. Although WebDB can easily reference existing *static* HTML pages by using virtual directories, these static pages cannot be dynamically generated from data in your database. On the other hand, there may be times when you want to combine some of your existing HTML code with data from your database, and this is where the flexibility of the Dynamic Pages Wizard comes in.

The real power of the Dynamic Pages Wizard is in the flexibility it offers you. Initially, the HTML text displayed in the main panel, as shown in Figure 12-3, is relatively simple. However, you are free to add your own HTML code into this window and replace the existing HTML code that WebDB suggests. If you are an HTML guru, you can simply starting typing over the HTML code that exists in the edit frame in Figure 12-3. If, on the other hand, you are not an HTML guru, you are free to use any visual HTML authoring tool, such as Symantec's Visual Page, to create your HTML. Importing this code into WebDB is as simple as cutting and pasting the HTML source into the Dynamic Page Content panel.

Before continuing on in this section, make sure that you have copied the NetU images to a directory accessible to WebDB, and that you have created a virtual directory for these images, as instructed in Appendix A.

The Dynamic Pages Wizard is designed to move quickly between development and testing modes. You will find it easy to add new HTML code in blocks and then test the code quickly before making any additional changes. Although dynamic pages do not provide for the use of templates, you can use your own blocks of HTML code to add headings as desired. For example, you can replace the default heading with a more descriptive heading using standard HTML.

In addition to making changes to the HTML, you can also make changes to the SQL code that is contained within the Oracle tags. You are free to use any valid SQL statement, PL/SQL statement, or function call just as if you were entering the code into SQL*Plus. You are, however, limited to entering a single SQL statement within each pair of <ORACLE> </ORACLE> tags, but WebDB enables you to enter multiple sets of tags, as you will see in the next section. For example, the default date selection on the example page does not provide much in the way of details, but it is easy to add some additional formatting using standard Oracle data functions.

1. Return to the Manage Component page for Dynamic Pages and edit the page you just created.
2. Select `<H1>Example of A Dynamic Page</H1>` in the text area and replace it with the code segment found in ch12_dynamic1.htm.
3. Replace the line:

```
<ORACLE>select sysdate from dual</ORACLE>
```

with the following code:

```
<ORACLE>select to_char(sysdate, 'Month DD, YYYY HH:MI A.M.')
from dual</ORACLE>
```

The net result of the changes to the page should be the code shown in Listing 12-2.

Listing 12-2: Modified HTML code

```
<HTML>
<HEAD>
<TITLE>Example</TITLE>
</HEAD>

<BODY>

<P><IMG SRC="/netu/netu_banner.gif" WIDTH="162" HEIGHT="81"
ALIGN="MIDDLE" BORDER="0"> <B><FONT SIZE="6">Net
University Web Page</FONT></B></P>

<P><B><FONT SIZE="6"></FONT></B>
<ORACLE>select to_char(sysdate, 'Month DD, YYYY HH:MI A.M.')
from dual</ORACLE>

</BODY>

</HTML>
```

It is possible to duplicate the functionality of any WebDB template in your own code simply by viewing the source for the template within the browser and copying the source into your Dynamic Page object. You have to selectively cut and paste the sections of the HTML code that reference the template, but this is not overly difficult. In fact, you can duplicate the functionality of almost any static HTML page by following this same technique.

The structure of the HTML code must still conform to the basic rules of HTML coding. However, you are free to add any parameters to the HTML tags, such as adding document information to the <HTML> tag. Typically, you would add document-indexing information into the HTML code via the <META> tag, but this information is not as useful in the WebDB environment. Document information can only be identified by a search engine when the HTML page is stored *externally* to the database. Because dynamic pages are stored inside the database, they are not indexed or accessible to standard Web search engines. They can however, be indexed by Oracle's inteMediaText database cartridge.

WebDB does not attempt to validate the HTML code you enter into a dynamic page, and the only indication that there is a problem with the code comes when you attempt to use the page at run time.

If you add images or links to other objects into the HTML code you use, you must be sure to make the links and paths accessible to WebDB. In Listing 12-2, note that the image name (`netu_banner.gif`) is preceded by a virtual directory path that is known to WebDB (`/netu/`). All links must be made relative to WebDB or point to a fully qualified URL in order for them to work within WebDB.

If you are importing code into WebDB from other visual HTML tools, you almost always need to check the images and links to be sure they are accessible from within WebDB.

4. Click the Finish button to save your changes and then use the Run link to test out the modified page, as shown in Figure 12-8.

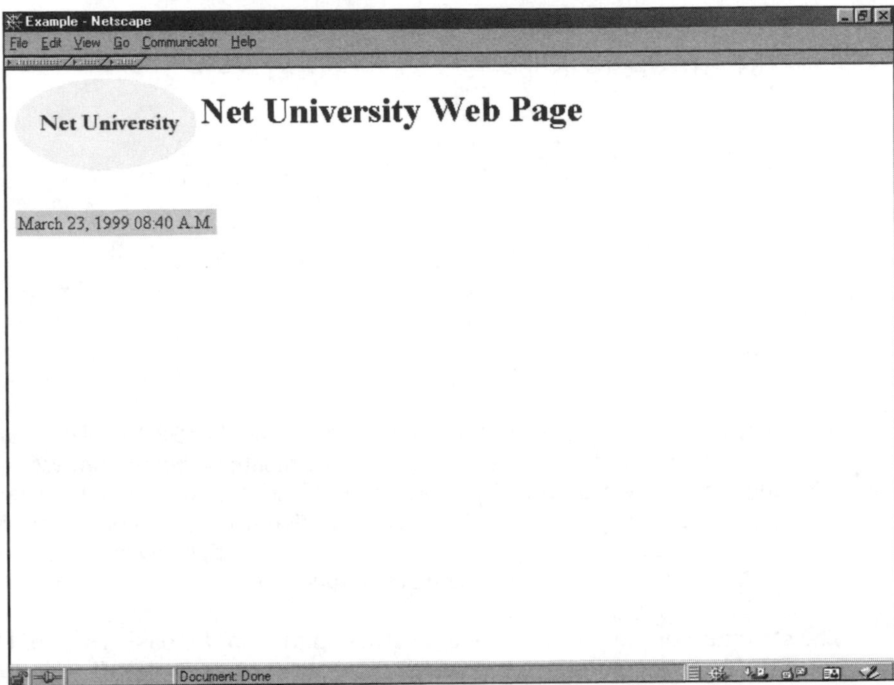

Figure 12-8: Dynamic page with custom HTML code

The modified page includes the banner graphic, a more descriptive block of title text, and a modified display for the date and time. The result is a customized HTML page that is much more flexible than the other WebDB components. Of course, the price for this increased flexibility is a lower level of productivity as you are responsible for manually formatting the HTML code. You will find that expert HTML programmers will be the most frequent users of dynamic pages, because they offer the ability to leverage HTML expertise directly.

Adding additional SQL code

When you built your initial Dynamic Page object, you noticed that the SQL code was surrounded by the Oracle tags <ORACLE> and </ORACLE>. Although the default page uses only one set of these tags, you are free to add as many pairs of these tags as you wish. This enables you to build pages that have multiple, separate SQL queries that are separated by custom HTML code. This can offer incredible opportunities for customization, because the various SQL statements need not have any direct relationship to one another.

1. Return to the Manage Component page for the dynamic page.
2. Edit the dynamic page using the Edit link.
3. Insert an additional set of tags and a new SQL statement, as shown in Listing 12-3.

Listing 12-3: Dynamic page with multiple SQL statements

```
<HTML>
<HEAD>
<TITLE>Example</TITLE>
</HEAD>

<BODY>

<P><IMG SRC="/netu/netu_banner.gif" WIDTH="162" HEIGHT="81"
ALIGN="MIDDLE" BORDER="0"> <B><FONT SIZE="6">Net
University Web Page</FONT></B></P>

<P><B><FONT SIZE="6"></FONT></B>
<b>Report Run Date:</b>
<ORACLE>select to_char(sysdate, 'Month DD, YYYY HH:MI A.M.')
from dual</ORACLE>
<br>
<b>NetU Students</b>
<ORACLE>select firstname, lastname, classyr, gender, photo from
netu.ugrads order by classyr</ORACLE>

</BODY>

</HTML>
```

The new code is shown in boldface text in the preceding listing. The first change is the addition of a block of bold text that displays a title for the date select statement. Next, an HTML break has been added after the date selection and a bold string of text has been entered after the break. Most importantly, an additional block of SQL code has been inserted that selects student records grouped by class year.

4. Enter the code as shown in Listing 12-3, remembering to preface the UGRADS select statement with the schema owner if you did not install the Net University database in the NETU schema as recommended.
5. Click the Dynamic Page Content tab to save your changes and display the PL/SQL code segments as shown in Figure 12-9.

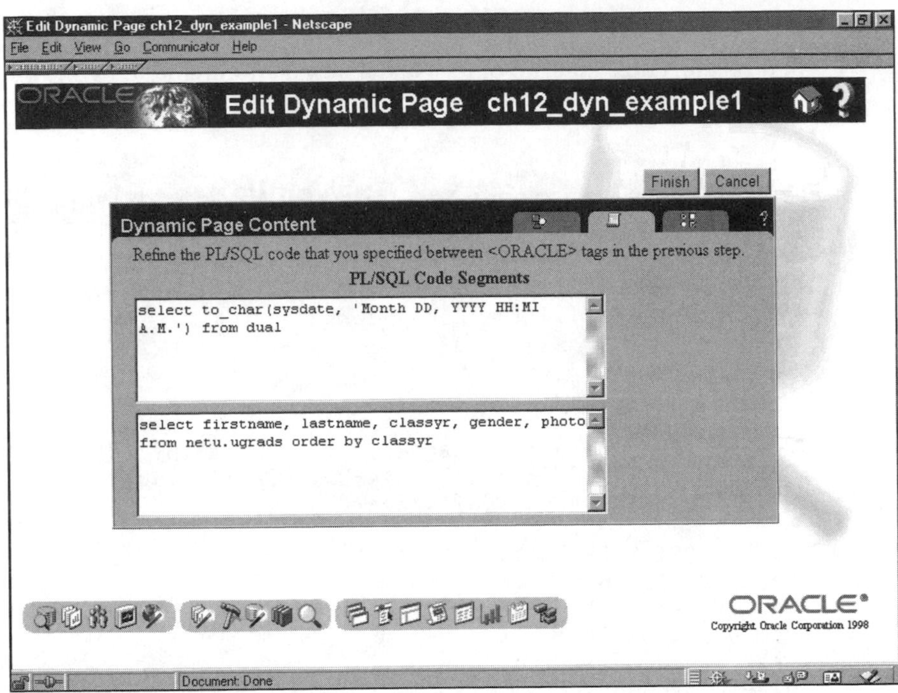

Figure 12-9: PL/SQL code segments

Notice that WebDB has built two text areas — one for each of the SQL queries that you entered using the <ORACLE> tag. WebDB extracts the text just as you entered it between the tags and it ignores any of the extraneous HTML code that may surround the tags. This gives you the opportunity to refine the SQL code without having your view obstructed by any HTML text.

When the page is executed, WebDB executes the code in the order that it was entered into the page, as shown on the panel in Figure 12-9. In this example, you are selecting the current date and time followed by a list of students in the Net University database. If necessary, you could insert new records into the database in one query and then select these records in a second query. You can also use this technique to populate a temporary table with one query and then display the results with a second query on the same page. WebDB displays the results in the order that they are executed, so update or insert queries are transparent to the end user.

You can enter almost any combination of SQL statements into the <ORACLE> tags, including INSERTS and DELETES, but you are not permitted to make use of DDL statements such as CREATE TABLE within the <ORACLE> tags. You are also prevented from using bind variables, because the Dynamic Pages Wizard does not allow for the passing of any parameters.

6. Save the changes to this page by clicking the Finish button and then use the Run link to test the modified version as shown in Figure 12-10.

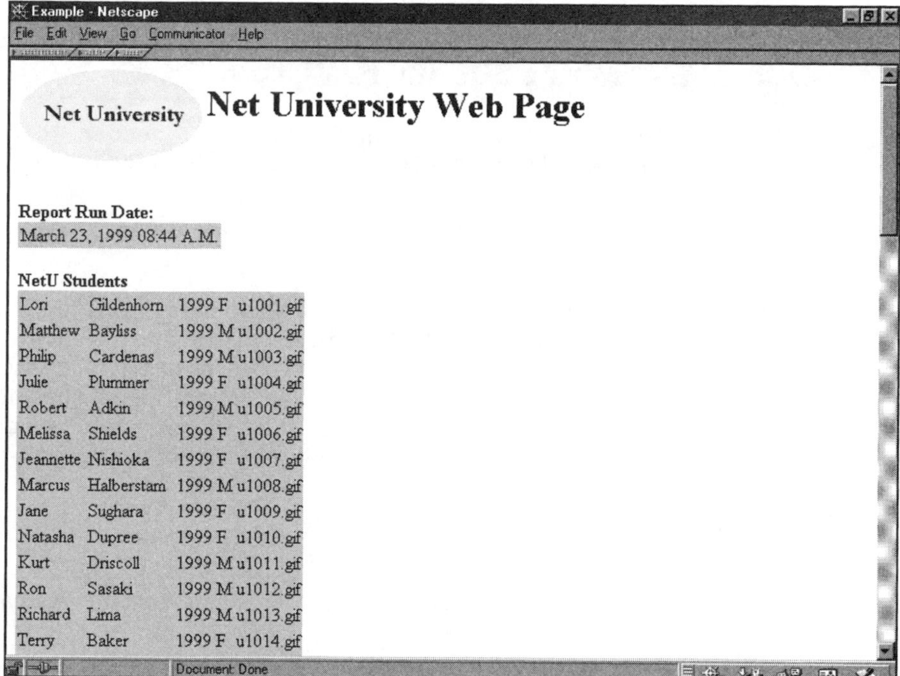

Figure 12-10: Dynamic page with two queries

The resulting page shown in Figure 12-10 is built using your exact specifications. Notice that the SQL query for the UGRADS records even lacks titles for the various columns. If you wanted titles for the columns, you would be forced to build the titles by hand using HTML. You can easily see that the increased flexibility comes at a price in terms of productivity. However, this flexibility can also be an important asset. Notice that the last field in the UGRADS list is a filename. This filename maps to a photo image of the student that is accessible to WebDB. Instead of pointing to the filename, you can actually mix HTML code with your SQL and get WebDB to render the image for you at run time.

Mixing HTML and SQL

WebDB enables you to mix HTML command syntax in with SQL when you are building queries. This feature enables you to provide some extra display formatting for your data that blends nicely with standard HTML formatting.

1. Return to the Manage Component page and edit your dynamic page one more time.
2. Modify the second SQL statement to use the code shown in Listing 12-4.

Listing 12-4: Mixing SQL and HTML code

```
<ORACLE>select firstname, lastname, classyr, gender,'<IMG
src=/netu/'||photo||'>' photo from netu.ugrads order by
classyr</ORACLE>
```

The critical change is highlighted in bold text. Instead of selecting just the filename as a text string, you are building an HTML IMAGE tag using some HTML code along with the value of the PHOTO field. Each UGRADS student has a pointer to a picture file that is stored within the database as a text field. The actual file is stored outside the database, but it could just as easily be stored inside the database. For each record, you are building an IMAGE tag that looks like the following snippet of HTML code:

```
<IMG SRC=/netu/u1001.gif>
```

When the browser processes this string, it generates an image link instead of the text.

Oracle provides a set of prebuilt functions that can generate complicated HTML syntax for you quickly and easily. Chapter 24 provides a detailed look at these utilities, which can be used inside dynamic pages.

3. Save the change by clicking the Finish button and then run the modified query using the Run link to display results, as shown in Figure 12-11.

This time when the query executes, the filename string is converted into the HTML IMAGE tag format and the browser displays the actual photo file for each student instead of displaying just plain text. Part of the power of using dynamic pages is that you are free to build HTML code *around* your SQL statements and produce very powerful, dynamic HTML code in the process.

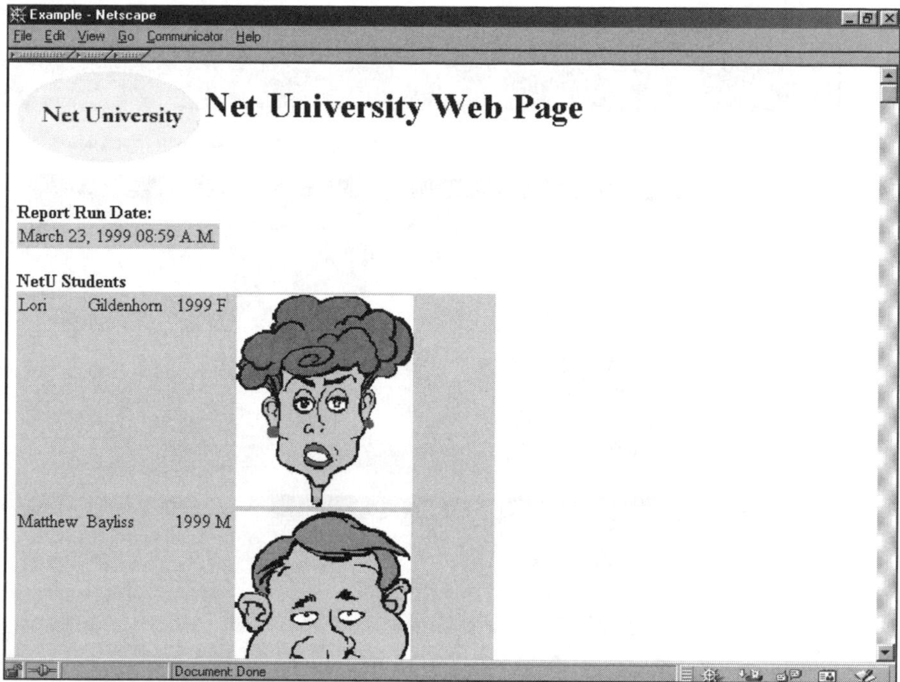

Figure 12-11: SQL output with advanced formatting

Despite this additional flexibility, dynamic pages behave in as consistent a fashion as the other content wizards in all other regards. WebDB provides a Manage Component panel for Dynamic Pages and you can set security, manage versions, and import and export pages just as you can with any other component.

Frame Drivers

WebDB provides an additional component builder that enables you to work more closely with HTML in the form of the frame driver. The frame driver enables you to create dual-paned windows based on the HTML frames extension that was pioneered by Netscape. Frames provide you with finer a level of control over the display of your components. Frames can be built using new components that are created along with the frame objects themselves, or they can be used to manipulate *existing* objects in a new way.

1. Use the Frame Drivers menu choice in the WebDB development menu bar to locate the Frame Driver Wizard. Click the Frame Drivers menu link to navigate to the main page of the Frame Driver Wizard as shown in Figure 12-12.

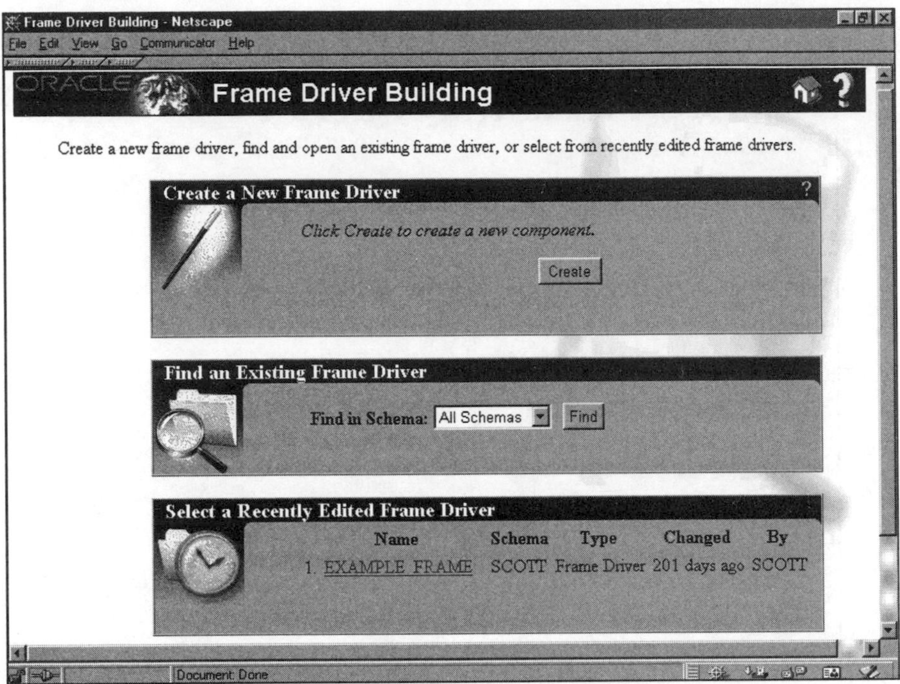

Figure 12-12: Frame Driver Wizard page

The main Frame Driver page offers three panels just like any of the other component builders. The top panel enables you to create new frames, the middle panel is used to find and edit existing frames, and the bottom panel lists the most recently edited frame objects.

2. Use the Create button to create a new frame.

The secondary panel of the wizard (shown in Figure 12-13) enables you to select an owner name for the forthcoming frame. As with the Dynamic Pages Wizard, the list of available schemas is built using the list of schemas in which your current logon is permitted to build. The frame driver name follows the same naming conventions and restrictions as any of the other component builders.

3. Select NETU as the owner of the new frame driver.
4. Enter the following name for the new frame: **ch12_fdr_example1**.
5. Click the Next arrow to continue.

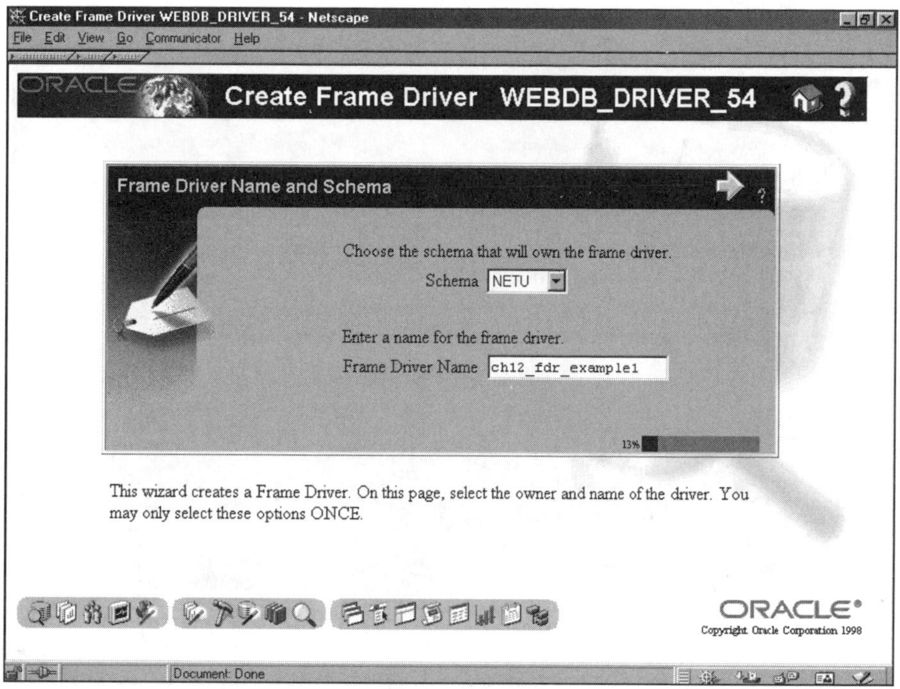

Figure 12-13: Frame Driver Name and Schema page

The main task in designing a frame is to build an SQL query that serves as the driving force for the frame. You may be familiar with building static HTML pages using frames. This is typically a fairly detailed but static process. You design a frame set and then you load pages into the frames. The frame driver is designed to automate this process by driving detailed frames from database data contained in the master frame. Figure 12-14 shows the basic components of the SQL Query panel used to construct the frame set.

The key to the frame object is a formatted query that is entered into the main text area. The SQL query is built using two columns that must be coded in a specialized format. WebDB frames are designed to be two-panel frames, and the SQL query columns map one to one with the two frames. From WebDB's perspective, the first frame in the frame set is considered to be the driving frame, and it maps to the first column in the SQL query. The column values in this frame drive the results in the second frame.

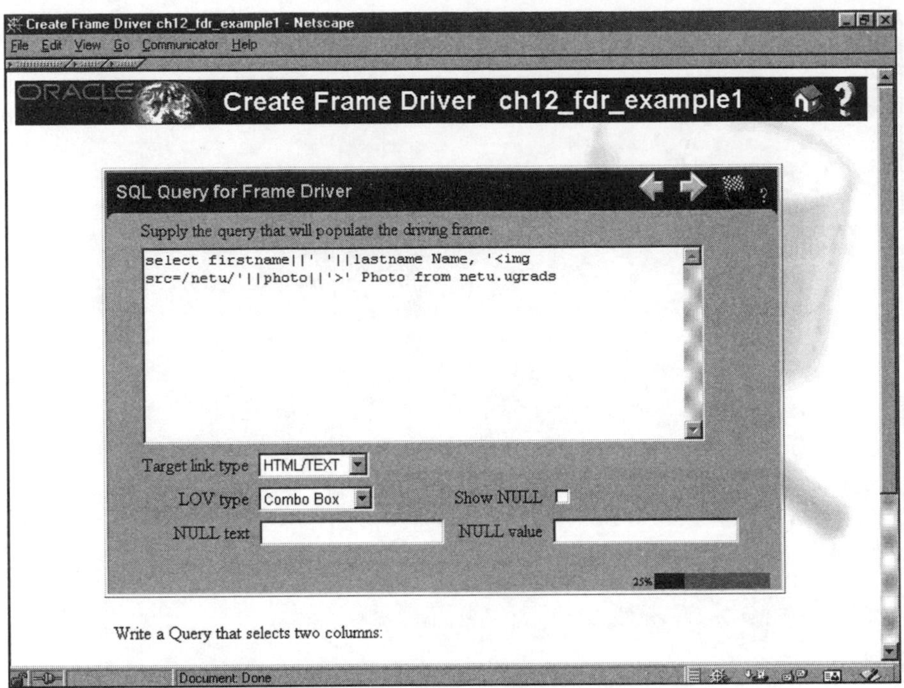

Figure 12-14: Frame Driver Query panel

The second frame in the set is the result frame, and the data that is displayed in the result frame is built by the data in the second column. You can think of this combination as a type of master- detail display with values in the master controlling the display of data in the detail frame. If you have previously used a WebDB report or form object to link to a second report or form, then you have the basic idea of what the frame driver is designed to do. The difference is that with the frame driver, both the parent and the child can be displayed in a *single* window. Consider the SQL query in Listing 12-5.

Listing 12-5: **Frame driver query format**

```
select firstname||' '||lastname Name, '<img
src=/netu/'||photo||'>' Photo from netu.ugrads
```

In this example, the first column is a concatenation of the FIRSTNAME and LASTNAME fields of the UGRADS table. The frame driver specifies that only two columns can be selected, but these columns can be coerced using any combination of fields, functions, and concatenation characters that are allowed by Oracle at the SQL level.

As with any long string of concatenation, WebDB requires that you provide a pseudo-column title for any string that exceeds 32 characters. The `Name` string literal is used as the column title for the combination of `firstname` and `lastname` in the first part of the query. For the result column, notice that the string is identical to the one used to display student photos in the example of the Dynamic Page object in the preceding section. As with the first column, the image string is given a pseudo-column title. The remainder of the SQL string uses standard SQL syntax, and you are free to make use of FROM clauses, WHERE clauses, and order by qualifiers in formulating your query. Typically, the first column in the query is based upon standard database data. The second column, however, can take three formats as shown in the Target link type drop-down list box.

The result frame can be HTML/Text, a URL, or a block of PL/SQL code. The simplest result frame format is the HTML/Text display. If the second column of data returns textual data or data that is mixed with HTML syntax, then the frame is considered to be of the type HTML/Text. The query shown in Listing 12-5 returns an HTML tag that builds an image link, and is thus considered to be of the format HTML/Text. If the second column points to another object via a URL, then the format of the query is considered to be of the type URL. You may find you need to build a list of addresses that a user can choose from for navigational purposes. In this case, the first column would be the list of addresses and the target column would be a URL that connects to the first column.

You can control the manner in which the first column is displayed by using the LOV Type field. The driver column can take one of three formats: a Combo Box, a Radio Group, or a List format. If you have a large number of choices, the List format is the best choice as it presents the most data in the smallest amount of screen real estate. Combo boxes are appropriate for up to about 50 entries and radio groups are only appropriate for a small number of choices.

The last type of result frame is the PL/SQL format. This format is used to connect to existing PL/SQL blocks that return HTML data, such as procedures that were built using the PL/SQL cartridge in the Oracle Application Server. The last chapter of this book is dedicated to advanced PL/SQL topics and there are several examples of using handcrafted HTP procedures such as those provided with the PL/SQL.

The remaining three fields on this panel all control the manner in which the frame handles NULL values in the database. By default, WebDB does not show null values in the target frame unless you select the Show NULL check box. If you elect to display NULL values, you can enter a constant value in either the NULL text or NULL value field. This text is displayed in place of the missing data whenever the frame encounters a database null value. The NULL text field literal is displayed for null values in the first column and the NULL value literal is displayed for null target column values.

6. Enter the SQL statement shown in Listing 12-5 as the SQL query for the new frame.

7. Select HTML/Text from the Target link type list box, and choose the Combo Box format for the LOV type.
8. Click the Next arrow to continue until you reach the initial page panel shown in Figure 12-15.

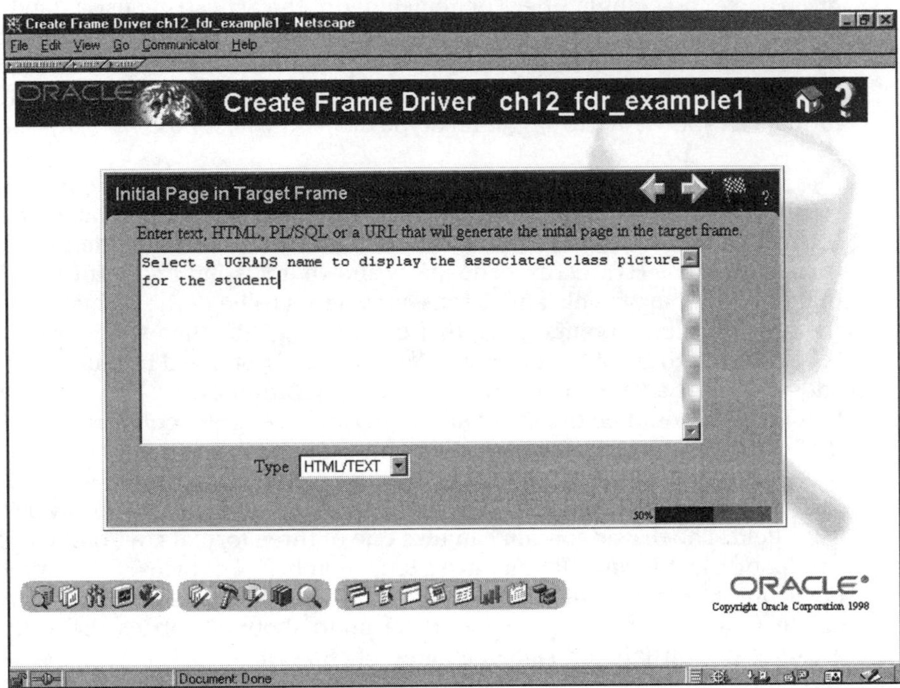

Figure 12-15: Initial Page in Target Frame panel

While the frames themselves can be dynamic, the initial display is static and you are permitted to specify a literal string of text, a PL/SQL procedure name, or a URL. Once you have entered the string into the text area, you need to select the Type for the string in the combo box just below the text area. WebDB has no way of determining whether the string you enter into the text area is HTML, PL/SQL code, or a URL.

The value you select determines how WebDB processes the string of text in the text area. If you choose to enter text, you are free to make use of HTML tags to improve the formatting of this text.

You must be sure that the Type value matches the text in the text area. WebDB has no way of determining on its own what the value that you entered into the text area is meant to be.

9. Enter **Select a UGRADS name to display the associated class picture for the student.** into the text area.
10. Select the HTML/Text option as the frame type.
11. Click the Next arrow to continue.

The next page in the Frame Driver Wizard controls the Display Options for the frame driver. The Display Options panel for frames serves the same purpose as with the Display Options panel in the other component wizards, but the choices are different, as shown in Figure 12-16.

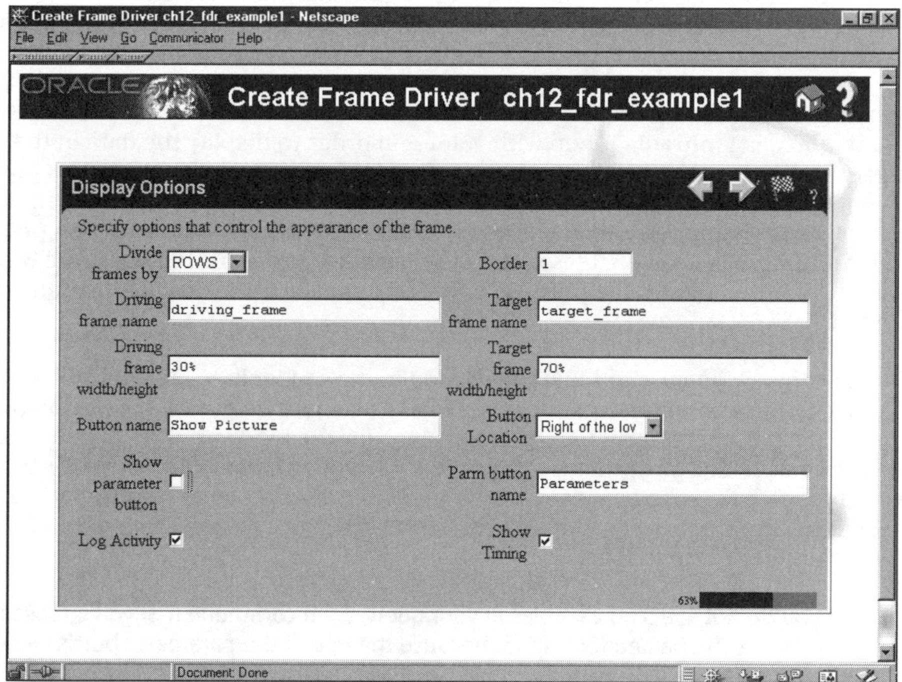

Figure 12-16: Display Options panel

The first choice is the basic layout of the frame set. You can choose between ROWS and COLS. Frames that are ROW-oriented show the driving frame on top and the result frame on bottom. Alternatively, frames that are divided as COLS display the driving frame to the left as a column and the result frame to the right as the column. You can set the width of the border between the two frames by entering larger integer values for the Border field. In order to address frames directly and display pages in a specific frame, you are required to provide a name for each frame. WebDB names the two frames for you automatically and you are not required to change the default names.

If you plan on nesting frame drivers, we recommend that you give the two frames more meaningful names (that match the frame driver name) in order to make them consistent with the naming conventions of your overall application.

WebDB expects that most of the data will actually appear in the target frame, and it allocates a larger amount of screen real estate to the target frame. You can change the default weighting by entering a specific value as either a percentage or as an absolute point size. Percentages must range from 1 to 99 and must be followed by the percent (%) character. Absolute values are entered as integers followed by the string "pt". If the frames are aligned as rows, then the setting determines the height of the frame. If the frames are displayed as columns, then the setting determines the width of the respective columns. WebDB assumes that the value that you enter is a percentage if you do not specify either the percent character or the point-size character (pt).

When the frame loads, WebDB selects the data in the first column and fills the combo box, list, or radio group with values. In order to display the data in the target frame, the end user is required to select a value in the driving frame. In order to minimize unnecessary processing, WebDB does not build the target when the user selects a value. Rather, the user is required to select a value and then press a submit button. WebDB enables you to set the label for the button using the Button Name field. You can set the position of the button using the Button Location combo box.

The SQL query you use to build the driving frame can include bind variables. If you choose to make use of bind variables, WebDB provides an additional button that displays a parameter form for entering values for the bind variables at run time. WebDB makes this an optional choice, because you can pass the values for bind variables as link arguments. If you wish to display the parameter button, you must select the Show parameter button check box, and you can enter a custom label for the parameter button as well.

If you do not use bind variables in your query, we recommend that you choose not to display the parameter button, because the use of the parameter button results in a blank page.

12. Divide the frame using ROWS and change the height percentages to 30% and 70% for the source and target.
13. Change the label of the button name to **Show Picture**.
14. Deselect the Show parameter button check box.
15. Click the Next arrow to continue.

Frame drivers also support the familiar Text Options panel shown in Figure 12-17.

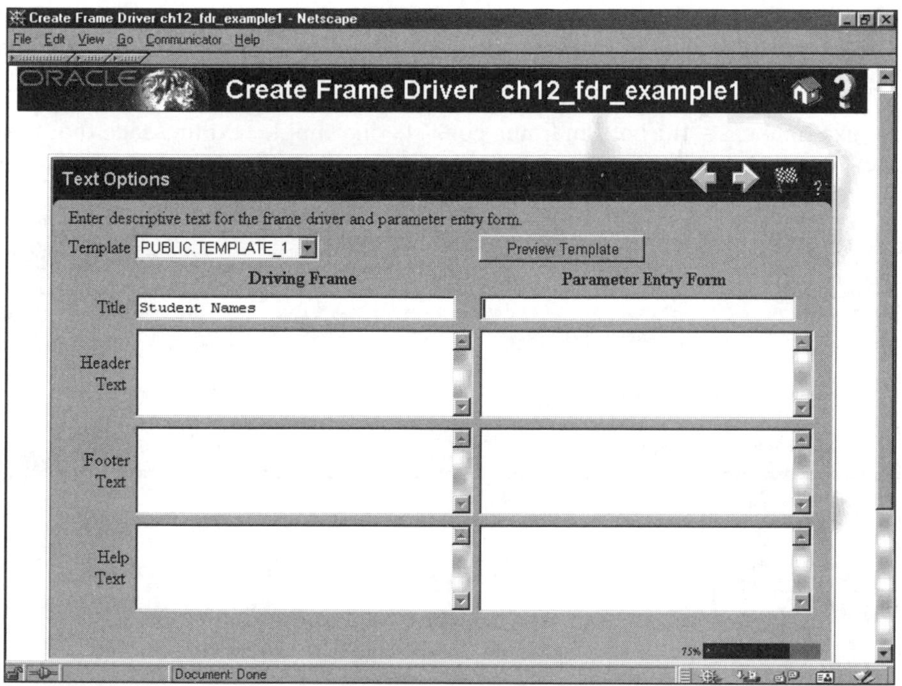

Figure 12-17: The Text Options panel

Text options within frame drivers only apply to the driving frame. You can choose a template, and set titles, headers, footers, and help text for the driving frame. The Template list box is populated by the templates that have been created within the Shared Component Library. WebDB renders the template only in the driving frame and you may find that your existing templates do not fit in the area that has been assigned to the driving frame. In such cases, you may wish to create a smaller version of the template that will fit in the reduced area. The remaining text fields can be filled with plain text and HTML tags as with the other component builders.

16. Enter a title for the driving frame and click the Next arrow to continue.

Frame drivers support the use of additional PL/SQL procedures that run at various points during the process of program execution. As with the text options panel, these settings only apply to the driving frame. If you wish to make use of PL/SQL blocks in the target frame, then you have to code them into the components that are called by the driving frame.

17. Skip over the PL/SQL options panel by clicking the Next arrow.
18. When WebDB displays the Create Frame Driver panel, click the OK button to save your changes and create the frame driver.

19. Test the frame driver by clicking the Run link.

WebDB displays the frame driver, as shown in Figure 12-18. Initially the bottom frame is filled with the data that was set by the Initial Page in Target Frame panel. In the example case, the bottom frame consists of a simple text message that tells the user to select a student name in order to display the associated image.

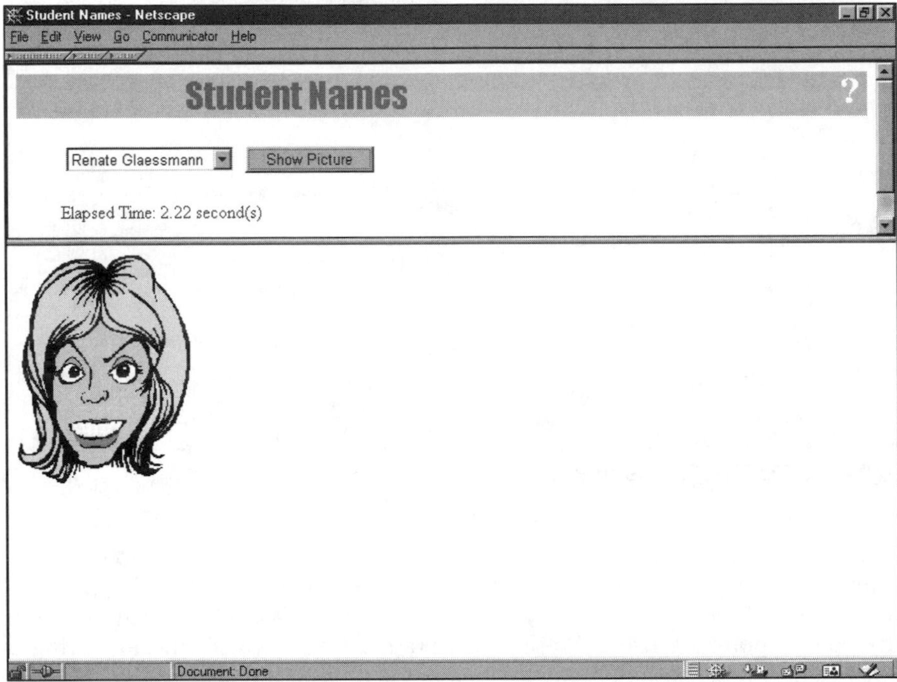

Figure 12-18: Executing the example frame

20. Select a student name and click the Show Picture button to display the bottom frame.

The bottom frame fills with the student picture to match the student name, similar to the way that the image was shown in the Dynamic Page object. The difference with the frame driver is that the user is able to individually select records as needed rather than displaying all of the data in one select statement. Alternatively, you could build similar functionality using a QBE form with a parameter entry form. You can also link an existing report, form, calendar, chart, or hierarchy to a frame by passing parameters from the driving frame to the linked component.

Connecting frame drivers to components with parameters

You can add parameters to the driving frame itself, and you can also link the driving frame to parameters in a component that displays in the target frame.

1. Load the ch12_rep_ugrads report from the companion CD-ROM into WebDB. Return to the Manage Component page and edit the frame driver again.

   In order to point to a component, you need to make two changes to the SQL Query panel.

2. First, you need to modify the SQL query text and change the target column to point to a component, as shown in Listing 12-6.

Listing 12-6: URL query format

```
select lastname||','||firstname,
'netu.ch12_rep_ugrads.show?p_arg_names=id&p_arg_values='||id url
from netu.ugrads where classyr = :classyr
```

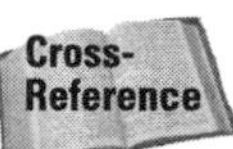

We advise you to read Chapter 17 on creating links to better understand the specialized structure of WebDB's link text.

The link text is composed of three pieces: the component procedure name, the parameters list, and the values list. The component procedure name is the schema owner followed by the object name and the procedure name. Every WebDB procedure, with the exception of dynamic pages, has a set of built in parameters along with parameters for any bind variables that have been defined. Parameter names are passed to the URL by entering the P_ARG_NAMES literally followed by an equal sign, the parameter name, and an ampersand for *each* parameter. In a similar fashion, argument values for the parameters are passed to the URL by entering the literal P_ARG_VALUES followed by an equal sign, the value of the parameter, and an ampersand for *each* value. You do not need to supply trailing ampersands, but the *number* of parameters and values must match. In addition, each pair of values must be sent in order—first an argument name, then an argument value.

The format of the target link type must match the format of the query. If you change the query to link to a component, then you must change the target link type to the URL setting. The drop-down list box setting for the link type must match the actual link. For example, if the page links to an external URL, then the target link type must be set to URL. Although you would think that the format would be the PL/SQL setting for a WebDB component, the call to the procedure is actually a URL. The PL/SQL setting is only used if you are calling a block of PL/SQL code, such as procedures that were created with the PL/SQL cartridge in the Oracle Application Server. Links to other WebDB components are considered to be URLs.

3. Change the code for your frame to match the code in Listing 12-6 and change the target link type to the URL setting.
4. Choose the Parameter Entry Form Display Options tab. Figure 12-19 shows the Parameter Entry Form Display Options panel. (You will need to use the Finish button and then re-edit the component in order to see this panel.)

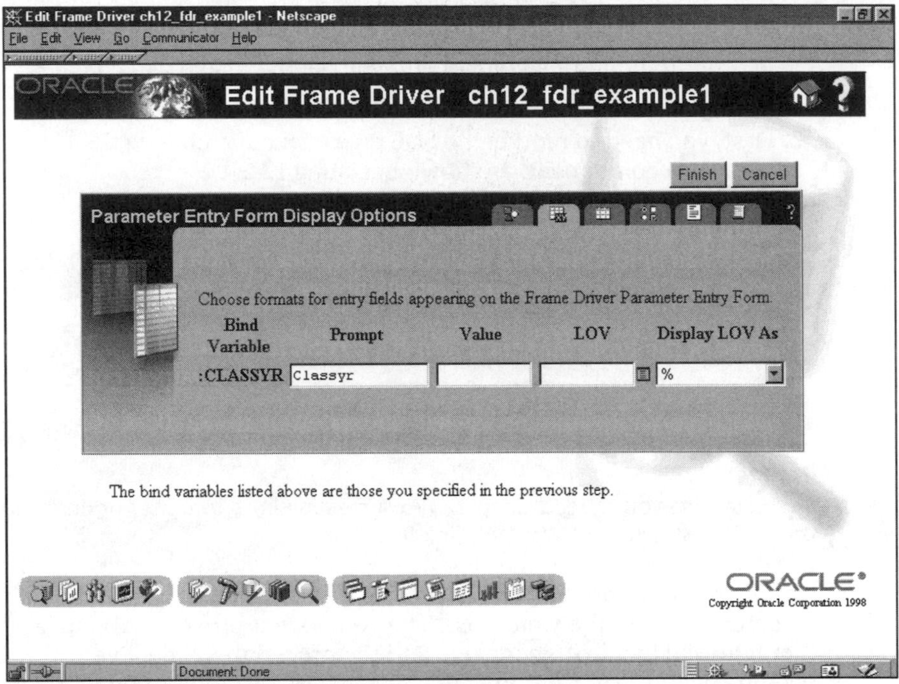

Figure 12-19: Parameter Entry Form Display Options panel

If you add bind variables to the query, such as the CLASSYR variable used in the code as shown in Listing 12-19, WebDB enables you to format the bind variable just as with any of the other WebDB components. If you have created lists of values, these can be bound to the variable as well, or you can specify a fixed value as a default value. The bind variable is applied to the driving frame and it affects the records that are shown as the source. In the example case, the CLASSYR variable restricts the student records to matching the CLASSYR value before building the combo box.

5. Navigate to the Display Options panel.
6. If you have not already done so, enable the show parameter button check box in order to display the parameter entry form for the bind variable.
7. Save your changes by clicking the Finish button and execute the modified frame by clicking the Parameters link on the Manage Component page.

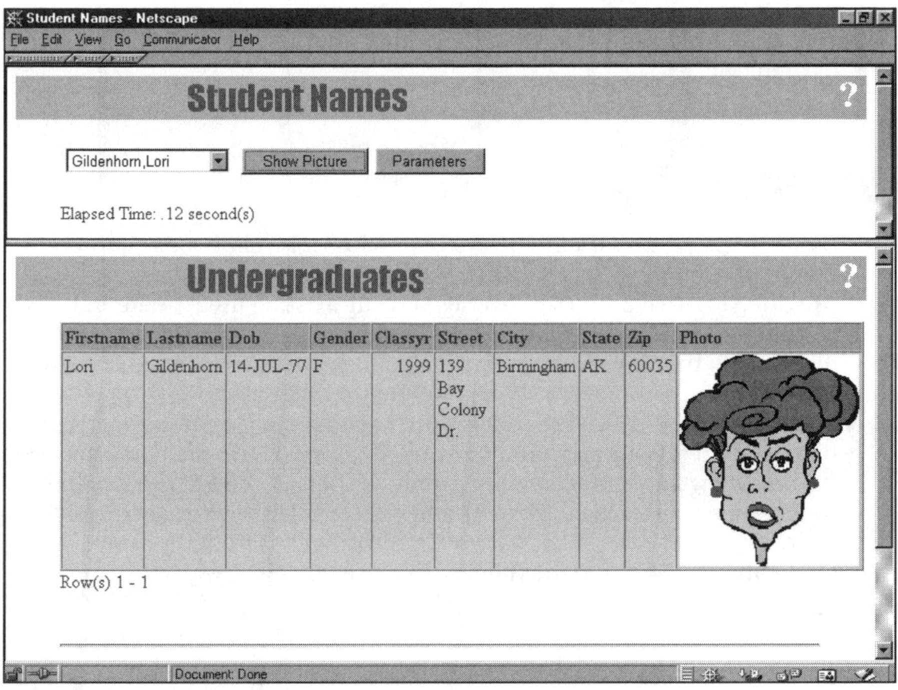

Figure 12-20: Example frame with links and bind variables

When you execute the modified frame object you will notice two differences. First, the combo box initially appears empty, as does the target frame. In order to fill in the combo box, you must select the parameter button and enter a valid class year value for the bind variable.

1. Choose the parameter button and enter a valid class year to fill the list box: **1999**, **2000**, **2001**, or **2002**. Use Run to fill the list.
2. Select a student name and click the Show Picture button, as shown in Figure 12-20.

Upon selecting a student name, the frame driver passes the ID number of the student to the report that runs in the target frame. The report accepts a single parameter that uniquely identifies a record and displays some basic background information about the student along with the same class picture. Although this example report only selects a single row from the database, you are free to build objects that accept multiple parameters as well as objects that retrieve multiple rows from the database.

3. Navigate back to the Manage Component page.

WebDB frames support the standard suite of manage component options, and you can import and export frames, set security options, and monitor the performance of them.

Wrapping Up

Dynamic pages and frame drivers offer a lower level of control than the other component builders you have worked with in previous chapters. Dynamic pages provide you with a tool for leveraging your existing investment in HTML code while working in the WebDB environment. You can use them to render complex documents that include complex HTML formatting and dynamic database data.

You can use frame drivers to link your existing components together in a parent/child format and allow your users to have an easier time accessing data. In Part III, we will introduce you to a suite of tools in the Shared Component Library that can be used to link various components together into a cohesive unit. These shared components will assist you in the process of building consistency into your applications, which makes them easier to use.

✦ ✦ ✦

P A R T

Building Web Sites and WebDB Applications

✦ ✦ ✦ ✦

In This Part

✦ ✦ ✦ ✦

Working with Lists-of-Values (LOVs)

✦ ✦ ✦ ✦

In This Chapter

Understanding the List-of-Values Object

Query Versus Update List-of-Values Objects

Building LOV Objects from Static and Dynamic Data

Deploying a Static LOV Object to Another Component

Creating a Dynamic LOV Object

Advanced Techniques for LOV Objects

✦ ✦ ✦ ✦

WebDB applications offer you the opportunity to use data from your Oracle database both for reporting and for building values into forms. In the days of client/server computing, user applications offered simpler navigation through the concept of drop-down combo boxes and list boxes. These objects provided a standardized interface for querying data by prompting the user with a simple list of possible values. When the user was given the opportunity to update data in the database, these objects served as the first line of defense in the endless struggle for data integrity. The usefulness of these objects carried them over from client/server computing into the realm of thin-client computing and HTML pages. WebDB provides a powerful wizard that enables you to create reusable lists of values that augment your reports, forms, and graphs.

Defining Lists of Values

The list of values concept has been with us since the earliest days of dumb terminal applications. Originally, lists of values were displayed by use of an overlaying, or pop-up, window in terminal-based applications. You can use lists of values to both limit user choices for data entry and make it easier for users to understand codes stored in the database. A list of values could display a descriptive name in the list, but insert an associated code for that name into the database. The simplest example of List-of-Values objects is the ubiquitous table of state codes and state names. An application could offer a simple listing of state codes, but it might be more helpful to offer a list of state names and then have the List-of-Values object translate the state name into the state code when the value is added to the database. Almost every application that stores address information for North America offers a look-up list or list of values display that shows some combination of state code and state name. In fact, many simple static HTML applications that support form-based entry of data provide you with some form of a list of values for state codes.

In general, list of values consist of two separate data elements: a code and a description. You often see List-of-Values objects referred to as *code and description* lists. The code is the data value that is used to link one table to another, and the description is the full-fledged name for the code. For example, in most data entry operations you select the value "PA" for the state of Pennsylvania. The application stores the value "PA" in the record, but the display shows you the full name, "Pennsylvania," when you view the record. Figure 13-1 shows a typical relationship between a code and description table and a data table.

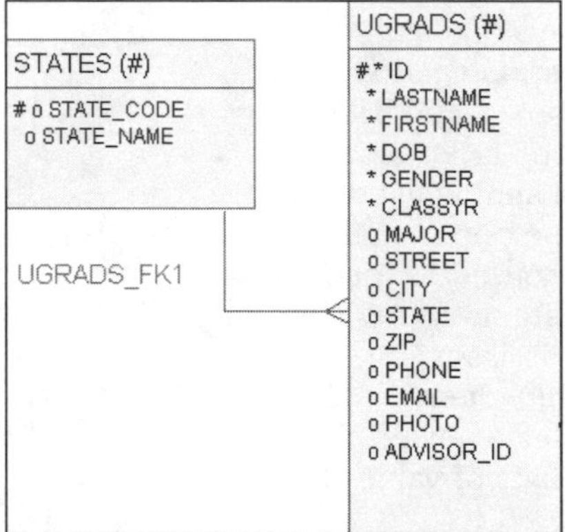

Figure 13-1: List-of-values sample data model from the NetU database

The STATES table joins to the UGRADS by means of the STATE_CODE and STATE fields. For consistency's sake, most applications use the same field name for the code in both the description table and the join table, but this is not mandatory. In many cases, LOV objects can be used to hide the fact that the join table uses a different name for the code column than the associated code and description table. In relational parlance, the code and description table acts as a master table to the join table, which is referred to as the detail table. This makes sense when you think about it, because there may be many undergraduate students for each state in the STATES table. In most cases, your list of values source table acts as a master table for database join operations.

From a strictly database perspective, you can use lists of values as part of a standard SQL join as shown in the query in Listing 13-1, which uses the example NetU database.

Listing 13-1: Sample join query for NetU database

```
select firstname, lastname, state_name from ugrads, states
where ugrads.state = states.state_code
```

Remember that you may need to preface a table name with the Oracle owner for that table if you did not use public SYNONYMS for the NetU database. If you connect to Oracle as owner of the NetU database, you need not worry about providing a preface or using a SYNONYM.

You may choose to run the preceding query using the dynamic pages capability of WebDB or you may choose not to. However, we recommend that you at least test out sample SQL statements using either SQL*Plus or the PL/SQL interpreter. As we discussed in earlier chapters, you may choose to create a single Dynamic Page object for testing purposes. In this case, you can simply replace the current SQL text of the Dynamic Page object each time you wish to test a new SQL statement.

It is not a strict requirement that the source for an LOV object come from a master table, and there are cases where you can derive a list of values from data directly out of a detail table. For example, if you take a look at the COURSE_CATALOG table by using the Browse function from WebDB's main menu, you see the data shown in Figure 13-2.

Notice that that CATNUM column has a combination of both letters and numbers as part of the catalog number. In this case, the alphanumeric field itself contains some additional information about the individual course record — the first three characters of the CATNUM column are also a code for the department that is offering the course. Run the query in Listing 13-2 to see the subpattern in the CATNUM field.

Listing 13-2: Finding the subpattern in the CATNUM field

```
select distinct substr(catnum,1,3) Department
from course_catalog
order by Department
```

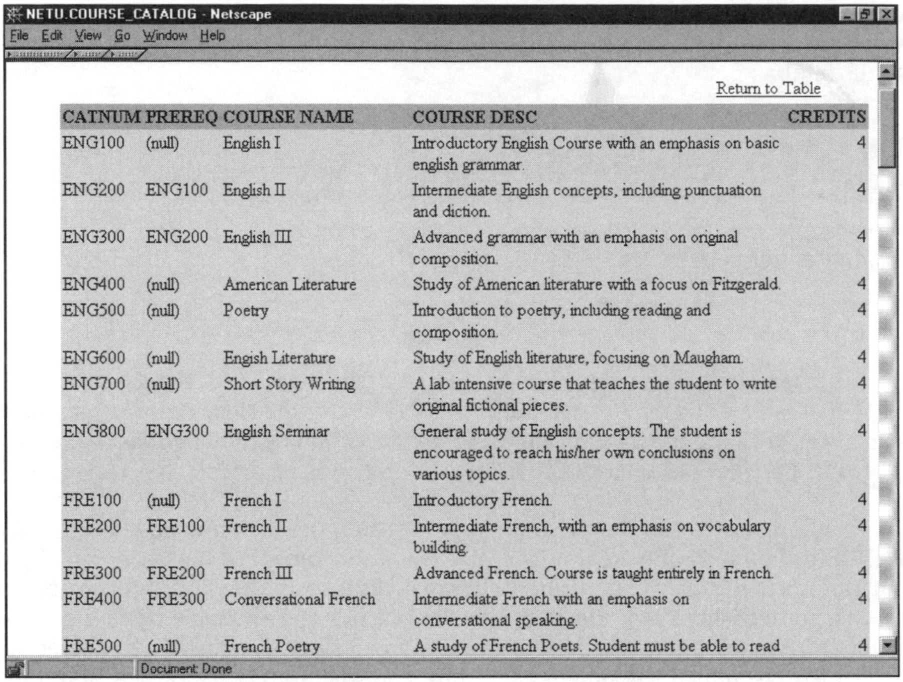

NETU.COURSE_CATALOG - Netscape

File Edit View Go Window Help

Return to Table

CATNUM	PREREQ	COURSE NAME	COURSE DESC	CREDITS
ENG100	(null)	English I	Introductory English Course with an emphasis on basic english grammar.	4
ENG200	ENG100	English II	Intermediate English concepts, including punctuation and diction.	4
ENG300	ENG200	English III	Advanced grammar with an emphasis on original composition.	4
ENG400	(null)	American Literature	Study of American literature with a focus on Fitzgerald.	4
ENG500	(null)	Poetry	Introduction to poetry, including reading and composition.	4
ENG600	(null)	Engish Literature	Study of English literature, focusing on Maugham.	4
ENG700	(null)	Short Story Writing	A lab intensive course that teaches the student to write original fictional pieces.	4
ENG800	ENG300	English Seminar	General study of English concepts. The student is encouraged to reach his/her own conclusions on various topics.	4
FRE100	(null)	French I	Introductory French.	4
FRE200	FRE100	French II	Intermediate French, with an emphasis on vocabulary building.	4
FRE300	FRE200	French III	Advanced French. Course is taught entirely in French.	4
FRE400	FRE300	Conversational French	Intermediate French with an emphasis on conversational speaking.	4
FRE500	(null)	French Poetry	A study of French Poets. Student must be able to read	4

Document: Done

Figure 13-2: Sample data from the COURSE_CATALOG table

The `substr` function extracts a substring from the column named in the first parameter from the starting position indicated in the second parameter for the length indicated by the third parameter. The word following the `substr` function, `Department`, is the name used as the column heading in the returned results. This query yields the following results when it runs from SQL*Plus:

```
DEP
---
ACT
ART
BIO
BUS
CHM
COM
ENG
FIN
FRE
GER
HIS
ITA
LAT
LAW
MKT
```

```
SCI
SPA

17 rows selected.
```

This may not be an optimal technique for providing department information for COURSE_CATALOG records, but you may find this technique in use in your existing databases.

Because one of the strengths of WebDB is its capability to leverage existing databases on the Web, you may find that you have a number of these hidden codes within your database tables. Later in this chapter, we make use of these hidden codes in a List-of-Values object.

Query Versus Update List-of-Values Objects

List-of-Values objects come in two types: the first type provides data integrity and the second type simplifies querying the database. You use data integrity LOV objects during the data entry process to ensure that a user only enters a valid value for a given field. The LOV object in this case typically matches a database integrity rule on the server side. For instance, in the NetU database, each UGRADS record includes address information, and the address information includes a field to indicate which state the student hails from. When you allow a user to enter new UGRADS records, you should prevent the user from adding a new record with a state value that does not appear in the STATES table. An LOV object can be attached to the data entry form in order to prevent the user from entering a value for a column that does not appear in the LOV attached to that column.

The second type of LOV object is more widely used throughout WebDB applications and serves as a means to improve ease of use for end users submitting queries to the database through WebDB. In this case, you can use the LOV object to simplify the query process by providing a quick choice menu for query by example. For example, if you build a query or report against the UGRADS table, you may wish to enable the user to select records by state. By providing an LOV object for states and attaching it to the parameter form, the user could quickly select UGRADS records by state. There are several examples of LOV objects within the NetU data model, and you will make use of them as you move ahead in this chapter.

The only difference between a data validation LOV and a query LOV is where the LOV object itself is used. You can use a single LOV object both for validation and for query purposes, and no distinction is necessary when you create a List-of-Values object. However, in most cases, you will use the LOV object to simplify the task of entering parameters for queries and reports. Table 13-1 shows you where LOV objects can be used within a WebDB application.

Table 13-1
Using LOV Objects with WebDB's Component Builders

Builder	*Validation*	*Query Parameter Entry*
Forms	X	X
Dynamic Pages		X
Reports		X
Charts		X
Calendars		X
Hierarchies		X

Building a simple, static LOV object

You can build List-of-Values objects directly off your data model, or you can build them by explicitly adding the values to a LOV object. If you choose to build a static LOV object, the display does not change when data in the database changes. The values only change if you manually edit the LOV object.

You can find WebDB's List-of-Values Wizard in the Shared Component Library builder off the main Build menu choice. Once you select the Shared Components menu choice, WebDB displays the menu shown in Figure 13-3.

The shared components portion of WebDB acts as a library, storing objects and preferences that can be used across various WebDB components and applications. Once you begin to build more complex applications with WebDB, you will find the Shared Component Library to be an invaluable tool for building consistency into your WebDB sites. Within the Shared Component Library, the Lists-of-Values Builder is somewhat unique in that it is the only shareable component that builds directly off data from your database.

After you select the Lists of Values link from the Shared Components menu, WebDB provides you with the panel of choices shown in Figure 13-4.

The panel WebDB displays has three sections, but you can ignore the two lower panels for now. These panels are primarily designed to help you work with existing LOV objects or search the library for matching objects. You will create the first LOV object for the NetU application, so you only need to interact with the first section.

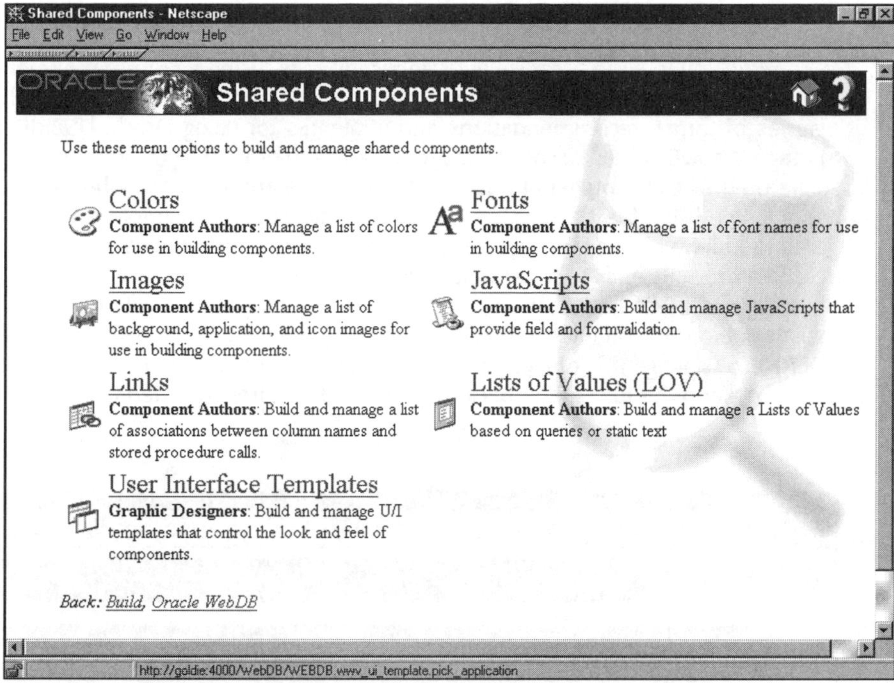

Figure 13-3: Shared Components main menu

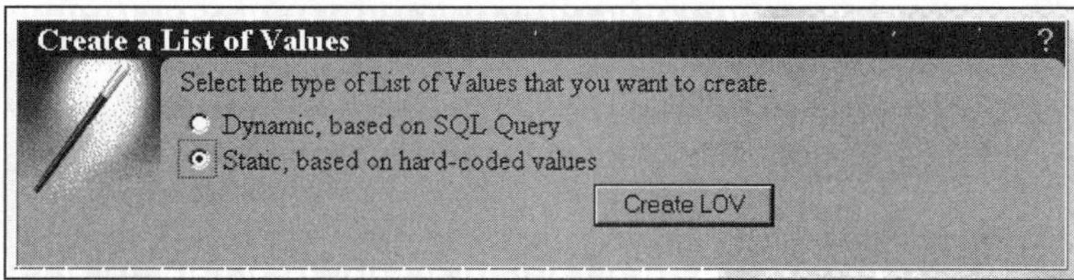

Figure 13-4: Creating a new LOV

WebDB enables you to create either a dynamic LOV object or a static LOV object. The simpler of the two types is the static LOV object, which you will create as your first List-of-Values object.

1. Select the Static, based on hard-coded values radio button and then click the Create LOV push button to continue building the LOV object.

   WebDB presents you with a simple panel you will use to create all the elements for your static LOV object. As Figure 13-5 shows, the top portion of the panel enables you to specify key information for the LOV you are about to create. In the list box next to the Owning Schema label, you select the owner for the LOV object.

2. Select your NetU USERID as the owner for the new LOV.

Tip

In general, you want to organize your applications by using a common owner for all the objects that are part of a single, logical application. In Part IV we introduce a series of formal recommendations and strategies for using Oracle USERIDs to manage WebDB content. LOV objects may be the exception to the rule of using a single USERID as the owner of a set of objects. There are occasions when you may use a single LOV object across a group of applications. For example, say you are going to build your first LOV object to provide the user with a choice of gender values: "M" for male and "F" for female. It is quite possible to use this List-of-Values object across several applications, as it has widespread applicability for all tables that track biographical information. In this case, you could create a single, "library" USERID to manage this object, and reuse it across multiple applications. For the moment, keep this idea in the back of your mind for later consideration.

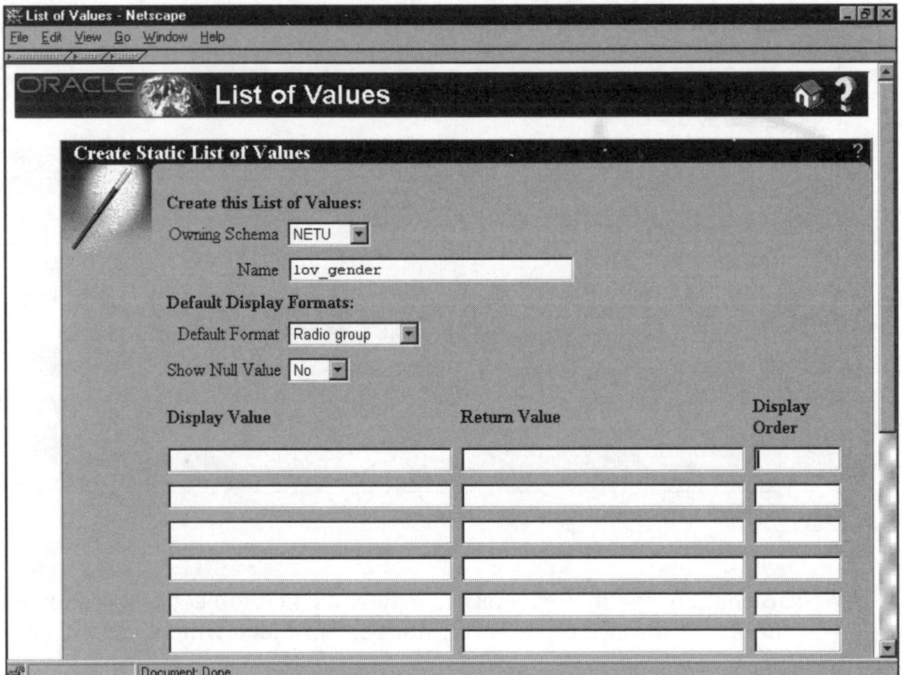

Figure 13-5: Static LOV entry panel

Note

In all forthcoming examples, we use the NetU USERID as the owner of all objects, and NetU as the owner of all tables. If you used a different USERID for either of these users, make sure you substitute your value for NETU in the following examples.

You now need to fill in the name of the new LOV object. Although WebDB tracks objects by type for your user name automatically, we recommend using a standard scheme for naming your objects in order to make applications easier to manage.

3. Enter **netu_lov_gender** as the name for your LOV object.

You needn't worry about mixing upper- and lowercase letters in the name, because WebDB converts all names to uppercase when it stores the object.

After you have named your new LOV object, the next task is to decide on a default format for displaying the values for the list. You have five choices for your default at this point: Check box, Combo box, Pop up, Radio group and Multiple Select. These choices roughly correspond to their equivalent display from the days of client/server:

✦ Check box causes the list of values to display as a series of labels with an associated check box next to each label. The user can select a value by clicking the check box. This display format is typically reserved for situations where you can select multiple values, and you will typically not use a check box display format.

✦ The next choice is the Combo box option, which displays as a drop-down list box. Combo boxes are most often used to display a long list of values, such as a table of states.

✦ If the list of data items you wish to display is extremely long, then you may wish to use the pop-up format, which causes WebDB to display the data in a pop-up window. When you choose this format, WebDB automatically provides a Find function, which enables you to quickly search a long list for a specific value. WebDB itself makes use of the pop-up window extensively for all of its object-search screens.

✦ The next choice on the list is Radio group. Radio groups are similar to check boxes, but the graphic display features a circle instead of a box. Radio groups are typically used to denote either/or–type choices, and are perfect for options such as yes/no, true/false, and on/off.

✦ The final format is the Multiple Select choice, which is similar to a list box style of display. One distinguishing characteristic of the Multiple Select format is that it enables you to select multiple choices from the list at once. This makes the Multiple Select format the ideal choice for query by example panels that can accept multiple values at the same time. For example, consider the course catalog list at the beginning of this chapter. If you wish to enable your users to select multiple departments at the same time for a query panel, you can display the list of departments using a Multiple Select format.

Radio groups and check boxes are appropriate only for limited lists of values, because they use up page real estate with an object for every individual choice. Conversely, the combo box and pop-up options are best for longer lists of values.

Multiple select boxes are reserved solely for situations in which the end user is permitted to select multiple values for a single field. You do not need to spend too much time choosing how to display your LOV at this point, because WebDB gives you the opportunity to change the display every time you use the list of values. It is convenient to enter a value here in order to enforce consistency, but you have a chance to override this choice later on.

For the example object you are about to create, the radio group is the most appropriate choice for the gender field, because there a small number of choices (two) and you can only be one or the other, not both.

4. Select the Radio group choice for your List-of-Values object.

The last decision you need to make on this portion of the panel is whether or not you wish to display NULL values. From a database perspective, NULL values are used to indicate that the data value for a given field is missing. For example, if you did not know the gender of a UGRAD when you entered them into the system, the gender field would be NULL. When you build a list of values, WebDB optionally displays an entry to indicate null or missing data. If you wish to allow users to enter new UGRADS records without entering a value for the gender field, change the Show Null Value option to Yes. One of the rules for NetU is that new student records must have a value for the gender field, however, so in this case you should take the default option for NULLs.

The bottom portion of the current panel offers you the ability to enter static values for your LOV object. The structure you use to enter these values is quite simple. For each row of the LOV, you are asked to provide three values. First, in the text box on the extreme left-hand side, enter the display value as shown in Figure 13-6. The display value is the text the end users see when they use the LOV object. In the case of our GENDER example, the text that users see is either Female or Male. The display value is often considered the "friendly" value for a list, because it is the portion that is shown on the screen when the user interacts with the data.

The return value is the actual data value passed along to the database as the data value for the column when the data is written or the table is queried against. In our example, the database itself stores the values (F and M) in the database for the column gender, so F and M become the return values for Female and Male. Figure 13-6 shows you the display value and return value for GENDER.

In addition to the display and return values, WebDB gives you the opportunity to choose the order in which the display values are shown. The default is the order in which the data values are entered. Notice that the user interface for adding and inserting new display/return values does not provide you with a way to insert values in the middle of a current list. This is due to the fact that WebDB uses straight HTML for its builders, which limits some user interface flexibility that you may have been used to in traditional client/server applications. The solution to this is always to insert a display order value as shown in Figure 13-6. As long as WebDB has a display order value, the order in which order you enter the display/return values does not matter.

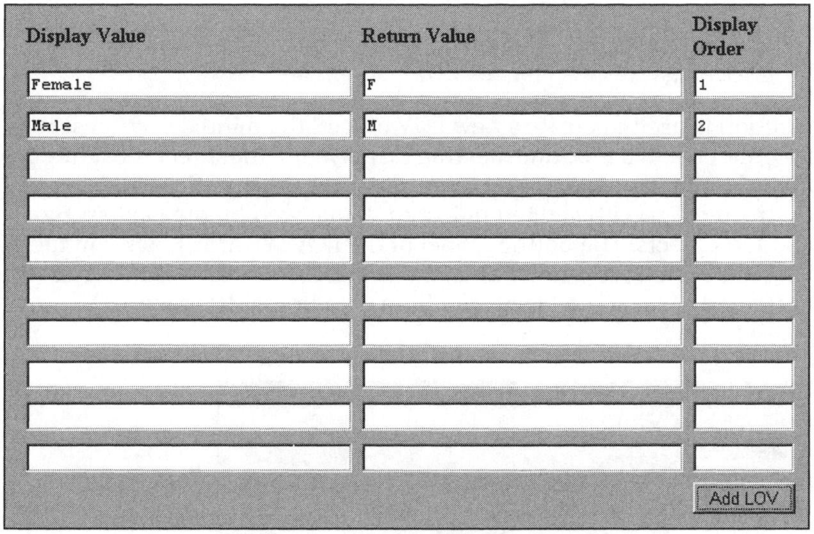

Display Value	Return Value	Display Order
Female	F	1
Male	M	2

Add LOV

Figure 13-6: Display values and return values for GENDER

5. Enter the following values for the static list of values shown in Figure 13-6:

```
Display Value - Female
Return Value - F
Display Order - 1

Display Value - Male
Return Value - M
Display Order - 2
```

6. Click the Add LOV push button to complete the List-of-Values object and return to the main LOV Wizard page.

You can see that initially WebDB only provides ten display/return text field combinations for you to work with. This makes it impossible to use the static LOV object if you have more than ten display/return combinations. However, you can fill in all the available slots and then save the LOV, and when you re-edit the list WebDB will provide additional entry slots for you.

While this may initially appear to be a limitation, it is actually a conscious design decision on the part of WebDB's developers. If you have more than ten LOV entries, you should probably store them in a database table as a dynamic LOV object. Later on in this chapter, we show you a technique for using a single table to store multiple LOV lists you can use situations where you may not feel that you need to create a dynamic LOV.

Testing your LOV object

There are three panels on the main page for the LOV Wizard.

The top section is used to create a new LOV object, the middle section serves as a component finder, and the bottom section displays the most recently edited LOV objects. This last section keeps track of recently created or edited objects by displaying the most recently edited object first, followed by the next six most recently edited objects. The bottom panel of the LOV Wizard shows you the type of the LOV object, so you are quickly able to tell whether the LOV object has been statically created or is built dynamically from data in the database.

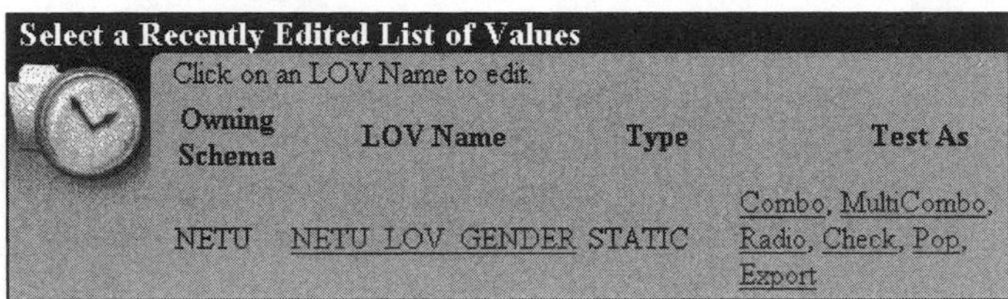

Figure 13-7: LOV Wizard test panel

To the right of the Type field is a series of links that enable you to test your new LOV object as a series of different display widgets. You have a number of choices for display, and each format has its pros and cons. Figure 13-8 shows the NETU_LOV_GENDER LOV in all five possible formats.

The top left-hand corner section of Figure 13-8 shows the NETU_LOV_GENDER object as a combo box. As you can see from the graphic, the combo box features a drop-down arrow for showing the display values, and the values themselves appear in a multiline text box. The combo box is an ideal format for a LOV object that has between 3 and 50 possible values, and it only allows the user to select a single value.

The middle graphic on the left-hand side shows the same LOV displayed as a multiple select box. The multiple select box is shown as a multiline text box and WebDB automatically adds a vertical scroll bar to the right-hand side if there are more than four entries for the LOV. One feature unique to the multiple select box and check box formats is the ability to select multiple entries from the list. You can select several entries by pressing the Ctrl or Shift key and clicking your mouse at the same time. This makes the multiple select display format ideal when you are using your LOV object to send parameters to a query or a report. In the case of data entry, however, it is the wrong format to use, because the database is only going to allow you to store *one* value in the field.

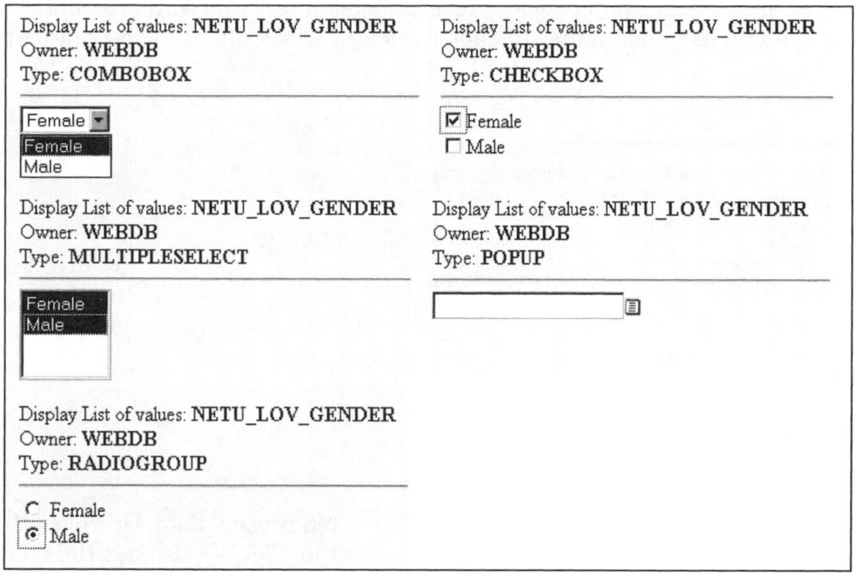

Display List of values: NETU_LOV_GENDER
Owner: WEBDB
Type: COMBOBOX

Female
Female
Male

Display List of values: NETU_LOV_GENDER
Owner: WEBDB
Type: CHECKBOX

Female
Male

Display List of values: NETU_LOV_GENDER
Owner: WEBDB
Type: MULTIPLESELECT

Female
Male

Display List of values: NETU_LOV_GENDER
Owner: WEBDB
Type: POPUP

Display List of values: NETU_LOV_GENDER
Owner: WEBDB
Type: RADIOGROUP

Female
Male

Figure 13-8: LOV display formats

The graphic in the lower-left corner of Figure 13-8 shows NETU_LOV_GENDER as a radio group. The radio group is traditionally used to distinguish among up to three distinct choices. Radio groups are suitable for both data entry and query entry and they give the user a fast visual cue as to the range of values for a given field. Unlike the combo box and multiple select box display formats, but similar to the check box format, you can see all the values of a radio group when you print the HTML page. This is a plus if the user is planning on printing a page for note taking before entering data into the system.

If you have a limited number of choices, but you still want the user to be able to select several values, then the check box format may be the best choice. You can see NETU_LOV_GENDER shown as a check box in the upper right-hand corner of the graphic. While the radio group only enables the user to select a single value, such as Female or Male, the check box format enables the user to select *both* values. This format is best when a data field has a default value of No and you want to give the user the choice of turning the option on. For example, assume that you change the UGRADS table to include a field called PUBLISH_GRADES. The default value at the database level is N, or null, for this field. You could display this field as a single-value check box. If the field is checked, the value of PUBLISH_GRADES is changed to Y, which causes a copy of the student's next report card to be sent to his or her parents.

Finally, on the middle-right side of Figure 13-8 you can see the NETU_LOV_GENDER List-of-Values object displayed in the pop-up format. Pop-up is short for pop-up window, and WebDB itself uses this format for most of its search screens. The display is simple enough to begin with, as it is just a text box with a small icon to the right. If you use your mouse to click the icon, WebDB displays the search panel in Figure 13-9.

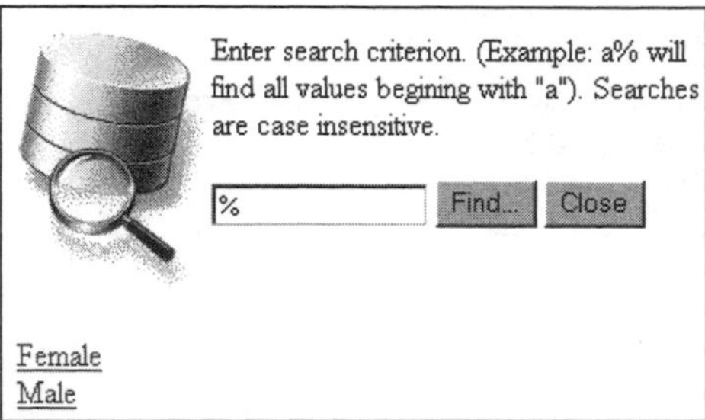

Figure 13-9: LOV pop-up format

Initially, the body of the panel is filled with up to ten rows of data. However, if you enter search criteria and press the Find push button, WebDB displays the complete list of display values that match your search criteria. Entering the "%" wild card as search criterion by itself returns the entire list. You can select a given entry simply by clicking the link displayed as part of the value. The pop-up format is ideal for long lists of values that are generated from data in the database, because you can easily restrict the list to only the values that you are interested in. Later in this chapter, you will create a dynamic list of values using this format so you can see it in action. Because the NETU_LOV_GENDER LOV only has two values, the pop-up format is overkill for this particular LOV object.

Use the links next to the NETU_LOV_GENDER LOV to test the display of your new LOV object.

The LOV Wizard does not attempt to validate any of the *data* that you enter into the display/return fields. The only indication that you have entered incorrect data comes when you attempt to use the LOV object to query or store data. For this reason, it is important to test your LOV lists carefully with other WebDB components before deploying them to users.

Deploy a Static LOV Object to Another Component

The default behavior for the LOV Wizard is to take you back to the first wizard page when you have finished building or modifying an LOV object. As you saw in the preceding section, you can test the visual display for your new LOV object directly from this page as well. However, the real test of whether you have designed your

LOV properly is to use the LOV object with another WebDB object such as a form or report.

Remember that you can use LOV objects for both updating data and submitting queries to the database. The simplest technique for making use of your new LOV object is to attach it to a report.

If you have completed Chapter 5, you may wish to modify the UGRADS report from that chapter. Otherwise, you can load the sample report ch13_rep_1 from the CD-ROM or from the Examples directory you loaded from the CD-ROM.

1. Select the Reports choice from the menu bar at the bottom of the form. Scroll to the bottom of the panel shown in Figure 13-10 and select the link for ch13_rep_1 to begin editing the report.

Select a Recently Edited Report

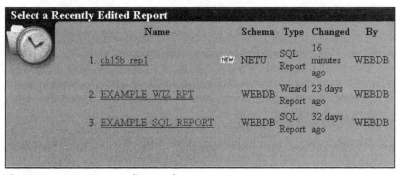

Name		Schema	Type	Changed	By
1. ch15b_rep1	NEW	NETU	SQL Report	16 minutes ago	WEBDB
2. EXAMPLE_WIZ_RPT		WEBDB	Wizard Report	23 days ago	WEBDB
3. EXAMPLE_SQL_REPORT		WEBDB	SQL Report	32 days ago	WEBDB

Figure 13-10: Report edit panel

2. Select the Edit link from the next panel.
3. Navigate to the Button Options panel, as shown in Figure 13-11.

   WebDB shows you a familiar panel that enables you to provide a query prompt for any field in the current report. The sample report already has an entry for the GENDER field, but the details of the prompt have not been entered.
4. Click the icon to the right of the LOV text field.

   This action causes WebDB to display a familiar search panel that enables you to search for matching objects. You can enter the name of your static LOV object directly, or you can use the FIND option to locate the object NETU_LOV_GENDER.

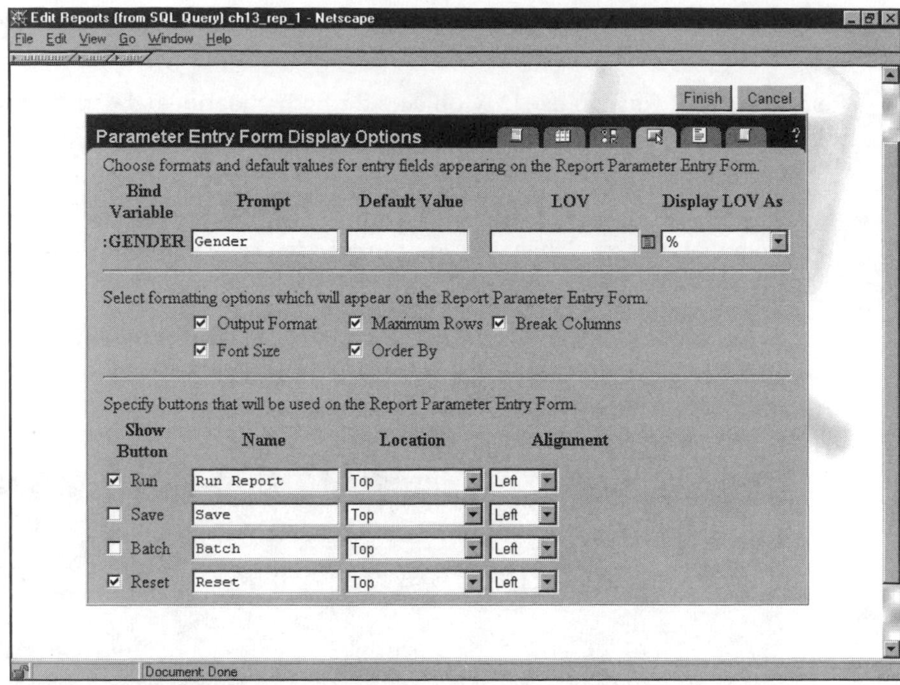

Figure 13-11: Report Wizard panels

5. Click the name of the NETU_LOV_GENDER object.

   WebDB has now attached your LOV object to the GENDER prompt in this sample report. Although you chose a display format when you created your static LOV object, you can override this formatting decision directly in this panel. The drop-down combo box to the right of the LOV field enables you to select a new format for this display.

6. Select the radio group for the LOV type combo box. The panel should now look like the panel shown in Figure 13-12.

   There is no need to view any of the remaining panels, because you are only concerned with modifying the report to use NETU_LOV_GENDER.

7. Click the Finish button to save your changes to this report.

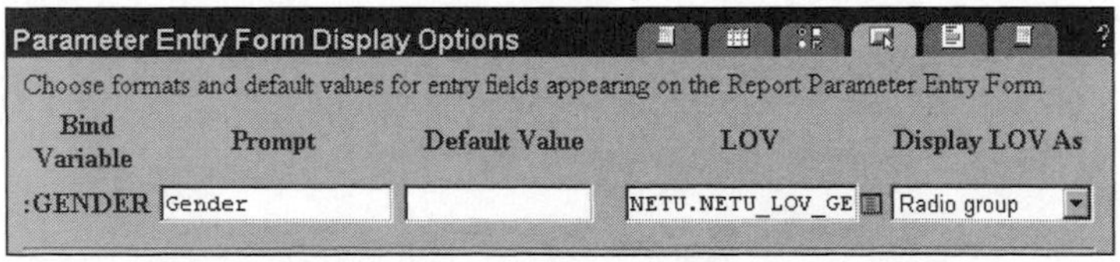

Figure 13-12: Gender prompt with associated LOV object

8. Return to the Manage Component menu.
9. Click the Parameters link and WebDB displays a parameter panel, as shown in Figure 13-13.

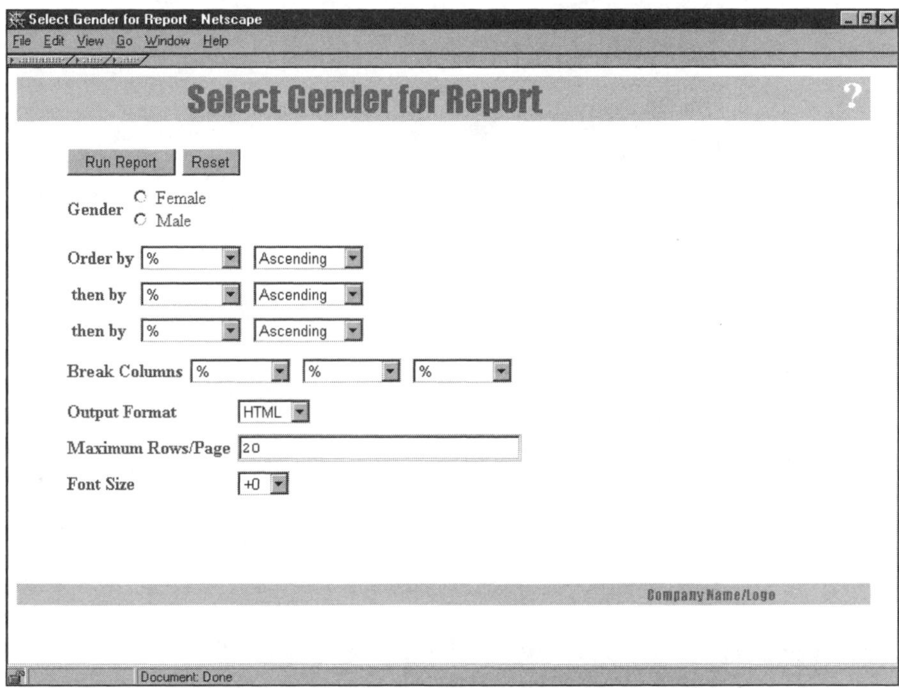

Figure 13-13: Parameter entry form with NETU_LOV_GENDER LOV

Notice that WebDB automatically uses the LOV object that you attached to the GENDER parameter field. All the end user needs to do is select either Female or Male by clicking one of the radio group options next to the Gender field. Once the end user makes a selection, he or she can click the Run Report push button to execute the query and review the results, as shown in Figure 13-14.

The Gender database column contains the values F and M, and WebDB's radio group automatically translates the user's selection into one of those two values for the query. The alternative to using an LOV object is to display the GENDER prompt as a text box. This may not make it clear to users just which values they are supposed to enter for the report. As you can see, the LOV object makes it much clearer to users just what the choices are for the GENDER prompt.

WebDB enables you to provide additional information on the parameter page to assist the user with making a selection. We cover these techniques in detail in the Chapter 6.

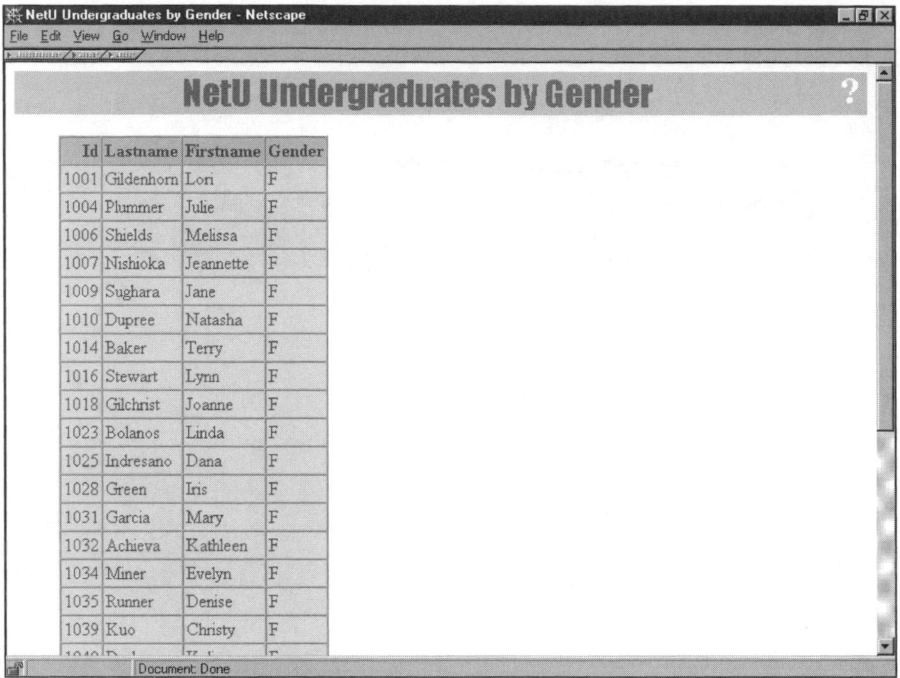

Id	Lastname	Firstname	Gender
1001	Gildenhorn	Lori	F
1004	Plummer	Julie	F
1006	Shields	Melissa	F
1007	Nishioka	Jeannette	F
1009	Sughara	Jane	F
1010	Dupree	Natasha	F
1014	Baker	Terry	F
1016	Stewart	Lynn	F
1018	Gilchrist	Joanne	F
1023	Bolanos	Linda	F
1025	Indresano	Dana	F
1028	Green	Iris	F
1031	Garcia	Mary	F
1032	Achieva	Kathleen	F
1034	Miner	Evelyn	F
1035	Runner	Denise	F
1039	Kuo	Christy	F

Figure 13-14: Gender query results

Creating a Dynamic LOV Object

While static LOV objects provide you with a tool for making your applications more consistent, they do have one major drawback. In order to change the values that are either displayed or stored, you must go into WebDB to change the values. In the case of the NETU_LOV_GENDER object, this is not really a concern, because it is unlikely that you will need to add a new gender value to your system. However, there are many cases when your list of values is more dynamic and you need to add and change data in the list more frequently. For example, in the Net University system, each student record has a MAJOR field, which contains that student's chosen field of study. The value in the MAJOR field joins to the table MAJORS. This table contains the master list of majors for Net University students. To see a list of the possible majors currently in the database, enter the query in Listing 13-3 in a SQL*Plus session.

Listing 13-3: Display a list of majors

```
select major, major_desc from majors
```

You should get the results shown in Figure 13-15.

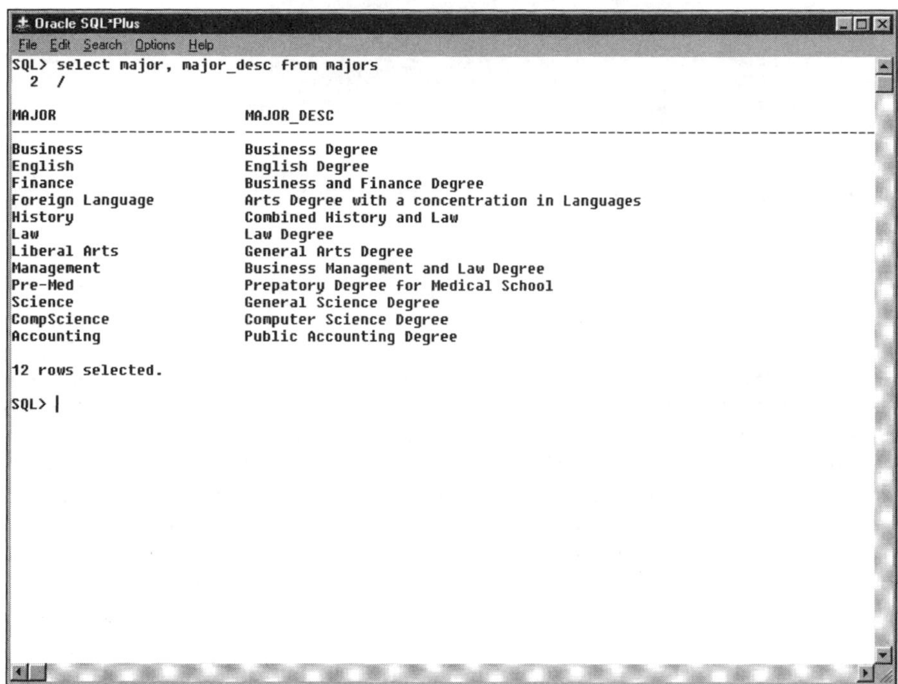

Figure 13-15: List of NetU majors

It is highly likely that NetU will need to change majors over the life of your WebDB application. In light of this, it doesn't make sense to hard-code these values into a static LOV object that you will then have to modify by hand each time the list of majors changes. A simpler solution is to build the LOV dynamically from the data in the database. WebDB offers you the dynamic LOV Wizard to help you create such an object.

1. Select the Shared Components menu choice from the menu bar at the bottom of the main WebDB form.
2. Click the Lists of Values (LOV) link to return to the LOV Wizard.
3. Select the Dynamic radio button for the LOV type.
4. Click the Create LOV push button.

   WebDB displays a panel similar to the one you used to create the static list of values object, as shown in Figure 13-16. The top part of the panel is identical to the one you used for the static LOV and provides you with the opportunity to name your object and select a display format.

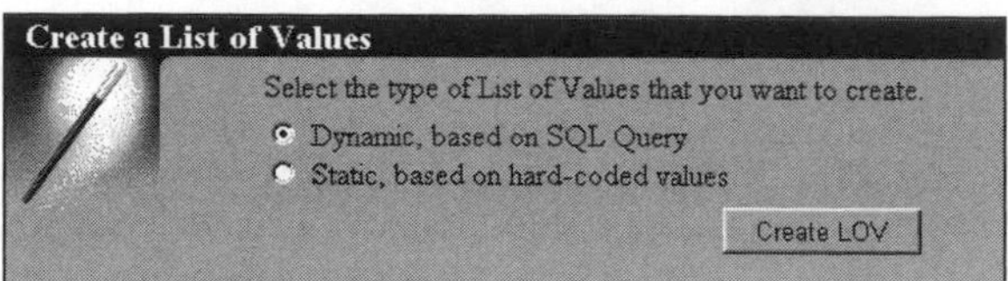

Figure 13-16: Dynamic LOV object

5. Enter the following information into the top portion of the panel:

```
Owning Schema - NETU
Name - NETU_LOV_MAJORS
Default Format - Combo
Show Null Value - No
```

The main difference between the static wizard interface and the dynamic wizard interface is the bottom portion of the panel. Whereas the static LOV object required you to input specific values into text boxes, the dynamic LOV object uses a SQL statement to create the data. The good news is that WebDB provides you with a simple multiline text box in which you can enter your SQL statement. The bad news is that you need to have a basic understanding of SQL SELECT statements in order to build your list of values. WebDB provides you with a sample SELECT statement so that you can see the format WebDB is looking for. Take a look at Figure 13-17, which shows this default query.

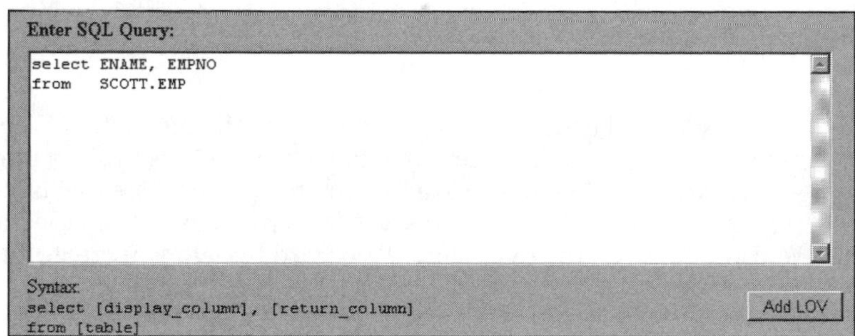

Figure 13-17: Dynamic LOV SELECT statement

WebDB displays the default query structure in two formats. Within the query text box you see a sample query using the default Oracle EMPS table. Just below the query text box, WebDB shows the same query statement in a default syntax format. In order to build a dynamic LOV object, you have to pattern your SQL SELECT statement after the default query WebDB provides. The key to building your LOV SELECT statement is to understand the three different portions of the SELECT statement:

✦ The first element to be aware of is the `display_column`. The `display_column` is the database column you wish to display in the LOV to the user. It correlates to the display column text box of the static LOV Wizard.

✦ The second element is the `value_column`, which is the value you wish to pass along to the database as part of the query or as part of the insert/update operation. The value column corresponds to the Value Column text box in the static LOV Wizard. For example, if you build an LOV against the STATES table, the STATE_CODE (AL, AK, and so on) is the value column and the STATE_NAME (Alabama, Alaska, and so on) is the display column.

✦ The final element of the query is the `table_name`, which corresponds to the name of the table on which you are basing this query.

While the `table_name` may initially appear to be the simplest portion of the query, you must enter your table name cautiously. If you have created a public synonym for the table name within your Oracle database, then you can simply enter the table name directly in the LOV query. However, if you have not created a public synonym, you need to preface the `table_name` column with the Oracle USERID that owns the table. Entering a USERID as part of the `table_name` affects the portability of your application, and you need to remember this if you attempt to move any object you create in this manner between systems or users.

Listing 13-4 shows the query that you should enter for the NETU_LOV_MAJORS LOV.

Listing 13-4: Query text for NETU_LOV_MAJORS

```
select major_desc, major
from netu.majors
order by major_desc
```

Note the addition of a clause that WebDB did not offer to you in the sample select statement in the form of an ORDER BY clause. When you created your static LOV object, you were able to input a display order value along with the display and value entries. If you do not specify an ORDER BY clause for your SQL query, the Oracle database returns the data back in an order of its own choosing, which may not be the order you were hoping for. In general, the Oracle database follows some basic rules for selecting data, and typically you will find that code and description tables are likely to be queried by default in code order. However, it is always best to build consistency into your objects, so you should always add the ORDER BY clause in your dynamic SQL statements.

If you wish to sort your data in a custom format, you may need to add your own display order field to your data table. You could then enter custom values in the display order field and sort your data based on these values, much as the static LOV automatically sorts on the numeric values in the display order field.

Although it does not initially appear as though you have much flexibility in the format of your SQL statement, this is a bit of a misconception. In actuality, you can enter *any* valid Oracle SQL statement that returns a *unique* set of rows in the `display_column`, `value_column` format.

For example, if you only wanted to include values in your NETU_LOV_MAJORS list that actually matched pre-existing NetU student records, you could enter the query shown in Listing 13-5.

Listing 13-5: Query text for NETU_LOV_MAJORS

```
select major_desc, major
from netu.majors where major in (select major from netu.ugrads)
order by major
```

6. Enter the query in Listing 13-4 and then click the Add LOV button to save the new LOV.

Once you have stored the object, you can test the display using the same links at the bottom of the panel that you used to test the static LOV. Figure 13-18 shows the NETU_LOV_MAJORS list-of-values as a combo box.

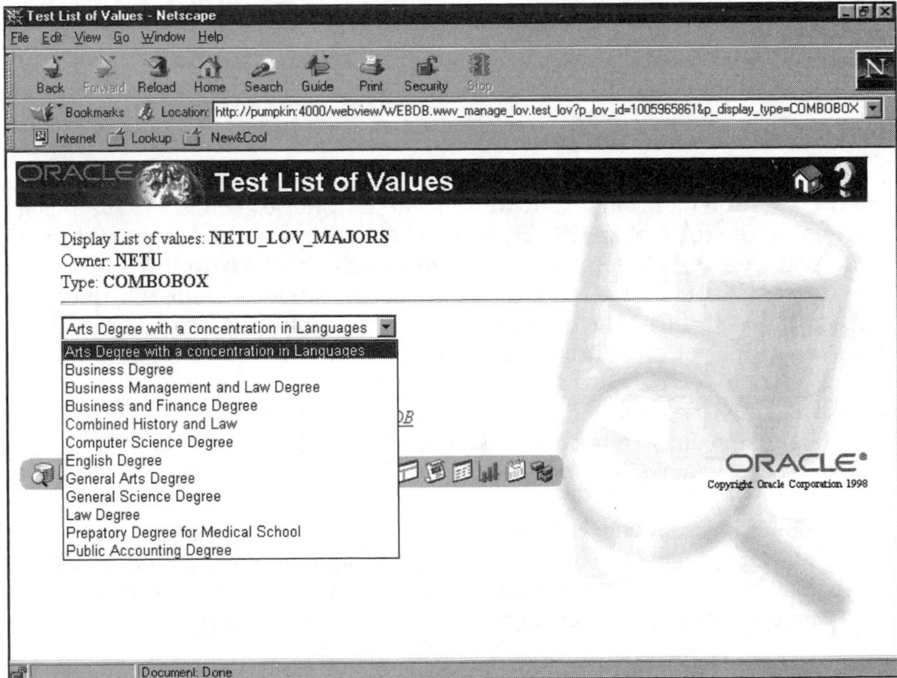

Figure 13-18: Majors LOV shown as a combo box

The value of building this list dynamically is that it is derived from the data in the database, so it changes as the data in the database changes. Once you have a system in production, you will likely provide your users with a set of forms for adding new majors to the MAJORS table. In this manner, the LOV object is self-maintaining, because it derives its data from the database each time it is executed. This saves you the trouble of having to edit the LOV manually each time your end users need to make a change to the data.

For the sake of simplicity, you can test this theory easily without having to use a data entry form for the MAJORS table.

1. Connect to your NETU USERID using SQL*Plus and enter the commands shown in Listing 13-6.

Listing 13-6: Inserting a new record in the majors table

```
insert into majors values ('ArtHistory', 'Combined Art and
History Degree','B.A.');
commit;
select * from majors where major like 'Art%';
```

The preceding code adds a new record to the MAJORS table, and then checks to make sure that the data has been entered into the database.

2. Select the Combo link from the test panel for the NETU_LOV_MAJORS object.

You can see that the new major shows up in the list automatically as the fifth entry. You may wonder why the entry did not show up with the *A*s in the list, but remember that you chose to sort this list by MAJOR_DESC and not MAJOR.

Using the Dynamic LOV to Update Records

In the previous sections you used our LOV object to simplify the process of inputting query parameters to a report. You can also use lists of values to improve the process of inserting or updating data in the database. The UGRADS table is the center point for our application, so you will use this table to test out the NETU_LOV_MAJORS object.

1. Open SQL*Plus, log in as WebDB, and import the script ch13_frm_1.sql.
2. Select the Forms icon from the shortcuts bar at the bottom of the panel to enter the WebDB Form Wizard.

3. Scroll down to the Select a Recently Edited Form panel at the bottom of the current page to the link for the ch13_frm_1 object that you just imported. Click the link and then select the Run link to execute this form.

You should see a page similar to the one shown in Figure 13-19.

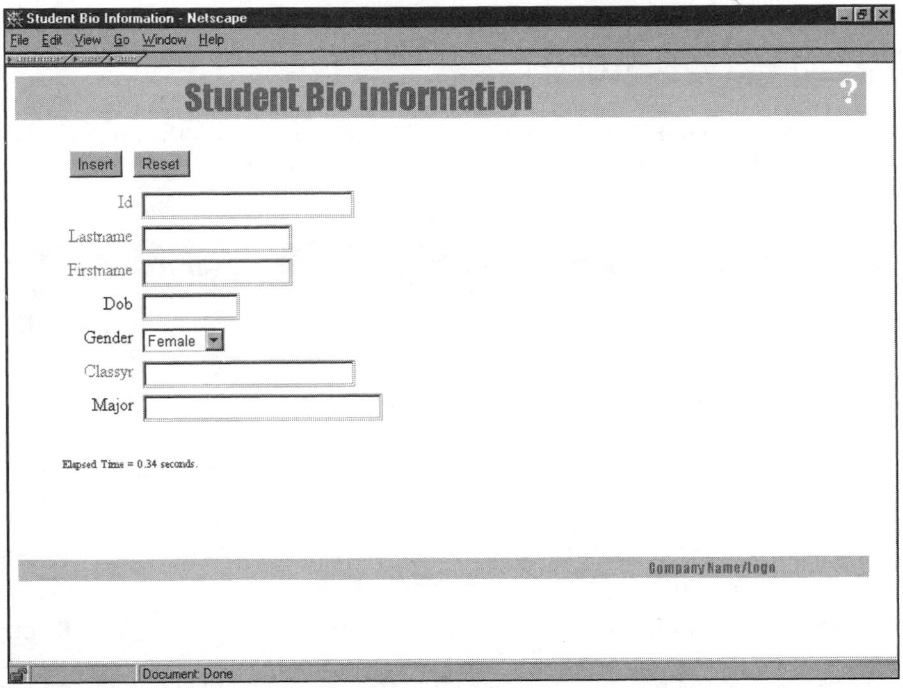

Figure 13-19: UGRADS form for modifying data

The first thing you might notice about this form is that WebDB is automatically using the NETU_LOV_GENDER LOV object you created earlier. The example form was coded to use a list-of-values object for the GENDER field named NETU_LOV_GENDER from the NETU account. If you created the static LOV object in the earlier section according to the instructions, then WebDB automatically uses this object for the recently imported form. However, this sample form does not include an association with the dynamic LOV you just created, so the MAJORS list of values does not appear.

You can correct the problem easily by editing the ch13_frm_1 form object.

1. Use your browser's back button to return to the Manage Component page and select the Edit option. The panel you need to adjust is the first panel WebDB displays for you, as shown in Figure 13-20.

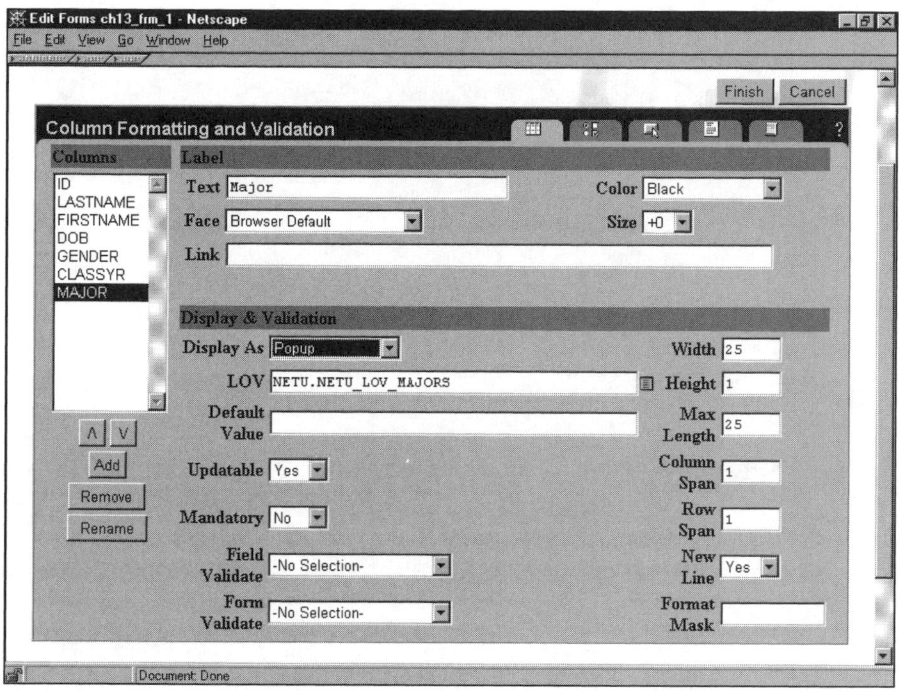

Figure 13-20: Column Formatting and Validation panel

2. Use the vertical text box on the left-hand side of the panel to select the MAJOR column as shown in Figure 13-20.
3. Select the Popup entry from the Display As combo box to set this particular form a pop-up format.

You have already seen what the combo box format looks like, and this gives you an opportunity to see the pop-up display format in action.

4. Click the icon to the right of the LOV text box under the Display As field. Use the Find button to locate your dynamic LOV (NETU_LOV_MAJORS) and click the link to return the item to the LOV field, as shown in Figure 13-20.
5. Click the Finish button at the top of the page to save your changes, compile the form, and return to the Manage Component page.
6. Click the Run option to test your form.
7. You can see that the Major field has the search icon next to it. Click the search icon to find the link for the Combined Art and History Degree and click it to return to the form.

Your page should look similar to the one shown in Figure 13-21.

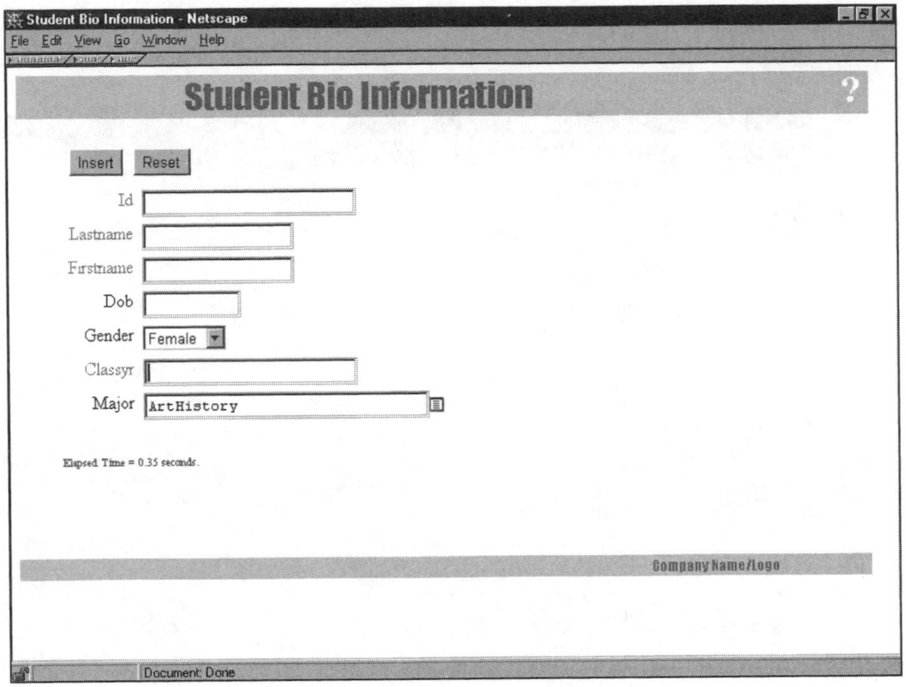

Figure 13-21: Returning a MAJOR to the student bio form

Although you selected the value Combined Art and History Degree, the system returned the value ArtHistory to the page. This is the automatic mapping that happens between the display codes and the return values.

Using Multiselect Lists-of-Values

So far you have used LOV objects to select and modify records. In all cases you have used a single value. Often, you will create reports or queries that enable your users to search for several values at the same time. For example, your users may want to create a report on UGRADS that selects students based on their current major, and your users may want to select several majors at the same time. Fortunately, you can use the LOV object to help users to enter query parameters for such a report.

1. Open SQL*Plus, log in as WebDB, and import the script ch13_rep_2.sql.

2. Return to WebDB and select the Reports icon. Scroll down to the Select a recently edited report panel and click the link for the ch13_rep_2 report.
3. Click the Edit link to work on this report.
4. Click the Parameter Entry Form Display Options tab to display the panel, as shown in Figure 13-22.

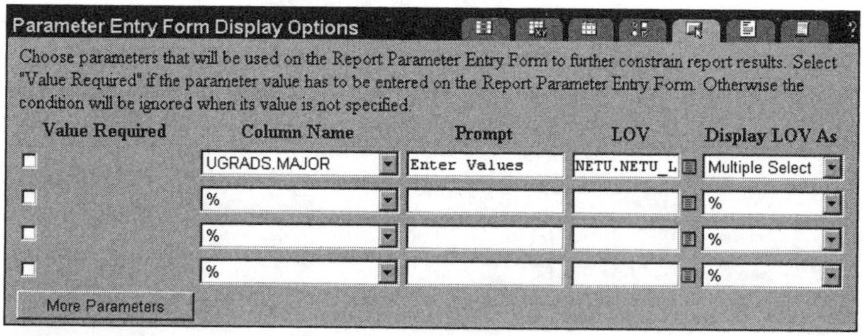

Parameter Entry Form Display Options

Choose parameters that will be used on the Report Parameter Entry Form to further constrain report results. Select "Value Required" if the parameter value has to be entered on the Report Parameter Entry Form. Otherwise the condition will be ignored when its value is not specified.

Value Required	Column Name	Prompt	LOV	Display LOV As
☐	UGRADS.MAJOR	Enter Values	NETU.NETU_L	Multiple Select
☐	%			%
☐	%			%
☐	%			%

More Parameters

Figure 13-22: Parameter prompt for MAJOR

You will remember from the chapter on building reports that you can enter a variety of search conditions for a given field prompt. This particular form is identical to the first report you created in Chapter 5 with one exception. The MAJORS field in the UGRADS table has been mapped to the dynamic LOV object you created in the preceding section.

5. Click the list icon in the LOV column to locate the NETU_LOV_MAJORS list box.

   The parameter engine for WebDB automatically associates this prompt with a value condition on the parameters form at run time. This enables users to select groups of UGRADS by their MAJOR. The use of the multiple select format enables end users to select multiple MAJOR codes for a single query.

6. Click the Finish button to save this report.
7. Execute this report by clicking the Parameters option, which shows you the page in Figure 13-23.

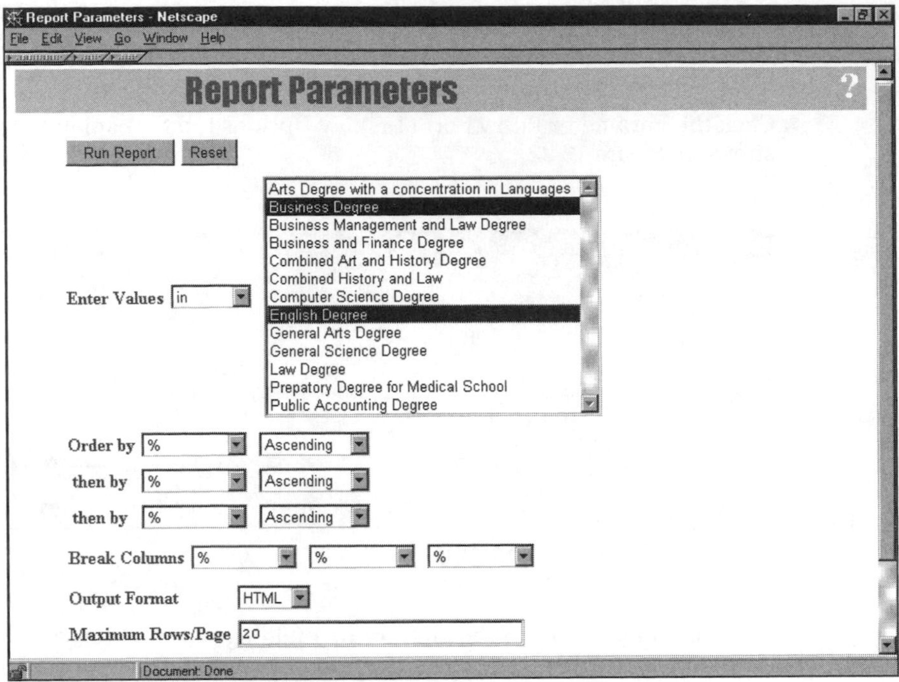

Figure 13-23: Entering multiple parameters

Notice that you can select multiple query parameters by using either Shift+mouse click or Ctrl+mouse click (for Windows users) within the Enter Majors multiple select box. To instruct WebDB to use multiple values in the query, you also have to set the Enter Values string to "in." WebDB uses the multiselected values and the "in" clause to create a dynamic query.

8. Select the Business Degree and English Degree majors as shown in Figure 13-23, choose the "in" qualifier, and click the Run Report button to execute your query. Figure 13-24 displays the results.

WebDB uses your selections to build a multiple select query against the data in the report. Notice that the parameter form shown Figure 13-24 enables you to specify a sorting option. When you give users the option to select multiple values for a query, it makes sense to enable them to sort the data as well. Typically, you will want to have the returned results sorted by the multiselect field to make the data easier to analyze.

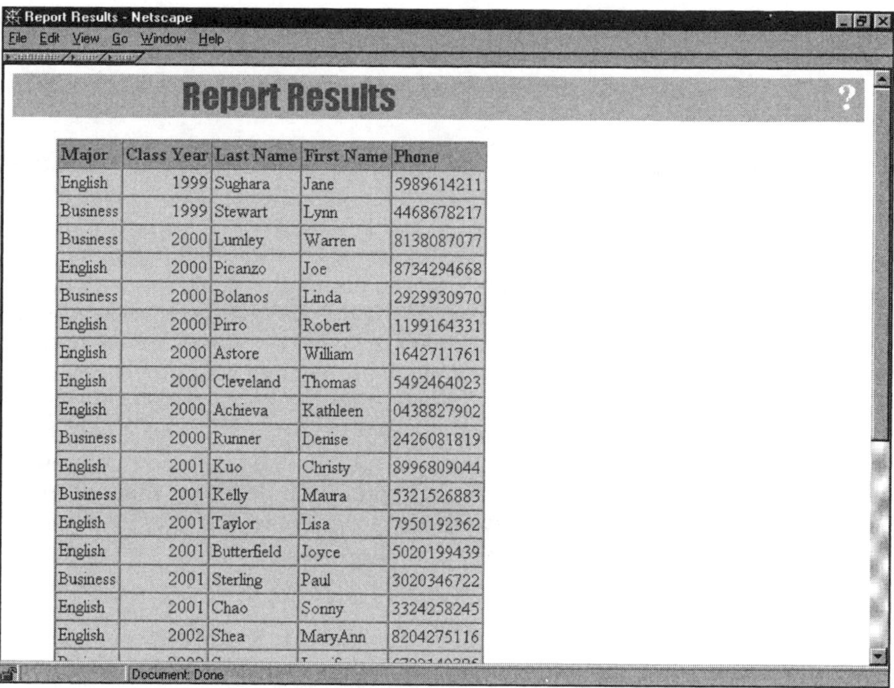

Major	Class Year	Last Name	First Name	Phone
English	1999	Sughara	Jane	5989614211
Business	1999	Stewart	Lynn	4468678217
Business	2000	Lumley	Warren	8138087077
English	2000	Picanzo	Joe	8734294668
Business	2000	Bolanos	Linda	2929930970
English	2000	Pirro	Robert	1199164331
English	2000	Astore	William	1642711761
English	2000	Cleveland	Thomas	5492464023
English	2000	Achieva	Kathleen	0438827902
Business	2000	Runner	Denise	2426081819
English	2001	Kuo	Christy	8996809044
Business	2001	Kelly	Maura	5321526883
English	2001	Taylor	Lisa	7950192362
English	2001	Butterfield	Joyce	5020199439
Business	2001	Sterling	Paul	3020346722
English	2001	Chao	Sonny	3324258245
English	2002	Shea	MaryAnn	8204275116

Figure 13-24: Multiple values for a query

Advanced Techniques for LOV Objects

In addition to the simple data structures we discussed in the preceding sections, there are often some additional LOV objects hiding within existing tables in your database. You can often use these lists to improve your data query process.

The three common techniques for deriving additional dynamic lists from your database are as follows:

- ✦ Derived columns
- ✦ Dynamic query lists
- ✦ Multivalue tables

Derived columns

Derived columns are probably less common than other formats, but they are very useful in building complex applications. Database columns often have useful information hiding within the single value stored inside a column. For example, in the PHONE field in the UGRADS table, the first three characters represent the area code of a student's phone number. That information may be useful information to have if you are planning a local fundraising event for the college and you are attempting to group people by a common area smaller than a state and larger than a city or town.

You have already seen another example of a derived value earlier in this chapter. You discovered that the department heading is the first three characters of the catalog number for each course. So if you were writing a report or query and you wanted to select courses by department, you could build a dynamic LOV object using the preceding query as part of the parameter form. In general, it would be better programming practice to store the department number as a separate field. However, you will often find that you are building WebDB applications on preexisting data structures that you cannot change, and you may need to use derived columns in order to build your queries.

There are also cases where you can find this hidden data in a nonunique column. For example, while there is no table in the NETU database that can give us a list of student advisors, we can derive the list from the UGRADS table itself as follows:

```
select distinct advisor_id from netu.ugrads
```

Derived LOV objects can often improve the flexibility of the applications you write with WebDB.

Dynamic query lists

Dynamic query lists are the least common LOV you are likely to come across, but they are very powerful and worth knowing about.

A dynamic query is similar to a dynamic list of values LOV, but it uses data from the detail table to restrict the query. For instance, suppose you wanted to use your MAJORS LOV, but you wanted to make sure every MAJOR on the list was actually being used. From a query perspective, you may not want to show a long list of values to the user if most of the values will not return any valid records. You could use a query such as the following to restrict the LOV to MAJORS that students are currently using:

```
select major_desc, major, from netu.majors where major in
(select major from netu.ugrads)
```

While this query incurs some additional overhead to build because it has to join to the UGRADS table each time it is executed, it guarantees that all values on the list return at least one UGRADS record. You should generally use dynamic query lists for queries and reports, not for data integrity purposes. This makes sense when you think about it. For example, if you only show lists of majors currently being used by students, you will never be able to select a new major for a student, because that major will not show up on the LOV unless it is already in use.

Multivalue tables

Multivalue tables offer a solution to one of the problems associated with static LOV objects. If you have a lot of short LOV lists, you may not want to incur the management overhead of creating tables in your database to store these values. At the same time, if these values turn out to be more dynamic than you thought, you may find yourself having to change them constantly within WebDB. A solution to this problem is to combine these lists into a single list that can be stored within a database. You do this by adding a third column that is the name of the list itself. Figure 13-25 shows a sample design and some sample entries for such a table.

```
Oracle SQL*Plus
File Edit Search Options Help
SQL> describe multilov
 Name                            Null?    Type
 ------------------------------- -------- ----
 CODE_VAL                                 VARCHAR2(10)
 DISPLAY_VAL                              VARCHAR2(20)
 MULTI_NAME                               VARCHAR2(10)

SQL> select * from multilov
  2  /

CODE_VAL   DISPLAY_VAL          MULTI_NAME
---------- -------------------- ----------
F          Female               Gender
M          Male                 Gender
Y          Yes                  YesNo
N          No                   YesNo
BLUE       Blue Eyes            EYECOLOR
GREEN      Green Eyes           EYECOLOR
BROWN      Brown Eyes           EYECOLOR

7 rows selected.

SQL> |
```

Figure 13-25: Code and description multivalue table

Each set of code and description values is tied together via the MULTI_NAME field. When you create your individual LOV objects as shown in Table 13-2, you use the MULTI_NAME column to organize each list.

Table 13-2
Multivalue LOV Objects

LOV Object	*Query*
NETU_LOV_GENDER	`select display_val, code_val from multilov where multi_name = 'Gender'`
NETU_LOV_YESNO	`select display_val, code_val from multilov where multi_name = 'YesNo'`
NETU_LOV_EYES	`select display_val, code_val from multilov where multi_name = 'EYECOLOR'`

This technique can save you time if you have lots of small code and description tables. The downside to using this approach from the database perspective is that you cannot automatically make use of declarative database integrity constraints. This is because the addition of the third column prevents the primary key from joining directly with the foreign key. However, you can get around this problem by using database triggers to enforce these requirements. In the end, you need to decide whether or not these code and description tables will be dynamic enough to warrant storing them as values in the database.

Wrapping Up

WebDB's Lists-of-Values Wizard provides you with a powerful tool for building parameter entry forms, look-up lists, and client-side data integrity checks. You will find they are most valuable if you create them at the beginning of the project in order to have them available as you create your reports, forms, calendars, and hierarchies. Static LOVs are the simplest objects to build, but we advise you to consider storing your lists as data in a database table. In the long run you will find that your applications are easier to maintain if your code and description data is stored within the database and is easily accessible from outside of program code.

✦ ✦ ✦

Creating WebDB Menus

WebDB applications are composed of different WebDB components. Initially, you may use WebDB to create content objects that can be used on their own, without relating them to other components to form an application system. WebDB provides shared components for fonts, colors, and images to give all the objects in a WebDB application a standard look and feel. While these elements help you make WebDB's HTML pages consistent in appearance, they do not necessarily assist you in the process of providing consistent navigation through an application. WebDB gives you a way to add a standard navigation interface to your application systems with the menu component. Menus provide you with a tool for building navigational flow into your WebDB applications — you can use menus to navigate between WebDB components and external pages. This chapter covers the creation and use of menus.

In This Chapter

Understanding Universal Resource Locators (URLs) and Menus

Using Simple Static Pages with WebDB

Building a WebDB Menu

Building a Menu from Scratch

Linking Root Menus

Managing the Menu

Universal Resource Locators

Web applications are built around three basic elements: Hypertext Transport Protocol (HTTP), Hypertext Markup Language (HTML), and Universal Resource Locators (URLs). HTTP is the protocol used to get content from the server to your browser. HTML is the system of tags that enable your browser to interpret the graphical display of content returned from the server as a page. URLs are the addresses used to get a particular HTML page from the server to your desktop. Initially, most Web applications were built around static, pre-existing HTML pages, which made the URL a fairly simple object to understand. The basic format of a URL is as follows:

```
protocol://servername:port/path
```

Each section of the URL represents a different portion of the location of the HTML page, just like each portion of your telephone number represents a specific portion of the telephone routing system. The first portion of the address is the protocol, which indicates to the browser the transmission technology that should be used for the address. Table 14-1 shows possible values for the protocol section.

Table 14-1
Protocol Values for URLs

Protocol Name	*Protocol Description*
HTTP	Hypertext Transport Protocol is the standard communications mechanism for Web applications.
HTTPS	Secure version of HTTP for encrypted data communications.
FILE	File access protocol that opens files from the operating system in your browser.
FTP	File Transfer Protocol transfers files from a remote system to your desktop.
NNTP	Protocol that connects your browser to shared bulletin board data.
MAILTO	Connects your browser to a user via an electronic mail address.
GOPHER	Makes a link to a GOPHER server.
TELNET	Provides a telnet session to the specified server. A telnet session is a terminal-based interface, typically to a UNIX server or mainframe computer.

In general, you will use the HTTP protocol type most often, because it is the standard communications protocol for communicating between your browser and the WebDB database. You may find that you need to use the other protocols on occasion, and you will find some examples of these other protocols later in this chapter. The `://` characters are required literal characters that separate the protocol name from the server address.

The second portion of the URL is the `servername`, which corresponds to the name of the machine the unique page is located on. When you are accessing pages in a WebDB application, the `servername` is the name of the server the WebDB listener is located on. The exact name of your server may not be readily apparent, so you may need to look in your local `hosts` file, which is located in the /system32/drivers/etc subdirectory under your Windows NT root directory. On most UNIX systems, the `hosts` file can be found in the /etc directory.

You may not even be able to find your host name on your local server machine. In many cases, your WebDB server uses a secondary server called a DNS (Domain Name Server) machine that resolves addresses for your server machine. In this case, you may need to contact your systems administrator in order to get the full name for your server machine. Table 14-2 shows the forms the machine name itself may take.

Table 14-2
Common Server Names

Server Name Style	*Description*
`pumpkin`	Simple machine name that is usually found within an intranet.
`www.pumpkin.com`	Commercial Web server application. Typically, official Web sites use this format.
`fred.server1.pumpkin.com`	Once you register a domain name such as `pumpkin.com`, you are technically free to add any number of "names" to the left of the domain name. Companies often use this format for secondary servers, especially if they have very large Web sites.
`Ftp.pumpkin.com`	File transfer services are typically offered on separate server machines from the standard World Wide Web server.

Common Server Extensions

In addition to the standard `.com` extension, you will find a number of standard server extensions such as `.org`, `.edu`, `.net`, `.mil`, and `.gov`. Each country also has its own server extension specific to that country.

The next section of the URL address is the port number (`:port`), which refers to the specific TCP/IP port on which the WebDB server listens. Most standard protocols such as HTTP and FILE are set to listen on a standard port number. In this case, you do not need to specify the port number explicitly. However, any links that you create *from* other Web applications to WebDB applications typically require you to specify the listener port number. (For a review of the listener's port configuration, refer to Chapter 2).

The final portion of the URL address is the `/path`, which refers to the specific object sent from the server to the client browser. The path portion of the address can be as simple as a singular HTML page or as complicated as a call to a WebDB procedure with parameter values. Later on in this chapter you will see just how sophisticated the path portion of the address can become. For the time being, consider the path section of the URL to be the name of the specific WebDB procedure you wish to run.

In general, you will find that the standard path of the links you build with WebDB are calls to WebDB components. However, when you link to existing Web components or other applications, you will encounter more complicated path definitions.

Using Simple Static Pages with WebDB

WebDB's link builder technology is based upon the standard linking capabilities of browser-based applications. Traditional HTML applications link pages through URLs embedded within the HTML text. For the most part, you will find that WebDB manages the URLs it needs automatically. This is an extremely powerful feature of WebDB and you will find that it makes developing applications much easier than building URLs by hand. This functionality is especially useful when you need to pass parameters between HTML pages, as you will see later in this chapter.

WebDB was designed to enable you to create completely self-contained applications systems. Despite this fact, you are likely to find that you need to link to other Web sites, servers and applications at times in order to take advantage of the wealth of information available on the Web and intranets. Your organization may already have Web applications in place, and you may need to integrate your WebDB site and components into these preexisting Web applications. The most common type of page you may need to link across applications is a static HTML page.

Listing 14-1: A simple, static HTML page

```
<!DOCTYPE HTML PUBLIC "-//W3C//DTD HTML 3.2//EN">
<HTML>
<HEAD>
<META HTTP-EQUIV="Content-Type" CONTENT="text/html;CHARSET=iso-
8859-1">
<META NAME="GENERATOR" Content="Visual Page 2.0 for Windows">
<TITLE>NetU Home Page</TITLE>
</HEAD>
<BODY BGCOLOR="white">
<P><BR>
</P>
<P ALIGN="CENTER"><I><B><FONT SIZE="6">Home Page
for:</FONT></B></I></P>
<P ALIGN="CENTER"><A HREF="netu_about.htm"><IMG
SRC="netu_logo.gif" WIDTH="176" HEIGHT="77" ALIGN="BOTTOM"
BORDER="0"></A>
</BODY>
</HTML>
```

Listing 14-1 shows a simple Web page in HTML source format. You could enter this text into a text editor and save the file with an HTML extension, or you could retrieve it directly from the directory where you loaded the course examples by its name — netu_home.htm.

1. Copy the HTML files from the ch14 directory to a working directory on your local hard drive.
2. Open the file netu_home.htm directly from your browser using the Open menu choice. The page that appears in your browser looks like Figure 14-1.

Figure 14-1: Simple, static HTML text as displayed by a browser

This particular HTML page contains very little information of value to an application; it is nothing more than a simple home page for Net University. However, we can still use this page format to illustrate how to create a simple link. The page is composed of a heading along with an image that displays the label of a URL link. If you allow your mouse to linger over the Net University logo, you see that the browser's message line displays a block of text much like the following string:

```
http://pumpkin/netu_about.htm
```

This line of text is the URL, or address, of the link associated with the text on the page. If you click the text link with your mouse, the browser automatically retrieves the associated HTML page for you. The browser assumes that the page exists and is located in the same directory path as the first page. The browser will be unable to locate the page unless they are both stored in the same physical file directory. Listing 14-2 shows the HTML source for the second, linked page.

Listing 14-2: **Linked static page source**

```
<!DOCTYPE HTML PUBLIC "-//W3C//DTD HTML 3.2//EN">
<HTML>
<HEAD>
<META NAME="GENERATOR" Content="Visual Page 1.0 for Windows">
  <META HTTP-EQUIV="Content-Type"
CONTENT="text/html;CHARSET=iso-8859-1">
<TITLE>Net University - About Page</TITLE>
</HEAD>

<BODY BGCOLOR="#FFFFFF">

<P><IMG SRC="netu_logo.gif" WIDTH="176" HEIGHT="77"
ALIGN="MIDDLE" BORDER="0"> <FONT SIZE="4"><B>Net University
A Progressive College for Higher Education</B></FONT></P>
<P>
<TABLE BORDER="0" WIDTH="100%">
  <TR>
        <TD WIDTH="49%" VALIGN="TOP">
              <P><B><I>Net University is a leading edge
University offering degree programs in science and liberal
arts. Students
              at Net University are encouraged to pursue
academic study using computer technology</I></B></P>
              <P><B>Contact Information:</B></P>
              <PRE>Admissions - 1-800-867-5309</PRE>
              <PRE>Hotline - 1-900-555-1212</PRE>
              <PRE>http://www.netu-university.com</PRE>
              <P>
              <ADDRESS><FONT SIZE="1">Net University<BR>
              <BR>
              1313-7 Ave of the Americas<BR>
              <BR>
              New York, NY 60609</FONT>
        </TD>
        <TD WIDTH="51%">
              <P><IMG SRC="netu_tabbycat.gif" WIDTH="377"
HEIGHT="336" ALIGN="BOTTOM" BORDER="0"></P>
              <P ALIGN="CENTER"><B><I>Net University TabbyCats
- Go Cats Go !</I></B>
        </TD>
  </TR>
```

```
</TABLE>
</BODY>
</HTML>
```

3. Click the link from the page in the browser and the second HTML page appears, as shown in Figure 14-2.

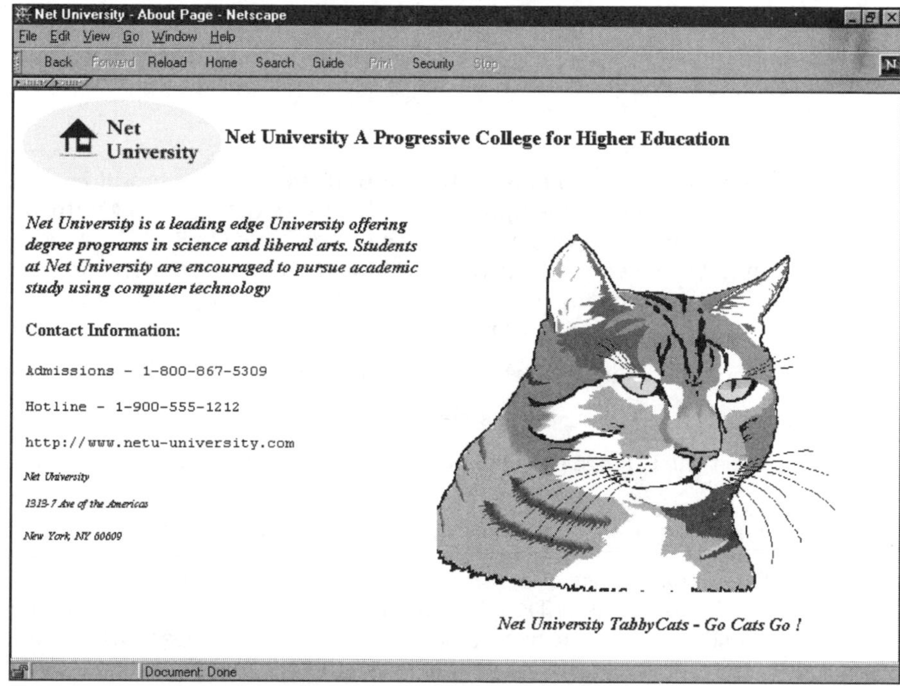

Figure 14-2: Linked page as displayed by the browser

The default behavior for your browser is to assume that a linked page can be found along the path of the calling page. You can override this behavior by specifying a complete URL for the link instead of specifying a simple page name as shown in Listing 14-1. While using the complete pathname as a URL makes it easy for you to view your Web pages, it is not the best way to deploy these pages to your users because it requires you to know the file structure on the machine where the files are stored. A better solution is to deploy these files to your Web server. The optimal solution is to store these files inside the WebDB database and enable WebDB to display them as requested by users. However, there may be times when you need to reference data from outside of WebDB, and WebDB enables you to use links to accomplish this task. You can easily take the two HTML files you created and deploy them to the WebDB server.

Adding a Virtual Path to the System

The first step in adding a simple, static HTML link from WebDB is to build a directory in which to store your external content. If you are combining your WebDB application with preexisting HTML pages, then this directory may already exist somewhere on your server. If it does not exist, you have to create a directory to manage this content.

1. Create a new directory called static_html under your NetU source directory and copy the following files to this new directory:

   ```
   netu_home.htm
   netu_about.htm
   netu_logo.gif
   netu_tabbycat.gif
   ```

   The static pages you just copied into the new directory will be integrated into your WebDB example application. Make sure the directory path you use is accessible to the WebDB server. Once you have created the new directory and copied the files into it, take note of the directory and drive you selected. The next step in the process is to add the directory that contains the HTML page files to the environment recognized by WebDB.

2. Select the Administer choice from the menu on the WebDB home page.
3. Click the Listener Settings menu choice.
4. Select the Change Listener Settings link from the top section of the page.
5. Click the Change Directory Mappings link from the top portion of the Change Listener Settings page to display the panel shown in Figure 14-3.

   WebDB makes use of a particular URL mechanism known as *virtual directories,* which enable an HTTP server to build links based on pseudo-names translated by the server at execution time. While these virtual directories are not strictly required for working with URLs, using them can drastically improve the portability of the menus and applications you create with WebDB. Most HTTP servers provide support for the use of virtual directories, and WebDB is no exception.

6. Enter the address of the physical directory path you created previously in left-hand text box in the first blank row.

Each directory mapping consists of two pieces of information: a physical directory and a virtual directory. The physical directory component refers to the actual file system path for the specific operating system on which the WebDB listener is running. In Figure 14-3 you can see that the physical directory uses a Windows file format. If you ran the listener on a UNIX-based system, you would need to enter the directory path in UNIX file format. The physical directory matches an operating system file directory, and all components must be valid, including the drive and the file directory. Any security settings on this path must enable the WebDB listener to have at least read access to the directory path and the files within the directory.

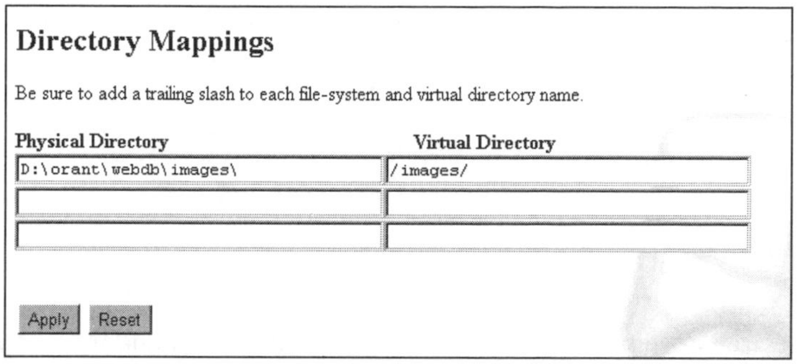

Figure 14-3: Initial Directory Mappings panel

The virtual directory is the shorthand notation by which the physical directory path is known to the rest of WebDB. The WebDB listener automatically translates the virtual directory into the corresponding physical directory for all other WebDB components, including the menu builder and the Link Editor. The value of using this virtual directory is that you can easily move the physical directory and its contents at any time. The only change you need to make is to map the virtual directory back to the physical directory. This insulates your applications from changes to physical file locations, and using virtual directories can save you lots of time when you move applications from development into production. You can see that the string format for virtual directories is very similar to actual file system directory paths, with the exception that the slash marks appear to be backward.

7. Enter the virtual directory name, **/static/**, which you will use in place of the physical directory name. Use the Apply button to save your changes.

You will typically create a number of such entries as a means of organizing your external content. If you had a number of different groups of content, it makes sense to locate them in different physical directories and provide each with its own virtual directory name. Although in Figure 14-4 it appears that WebDB only gives you space for four virtual directory entries, this is not true. As you add entries to the panel and press the Apply push button, WebDB adds new blank lines to the list for you. In fact, WebDB enables you to add as many virtual directories as you like.

Directory Mappings

Be sure to add a trailing slash to each file-system and virtual directory name.

Physical Directory	Virtual Directory
D:\orant\webdb\images\	/images/
d:\college\ora\	/netu/
d:\college\ora\static\	/static_html/

Apply Reset

Figure 14-4: Modified Directory Mappings panel

However, we advise you not to use a virtual directory as a standard way to store external data for WebDB. WebDB's site-building tools provide you with routines to move external content from the file system into the WebDB repository, and they should be your first choice for working with external content. You should use virtual directories when you are getting content from another source (or department) that may not be able or willing to have content stored within WebDB. For example, you may have a group within your organization using an automated system to refresh a set of HTML pages on an hourly basis. Further, they are creating this content primarily to serve a different constituency. It may not be possible for this group to use the WebDB repository to store their pages or modify their preexisting publishing strategy to push content into WebDB. In this case, it may make sense to reference the material from within WebDB using virtual directories.

One additional situation may call for the use of virtual directories. WebDB has a built-in facility for indexing content based upon Oracle8*i*'s interMedia Text searching and indexing technology. Oracle8*i* interMedia Text automatically indexes content stored within the database for you, and access to interMedia's search engine is built into WebDB. While this makes your searches for specific content fast and easy, it does have one significant drawback. Content stored within the database cannot be automatically searched and indexed by external search engines such as Yahoo!, AltaVista, Lycos, and Excite. This may make it difficult for external users to find your content if they are not already on your site. This is true even if you are deploying your application on an intranet where groups of users may be linking from their site to yours.

One solution to this problem is to create a series of external pages to use as entry points to your application. These pages can be stored externally and accessed by WebDB by means of a virtual directory. This way, an external search engine can index the external pages and these external pages can serve as portals into your WebDB application.

Once you have created your virtual directory entry and copied HTML source files to this new directory, WebDB has all the information it needs to use the content.

Accessing this new content is as simple as providing your browser and WebDB with the proper URL. Figure 14-5 shows the standard URL format for a WebDB object.

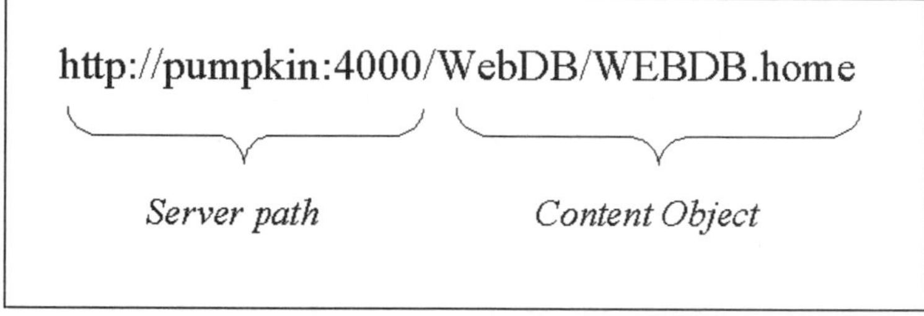

Figure 14-5: URL format for WebDB content objects

The left-hand side of the URL is the server path portion of the complete URL address. The URL address has a content-type indicator (`HTTP://`), a server name (`pumpkin`), and a port number (`:4000`). The server name and port number may be different on your WebDB test machine, and you may have a number of server name and port number combinations for a larger site. WebDB allows you to have as many servers and ports as you need to service your sites. Typically, you will have a separate server for each autonomous environment you build with WebDB. If you install WebDB on multiple servers, you will certainly have multiple server names in place for each of the servers. Because WebDB has built-in version control, it is not necessary to have separate environments for development and testing, although we recommend a separate test environment for large applications and environments.

The second half of the URL address for WebDB is the content object, which is itself composed of two basic pieces: the owner name (`/WebDB/`) and the procedure name (`WEBDB.Home`). The owner name corresponds to the Oracle USERID that owns the particular WebDB installation. The default owner name is WebDB, but you can use any valid Oracle USERID for your WebDB owner name, which you specified when you installed WebDB. The rightmost portion of the content object, the object name, is the most complicated portion of the WebDB address and it varies widely by content type. The object name is itself a compound object that includes an Oracle package name, an Oracle procedure name, and an optional list of parameters.

If you are linking to an external page, you only have to know the name of the page and the name of the virtual directory.

The key portion of the address to understand in order to use your recently created virtual directory is the server name. External virtual directories are connected with the WebDB listener, and are therefore associated with the *server.* If you choose to create multiple WebDB installations, they can all share a single listener and a common set of virtual directories.

If you are connecting to WebDB via an external HTTP listener such as Microsoft IIS, Netscape Enterprise Server, or Apache Server, you may choose to use the external HTTP server's virtual directories capability. In this case, ignore WebDB's virtual directories altogether and use your HTTP server to manage external content. (See Chapter 22 for more details.)

Test using WebDB to access to the static external pages by entering the following URL in your browser's address window (substitute your server name and port number for `pumpkin:4000`):

```
http://pumpkin:4000/static/netu_home.htm
```

If you have connected the virtual directory properly and moved the content to the associated physical directory, WebDB returns the page shown in Figure 14-6.

Figure 14-6: Retrieving a static page from a virtual directory

Your browser automatically associates the linked page to the same path, so choosing the Net University Logo link produces the correct page as well. If you choose to move the linked page to another location, simply edit the link as you would any other HTML page link.

Building a WebDB Menu

Up until this point, we have not discussed building an actual menu with WebDB. The key to understanding WebDB's menus is to have a thorough understanding of URLs, because the WebDB menu builder is entirely based upon URLs. You can even deploy WebDB's menus to a Site Builder site just like any other WebDB component. However, you do not need to create a Web site in order to use WebDB's menus. In fact, the simplest strategy for building and deploying a WebDB application is to start out by building content and menus without creating an entire site. In many cases, you will already have some type of Web application in place, even if this application is nothing more than a series of static Web pages. You can easily create some new, dynamic content and deploy this content to your existing environment by using WebDB's menu builder wizard.

Understanding the menu hierarchy

Initially, the WebDB menu builder wizard can be challenging to work with if you are starting from ground zero without any menu structure in place. While it does provide you with incredible flexibility, the wizard interface does not exactly guide you through the process as seamlessly as WebDB's other builders do. The fastest way to come up to speed with the menu builder wizard is to take a look at an existing menu in action.

1. Load in a precreated menu by importing the file ch14_mnu_example1.sql into your WebDB application.

If you don't know how to import an object, or if you haven't imported the components from the previous chapters, please see Appendix A for instructions.

2. Enter the following URL in your browser window, substituting your server name and port for the `pumpkin:4000` address. (You may also need to replace the USERID and owner name if you used a different USERID for your WebDB installation.)

   ```
   http://pumpkin:4000/WebDB/NETU.ch14_mnu_example1.show
   ```

WebDB displays a menu similar to the one shown in Figure 14-7.

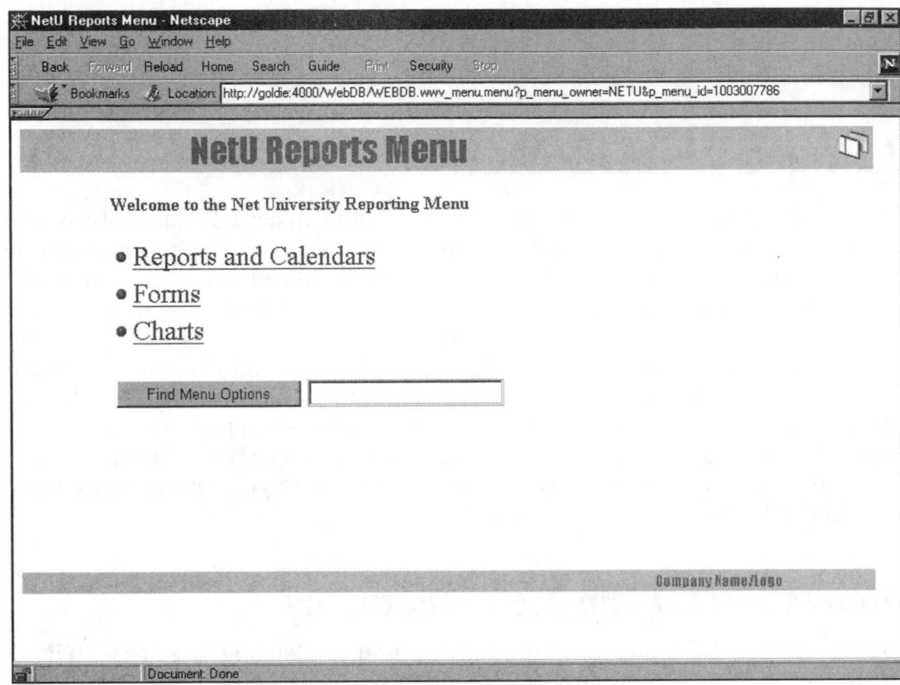

Figure 14-7: Sample WebDB menu

WebDB menus work very much like any other WebDB-formatted page. The template used to create the page determines the graphic display of the menu. Both the header and footer of the page can include different color schemes and fonts depending upon how extensively you have edited the template. Changing the template changes all the menus without requiring you to change the menu itself. This makes it very easy to customize the menus without having to agonize over items such as color schemes when you create the initial menu. The core menu area in the middle of the panel is divided into four sections:

- ✦ Header
- ✦ Menu body
- ✦ Search function
- ✦ Footer

The header is the text area at the top of the page just below the title bar. The header is a block of HTML text that WebDB formats for you as the introductory text for the menu. As with most other blocks of text within WebDB, you can include any combination of text and HTML tags to construct the header.

Just below the header is the menu body, which is the actual link text that creates the menu itself. This body is entirely composed of menu choices in the form of text, links, and images. The menu body in Figure 14-7 was built solely from links, which is the default format for menus. Later in this chapter, you will modify this menu to include additional menu choices as well as some additional text and images.

Just below the menu body is a text box and a push button, which together provide a search option for the menu. Typically, a WebDB menu is a hierarchy of options, and the search function provides you with a tool to search for menu options for all submenus below the current menu. This feature makes it very easy to provide a deep hierarchy of menus you can quickly search for matching menu options. While deep menus appeal to the novice application user, the search function enables the more experienced user to jump to a lower-level menu without having to remember the exact menu hierarchy. This feature is also ideal for situations where a developer has moved a menu hierarchy from one area to another, as a user can find the new location by executing a search from the upper menu. You can use the Find Menu Options search by entering any text string in the text box and then clicking the push button. The search uses a LIKE comparison, so you do not need to worry either about CASE or surrounding your search string with wild card characters. (You cannot perform compound searches, as the search command uses an implied LIKE comparison.)

The last section of the panel is the footer text. Footer text offers the identical functionality for the bottom of the form that the header offers for the top of the form. You can embed text, HTML tags, Oracle PL/SQL commands, and graphics within the footer to provide additional information on a menu.

Before moving on, you probably want to play around with the menu you just imported. Select any of the links in the menu and click down through the various submenus.

Editing an existing menu

Once you have navigated through the various submenus, you can start to modify the menu to get a better understanding of how WebDB menus work.

1. Return to WebDB's home page and select the Menus choice from the shortcuts toolbar at the bottom of the page.
2. Scroll down to the Select section and click the ch14_mnu_example1 menu to begin working with the menu you were recently testing.
3. Click the Edit link to start the modification process.

You will undoubtedly find it easier to begin work with an existing menu rather than starting from scratch. The menu builder wizard is incredibly flexible, as you will see, but working with it is slightly less intuitive compared to some of the other wizards. Once you have chosen the Edit option, WebDB presents you with a panel much like the page shown in Figure 14-8.

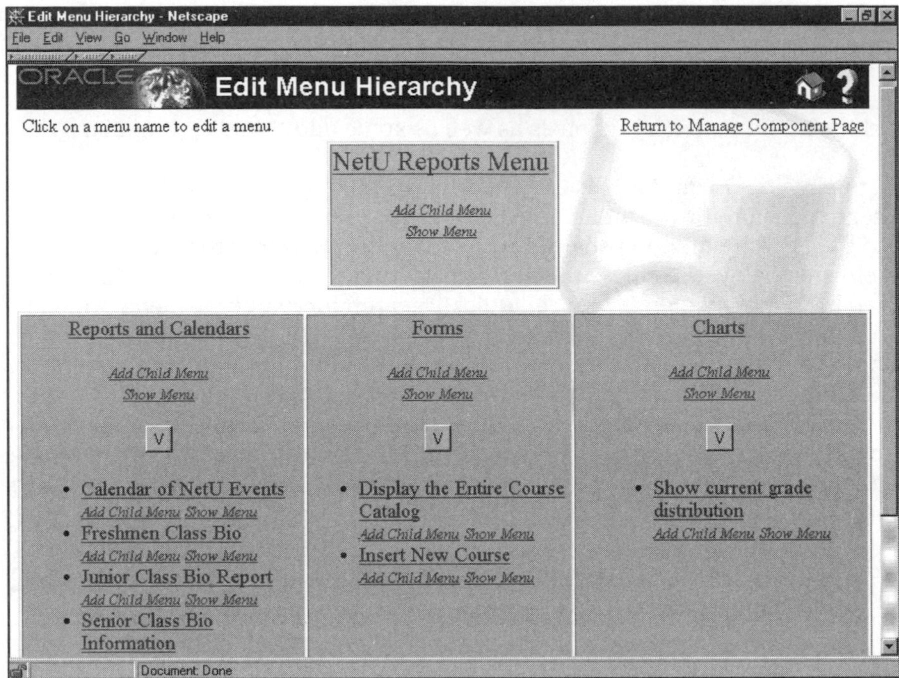

Figure 14-8: Editing the ch14_mnu_example1 menu

WebDB automatically builds a hierarchy of menus and submenus starting with the menu you selected to edit. Although you initially selected only a single menu to edit, menus themselves are compound objects in the WebDB world. Selecting a single menu opens that particular menu and all of that menu's submenus. This is because the menu builder wizard considers the hierarchy of menus to be one large menu object. Combining menus and submenus into a single object makes it much easier to import, export, and manage the individual menus, as they are always carried together as a group.

When you read a WebDB menu tree, you read it from the top down. The lowest items on the menu page always correspond to a URL, static page, or component object, such as a dynamic page, report, form, chart, hierarchy, or calendar. All items above the lowest items are either menus or submenus. In this example menu, there are two levels of menus: a main menu called NetU Reports Menu, and three submenus called Reports and Calendars, Forms, and Charts.

Each menu or submenu is contained within a block on the panel, and the blocks are arranged in a hierarchy that matches the flow of the menus. The particular view shown in Figure 14-7 is designed to maximize your ability to edit and test the individual menus. WebDB provides a second display format in the management panel for menus that provides you with a simpler format for viewing the hierarchy and its individual menu choices.

You can reach this alternative view using the About link on the Manage Component panel.

In every menu building block, you will find a standard format and a consistent set of objects as follows:

- ✦ Report Title
- ✦ Add Child Menu function
- ✦ Show Menu function
- ✦ Directional arrow
- ✦ Menu Title(s)

The Report Title is the English-language name of the menu itself. The only portion of a menu hierarchy that has an actual component name, such as ch14_mnu_example1, is the highest level menu. You only see this name when you either create a new hierarchy or select the menu from the main edit panel for menus. The Report Title is the phrase displayed when you run the menu, and you are free to use any combination of characters to create a Report Title.

The first function below the menu title, which is implemented as a link to another page, is the Add Child Menu function. Selecting this link creates a new menu under the current menu panel. This new menu is part and parcel of the main menu object you are working on, but it is displayed under the parent menu on which it was created. You use the Add Child Menu function to build the hierarchy, and you will delve into this menu shortly.

In order to test any menu while you are working on it, you can select the Show Menu function, which causes WebDB to display the menu as it currently exists. Unlike some of the other builders within WebDB, menus can be tested without compiling them into procedures. WebDB uses the source records for each menu to test the menu interactively, and only compiles the menu into a procedure when you create the menu initially, or when you run the menu from the Manage Component menu.

Directly below the Add/Show functions is a directional arrow. The directional arrow is displayed either in the up or down direction, depending upon whether you are at the bottom of the hierarchy or not. Once you get to the lowest level of a hierarchy, WebDB reverses the direction of the arrow to enable you to move back up the hierarchy.

4. Select the down arrow on the Reports and Calendars panel to move down to the next level of the menu.

   Notice how the Reports and Calendars menu becomes the first-level panel and the directional arrow changes to point upward.

5. Click the upward arrow to return to the previous panel with NetU Reports Menu as the top panel.

At the bottom of the lower panels are the Option Titles. Each Option Title is a link to a specific component or URL in your application. These are the actual objects that your menu is designed to provide access to, and you will link the components you build with WebDB to your menus with Option Titles. The title itself is formatted as a phrase and it serves as the display link on the menu body. The title text is also the data used by the search function to locate menu options, so it is imperative that you use descriptive, unique, and accurate titles for your menus.

Your work with menus will start by adding a new option to one of the existing menus. As it now stands, the Charts menu choice has only the one option, so you will add a new chart option to the Charts menu.

6. Click the Add Child Menu link under the Charts header.

WebDB uses the same page for editing every menu, regardless of whether it is an actual component or merely a submenu. The page is divided into three panels:

✦ Menu Heading and Parent Information

✦ Menu Entry Links-To:

✦ Menu Text Descriptions

The first of these panels is shown in Figure 14-9.

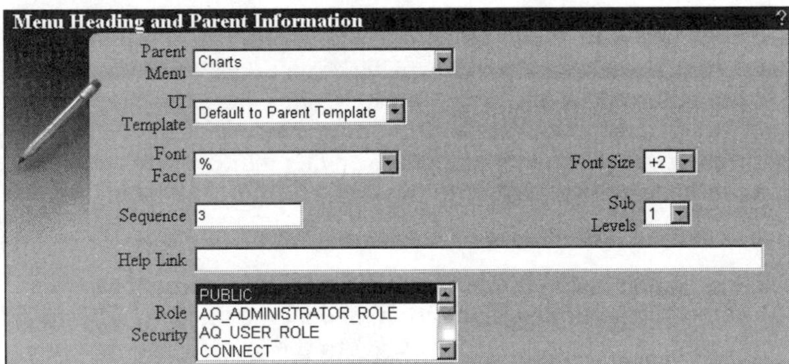

Figure 14-9: Menu Heading and Parent Information panel

The top part of the panel contains formatting options that apply to the entire menu object, most of which you do not have to deal with initially. However, as you work with the menu builder wizard, you will find that this simple panel is incredibly powerful and elegant.

The first field on the panel is the Parent Menu option, which is implemented as a drop-down list box. If you are editing an existing menu or submenu, this entry initially defaults to the current parent menu as it existed when you selected the Add Child Menu option. WebDB fills the drop-down list box with all the entries within the current menu hierarchy. If you click the drop-down list box, you see all the menu choices that exist within the NetU Reports Menu hierarchy.

Selecting a different choice from this menu causes it to align under a different parent menu. Once you have created a menu choice, moving it to another level or position within the hierarchy is as simple as selecting a new choice from this drop-down menu. Notice that the drop-down list includes both menus and option titles. This can make it confusing, because it is possible to move a menu below an actual menu choice. To avoid this problem, it is a good idea to develop some naming conventions to indicate which choices are menus and which choices are actual option titles.

Note WebDB does not allow you to move options across menu objects, and it only displays menu choices found within the same component object. When you are planning your menu structure, you should place related menu choices within the same menu object if you plan on moving these choices around.

The next item on the top panel is the UI Template, which is also implemented as a drop-down list box. The UI Template affects how the menu is displayed at run time, just like it controls any of the reports, forms, charts, calendars, and hierarchies. You will learn more about templates in the next chapter, so for the time being, just accept the default value.

Just below the UI Template field is the Font Face combo box, which enables you to set the font face for the text of the menu. The list of available fonts is derived from the list of available fonts you have entered in the Shared Component Library.

To the right of the Font Face combo box is the Font Size field, which is also implemented as a drop-down list box. Font Size values range from –3 to +4 and correspond to the `<Font Size=#>` HTML tag. Selecting any of the positive values causes your menu's title to be displayed in a font size larger than the current default font size for the page. Choosing a negative value causes your menu's title to be displayed smaller than the default font size of your page. The WebDB developers limited the range of values you can enter in this field to match HTML best practices. In general, take the default value for this field unless you have a particularly dense menu page, in which case you may wish to use a smaller font size.

Note If you are generally not going to increase the font size, then you may ask why WebDB gives you the option to do so. One of the advanced menu options you can take advantage of is the ability to attach a graphic image to the menu choice. You may find that the image overpowers your menu text, and increasing the font size helps to balance the two visually.

You use the next major section of this panel to manage the ordering and positioning of your menus. The Sequence field is a numeric text field that determines the order of the elements on the menu. The particular number generated by default varies depending upon how you launched the menu builder. The numbers for the menu item match the display order (for example, 1 is first, 2 is second, and so on). Changing the order of a menu item is simple, and it does not matter if you duplicate entries.

One trick to keep in mind with menu sequencing is to leave intentional gaps in the orders you create. For example, starting all of your menus with 10 and adding new items in increments of 10 gives you plenty of freedom if you need to add items in between at some point in the future.

7. Enter **20** as the sequence for the new menu you are working on.

The Sub Levels field to the right of the Sequence field controls how many menu levels display at any given time. This particular feature is best understood by example.

8. Scroll to the top of the current page and click the Insert button to save your new child menu.
9. Click the up arrow in the Charts panel to return to the main menu builder.
10. Click the NetU Reports Menu link to edit the main menu.
11. Change the Sub Levels field to **4** and click the Update button at the top of the page.
12. Click the Show Menu link in the NetU Reports menu to test out your change.

WebDB changes the menu display to show up to four levels of the menu hierarchy at the same time. Figure 14-10 shows an example, but you can only see two levels of menu choices in the figure because there are only two levels of menu defined. When you changed the value of the Sub Levels field, you allowed up to four levels of menu to be displayed, if they existed. In the example case, there are only two levels of menus for you to see.

You may find it easier to display a deep hierarchy of menus using sublevels. This makes the navigation simpler for your end users. As you add menu options, using sublevels may make your pages too cumbersome, at which point you can change the sublevel entry back to a smaller number.

WebDB enables you to set this option on a menu-by-menu basis, and submenus can use a different setting than their parent menus for maximum flexibility.

1. Return to the Edit Menu Hierarchy panel and click the Child Menu link in the Charts box to resume editing your menu.

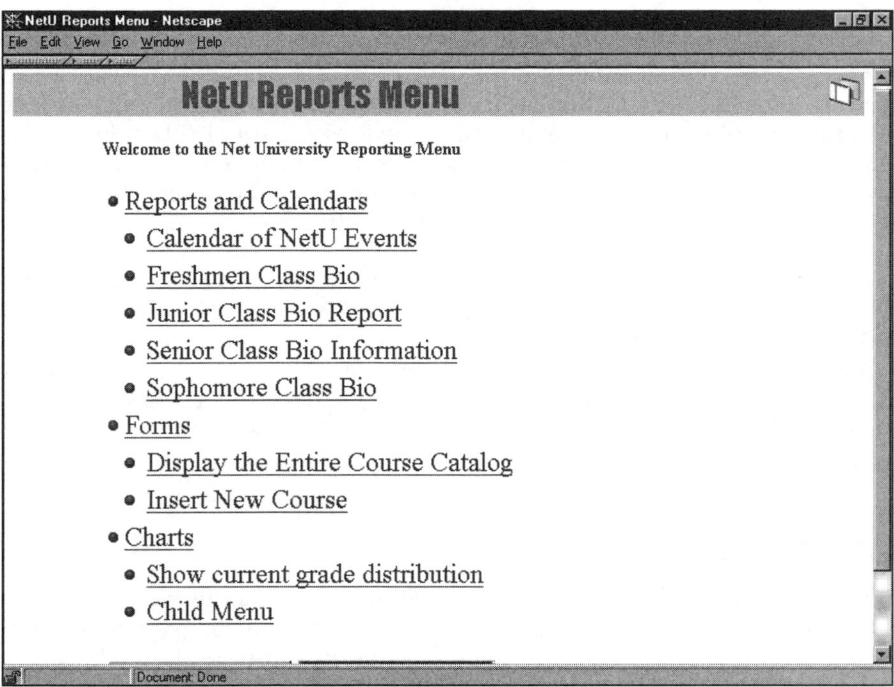

Figure 14-10: Multi–Sub Level menu display

The next item in the top panel is the Help Link, which is displayed as a single, long text box. You can provide help for your menu by entering a URL into this field. When you execute this menu, the URL is activated when the user clicks the question mark image in the upper-right corner of the page. You are free to enter any valid URL in this text box, including calls to other HTTP servers. In general, you probably want to create some static HTML pages that explain your particular menus and reference these pages from the Help Link. WebDB's site-building component provides tools for uploading HTML content, and we will take a closed look at uploading pages later in this book.

While it is possible to reference help as external URLs, it is not a good idea to store help pages externally when working with WebDB. A good part of the value proposition of the product is to store as much of your content as possible within the database.

This particular menu item is going to link directly to another component and not a submenu, so you should leave the Help Link field blank for now. You will add help to the Charts menu in the next section.

The final item in this top panel is the Role Security assigned to this menu choice. We cover security in detail in Chapter 20. For the time being, understand that

WebDB applications consist of USERIDs (with passwords) and ROLES. This matches the normal database security scheme implemented by Oracle, which should come as no surprise, because WebDB is based upon the Oracle database. The default security behavior for any WebDB object is public access. You can restrict access by selecting any of the entries that appear in the Role Security list box. In fact, you can select multiple entries from this list box by using the Windows Ctrl key along with your mouse. You can also use the Windows Shift key and mouse combination to select a range of roles, which are sorted alphabetically.

Once you select a value for this field, any user that requires access to this object will have to be granted the associated role. WebDB highlights the roles you select and keeps them highlighted each time you return to this panel to edit the menu. You can reset security for an object to the default value by selecting the CONNECT role, which is the lowest level of access granted by Oracle. (A user is automatically given the CONNECT role when they are added to the Oracle database through WebDB.)

Menu links

The middle panel of the Edit Menu Items Wizard connects the menu item to an actual component object. Menu items not connected to a component object are assumed to be submenus or placeholder menus. Figure 14-11 shows the Menu Entry Links To: panel for the chart menu you are working on.

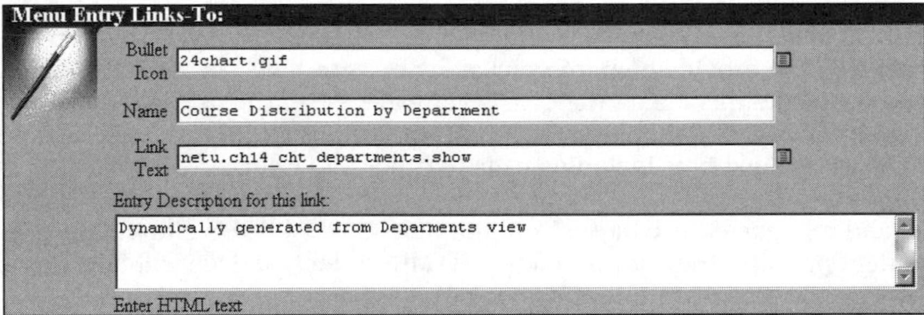

Figure 14-11: Menu links for the chart menu

You need to carefully consider four items when specifying menu links. The order in which these four items are listed in the panel does not reflect their relative importance for a menu choice. The first item is the Bullet Icon, which is a placeholder for an image displayed to the left of your menu link when the menu is executed. The Search icon to the right of the field enables you to search WebDB's repository for images to use. In the next chapter, you will see how you can add your own images to the system. Careful use of images can help build consistency into your applications by giving the user a quick visual cue as to what type of object the menu choice connects to.

Although WebDB shows you a link name when searching for images, it returns the actual GIF file name to the text field. Because the link name is not used in attaching the GIF to the menu choice, if the link name is later modified, this change does not propagate to the menu. We recommend that you design all of your icons for a site before you begin deploying them to menus in order to avoid this problem.

2. Click the List icon to the right of the field to search for the image **chart** and accept the value back into the Bullet Icon field.

The next item on the list is the Name field whose entry corresponds to the text that appears on the page as either the name of the menu or the name of the link. If the menu is a master menu for a list of submenus, this value simply appears at the top of the panel. If this menu choice links to a WebDB component object, the text you enter for the name becomes the link name on the panel. It makes good sense to include some hint as to the type of object this menu connects to directly within the Name field — it makes menu searches and navigation easier. For example, if this is a master menu for a group of submenus, include the word *menu* somewhere in the name. In this example menu, we have included the word *chart* in the name. Even if you attached a chart icon to the left of the menu choice, you should still include a phrase in the name field so menu searches can find these entries in submenus.

3. Replace the text Child Menu with Course Distribution by Department Chart in the Name field.

The key to the entire menu system is the Link Text, which appears just below the Name field. If this field is blank, WebDB assumes this menu is going to be a parent menu for a series of submenus. *The "root" menu of all menu objects will always have this field blank*. If the menu choice is intended to connect to a specific object, then the value of the Link Text field is used as the command string for the link. By default, WebDB expects the entry you make in this field to be a WebDB link, which is part of the Shared Component Library. If you click the List icon to the right of the text field, WebDB enables you to search for matching links. Chapter 15 will introduce you to links in detail, and it is not necessary to use links to build menus. In fact, you should probably initially avoid links when building your menus until you master the basics of the menu builder wizard.

At this point, you are better off considering the link text to be a call to another WebDB component. The last part of this chapter will show you how to connect WebDB to an external URL from the menu builder wizard.

As you learned in the previous chapters on reports, forms, charts, calendars, and hierarchies, you can access each one of the objects you create with WebDB directly by a URL. If you want to figure out the exact URL for a given component, simply choose the component from any Manage Component menu and select either the Run link or the Parameters link. WebDB builds two procedures for each object you create: one for the object itself and one that provides a parameter window for the object. The format of the URLs that WebDB creates looks much like the following line of code:

```
http://pumpkin:4000/WEBDB/netu.ch14_cht_departments.show
```

Remember from the earlier section in this chapter, the first part of the URL varies according to the server name and port number you are using for your WebDB server. The second portion of the URL is composed of the WebDB USERID and the procedure name of the individual component.

You can specify any valid component line and parameter set for the Link Text of a menu item. Review Chapter 17 to understand how WebDB formats its URL arguments.

Of course, this makes it very cumbersome to move this application to a different server, because you are forced to change the server and port number for every entry. Never fear, however, as WebDB works off standard URL technologies. In the first part of this chapter, we talked about standard URLs and how the browser automatically assumes that the root path for a page matches the parent page. The only portion of the URL you need to enter for the Link Text is the last portion of the URL—the part *after* the last slash / character.

4. Enter the following URL into the Link Text field:

   ```
   netu.ch14_cht_departments.show
   ```

You can enter some additional descriptive text for the menu link in the last text entry field provided. WebDB automatically formats the block of text to fit under the menu link. This text is *only* displayed if the menu option is linked to a *specific* component, and it is not displayed if the menu choice is a parent menu for a series of submenus. WebDB provides a third panel for you to use if you are creating a parent menu. For the moment, you can skip over this last panel until we create a new root menu later in the chapter.

5. Enter the following text in the Entry Description text box: **Dynamically generated from Departments view**.
6. Click the Update button at the top of the page to update your menu.
7. Load the ch14_cht_departments.sql script into your WebDB account using SQL*Plus (if you have not already done so).
8. Click the Show Menu link in the Charts box to test the changes to your menu. WebDB displays the menu shown in Figure 14-12.

Notice how WebDB shows the new link for the course distribution chart, with a graphic icon to the left and the extended description below the menu link.

9. Click the new link to test the chart. When you have finished, click the Return to Manage Component Page link.

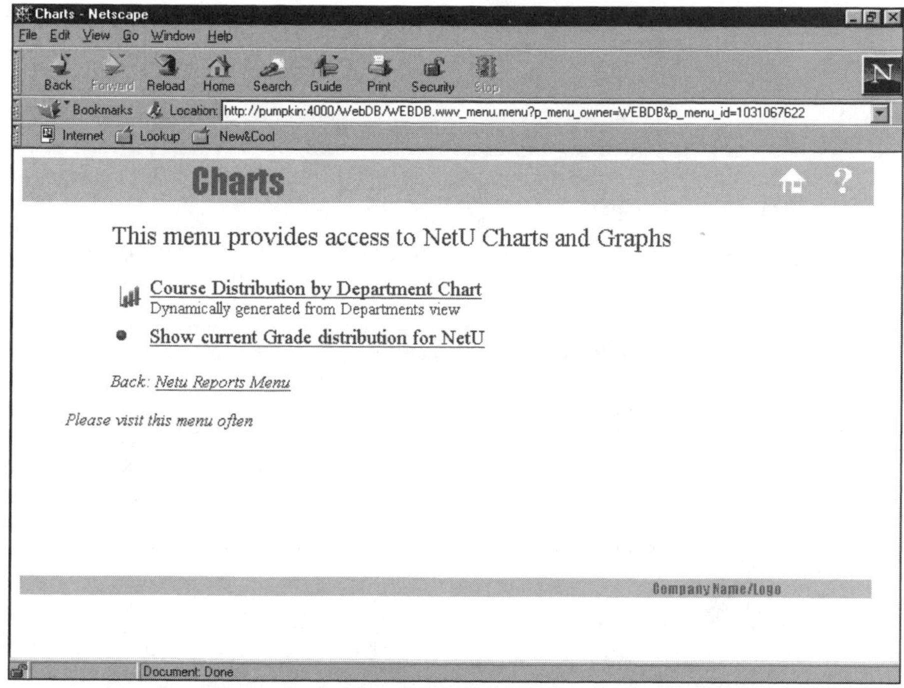

Figure 14-12: Viewing the modified chart menu

Building a Menu from Scratch

Now that you have explored an existing menu, you are ready to build a WebDB menu from scratch. The wizard that enables you to create a new menu is somewhat counterintuitive, and you will find that all you really need to worry about is creating the basic structure with the wizard. Because WebDB makes it so easy to edit a menu object, you only need to use the wizard to create the component itself.

1. Select the Create button from the Menu Building panel. WebDB displays the panel shown in Figure 14-13.

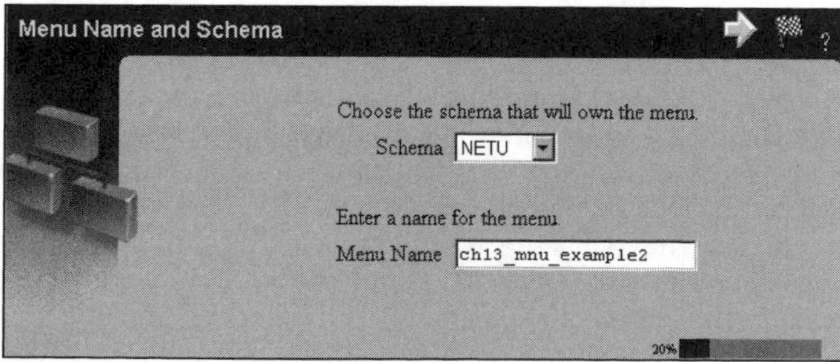

Figure 14-13: Create menu wizard

2. Select your WebDB developer account as the owner for the WebDB menu, and enter the name **ch14_mnu_example2** as the new menu object. Click the Next arrow to continue.

   The next panel WebDB displays enables you to enter a user-friendly title string for your new menu, as well as some header and footer text. Do not bother to add this information now — it is easier to edit this information when you modify the menu.

3. Click the Next arrow to go to the Text Options page, as shown in Figure 14-14.

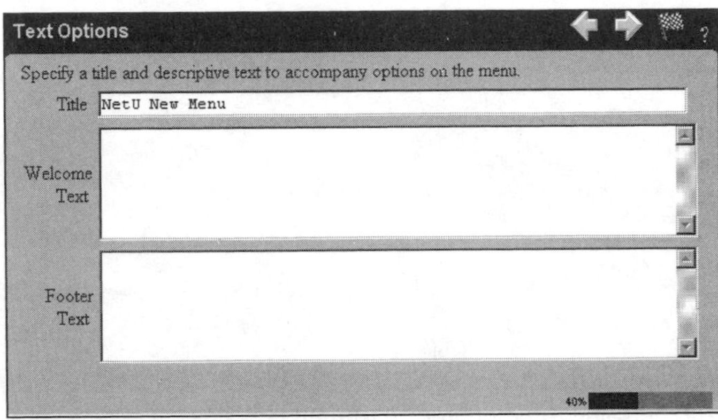

Figure 14-14: Text Options page

   You can specify three items on the Text Options panel: a title, welcome text, and footer text. The title text displays in the title bar for the menu and appears wherever the title text is defined in the template applied to the menu. (You specify the template further on in the process.) Any welcome text you enter is displayed above the menu choices, and footer text is displayed below the menu choices. You can enter text as well as HTML tags inside either of these two text blocks.

4. Enter **NetU New Menu** in the Title field, and leave the Welcome Text and Footer Text fields blank for the moment.

5. Click the Next arrow to continue to the Root Level Menu Items panel shown in Figure 14-15.

   WebDB provides two text boxes for you to enter root level menu items and their associated URLs. Root level menus are menu choices that appear on the topmost panel for the menu on this main menu. If your root level menu needs to connect directly to a component, then you enter the menu item and its associated URL in this panel. If the root menu needs to connect to a series of submenus, then you only need to enter the menu item title in the left-hand column. It is much easier just to leave this panel blank when you create the menu, and then fill in the choices during an edit session.

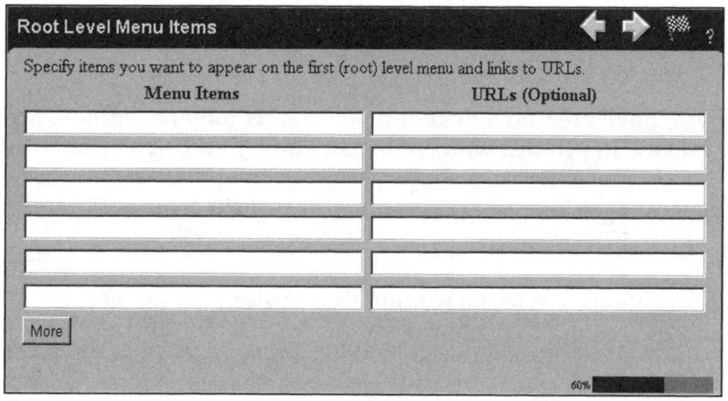

Figure 14-15: Root Level Menu Items panel

6. Skip over the root menu items panel by using the Next arrow to show the Display Options panel in Figure 14-16.

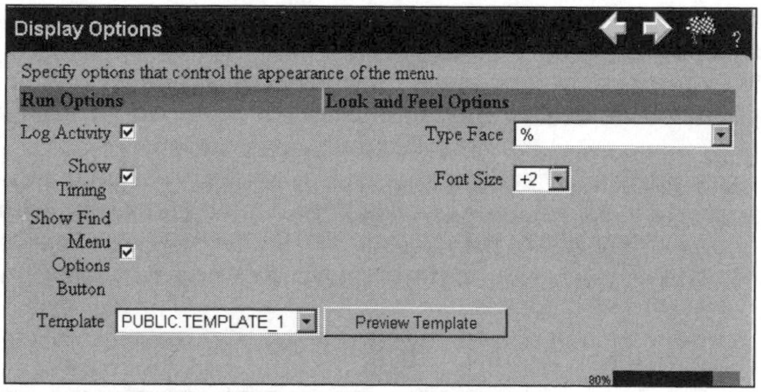

Figure 14-16: Display Options for a new menu

There are fewer choices on the Display Options panel for a menu component compared to the same page in the form or report builder wizards. You can choose a template for the menu and set the typeface and font size for the menu choices. These are the same choices you had when you were editing a preexisting menu in the preceding section. You can also select whether or not to log activity to the activity logs and whether to show the menu timing on the face of the menu. In addition to these familiar choices, you can elect to display the Find Menu Options button on the face of the new menu. If you accept the default value and enable this setting, WebDB enables users to search for submenu strings from the main menu panel. This Find Menu button is a powerful feature for your users, especially if you have deeply nested menus. We recommend that you make use of this capability on the menus you build.

7. Click the Next arrow to continue.
8. Click the OK button to create the new menu.

At this point you have created a default menu that is fully functional. However, the menu object lacks entry items, which you can add by editing the new menu object.

1. Go to the Manage Component panel and select the Edit option to begin editing the panel you just created.

The interface for editing the menu resembles the previous session where you edited the example menu. This interface is easier to work with than the Create interface and it gives a finer grain of control over process of editing the menu.

2. Click the NetU New Menu link to edit the root menu.
3. Go down to the bottom panel for this menu.

Because you are working on a root menu, this panel is activated when you run the menu. The two text boxes on this panel represent the header and footer for the root menu page. These text boxes are highly specialized fields. You can add free-form text to these boxes, and you can also enter any valid HTML tags directly into this panel. WebDB passes along the HTML tags to the browser along with the text when it passes the HTML stream to the browser window. This enables you to add highly specialized syntax for the header and footer of any menu.

It is not necessary for you to handcraft the HTML. In fact, you can use any given visual HTML tool (such as Symantec's Visual Page, which is bundled with WebDB) to create the page. Simply create the page and then cut the HTML source and paste it into either of two text boxes. Figure 14-17 shows a sample block of HTML text for the current menu.

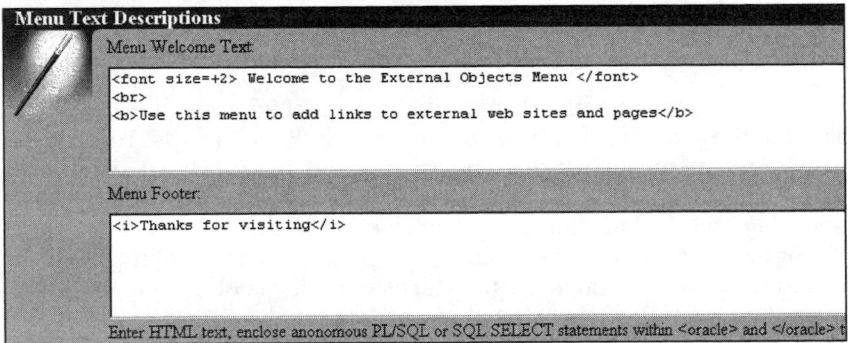

Figure 14-17: Extended header and footer HTML text

In the example text, we used some additional tags such as <font>, <b>, and italics (<i>). You can choose to use HTML formatting tags or not, as you wish.

4. Enter some text for your header and footer and then choose the Update button at the top of the page to store the menu changes.
5. Use the Add Child Menu link to add two child menus to your new menu.

```
Change the name of the first Child Menu to "Netu Home Page"
and enter "/static/netu_home.htm" into the Link Text field.
```

You should remember this particular page from the first portion of the chapter when we covered the use of URLs and virtual directories. Because the browser accesses this page from within the menu page, you do not need to specify the server name and port number.

6. Click the Insert button to save the changes to the menu.

Notice how the box for your menu item no longer displays the Show and Add links. WebDB detects the fact that you have entered a component for the link and so it knows that the menu is not acting as a root menu and therefore it removes the unnecessary links.

7. Edit the second child menu and change the name to any value you like.

WebDB enables you to enter any valid URL as the destination for a menu item. This allows you to use WebDB's menus to integrate data from other Web sites into your WebDB application. The only catch is that you must remember that the link you provide connects you to a site accessible from the *browser,* not the *server.*

When WebDB serves up the menu with your external link, it is merely passing the address within the HTML page as part of the link. The WebDB server is not processing this link when you use the menu; your browser is processing the link. This gives you lots of flexibility to link other content to WebDB. Your server does not need to have authorization and access to connect to external sites — only the browser needs authorization. This is particularly powerful when you have stored your WebDB server behind a firewall and plan on limiting its access to the outside world.

It is possible to use the WebDB server to connect to external Web pages, but you have to make this connection inside of a content component such as dynamic pages.

Edit the Link Text and enter a complete URL for any other Web site you have access to.

8. Select the Update link to save your changes.
9. Click the Show Menu link on the root menu to test your changes. Test your links to the static pages and the external Web site.

Linking Root Menus

The last major task remaining is to link the two root menus. Although WebDB does not allow you to separate out submenus, it does allow you to link from one root menu to another. To take advantage of this capability, it makes sense to organize your menus into groups of menu choices that exist as linked root menus. You will be able to modify the structure of each of the root menus easily and still be able to link them.

Try to strike a balance between too many and too few root menus when you design your menu structure. If you create too many root menus, you could have trouble keeping track of all of them. And if you create too few menus, you may encounter locking problems if there are a lot of developers working on the menu system simultaneously.

1. Return to the main menu page, select your new menu once again, and then click Edit.
2. Click the Add Child Menu link in the NetU New Menu box to create a new submenu off the root menu.
3. Change the Name on the new child menu to **NetU Reports Menu**, and change the link text to **netu.ch14_mnu_example1.show**. (This links your new menu back to the first menu you worked with in the preceding section.)
4. Click the Insert button to save the menu changes.
5. Test the root menu again by clicking the Show Menu link, and WebDB shows you the panel in Figure 14-18.

If you choose the NetU Reports Menu link, you are connected to the menu that you imported in the first part of this chapter. Because you are calling another root menu, any root menu settings you may have modified for the initial menu apply when the menu is run. For example, if you choose to use different templates for the two menus, they display with their specified template, even when the menus are nested. This is because the menus are considered to be separate objects and they are only linked through a URL link.

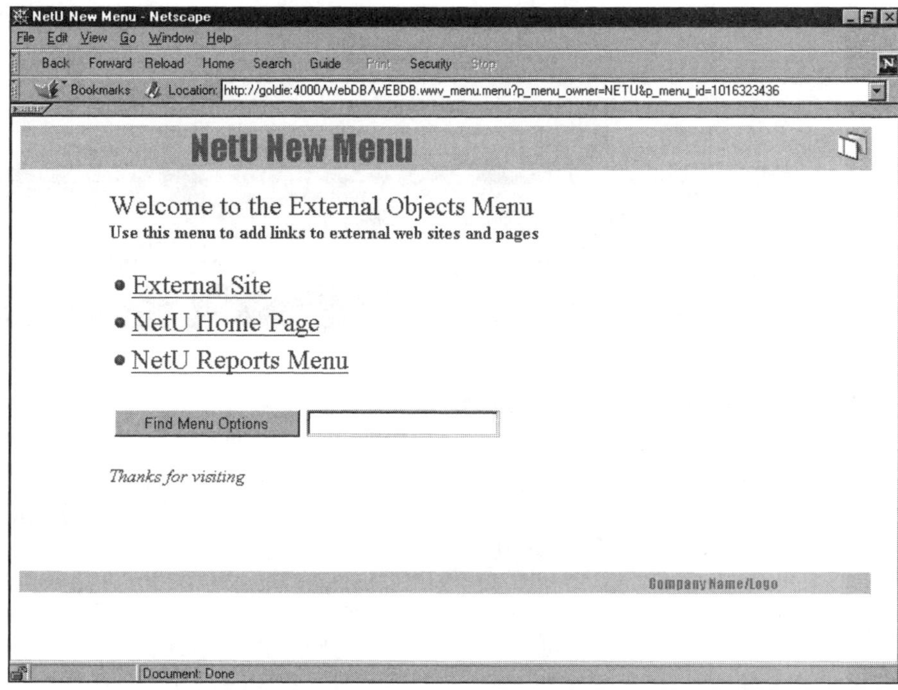

Figure 14-18: View modified menu

Managing the Menu

WebDB provides you with the standard Manage Component option for menus so that you perform routine tasks such as copying, renaming, and exporting menus. In addition to these standard functions, the About link on the Manage Component page for menus offers you an additional viewing format for your menus as we mentioned earlier in this chapter.

Use the About link on the Manage Component page to display the panel shown in Figure 14-19.

WebDB shows you a hierarchical display of the root menu you selected. Included in this display is the sequence for each menu and submenu, and the data itself is sorted on this sequence number. You can see the security settings for each of the menu choices as well as the actual links to WebDB components for the lowest-level menus. The Link field remains blank for root menu pages and options, and because WebDB manages these items internally there is no addressable component link for you to view. You can also edit the menu directly from this interface by clicking the link numbers in the far-left column. Choosing one of these links returns you to the standard menu editor with the selected menu item opened and ready for modification.

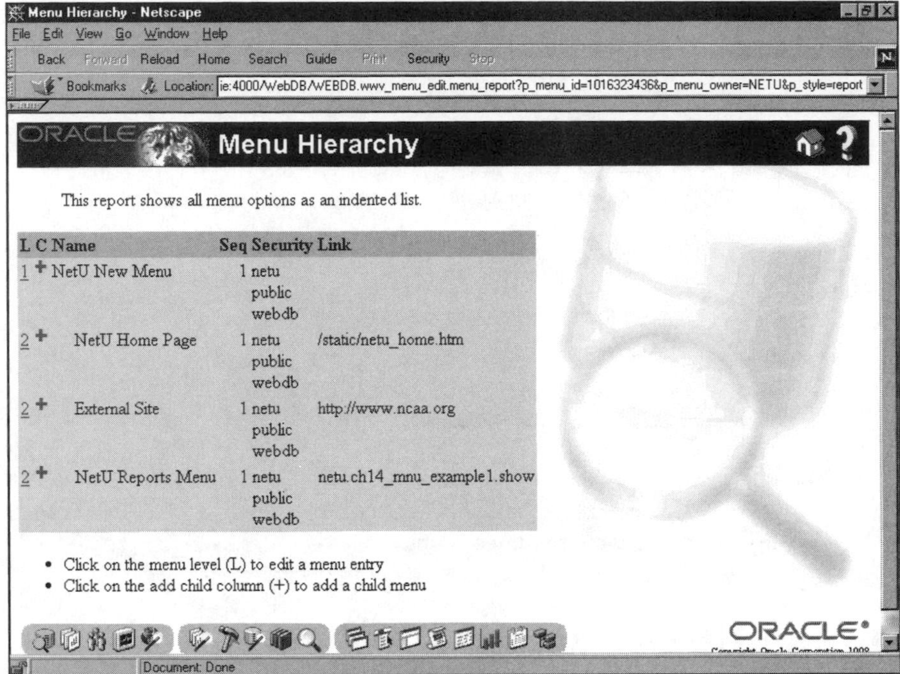

Figure 14-19: Menu hierarchy display

Wrapping Up

WebDB works in conjunction with existing Web technology and HTML standards to help you create Web applications. You can use the menu objects in WebDB to provide the basic navigational path through your application system with standard links and URLs. WebDB itself communicates between all of its own components using URLs. WebDB's menu builder wizard offers a very powerful interface for rapidly creating and modifying menus. You can easily incorporate external HTML pages and Web sites by embedding links into WebDB's menus.

✦ ✦ ✦

CHAPTER 15

Building Consistency into WebDB Web Sites

✦ ✦ ✦ ✦

In This Chapter

Content Creation and Standards Enforcement

Creating Standardized Colors and Fonts

Fonts, Images, and Templates

Importing Custom Images into WebDB

Building User Interface Templates

✦ ✦ ✦ ✦

In Part II of this book, you learned about the various build wizards WebDB offers for creating content objects for your Web sites. Each of the wizards for creating components is designed to ensure some consistency between objects. The Report Wizard, for example, provides the same customization options for each and every report you create in order to ensure that groups of related reports look and behave in a similar fashion. Furthermore, many of the options for a single wizard are shared amongst the other tools. For example, you will find the same page for adding PL/SQL code in many of the various builders. This feature helps you share a common set of features and functions across objects.

If you survey a number of public Web sites across the Internet, you will find that the most useful and well-organized Web sites offer a basic consistency in their design and appearance. When you build consistency into groups of related pages, you deliver two advantages to your site. First, you make the site easier to navigate by offering a consistent set of options and functionality. Second, you create a type of informal brand recognition by making the content for a logically related group of objects appear in a similar format. WebDB provides an additional set of tools for building an enhanced level of consistency into your objects in the form of colors, fonts, images, and user interface templates. The content wizards use these components to create a consistent, visual theme for your applications.

Content Creation Versus Standards Enforcement

WebDB provides a set of tools in the Shared Component Library for building standards and consistency into your applications. The library is a series of utilities and wizards that create objects, which are then used by the other content builders within WebDB. You were exposed to the Shared Component Library when you used the Link Editor to build links between content objects. The utilities within the Shared Component Library are divided into two separate categories: those that produce content and those that enforce visual standards. The main menu for the Shared Component Library appears in Figure 15-1.

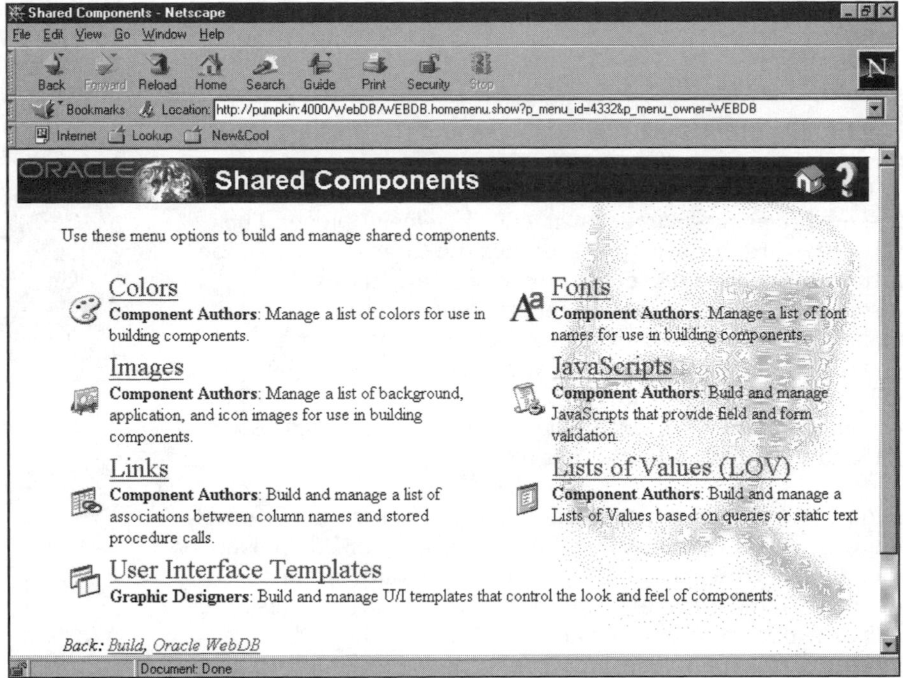

Figure 15-1: Main menu for the Shared Component Library

Looking at the menu, you do not find any indication that any one particular utility is used to create content or to enforce visual standards. In fact, the utilities are evenly divided between content creation and standards enforcement, with one utility straddling the fence between both camps. The content creation tools consist of the following:

- ✦ Links
- ✦ JavaScripts
- ✦ Lists-of-Values (LOV)

You use each of these utilities either to interact with data in some way, or to transfer data and control between WebDB objects at run time. Because the other content objects within WebDB can share these objects, they are included as part of the Shared Component Library. Within the Shared Component Library, they represent a subset of objects that interact directly with data on the form. Each is a sophisticated piece of content in and of itself, and this book includes a complete chapter dedicated to each of these tools.

The remaining tools in the Shared Component Library are geared toward creating visual consistency within your WebDB applications. These utilities also build objects used by the other wizards, but by and large they are not used to interact with data directly. The following utilities fall into this category:

✦ Colors

✦ Fonts

✦ Images

✦ User Interface Templates

You use each of these utilities to enforce visual standards for your WebDB applications in some way. Images are the exception to the rule, because they are actually content in and of themselves. Within the Shared Component Library, you should consider images to be part of the tools for building consistency into your applications. Image files that provide data for your application should be either stored in the database or referenced from entries in database tables.

Colors

Colors can have a profound impact on the way your data is displayed within a browser. In many cases, the use and abuse of color determines the level of user satisfaction of your site. Since the dawn of the client/server age, color displays have been a standard for users. End users expect color screens for their applications, and monocolor sites are unacceptable. However, there are countless examples of Web sites that are difficult to use solely because the designers made gratuitous use of color to the detriment of the overall site. Users do not want screens that read like a black-and-white newspaper and they do not want screens that remind them of a psychedelic trip back to the sixties.

WebDB enables you to make frequent use of colors throughout the various wizards. In most cases, you can provide a color value for many of the visual settings for each of the builders. If you are familiar with the way in which colors are used within a Web browser, then you will find WebDB's Color Editor easy to work with. The WebDB color palette is based upon the colors typically found in Netscape Navigator and Microsoft Internet Explorer.

Video display

The colors displayed by your computer are based upon the video card installed in the machine and the video display driver that controls the interface between the computer and the video card. On most PC desktops, the standard video card is either a Video Graphics Adapter (VGA) or Super Video Graphics Adapter (SVGA) compatible card.

The particular video card installed in a given desktop computer has an effect on two aspects of the way in which your WebDB applications are displayed. The first attribute is the resolution of the display, which controls the amount of information on a single screen. The decision of level of resolution to use is a critical one and it can have a dramatic effect on the usability of your applications. Because WebDB cannot automatically convert content from one level of resolution to another, it does not provide you with any tools for changing the screen resolution. In general, most computer desktops support 800 × 600 pixel resolution, and this setting is typical for desktop applications. WebDB itself was designed with this resolution in mind, and you will find that most of WebDB's pages fit nicely onto a screen of this size. If you choose to develop using a higher level of resolution, you may find that your pages are too large to view comfortably at the lower settings. Figure 15-2 and Figure 15-3 show the WebDB home page at two levels of resolution for comparison purposes.

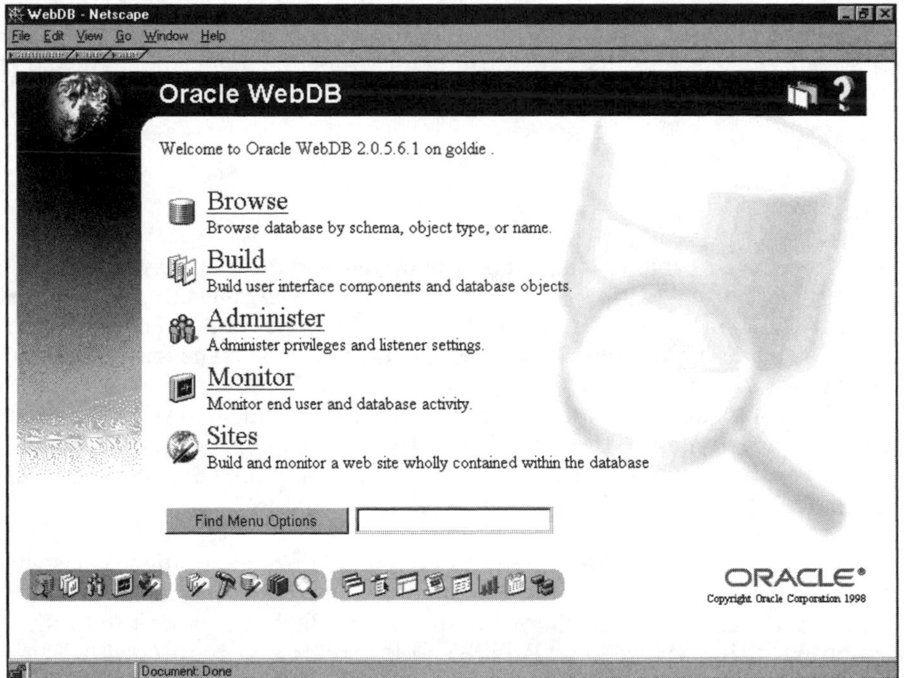

Figure 15-2: WebDB home page at 800 × 600 resolution

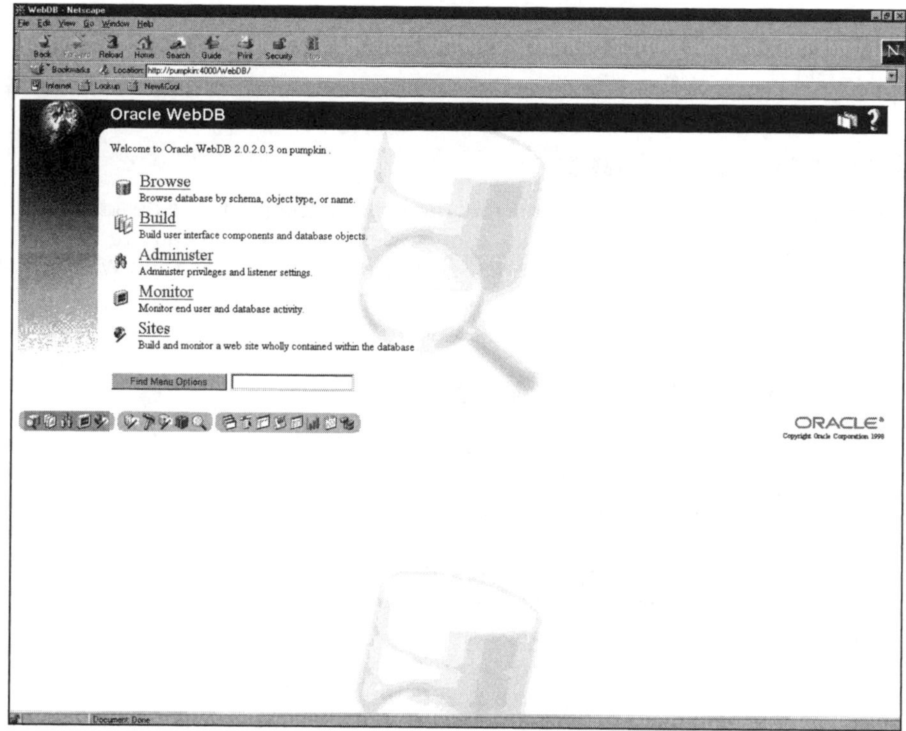

Figure 15-3: WebDB home page at 1280 × 1024 resolution

The WebDB home page comfortably fits in the 800 × 600 window, but it is too small and hard to read at the higher resolution. Extra large display monitors can display higher resolution output in a readable format, but very few users have such large monitors because they are prohibitively expensive. In general, your WebDB applications should be designed to fit on 800 × 600 screens unless you are sure that your user base is able to support the higher resolution.

Tip

You should design your pages to aim for the lowest common denominator of resolution in your target audience. If your pages constantly require a user to scroll through them, it makes your system significantly harder to use. Therefore, the downside of using too high a resolution outweighs the upside of pleasing some of your target audience with a larger-sized page.

The higher resolution displays enable you to show more information on a single page, and some applications may require this level of resolution. WebDB automatically uses the additional screen real estate at application run time. On Windows desktops, the control panel sets the resolution of the display, and the user can change it from his or her desktop. The examples for resolution settings in this chapter are taken from Windows, but the same principles apply to other desktop operating systems. If the user changes to a higher resolution, the objects you create with WebDB automatically use the additional space. The WebDB development environment itself will *not* necessarily use this additional real estate, however, because most of the wizards have been designed to show a fixed amount of information.

Video color settings

The video display adapter also controls the color settings for the desktop. Although WebDB does not specifically provide tools for managing the display resolution, Figure 15-4 shows the control panel's Display Properties screen for a Windows desktop.

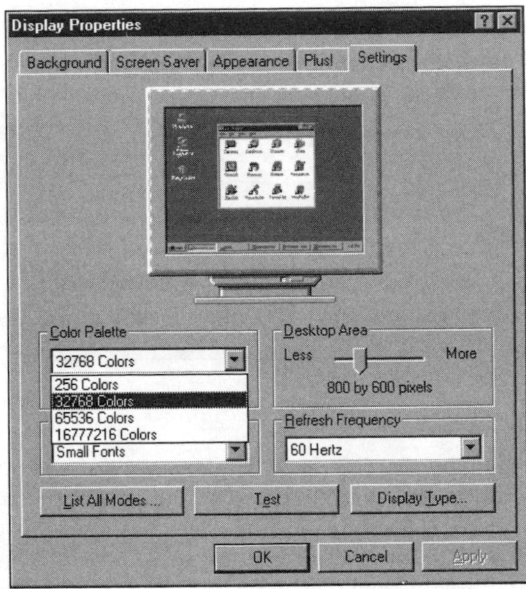

Figure 15-4: Display settings for video adapter

The Desktop Area setting controls the resolution of the display as discussed in the previous section. To the right of the Desktop Area is the Color Palette, which controls the color settings for the computer's display. The setting for the Color Palette is typically a number between 256 and 16 million, and it refers to the number of unique colors the video adapter can display. Older video cards may not support the higher settings, and the valid range of values appears in the list shown on the Display Properties page. The desktop operating system attempts to compensate for missing colors when running an application that uses more colors than the computer can handle. Although applications run them, the colors and images displayed are often very hard to read and ugly.

WebDB leaves the rendering of colors to the browser and operating system, and it works well with 256 colors. If you deploy your applications to machines using a lower setting, the results for these users may be less than satisfying. It is possible to build applications that use only 16 colors, but you will probably find that your applications appear less attractive if you do. If you set your display adapter to a higher Color Palette setting, you are able to add many more colors and variations to your applications. However, if you build applications using these additional colors, your applications do not display the same on lower resolution machines.

The operating system compensates for you by attempting to simulate the missing colors, but the display itself appears fuzzy. This phenomenon is much easier to understand once you have seen it, and the easiest way to see it is by using the control panel and your browser.

Note

We used Netscape Navigator for the following example, but Microsoft Internet Explorer has a similar setting under the Internet Options menu.

1. Exit your browser.
2. Using the Windows control panel Display icon, set the Color Palette on the Settings tab to 16 million, or the highest number your desktop supports.
3. Select the Edit/Preferences menu on the Navigator menu bar and select the Color keyword in the Category panel on the left-hand side.
4. Double-click the box next to the field labeled Text in the Colors group and click the Define Custom Colors push button to display a panel similar to Figure 15-5.

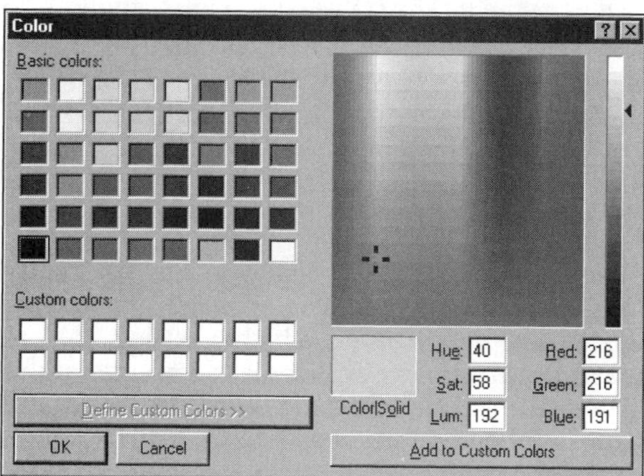

Figure 15-5: Define Custom Colors panel

Colors are determined by particular a combination of the three primary colors: red, green, and blue. The amount of each of the primary colors contained in any one combination determines the final color.

The Define Custom Colors panel enables you to build a color using a combination of red, green, and blue. The resulting color is known as the *RGB value*. The maximum value for any one of the colors is 255 and the minimum value is 0. The various combinations of red, green, and blue values can produce just over 16 million different colors when the complete range of values are used. Higher values indicate heavier weighting of one of the primary colors and lower values indicate lighter weighting.

5. Enter the following values into the text fields next to the labels for the red, green, and blue colors:

   `Red=216, Green=216, Blue=191.`

   Once you have entered a value for each of the primary color fields, the browser produces the resulting color in the box labeled Color | Solid. The resulting color from the combination of RGB values you entered in the preceding step is a pale tan that might be called "Wheat." Also notice that the color spectrum displayed above the Color | Solid field is a clean, crisp display of colors for the entire spectrum from white to black. Almost any combination of RGB values produces a solid color with clear definition.

6. Cancel this custom color and exit the browser.
7. Use the Control Panel to change the Color number back to 256.
8. Restart the browser and follow Steps 1–4 to produce the same color (Wheat).

This time, the Color | Solid field is split into two sections. The left-hand section shows a combination of white and gray pixels that looks like an impressionist painter's rendition of the color Wheat. The right-hand section shows a solid gray color. When your display adapter is set to show only 256 colors, the computer attempts to simulate a given combination of RGB values using the colors it has available. At the higher setting, the Wheat color is much sharper and pleasing to the eye. In effect, at the lower color setting you are eliminating some of the numbers between 0 and 255 for each of the three primary colors. Fewer numbers yields fewer unique combinations.

WebDB itself uses 256 colors as the basis for all of its wizards. You can set your display resolution for a higher number of colors and WebDB still displays just fine. However, if you build Web sites while running at a higher setting, you are likely to use colors and images that may not show as well under a lower color setting. Ideally, you should build your WebDB applications using the same color settings the majority of the end users of the application use.

Defining WebDB colors

Because the use of color has such a significant impact on the visuals of your applications, WebDB provides a wizard to assist you in the process of defining colors. As we mentioned earlier in this chapter, the Color Wizard is part of the Shared Component Library.

1. To start the Color Wizard, select the Colors link from the Shared Component Library menu.

Before you can add a new color to the system, you need to understand how WebDB assigns a color value to an RGB color combination. The lower panel of the Manage Colors page is the Edit Color Definition panel and, as the name implies, it enables you to modify the settings for a color definition. Figure 15-6 shows the default Edit Color Definition panel.

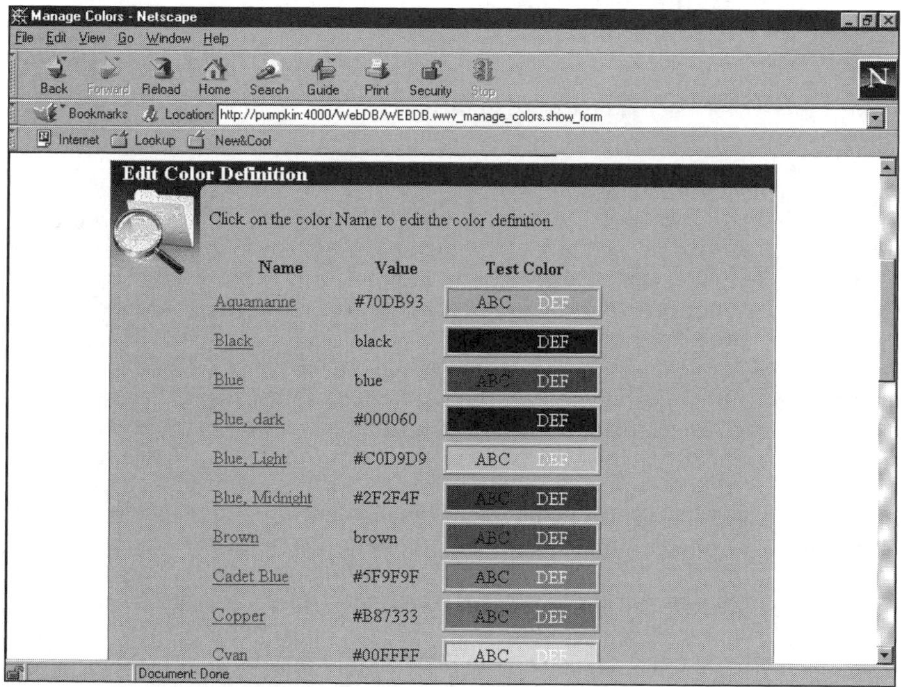

Figure 15-6: Edit Color Definition panel

The edit panel is composed of three pieces of information: the color name, the color value, and the test color display. The color name is the user-friendly name for the color combination, and it is the name by which you refer to the color from within any of WebDB's other wizards. The color value column contains two types of values that match the two formats used by Web browsers. Servers pass HTML pages to the Web browser, and the browser intercepts color tags (such as BGCOLOR) and uses the associated value to set a color for the designated object. Some browsers can accept a limited number of color names as the color value, such as those shown in Figure 15-6. Alternatively, the color setting can be provided using the RGB value in an encoded format. The format string is a seven-character string starting with a hexadecimal code indicator followed by three two-character fields for each of the three primary colors, as shown in Figure 15-7.

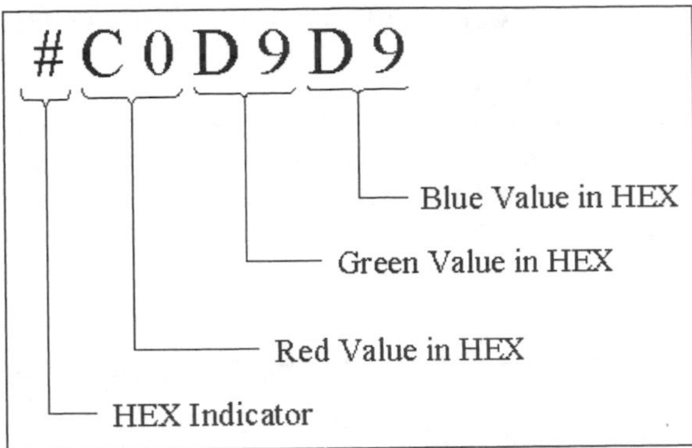

Figure 15-7: Color values in encoded format

The developers of the HTML standard decided to use hexadecimal (HEX) values to represent colors, not the developers of WebDB. If you are not familiar with HEX, all you really need to know is that it is a number system based on powers of 16. You need not be familiar with HEX in order to define color settings as this is the only place in which HEX is used, and you only need to convert small numbers between 0 and 255.

A random tour of almost any corporate home page will show that the vast majority of color settings are made using this HEX format. If you are familiar with HEX values from other applications, you may be surprised to note that the color format lacks the leading 0X HEX indicator. The designers of HTML replaced the standard hexadecimal identifier with the # character. The center column of the Edit Color Definition panel shows a mix of HEX color codes and literal color names.

Although WebDB provides a set of limited colors using color names, we advise you to build your applications using colors based upon HEX codes. Literal color names are subject to interpretation by the browser and may lead to inconsistent results when your applications are deployed.

The right-hand column shows the color value inside of an image block so you can see how the color appears when it is used. WebDB overlays black and white text on the color so that you can see what standard lettering will look like when contrasted with the background color. The colors you create are not limited to backgrounds. In fact, you can use them anywhere WebDB enables you to define a color setting. In general, colors are most often used for backgrounds, which is why WebDB shows the color as a sample background on the panel.

2. Scroll down until you reach the setting for Blue, Light.

The color defined for the color named Blue, Light probably appears to be more gray than blue. This is the result of two separate phenomena. First, WebDB enables you to use any valid string for the name of a color, and there need not be any direct connection between the name and the color value. You can name the color "white" but enter a color code for "black" if you choose to do so. In the case of Blue, Light, the color value does not match the color name for a different reason. The color was defined at a higher color palette setting than the machine is currently using. If you were to reset your display adapter to show more than 256 colors, you would find that the color definition is indeed a shade of light blue. At the 256-color setting, the machine does not have enough colors to render the particular combination of red, green, and blue needed to display the true coloring. The browser and the operating system renders the color on the panel at the *current* color setting so that you can see exactly what the color looks like when it is displayed. If you reset your computer's resolution to a higher color setting, the correct color displays when you restart your browser.

Defining a new color

At the top of the Manage Colors page is a panel for adding new colors. This is the simplest wizard WebDB offers. The wizard is nothing more than the two fields at the top of the panel called Color Name and Color Value.

The real key to defining colors is creating a consistent color naming convention for your applications. There are three factors you need to consider when you define your colors: the color value, the usage of the color, and the color setting for the color. The *color value* is the common name for the color such as Blue, Light Blue, Powder Blue, and so on. It is easy to see what a color looks like when you are using the Manage Colors page, but the other wizards do not show colors, only the color names. If you use a color *name* that does not accurately reflect the actual color *value,* you may find that the rest of your development team is selecting incorrect colors. If the actual color is some shade of blue, then the name should typically give some indication of the value.

The exception to this rule is to assign the color name based upon the color usage. For example, Net University has its own "college colors" that are used to enforce branding on their Web site. The standard color scheme for NetU is light gray with gold highlights. It makes sense to use a gray background for most components in light of this fact. Rather than creating a color called gray, it might be better to define a color named netu_standard_bg to indicate that the color is the standard background color for NetU. In this case, the name of the color indicates *usage* rather than color *value*.

The last factor in choosing a color naming convention is considering the color setting used when defining the color. You may choose to create colors at a higher setting, such as 16 million colors, in which case you may want to provide some hint as to this fact in the name of the color. If NetU has a particular shade of gray that is better shown when the desktop is using a higher color setting, you may choose to label your color with the color setting included, for example, netu_standard_bg_255 and netu_standard_bg_16m. The WebDB data dictionary enables you to use up to 400 characters for each color name you create, giving you plenty of room to implement a meaningful naming convention.

We recommend that you create two types of colors: one set based upon the color value and one set based upon usage. This gives your developers guidance as to which colors to use directly within the name of the color. In both cases, you should include the color setting number in the name.

Once you have decided on a color name scheme, the only remaining step for creating colors is to calculate the color value code. The color value is a HEX string in the format shown in Figure 15-7. WebDB does not provide a translation facility of its own, but we have included two different tools for converting numbers to HEX color values.

There are two separate utilities for converting color numbers on the CD-ROM. First, ch15_tohex.htm is an HTML page for converting colors onscreen. In addition, there are two PL/SQL functions, ch15_listing1.sql and ch15_listing2.sql, that also convert to and from HEX. Copy the HTML page to your desktop and install the PL/SQL functions using SQL*Plus.

Before you create the HEX color code, you should decide on the mix of red, green, and blue you want to use for the color. The easiest way to do this is to use the color definition screen in your browser, as shown in Figure 15-5. Once you have selected the values for the color you wish to create, the HEX conversion is relatively straightforward.

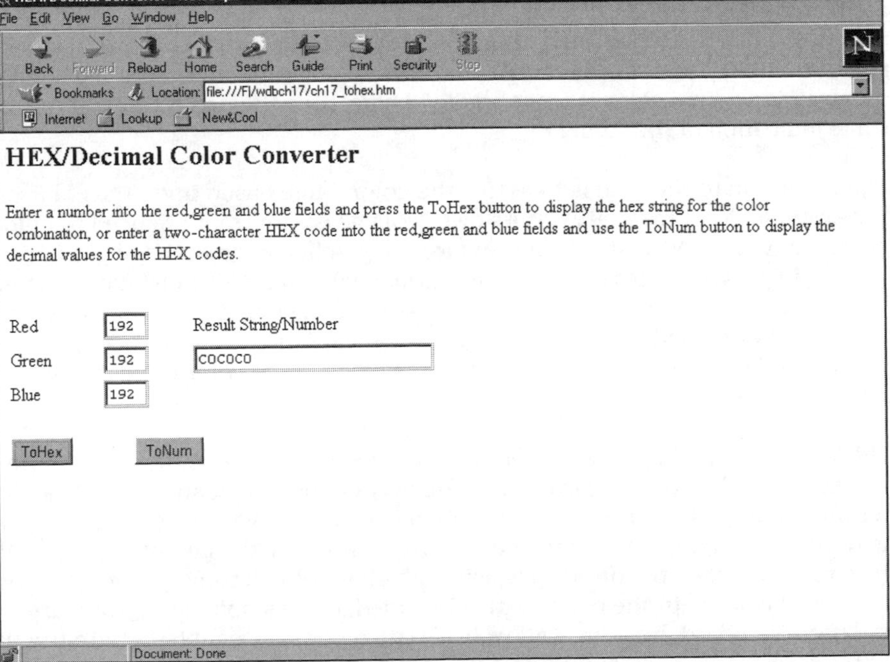

Figure 15-8: HEX conversion HTML page

1. Open the ch15_to_hex.htm file in your browser as shown in Figure 15-8.

You can enter any numbers between 0 and 255 in the fields labeled red, green, and blue. Once you have entered the values into the page, you can use the ToHex button to convert the numbers to a HEX string. Conversely, entering uppercase two-character HEX codes into the red, green, and blue fields and using the ToNum button converts the HEX codes to a string of comma-delimited RGB values. Alternatively, you could use the PL/SQL function to convert the values for you as follows:

```
select short_to_hex(205) from dual
```

You are going to create a header background color for the NetU application. The color will be a standard gray with an equal weighting of red, green, and blue of 205.

2. Use the conversion page to create the HEX string (CDCDCD).
3. Enter a new color for the NetU application by using the name netu_heading_255 as the Color Name on the Manage Colors page in the Add Color Name panel.
4. Enter the value for the new color by entering a number character (#) followed by the six HEX characters for the color name as indicated from the HEX conversion HTML page.
5. Click the Add Color button to save the new color.

Once you have created a new color, it appears in the Edit panel, and you can simply edit the color by clicking its name link. WebDB enables you to create duplicate color values with different names, but the color name itself must be unique. You can also use the Edit panel to delete any colors you create. A color that appears in the Edit panel also appears in all of the other wizards wherever you are allowed to enter colors. Later on in this chapter you will use a set of custom colors as part of a template.

6. Add three additional colors for NetU through the Manage Colors panel as follows:

```
netu_text_255 / #000000
netu_bold_255 / #FFFF00
netu_bg_255 / #FFFFFF
```

WebDB does not automatically cascade color changes throughout your application. If you change the color value for a given color, you have to regenerate your objects manually in order to use the new color value. Early versions of WebDB were known to have constraint violations when adding colors.

Fonts

Fonts are managed in an identical fashion to colors within WebDB, and you will find the interface for working with fonts to be a familiar one. Fonts control the manner in which text is rendered on the HTML pages, and they can have a dramatic impact on the way data is displayed. The simple choice of a particular font can transform an HTML page from a conservative look into a bold, lighthearted look, or vice versa. WebDB provides you with many opportunities to use specialized fonts within all of the content wizards.

Fonts are also part of the Shared Component Library and they should be universally defined for your application in the same way you define colors. Like colors, fonts are supplied to the browser by the operating system, and it is possible to define fonts within WebDB that are not found on the end user's desktop. Web browsers automatically substitute a missing font with a replacement font available on the desktop for the user, but the results of this automatic substitution may not be aesthetically pleasing. It is best to choose a range of fonts that are generally available to your end users when you create your WebDB fonts. Although you need to access the operating system to determine your machine's color settings, the browser automatically prepares a list of fonts available to you. The font settings are usually found in the Preferences section of the browser in the same general area as the color setting, as shown in Figure 15-9.

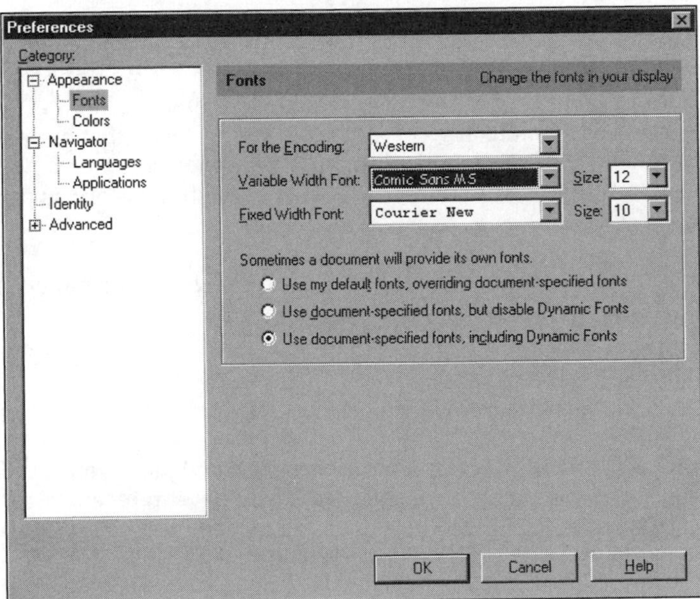

Figure 15-9: Font settings

Your browser uses two types of fonts to render HTML pages: variable width fonts and fixed width fonts. *Variable width* fonts, also known as *proportional* fonts, use characters that vary in dimension. Each letter is not guaranteed to use a fixed amount of display real estate. Proportional fonts are the standard for displaying text on HTML pages and within most desktop office tools such as Microsoft Word and PowerPoint.

Fixed width fonts display all letters and characters using a consistent amount of real estate. Data entry fields on HTML pages, such as text boxes and text areas, are typically displayed using fixed width fonts. Data entry fields are usually tied back to database fields that have a fixed size within the database. However, using a proportional font for the data entry box for these fields does not allow a user to enter more data into the form than can be stored within the database. A fixed width display font for a data entry field enables the user to see all of the characters that have been entered up to the maximum number of characters allowed. Most HTML tools prevent you from using proportional fonts for input fields, and WebDB honors this standard.

The Web browser provides combo boxes for both variable width and fixed width fonts, as shown in Figure 15-9. The browser builds the list of available fonts from the operating system each time the browser starts. If the font appears in the combo box, the system has the font available for display. Of course, you cannot be sure that every user's machine has this same set of font files. If a user does not have access to a specified font, the browser makes a substitution automatically as shown by the radio buttons in Figure 15-9. However, the substitute font may not display your data properly. Fonts are organized into families of fonts and the operating system attempts to substitute for a missing font using a font from the same family. The fonts themselves are typically broken down into two broad classifications, TrueType and PostScript. TrueType fonts are the standard format supported by the Windows operating system, while PostScript is the more common format for UNIX operating systems. When your browser is running under Windows, you need to have software from Adobe if you plan on using PostScript fonts.

Typically, many variable width and fixed width fonts are available on the browser desktop as shown in the two combo boxes. All of these fonts can be made available to WebDB as part of the Shared Component Library.

Adding fonts to WebDB

WebDB's font management facility is part of the Shared Component Library. Selecting the Fonts link from the Shared Component Library main menu displays the Manage Fonts page shown in Figure 15-10.

The Manage Fonts page looks almost identical to the Manage Colors page, and is composed of two panels. The top panel enables you to add a new font to the system and the lower panel displays a list of the existing fonts. The Edit Fonts panel is divided into two columns: the left-hand column is the font definition name and the right-hand column shows how the font will display at run time. The Edit Fonts panel differs from the Edit Colors panel in one key manner. Remember that you can provide WebDB with logical color names that resolve down to HEX codes for a physical color.

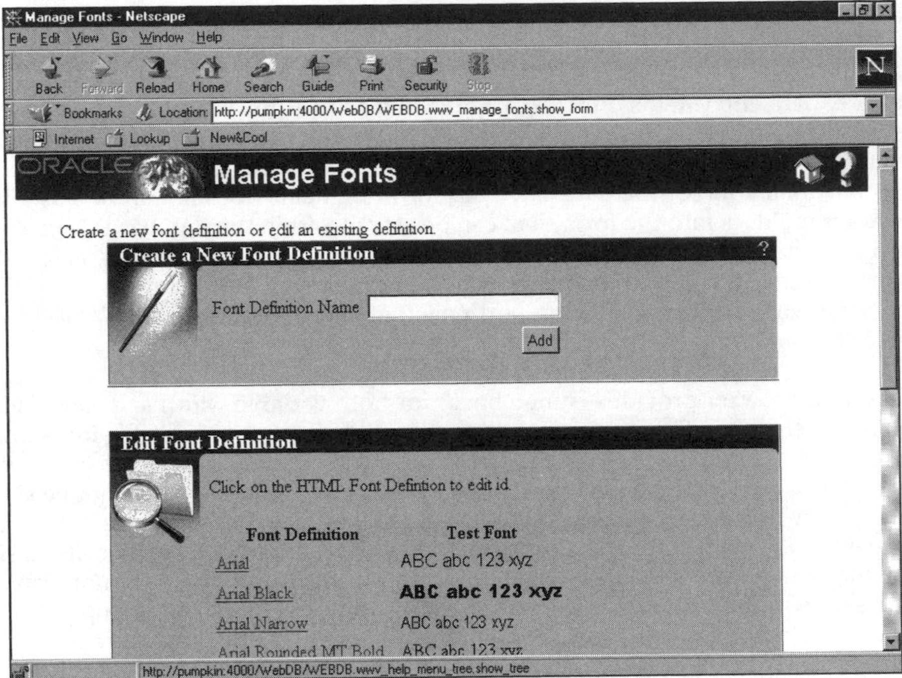

Figure 15-10: Manage Fonts page

The color name need not have any direct connotation with the color number. WebDB's font definitions, however, must map *exactly* to the name of the physical font, as it is known to the operating system. You are unable to use logical names for your fonts, as you were able to with colors. In order to add a new font to the system, you need to obtain the actual font name from the operating system. The fastest way to do this is to use the browser preferences, as shown in Figure 15-9.

1. Return to the main Shared Components page.
2. Click the Fonts menu choice.
3. Use the Create a New Font Definition panel on the Manage Fonts page to add a new font to the system. A popular choice is the Garamond font.
4. Use the Add button to store the new font.

WebDB does not attempt to validate the font when you enter the value. If you enter an invalid font, WebDB simply displays a default font value for the invalid font name. You can verify that the font had been added successfully by viewing the Test Font display on the Edit Font Definition panel.

WebDB may display constraint violations when you attempt to add fonts due to a long.

Editing fonts

Editing font definitions is easier than editing colors, because the only edit you can make is to delete the font. You can select the font name from the Edit Font Definition panel and then delete the font on the Edit Font page by replacing the font name with blanks. In effect, the only changes you can make are either to add fonts or to delete fonts. The following list shows all the standard fonts preinstalled by WebDB.

Standard WebDB Fonts:

Arial

Arial Black

Arial Narrow

Arial Rounded MT Bold

Arial, Helvetica

Book Antiqua

Century Gothic

Century Schoolbook

Comic Sans MS

Courier

Courier New, Courier

Haettenschweiler

Helvetica

Impact

Marlett

Monotype Sorts

Times New Roman, Times

Verdana

Most of the fonts you add to the system will be variable width fonts. WebDB uses the fixed width font defined by the browser to display text data entry fields. You cannot set the fixed width font from within WebDB. If you need to change the fixed width font, you need to use the browser Preferences page shown in Figure 15-9.

Images

Most Web sites are composed of a mixture of HTML text and images. HTML in and of itself often does not offer a fine grain of display formatting for certain types of information. It is often impossible to even display certain text formatting due to the limitations of how HTML formats text. Many popular Web sites such as Oracle's home page use a mix of HTML and images in order to display data in the desired format. WebDB offers advanced formatting options for display, but the final output is always in HTML format and is subject to the same display limitations as static HTML text. Graphic images, on the other hand, are displayed as rendered by the browser, and they can offer you a much higher resolution of display when compared to standard HTML text. The downside of images is that, unlike HTML-rendered text, a graphic is static — you cannot easily change it on the fly.

Web images are typically stored in one of two formats: GIF or JPEG. Graphics Interchange Format, or GIF, is one of the most popular Web graphics formats. Joint Photographic Expedition Graphics, or JPEG, is the other common type of Web graphics file. JPEG files are considered to be vector graphics files, and can be enlarged easily without losing the crispness of the image. GIF files are typically used as simple images on a form, and JPEG files are typically used to display photographs and wallpaper backgrounds. WebDB itself makes use of both types of image file formats.

Images are subject to the same color reduction problems that affect text colors. If you create images that use a large number of colors, you may have problems viewing these images at lower color settings.

The Oracle database can store images directly within the database itself, and you can build SQL queries that retrieve the data in graphic format from the database. However, WebDB itself stores its standard images outside the database in the file system of the host machine. Initially, you should plan on storing the images you create for use with WebDB in a file system directory as well. The exception to this rule is the Site Builder component of WebDB, which has been designed to help you store content (including images) directly in the database.

Chapter 2 discusses the process of adding file system directories so that WebDB can use objects in them. Before you proceed with the examples in the following sections, you need to create these file system directories and be familiar with WebDB's /images/ directory hierarchy.

WebDB image types

WebDB images are stored as either a GIF or JPEG file, which is considered to be the physical type of the file. WebDB organizes its images in a series of logical image categories and this distinction is made only inside WebDB. You can find the Manage Images menu for WebDB under the Shared Component Library menu, as shown in Figure 15-11.

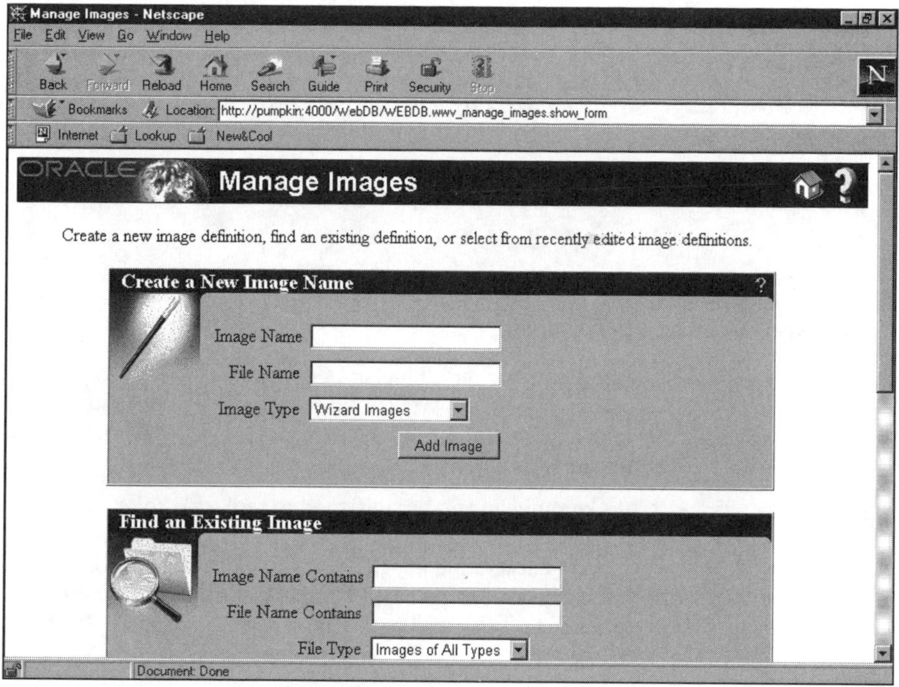

Figure 15-11: Manage Images dialog box

The Manage Images page is divided into three panels: a creation panel, a find panel, and an edit panel. Of all of the shared component builders, it most closely resembles the standard WebDB builders, in that you can search for images based on a matching name for the image, as well as create images or edit existing images. WebDB images are comprised of the following three pieces of information:

✦ Image name

✦ File name

✦ Image type

The *image name* is the logical name that developers use to refer to the image from within WebDB's content wizards. Image names work the same way as color names — they are a logical association between a particular graphic image and a reference name. In most cases, WebDB's own images use the filename as the image name, but this is not a requirement. Consistent use of logical names can make your images much easier to find and remember. The filename is the physical operating system file name for the image. WebDB stores image files in operating system directories and needs to have access to the actual physical filename in order to load the specified image. If you store all of your application images within WebDB's standard images file system directory, then the filename is nothing more than the name and a file extension. If you locate your own graphic files in a separate directory tree, then the filename includes a virtual path definition as part of the filename.

Within WebDB, images are organized by a usage indicator, which is referred to as the *image type*. Table 15-1 lists the various image types defined by WebDB.

Table 15-1
WebDB Image Types

Image Type	*Description*
Arrows	Arrows are the directional arrows displayed at the top of the panel within the wizards. WebDB supplies these images and you are free to use them, but you will typically not create new images under this heading.
Backgrounds	Background images are designed to replace a color as the backdrop for a Web page. WebDB comes equipped with some sample background images, and you can add your own backgrounds. The pale gray database and magnifying glass picture that appear behind all of WebDB's pages is an example of a background.
Database Browsing	These are images used by the database browsing tool. WebDB supplies these images and you are free to use them, but you will typically not create new images under this heading.
Database Objects	WebDB associates these images with the various database objects (tables, views, triggers, and so on) within the database browser. WebDB supplies these images and you are free to use them, but you will typically not create new images under this heading.
Heading Icons	Heading icon images appear in the top-line header of the page within the various templates. The Oracle logo and globe picture shown on WebDB's panels is an example of a heading icon, as are the home and help images.
Icons 24×24	Icons are used throughout WebDB as menu choices and as links. The menu bar at the bottom of WebDB is built using icons. WebDB itself uses three different size icons, 16-pixel, 24-pixel, and 32-pixel. The 24×24 size is the middle size, and all the images in this category are 24 pixels by 24 pixels square, as implied by the name. You may add your own icons to this category, and you can use these icons in your own applications as menu choices within the menu builder.
Icons 32×32	This is the largest icon size and it is used for the same purpose as the 24×24 size icons. The larger size is more appropriate for less densely populated menus and forms.

Image Type	*Description*
Logos	Logo images are designed for storing company logos and trademark images. Oracle's standard red and white trademark is stored as a logo image. Although you may use the company logo within other images, the standard logo is meant to be stored in this category.
Miscellaneous	This artwork does not specifically fit into other categories and can be stored here. WebDB's miniature "new" image is stored in this category.
Public Template Art	Templates provide a complete structure for displaying content in a standard and consistent format. Templates are composed of colors, fonts, and images. Graphics to be used in the building of templates are stored in this category.
Icons 16×16	Icons 16×16 are the 16 by 16 pixel graphics that WebDB uses on panels within the wizards to provide visual cues. These are the smallest graphic objects used by WebDB.
Wizard Images	Wizard images are the purple and gray styled images shown at the top left on each wizard panel within a wizard page. These images are specific to WebDB, and you will not need to add images to this category.

WebDB uses the image type categories to limit searches when you are creating templates and using graphics. If you wish to add a background image to a template, for example, WebDB only shows you background images when you perform an image search.

Adding images

Adding images to the WebDB system is a simple two-part process. The first part of the process is to locate the GIF or JPEG image files you plan to use and copy them to a directory tree accessible by WebDB. WebDB can store images within its own images subdirectory in the file system, or within a virtual directory that has been made accessible to WebDB. Graphic images used as data items can be stored either in the database or, with the pathname of the image stored in the database, in a separate file system directory. Shared component images can be stored in the standard WebDB images subdirectory, however, because these are likely to be fewer in number and more consistent. Images associated with a particular application should have some indication of this fact in the image file name so that these files can be easily identified at the operating system level. The Net University application uses a number of standardized images, as shown in Table 15-2.

Table 15-2
NetU Images

Image Name	*Image Type*	*Description*
netu_bg	Background	Stucco background for use as a backdrop for report pages.
netu_campus	Miscellaneous	GIF image of the NetU campus buildings.
netu_heading	Heading Icon	University image for upper-left corner of page.
netu_help	Heading Icon	Graphic image of a question mark for use with templates.
netu_home	Heading Icon	Home image for navigation back to the NetU home page within templates.
netu_internal_use	Background	Small background image with light gray text for use as a backdrop on sensitive report pages.
netu_ivy	Miscellaneous	Ivy image suitable for use as a border.
netu_logo	Logo	Net University corporate logo.
netu_notes	Background	Large background with the ivy image displayed to the right. This image is large enough to fill the entire background, and it is not be tiled when displayed.
netu_tabbycat	Miscellaneous	Picture of the NetU mascot, the TabbyCat.

Each of the images in Table 15-2 includes "NetU" within the name of the graphic file. This helps keep the images grouped together when you transfer the files or edit the images.

1. Go to a file manager that can access the directory structure on the machine hosting WebDB.
2. Copy the image files listed in Table 15-2 to your WebDBimage directory. You may need the assistance of your system administrator to gain permission to write to this directory.

WebDB supports the use of animated GIF files. You can copy animated GIFs into WebDB's image directory just like any other image. WebDB displays the animation at run time for you. The image file netu_heading.gif is an animated GIF file.

Once you have moved the files to a location WebDB has access to, the rest of the image creation process is simple. From the Manage Images page, enter the information for your image as shown in Figure 15-12.

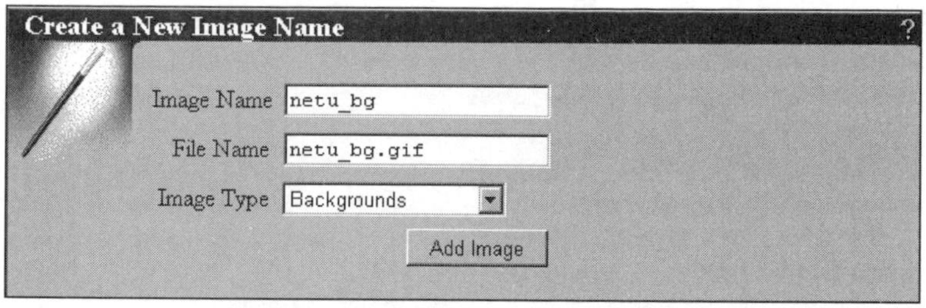

Figure 15-12: Adding a new image

The Image Name is the name you wish to use to refer to the graphic from inside WebDB, and the File Name is the physical name of the image file, including the file extension. You can use virtual directory paths for the File Name by preceding the name with a virtual directory path known to WebDB, such as `/my_images/`. WebDB does not verify that the physical file name you enter is correct, or that the image exists when you add the entry. WebDB verifies that the file exists only when you attempt to display the image.

3. Enter the information shown in Figure 15-12 for the first NetU image. The Image Name is netu_bg, the File Name is netu_bg.gif and the Image Type is Backgrounds.

Once the image has been added to the system, WebDB includes the image in the Find panel and the Edit panel. You can search for images using the Find panel and narrow your search to include specific image types, filenames and image names. The find function supports wildcard searches using the "%" search character. Entering the search criteria shown in Figure 15-13 locates all image types that include the string netu as the first part of the image name.

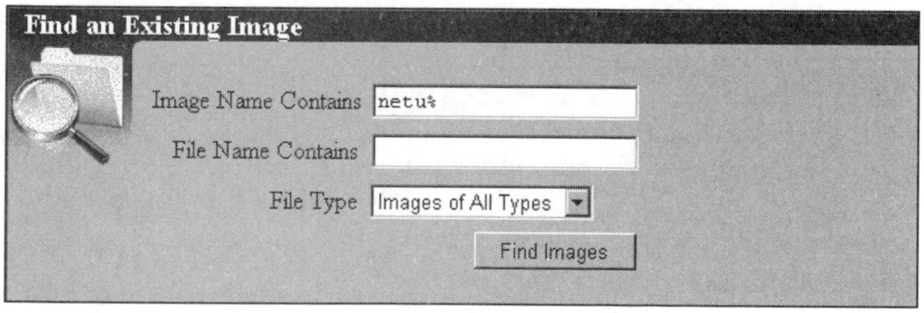

Figure 15-13: Image search

The results of an image search are presented in the same format as the Edit panel on the Manage Images page. Figure 15-14 shows the results of searching for image names with the net% search string.

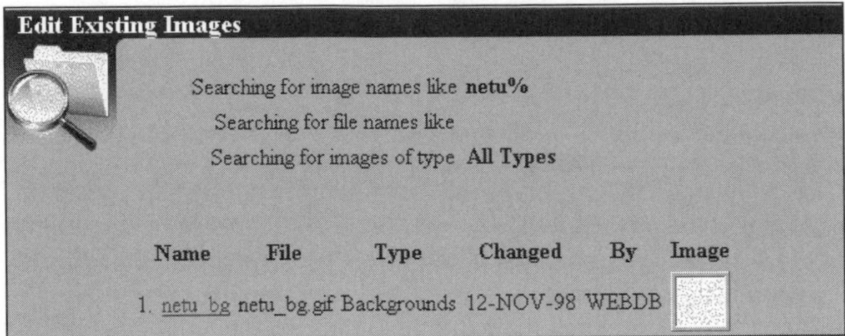

Figure 15-14: Edit Existing Images panel

The Edit panel provides you with a wealth of information about your image. On the left-hand side of the panel is a link that you can use to edit the image. You are only able to edit three things about the image: its name, the filename, and the image type. Removing an image requires you to edit the image and delete the name from the edit panel in the same manner you delete colors and fonts. In addition to the filename and image type, the Edit panel displays the date when the image was last changed, and the Oracle USERID of the user who made the change.

The actual image files are stored outside WebDB and you can only edit the image itself from outside WebDB. If the image is changed, WebDB does not give you any indication that the image has been modified on the Edit panel. WebDB does not attempt to use the contents of the image and it does not track file system dates on images.

On the right-hand side of the panel is a thumbnail sketch of the image. This provides you with a simple view of what the image looks like when viewed. You can view the full-size image by clicking the image itself in the Image column of the Edit panel. The full-size view gives you an accurate look at the image just as it appears in your applications. The exception to this rule is the Background image type, which is only fully rendered when it is used as a background. Backgrounds are used exclusively in public templates, as you will see in the next section.

4. Add the remaining images for Net University using Table 15-2 as your guide. You can bulk load the images using the PL/SQL script ch15_images.sql.

Templates

Templates are the organizers for your colors, fonts, and images. Templates provide a complete structure for your content objects and ensure that your reports, forms, charts, menus, calendars, and hierarchies look and behave consistently. The template object is comprised solely of the three object types that you have worked with thus far in this chapter. In effect, templates are used to mix and match colors, fonts, and images to produce a particular look for your applications.

You can build a single application entirely on a single template, and one template can be used by many applications. Applications are more likely to be built using several templates, unless the application is targeted at a single class of user. For example, divide the contents of the NetU Web site into the following three categories: students, faculty, and alumni. You could create a separate template for each of the three different groups and use it when building a component for the associated group. In this manner, every piece of content for each group looks and behaves consistently.

You can call the Manage U/I Templates page from the User Interface Templates link on the Shared Components page, as shown in Figure 15-15.

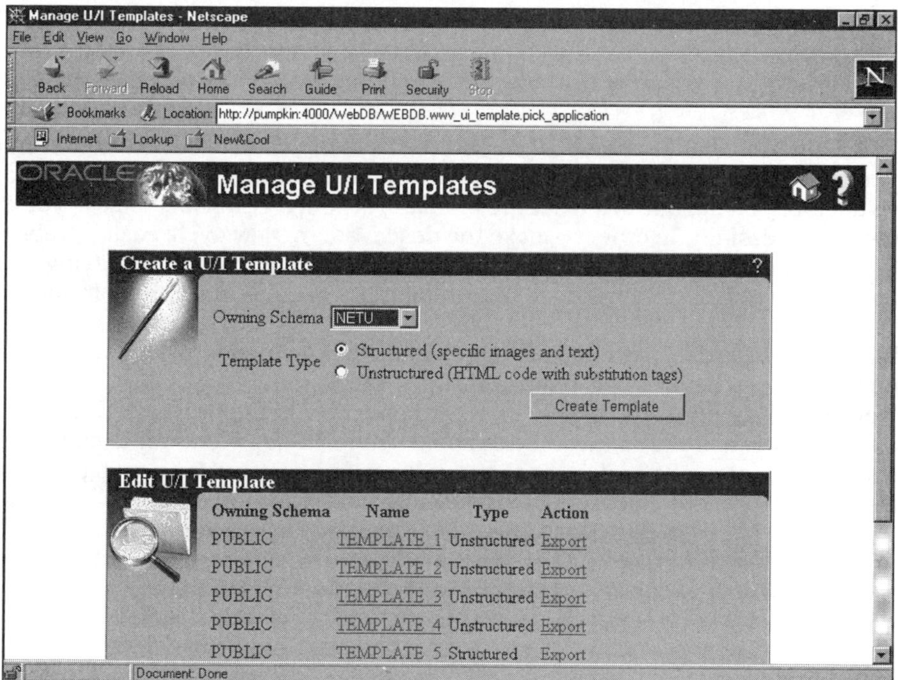

Figure 15-15: Manage U/I Templates page

Adding a new template

The template builder is closer to a wizard than the equivalent builder for colors, fonts, and images. The top panel on the Manage U/I Templates page enables you to create a new user interface template. Templates are owned by a particular USERID as is the case with WebDB's other components.

Because colors and fonts are dependent on the browser and operating system outside the control of WebDB, colors and fonts do not have specific owners.

Templates come in two basic types: *structured* and *unstructured.* Structured templates use a fixed format for positioning content, loading images, and setting colors and fonts. They are simple to build, and the structure ensures that you use all of the capabilities of the template skeleton. Unstructured templates are based upon HTML and enable you to have a much finer grain of control over the layout and behavior of your templates. Unstructured templates assume a firm knowledge of how structured templates are meant to work, and you should avoid using unstructured templates until you have sufficient experience with the structured version.

1. Return to the main Shared Components page in WebDB. Click the User Interface Templates choice.
2. Set the owner for the new template to your NetU USERID and create a structured template.

The Structured U/I Template page is unique as compared to WebDB's other build wizards because it uses a framed display format. Designing templates is primarily a visual job; you need to see what the template is going to look like before you can use it successfully. In order to make the design and review cycle easier, WebDB uses the top frame for editing the template and the bottom frame for displaying the results dynamically. Figure 15-16 shows the top portion of the editing frame.

The various parts of the template editor frame are divided into sections using bold text. The top section is the Template Owner and Name, and it is identical to all of WebDB's other content creation wizards. The owner is the Oracle USERID that owns the template, and the name of the template is the unique identifier used to work with the template. You will want to use a consistent method for naming templates, just as with any other content object.

3. Enter your NetU USERID as the owner for the template, and use the name **netu_tmp_standard** as the name of the new template.

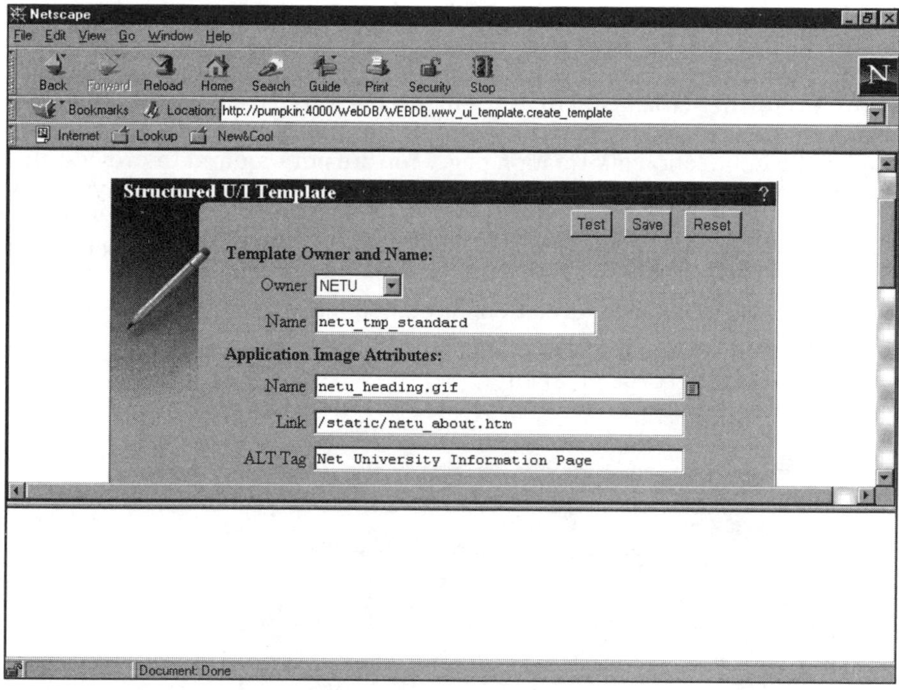

Figure 15-16: Top section of the edit template frame

Structured templates are composed of a series of objects as shown in the following list. Every structured template contains each of these components.

- ✦ Application image
- ✦ Home link
- ✦ Help image
- ✦ Template title
- ✦ Heading
- ✦ Background

The first content section in the top frame is the Application Image section, which refers to the top left-hand section of your pages. Within WebDB itself, the Oracle logo and globe in the upper-left corner of all of WebDB's pages is considered to be the application image. You are able to specify three attributes for the application image. First, you can specify a WebDB image to be displayed. You can use the icon to the left of the image name field to search for a particular image by name, but WebDB only displays images that have been entered as heading images as results of this search.

Just below the image field is the link field, which enables you to specify a link to be followed when the end user clicks the image. You are permitted to enter any valid URL into this field, including links to other WebDB components. Because this link is shown everywhere the template is used, this link is typically used to connect the end user to a standard information page. Within WebDB itself, this link is used to display the Connection Information page. You are not required to provide an application image in the template, but if you provide a URL link, then you *must* provide an image for the link. The ALT Tag entry field is used for entering text that is displayed when the user hovers over the application image with their mouse.

4. Enter the following information into the Application Image section:

```
Name: netu_heading.gif
Link: /static/netu_about.htm
ALT Tag: Net University Information Page
```

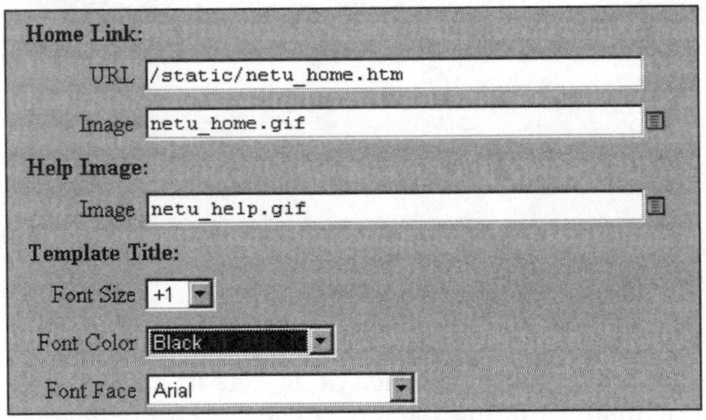

Figure 15-17: Help Link, Help Image, and Template Title entries

The next data entry section is the Home Link section, as shown in Figure 15-17. The Home Link section defines whether an image exists on the upper-right corner of the page. WebDB uses the miniature house image as its Home Link. The Home Link is composed of two pieces of data: the URL and the Image. The URL points to a valid Web address in either a full or relative format. In many cases, the home page for your application may be located on a separate HTTP server. You can link to this server by entering a URL in this field. If the link is a relative link, then the browser uses the WebDB listener to locate the page. You can also search for an image to represent the link by using the search button in the Home Link section. Only images that were filed in the headings category can be used. It is possible to circumvent this check by entering a filename directly, but we recommend against doing so, as WebDB is liable to enforce this check in the future.

5. Enter the following information into the Home Link section.

```
URL: /static/netu_home.htm
Image: netu_home.gif
```

Below the Home Link section is the Help Image section, which is also shown in Figure 15-17. Much like the Home Link section, it enables you to select an image to be displayed next to the home link in the upper-right corner of the page. The help image does not have an associated URL link because WebDB determines the link at template execution time. If the run-time object has help associated with it, WebDB links to that help dynamically from this image.

6. Enter the following information into the Help Link section:

```
Image: netu_help.gif
```

The last section shown in Figure 15-17 is the Template Title. The information you provide in this section is used to display the title text, which appears to the right of the application image. The Template Title has three components: Font Size, Font Color, and Font Face. Font Size is a relative setting and you should enter a plus sign followed by an integer value (+1, +2, and so on). WebDB uses the number as a relative number to the size of the font used to display the text on the body of the page. This ensures that the title is always larger than the data on the page. You can select the font face and font color from combo boxes built from your WebDB font and color tables.

WebDB uses the color name to search for colors and the image name to search for images, but it always copies the actual color number and image filename to the calling field. If you later change the color definition or image, the change will not be carried into your template, and you will have to make the change manually.

Font Face is the last entry in the Template Title section, and it determines the font used to display the title text. The text itself is provided inside component objects such as forms, reports, and charts. WebDB extracts the title from these components at run time and renders it in the font, size, color, and location you specify in the template.

7. Enter the following information for the Template Title:

```
Font Size: +2
Font Color: black
Font Face: Arial
```

Heading Background:
Color Gray, Light
Image
Background Color and Image:
Color White
Image netu_bg.gif

Figure 15-18: Heading and background settings

The final two sections of the template layout are the heading and background sections, as shown in Figure 15-18. The heading background is the area at the top of the page behind the application image, template text, home link, and help image. The heading background supports two settings: a color name and an image name. The color setting is a standard WebDB color value and the image is a standard WebDB image, but only one of these is used at run time by WebDB. The image field takes precedence and overlays the color value when the template is used. If you supply a color value instead of an image, the color appears behind all of the images and text in the template header. The color of the heading shows through your images if they have been created with a transparency setting.

Alternatively, you can choose an image name from the headings category. WebDB tiles the image across the entire heading area if the image is smaller than the designated heading space. If the image size matches the space allotted to the header, then the image displays only once.

8. Enter the following information into the Heading Background section:

```
Color: Gray, Light
```

The final portion of the structured template page is the Background Color and Image section. The background of the page is the area shown behind the text on the body of the page. As with the heading section, the background can be either a color or an image. The pale gray database and magnifying glass that appears in the background of WebDB's pages is an example of an image background. WebDB automatically tiles images that do not fit uniformly in the background using a wallpaper effect. The sample images you loaded as part of the previous section included several examples of this type of background image.

9. Enter the name **netu_bg.gif** in the Image field of the Background Color and Image section. Alternatively, you can search for the background from the search list. WebDB only shows images that are loaded as backgrounds.
10. Use the test button at the top of the page. The Test function causes WebDB to render the template as shown in Figure 15-19.

WebDB implements the template specifications you entered in the top frame in the bottom frame of the page. Notice how the background image is tiled to fill the entire backdrop of the page with a pebble effect. WebDB displays icons for the application image, home page, and help as indicated and sets the background color for the heading. You can achieve different background effects by using different types of images. There are two additional backgrounds included in the sample application that you can test: netu_internal_use and netu_notes. The internal use image displays a white background with faded gray text showing the phrase "internal use only." The notes background shows a collegiate branch of ivy down the left-hand side of the page. This particular image is large enough to cover the entire backdrop, so WebDB does not attempt to tile this image.

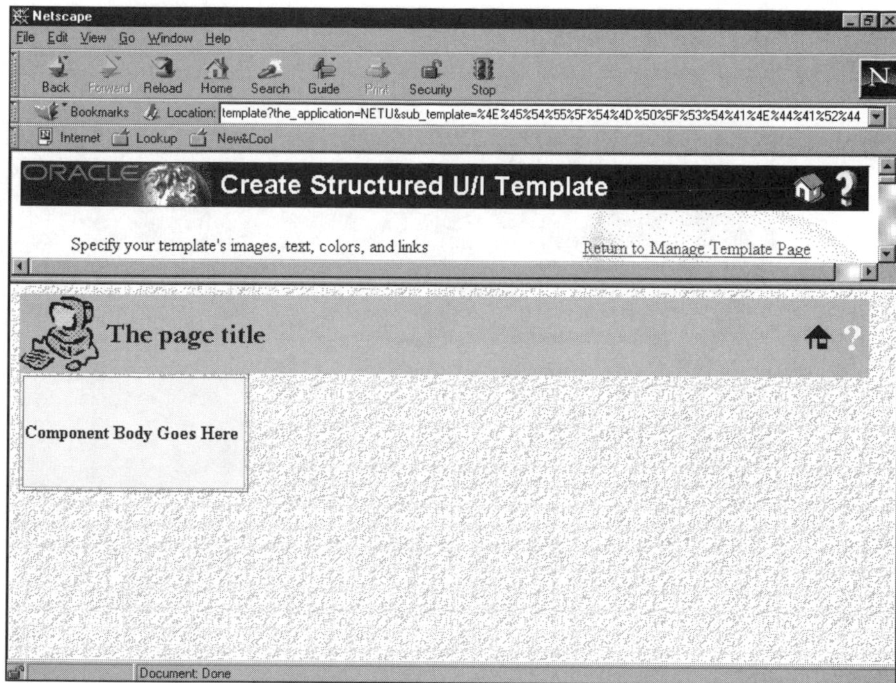

Figure 15-19: Template rendering frame

11. Change the background image to **netu_bg**.
12. Save this new template using the Save button at the top of the form.
13. Return to the Manage Template page.

Using unstructured templates

While structured templates provide you with the ability to add advanced formatting to your WebDB components, you are limited in the type of interface you can build. If you are an advanced HTML author and you find that you need to provide additional flexibility for your applications, WebDB offers the unstructured template format.

1. Click the User Interface Template link on the Shared Components menu to create a new, unstructured template as shown in Figure 15-20.

The Unstructured U/I Template page lacks the individual fields and sections found in the structured template builder. An unstructured template is nothing more than a block of HTML in a certain format. Underneath the covers, the structured template format is actually nothing more than a block of HTML text as well. Listing 15-1 shows the source of the structured template you created in the previous section:

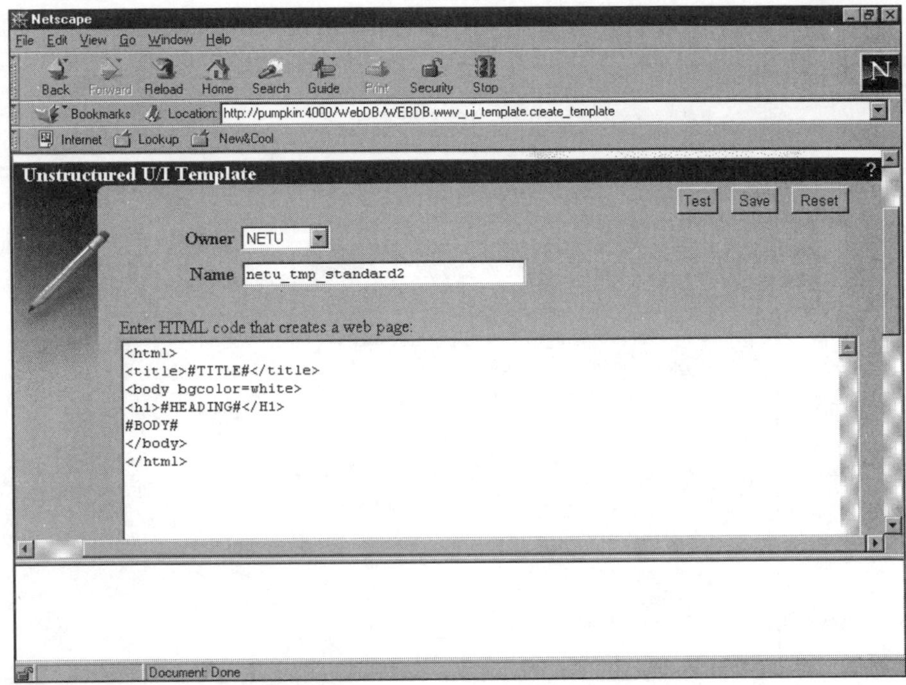

Figure 15-20: Unstructured template

Listing 15-1: **Structured template format**

```
<HTML>
<TITLE>The page title</TITLE>
<BODY bgcolor="#FFFFFF" background="/images/netu_bg.gif">
<SCRIPT LANGUAGE="JavaScript">
<!-- Comment out script for old browsers
 //onClick event handler
 function show_help(h) {
 newWindow = window.open( h, "HelpPage",
"scrollbars=1,resizable=1,width=600,height=400");
}
//-->
</SCRIPT>
<TABLE  width="100%" height="40" cellpadding=0 cellspacing=0
border=0 bgcolor="#CDCDCD" >
<TR>
<TD width="1%" align="LEFT"><A
HREF="/static/netu_about.htm"><IMG
SRC="/images/netu_heading.gif" ALT="Net University Information
Page" border="0"></A></TD>
<TD width="97%" align="LEFT"><FONT COLOR="#000000"
FACE="Garamond"
SIZE="+2"><B> The page title</B></FONT></TD>
```

```
<!—- frame_link =  —->
<TD ALIGN="right" width="1%"><A
HREF="WEBDB.wwv_ui_template.example_home_link"
target="_top"><IMG SRC="/images/netu_home.gif" valign=top
ALT="Application Home" border=" 0"></A></TD>
<TD ALIGN="right"><A
HREF="WEBDB.wwv_ui_template.example_help_link"><IMG
SRC="/images/netu_help.gif" valign=top ALT="Help"
border="0"></A></TD>
</TR>
</TABLE>
<table border=1 bgcolor=yellow><tr><td><p> <p>
<B>Component Body Goes Here</B>
<p> </td></tr></table>
```

You can see the data that you supplied in the structured template embedded in the text of the HTML source for the template. WebDB implements the heading block using HTML tables. This enables you to align the application image, title text, Home icon, and Help icon along the same line. The equivalent HTML source in the unstructured format is much simpler, because you are expected to "roll your own" HTML.

The secret to building an unstructured template is a series of keywords WebDB provides. The WebDB run-time system replaces the keywords with generated data when the template is used. Table 15-3 lists the keywords and their usage.

Table 15-3
Template Keywords

Keyword	*Usage*
#TITLE#	The title is the text that appears at the top of the browser and is transmitted by the component object to the template at run time. When you create a WebDB report, form, chart, calendar, and so on, you include title text on the Add Text panel. WebDB replaces the string #TITLE# with this text.
#HEADING#	The heading text is supplied on the same panel as the title, and it appears just below the title text.
#HELPLINK#	Help links connect to the help text of the component.
#HOMELINK#	The home link connects back to the home page for your application. WebDB maps this back to a standard WebDB component.

Continued

Table 15-3 *(continued)*

Keyword	***Usage***
#FRAMELINK#	Frame links are used exclusively by menus and serve as a target for menu navigation.
#BODY#	The body of the template is replaced with the data generated by the WebDB component when it is executed.
#TIMING#	The timing keyword is replaced with timing information when an object executes. Timing information is typically displayed at the bottom of the page.
#IMAGE_PREFIX#	Normally, WebDB looks for images in a standard image directory, but you can replace the path by using the image prefix keyword.

You can add any of your own HTML code to the HTML shown by default for the unstructured template.

2. Return to the main Shared Components page. Click the User Interface Templates choice.
3. Set the owner for the new template to your NetU USERID and change the name of the new template to **netu_tmp_unstructured**.
4. Delete the HTML from the text box and replace it with the code found in the file ch15_unstructured.htm using cut and paste.
5. Save and test the template.

Figure 15-21 shows the results of importing the customized HTML code. The main changes to the code are the italics around the page header and the heading line is displayed below the body of the document. The critical keywords to include within the template are the TITLE, HEADING, and BODY.

Unstructured templates offer more advanced capabilities than the simpler, structured templates. If you have existing static HTML code, you can often use it to supplement your WebDB applications using unstructured templates. Initially, it is easier to begin working with structured templates. As you become more familiar with the capabilities of templates, you can begin to branch out into using the unstructured variety. WebDB's own menu bar is built using an unstructured template.

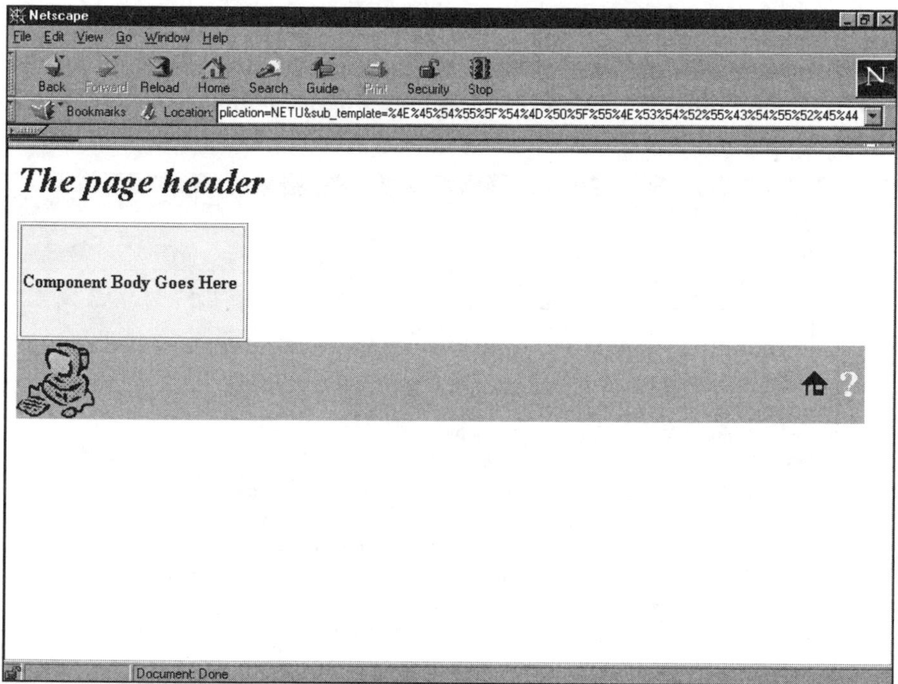

Figure 15-21: Testing unstructured display template

Deploying Templates into Your Components

The power of templates becomes apparent when you deploy them to your applications. Deploying templates is as simple as making a combo box selection within any one of the builders.

Please refer to Appendix A for information on importing components.

1. Choose any report, chart, form, calendar, hierarchy, or menu you have already built, or import the file ch15_rep_catalog.sql.
2. Edit the report (or any other object you choose) and select the Add Text (or Text Options) tab within the wizard.
3. Select the netu_tmp_standard template from the Template combo box.
4. Save the changes and run the report.

Figure 15-22 shows a simple report for the course catalog table with your structured template applied to the report. You can click the application image, the home image, and the help image, and WebDB displays the linked objects automatically.

5. Navigate through the report and test out the remaining template features.

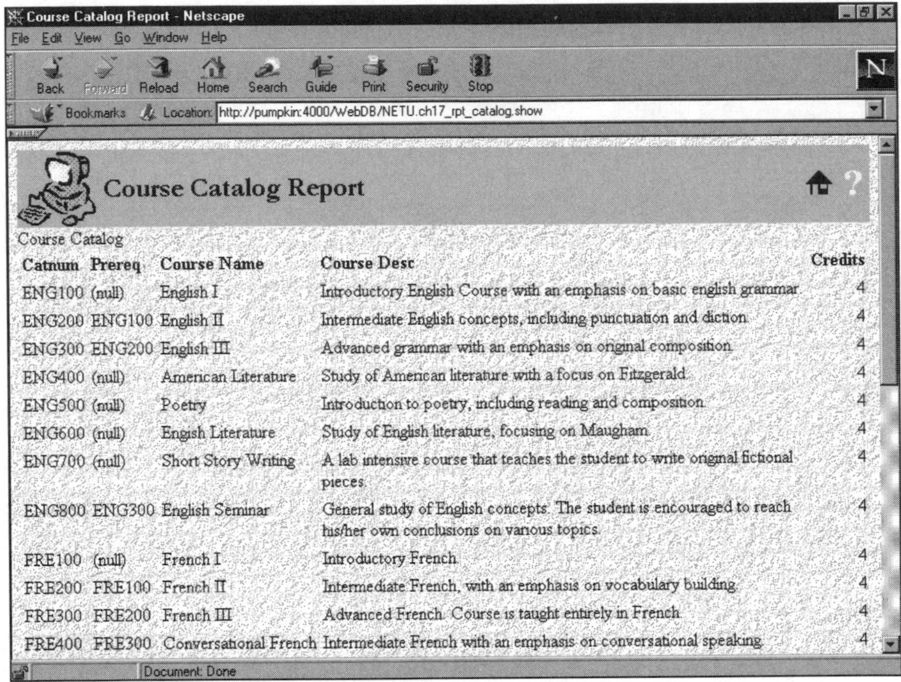

Catnum	Prereq	Course Name	Course Desc	Credits
ENG100	(null)	English I	Introductory English Course with an emphasis on basic english grammar.	4
ENG200	ENG100	English II	Intermediate English concepts, including punctuation and diction.	4
ENG300	ENG200	English III	Advanced grammar with an emphasis on original composition.	4
ENG400	(null)	American Literature	Study of American literature with a focus on Fitzgerald.	4
ENG500	(null)	Poetry	Introduction to poetry, including reading and composition.	4
ENG600	(null)	Engish Literature	Study of English literature, focusing on Maugham.	4
ENG700	(null)	Short Story Writing	A lab intensive course that teaches the student to write original fictional pieces.	4
ENG800	ENG300	English Seminar	General study of English concepts. The student is encouraged to reach his/her own conclusions on various topics.	4
FRE100	(null)	French I	Introductory French.	4
FRE200	FRE100	French II	Intermediate French, with an emphasis on vocabulary building.	4
FRE300	FRE200	French III	Advanced French. Course is taught entirely in French.	4
FRE400	FRE300	Conversational French	Intermediate French with an emphasis on conversational speaking.	4

Figure 15-22: Report deployed with a template

Wrapping Up

WebDB's shared objects provide you with a suite of tools for building consistency into your applications. A single application likely has several templates to match the different classes of users and component types. Certain objects may require additional formatting, which templates can provide. Consistent use of colors, fonts, and images can help build commonality into your applications and make them easier to use. Training costs will decrease as users find that individual objects look and behave the same way.

Templates are so easy to create and use that you will find them indispensable when you are creating applications. Even if individual reports, charts, calendars, menus, forms, hierarchies, and pages are built inconsistently, you can use templates to tie them together at run time.

✦ ✦ ✦

Data Validation with WebDB

In This Chapter

Data Validation Concepts

JavaScript

Creating JavaScript Validations with WebDB

Testing the JavaScript

Building More Complicated Scripts

Attaching Validations to Forms

Cross-field Validations

Cross-record Validations

Server-side Validations

In the days of mainframe computing, the user was often forced to wait until a screen was filled completely before the system provided any feedback on the data the user entered. One of the keys to the success of client/server applications was the capability to provide the user with rapid feedback on the validity of data that was input to the system. By using the computing power of the desktop, it was possible to validate data entry values directly from the client workstation, giving the user immediate feedback on the data.

As client/server systems spread, developers quickly realized there was a problem with this solution. They found that different developers working on separate projects that accessed the same data were often using different validation rules. On one screen, the user was allowed to enter one value and on another screen, a different value was permitted for the same column. The solution to this problem was to embed rules in the database that would verify the correctness of the data before it was stored in the database. These rules acted as a last line of defense against improper values being written to the database. Application developers made use of both types of rules: client-side validation for making forms easier to use, and server-side rules for ensuring that data entered into the database was valid and logical. Browser-based applications have continued this tradition by using the same two technologies for data validation, albeit with a slightly different implementation. Web browsers use JavaScript to validate data entry on the client side, and they rely on the same database constraints and triggers from the days of client/server computing to validate data on the server side.

Data Validation Concepts

Data values must be validated against a set of rules before data is stored within a database in order to ensure the consistency of the resulting information. There are cases in which database columns do not require validation, such as comment fields or notes fields. However, the vast majority of database columns require some sort of basic validation in order to be sure they contain values consistent with the needs of the organization. Data validations fall into a set of six basic categories as follows:

- Null/Not Null
- Exact match
- Referential integrity
- Ranges
- Pattern matching
- Cross-field validation

The simplest form of validation is the *Null/Not Null* validation. If your applications require that a user enter a value for a given column, the field is considered to have a Not Null validation. On the other hand, if the user is not required to enter a value for the field, the column is considered to be nullable, and a column that lacks a value for a record is considered to be null. In the NetU database, the LASTNAME and FIRSTNAME fields in the UGRADS table must be filled in, so they have been given the Not Null validation. You would not want to create a student record if you did not have a first name and last name for the student. On the other hand, you can leave the gender field blank, or null. You would certainly want to know the gender of the student, but it is not a requirement for entering a record into the system. Values that are critical to a given record should be given a Not Null validation test, and values that are optional can accept null values.

In the case of the gender field, it is permissible that the value for this field be left as null. However, if the user supplies a value for this field, you will want to be sure the value entered is consistent across records. The gender field is a single-character field and the intent is for the user to enter either an **F** for female or an **M** for male into this field. This type of validation is an *exact match* requirement. Users can leave the gender field blank, but if they enter a value, it can only be the letters F or M. Exact match validations are typically case sensitive because you do not want to permit your users to enter both uppercase and lowercase letters for the same intended value. Doing so makes querying the database much more difficult, because you are forced to check for the presence of both case values (F/f, M/m) every time you execute a query.

If the exact match validation value for a field is stored in a column in another table, the validation is considered to be a *foreign key* or referential integrity validation. The value in the column matches a primary key value in another table, and in relational jargon this is called a foreign key. Within the UGRADS table, the CLASSYR field requires a foreign key validation that matches the CLASSYR field of the CLASSES table. You cannot enter a value for the CLASSYR field in the UGRADS tables that does not already exist in the CLASSES table. After all, you do not want to associate a student with a graduation year that does not exist. Using a foreign key validation ensures that your user only enters student records with valid class years. You may also wish to enforce uniqueness using references to keys across tables, and this type of validation falls under the broad category of referential integrity as well. Typically, you perform these validations at the server level as well as the client level to ensure that bad data does not find its way into the database. Although this may seem like a duplication of work, the two sets of validations serve different purposes. Server-side validations, which are typically written in PL/SQL, protect the data. Client-side referential integrity constraints make it easier for the user to work with the data on the form.

Some fields within your database allow for a large number of values that do not match fields within a parent in a table. Nevertheless, these same fields may only permit a limited number of values. The most common column format for this type of validation is dates. While you will often allow your users free rein to add a date value, you should still validate the value entered in some way. For example, within the UGRADS table, the user is allowed to enter a date of birth for each student in the DOB field. NetU does not discriminate on the basis of age, and you are free to add students of any age, within reason, to the system. *Range* validations determine what "within reason" means for a given column. For example, you would not want enter a student into the system who was less than 17 years old. Furthermore, the birth date you enter should be a valid birth date—you cannot be born on September 41, for example. These are both examples of range validations; the value for the day of the month ranges from 1 to 31 and the value for the range of years should correspond with students being at least 17 years old. The width of the range is based upon the type of data that you are capturing. If you were storing the daily Fahrenheit temperature in a table, then the logical range of values might be from –100 to +200. On the other hand, if you were storing the date of a gift record in the DONATIONS table, then the AMOUNT field would range from one dollar to one million dollars. One of the most common forms of range validations is the datatype validation. Datatype validations ensure that character data is not entered into numeric fields and vice versa. For example, this type of validation is considered to be part of the range validation for a number because the implied range of values for numeric fields are numbers.

There are times when the validation you need to enforce upon a field does not follow a set of values, but rather it follows a set of rules. Postal codes in most foreign countries are a mix of a certain number of letters and numbers, and the particular mix is almost always a pattern. In this case, the data validation for the column is a *pattern matching* validation. The data for the field contains a fixed combination of numbers and characters. Pattern matches are common for fields in which the individual characters within a field have their own particular meaning. The CATNUM field in the COURSE_CATALOG table is an example of one such field in the NetU database. The catalog number is composed of three letters indicating the department followed by three numbers indicating the course number for the department. The pattern is three uppercase characters followed by three lowercase characters.

The last category of data validation is the most complicated. *Cross-field* validations check the value of one column against a value in a subsequent column. For example, in an order entry system, the value you enter for the tax rate may be based upon the state from which the customer is ordering. In this case, the valid value for the tax field cannot be determined without checking the ship-to state field. Sometimes you enforce a cross-field validation by looking at a range of records. For example, the valid discount percentage may require that you add up the amount the customer has spent.

Each validation type can be performed at either the client side or the server side, and in most cases it is performed at *both* levels. WebDB enables you to easily handle all of the preceding types of validations at both the client side and the server side. Only cross-field validations prove more difficult to enforce at the client side. If the cross-field validation requires you to access database values that are not part of the current page, you are not able to enforce the validation at the client side. However, you are still able to enforce the restriction at the database server level. Client-side validations are made with JavaScript and server-side validations are enforced with Oracle constraints and triggers written in either PL/SQL or Java.

Normally you build database validations from the server out to the client. This means that you create your database constraints and triggers first, and then you create the client-side validations to match these constraints later on. With WebDB, you may find that you can skip over the server-level validations if you have a preexisting database, because the database is likely to already have these validations in place.

JavaScript

JavaScript is a client-side scripting language for your browser created by Netscape Communications Corporation. JavaScript was originally named LiveScript. The language's name was changed to JavaScript in 1995 after Netscape entered into a marketing agreement with Sun Microsystems to sublicense the Java prefix. JavaScript is often erroneously thought to be a version of the Java language for your browser. While it is true that both JavaScript and the Java programming language share some common syntax and style, they are not equivalent. JavaScript was intended to be a programming language for working with HTML documents, while Java is a full-fledged object-oriented programming language.

The two languages require a completely separate processing engine within the browser, and they are more different than they are the same. Programmers have attempted to draw the distinction that Java is primarily for the server and JavaScript is primarily for the client. As it turns out, both assertions are false. The Java programming language is equally good at building client-side applications and server applications, and Netscape offers a version of JavaScript called LiveWire that runs at the server level. From the WebDB perspective, JavaScript is a scripting language for working with HTML on the client side. WebDB uses JavaScript scripts to enforce data validation logic at the browser level.

JavaScript compatibility

Netscape Navigator and Microsoft Internet Explorer both support a version of JavaScript, although Microsoft has historically lagged behind in its support for JavaScript. As of this writing, the current release of the JavaScript language is version 1.2 and both Netscape Navigator 4.*x* (and subsequent releases) and Microsoft Internet Explorer 4.01 support the 1.2 version. Microsoft has run into licensing issues with Sun Microsystems over the Java language and with Netscape over the name JavaScript. The result is that Microsoft calls their version of JavaScript JScript, but it is basically compatible with JavaScript 1.2. Microsoft offers a client-side scripting language of their own called VBScript, which is based upon Microsoft's Visual Basic Language. Although JavaScript is not derived from Java, VBScript is derived directly from Visual Basic. The designers of WebDB specifically chose to use JavaScript as the client-side data validation tool for WebDB because JavaScript is supported by a wider variety of browsers. While it may be possible to use VBScript with WebDB, we discourage you from doing so because it limits your users to running Internet Explorer as their browser.

JavaScript is a much simpler language to learn compared to Java, but that does not mean that JavaScript is limited in functionality. In fact, you can build some very complex and sophisticated user interfaces if you make use of all of JavaScript's capabilities.

In order to make applications easier to develop, both Netscape and Microsoft have created a hierarchy of objects within their browsers. This hierarchy determines the names, addresses, and attributes of the objects within an HTML page. This hierarchy is commonly known as the *document object model* for the browser. If you were developing HTML applications from scratch with raw HTML text, you would find that a complete understanding of the document object model might be necessary. However, because WebDB is managing and creating most of the HTML that you generate, it is not necessary for you to understand all the ins and outs of the document object model in order to use JavaScript within WebDB applications. Table 16-1 shows you the four key elements of the document object model you may use within WebDB.

Table 16-1
Document Object Model Elements

Element	*Description*
Window	The top of the document object model hierarchy is the Window object, and it represents the browser in which the application is running. For the most part you will work with a single window unless you make extensive use of frames, in which case you need to work with multiple windows because each frame is displayed within its own window.
Document	Each HTML page created and loaded into your browser by WebDB is a document. It is very rare to work with multiple windows, but it is possible that you will work with multiple documents. Documents are also the *container* object for any of the form elements you create.
Form Object	HTML forms are created by using the <FORM> and </FORM> tags within an HTML page. It is possible to create more than one form within a document, and thus forms are one level below documents in the hierarchy. The Form Object is a container for all the display fields that are shown on a data entry page.
Form Elements	Form Elements are the individual form fields that appear on an HTML page (for example, text boxes, check boxes, and radio groups). By and large, you will find the JavaScript validations you build for WebDB concern themselves with Form Elements, which are described in more detail in the next section.

Form Elements

Form Elements have a number of associated events you are probably familiar with if you have programmed in JavaScript before. JavaScripts define *what* to do and events define *when* to do it. For example, you want to make sure the date of birth for a student is at least 17 years ago. The event determines when you enforce this validation. Do you want to enforce this when the user tabs out of the field? How about when the mouse passes over the date of birth field? The document object model provides many opportunities for firing off this validation, but you can only use two of them within WebDB: the onBlur event and the onClick event.

WebDB uses the List-of-Values Wizard to create validations based upon data values in the database, as you learned in Chapter 13. Lists of values can take many different display formats. However, the only format you can use for JavaScript validations is the Textbox format. The reason for this relates back to the nature of the display formats. You cannot display a database field as anything other than one of the following formats unless you use a List-of-Values object:

✦ Hidden Field

✦ Textbox

✦ TextArea

✦ Password

Each of these field types is a variation of the textbox form element, and the event rules that apply to text boxes apply to these elements as well. The document object model allows for the following events to be defined for text boxes as listed in Table 16-2.

Table 16-2
Textbox Events

Event Name	*Description*
onBlur	Signaled when the user leaves the field either using the keyboard or the mouse.
onChange	Fired when the user begins to change a value within a form field.
onFocus	Called when the user enters the field either using the keyboard or the mouse.
onSelect	Fired when the user uses the mouse to select a block of text within the field as in a copy operation.
onKeyDown	Signaled when the user presses a key on the keyboard within the field. This event fires for each keystroke within a given field.
onKeyUp	Signaled when the user releases a key that was previously pressed on the keyboard. This event fires for each keystroke within a given field.

The browser enables you to attach a block of JavaScript code to each of the events listed in Table 16-2. In fact, the actual list of events is much larger, because JavaScript supports events for all of the other form element types including check boxes, radio groups, combo boxes, multiple select boxes, images, and labels. This enables you to have an incredible amount of control over the data validation within form elements, because you can add code for each event. However, you can ignore these additional events entirely for the purposes of working with WebDB because WebDB supports only two JavaScript events: the text box onBlur event and the push button object onClick event.

The document object model and the event model for JavaScript are much more complicated than portrayed in this chapter. However, because WebDB hides most of this complexity from you, it is unnecessary for you to dive into the details of the event model in order to use JavaScript with WebDB for data validation purposes.

If you are not familiar with building JavaScript validations, you are probably slightly confused, because you are not even sure what a JavaScript script looks like, never mind how to attach one to a form. Never fear, you will be introduced the basic elements of JavaScript later in this chapter.

JavaScript elements

While you can build sophisticated programs in JavaScript, the basic script type for performing data validation is a function. Functions are composed of a series of JavaScript syntax statements, as shown in Listing 16-1.

Listing 16-1: Simple JavaScript function

```
//
// Comment Text
//
function netu_showvalue (theElement)
{
var my_vaiable = 5
if (theElement.value > 10) {
     alert("The value is greater than 10")
} else {
     alert("The value is less than 10")
}
return true
}
```

The preceding block of code is fairly simple, but it shows off the basic components of a JavaScript function. JavaScripts are much like any other program and they have a number of component pieces as follows:

- ✦ Comment text
- ✦ Function declaration
- ✦ Name
- ✦ Parameter list
- ✦ Variable declarations
- ✦ Control structures
- ✦ Methods
- ✦ Return values

The key to any complex system is proper documentation. JavaScript supports a comment indicator using the double slash character (//). Although it is not a requirement of JavaScript itself, it is a good idea for you to start all of your scripts with some comment information. Doing so makes the task of maintaining these scripts much easier for the programmer who has to support your code later on. The function shown in Listing 16-1 includes three lines of comment text to identify the function.

The first requirement for a JavaScript program unit is the *function* statement. The job of the function keyword is to name the following block of code as a JavaScript program unit. The function statement starts with the keyword *function* and includes the name and the parameter list for the function.

The *name* of the JavaScript function follows the function keyword. The name is a string of up to 32 characters that must start with a letter and may not contain any punctuation characters other than the underscore character (_). WebDB adds a restriction that the function name must match the name that you use to identify the script to WebDB, as you will see later on in this chapter.

Note JavaScript passes the element handle by default and you must use method calls within the function to extract the information you need from the element. JavaScript offers a great deal of flexibility in this area, but you do not need to concern yourself with most of the details in order to build data validation routines into WebDB.

The next item is the *parameter list,* which is a list of elements passed to the function when it is called. The parameter you pass from your page to the JavaScript is a type of pointer to the field on the page. WebDB handles the transformation of the parameter for you and gives you access to the various parts of the parameter through a series of standard method calls. These method calls are a series of keywords appended to the name of the parameter that produce some output for you to use.

For the most part, you will use a single method in your WebDB JavaScript functions — the VALUE method, which refers to the value of the parameter. You could also get access to the number of characters stored in the parameter by using the LENGTH method.

JavaScript uses dot-based notation similar to what the Internet uses for separating URL addresses (for example, `www.netu-college.com`). For instance, if you pass an element called MY_PARM to a function, you can derive the value of MY_PARM by making a method call within the function as follows:

```
var my_variable
my_variable = MY_PARM.value
```

Parameters can be a very complex topic, but WebDB simplifies the process by controlling the manner in which the function is called at run time. WebDB only allows you to pass a single parameter to the function, and WebDB always translates the field name that calls the script into the element name that you use. In other words, the only parameter you can pass into a JavaScript is a pointer to the calling field. For the moment you do not need to worry about the specifics of the parameter name, only that you can pass a parameter to the script.

The next item in the function is the *declaration* of variables. Just like any other programming language, JavaScript supports the declaration of variables. Unlike most other languages, it automatically converts data between one datatype and another. Variables can be declared anywhere within the body of a JavaScript function. Table 16-3 lists the base datatypes JavaScript supports.

Table 16-3
JavaScript Datatypes

Datatype	*Description*	*Sample*
String	Any series of characters surrounded by double quotes	"Joe" "Joe Smith"
Number	Any set of numbers and punctuation separators not surrounded by quotes	10 4.5
Boolean	A logical true or false	true false

You must declare variables by using the *var* keyword, and the names of your variables must follow the same restrictions as the name of functions. In addition, you must be careful to avoid using JavaScript keywords in the names of variables. It is often a good idea to use mixed case variable names and underscore characters in order to avoid the likelihood of running into keywords inadvertently. Notice that there is no declaration of the datatype for a variable, because the variable type is set whenever you use the variable in an expression. Expressions are composed of variables and operators, and JavaScript supports a standard set of operators, as shown in Table 16-4.

Table 16-4
JavaScript Operators

Operator	*Name*	*Type*	*Works On*
=	Set Equal to	Value	Numbers, Strings
+	Plus	Value	Numbers, Strings
-	Minus	Value	Numbers
*	Multiply	Value	Numbers
/	Divide	Value	Numbers
%	Modulo	Value	Numbers
++	Increment	Value	Numbers

Operator	Name	Type	Works On
–	Decrement	Value	Numbers
==	Equality	Comparison	Numbers, Strings
!=	Not Equal	Comparison	Numbers, Strings
>	Greater Than	Comparison	Numbers, Strings
>=	Greater Than or Equal to	Comparison	Numbers, Strings
<	Less Than	Comparison	Numbers, Strings
<=	Less Than or Equal to	Comparison	Numbers, Strings
&&	And	Boolean	Numbers, Strings
||	Or	Boolean	Numbers, Strings

The top portion of Table 16-4 holds the *value* operators that are used to set the value for a variable or expression. The bottom half of the table contains the *comparison* operators and *Boolean* operators, which are used for the purpose of decision making. In addition to the standard operators, JavaScript provides the additional null keyword used to set the value of a variable to an empty state, much like a database NULL value. JavaScript automatically converts variables between types, as the following lines of code demonstrate:

```
"Joe " + "Smith" // result  = "Joe Smith"
9 + 9            // result  = 18
"9" + 9          // result  = "99"
"9" - 1          // result  = invalid, "9" is not a number
```

The comparison operators are primarily used in *control structures,* which are the sixth element of a JavaScript function. Control structures provide you with decision-making processes for your JavaScript functions. JavaScript offers a very powerful set of control structures, including commands to step through the properties of an object at run time. JavaScript provides five different types of control structures that you will find useful in working with WebDB:

- ✦ If-Else
- ✦ Switch
- ✦ For loop
- ✦ While loop
- ✦ Do-While loop

The If-Else control structure is a standard set of syntax for basic decision making and it is structured as follows:

```
if (condition) {
     code if true
} else {
     code if false
}
```

The condition is an operator-based expression that evaluates to a true/false condition and it can contain any number of variables, value operators, and comparison operators. You are free to nest If-Else statements and you can have any number of lines of code within the curly braces as shown in the following code sample:

```
var var_a = 10
var var_b = 20
if (a > b) {
     alert("a is larger than b")
} else {
    alert("b is larger than a")
    a = a + b
}
```

You must use the *equality comparison* operator "= =" for comparisons in expressions; the *set equals* operator "="causes the comparison value to be set to the comparison value.

JavaScript enables you to nest multiple levels of If-Else statements, but you will want avoid excessively deep hierarchies of If-Else loops because they are harder to read and maintain. JavaScript provides the *switch* statement as an alternative for lengthy If-Else statements. The switch statement uses the following syntax structure:

```
switch (expression) {
     case label1:
          code
          [break]
     case label2:
          code
          [break]
      ...
     default:
          code
}
```

The expression can be any valid variable or combination of operators that evaluates to a value. The `case/label: structure` gives you a place to list a value for comparison, and the code below the value gets executed only if the expression evaluates to a value that matches the label. In the following example code fragment, the switch statement is used to test for a specific value of class year:

```
var some_year = "2002"
var my_class = null
switch (some_year) {
     case "1999":
           my_class = "Senior"
           break
     case "2000":
           my_class = "Junior"
     case "2001":
          my_class = "Sophomore"
     default:
         my_class = "Freshman"
}
```

In the preceding example, the switch statement falls through to the default value because it does not match any of the strings beside the other case statements. JavaScript provides a *break* command to enable you to break out of a switch statement once a match has been found. By default, switch statements continue to process even after a match has been found, enabling you to modify the value of the expression in the *body* of the switch statement. Adding a break statement after a command statement as shown previously for "1999" causes the switch statement to end once a match has been found. You must add the break statement to each case substatement you wish to break out of.

If you need to cycle through a fixed number of expressions several times each the For loop is probably a better choice. For loops follow a fixed number of cycles through a set of code and they work much like For loops in C, Java, and PL/SQL.

```
for (initial expression; condition; update expression) {
      code
}
```

The loop processes until the conditional expression becomes false, and the loop starts with a value for the initial expression as set by you in the For statement. Each complete cycle results in the update expression being executed, and the value for the expression can be used in the body of the loop as follows:

```
for (var i= 1; i< 10; i++) {
     alert ("The Value of i is :" +String(i))
}
```

The For loop is ideal for parsing through a string searching for a set of characters or for enforcing a pattern.

Note

String indexes start with the zero (0) position in JavaScript, and you need to keep this in mind if you use For loops to parse strings of values. The first character position of a string is always zero.

JavaScript permits you to embed functions within For loops, and you can combine conditions with the Boolean and/or operators to produce compound expressions with For loops. For example, the comparison operation can itself be a function call to another procedure, which returns a Boolean result. You can use this feature to build a loop that is equal to the length of a string field for parsing.

If you need to build a more general-purpose looping routine, JavaScript offers the While loop and the Do-While loop. Both of these control structures loop indefinitely until a given condition becomes false. While loops check the condition at the beginning of the loop, and Do-While loops check the condition at the end of the loop. Do-While loops always execute at least once, and While loops may or may not execute at least once depending upon the condition. The format for the two structures is as follows:

```
// While Loop
while(condition){
     code
}

// Do Loop
do {
      code
} while (condition)
```

The While loop evaluates the condition before cycling through its code. In the following example, the body of the loop never gets executed because the expression is false to begin with:

```
while (1<0) {
     alert("Did you know one is less than zero?")
}
```

If you changed the While loop to a Do-While loop, then the code within the loop executes at least once:

```
do {
     alert("One is less than zero for one time only!")
} while (1<0)
```

Because of this, you use a Do-While loop when you want to guarantee that a given block of code is executed at least once, and a While loop when you only want to execute a block of code when a condition is true.

There are many subtleties to JavaScript's control structures and you will want to have a copy of a more detailed text on JavaScript if you plan on building very complex JavaScript procedures. IDG Books Worldwide offers *JavaScript Bible* for those of you who want to learn more about JavaScript in detail. Netscape has added a great deal of built-in functionality to JavaScript in the form of methods and functions that are included directly within the language. These methods can be invaluable in helping you build more complex functions and programs. *JavaScript Bible* provides detailed examples for all the built-in JavaScript functions and methods. You have seen fragments of some of these methods in the previous sample code blocks and Table 16-5 shows a partial table of these functions.

Table 16-5
JavaScript Methods and Functions

Method	Description	Example
`alert(string)`	Alert displays a message to the user. The alert method is part of the Window object, but you can use the method all by itself without prepending the window keyword, because the window is the highest part of the document hierarchy.	`alert("Hello World!")`

`confirm(string)`	Confirm is an advanced form of the alert method. The syntax is almost identical, but the confirm method gives the user two response choices: ok and cancel. The confirm statement evaluates to true or false, depending on the user's interaction with the confirm box. You typically wrap a confirm method call in an If-Else statement to test for a response.	`if (confirm("Are you ok?")) {`
		`    // Yes`
		`} else`
		`   // No`
		`}`

`prompt(string, default)`	The prompt method is related to alert and confirm and is the most powerful of the three message structures. Prompt opens a text box and enables you to insert a manual value. You can also pass a default value for the text prompt, and prompt also offers the user the same pair of ok and cancel options as the confirm method. If the user chooses the ok button, then the variable contains the value in the text box. If the user clicks the cancel button, the reply variable is null.	`var my_reply = prompt ("Are you ok?","Yes")`

Continued

Table 16-5 (continued)

Method	***Description***	***Example***
`focus( )`	Sets the focus on the HTML page to the specified FORM object.	`my_textfield.focus()`
`select( )`	Selects the text entered into the field on the form.	`my_textfield.select()`
`indexOf(string)`	Finds the starting position of a substring within a string.	`var string_x = "ABCDEF"`
`var num_y = string_x.indexOf("B") // result = 1`		

`charAt(position)`	The charAt method returns the single character at the specified numeric position within a string. JavaScript strings all start at position zero (0). The charAt function is part of the string object and it is called by appending it to the string name.	`var my_string = " ABCDEF"`
		`my_string.charAt(1)`
		`// result = "B"`

`Number`	Number converts a string of numeric characters to a number. The Number method is part of the window structure and it can be called directly.	`var my_value = "123"`
		`Number(my_value)* 10`
		`// result = 1230`

`String`	String converts a number to a string value. The String method is part of the window hierarchy and it can be called directly.	`var my_value = 123` `String(my_value) + " Oak St."// result = "123 Oak St."`

JavaScript functions and methods are case sensitive. Take note of the mixed case characters above when you attempt to use *any* of the preceding methods in your own code.

JavaScript has literally hundreds of prebuilt methods for windows and pages you can use to accomplish a variety of tasks. You only need to know the basics in order to perform validations with WebDB, but we recommend that you get a copy of *JavaScript Bible* if you plan on doing any complex JavaScript coding. In many cases, JavaScript already has a method or function that handles the complex problem you are trying to solve by writing your own routine. One such example is the date object, which offers well over a dozen functions, as you will see in the next section.

JavaScript dates

You are likely to want to manipulate dates on the client side frequently. After all, you can perform simple checks such as making sure the product shipment date is later than the order date on the client side. This type of validation makes your applications easier to use and it saves your browser from having to make unnecessary trips back to the database server to validate "bad" data. JavaScript implements dates as objects within the page, and you need to reserve a variable and create a date using the new keyword in order to work with dates.

```
var my_date = new Date( )
```

If you create a date without passing it any parameters, JavaScript uses the current date and time from the browser as the value for your date. Most of the methods associated with dates are used to either extract values or to set values as shown in Table 16-6.

Table 16-6
JavaScript Date Methods

Method	*Description*
GetTime( )	Milliseconds since 1/1/70 00:00:00 in GMT.
GetYear( )	Year minus 1900.
GetMonth( )	Month within the year as a number starting with month number zero (0).
getDate( )	Day number within the month, starting with 1.
getDay( )	Day of the week starting with Sunday as the first day. As with months, days of the week start numbering at zero (0).
GetHours( )	Returns the hour of the day in 24-hour time starting at hour zero (0).
GetMinutes( )	Returns the minute of the hour starting with minute zero (0).
GetSeconds( )	Returns the seconds within the minute starting with second zero (0).

Each of the *get* methods has an associated *set* method that enables you to change the value of the specified unit of the date and time. JavaScript provides a shorthand method for setting the date and time so you only need to use the set methods if you want to change a value that you have already set.

```
var my_date = new Date("September 25, 1998")
my_date.setYear(97)
```

The preceding block of code sets the initial value of date to September 25, 1998 and then changes the value of the year to 1997. Dates can be one of the more complicated types of validation you need to perform, and JavaScript's date functions come in handy for performing date validations with WebDB.

Creating JavaScript Validations with WebDB

WebDB uses JavaScript functions to validate data on the client side of the application. JavaScripts are part of the Shared Component Library shown in Figure 16-1.

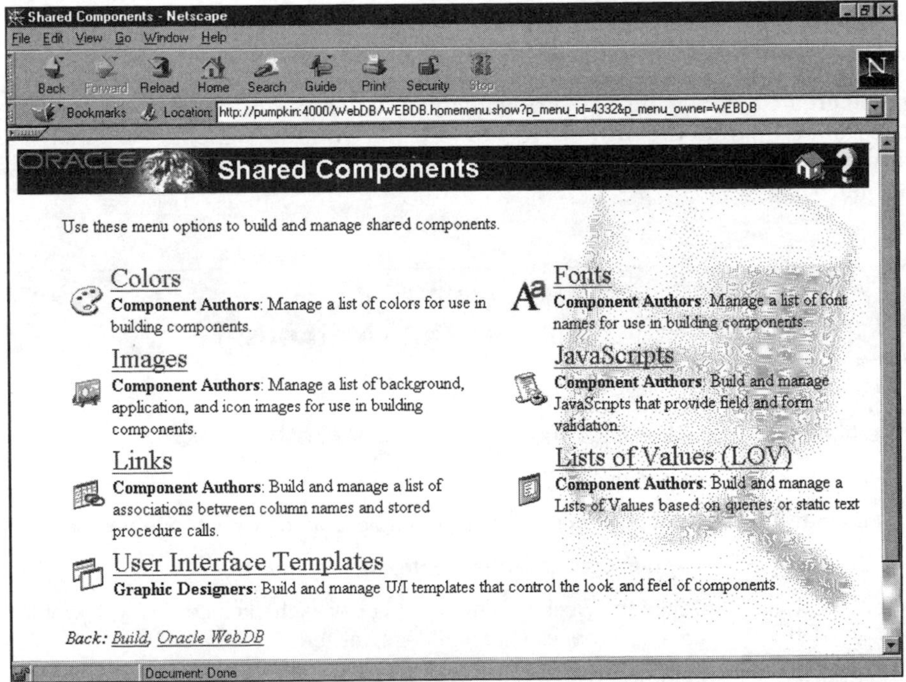

Figure 16-1: Shared Component Library

Both JavaScripts and lists of values can be used for validating data at the browser level. JavaScripts are used to validate the data that users have entered into fields, while lists of values limit the choices a user has when they enter data into a field. List-of-Values objects are covered in detail in Chapter 13 of this book, but it is important to understand a little about them when you are deciding which technique to use when validating data at the browser level. LOVs build lists of acceptable data values based upon records in your database and they require some communication with the database. JavaScripts, on the other hand, do not require any communication with the user but they do not provide the user with any visible clue as to the valid values for a given field.

1. Select the JavaScripts link from the Shared Component Library page to begin creating a JavaScript validation.

The WebDB wizard for creating JavaScript validations is one of the simplest interfaces that WebDB provides. The developers of WebDB have made no attempt to guide you through the process of writing JavaScript code with the JavaScript Wizard. If you are building JavaScript validations, WebDB assumes that you have a working knowledge of JavaScript. The initial panel for constructing JavaScript validations appears in Figure 16-2.

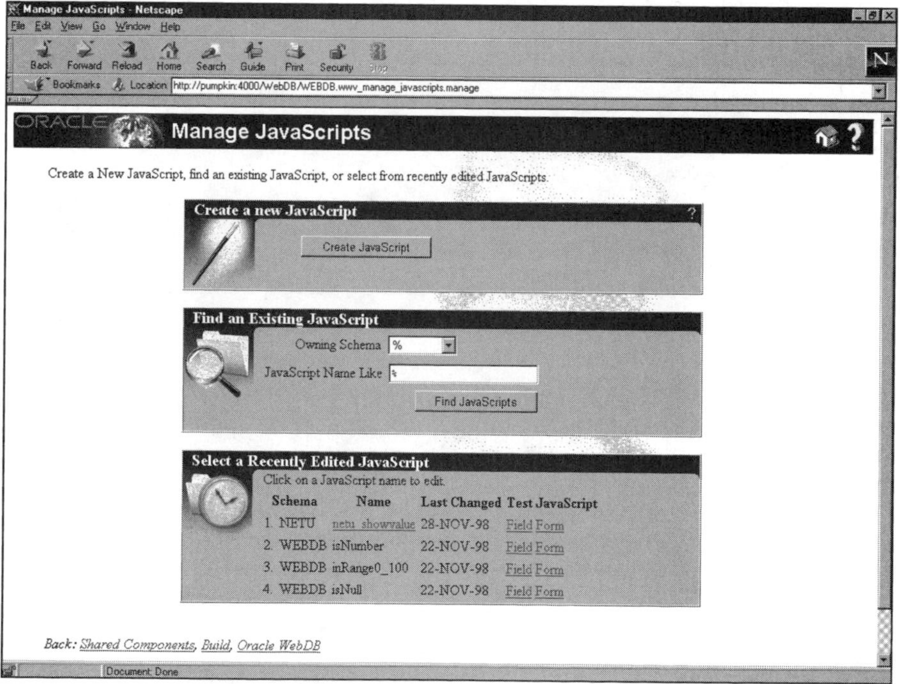

Figure 16-2: Manage JavaScripts panel

The management page is very similar to that of the other Shared Component Library objects. You can create a new JavaScript using the top panel, search for existing scripts using the middle panel, or edit and test scripts using the bottom panel.

2. Click the Create JavaScript button in the top panel to create a new JavaScript validation.

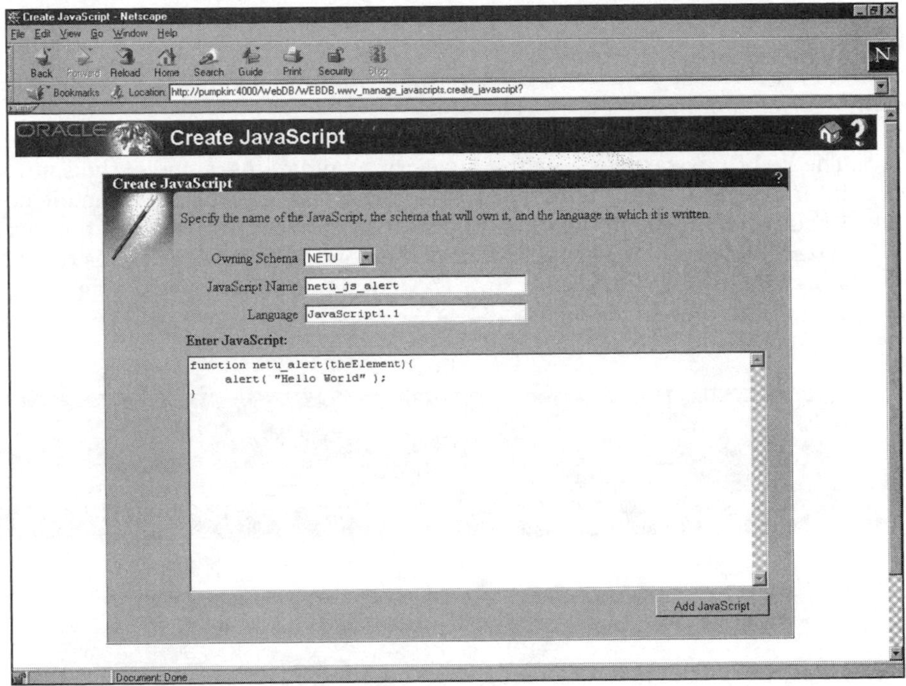

Figure 16-3: Create JavaScript panel

The Create JavaScript page is the complete interface for building JavaScript validations. It is composed of the following four components:

- ✦ Owning Schema
- ✦ JavaScript Name
- ✦ Language
- ✦ Script Code

The *Owning Schema* is the Oracle USERID that owns the resulting script, and it is used just like the owner of any other WebDB components. The script owner determines the account that controls the object once it has been created.

The *JavaScript Name* is the name you use to refer to the component, and once again it follows the same naming convention and requirements as any other WebDB component. However, the JavaScript Name serves one additional function in that it is also used as the name for the function within the code itself. The name you provide for the script must match the name as it is entered into the body of the code itself.

A single JavaScript validation may be used throughout many applications, or it may apply to a single field in a single table. The name you give to your JavaScript should reflect your planned usage of the validation. You may want to consider creating a common set of routines for general validation, which you can then augment with some additional application-specific validations. JavaScript enables you to call functions from functions, so it is theoretically possible to build general-purpose routines that you can refer to from field-specific validations. WebDB, however, only transfers the code for individual validations within a Web page. This prevents you from calling out of one function into another. Furthermore, it is not possible to attach multiple validations to a single field. The net result is that you are likely to create specific-field validations just like you would create specific database constraints: on individual columns. The naming convention you use for your JavaScripts should reflect this policy, and it makes it easier to find the validation you are looking for when you build data entry forms.

If you leave the name blank or change an existing name to all blanks, WebDB deletes the JavaScript. WebDB does not offer a separate interface for managing and deleting JavaScripts.

Note

WebDB does not validate the data in the Language field, and it is possible to change the language setting to VBScript. Although this may work, WebDB does not support changing the language setting, and VBScript will *only* work with Microsoft Internet Explorer. Technically, it is possible to change the language setting to VBScript and then code your script using VBScript code instead of JavaScript. This is not supported, however, and we do not advise you to change the language setting for this release of WebDB.

JavaScript itself has gone through several iterations of development, and this is reflected in the *Language* field. The current revision of JavaScript is JavaScript 1.2, but many older browsers do not support this version of the code. WebDB defaults to using JavaScript 1.1, and that is the value that you see loaded into the Language field by default. When WebDB renders your HTML pages, it loads your JavaScript validations into the page using the <SCRIPT> and </SCRIPT> tags. One of the parameters of the <SCRIPT> tag enables you to set the client-side language, and WebDB uses the Language value on this page to set this parameter at run time. The browser reads the language tag before it executes the script, making it possible to use different scripting languages for validation routines. At the current time, WebDB only supports JavaScript 1.1 as its validation language for the browser, but the presence of the Language identifier allows WebDB to support other languages and versions in the future. For this release of WebDB, you should leave the Language setting to the default value as provided by WebDB.

The last item on this page is the *Script Code* field, which is a large text area used for inputting the actual JavaScript validation code. The Script Code field is not a full-functioned editor, and you may find that as you use JavaScript more often, you will want to create your code in a more powerful desktop editor and paste it into this window. You are certainly free to do so, as WebDB does not provide any help in building the JavaScript procedure itself. You must enter your JavaScript code into the Script Code text area as a complete JavaScript function, including the function declaration, function name, and body as shown in Listing 16-2.

Listing 16-2: **Sample JavaScript function**

```
function netu_js_alert(theElement){
     alert( "Hello World" );
}
```

Although this particular block of code is artificially simple, it includes all the basic components you must include in the JavaScript code that you enter in the Script Code text field. WebDB does not provide any of the JavaScript primitives and you must enter all the required functional elements yourself.

The name value that you enter to the right of the function keyword must match the value that you enter into the JavaScript Name field. If you use two different name strings, or if you change the case of any of the characters from one name to the next, WebDB will be unable to locate the function at run time.

The parameters for the function you create are shown between the two parentheses. If you are familiar with JavaScript from building previous applications, you know that the name you use for the parameter is typically specific to the script. In this case, WebDB automatically coerces the HTML field to the proper parameter value at run time, and you need not concern yourself with the specifics of the parameter name you use. WebDB's own scripts use the mixed case name theElement as the parameter value name, and you can either follow this standard or choose your own name. The parameter name is case sensitive, so you need to refer to the parameter using a consistent set of uppercase and lowercase letters.

Select a single consistent name to use as the function parameter name. WebDB converts the associated field into the parameter at run time for you and it does not matter what you call the parameter. However, using a consistent parameter name helps your junior programmers along by giving them consistent examples they can follow. If you use a single parameter name, they are able to cut and paste from your example code directly into their own routines as necessary.

The Manage Component page for JavaScripts provides a test panel so that you can see your JavaScripts in action before you deploy them into applications. However, WebDB does not provide you with any tools for verifying that an individual line of

JavaScript is working properly. If you are using Netscape Navigator as your browser, you will find that there is a workaround for this problem.

1. Use the File/Open Page menu choice on the pull-down menu bar for Navigator and enter the string **javascript:** as the URL and press the Open push button.

   Navigator opens up a two-pane window that enables you to enter single lines of JavaScript and test them immediately within the browser as shown in Figure 16-4. Although this is a far cry from the interactive debug windows provided with other integrated development environments, it does provide a basic test capability for your JavaScript functions.

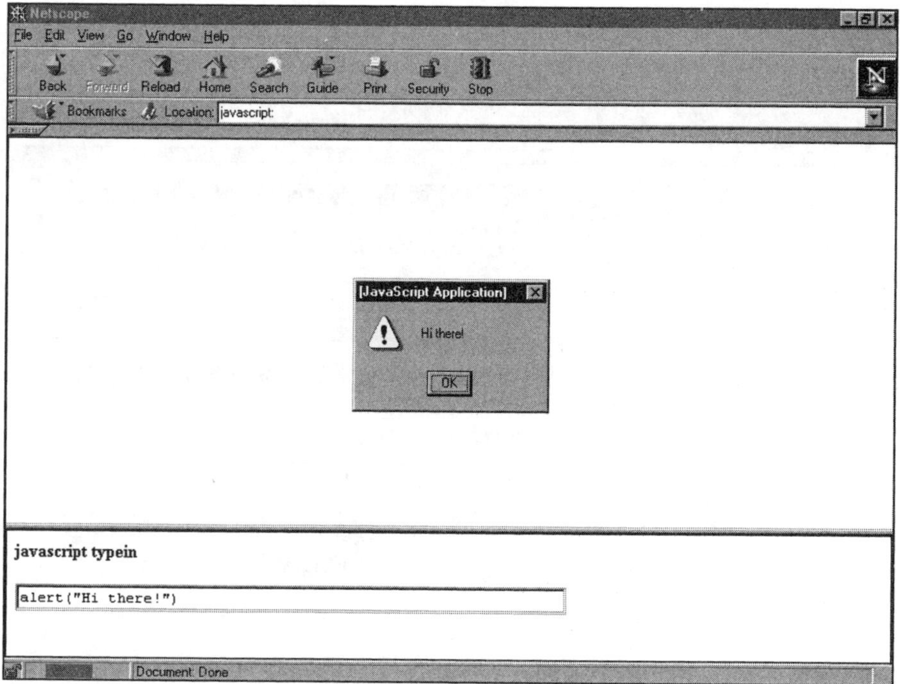

Figure 16-4: Navigator JavaScript test window

2. Navigate back to the Create JavaScript page.
3. Enter the following information as your first JavaScript:

```
Owning Schema: Netu
JavaScript Name: netu_js_alert
Language: JavaScript 1.1
```

4. Enter the script code in Listing 16-2.
5. Use the Add JavaScript button to save your JavaScript.

Netscape provides a true JavaScript debugger on the Netscape Web site for working with JavaScript interactively. You can use this JavaScript debugger with WebDB code, and you may find that you need to do so if your scripts are either long or complicated.

Testing the JavaScript

WebDB provides a management and test panel for JavaScripts at the bottom of the Process Change for JavaScript page shown in Figure 16-5.

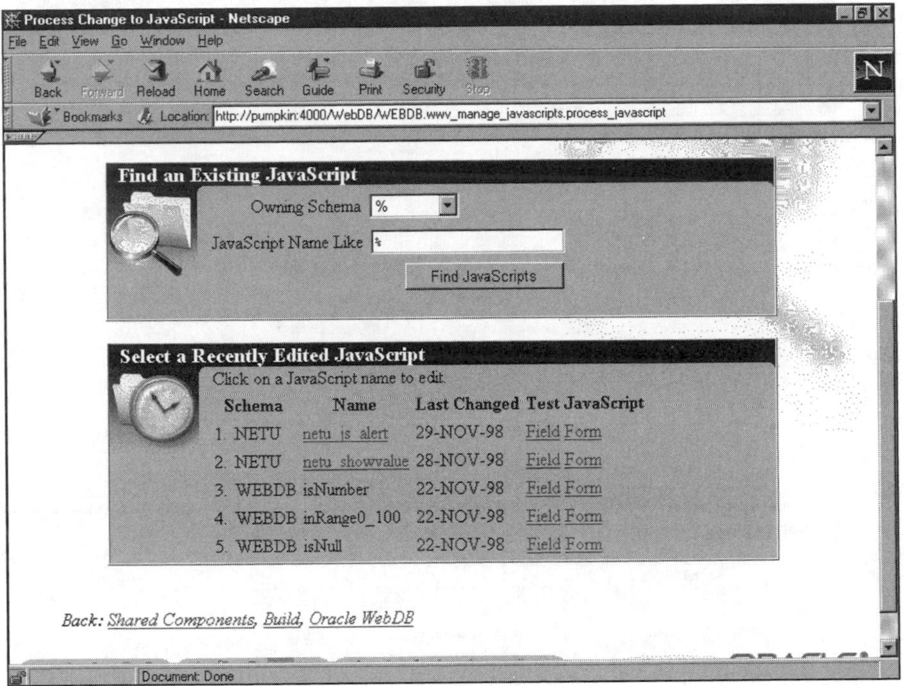

Figure 16-5: Edit JavaScript panel

The edit panel provides you with three choices. You can choose the Name link to edit the component, or you can choose either the Field link or the Form link to test the component. You can attach JavaScripts to many events on a form field within an HTML page. WebDB currently restricts you to using only two of the possible events within the HTML pages it generates. The first event is the onBlur event, which is fired when the user leaves a field on a form. The second event is the onClick event, which is fired when the form is sent back to the server. Although there is certainly value in being able to use the other events, you only really need these two events to validate data in a form. If the item you are trying to validate is a single field, then you can use the onBlur event to enforce your restriction. On the other hand, if the value you are trying to enforce is based upon a value in another field, then the onClick event is the better event to use. You would not want to attempt to validate cross-field data until all of the required fields are filled in, and the onClick event determines the moment when the data entry fields are expected to be complete. WebDB provides you with the two links on the edit panel so that you can test a single JavaScript with either the onBlur event or with the onClick event.

1. Use the Field link to test your simple JavaScript.

WebDB presents you with two text boxes, a Submit button, and the source code for your JavaScript on the generated test page.

2. Enter some text into the first text box and then tab to the second text box. WebDB displays a pop-up message window over your page as shown in Figure 16-6.

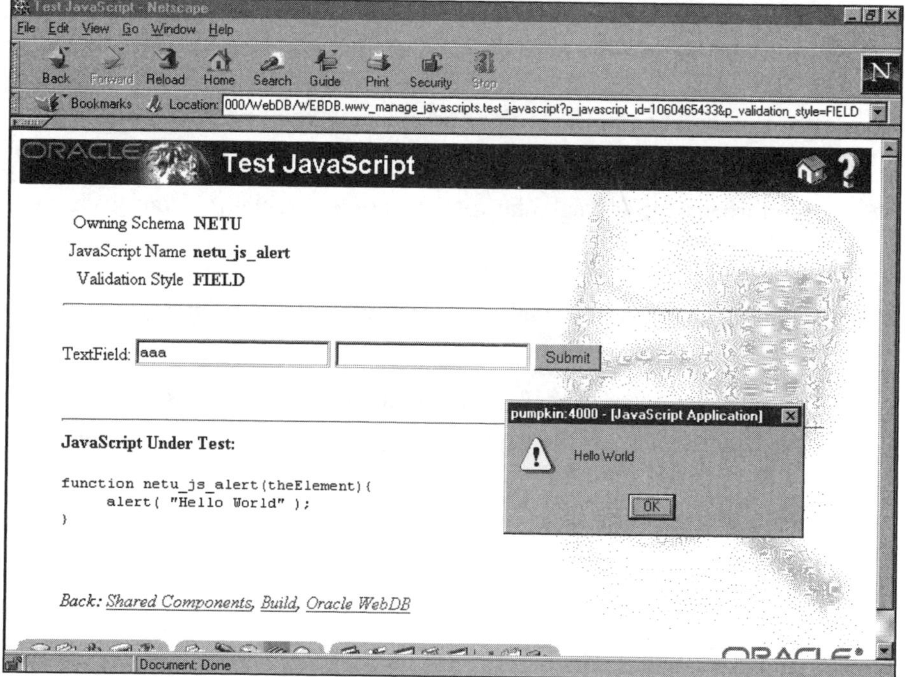

Figure 16-6: Testing a JavaScript function

WebDB associates the JavaScript code with the first text box within the HTML that it generates for the test page. If you were to look at the source HTML for the test page, you would see the following fragment of code embedded within the <FORM> and </FORM> blocks:

```
<INPUT TYPE="text" NAME="TextField" onBlur="netu_js_alert(
this, 'TextField' )">
<INPUT TYPE="text" NAME="TextField2">
<INPUT TYPE="submit" VALUE="Submit" onClick="return
netu_js_alert( TextField, 'TextField' )">
```

Notice that WebDB ties the JavaScript to the onBlur event of the first text box. The parameter value is passed to the function by using an advanced feature of the JavaScript language. JavaScript enables you to use a shorthand name for any object using the keyword "this." WebDB uses the field name and the this keyword to pass a handle to the text box object to the function. In this manner, the function has access to all of the properties of the original object, which is how you are able to access the data within the field while running your JavaScript functions. You may also notice that WebDB has tied the same procedure to the Submit button that it has generated for you so you can test the function at the form level as well as the field level from this one test page.

Building More Complicated Scripts

The JavaScripts you create for field validations are based upon the needs of the forms you create and the tables and columns you use. You will find it easier to create and manage JavaScripts by driving them from the data in your applications. In Chapter 8 of this book, you built a data entry form based upon a stored procedure, and that particular form makes an excellent example case on which to build some validations.

If you are not familiar with how to import scripts to WebDB, please see Appendix A.

1. Import the script ch16_lov.sql to load in a set of List-of-Values objects.
2. Import the script ch16_frm_donations.sql to create a copy of the donations form from Chapter 8.
3. Test the form to display the page shown in Figure 16-7.

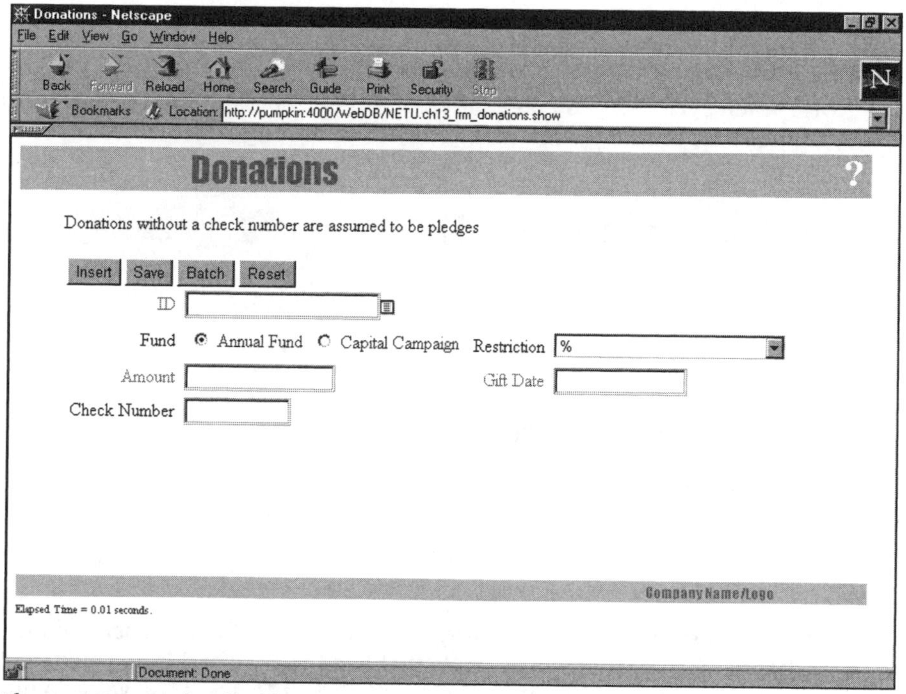

Figure 16-7: Reviewing the Donations form

Although this form is quite simple, it can be difficult for the user to work with at run time. The form is based upon a stored procedure and the procedure is particular about the number and format of the data that is passed to it at execution time. A few client-side validation routines can make this form much easier to work with. Before you start building these JavaScript validations, take a close look at the existing data on the form. Notice how the fields ID, FUND, and RESTRICTION all have List-of-Values objects associated with them. If your database makes use of foreign key validations or exact match values, you should implement these validations as lists of values and not as JavaScript validations. JavaScript validations require your users to enter data into the fields on the form, which could be incorrect, and having error boxes pop up continually for a novice user can be a time-consuming and frustrating process. It is better to provide the user with data directly.

JavaScript validations are better suited to cases where the data cannot be presented to the user as a list. For example, the fields AMOUNT, GIFT DATE, and CHECK NUMBER are all free-form fields. It would be all but impossible to build a List-of-Values object that would cover all of the possible values for these fields. JavaScript validations are the better choice for these items.

Return to the Shared Component Library.

The import script creates four JavaScript validations for use with the Donations form. Each script shows you a different type of validation and illustrates a different technique for working with data, as shown in Listing 16-3.

Listing 16-3: **Replace missing data with NULL**

```
function netu_js_makenull(theElement){
//
// Replace blanks with NULL
//
if (theElement.value == null || theElement.value == "") {
     theElement.value = "NULL"
     }
return true
}
```

Listing 16-3 shows you several ways to work with NULL or missing data. The Value method is used to extract the value that has been passed from the data entry field to the parameter of the script. The script checks to see if the value is null, or if it has been deleted. If the user never enters the field, it will be null, but if the user enters a value and then uses the Delete key, then the field is technically not null according to JavaScript. To circumvent this problem, the routine checks for both situations. Normally, you could simply leave a null value as null, but in the example case, the stored procedure requires you to pass the NULL value as a keyword string to the procedure. The JavaScript routine converts missing data into the string NULL. You can just as easily strip characters out of the field entry as you can check for null, as Listing 16-4 demonstrates.

Listing 16-4: **Range check**

```
function netu_js_range_1_to_50000(theElement){
var num_x = 0
//
// Check for blank or zero
//
if (theElement.value == null || theElement.value == "" ||
theElement.value == "0") {
     alert("Field " + theElement.name + " must be > 0 and
<50001");
     theElement.focus()
     return false
     }
```

```
//
// Not blank or zero, eliminate character values
//
var string_y = theElement.value
var string_z = ""
for (var i = 0; i<string_y.length; i++) {
      var single_char = string_y.charAt(i)
      if (single_char < "0" || single_char > "9"){
          continue
      } else {
          string_z = string_z + single_char
      }
}
// Check value range
//
num_x = Number(string_z)
theElement.value = num_x
if (num_x < 1 || num_x > 50000) {
       alert("Value is out of range (1-50000)")
       theElement.focus()
       return false
} else {
       return true
}
}
```

In this case, the routine performs three different types of validation. First, it checks to be sure that the field is not either blank, zero, or null. Next, it uses a For loop to step through the individual characters using the charAt() function to eliminate any nonnumeric characters. This part of the JavaScript function is where you cross over the line from simply validating data to improving the usability of the application. You could simply look for nonnumeric values and then signal an error when you find them. However, it is better to search for a light than to curse the darkness, and it is correspondingly better to attempt to eliminate common user errors and make the form easier to use. The JavaScript function is meant to search for numeric values out of range, and it makes sense to strip out any nonnumeric characters. If a user should inadvertently enter punctuation into the field, this routine quietly removes the errors. The final task for this validation is to check that the remaining numeric data is within the range of valid values. Notice that the function actually changes the value of the field with the code:

```
theElement = num_x,
```

If the resulting value is out of range, the cursor is returned to the field, and the user is given the "clean" version of the field to work with. In some cases, you may find it is too complex to try and repair the data a user entered into a field. For example, Listing 16-5 shows a simple date-checking script.

Listing 16-5: **Simple date check**

```
function netu_js_currentyear(theElement){
//
// Check date. Assumes input date of dd-mmm-yyyy
//

var string_x = theElement.value
//
// Check the length first
//
if (string_x.length != 11) {
      alert("Date does not appear to be in the correct dd-mmm-
yyyy format")
      theElement.focus()
      return false
}
// Check the year
//
var thisYear = (new Date()).getYear()
var year_y = Number(string_x.charAt(9) + string_x.charAt(10))
if (year_y != Number(thisYear)) {
      alert("Date year must match current year")
      theElement.focus()
      theElement.select()
      return false
} else {
      return true
}
}
```

You could write a complete routine to check for a valid date value, and attempt to repair the data if the user entered it incorrectly. However, it may be enough just to show the user the correct format for the date and perform a rudimentary check of the data.

This function first checks to see if the length of the date field is 11, which is the correct length for a date in the dd-mmm-yyyy format. Next, the script finds the year of the current date by using the Date function and then compares it to the last two characters of the date entered by the user. If the two numbers match, then the date entered by the user is in the current year, otherwise the date is invalid. The Select function is used to cause the browser to lasso the date field when the user is returned to the page. This makes it easier for the user to change the value of the field.

Use the JavaScript Wizard to create three functions for each of the Listings 16-3, 16-4, and 16-5. Be sure to match the name of the function to the WebDB name for the function.

The JavaScript source code is included as part of the examples for the book on the CD-ROM and can be opened, cut, and pasted into WebDB. Once you have created the three sample functions, the next step is to attach them to fields on a data entry form.

Attaching Validations to Forms

Once you have created your JavaScript validations, you can easily attach them to any WebDB form.

1. Use the Manage Form page to edit the ch16_frm_donations form.
2. Navigate to the Argument Formatting and Validation page. The formatting panel for the Donations form looks like Figure 16-8.

   You are probably familiar with this panel from building forms in previous chapters of this book. The column selector on the left-hand side of the form enables you to click a field name and display the formatting options for the form. The two combo boxes at the bottom of the page labeled Field Validate and Form Validate are the places where you attach your JavaScript validations to your fields. WebDB loads all of the validations into each of the combo boxes and you can select the script you wish to use from the list of available validations. If you attach a JavaScript validation to the Field Validate item, WebDB associates the JavaScript with the onBlur event. If you associate a script with the Form Validate combo box, WebDB associates the validation with the onClick event for the Insert/Update buttons added to the form on the Button Options page.
3. Add the netu_js_1_to_50000 validation to the P_AMOUNT field as a field validation.
4. Add the netu_js_currentyear validation to the P_GIFT_DATE field as a field validation.
5. Add the netu_js_makenull validation to the P_CHECKNO field as a field validation.
6. Click the Finish button to store your changes.

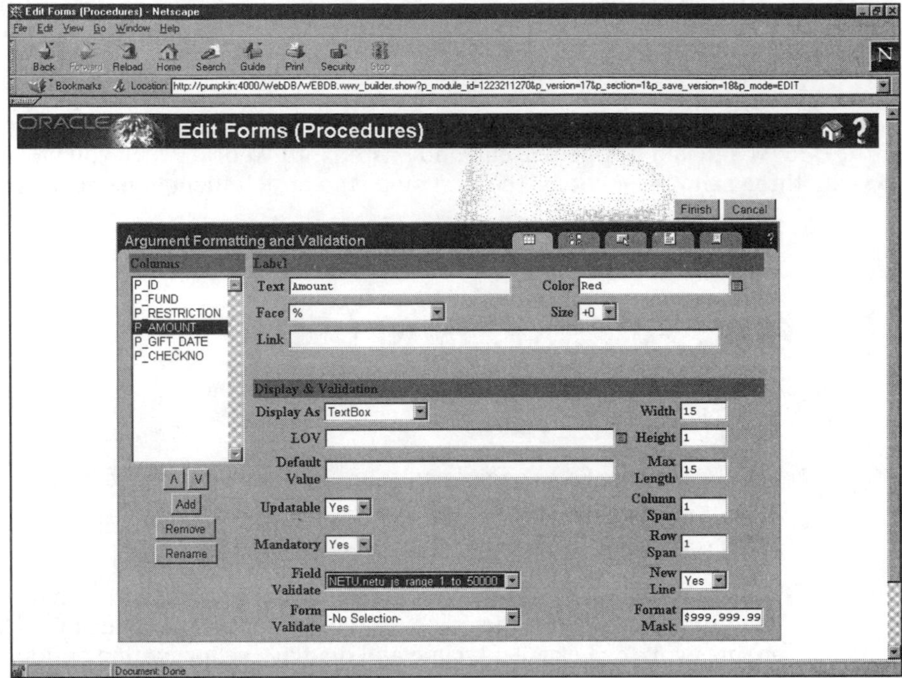

Figure 16-8: Formatting options panel

7. Use the Run link to test the modified version of your form. WebDB renders the form and adds the specified validations to yield a new copy of the form, as shown in Figure 16-9.

The form does not look any different from the previous version of the form, but you will see that it behaves differently if you try to enter invalid information into the Amount, Gift Date, or Check Number fields. The browser displays alert boxes as shown in Figure 16-9, and prevents the user from leaving the form.

It is possible to get yourself into an endless loop with validation scripts, even if it appears that the validation code is properly designed. We recommend that you provide acceptable default values for form fields if you plan on attaching validation scripts to these fields. This ensures that the user does not get caught in an error loop from which they cannot escape.

8. Enter improper values into the AMOUNT and GIFT DATE fields to see how the validations operate.

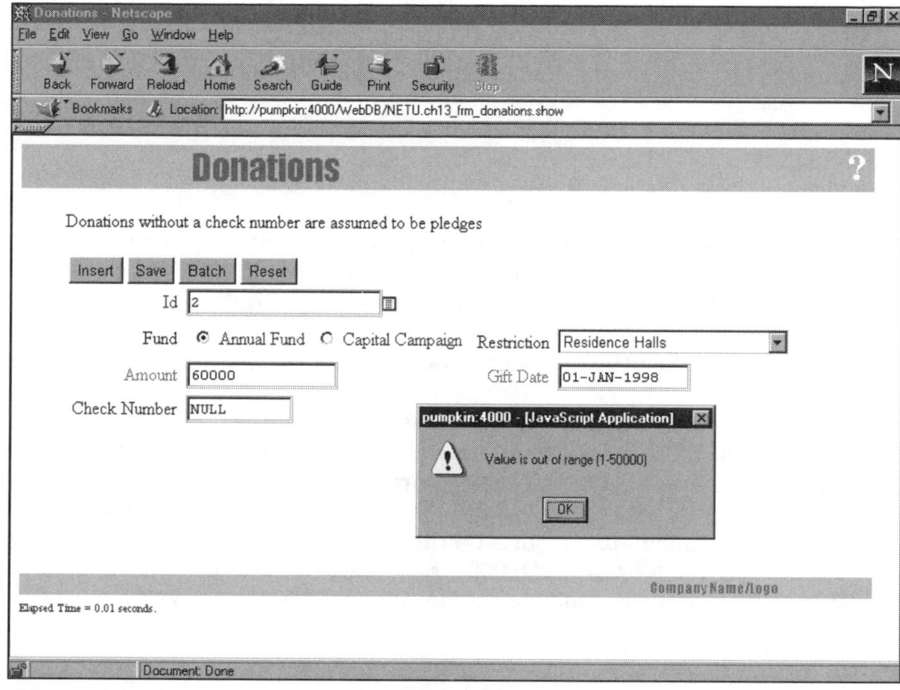

Figure 16-9: Donations form with validations

Although all of the fields are protected in some way on this form — either through JavaScript validations or list of values entries — you can still do more to this form. There will be cases where you want to warn your users about an improper value, but still allow them to proceed with the transaction. There are also cases where the validation for one field is dependent upon the values in a subsequent field. WebDB enables you to add JavaScript code that can handle both of these problems.

Cross-Field Validations

Cross-field validations are those validations that compare the data in one field to the data within a second field. The secret to working with cross-field validations is to understand how WebDB identifies fields within a form. The document object model that applies to your browser determines the hierarchy of components on a page of HTML. For the purposes of form validation, this hierarchy is composed of three elements: the document, the form, and the fields. In Figure 16-8, you can see a list of fields that are part of the Donations form. The name of the field as shown in the left-hand column is the name of the field as it appears in the form itself. The full name for the field is the keyword "document" followed by the name of the form as shown on the Manage Component page for the form and the field name on the Column Formatting page. In the example form you have been working with, the names of the three fields you have been validating are as follows:

```
document.ch16_frm_donations.P_AMOUNT
document.ch16_frm_donations.P_GIFT_DATE
document.ch16_frm_donations.P_CHECKNO
```

The names are case sensitive and both the document keyword and the form name are in lowercase, and the field names are all in uppercase. You can access the data for any field using the *value* method, just like you could when using a parameter. The biggest issue with this type of coding is that it is very form-specific and you will not be able to test the JavaScript code without actually executing the form itself.

In the example Donations form there is the additional need to check for large pledge records. The form itself uses a stored procedure to write data into the database as either a DONATIONS record or as a PLEDGE record. Donations that have a null value for the check number are assumed to be pledges. Although the form enables users to add gifts up the amount of $50,000, it is unlikely that you would have pledges over $10,000. You can use a form-based JavaScript to check for large gifts that have a null check number by using the following code in Listing 16-6.

Listing 16-6: **Cross-field validation**

```
function netu_js_donation(theElement){
//
// Get value of amount and check number
//
var idx;
idx = findItem(document.ch16_frm_donations, "P_AMOUNT");
var num_x =
Number(document.ch16_frm_donations.elements[idx].value)
idx = findItem (document.ch16_frm_donations, "P_CHECKNO");
var string_y = document.ch16_frm_donations.elements[idx].value
if (num_x > 10000 && string_y == "NULL") {
 if (confirm("This looks like a large pledge, are you sure?")){
        return true
     } else {
        return false
     }
}
return true
}
```

In Listing 16-6, the parameter value is ignored completely, because you are not actually using the field parameter. Within the body of the script, two variables are defined that extract the value of the P_AMOUNT field and the P_CHECKNO field.

Unlike the field-level validations, you do not have to make extensive alterations to the data in the fields themselves, because the field-level validation code assures you that the values are already within limits for the field. The actual validation is simple: If the amount of the gift is over $10,000 and the check number is null, then the user is asked to confirm the entry. Instead of preventing the user from storing the data, the use of the CONFIRM method of the window object enables the user to accept the item or reject the entry. After all, it is possible that a donor will make such a large pledge to the university, even if it is unlikely.

1. Use the JavaScript Wizard to add the validation netu_js_donation. You can copy the JavaScript code from the CD-ROM.
2. Edit the ch16_frm_donations form and add the validation netu_js_donations to the Form Validation for the P_CHECKNO field.
3. Save the changes and test the form.
4. Enter the values shown in the Figure 16-10, and attempt to store the record by using the INSERT button.

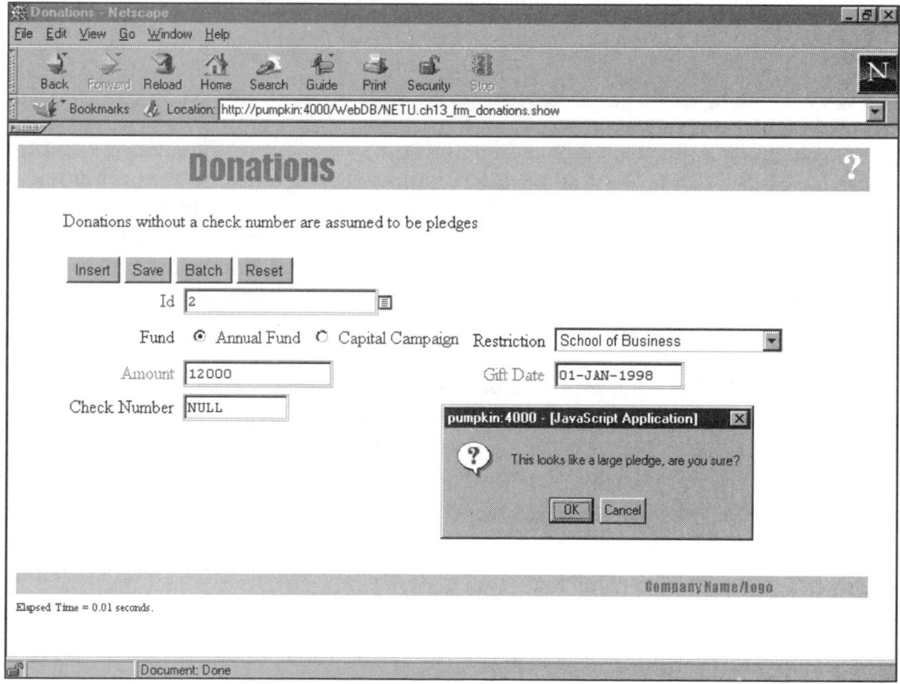

Figure 16-10: Form-level validations

If you enter a gift amount over $10,000 and leave the check number as null, the script prompts you to accept or reject the data with a dialog box. The user can accept the change with the OK button, or reject the data with the Cancel button. If the user elects to cancel the operation, the cursor returns to the last field on the form. You can change this behavior simply by adding some custom code to the else block of the if-then code. Because this validation is attached to the form itself, it fires whenever the user attempts to save the form. The validation fires even if the user did not enter the field on the form.

You will find that end users often prefer this type of validation as it gives them some additional control over the process. Large, complex data entry forms can be frustrating for users if they are continually forced to re-enter data that is rejected based upon unclear data entry requirements.

Form-level validations that ask the user for confirmation of questionable data can make the user more comfortable with your applications, while also ensuring that your data remains consistent. The downside to building this type of validation is the need to build and test your JavaScripts directly against the data entry form.

WebDB dynamically loads the JavaScript code into the form when you run the form, so it is not necessary to recompile your forms each time you change your script code. Once you have attached the JavaScript to a field, you can simply edit the script and retest the form without recompiling the form.

Cross-Record Validation

There is one additional type of validation you may find necessary to implement on the client side of your application: cross-record validation. When you create master-detail forms with WebDB, you are allowed to enter multiple detail records for each client record. By definition, the database rejects duplicate child records for a given parent record. However, the browser does not validate the data against the database until you exit the field. This enables the user to enter duplicate records in the browser that will not be rejected until the page is stored.

The solution to this problem is to make use of two additional features of the JavaScript language, as shown in Listing 16-7. It is important to note that WebDB does not currently allow for master-detail validations. However, for the purpose of fully understanding the potential of JavaScript and WebDB, we have provided the following code.

Listing 16-7: Elements and global variables

```
var my_elements = ""
function netu_js_elements(theElement){
   var form = document.forms[0]
   for (var i= 0; i <form.elements.length; i++) {
     if (i == 0) {
        my_elements = form.elements[i].name + "="
+form.elements[i].value+"|"
```

```
      } else {
         my_elements = my_elements + form.elements[i].name + "="
+form.elements[i].value+"|"
      }
   }
alert(my_elements)
}
```

Up until this point, you have worked with entirely self-contained functions. By default, variables you define within JavaScript functions are local to that function. However, if you create a variable outside of the JavaScript function keyword, then the variable becomes global to the entire HTML page. In Listing 16-7, the variable my_elements has been declared outside of the function definition and it is therefore usable in any other JavaScript function on the same page. The second item of note is the use of the *elements* object within the *form* object. Your browser automatically keeps track of the fields on the forms you create, and you can access them by navigating through the *elements* array. The document object model enables you to extract the following three key items from each element:

✦ Name

✦ Type

✦ Value

The *name* of the element is the label that has been assigned to the field within the page, and you can use this name to set the value of the field. The *type* property is the format of the field, for example, it may be a text box or a check box. The *value* property is the data that has been currently stored in the field on the page at run time. As long as you know the base name for the field item, you can build a loop that steps through all of the fields of that type looking for a duplicate value. You can attach this item to the Form Validation for the designated field and build up a list of name/value pairs that can be searched for duplicate values.

You can only declare global variables once, and you should create them with a short function attached to a field used at the top of your form. Once you have defined the variable, you will be able to use it within any other function on the same page later on.

You do not actually need the global variable to perform the data check, because you can perform the entire validation at the form level. The global variable can be useful if you want to store a value in one script and use that value later on. Cross-field validations that check for duplicate values across records should be attached as form-level validations. Master-detail forms do not even allow for validations in consideration of this fact. Users may find this a bit disconcerting, because they will not be told of a conflict until they attempt to save their changes.

Server-Side Validations

You will find that users are much more satisfied with your applications if you provide them with clean, user-friendly data validation within the browser. However, the primary line of defense for your data is the constraints and triggers provided inside the Oracle database. Oracle permits you to define simple rules called CONSTRAINTS that are associated with fields and tables within your database. There are three types of constraints found in the typical database:

✦ Primary key

✦ Foreign key

✦ Check Constraints

Primary key constraints define the primary key for a table and are typically used to enforce uniqueness on a table's key field. Within the NETU database schema, every table has a designated primary key constraint that ensures uniqueness.

Foreign key constraints are the server-side equivalent of lists of values and they associate a field in one table with the primary key of a second table. A foreign key constraint prevents you from entering data into a field on one table that does not match pre-existing data in a field on a second table. For example, you cannot add or modify a UGRADS record with a value for the CLASSYR field that does not match a CLASSYR value in the CLASSES table. This prevents you from entering students for a class year that does not yet exist. In most cases, you will want to provide a List-of-Values object for foreign key field validations within WebDB forms.

Oracle's *Check Constraints* provide a more general-purpose tool for limiting the allowable data values for a field. Check constraints enable you to set a range of values for a field at the server level. Within the NETU database, the FUND field in the DONATIONS table has a check constraint that limits the allowable entries in the FUND field to either "Annual Fund" or "Capital Campaign." Check constraints are used when a foreign key table does not exist, or wherever a *range* of values is to be permitted.

Check constraints are limited to comparing data within a single table. If you need to compare the value of one field to a value in another table, then Oracle provides an additional tool in the form of database triggers. Oracle *triggers* are blocks of PL/SQL code that are processed whenever a change to a table is performed such as inserts, updates, or deletes. You can use triggers to make silent modifications to your data or to stop completion of the changes you make. For example, you could create a trigger on the ALUMNI table that would prevent any record from being deleted if the alumni had given more than $10,000 to the university. You can also use triggers to massage your data, such as converting the first letter of every last name to an uppercase value when the record is either updated or inserted.

If you are building a WebDB application on top of an existing Oracle database, you are likely to find that the database already has constraints and triggers in place. Be sure to create a client-side JavaScript data validation for these existing database rules within WebDB. This ensures that the data entered into your forms satisfies the database requirements when it is passed from the browser to the database.

Wrapping Up

Data validations can make your applications much easier to use and improve the quality of the information stored within your database. You will find that typical applications are a mix of List-of-Values objects and JavaScript validations and that each object serves a distinct purpose. End users will be more comfortable with applications that attempt to solve data entry problems rather than applications that merely point out the inconsistencies. Keep this in mind as you build your JavaScript validation functions, and consider making an extra effort to simplify the overall process for your users. If you find that you need to build larger JavaScript validations, we recommend that you invest in a more complete guide to the JavaScript language, such as IDG Books Worldwide's *JavaScript Bible*.

✦ ✦ ✦

CHAPTER 17

Using Links to Connect WebDB Objects

✦ ✦ ✦ ✦

In This Chapter

✦ ✦ ✦ ✦

In Chapter 14 you learned how to use menus to create complete application systems using WebDB's component objects. One of the problems you may have encountered when building your menus is the difficulty in determining which WebDB component should connect to a particular menu choice. WebDB provides a second utility in the form of the Link Builder that can help you create reusable connections between WebDB components. In this chapter, you will learn how to build links based on WebDB components and how to use these links to provide parameter passing for your applications.

Defining Links

In its simplest form, a link is nothing more than a standard URL string, as we discussed in Chapter 14. Links are the backbone of navigation for Web applications, and the WebDB Link Builder is designed to assist you in the process of creating custom URL links for your WebDB content. As you also saw in Chapter 14, WebDB enables you to link to components from menu items, so at first it may seem as if a separate link builder is not necessary. The Link Builder provides you with access to links in places where WebDB does *not* allow you to directly connect to other components or menu items, but this is not the most important reason for using links.

A WebDB link provides you with the capability to drill up or drill down to other WebDB component pages containing related data. Browser users have learned to make use of links in static Web pages as means of navigating through content. WebDB links provide a similar experience for dynamic, database data. For example, a user who is looking at high-level summary data may wish to have the capability to drill down to more detailed transactional data. You can use links to determine which specific summary data the user is viewing and then connect that data to the appropriate, detailed transactional data. Conversely, a user that is looking at transactional data may also wish to jump up to a higher level of abstraction, and WebDB links can address this requirement as well.

The Link Builder is specifically designed to enable you to link a WebDB component such as a report, form, chart, calendar, or hierarchy to an individual target component. The presence of a link on a database column enables a WebDB application user to click through from one component to another automatically.

Linking from an Existing Component

Links are easy to understand once you see them in action. Every one of the eight user interface components can be linked directly to another WebDB component using links. In fact, you can link any WebDB component to any other URL-based application using links. The simplest way to create a link is to attach a target component to a specific column in a source component.

1. Load the view netu_class_totals into the NETU account via SQL*Plus.
2. Load the sample reports ch17_rep_students and ch17_rep_classes using SQL*Plus into the WebDB account.

   The sample report creates a list of UGRADS students that is organized by class year and last name, and it shows off the various majors for each of the students.
3. After you have loaded the report into the database, navigate to the Reports menu, select the ch17_rep_students, and execute it.

   Figure 17-1 shows the results of running this simple report. This body of this report shows student records organized by class year and includes the major for each student.
4. Exit the ch17_rep_students report.
5. Run the ch17_rep_classes report as shown in Figure 17-2.

The Class Years report shows a summary of class information from the UGRADS table and the CLASSES table. This report counts the number of students per class year and prints the total along with the class year and associated class code.

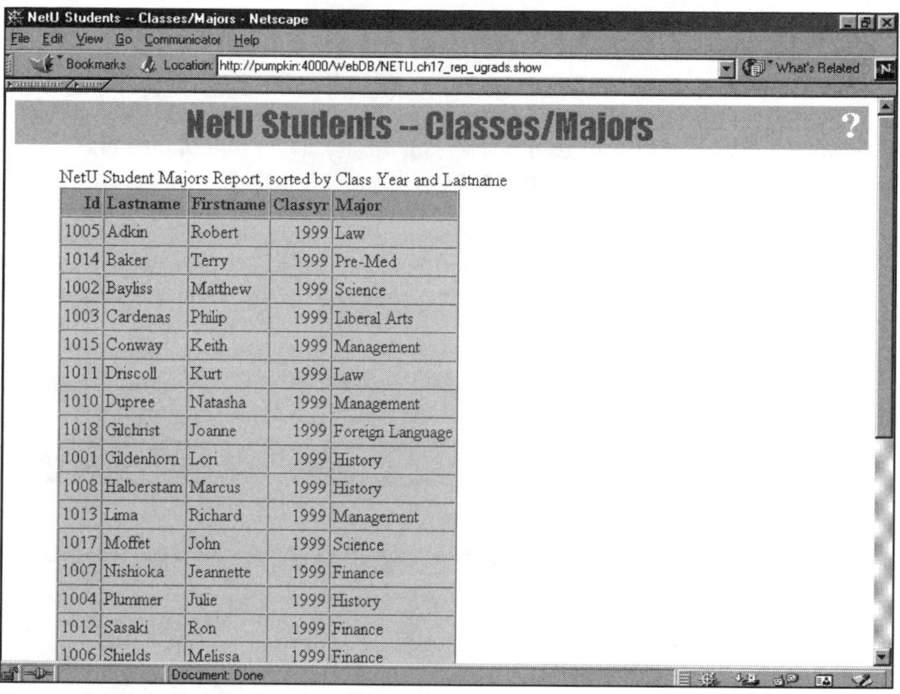

Figure 17-1: UGRADS report by class year

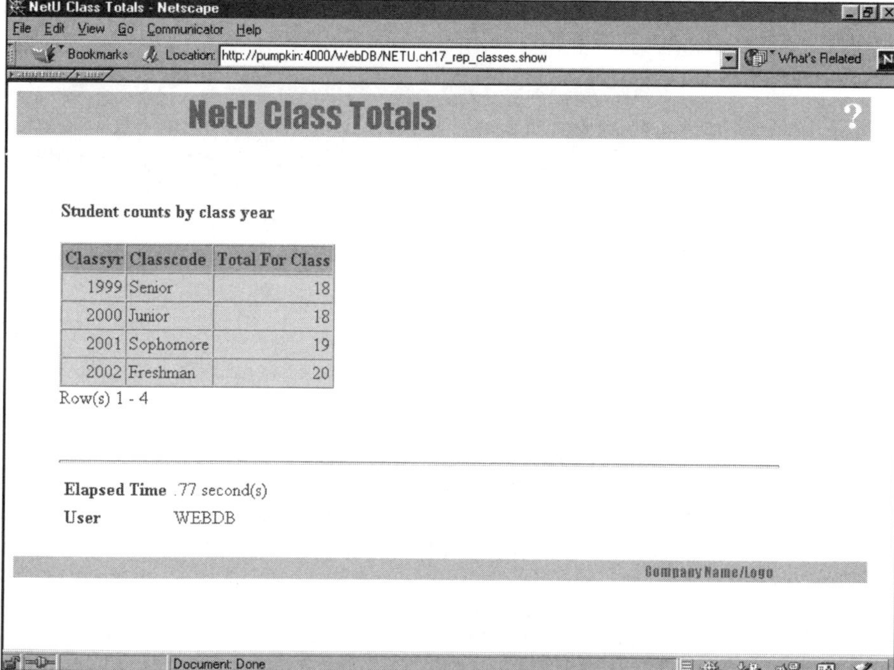

Figure 17-2: Class Years report

Link the UGRADS report to the CLASSES report

It would be useful to automatically associate the UGRADS report with the CLASSES report so users can automatically drill up from the Class Years column to a summary of the class years at Net University. The Link Wizard is the tool WebDB provides to make such a connection.

1. Navigate to the Shared Component Library and select the Links menu choice to display the panel shown in Figure 17-3. WebDB displays the familiar three-panel page that enables you to create, find, and edit recently created links.

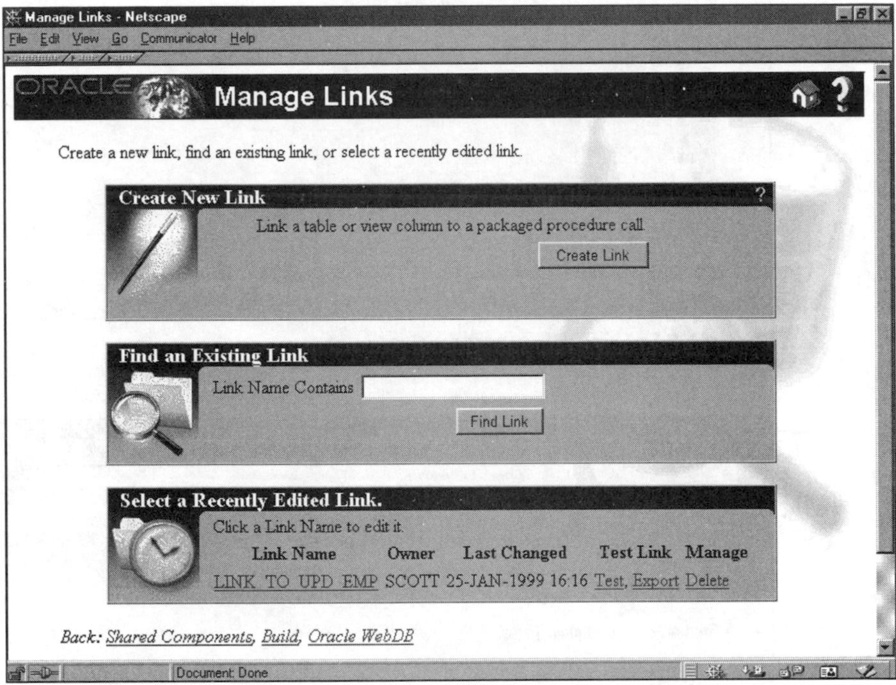

Figure 17-3: Creating a link

2. Select the Create Link button to create a new link and display the panel shown in Figure 17-4.

Links are owned by USERIDs just like any other WebDB component, and you should create links in the same USERID as the linked components. It is possible to link together objects from separate schemas, but it is more common to link objects within a single schema. If you are linking components across schemas, we recommend that you create the link in the same schema as the target component. For example, if the UGRADS report and the CLASSES report were in separate schemas, you would create the link object in the same schema as the CLASSES report, because the UGRADS report links *to* the CLASSES report.

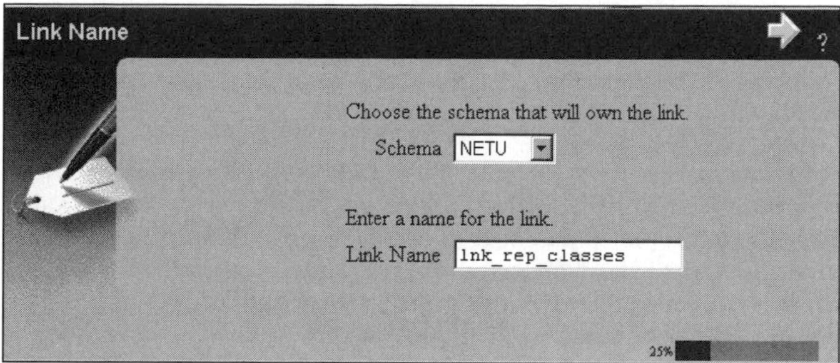

Figure 17-4: Naming a link and setting the owner

Links follow the same naming conventions as any other WebDB component, and you are free to name links using any scheme you choose. You may find it more difficult to adequately name link objects, because a descriptive name should include a reference to both the calling component and the linked component.

3. Select the NETU account as the owner of your new link and enter **lnk_rep_classes** as the name of the link.
4. Click the Next arrow to display the page shown in Figure 17-5.

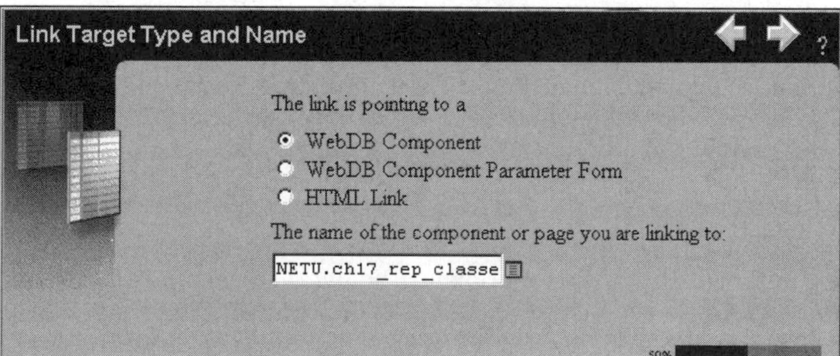

Figure 17-5: Link Target Type and Name page

Links are designed in reverse order: the target link is selected first, and then the source link is defined. Although this may seem illogical to begin with, it actually makes the overall process much easier. The key to building a link is the passing of parameters between the source component and the target component.

By selecting the target component first, WebDB can interrogate the target component and build a list of possible parameters for you. There are three possible link types as defined by the Link Wizard:

- ✦ WebDB Component
- ✦ WebDB Component Parameter Form
- ✦ HTML Link

WebDB components are the most common type of link and they include any of the other WebDB component objects such as forms, reports, charts, menus, calendars, hierarchies, and dynamic pages. In effect, by selecting the WebDB Component type, you are connecting to the SHOW procedure of the target. It makes no difference at this point whether you are passing parameters to the target or not, as the SHOW procedure is called in either case.

However, if you do not plan on passing parameters to a target object, but you want the end user to be able to specify parameters manually, then you would select the WebDB Component Parameter Form link type. This causes WebDB to call the SHOW_PARAMETER procedure instead of the SHOW procedure for a given component. End users of your application are shown the parameter form for the target component and they are able to enter parameters interactively.

In most cases, you will connect links from columns to the SHOW procedure. One of the most common intents of a link is to provide a drill up or a drill down from a column to a detailed user interface object. Therefore, you are more likely to create these links using parameter values in order to invoke the SHOW procedure with appropriate data. Because links are most often used to drill down or drill up through data, the SHOW procedure, which can accept parameters without user intervention, is the most likely destination of a link.

WebDB links can also connect to external components using the HTML Link type. You can link external Web sites and applications as the target component with URLs within the Link Wizard using HTML links. For example, you might want to link a Net University sports calendar to the NCAA Web site using the HTML Link type.

Once you have chosen the link type, you can specify the name of the component to which you are linking in the text box just below the radio buttons. If you are linking to either a WebDB Component or a WebDB Component Parameter Form, you can use the search icon to search for a listing of components, as shown in Figure 17-6.

The search panel displays a list of WebDB components sorted by USERID and component name. You can enter a partial search string such as netu.ch17% to search for components that are specific to a certain schema or application name. The Search Dialog box lists only those packages that have been built with WebDB. If you have created other packages within Oracle, they will not appear in the Search Dialog even though they are valid packages from the database's perspective. If you need to link to an external PL/SQL package (such as one built for OAS), you must do using the HTML Link type.

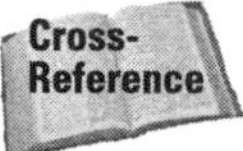

Chapter 24 contains a detailed look at using PL/SQL packages with WebDB.

The text box should be filled with the name of the external URL link or external PL/SQL package name for the HTML Link type. For example, if you wanted to connect the UGRADS report to the virtual Web campus at `college.com`, you would enter `http://www.college.com` in the name text box. You are free to add parameters to any external URL that you enter as additional strings on the command line.

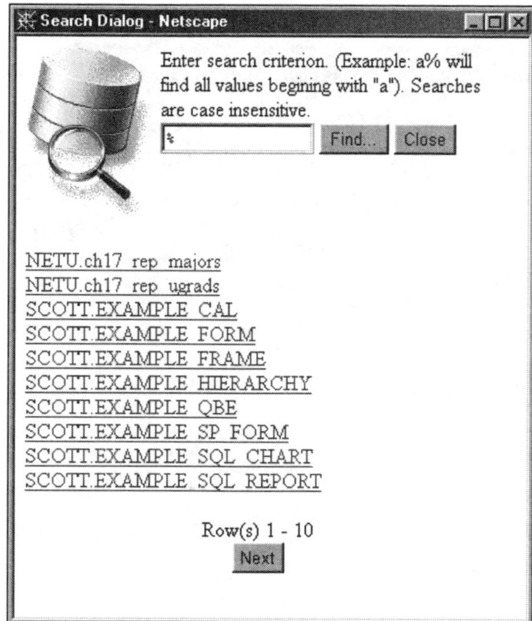

Figure 17-6: Search Dialog for WebDB components

5. Select the WebDB Component radio button for your new link.
6. Use the search icon to locate the report NETU.CH17_REP_CLASSES as the component name.
7. Click the Next arrow to display the panel shown in Figure 17-7.

   The Link Target Inputs panel is constructed by interrogating the component procedure and building a list of possible parameters. Notice that there are two groups of fields: parameters and display options. Both groups of fields are actually parameters, but those marked as parameters are the formal parameters that have been created as part of the component. For example, assume that the Class Years report included a bind variable that allowed the user to select a class year as a parameter for the report. In such a case, the

Link Wizard would display that bind variable as a parameter option on the link panel. In this particular example, because there are no bind variables as part of the Class Years report, the parameters group does not contain any values.

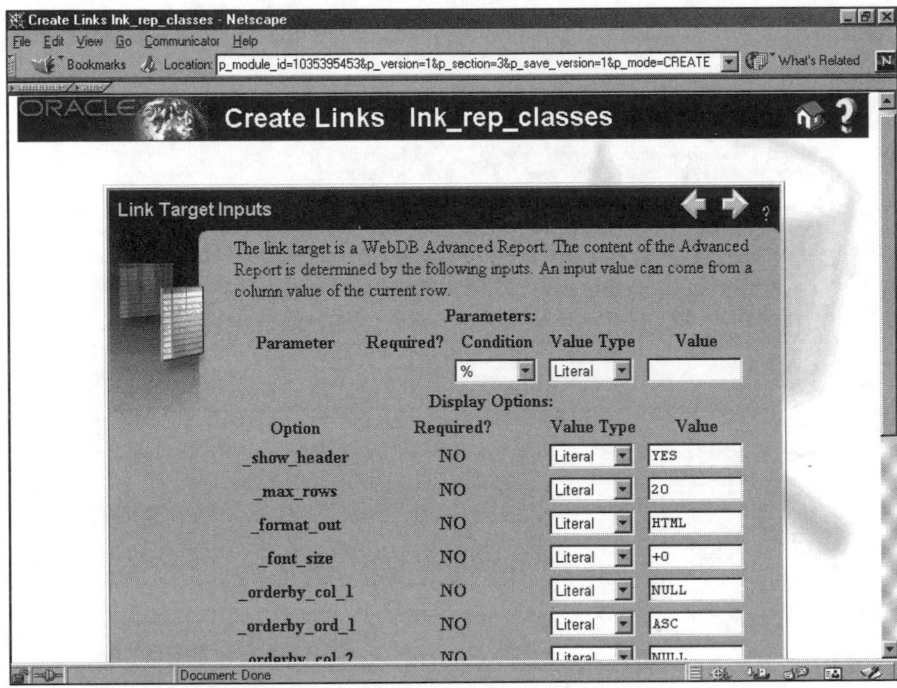

Figure 17-7: Link Target Inputs panel

Display options parameters

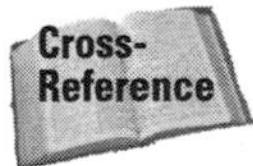

The parameter option is discussed in more detail in the next section of this chapter.

The second group of parameters is the display options parameters group. This group represents display parameters you can use to affect the execution of the component in some way or the other. The specific list of parameters is somewhat consistent between all of the various user interface objects: forms, reports, dynamic pages, calendars, and hierarchies. The parameters themselves are taken from the Display Options page in each wizard. Table 17-1 lists the most common parameters along with their function.

Table 17-1
Common Display Parameter Names and Functions

Parameter Name	*Description*	*Submit Values*
_show_header	Indicates whether the component should display the header section of the report (including the title).	YES, NO
_curr_sums	Indicates whether WebDB should create numerical counts on the break fields.	YES, NO
_font_size	Font size for output data. Determines the size of the font used to render the body of the report, form, chart, calendar, or hierarchy.	−3,−2,−1,0,+1,+2,+3
_format_out	Determines how the data is displayed. There are three possible formats: HTML, ASCII, and Excel spreadsheet.	HTML EXCEL ASCII
_max_rows	Maximum number of rows that should be displayed on a single page.	Positive integer value
_orderby_col_1		
_orderby_col_2		
_orderby_col_3	Three separate parameters used to indicate the sort order for the report. You must use these parameters in order—you are not allowed to supply a value for COL_2 without first supplying a value for COL_1.	Tablename. Column-name (For example: UGRADS.LASTNAME)
_orderby_ord_1		
_orderby_ord_2		
_orderby_ord_3	Sort order for selected columns.	ASC, DSC
_break_cols	Literal value for the name of the column on which the report should break.	Tablename.Column-name (For example: UGRADS.CLASSYR)
_row_id	Parameter name that matches the ROWID of the record in the table. ROWIDs are an internal column that Oracle uses to uniquely identify records.	N/A
_alt_rowid	Alternative ROWID value usually associated with a unique key field for a table, such as the primary key.	Column name (such as ID).

The specific display options parameters that appear depend on the type of component you are linking to and the specific built-in features of the component. For example, although _break_cols is a standard parameter for reports, it will not appear if you have not specified break columns in the report to which you are linking. (In particular, the Chart Wizard features a number of additional parameters that are specific to the chart object.)

Generally, every WebDB parameter begins with the underscore(_) character to distinguish the name from other types of data within a procedure. While you never have to look at the detailed PL/SQL source for your procedures, the internal parameter names of these procedures appear in the header. WebDB uses the procedure declarations to create the pick lists for the Link Builder and the result is that you are presented with parameter names that begin with the _ character.

8. Click the Next arrow to continue, and then click the OK push button to save and compile the new link.

Testing a Link

Once you have saved the new link, WebDB returns you to the main link page. You can view the link by using the TEST link in the bottom panel on the Manage Links page.

1. Use the TEST link for lnk_rep_classes to display the panel shown in Figure 17-8.

The Manage Link page has three panels that enable you to create a link, find a link, and test or export a recently created link. However, it is important to test out your newly created link before you start deploying it to other objects. WebDB makes the testing part easy by giving you a prebuilt link to test out your code at the bottom of the Manage Link page.

The Test Link page displays the results of the link test in four sections. First, the internal name of the link destination is displayed. You will recognize the link as the concatenation of the USERID, the package name, the procedure name, and all of the possible parameters. Second, WebDB displays the HTML anchor text as it is embedded within the source Web page. Typically, you do not have to worry about the anchor text, and you are unable to change the anchor if it is incorrect. The only real value in seeing the anchor text is to report the information to technical support if WebDB is generating incorrect results. The next section is the SQL query that WebDB generates to produce the anchor text and data. WebDB attempts to generate some test data from any parameter columns that were created as part of the report, using the base table for the component as the source for the data.

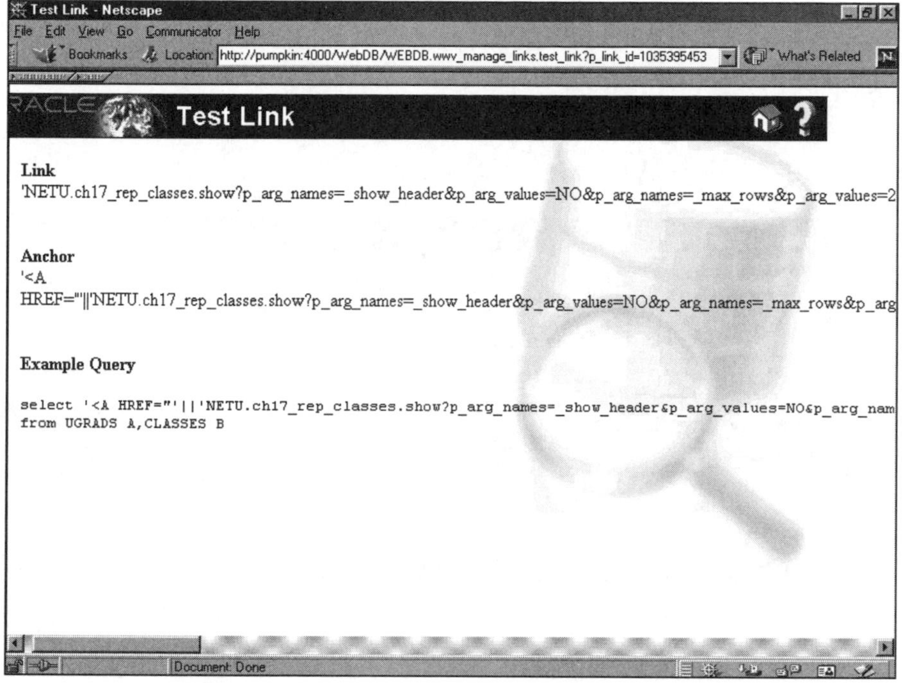

Figure 17-8: Test Link page

If all goes as planned, the last item on the panel is the results of the link query. The display value for the query matches the display column you specified when you entered the link source information. Components that do not display parameters do not necessarily display any test data, but the link still executes when it is attached to a column. The most useful way to test your link is to connect it to another component. In the example case, you can connect the new link to the pre-existing UGRADS report.

1. Navigate back to the main Report Wizard and select the ch17_rep_students report.
2. Edit the report and navigate to the Columns Formatting panel, as shown in Figure 17-9.

   Links are normally connected to columns unless you are using a link within a menu item. When you connect a column to a component, WebDB can pass the value of the column to the component as a parameter. This is where you can see the real power of links. The example Class Years report does not take any parameters itself, but you can still connect it to a column in the UGRADS report.

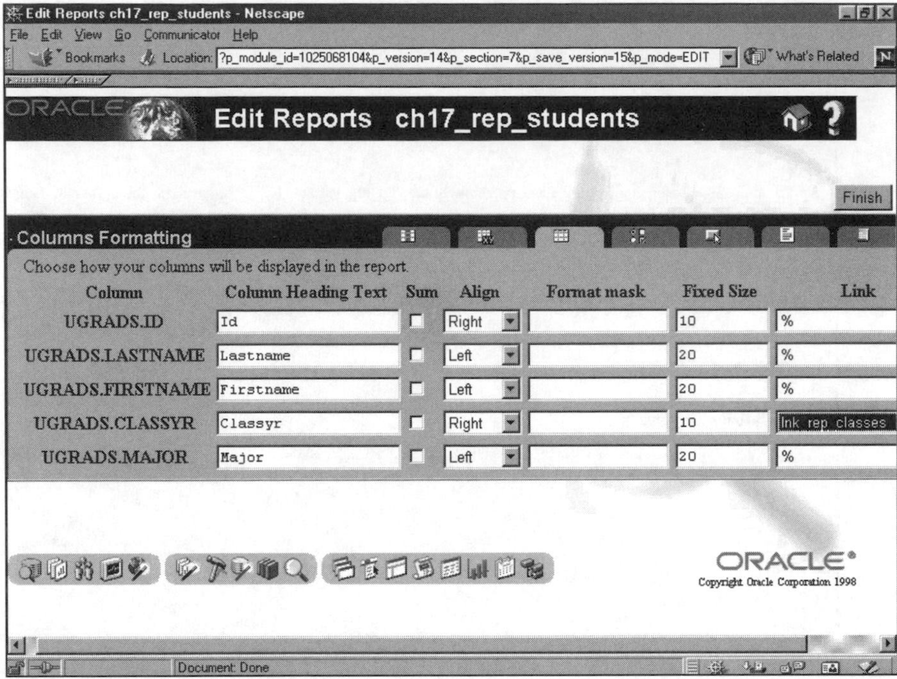

Figure 17-9: Adding a link to a report

3. Find the CLASSYR column and select the lnk_rep_classes link in the link combo box, as shown in Figure 17-9.
4. Use the Finish button to save this change and compile the modified report.
5. Choose the Run link to display the page shown in Figure 17-10.

   This time when you run the UGRADS report, the CLASSYR field appears as an HTML link. From the HTML perspective, the field is a link, and the link is built by WebDB when the page is rendered using the link object you created with the Link Wizard.
6. Click the CLASSYR field in any row to display the total, as shown in Figure 17-11.

When you use the link on the CLASSYR field, you connect to the CLASSES report. No matter which row you click through, however, you are always taken to the same report because the link itself is a *fixed* link. Although the link is dynamically created by WebDB for you, the destination point is fixed to a single location — the netu.ch17_rep_classes.show procedure.

Note

If you change a link, you need to edit and recompile any objects that reference the link in order for your change to take effect.

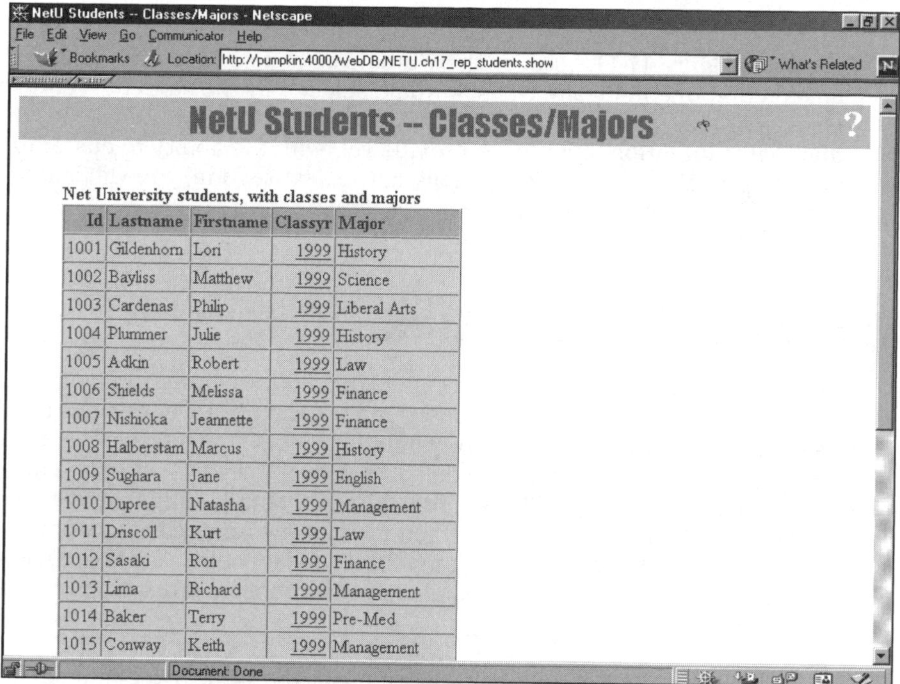

Id	Lastname	Firstname	Classyr	Major
1001	Gildenhorn	Lori	1999	History
1002	Bayliss	Matthew	1999	Science
1003	Cardenas	Philip	1999	Liberal Arts
1004	Plummer	Julie	1999	History
1005	Adkin	Robert	1999	Law
1006	Shields	Melissa	1999	Finance
1007	Nishioka	Jeannette	1999	Finance
1008	Halberstam	Marcus	1999	History
1009	Sughara	Jane	1999	English
1010	Dupree	Natasha	1999	Management
1011	Driscoll	Kurt	1999	Law
1012	Sasaki	Ron	1999	Finance
1013	Lima	Richard	1999	Management
1014	Baker	Terry	1999	Pre-Med
1015	Conway	Keith	1999	Management

Figure 17-10: UGRADS report with links on the CLASSYR field

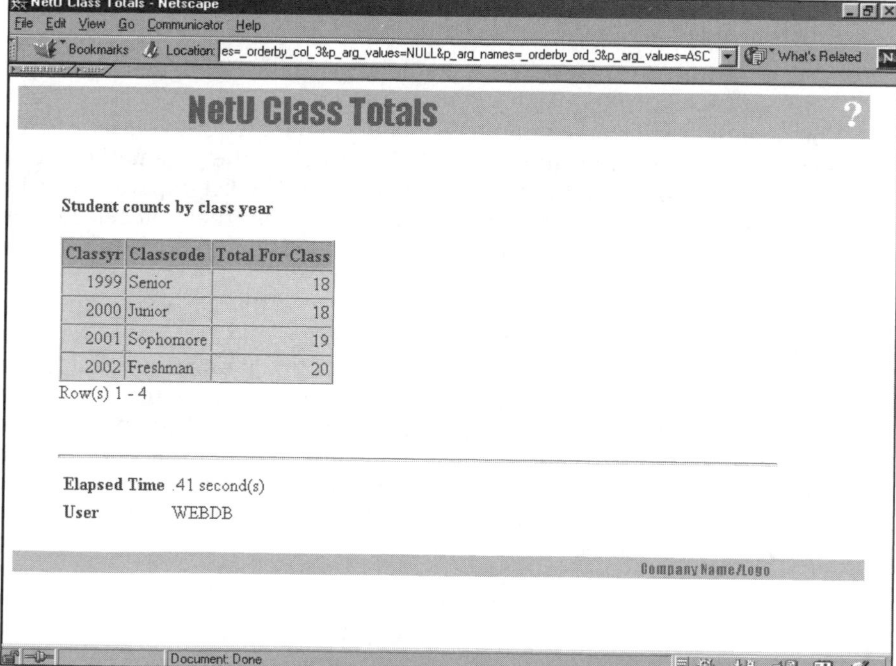

Classyr	Classcode	Total For Class
1999	Senior	18
2000	Junior	18
2001	Sophomore	19
2002	Freshman	20

Figure 17-11: NetU Class Totals report

No matter which record you choose, you will see HTML output similar to the data shown in Figure 17-11, because there are no selection parameters passed to the linked component. Ideally, the link would select *only* the student records for the class year that you chose from UGRADS report. WebDB has no way in which to divine this intention, but it does provide you with the ability to customize the link in order to achieve the desired result. In the next section, you will learn how to use parameters to limit the rows shown in a linked report.

Making a Dynamic Link

The difference between a fixed link and a dynamic link is as simple as the use of parameters. Every WebDB component can potentially accept values through the use of parameters. The SHOW procedure for WebDB objects expects to be passed parameters, but it executes with default values if the parameters are not supplied. When WebDB creates the SHOW procedure, it includes sufficient information within the body of the procedure for it to run by itself, without using any parameters. For parameters created as part of a component, a placeholder for these parameters exists, and the Link Builder automatically finds them and displays them for you as necessary.

1. Load the ch17_cht_gender chart file into the WebDB account using SQL*Plus.
2. Return to the Manage Links menu and create a new link called lnk_cht_gender.
3. Select the WebDB Component radio button as the link type.
4. Locate the netu.ch17_cht_gender chart as the component name.
5. Click the Next arrow to display the page shown in Figure 17-12.

The only difference between the fixed link you created previously and a dynamic link is the use of parameters. WebDB displays all of the parameter fields for the selected component at the top part of the form. The list of parameters is constructed by interrogating the WebDB component that you selected on the preceding panel in the wizard. (If you select the HTML radio button, the wizard will not even display the current panel.) The chart you loaded compares the number of males and females for a given class year, and accepts the class year as a parameter. Each parameter has three settings: the condition, the value type, and the value. The condition field is the comparison operator for the parameter and it is displayed as a combo box. The setting that you make for the condition determines how WebDB manages the comparison of the parameter and the list of comparison operators matches the standard Oracle PL/SQL comparison operators. For example, if you want to make an exact match, select the equality (=) operator. On the other hand, if you want to locate all records greater that a certain value, select the greater than (>) operator, and so on.

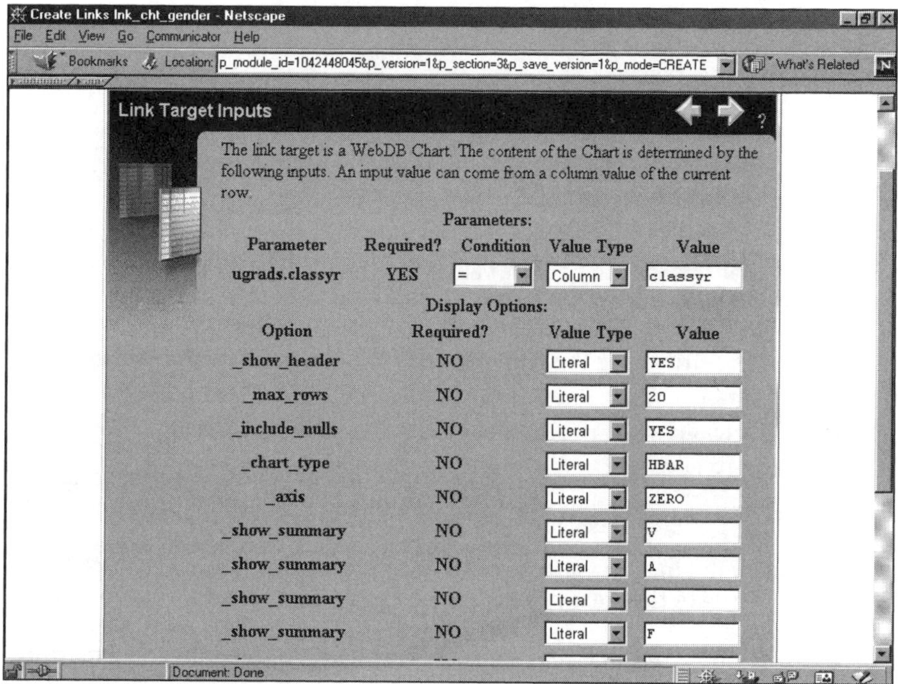

Figure 17-12: Link parameters

The value type field provides two settings — Literal and Column. If you are comparing your parameter to a fixed value, then you use the Literal value type. The value type is set in conjunction with the value field to form a comparison. The value field is a text box, but it accepts two types of values: literals and column names. For example, if you want the gender chart to display only the juniors and seniors, set the following options:

```
Condition - <
Value Type - Literal
Value - 2001
```

At run time, WebDB passes the parameter values to the chart object and selects only Juniors and Seniors (class years less than 2001). However, this particular example is still a fixed link, because the link will never change no matter where it is called. The underlying data may change as students are added and removed, but the link always shows only the Juniors and Seniors. To have the link vary along with the data, you need to use the Column value type.

When you set the value type combo box to column for a given parameter, WebDB assumes that the string you enter into the value field corresponds to a column name. In such cases, WebDB uses the value of the column at run time as a variable for the parameter. For example, assume that you wish to chart the number of males and females in a given class year. The ch17_cht_gender report already accepts the classyr as a parameter, so all that you need to do is pass the current class year value to the classyr field at run time. You can use the following parameter settings to accomplish this task:

```
Condition - =
Value Type - Column
Value - classyr
```

In order for this link to work, you have to be sure to connect the link to a component that passes the correct values for the classyr column, using the same datatype as in the chart object.

6. Enter the settings for the ugrads.classyr field as shown previously and in Figure 17-12.
7. Click the Next arrow to continue.
8. Click the OK button to store and compile the new link. In order to pass the correct value to the link, you need to edit the link source object.

The process of linking the variable to the link parameter is very simple. All you need to do is locate the classyr field on the report and select the proper link.

1. Edit the ch17_rep_classes report and navigate to the column formatting panel, as shown in Figure 17-13.

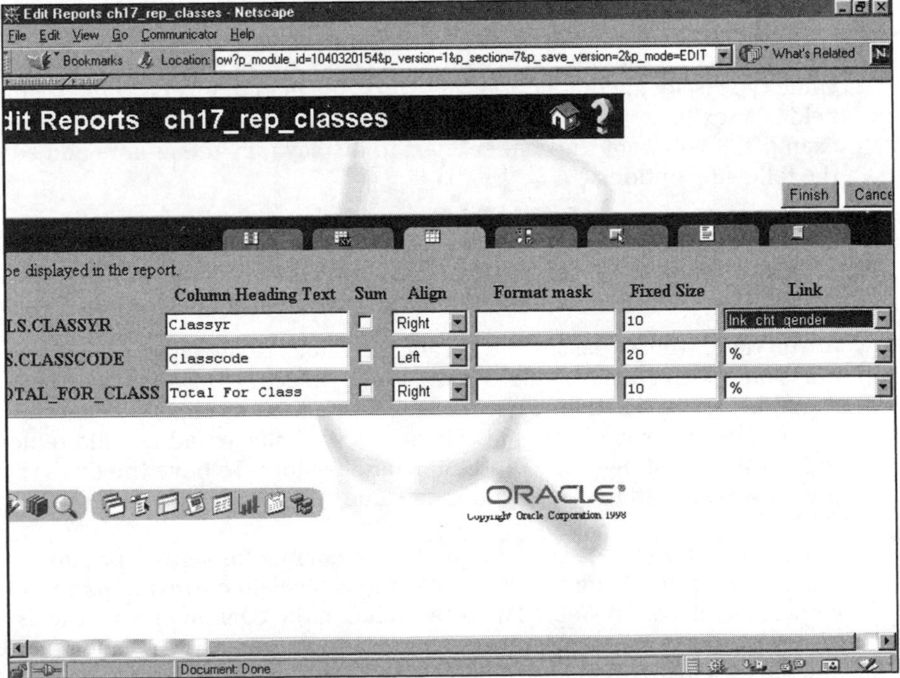

Figure 17-13: Passing column parameters

2. Navigate to the classyr field and select the entry lnk_cht_gender link.
3. Click the Finish button to save your changes.

   The real power of links is the ability to chain them together and allow your users to drill through your Web applications. Although you connected the chart object to the CLASSES report, you can get to the chart object by starting with the very first UGRADS report and drilling through to the chart.
4. Locate the ch17_rep_students report and use the Run link to test it.
5. Click any classyr field to display the ch17_rep_classes report. Notice that the classyr field on the report is now displayed as a link itself.
6. Click any classyr field to display the chart shown in Figure 17-14.

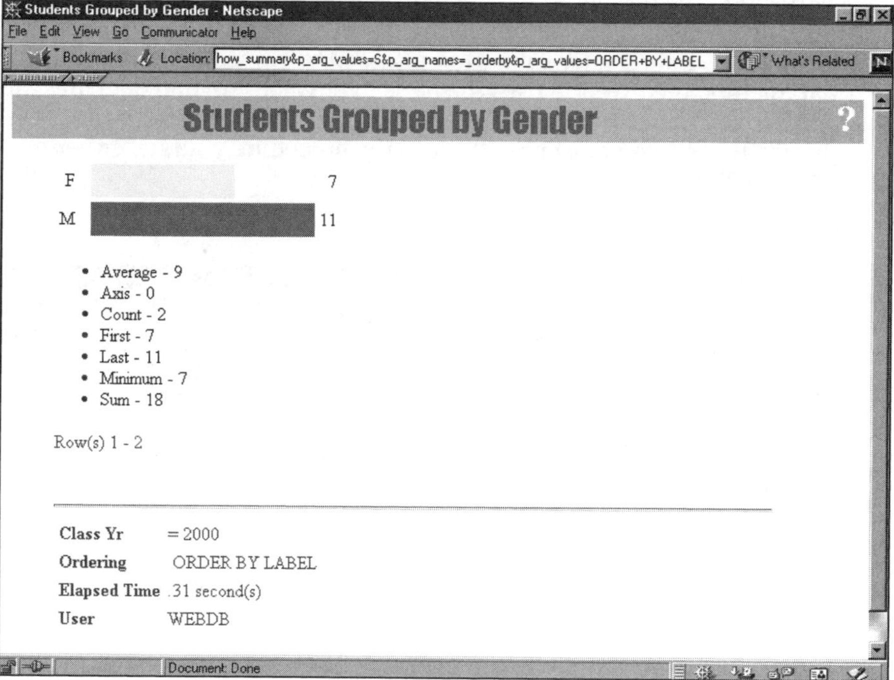

Figure 17-14: Students Grouped by Gender chart

This time, notice that the results for the chart change with each classyr value. You can even see the value that is passed to the chart in the footer section at the bottom of the chart itself.

Using Links to Update Data

WebDB's Link Wizard provides one additional piece of functionality that is critical in building interactive applications. In the Part II of this book, you learned how to build reports to display data, and forms to both read and write data. WebDB uses the link object to drive data entry forms by passing key values to form objects. When you build a data edit form, WebDB does not display any data in the form, nor does it provide update buttons unless the form object is passed key values when it is executed.

1. Load the form ch17_frm_students using SQL*Plus.
2. Run ch17_frm_students to display the page shown in Figure 17-15.

Notice that the form does not appear with any data loaded into it and the only options are INSERT and RESET. Internally, the procedure that renders the form looks for two parameter values to be passed to procedure. If it finds these parameters, then WebDB uses the parameter values to load data into the form and display additional buttons. By default, none of these values are passed to the procedure and you must pass them to the procedure yourself either manually or by using links.

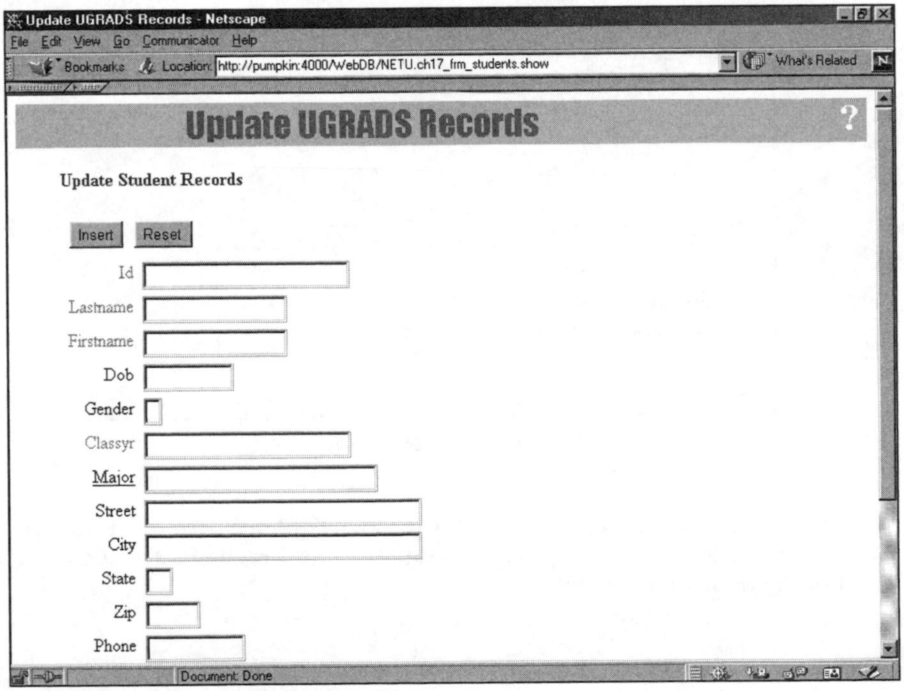

Figure 17-15: Update UGRADS form

3. Return to the Link Wizard and create a new link owned by the NETU account called lnk_frm_ugrads.
4. Choose the WebDB Component radio button.
5. Load netu.ch17_frm_students as the component name.
6. Navigate to the Link Target Inputs panel.

All of the fields for the form are available as parameters, so it is possible to restrict the display of the form by entering query parameters directly. However, in order to map the form to a given record you need to use two particular fields, as shown in Figure 17-16.

Display Options:			
Option	Required?	Value Type	Value
_show_header	NO	Literal	YES
_rowid	NO	Column	id
_alt_rowid	NO	Literal	ID

Figure 17-16: Link Target Inputs for a form

WebDB uses the _rowid and _alt_rowid fields to map the primary key values of a field to a form object. The value for the _rowid field is a column type, and it maps to the primary key field of the table. Strictly speaking, WebDB does not specifically require that the _rowid value be the primary key, but it must be a field that uniquely identifies an individual record. The value type is Column and the value field is the name of the unique column. The _alt_rowid field is a literal value in the link and it also maps to the same unique column string. At run time, WebDB uses the _rowid parameter to pass the value and the _alt_rowid parameter to pass the name of the value.

7. Set the following values on the Link Target Input panel:

```
_rowid
Value Type - Column
Value - id

_alt_rowid
Value Type - Literal
Value - ID
```

8. Click the Next arrow to continue, and then use the OK button to save and compile the link.
9. Use the TEST link to display a test page as shown in Figure 17-17.

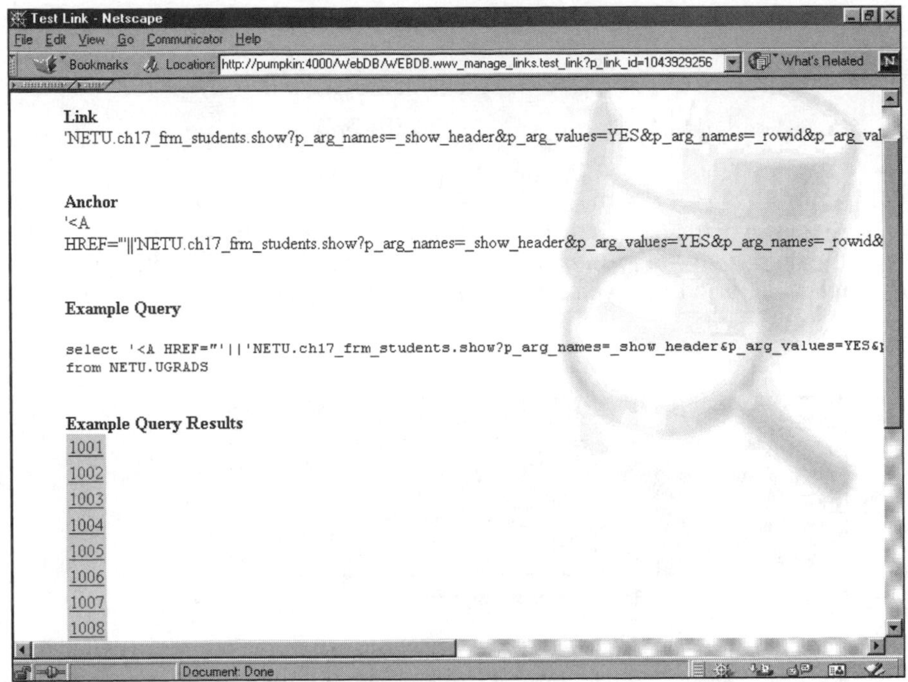

Figure 17-17: Testing the form link

10. Click through the link for any ID number to display a panel similar to Figure 17-18.

Note If the update and delete buttons have been deselected in the form object, they will not appear even if the _rowid parameters have been properly passed.

When the form appears this time, it is filled with data as shown in Figure 17-18. The procedure that renders the form has been passed the proper parameters and it therefore displays the data and additional form buttons. Once you have successfully tested the link, you can then deploy the link to the UGRADS report.

1. Exit the form and return to the main menu for the Report Wizard.
2. Edit the ch17_rep_students report.
3. Navigate to the Columns Formatting panel.
4. Connect the lnk_frm_ugrads link to the ID column.
5. Connect the lnk_frm_students link to the LASTNAME column.
6. Use the Finish button to save the report.
7. Run the report as shown in Figure 17-19.

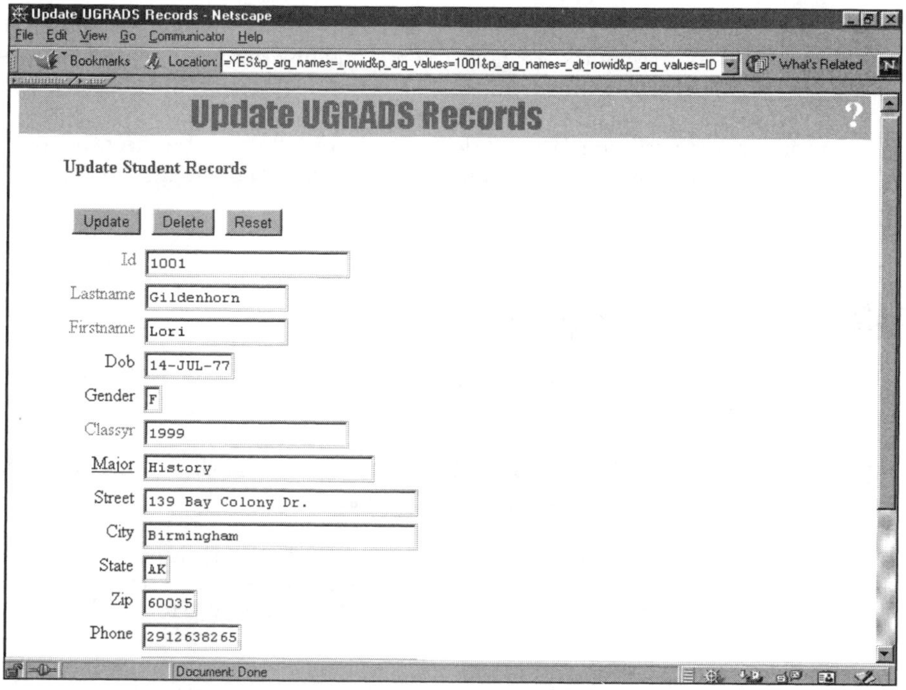

Update UGRADS Records - Netscape

Update UGRADS Records

Update Student Records

Update | Delete | Reset

Id 1001
Lastname Gildenhorn
Firstname Lori
Dob 14-JUL-77
Gender F
Classyr 1999
Major History
Street 139 Bay Colony Dr.
City Birmingham
State AK
Zip 60035
Phone 2912638265

Figure 17-18: UGRADS form with data

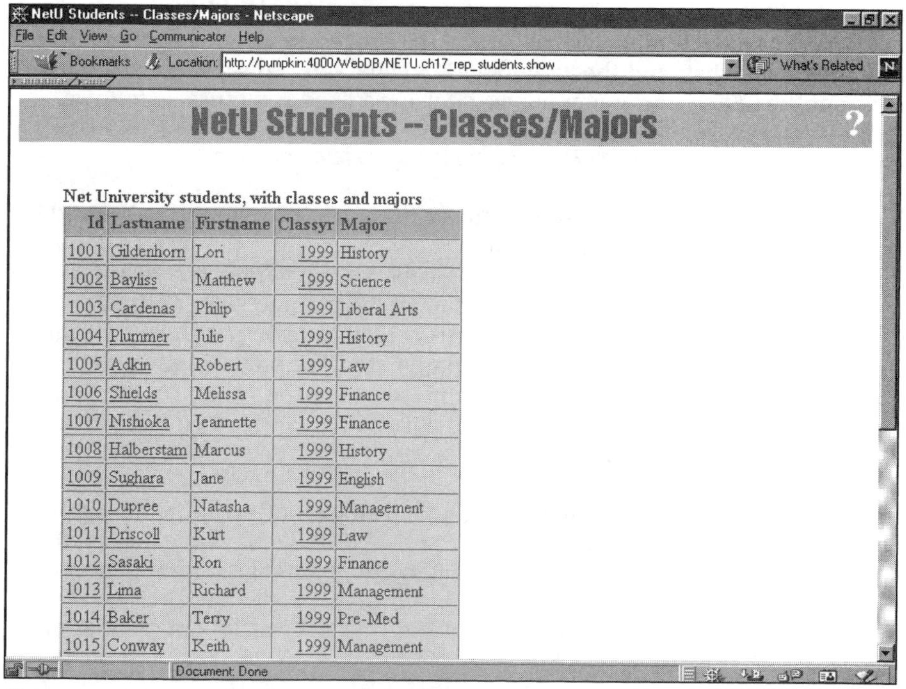

NetU Students -- Classes/Majors - Netscape

http://pumpkin:4000/WebDB/NETU.ch17_rep_students.show

NetU Students -- Classes/Majors

Net University students, with classes and majors

Id	Lastname	Firstname	Classyr	Major
1001	Gildenhorn	Lori	1999	History
1002	Bayliss	Matthew	1999	Science
1003	Cardenas	Philip	1999	Liberal Arts
1004	Plummer	Julie	1999	History
1005	Adkin	Robert	1999	Law
1006	Shields	Melissa	1999	Finance
1007	Nishioka	Jeannette	1999	Finance
1008	Halberstam	Marcus	1999	History
1009	Sughara	Jane	1999	English
1010	Dupree	Natasha	1999	Management
1011	Driscoll	Kurt	1999	Law
1012	Sasaki	Ron	1999	Finance
1013	Lima	Richard	1999	Management
1014	Baker	Terry	1999	Pre-Med
1015	Conway	Keith	1999	Management

Figure 17-19: UGRADS report with update links

Notice that both the ID and the LASTNAME fields are highlighted and you can select either field to display the form with data. The link has been coded to pass the ID value, regardless of which field the link is connected to. This means that you can leave the ID number off the display of the report, yet still be able to pass the value to the form at run time. WebDB does not require links to be directly connected to their data item counterparts, and this makes your reports and forms much more flexible.

WebDB Parameter Arrays

You might notice that when you select a particular link, WebDB builds a URL based on the data value you selected.

Click the link for ID 1001 in the UGRADS report and then view the link that appears in the location bar in your browser:

```
http://pumpkin:4000/WebDB/NETU.ch17_frm_students.show?p_arg_nam
es=_show_header&p_arg_values=YES&p_arg_names=_rowid&p_arg_value
s=1001&p_arg_names=_alt_rowid&p_arg_values=ID
```

The _rowid and _alt_rowid parameter sections are shown in boldface and you can see how WebDB passes these values to the component. All parameters are passed to WebDB components using a series of p_arg_names and p_arg_values fields. Any WebDB component that accepts parameters (including display options parameters) can accept a formatted parameter string as a URL. WebDB uses the question mark (?) character to indicate the end of the procedure name and the start of the parameter list, and the ampersand (&) character to separate parameters from one another. Each parameter is passed using a fixed structure as follows:

```
p_arg_names=name&p_arg_values=value
```

The `p_arg_names=` portion of the string is a fixed required value and it denotes that the next value WebDB finds should be read as a parameter name. The `name` portion of the string is read as the name for the parameter. Next up is the `&` character, which separates the name of the parameter from the value of the parameter. The `p_arg_values=` string tells WebDB that the next value WebDB finds should be read as the value for a parameter. The value itself is matched up with the parameter name that was passed just ahead of the value. So, in plain English, the substring tells WebDB that the next parameter is the *`name`* parameter and the value for this parameter is *`value`*.

The result is an incredibly powerful and elegant means of allowing procedures to accept a dynamic array of parameters. WebDB displays the complete list of parameters for any component as part of the Manage Component menu.

1. Navigate to the Chart Wizard and select the ch17_cht_gender chart.

2. Click the Manage link and then click the Show Call Interface link to display the page shown in Figure 17-20.

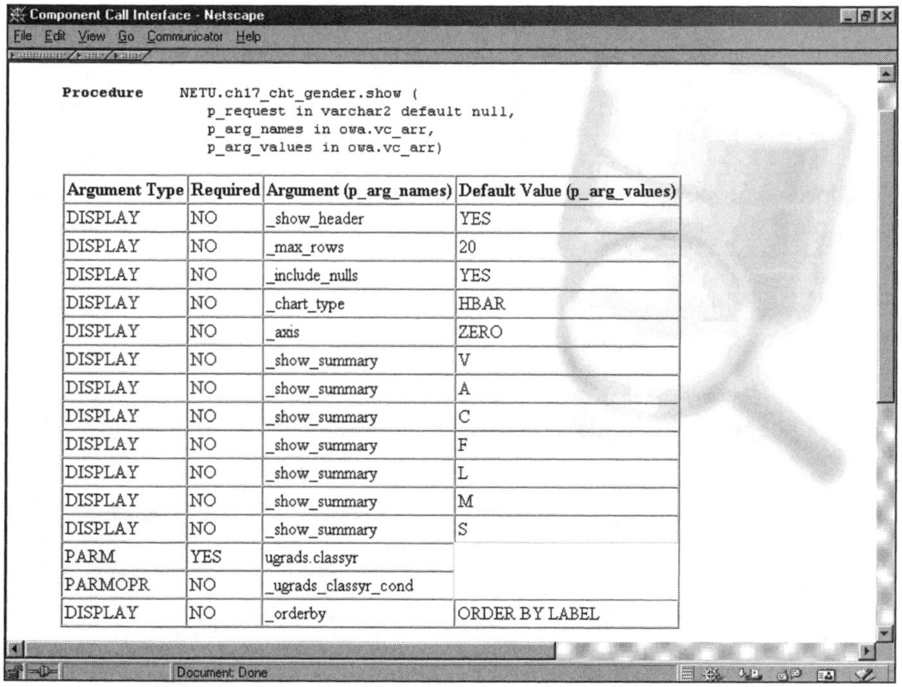

Component Call Interface - Netscape

File Edit View Go Communicator Help

```
Procedure     NETU.ch17_cht_gender.show (
                  p_request in varchar2 default null,
                  p_arg_names in owa.vc_arr,
                  p_arg_values in owa.vc_arr)
```

Argument Type	Required	Argument (p_arg_names)	Default Value (p_arg_values)
DISPLAY	NO	_show_header	YES
DISPLAY	NO	_max_rows	20
DISPLAY	NO	_include_nulls	YES
DISPLAY	NO	_chart_type	HBAR
DISPLAY	NO	_axis	ZERO
DISPLAY	NO	_show_summary	V
DISPLAY	NO	_show_summary	A
DISPLAY	NO	_show_summary	C
DISPLAY	NO	_show_summary	F
DISPLAY	NO	_show_summary	L
DISPLAY	NO	_show_summary	M
DISPLAY	NO	_show_summary	S
PARM	YES	ugrads.classyr	
PARMOPR	NO	_ugrads_classyr_cond	
DISPLAY	NO	_orderby	ORDER BY LABEL

Document: Done

Figure 17-20: Component Call Interface panel

The top part of the panel shows a table with all of the valid parameters for a given component organized according to four values: argument type, required indicator, argument name, and default value. Display options argument types control things such as the header and font size. (The specific list of display options varies by component object type.) Argument types marked as PARM elements indicate that the parameter is used as part of a query or bind variable. In the case of the GENDER chart, the CLASSYR field in the UGRADS table is used a query parameter, and it is marked as a PARM value. WebDB creates a matching parameter for each PARM type called the PARMOPR, which is short for Parameter Operator. WebDB enables you to pass the comparison operator as a parameter to the component using the PARMOPR string.

So, although the example GENDER chart accepts a CLASSYR parameter using an equality comparison, you can override the equality operator = and use the greater than > operator if you wish.

The Required column indicates whether any particular parameter is required to execute the component, and you will find that most bind variables are required parameters. The final two columns show the P_ARG_NAMES and the default P_ARG_VALUES for each parameter. Although the GENDER chart does not provide defaults for the PARM and PARMOPR parameters, you could have specified default values within the Chart Wizard. You can also view alternative values for any of the display parameters by changing values on the Display Options panel in each wizard and then redisplaying the call interface for the resulting component.

WebDB displays a sample call interface just below the table of parameters in two formats. First, WebDB shows the call interface as a stored procedure call, so that you can embed the component inside of another PL/SQL procedure. WebDB also shows the same procedure as a URL string, which you can use to embed the component as a manual link within any Web page. For example, take the following URL string:

```
http://pumpkin:4000/webdb/NETU.ch17_cht_gender.show?p_arg_names
=ugrads.classyr&p_arg_values=1999
```

If you were to enter this string into the location field of your browser (substituting your server, port, and DAD entries) you would get the results shown in Figure 17-21.

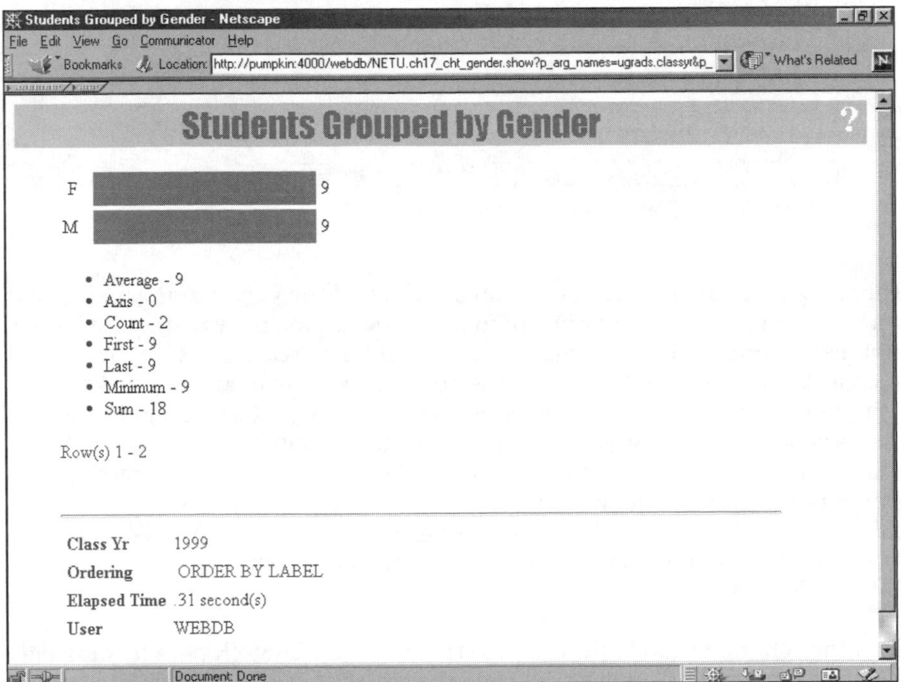

Figure 17-21: Gender chart using a manual URL entry

WebDB renders the chart by using the CLASSYR parameter that you passed on the command line. You can even change the chart entirely by passing in a different comparison operator as follows:

```
http://pumpkin:4000/webdb/NETU.ch17_cht_gender.show?p_arg_names
=ugrads.classyr&p_arg_values=1999&p_arg_names=_ugrads_classyr_c
ond&p_arg_values=>
```

In this case, the CLASSYR parameter of 1999 was used as a greater-than comparison to yield the output shown in Figure 17-22.

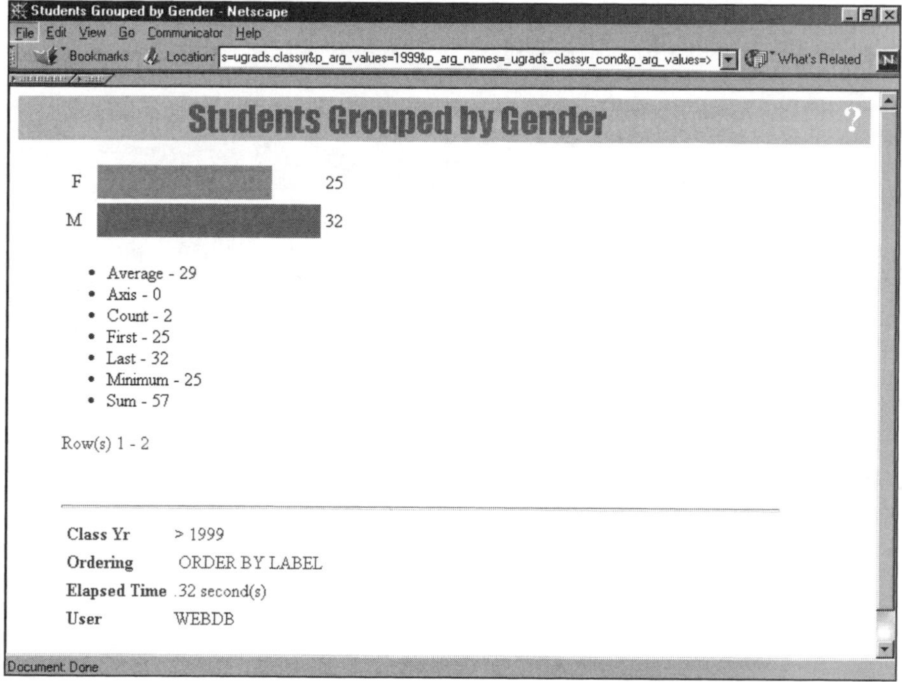

Figure 17-22: Gender chart with a greater-than operator

You are free to pass parameters in any order, but they must always be passed using the same format, with the p_arg_names string first and the p_arg_values string second. Conditions can be passed ahead of comparison operators and display options can be mixed in with PARM parameters as long as you follow the required format.

You can use these URL strings wherever URL values are permitted, and you will find them especially useful for menus. For example, you could build a WebDB menu with four options for the GENDER chart, one for each class year. The link text for each menu item would be a URL string with the proper parameter for the class year as shown in the preceding URLs.

Wrapping Up

WebDB's Link Builder is a useful tool for providing drill-up and drill-down access for your dynamic database data. Consistent use of links can make your data much easier to navigate through and can help your users make information out of raw data. Parameters enable the links to respond appropriately to specific end user requests, which can make your Web application much more intuitive. Parameters also have the effect of making the data on your site appear fresher and more up to date, as each new interaction by a user may take him or her down a new path. It's best to add links to your application after you have built most of your user interface objects, because they are derived from these objects. When used in conjunction with menus, you can quickly bundle blocks of database content together into a cohesive application in record time.

✦ ✦ ✦

CHAPTER 18

Using Site Builder — Part I

✦ ✦ ✦ ✦

In This Chapter

Introduction to Site Builder

The Site Builder Architecture

Site Builder Elements

Building Your First Site

Modifying the WebDB Site Using the Administration Tools

Content Managers

Content Types

✦ ✦ ✦ ✦

Chapter 14 introduced you to the WebDB Menu Wizard, which you can use to build a structure for your WebDB components and deploy applications to end users. WebDB also provides a tool for generating Web sites with a more rigorous structure through Site Builder. Site Builder provides a complete methodology for deploying data to users through a Web interface. Although there are a number of tools that provide similar functionality, Site Builder is unique in its ability to enable end users to contribute content to your Web sites directly through the Web interface. You can deploy structured data to your users through the various WebDB component wizards, and Site Builder provides the access points for connecting these objects to the Site Builder framework. However, users can also upload unstructured content to your Web sites, and Site Builder provides the structure to organize and manage this content. Site Builder can often be the glue that holds your Web site together. Site Builder is an integral part of WebDB, but you can use it without using any of the other component wizards. In this chapter, we will introduce you to Site Builder and walk you through the process of building and modifying a site.

The Site Builder Architecture

Site Builder has two main components: the Site Builder environment and the Site Wizard. The Site Wizard represents a very small part of the overall solution, but is the portion of Site Builder that generates the site framework on your behalf. The Site Wizard is a very simple wizard to use, especially in comparison to some of the other component wizards within WebDB. However, when you have finished navigating through one of the content wizards within WebDB, your work is often done. With Site Builder, creating the site and using the Site Wizard is just the tip of the iceberg. Site Builder contains numerous utilities for modifying both the structure and the user interface of your site. The key to understanding how Site Builder works is through the three mechanisms that Site Builder uses for organizing content:

✦ Folders

✦ Categories

✦ Perspectives

A *folder* represents a distinct organizational area of a Web site. Each folder has one or more owners who define the components and content that appear in the folder. A Site Builder Web site can have a hierarchy of folders, where one folder acts as a subfolder of another.

A folder owner can assign security on a folder, based on either user names or groups, which can represent many users. The security assigned to a folder cascades to the items contained in the folder. Through the folder security settings, you can determine whether an individual user can view, modify, delete, or create items within a folder. With the use of folder security, a single Site Builder folder can serve the needs of a wide variety of users. Folder access is implemented through Oracle database security just as it is for WebDB component objects. Site Builder users are assigned Oracle USERIDs and ROLEs, although Site Builder itself manages access to the folders within the site. In the Net University database, you might create folders for each of the main constituents of the site: Faculty, Alumni, and Undergraduates.

The content in a Site Builder Web site is classified in two basic ways: as a member of a *category* or a *perspective.* A category is a way to classify what an item is. For example, in the Net University database, the categories might include such items as academics and sports. Categories are classifications applied to content within folders. All folders in a given WebDB site have the same set of categories, although it is not necessary for each folder to have entries for each category.

A perspective is a way to classify who would be interested in a particular item. For example, you might create perspectives that are specific to each undergraduate major, or that identify "hot" topics. A perspective can span multiple categories. All items are assigned to one and only one category and zero or more perspectives when they are added to a Site Builder site. Perspectives, as well as categories, can be used as search criteria when a user searches a Site Builder Web site for content.

Folders can use categories and perspectives to organize the content of the entire folder or to target different users. The use of these powerful organizing classifications, coupled with the ability to define users and user roles, makes it easy to create Web sites that automatically deliver a customized view of the information available in your WebDB site. Most of the work you do in setting up a Site Builder Web site is creating the folders, categories, and perspectives, and assigning attributes, ownership, and styles to each of these objects. Once these objects are in place, the site continues to organize the new information added to the site according to the folders, categories, and perspectives you created during the configuration process. You can add new folders, categories, and perspectives to production sites as the need arises.

Site Builder Elements

The WebDB wizards that you have worked with up to this point have all guided you from start to finish using a series of panels. The Site Wizard operates differently, although the site creation process does make use of a series of panels. When you use a component builder wizard, the edit panels mirror the create panels. There are no options on the edit panels that were not presented to you during the creation process. With the Site Wizard this is not true, because many additional options only appear during the edit phase. In fact, so many options are available within the Site Editor that displaying them within the build wizard would make the entire process unproductive. Because the Site Wizard operates differently, the approach that you take in working with Site Builder is different as well.

It is important to understand the ultimate shape and form of a site before you try to create your own sites. To help you with this process, WebDB includes a sample Site Builder Web site you can install during the build process. Figure 18-1 shows the main page for this sample site.

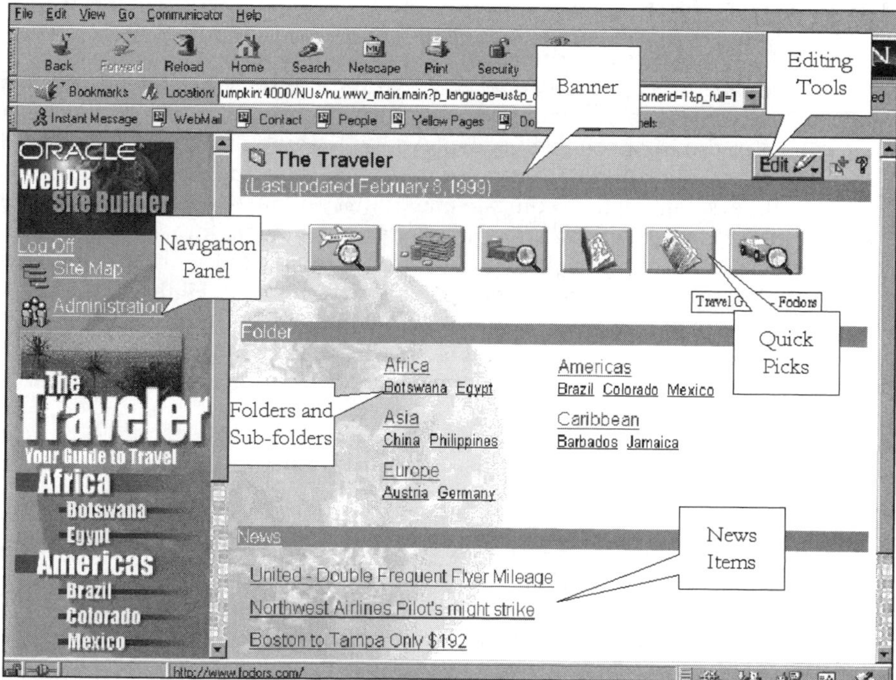

Figure 18-1: The Traveler Web site

The Traveler Web site shows off all the elements of a Site Builder site in a reasonably small package. When you create a new site, it will never look as complete as this sample site because the sample comes complete with data as well as structure. This sample site can be an invaluable tool when you are learning to work with Site Builder because you can see folders, categories, and perspectives in action. You can also see the various display options and structure options provided for the site. The Site Builder framework provides increased productivity as compared to building your own site from scratch, but you are also forced to work within this framework. You will find that you can create powerful, interactive Web sites very quickly with Site Builder, but you must be willing to work within the confines of the framework.

Six basic elements make up the Site Builder framework:

- Navigation Bar
- Banner
- Edit menu
- Quick Picks
- News and announcements
- Folders, subfolders, and items

Navigation Bar

The Navigation Bar serves as the menu for a Site Builder Web site and is implemented as a frame, which appears by default on the left-hand side of the page. You can move the elements that appear on the Navigation Bar to other parts of the framework, but the bar itself can be displayed in a frame on the right or left side of your pages. The Navigation Bar provides two services: administration tasks and navigation. Users can log on to the site and adjust administrative information, such as passwords and user information, from links on the Navigation Bar. You can also include navigation options such as folder links, category links, and perspective links within the Navigation Bar. In the example site shown in Figure 18-1, the Navigation Bar includes links to all of the travel destinations, which are shown as folders and subfolders. Each continent is a folder and all the countries within that continent are subfolders. You can see the details of how this is laid out in the next section.

Banner

The Banner is the ribbon area at the top of the page used for displaying page titles, messages, edit options, and the announcement area. You will normally use the Banner for site messages and options that apply to the current folder, because the Banner contents can vary by folder. For example, in Figure 18-1, the Banner includes a title for the site along with the current date. You can reserve the bottom portion of the Banner for special options and messages. You can also use it for linking to other content called Quick Picks. The right-hand corner of the Banner holds the Edit menu, which may or may not appear depending upon the level of security you have implemented for your site.

Edit menu

One of the features that make the Site Builder product unique amongst the many site creation tools is its ability to build Web sites interactively. During the site modification process, the site administrator uses the Edit menu to adjust folders and modify the site's parameters. You can enable end users to submit content for the various folders on your site through the Edit menu. If you give users the ability to modify information on your site, the Edit menu appears within the Banner area when these users log on to the site.

Quick Picks

Quick Picks are URL links that are embedded in the reserved space just below the Banner. These links can vary on a folder-by-folder basis and are used as menu choices specific to a given menu. In the Traveler example site, the Quick Picks items link to a variety of external sites such as an airline fare-finder site and the government passport agency. However, they could just as easily point to other items stored within your Web site. Their main purpose is to provide a visible and fast mechanism for reaching popular items that may be folder-specific, but are not necessarily associated with any of the categories within that folder.

News and announcements

WebDB reserves a special area of the page for news and announcement items, which are similar in concept. News items are pieces of time-sensitive information stored within a special section in the folders on your site. News items are generally short messages that have a specified shelf life. In Figure 18-1, you can see the news items at the bottom of the page announcing special fares on various airlines and routes. Announcements provide a similar service, but WebDB gives them a higher profile by placing them below the Quick Picks items at the top of the screen.

Folders, subfolders, and items

All of the preceding structural items support this last group of elements: folders, subfolders, and items. Site Builder content objects are called items, and items are stored within folders or subfolders. You can see each continent implemented as a folder, and each country implemented as a subfolder in Figure 18-1. Folders provide the organization, but items are the *leaf* objects within a Site Builder site. If you were to drill down in the Traveler site within a particular country, you would a see a page much like the one shown in Figure 18-2.

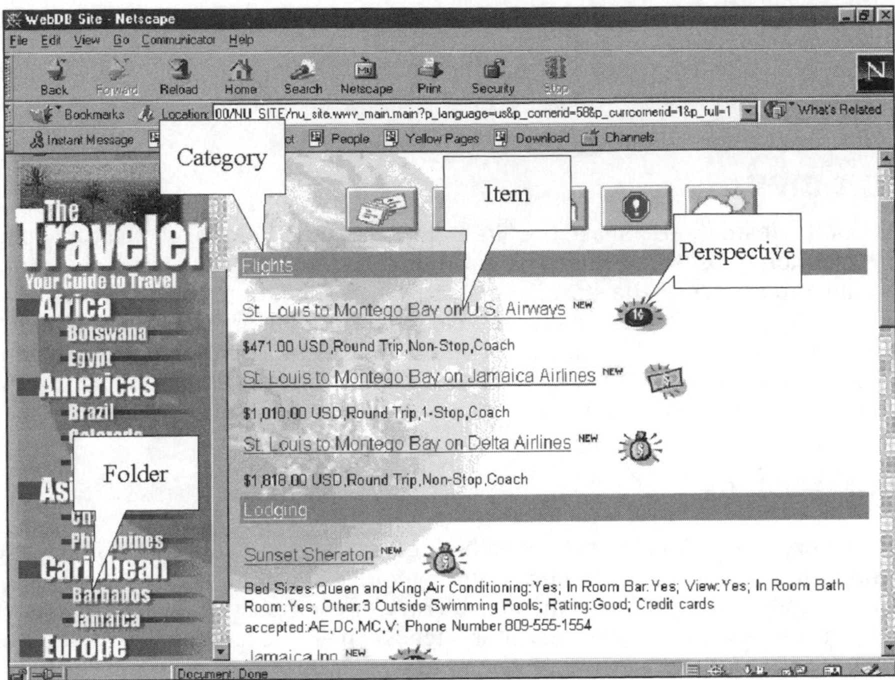

Figure 18-2: Folders and items in the Traveler site

Through the Navigation Bar, you can drill down into the details of a particular subfolder, as shown in Figure 18-2, and within the subfolder are a number of categories such as Flights and Lodging. The layout of the categories for this example site are not particularly important, because the key concept to understand is that the folder is divided into categories as a means of organizing the content. Within each category are a number of entries that are the leaf elements for the site. Chapter 22 provides a more detailed look at items, because they are more relevant to using a site than to building one.

At this point, it is only important to understand that items are content objects either stored in the Site Builder Web site or addressed through a URL. In Figure 18-2, the identified item is a particular flight from St. Louis to Montego Bay on USAirways. All of the entries within the Flights category are links to flights, just as all of the entries in the Lodging category are entries for hotel accommodations. Also notice that each item has an image icon displayed to the right of the text link. This image corresponds to a perspective, and three different perspectives appear within the Flights category. The penny image denotes an inexpensive flight, while the dollar bill icon identifies a more expensive airfare. Really expensive flights are marked with the bag of money icon. Perspectives provide the user with a visual clue about the content, and later you will see that users can also search for content by perspectives as well. Folders, categories, and perspectives are implemented during the design phase of a site, but items are added only when the site is put to use. With the Site Wizard, you will create the basic structure for your site utilizing these six basic elements.

Building Your First Site

The Site Wizard interface is less elaborate than the other content creation wizards, but the end result is quite impressive. You can find the Site Wizard on the main WebDB page and in the menu bar at the bottom of the WebDB page. However, your logon account must have DBA privileges in order to have access to the Site menu item. You must address the following five items within the Site Builder Wizard:

- Site Name
- Owning Schema
- Tablespaces
- Language
- Demos

The site name is the logical name used to identify the site within WebDB, and the site name is also used as the main title page for the new Web site. Because the site name serves as the title string, WebDB permits you to use spaces and mixed case characters for the name string.

The owning schema is the Oracle USERID that owns all of the content and contains the structure for the Web site. This USERID acts as a component building schema and this account should only be used for storing content. End users should never log on to this USERID directly. When you create your new site, the Site Wizard creates this USERID as part of the build process, so the USERID must not exist already in the target Oracle database. The Site Wizard also creates a series of data access descriptor entries to match this USERID, which are to be used when connecting to the new site. Because the Site Wizard creates a new user account to hold the content, you must also provide tablespace entries as part of the build process. The Site Wizard requires two tablespace settings: one for the primary storage area and one for temporary sorting operations. Once you have created the site, you are free to change these definitions and split tables between multiple tablespaces just as you would for any other Oracle account. Initially, the new site takes approximately 20MB of database space, but you will want to make sure that the selected tablespace entries can be expanded as you add content and items to the site.

WebDB builds upon the settings for your Oracle database, including the language settings. The Site Wizard can create Web sites using any of Oracle's many national language setting (NLS) values, so you are prompted to select a language setting during the build process. You must choose this setting carefully, because you cannot change this setting once the site has been created.

The menu panel in the wizard enables you to install the Traveler demo inside the new Web site. The Traveler is implemented as a subfolder within your site, so it is easy to delete this demo from your site at any time. The Traveler demo is filled with examples of the various features of Site Builder, and you may find these examples useful for comparison purposes.

We recommend that you install the Traveler demo into its own site and keep it separate from your own Web sites. Doing so enables you to keep the Traveler online for reference purposes without it interfering with your custom work.

The six panels in the Site Wizard correspond to the preceding five elements along with the familiar OK panel used to build the final stored procedure. The entire process should take only a few minutes to complete, depending upon the speed of your Oracle database server machine.

1. Navigate to the main menu for WebDB and choose the Sites link.
2. Click the Create button to begin creating your site.
3. Enter **Net University** as the name for your site, and click the Next arrow to continue.
4. Enter **nu_site** as the name of the Owning Schema and click the Next arrow to continue.
5. Select a language setting for your site from the drop-down list box. (The examples in this chapter are based upon the American language setting.) Click the Next arrow to continue.
6. Choose a tablespace entry for the User Tablespace that the NU_SITE account will use for storing the site, and select a tablespace for temporary storage. Click the Next arrow to continue.
7. Deselect the Traveler demo check box if it has been selected by default. You can repeat this entire build process using a second site if you want to have access to the Traveler demo later on. Click the Next arrow to continue.
8. The last panel in the wizard redisplays the information you entered and prompts you to click the Finish button to complete the process and build the site. Click the Finish button to commence with the install process.
9. When the installation completes, click the Done push button to acknowledge the message that the site has been built.

Viewing the generated site

After you have finished filling in all the pages in the Site Wizard, WebDB generates a page, as shown in Figure 18-3. From this page you can either view the site or proceed to the administration menu where you can begin modifying the generated settings.

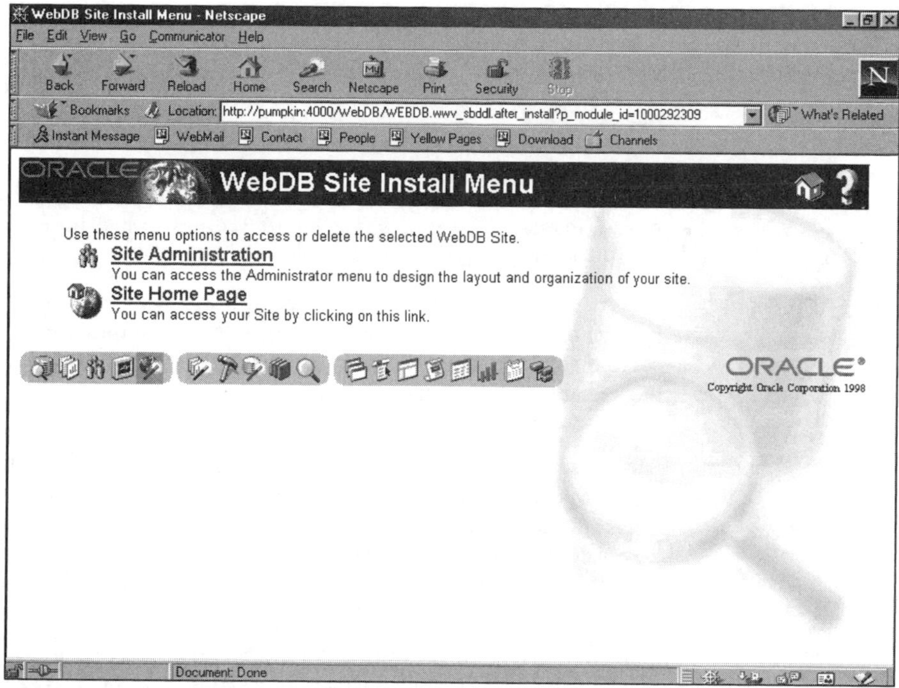

Figure 18-3: WebDB Site Install Menu page

During the generation process, the Site Wizard creates approximately 50 tables inside the schema you identified as the owning schema during the parameter entry phase of the process. WebDB uses these tables and views to store the site information as well as the content for the site when you begin adding items to the site. An entry for the site is made in the WebDB schema within the WebDB account, but most of the source information for your site is stored directly inside the site schema itself. In addition to the tables, the Site Wizard also creates some additional user accounts along with several data access descriptors (DAD) entries for the WebDB listener. The user accounts and DAD entries are based upon the owning schema name you provided. In the example case, the Oracle USERID that owns the Net University site is called nu_site. Table 18-1 lists the additional user accounts and DAD entries created by Site Builder.

From the WebDB site install menu, you have two choices: you can begin using the new site with the Site Home Page link, or you can select the Site Administration link to begin modifying the site. Once you have completed using the Site Wizard panels, you are finished working with the wizard interface, at least as far the current Web site goes. This point marks the transition between the Site Wizard and the Site Builder interface. Because you are just beginning to work with Site Builder, it makes sense to start by viewing the site as is.

Table 18-1
User Accounts and DAD Entries Created by Site Builder

Entry	*Description*
NU_SITE	Site Wizard creates a site schema using the name you provided during the parameter entry process. This account appears as an Oracle USERID, but it should only be used as a storage schema for the site. Users should not be given direct access to this account.
NU_SITE_*admin*	Site Wizard creates a second Oracle USERID that is a concatenation of the owner schema name and the string _admin, and the password is set to match the name. This account is given special privileges within the site and should be used by the site administrator to modify settings for the site.
NU_SITE_*public*	Site Wizard automatically creates a public USERID that is given end user privileges within the site. This logon can be used by end users to access to the content within the site. You may create additional accounts for end users to use on an individual basis, but this account serves as the default account. The default password for this account matches the user name as well.
NU_SITE (DAD)	WebDB maps the public USERID for the site to a new DAD entry that matches the name of the owning schema. This entry can be used to access the site directly from the browser through the following URL: `http://servername:port/NU_SITE/` WebDB automatically plugs the public USERID and password into this DAD entry so that end users can navigate to the site without having a user name or password.
NU_SITEs (DAD)	In addition to the NU_SITE DAD entry, WebDB creates a second DAD that the administrator uses when connecting to the site. This second DAD has the same name as the owning schema with the letter *s* (for secure) appended to the end of the name string. Administrators can connect to the site using this secure connection with the following string: `http://servername:port/NU_SITEs/` This DAD does not have a USERID and password assigned, so the administrator is prompted for the admin account and password in order to log on as the administrator.

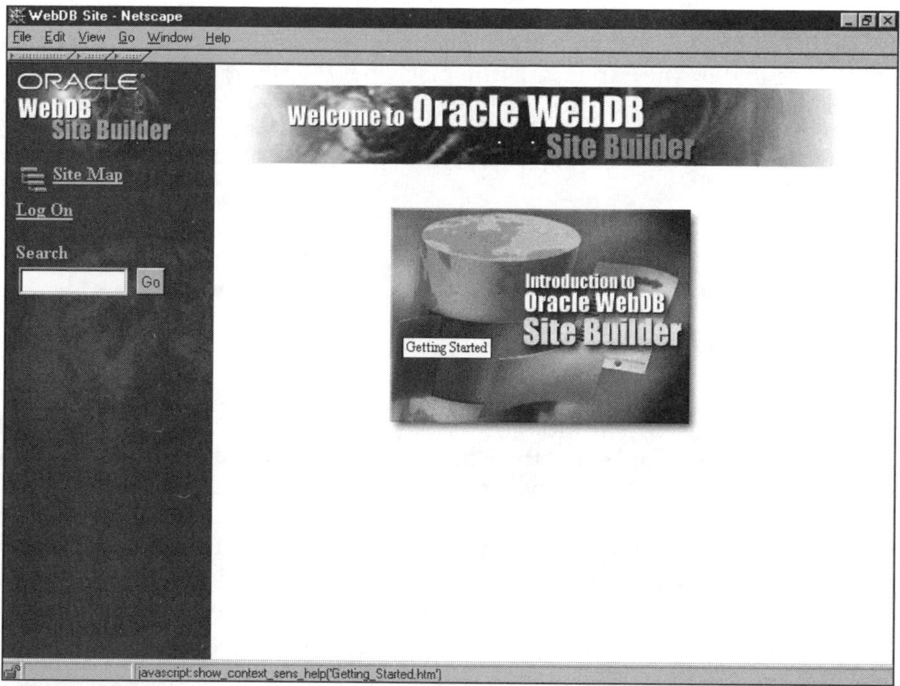

Figure 18-4: Net University site home page

1. Use the Site Home Page link to navigate to the home page for the new site as shown in Figure 18-4.

   The default site generated does not contain any data, but it does provide all of the basic framework components you need to customize your site. The two image panels in the center of the page point to help information for Site Builder. The left-hand image provides a link to general information on the interface itself, while the right-hand image shows you how to add content to your site. The Navigation Bar has entries for logging on, viewing a map of the folders, and searching for content items. At this point, the site is empty except for the structure, so the next logical step is to modify the site and prepare it for use.

2. Use the Log On link to connect to the site. If you are prompted for logon information, use the following default secure user name and password combination: nu_site_admin/nu_site_admin.

We recommend that you change the password for the administration account as soon as the site has been created. This keeps unauthorized users from gaining entry to the site while you are working on it. The site administration menu has tools for modifying user names and passwords, or you can use the familiar administration menu to make this change.

Once you have logged onto the site, the home page contains two additional links: one for accessing the administration functions and one for accessing the default WebDB site folder. The framework is in place, but the site is effectively empty because there is only a single folder and that folder contains no content. The key to getting your site rolling is to modify the look and feel and add some folders and subfolders.

Modifying the WebDB Site Using the Administration Tools

The Site Builder Wizard makes it is easy to create the framework for your site, but it does not make the site ready for access by your end users. You need to add folders and modify the look and feel of the site to match your requirements. To help you with this process, Site Builder includes a suite of administration tools.

The site administration tools consist of four basic classes, as shown in Figure 18-5: Web Site Managers, Content Managers, Access Managers, and Toolbox.

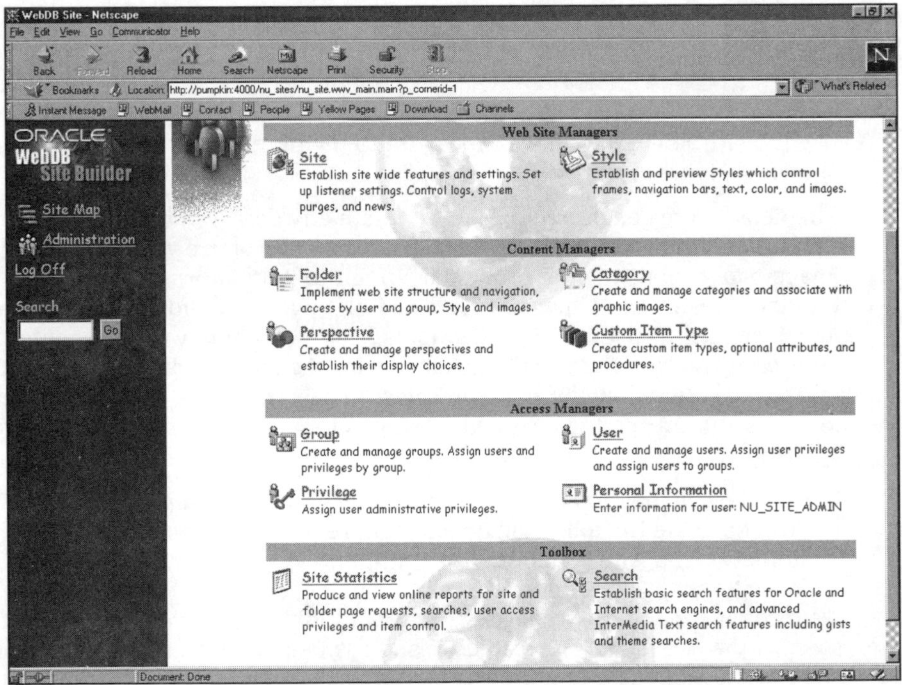

Figure 18-5: Site administration menu

Use the Administration link to display the site administration menu. (Use the default administrative user name and password to logon — nu_site_admin/nu_site_admin — or the new values you assigned for them if you are prompted for logon credentials.)

Web Site Managers

The Web Site Manager tools control the look and feel for your site as well as the basic operation of the site. The Site link provides access to a series of edit panels that enable you to control the operation of your site. From this panel, you can determine how long the site activity logs are kept and whether or not individual items are managed using version control. The Style link provides a complimentary suite of editors that determine the look and feel of your site. From this panel, you can set the color scheme for your site and lay out the items that appear on the Navigation Bar. You will typically use the Web site managers to configure your site properly, but you can make changes using these tools at any time over the life of your site. For example, if your company changes its corporate colors, you can use the Style link to change the Web site to match.

Content Managers

The Content Managers are the meat and potatoes of your site, for they control the folders, categories, and perspectives used by the site. The main navigation mechanism for a Site Builder Web site is the folder hierarchy that you create with the Folder link on this panel. This hierarchy forms the basis for the organization of your content. The folders themselves are divided into sections using the Category editors and the items within the site are indexed with the Perspectives Editor. You can add new folders, categories, and perspectives to your site at any time over the life of the site. However, WebDB does not provide any tools for automatically moving blocks of content items to new folders. Given this restriction, it makes sense to devise an overall plan for these items before you begin adding content to the site. The Content Managers contain an additional link you can use to design custom item entry panels. You will learn more about using this feature in Chapter 23.

Access Managers

The Access Managers control the users and groups permitted to access the Web site, and they also control the privileges granted to these users and groups. User accounts become Oracle database users just as if these accounts were entered into the database using Enterprise Manager or the WebDB administration panels. WebDB provides these utilities inside Site Builder in order to make it easier for you to manage a Web site without ever having to leave the Site Builder interface. Site Builder identifies the administrative user of each site as a special account, and through the access manager Personal Information link you are permitted to provide additional descriptive information for the administrative account user.

Toolbox

The Site Builder Toolbox controls the site statistics views and search capabilities for the overall site. Site Builder captures its own statistics using a custom installation of the activity log tables. You can view these customized charts and tables by using the Site Statistics links in the Toolbox.

Site Builder is integrated with the search capabilities of the Oracle8*i* database, and it can make use of the interMedia search facilities of the Oracle database. Through the Search link, you can control the features of the search interface within your site.

We recommend that you review Chapter 21 for a complete description of the WebDB monitoring utilities. Site Builder's logs are compiled using the same technology that WebDB uses to monitor component objects, but they are stored within the component building schema that owns the account.

Establishing your site

Now that you have created your site, you need to modify it before you can release it to your user base. The first step in this modification process is to establish the overall site features and settings using the Site link.

Use the Site link to display the panel shown in Figure 18-6.

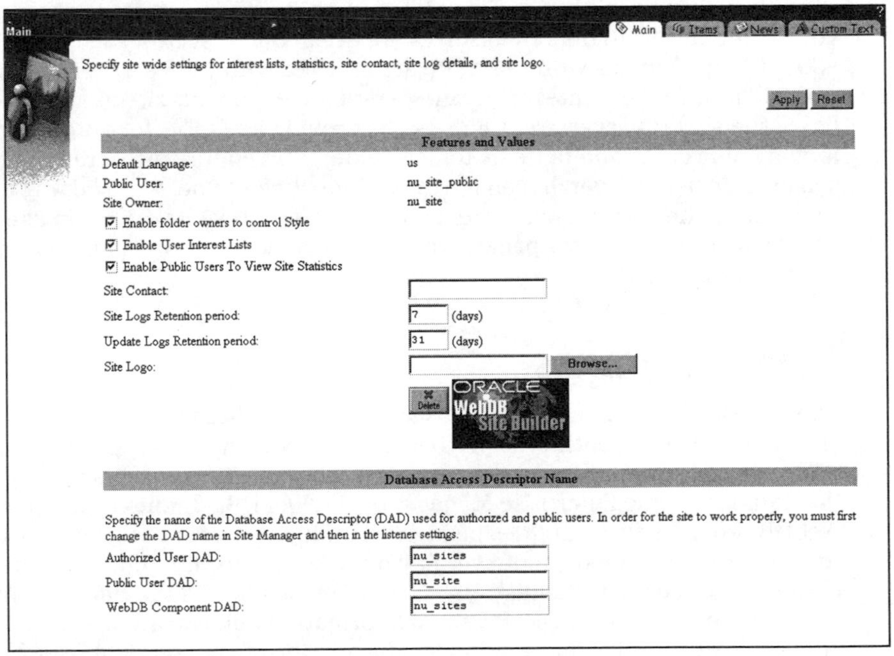

Main | Main | Items | News | Custom Text

Specify site wide settings for interest lists, statistics, site contact, site log details, and site logo.

Apply | Reset

Features and Values

Default Language: us
Public User: nu_site_public
Site Owner: nu_site
☑ Enable folder owners to control Style
☑ Enable User Interest Lists
☑ Enable Public Users To View Site Statistics
Site Contact:
Site Logs Retention period: 7 (days)
Update Logs Retention period: 31 (days)
Site Logo: Browse...
Delete | ORACLE WebDB Site Builder

Database Access Descriptor Name

Specify the name of the Database Access Descriptor (DAD) used for authorized and public users. In order for the site to work properly, you must first change the DAD name in Site Manager and then in the listener settings.

Authorized User DAD: nu_sites
Public User DAD: nu_site
WebDB Component DAD: nu_sites

Figure 18-6: Site Manager page

The Site Manager has four main functions that are implemented with a series of panels, as shown in Figure 18-6. All of the editors within the Site Builder administration editor are built using a similar design. Once you have mastered one editor, you will find working with the other editors to be much easier, because they all make use of the same paradigm.

The Main tab controls the overall settings for your site, and the default language, public user, and site owner appear on this panel for reference purposes. You cannot change these settings from this page.

The three check boxes in the middle of the panel control the level of access that your end users are permitted within the site. Site Builder enables you to delegate the authority of your site to a series of folder managers. For example, in the Net University site, you probably want to create folders for each of the major end user stakeholders accessing this site: alumni, undergraduates, and faculty. Because lots of activity is likely in each of these segments, it makes sense to have a series of administrators rather than just a single site administrator.

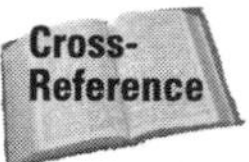

Chapter 21 discusses folder administrators and end user security in more detail. Security is one of the features of Site Builder you can change at any time over the life of your site, and it is not necessary to make all of your security decisions up front.

If you decide to pursue the strategy of using folder managers, you can enable these managers to change the look and feel of their folders themselves by using the Enable folder owners to control Style check box. We recommend against allowing your folder managers to have this capability at the outset, because this can cause the look and feel of your site to vary widely between folders.

Within Site Builder, you can further extend your Web site and enable your end users to have their own individual accounts within your site. Should you choose to pursue this strategy, you need to provide an Oracle logon for each and every end user of your site. While this may make sense for an intranet application, it may not make sense for an Internet application. However, if you decide to follow this strategy, you can permit your users to create their own individual interest lists on your site by selecting the Enable User Interest Lists check box. Site Builder provides the interest list function that enables users to mark folders with an individual marker to denote an interest in a particular folder. When the user logs onto the Web site, Site Builder displays the interest list as part of the main page for that individual user. If you do not plan on providing your users with individual accounts, the interest list can be difficult to manage, because multiple users can manipulate the same interest list. You can also choose to make the site's access statistics available to your users by selecting the Enable Public Users To View Site Statistics check box. The site statistics provide powerful insight into the popularity of items and folders within your site, but you may not want to make this information available to your users directly. This is especially true if you are implementing a public Internet site, because your competitors will be able to quickly determine which parts of your site are the most popular and copy the functionality.

1. Disable these advanced functions by unchecking the three check boxes for Enable folder owners to control Style, Enable User Interest Lists, and Enable Public Users To View Site Statistics.

The next block of settings control the administration of the site. You can supply a contact name for your site by entering an Oracle USERID into the Site Contact field. This entry should match a user security record that has been modified with the User link from the Access Settings panel. Site Builder uses the site contact name to display site contact information attached to the security record at run time.

2. Enter nu_site_admin as the site contact for Net University.

Although Site Builder uses its own activity logs, the structure of these files matches the standard WebDB activity logs. As with WebDB, the activity logs are built in pairs and you can control the period between rollovers of these logs by entering a value in the Site Logs Retention period text field. You can also determine how long Site Builder keeps activity log information stored by entering a value for the Update Logs Retention period text field.

Site Builder also permits you to change the logo for the overall site. The vast majority of the look and feel settings for your site are in the Style Editor, but the site logo is the exception to this rule. By default, all Site Builder sites have the default WebDB Site Builder logo installed as the logo for the site. You can change this setting by selecting a new image file using the Browse button on this panel. Net University has its own logo, so it makes sense to replace the Site Builder logo with the custom NetU image.

3. Use the Browse button to locate the netu_logo.gif image on the CD-ROM and load it in as the new logo for your Site Builder site.

The default behavior for all of the Browse buttons within Site Builder is to search for HTML files. If you want to use a simple logo image, you have to change the list box on the file search dialog panel to include all files.

The last section of the Main panel displays the Database Access Descriptor settings for your site. The first two entries will be familiar to you because the wizard displayed them when the site was created. The Authorized User DAD field directs end users to a logon screen when they access the site, and Public User DAD directs public users to your site. You will typically leave these values unchanged. The last entry in this section refers to the DAD entry used within Site Builder to gain access to your WebDB components.

4. If you deploy your WebDB components inside a Site Builder application, you can often dispense with component-level security. You can use the security framework of Site Builder to protect your WebDB components from unauthorized access.

5. Save your changes on this panel by clicking the Apply button in the upper-right corner of the page.

Even public users make use of an Oracle username and password to connect to the site. The difference is that the public DAD has the username and password hard-coded into the DAD record.

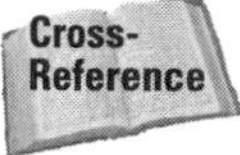

Chapter 22 contains a detailed discussion of DADs. We recommend that you read Chapter 22 carefully to understand how DAD entries are used to connect to WebDB components.

Site Manager – Items

The second panel in the Site Manager Editor is the Items panel, which controls how items that you upload to the site are managed.

Navigate to the Items panel by clicking the Items link in the tab panel at the top of the page to display the panel shown in Figure 18-7.

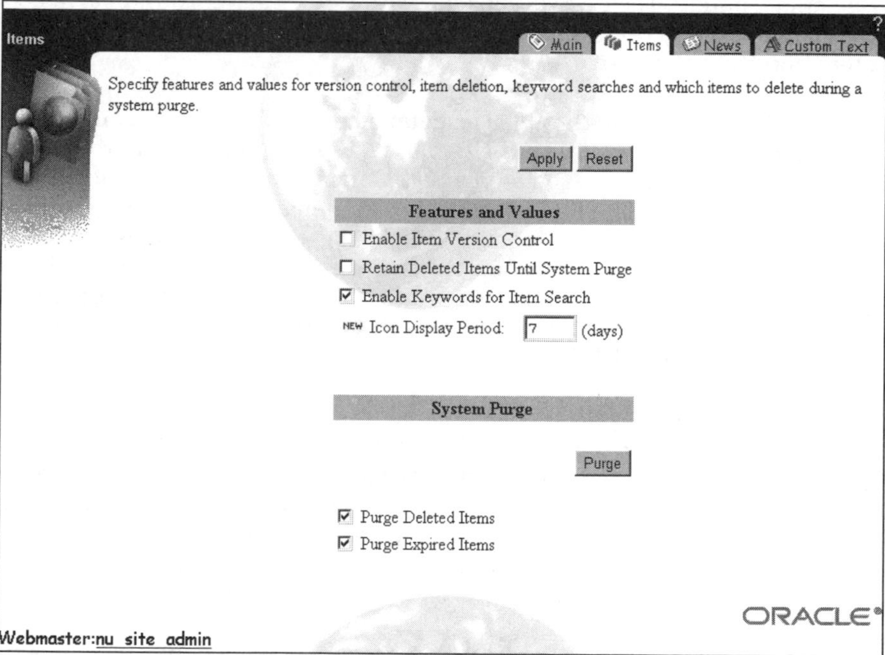

Figure 18-7: Site Manager – Items panel

There are two main functions on the Items panel: features and values settings, and system purge. The Items panel does not control how the items are displayed in the site, as the Style Editor is solely responsible for the formatting of items. The Site Manager Items Editor controls how the items are managed by the system.

First, you can set whether or not Site Builder tracks the versions of items that are added to the site through the Enable Item Version Control check box. You will remember from working with the other wizards that WebDB can automatically track the various versions of a component. Site Builder can perform the same service for uploaded items, but it is not enabled by default. Should you choose to enable this setting, Site Builder maintains versions for each revision of an item that is added and edited on your site. Site Builder only displays the most recent version, but you have access to previous versions when you edit the item.

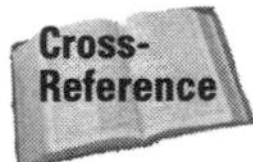

Enabling version control on items is especially useful if you allow your end users to submit content to the site. Refer to Chapter 23 for a more detailed discussion of allowing end users to have write access to Site Builder Web sites.

When you delete items from your site, WebDB can place these items into a pending delete state without actually removing them from the system. This is similar in concept to the operating system trash can on your desktop, and it can save you from inadvertently removing items from your site by employing a two-stage method for deleting content. The default behavior within Site Builder is to remove content immediately, but you can change this by enabling the Retain Deleted Items Until System Purge check box.

In Chapter 23, we take you through the detailed process of adding content to the folders that you create within your site. During the content upload process, you can add keywords that will be associated with the item after it has been uploaded to the site. In order to permit Site Builder to search for items using these keywords, you must enable the keyword functionality by selecting the Enable Keyword For Item Search check box. During this same upload process, Site Builder marks all new entries with a special built-in image item called “new.” This image automatically expires after seven days, but you can adjust this setting higher or lower by entering a value for the Icon Display Period text field associated with this perspective.

The lower panel on this page provides an interface for actually deleting content that has been marked as deleted. Folder owners, or users with that permission, must explicitly mark items for deletion within the folder interface. If you have enabled the Retain Deleted Items Until System Purge check box, Site Builder marks the items as deleted rather than simply deleting them. In order to actually delete items marked in such a manner, you must enable the Purge Deleted Items check box and then click the Purge push button.

Site Builder automatically marks News items as deleted once they have reached their expiration dates. You can physically remove them from the database by selecting the Purge Expired Items check box and then clicking the Purge push button. Site Builder does not provide an interface for automatically performing these two tasks according to a set schedule — you must use the Items interface to effect the delete and purge operations.

Enable only the Enable Keywords for Item Search check box and click the Apply button to save your changes.

Site Manager – News

Site Builder considers News items to be a particularly special type of content, so the Site Manager Editor has a panel dedicated solely to News.

1. Navigate to the News panel by using the News link in the Site Manager as shown in Figure 18-8.

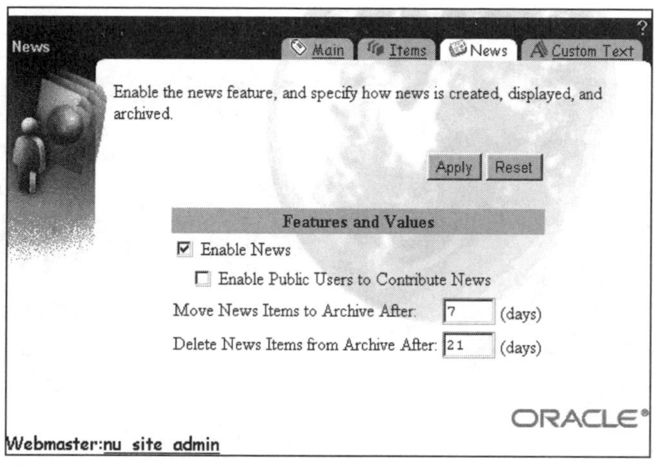

Figure 18-8: Site Manager – News panel

There are three settings for news items within your site, but you are not required to provide news as a feature. News items are special, time-sensitive items that appear in a certain section of each folder. If you do not plan on having news on your site, you can disable it entirely by deselecting the Enable News check box on this panel. However, should you decide to provide news items on your site, you will almost always want to enable your end users to contribute news items. The Enable Public Users to Contribute News check box determines whether or not users have this ability on your site.

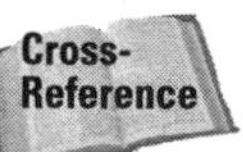

News items are essentially unstructured blocks of text added as content items to your site. Chapter 23 includes a more detailed discussion of news items.

If you permit news items on your site, WebDB automatically archives the items after a certain period of time. Furthermore, these news items are deleted from the archive after an additional period of time. You determine the time period for both settings by entering the value in days as an integer into the two text fields on this panel.

Remember, if you have enabled the two-stage delete mechanism on the Items panel, your news items will not be physically removed from the archive until you manually invoke the purge function.

2. Select the Enable News and the Enable Public Users to Contribute News check boxes and click the Apply button to save the changes.

Site Manager — Custom Text

The Site Manager contains one additional panel called the Custom Text panel.

1. Navigate to the Custom Text panel using the Custom Text link, as shown in Figure 18-9.

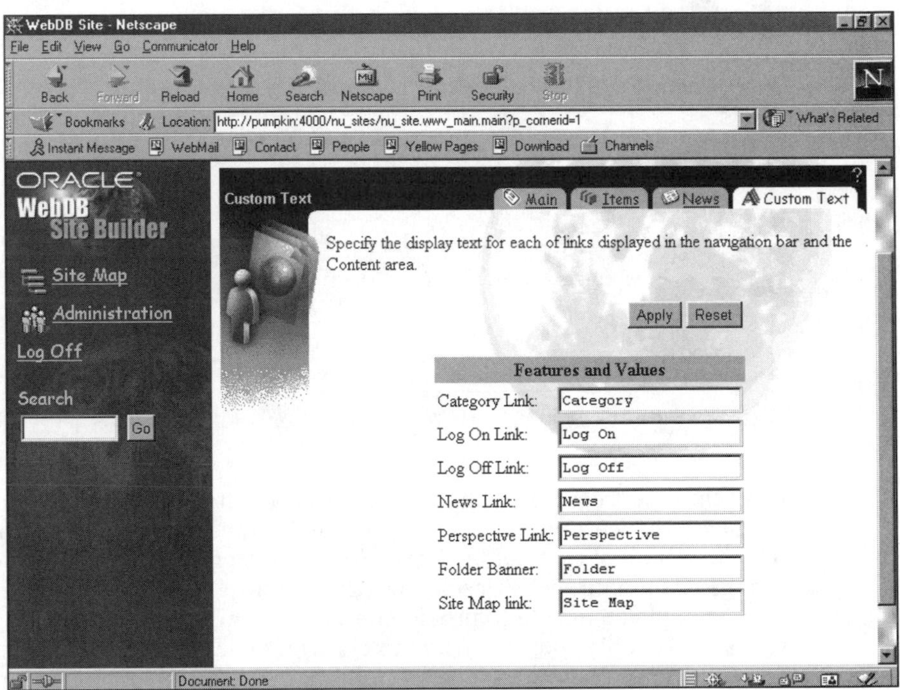

Figure 18-9: Site Manager — Custom Text

Site Builder includes seven basic links in all Web sites regardless of the number of folders, categories, perspectives, or items. Four of these links — news, folders, categories, and perspectives — point to content. The remaining three links display a map of the site and enable users to either log on or log off the system. WebDB provides default text for each of these links, but you can change this text on the Custom Text panel. Notice that you cannot change the color or font for these links on this panel, but you can change these items within the Style menu.

2. Change the Log On Link text to **LogOn to NetU**.
3. Change the Log Off Link text to **LogOff of NetU**.
4. Click the Apply button to save your changes.

Changes that you make on the individual panels are stored in the database when you click the Apply button. When you are finished using the Site Manager, click the Finish button to return to the main administration menu.

5. Navigate back to the main site administration menu using the Finish button.

Notice that the changes are not reflected in the display of your site. Although the changes have been saved to the database, you must exit the administration menu entirely in order for them to take effect.

Changing the style of your site

The Site Manager panel provides control over the inner workings of the site, but it does not enable you to adjust the look and feel. Site Builder provides a companion facility called the Style Manager that provides you with the editing tools for making user interface changes.

1. Use the Style link on the administration panel to navigate to the Style Manager as shown in Figure 18-10.

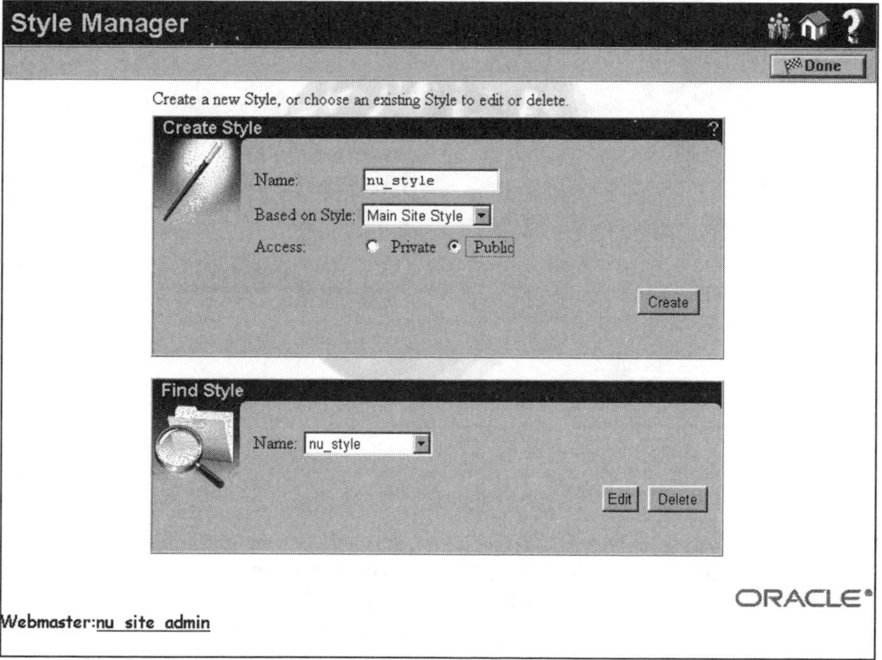

Figure 18-10: Style Manager – Create Styles panel

The Style Manager has two main panels: the Create panel in the upper section of the page, and the Find panel in the lower section. Site Manager Styles serve the same function for Web sites as the WebDB templates serve for components. They provide a consistent color scheme and font layout, and they control the navigation options for your folders.

Site Builder comes equipped with four Style schemes you can use out of the box. You will always want to create your own style for your site in order to insulate yourself from changes that Oracle may make to the built-in styles in subsequent releases.

2. Enter **nu_style** as the style name for your site in the name field and base this new style on the Main Site Style setting, as shown in Figure 18-10.
3. Set the Access for this new style to Public.
4. Use the Create push button to create the style.

   Once you have created the style entry, it appears in the Find panel at the bottom of the page. From this panel you can either delete a style or edit a previously created style.
5. Select the nu_style entry in the Name list box and use the Edit push button to begin modifying this style.

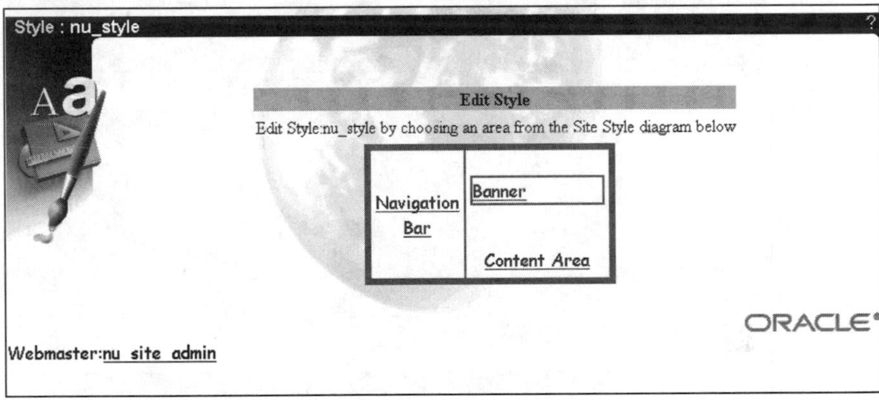

Figure 18-11: Style Manager — Edit Style

There are three aspects to every style, as shown in Figure 18-11. The first element of the site style is the Navigation Bar, which serves as the primary menu tool within a Site Builder application. The Navigation Bar appears on the left-hand side of the page as shown in Figure 18-1, and it can include links to folders, categories, and perspectives. The second element is the Banner, which appears at the top portion of every page as shown in Figure 18-1. The last section is the Content Area, which displays the items uploaded into the Site Builder application. The detailed panels for each of these items are similar, and you should generally start with the Navigation Bar as the anchor for your style.

Click the Navigation Bar link to display the edit panel in Figure 18-12.

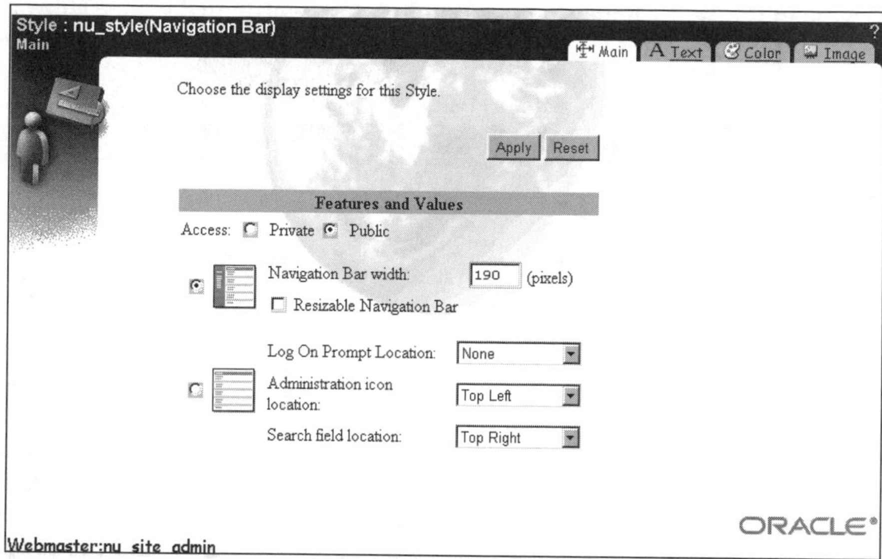

Figure 18-12: Style Manager – Navigation Bar panel

Style Manager – Navigation Bar

This panel can be particularly confusing when you first work with it due to the layout of the radio buttons. First, you must decide whether you should make the Navigation Bar in this style available to the public. The only reason not to do so is when you wish to create a style that does not provide a Navigation Bar. Once you have decided whether or not to make the Navigation Bar public, you can either set the width to a fixed size, or make it resizable. You can set the size of the bar by entering a width in pixels and you can enable the Resizable Navigation Bar check box to permit end users the ability to change the width of the bar at run time.

Note If you use a fixed width Navigation Bar and do not permit resizing, WebDB truncates any strings or images wider than the pixel setting.

If you wish to change either of these settings, you must select the radio button next to the first icon and enter your values for the text field and check box. Clicking the Apply button saves these changes to the database.

Three standard elements appear on every Navigation Bar: the Log On Prompt, the Administration icon, and the Search field. You can position these items by choosing the second radio button, and then selecting the desired positions using the three combo boxes.

Note Moving these three items outside their default positioning can cause the Navigation Bar to disappear. We recommend that you leave the log on prompt, Administration icon, and search field in their default positions.

Navigate to the Text panel using the Text link tab to display the page shown in Figure 18-13.

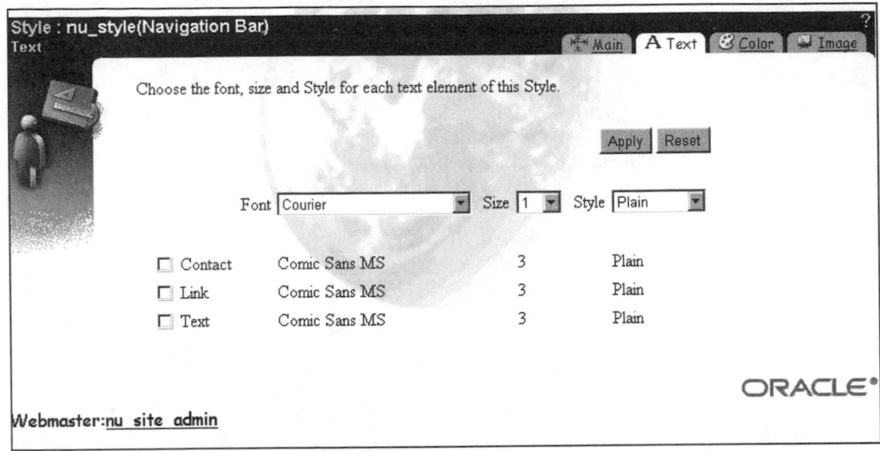

Figure 18-13: Navigation Bar Text panel

The Text panel sets the font face, size, and style for text items that appear in the body of the Navigation Bar. All of the text panels and the color panels throughout the Site Builder Editor interface work the same way, and it can be slightly confusing at first. In order to set a color or a font for any item you have to follow four steps.

1. Select the item.
2. Deselect all other items.
3. Choose your settings.
4. Click the Apply button.

As you can see in Figure 18-13, each of the text items has an associated check box. The three rows of text items — contact, link, and text — are the three different types of text entries within the Navigation Bar. In order to change one of these entries, the first step is to select the entry using the associated check box.

The second step is to deselect any other selected rows that should not be affected by the changes you are about to make. By default Site Builder displays each panel without any of the items checked, and it automatically deselects any rows when you use the Apply push button. When Site Builder applies a change, it applies the same change to every row that has its check box filled in. A good rule of thumb is to make sure that you have deselected any previously checked values before proceeding.

The third step in the process is to change the settings using the combo boxes that sit above the text items. The Font list is constructed from the default fonts list of WebDB, and the Size setting is a relative setting to the standard font size for the page. If you want to use a larger font, select a progressively larger number in the size combo box. Once you have selected the font name, size, and style, you can save these changes to the database by using the Apply push button.

1. Select the TEXT line item and change the font to Century Gothic, size 2.
2. Click the Apply key to save the changes.
3. Use the Color link on the Color tab to navigate to the Color panel, as shown in Figure 18-14.

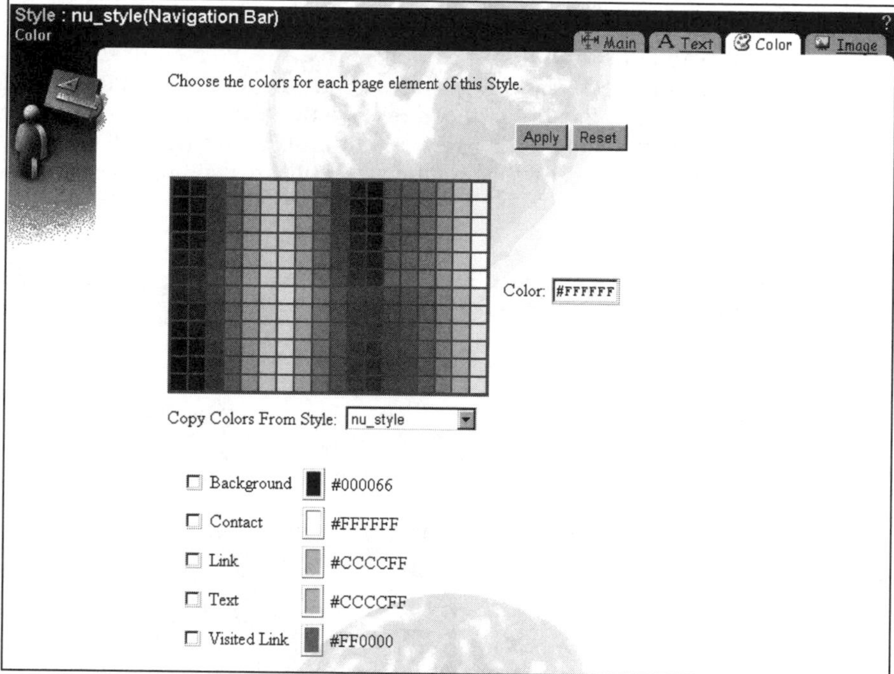

Figure 18-14: Navigation Bar – Color panel

The Color panel works in a similar fashion to the Font panel — you select a color setting using the check box and apply a color using the Apply button. The main difference is the manner in which you select the color. Site Builder gives you two choices: You can either select the color by clicking the color in the color chart, or you can enter the color code directly into the Color text field using the hexadecimal representation of the color.

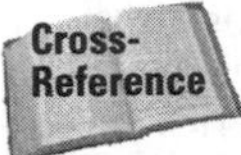

Chapter 15 includes a detailed discussion of how to convert between RGB color codes and the hexadecimal format required by WebDB and your Web browser.

The colors in this panel apply to the various types of text in the Navigation Bar. To set the following color codes for the Navigation Bar, use the four-step process:

```
Background — #FFFFFF
Contact — #000000
Link — #000000
Text — #000000
Visited Link — #0000FF
```

1. Use the Image link on the Image tab to display the panel shown in Figure 18-15.

   Site Builder gives you the opportunity to set the background for the Navigation Bar to an image as well as to a specified color. The default installation of Site Builder includes a purple globe shown in the background of the Navigation Bar, but you can replace this with your own image using the Image panel. You are free to use either a GIF image or a JPEG image, and Site Builder automatically tiles the image to fit the available space of the Navigation Bar.

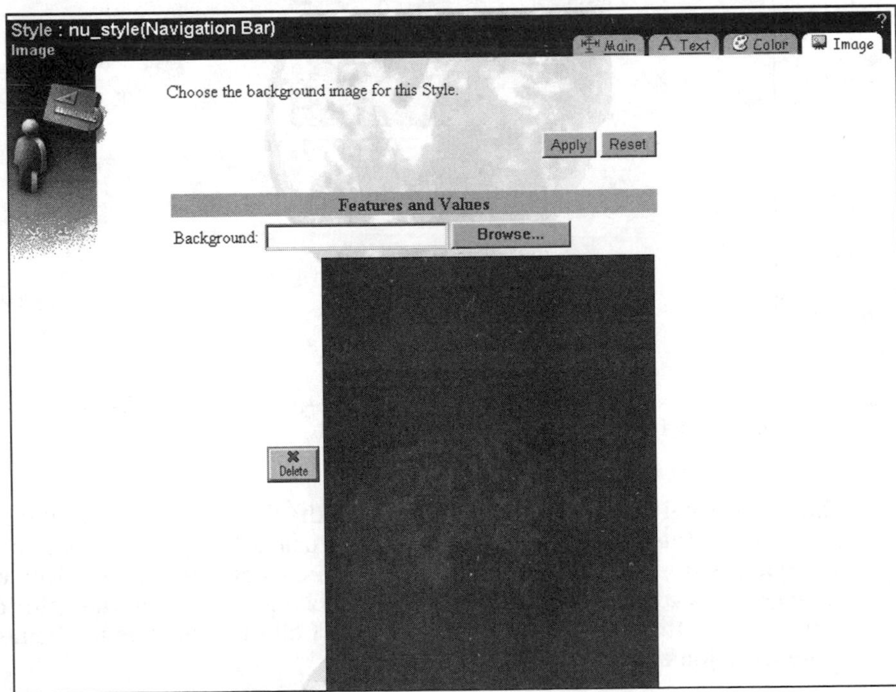

Figure 18-15: Navigation Bar – Image panel

2. Set the background image to the file netu_bg.gif using the Browse button and save this change using Apply.
3. Click the Finish button to return to the main panel of the Style Editor.

Style Editor – Banner

The Banner is the second major object in the Style Editor. Banners are the ribbons of color and text displayed at the top of pages, folders, and subfolders. Site Builder labels the various sections of a page using these Banners and they form the borders that separate content.

1. Select the Banner link to display the Banner Editor shown in Figure 18-16. There are five different Banner types displayed on Site Builder pages, as listed in Table 18-2.

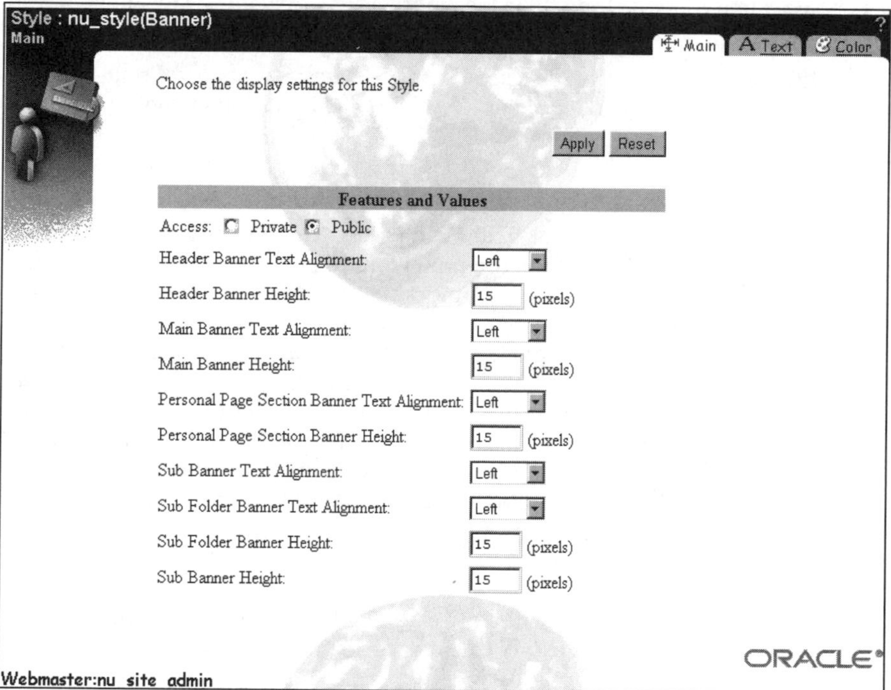

Figure 18-16: Style Editor – Banner

Table 18-2
Banner Types

Banner	*Description*
Header	The Header Banner is a ribbon that displays at the top of each category within each folder. The header separates one category from the next within the folder. The header does not appear unless you have added categories to your Site Builder site.
Main	The Main Banner is the ribbon of color that appears at the top of every Site Builder page. The Main Banner serves as the title bar.
Personal Page	The Personal Page Banner displays at the top of the personalized section of each Web page. It only displays if personal pages are permitted on the Site Builder site.
Sub Banner	The Sub Banner appears just below the Main Banner on each page, and it contains the subtitles for a page.
Sub Folder	The Sub Folder Banner appears as a ribbon of color at the top of each folder and its subfolders, and it separates folders from categories.

The Style Editor for Banners displays on three tab panels: the Main panel, the Text panel, and the Color panel. The Main panel, which is shown in Figure 18-16, is used to set the display height for the panel and to set the justification for the text displayed in each panel. The Banners themselves stretch from left to right and the pixel setting determines how much real estate the panel takes in the vertical dimension. For the most part, you need not change the pixel height unless you wish to use an extra-large font face for the text that displays in any particular Banner. The exceptions to this rule are the Main and Sub Banners, which display together at the top of the page. You will often wish to set the Main Banner slightly larger and the Sub Banner slightly smaller in order to emphasize the title and subtitle nature of these two ribbons. By default, Site Builder left-justifies the text in the Banners, but you can change this to right justification or center justification as desired using the combo boxes on the Main panel.

1. Set the Main Banner height to 20 pixels and the Sub Banner height to 20 pixels and click the Apply key to save these changes.

The text panel enables you to set the font face, size, and style for the text displayed within each Banner area. The Text panel operates exactly the same as the text panel in the Navigation Bar Style Editor, using the now-familiar four-step process. If you set the font size for any particular Banner to a value that exceeds the pixel height, then Site Builder automatically increases the pixel height at execution time to match the selected font size.

The last tab panel in the Banner Editor enables you to set the color for each of the Banner areas. You can set both the background color and the text color from this panel, which works exactly the same as the Color panel in the Navigation Bar Editor. Although you can set each Banner background and text to a different color, it is probably not wise to do so. Site Builder includes default color schemes that make use of similar colors, and this is often the best strategy. For example, you can set each Banner to be a slightly different shade of the same color. This creates a visual clue to the differences of each Banner, but it is unlikely to be as hard on the eye as setting each Banner to a completely different color.

2. Change the Banner backgrounds to a single grey color — #C0C0C0.
3. Change the Banner text to black — #000000.
4. Use the Finish button to return to the main Style Editor panel.

Style Editor – Content Area

The Content Area is the third and final section of the Style Editor, and it covers the actual display area for objects that are loaded into the site.

1. Use the Content Area link to display the panel shown in Figure 18-17.

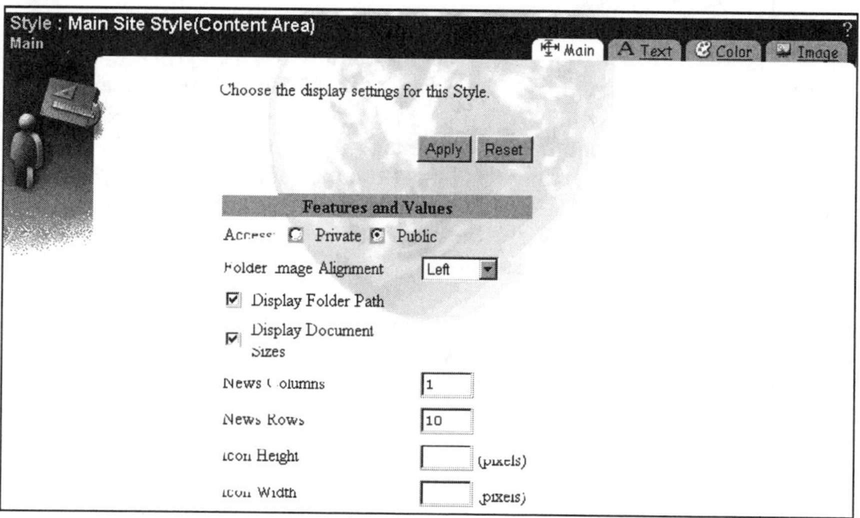

Figure 18-17: Style Editor – Content Area panel

There are five basic options you can set for the main area of your content: the alignment, the folder path, the document size, the layout of the news section, and the size for icon images.

When you upload content into your Web site, you can add customized images to each content object as a means of drawing attention to the content. You have a choice as to where the image is aligned: to the left, to the right, or in the center. The images on this panel are different than those referred to on the Image tab. The images on this tab panel refer to the images that you assign to a particular piece of content uploaded to the site by a user. For example, you might add a content item about an upcoming concert event to the Net University site. As part of adding this new content item, you could upload a GIF file of the band's current album cover to be displayed alongside the title of the item. As you add folders to your site, the hierarchy can get quite deep, and you can make the site easier to navigate through by displaying the complete hierarchy in the folder name. If you check the Display Folder Path check box, Site Builder displays the complete lineage of each folder as part of each folder link. Each layer in the history is separated from the previous layer by a colon character.

Content can include links to other sites and it can also include documents and images that are uploaded into the site. Because you may have users connecting to your site with a slower-speed connection such as a 28.8 modem, Site Builder gives you the option to display the object size for each upload. If you enable the Display Document Sizes check box, Site Builder includes the size of each content object (in bytes) to the right of the title for the object.

Site Builder ignores the Display Document Sizes setting for URL links and WebDB components, because the size of the object cannot be accurately measured for these object types.

The final two options are shown as groups of two. First, you can set the dimensions for the News folder by providing a value for the News Columns and News Rows text fields. If you set the column number to a value greater than 1, Site Builder wraps the news into multiple columns. It will be more common for you to set the number of news rows, which determines the maximum amount of vertical page real estate that Site Builder reserves for news items. In cases where the number of news items exceeds the available space, Site Builder provides navigation menus that enable you to scroll to the hidden entries.

The last setting is concerned with the page real estate reserved for images that are attached to content items. A null value for Icon Height and Icon Width tells Site Builder to display images at their actual size. A positive integer setting for these fields causes Site Builder to compress the image to fit the allotted page real estate. Normally you will want to provide a setting for these fields in order to prevent images from using excessive amounts of screen space.

1. Enable the Display Folder Path and the Display Document Sizes check boxes.
2. Set the Icon Height and Icon Width to 50 pixels.
3. Click Apply to save your changes.

Site Builder enables you to set the font face, size, style, and color for each section of the content using the same panels used in the Navigation Bar. See the "Style Editor – Navigation Bar" section of this chapter for details on how to use these two panels.

The Content Area matches the Navigation Bar more closely than it does the Banner section, as you can include a background image for display behind the content. You will want to use background images of a lower intensity than the main content of the page so as not to interfere with the display of the content. For example, use an internal use only image to mark pages as being company confidential, or use a monocolor version of the company logo to reinforce your brand on the Web site. In the Net University example, you can use a pale gray version of the NetU TabbyCat as a background.

1. Navigate to the Image panel of the Content Area.
2. Use the Browse button to locate the netu_content.gif file.
3. Save the image as a background using the Apply button.
4. Click the Finish button twice to return to the main Style Manager panel.
5. Click the Done button to exit the Style Editor.

Site Builder tiles the image in the background, you cannot change this behavior. If you have an image that you do not want tiled, you have to surround the image with white space and enlarge it to prevent the tile effect from appearing.

Content Managers

In the first part of this chapter, we introduced you to the concept of folders, categories, and perspectives. These three objects enable you to organize the content that is uploaded to your site. Site Builder provides an editor for each of these objects inside the Content Manager section of the main editor menu.

Folder Manager

The Folder Manager is the starting point for organizing your site. Folders provide the hierarchy into which your content is loaded. One of the major features of Site Builder is the ability to change almost any of the aspects of your site at any time and have these changes cascade throughout the site. This same capability extends to folder objects — you can add or remove folders to a production site as needed. Site Builder provides tools for moving subfolders around, but you cannot move groups of content items within a folder as a single operation. Because of this restriction, we advise you to plan your folder hierarchy out in advance.

The example Net University database contains three main constituencies: Alumni, Undergraduates, and Faculty. Within the Undergraduates category, you can define four additional subfolders for each of the Undergraduate classes: freshmen, sophomores, juniors, and seniors.

Click the Folder link to display the editor as shown in Figure 18-18.

You can perform four main operations on a folder: Add, Delete, Move, and Edit. Site Builder provides an icon next to the name of the folder for each of these tasks. You can access the function by clicking the icon associated with the task.

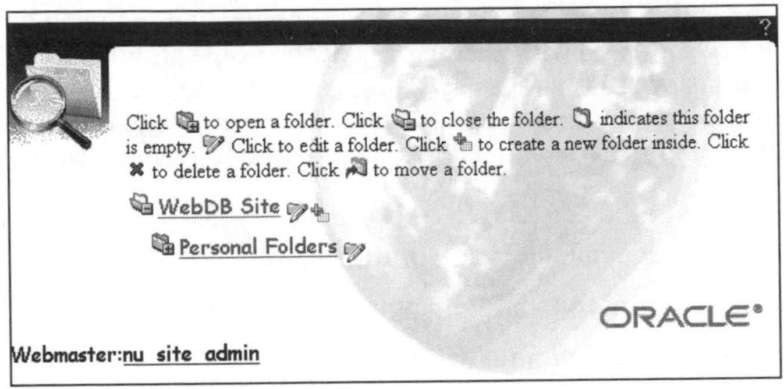

Figure 18-18: Folder Manager

The first step in the folder management process is to edit the attributes associated with the main folder for the site. When you create a new site, Site Builder creates a single master folder called WebDB Site within the site.

Click the pencil and folder icon to display the Edit menu for the WebDB Site folder as shown in Figure 18-19.

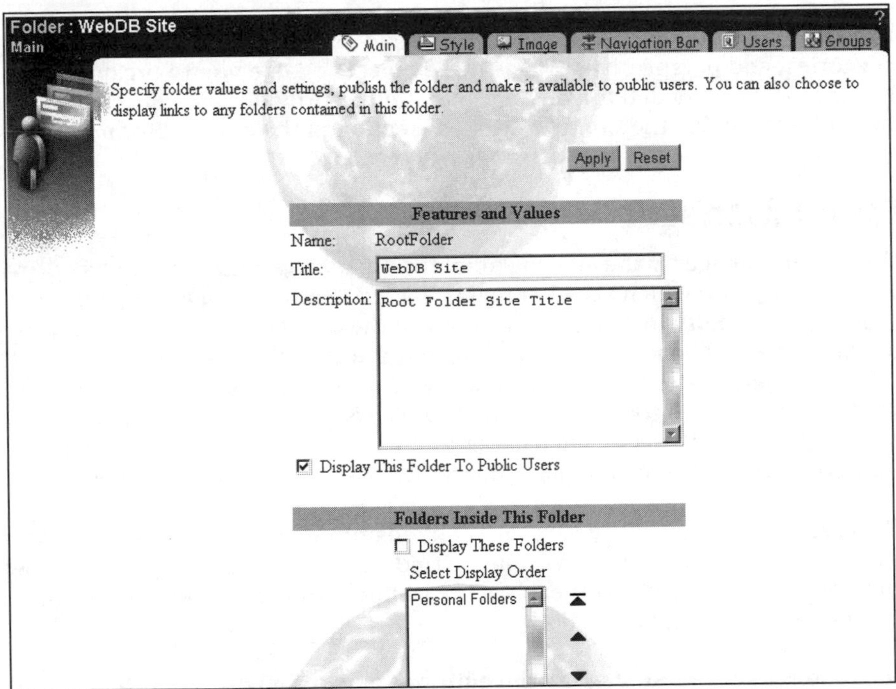

Figure 18-19: Edit Folder – Main panel

Site Builder enables you to make six types of changes to your folders, and the Folder Manager provides an Edit panel for each of these changes. The Main panel enables you to change the title and description for the current folder. Initially, your site will have a single master folder called WebDB Site as shown in Figure 18-19. You will want to change the title and description for this folder to a more meaningful name for your site. Internally, WebDB refers to this site as the RootFolder, and you are not able to change the name of this folder. However, as you will see shortly, WebDB permits you to provide names for the subfolders you create inside of the RootFolder. In the lower section of the main panel, you can select the subfolders you wish to display as part of the RootFolder. When you create your site, this lower panel is meaningless until you have created your subfolders.

1. Change the title of the RootFolder to **Net University**.
2. Change the description of the RootFolder to any block of text that you wish to use as a description for Net University.
3. Use the Apply button to save your changes to the database.
4. Use the Style link on the tab panel to display the page shown in Figure 18-20.

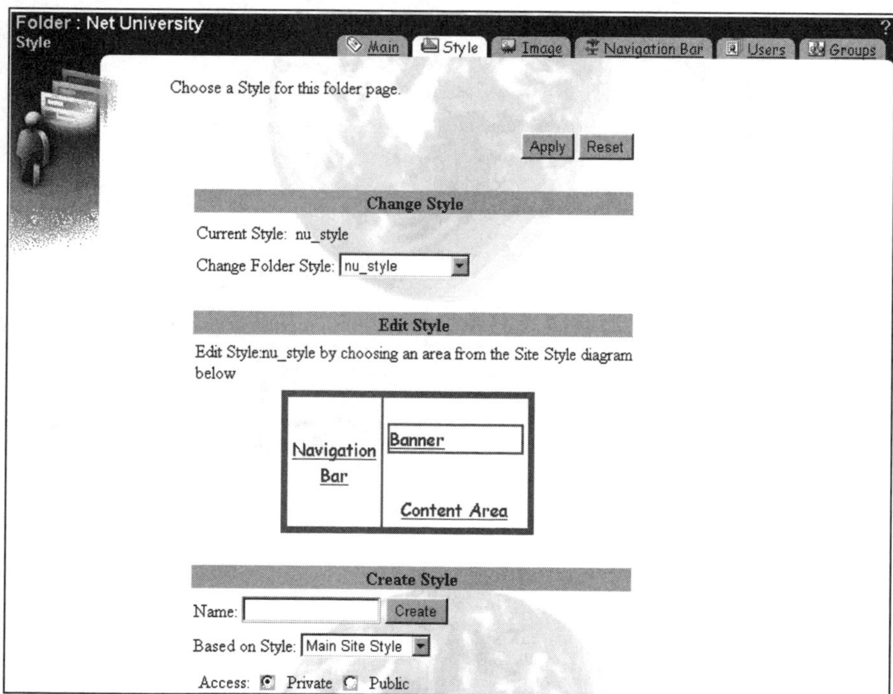

Figure 18-20: Folder Manager Style panel

The second panel in the Folder Editor will look familiar, because it is a smaller version of the Style Editor. Site Builder enables you to use a different style for every folder and subfolder within your site. In most cases, you will want to use the same style for each of your folders, but there may be times when you want your subfolders to use a different style. For example, assume that one subfolder in your site has been reserved for privileged information. In addition to setting an extra level of security for this folder, you might also choose to use a confidential background for the content in this site. Site Builder assigns the Main Style settings to the RootFolder by default, and it cascades the style setting for a parent folder down to its child folders. You can change the style setting for a folder by selecting a style in the Change Folder Style combo box and pressing the Apply button. The remainder of this page is a series of shortcuts to the Style Editor that was discussed in detail in the preceding section.

1. Change the style for the RootFolder to nu_style and press the Apply button to save your changes.
2. Use the Image link in the tab panel to navigate to the page shown in Figure 18-21.

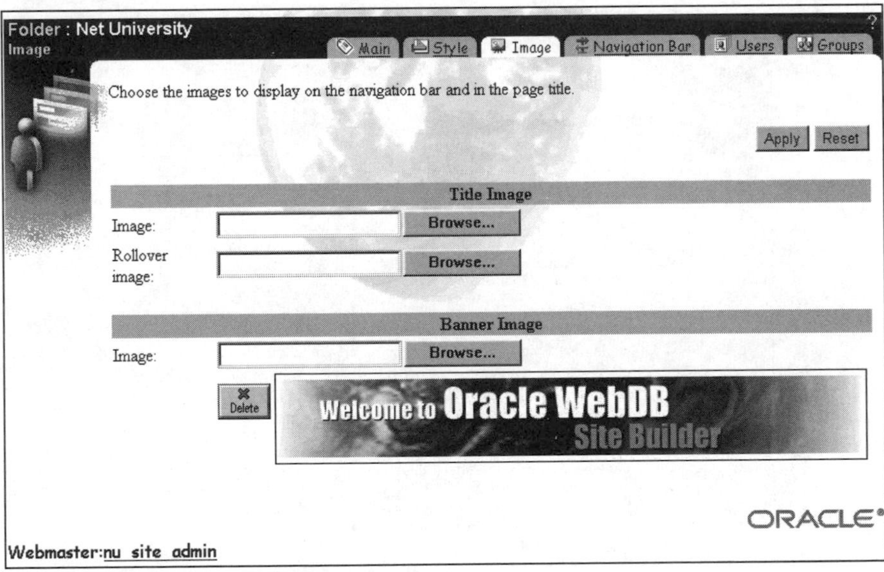

Figure 18-21: Folder Image panel

Three images can be associated with a folder. You can include two images for the title of your folder: one as the main image and one as a rollover image. Site Builder automatically switches from the first image to the second image when the user passes over the image. As with the images associated with content items, you should be careful not to use overly large images, as they cause the title bar to use a large amount of screen real estate.

In addition to the title images, you can set an image for the Banner area below the Main Banner for each folder. The Banner image serves as an additional layer of separation and identification.

1. Select the image file netu_banner.gif as the Banner image for the main folder.
2. Use the Finish button to navigate back to the main folder panel.

You can make three additional tab settings for each folder: Navigation Bar, User Security, and Group Security. The Navigation Bar options are easier to understand once you have created some categories and perspectives, and we circle back to this panel at the end of this chapter. Chapter 23 covers user and group security for folders because it makes the most sense to consider these two options in light of adding content to your site.

Adding folders and subfolders

Once you have set the RootFolder options, you can then begin adding folders and subfolders for the site. The green cross and folder icons are shortcuts for adding folders.

1. Click the Add icon to display the panel shown in Figure 18-22.

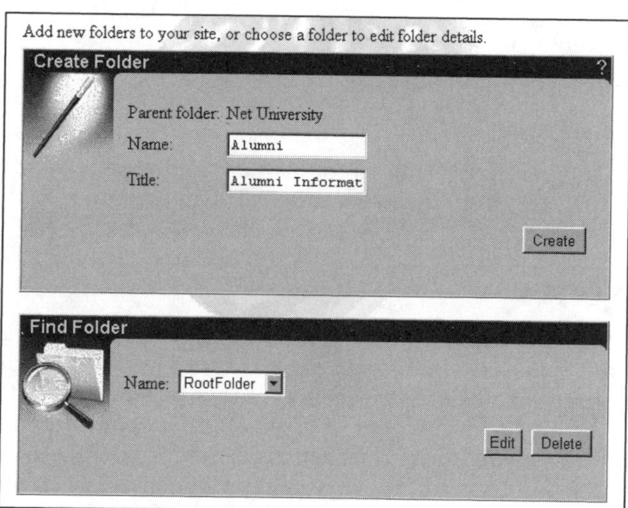

Figure 18-22: Add Folders Panel

The Create Folder panel uses a simple interface for adding new folders, or editing a folder. Site Builder displays the parent folder title for the current folder in the top panel. When you first create a site, the parent folder is the root folder for the site. As you begin to add subfolders, you can be sure that you are creating them within the correct parent folder by checking the display name in the title of this panel. You can add folders by entering a name and a title in the two text fields and then using the Create push button to save your changes. The name for the folder is the internal handle for the folder, and it should be a simple string without spaces or other punctuation. The title field is a free-form text field and you can enter a more descriptive string as the title.

2. Add three folders for Net University as follows:
   a. Alumni — Alumni Information
   b. Students — Undergraduate Information
   c. Faculty — NetU Faculty and Staff
3. Use the Done button to save your changes.
4. Use the Plus/folder icon to the left of the Net University folder to expand the list of folders.

Once you have created a set of folders under the root folder, you can use the Add icon for any of these folders to add subfolders to them.

5. Add four subfolders to the Students folder as follows:
   a. Seniors — Senior Class
   b. Juniors — Junior Class
   c. Sophomores — Sophomore Class
   d. Freshmen — Freshman Class
6. Click the Done push button to return to the main folder panel, and then click Done once more to return to the main administration menu.

Adding categories

Once you have created your folders, you can further organize them by adding categories and perspectives. Site Builder displays content items by loading them into categories, and users can elect to view content by category instead of just by folder. In effect, categories serve as a type of cross-reference for folders. When you create categories for a Web site, they appear in every folder contained in that site. You are not required to add content for every category in each folder, but once you create a category, it appears in every folder and subfolder in your site, provided the folder has content stored within each category.

In the example case for Net University, four basic categories have been identified: General Information, Academics, Events, and Athletics. Site Builder builds the general category when the site is created to deal with the restriction that all content must be loaded into a category.

News items are the one exception to this rule, as news content is in effect a category all its own. However, Site Builder does not list news as a separate category. We advise against creating your own category called "news," and instead recommend that you use the built-in news interface to add content of this type. News is discussed in detail in Chapter 23.

1. Use the Category link to display the page shown in Figure 18-23.

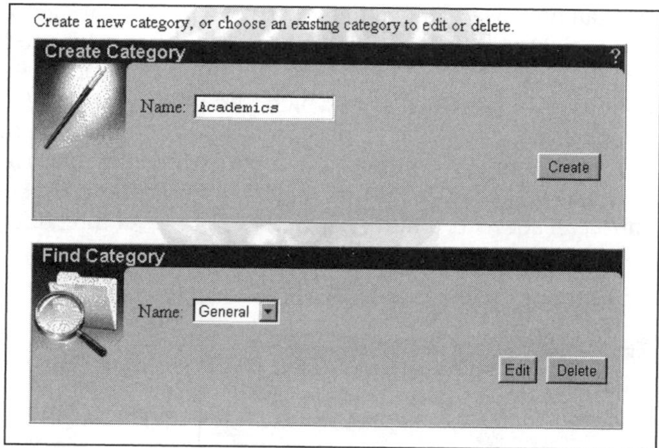

Figure 18-23: Create Category panel

The Add Categories panel is even simpler than the Add Folders panel. The only function the interface supports is the ability to enter a new category name and save it using the Create button. If you inadvertently enter a duplicate value, Site Builder displays an error message, and you can use the combo box in the lower panel of the page to list the current categories.

Once you have added a category, you can use the Edit button on this panel to display a page that enables you to add an image to be displayed with the category. Site Builder displays a Banner for each category within a folder, but you may to choose to add an image to better identify each category.

Remember, it is not necessary to fill in all of the options for each folder, category, or perspective up front. You can always work with the site for a bit and then go back and add in these extra settings once you have a better idea of how your site will be used.

2. Add three categories for Net University as follows:
    a. Academics
    b. Events
    c. Athletics
3. Navigate back to the main administration panel using the Done button.

Adding perspectives

Perspectives are the third and final mechanism for organizing content on your site. Perspectives are associated with individual content items, but unlike categories, you can assign multiple perspectives to a single item. An item also does not need to be associated with any perspective, while every item must be associated with one and only one category. End users can even search your site for items that have been assigned to a particular perspective.

The Net University example case has two perspectives: one to mark a particularly hot topic and one to indicate that the particular event requires advance ticketing. You can add perspectives any time, and you may find that your end users are the best source for generating suggestions as to which perspectives to add. Although you can add search criteria for any object, perspectives provide a type of organized search. When folder managers add content to your site, they may choose to index entries based upon keywords or phrases that may be inconsistent. Perspectives are defined centrally, and can serve as a more consistent high-level indexing scheme.

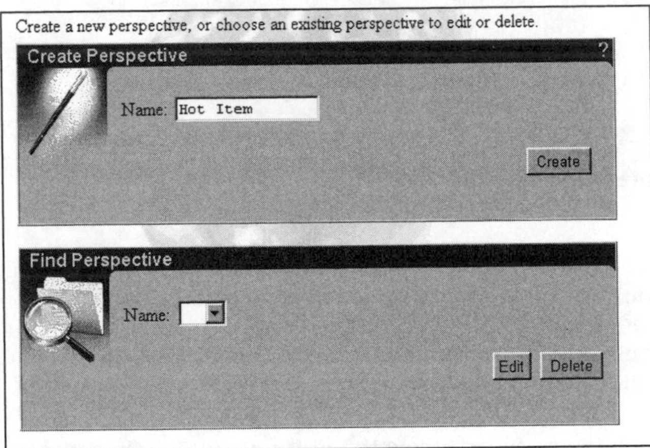

Figure 18-24: Create Perspective panel

1. Use the Perspectives link to navigate to the panel shown in Figure 18-24.
2. The Create Perspective panel works in an identical fashion to the Categories panel. Add two new perspectives as follows:
   a. Hot Item
   b. Tickets Required
3. When you have finished creating the two perspectives, select the Hot Item entry in the lower panel and click the Edit push button to display the page shown in Figure 18-25.

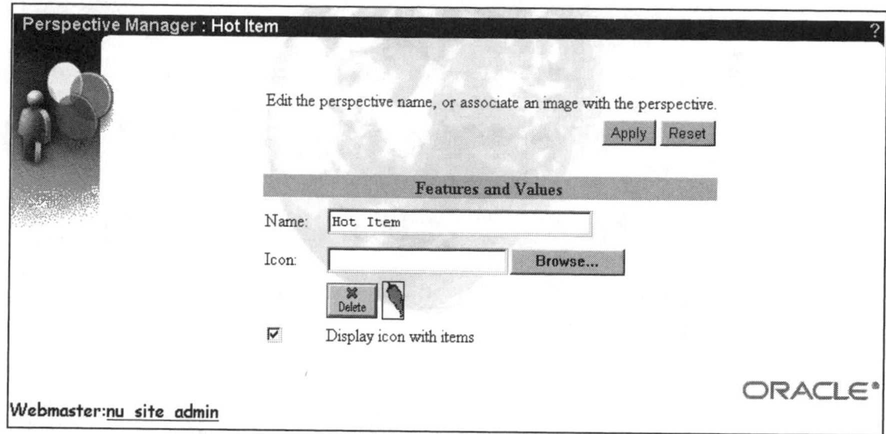

Figure 18-25: Perspectives detail panel

Although you may choose not to display icons with categories, you almost always choose to do so for perspectives. You can add icons for each perspective by using the browse function to locate an image file that will be associated with the perspective at run time. Images used with perspectives should be of a consistent size so that they appear evenly when multiple perspectives are added for a single item of content. Because perspectives serve as indexes, you may choose to create certain perspectives without an associated image. Users are able to search for matching items using this perspective, but there is not a visual cue that the perspective is associated with a content item on the page.

4. Edit the Hot Item perspective, attach the image netu_hot.gif, and set the Display icon with items check box to true.
5. Edit the Tickets Required perspective, and attach the image netu_cost.gif, and set the Display icon with items check box to true.
6. Navigate back to the main administration menu.

Link categories and perspectives to the Navigation Bar

The last major step in the edit process is to connect the categories and perspectives to the Navigation Bar on your site. These categories and perspectives are automatically displayed when users or folder managers add content to your site, but they are not displayed in the Navigation Bar unless you add them to the panel using the Style Editor for the RootFolder.

1. Use the Folder link from the administration page to navigate to the edit page for folders.

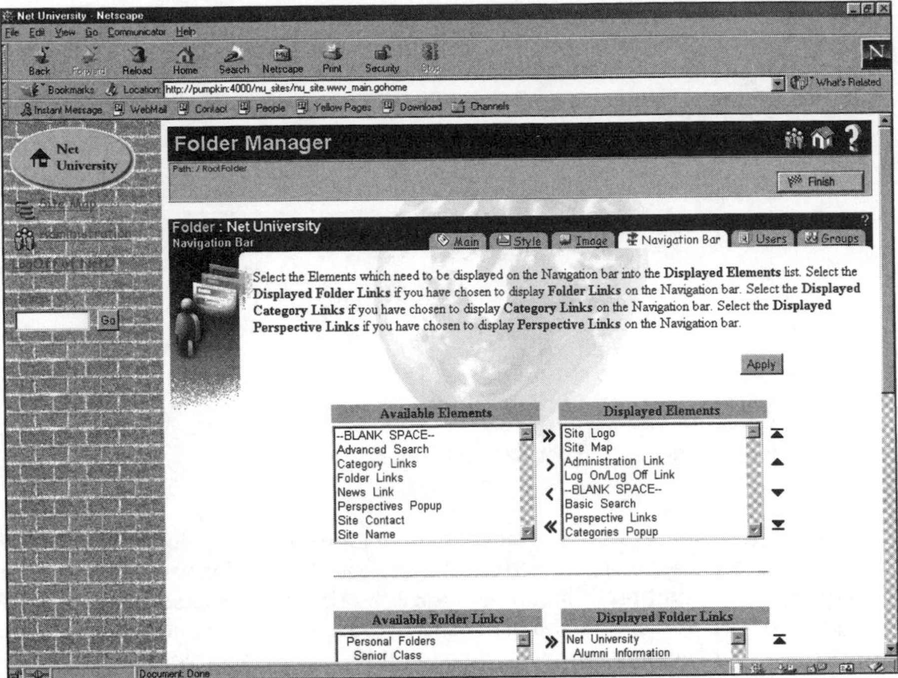

Figure 18-26: Navigation Bar options for folders

2. Edit the Net University Folder and use the tab panel for the Navigation Bar to display the page shown in Figure 18-26. Table 18-3 shows the 15 items that can be displayed within the Navigation Bar for a folder.

Table 18-3
Navigation Bar Items

Item	*Description*
Administration Link	Link to the administration interface. Certain items within the administration panels are open to all users. Site Builder automatically removes any links that are not accessible to unprivileged users.
Advanced Search	Link to an advanced search page that enables Boolean searches.
Basic Search	Displays a text box and GO button that searches for content items based upon individual keywords.

Item	*Description*
Site Logo	Displays the logo image for the site in the upper-left corner of the site if such an image has been loaded.
Site Name	Displays the name of the site as it was entered during the site creation process.
Site Contact	Displays a text string with the name of the Webmaster for the site. This name links to an e-mail address if one has been provided in the site profile.
Site Map	Displays a panel with a hierarchical listing of folders and subfolders within the site.
Categories PopUp	Provides a combo box of the categories created for the site. The user can select a category and Site Builder builds a list of the content items for that category.
Category Links	Provides the same functionality as the Categories PopUp, except that the categories are shown as text links instead of in the combo box format. You will generally use only one of these two formats.
LogOn/LogOff Links	Links to pages that log users on and off the site.
Folder Links	Text links that navigate the user to the selected folder.
Perspectives PopUp	Provides a combo box of the perspectives created for the site. The user can select a category, and Site Builder builds a list of the content items for that perspective.
Perspectives Links	Provides the same functionality as the Perspectives PopUp, except that the perspectives are shown as text links instead of in the combo box format. You will generally use only one of these two formats.
News Link	Text link to the news panel.
BLANK SPACE	The blank space item is a placeholder, it inserts a blank row between the entries immediately above and below it.

The list boxes on this page are displayed in pairs. The arrow buttons move items in the Available Elements list box on the left-hand side to the associated Displayed Elements list box on the right-hand side. The lower three pairs of list boxes on this page are associated with the Folders Link, Category PopUp/Link and Perspective PopUp/Link items respectively. If you add any of these elements to the Displayed Items list, then you can use the associated pairs of list boxes for that particular element to determine which subitems to display. For example, if you choose to display Folder Links as a displayed element in your Navigation Bar, then you can use the Available Folder Links/Displayed Folder Links list boxes to determine exactly which folders to display. This same methodology applies for the category and perspectives elements.

Site Builder enables you to set a different style for each folder and you may choose to display certain folder, category, and perspective links in one folder, but not in other subfolders. For example, you may not want to publish links to secure folders in the Navigation Bar for public folders.

3. Add the following elements to the Displayed Elements list:
   a. Folder Links
   b. Category PopUp
   c. Perspective Links
4. Save your changes with the Apply button.
5. Move all of the folders, categories, and perspectives from the Available lists to the associated Displayed lists.
6. Save your changes with the Apply button.
7. Click the Finish button to exit the Folder Editor.
8. Click the Done button to return to the administration page.
9. Click the Home icon in the upper-right corner of the page to display the home page for Net University. The result of all of your efforts is the Web site shown in Figure 18-27.

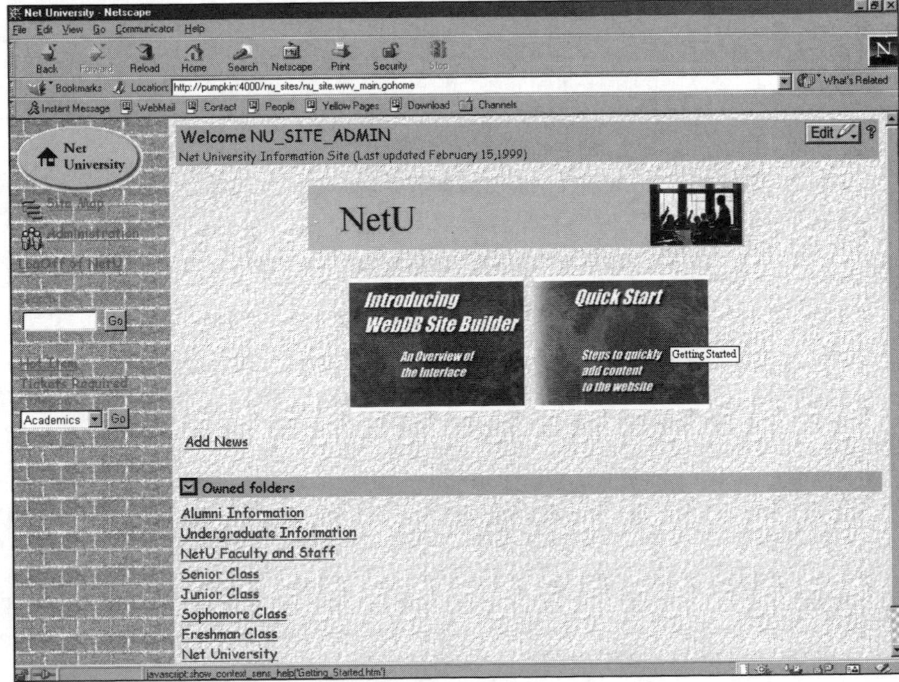

Figure 18-27: Net University Web site

At this point, the site has all of the features required for deployment to end users with the exception of some security settings. However, you will likely make some changes to the site once you have worked through the process of adding content to it. In particular, you will most likely assign responsibility for your folders to power users within your site. For example, in the Net University system, it makes sense to give the class officers of each of the undergraduate classes some control over the items in the class year subfolders. In order to grant such authority, you need to spend a little time understanding how WebDB implements the Oracle security mechanisms, which Chapter 20 covers in detail.

Wrapping Up

This chapter covered the basics of building a Web site with Site Builder and how the various site editors work. You are no doubt a bit confused at this point because your site does not actually contain any content. The only thing you have managed to accomplish is to create the structure for your site and adjust some of the look and feel of the site.

Before you tackle the next phase of Site Builder, it is important that you understand the WebDB security and deployment mechanisms covered in Chapters 20 and 22. You must create the security scheme for your site before you can turn access to your site over to your users. In the next section of this book, we introduce you to the administration tools of WebDB. In the final part of this book, you will return for a second look at Site Builder, and begin deploying content and assigning folder privileges to users.

✦ ✦ ✦

P A R T

IV

Administering WebDB

✦ ✦ ✦ ✦

In This Part

✦ ✦ ✦ ✦

Administering WebDB Components

✦ ✦ ✦ ✦

In This Chapter

Using the Component Finder

Using WebDB Version Management

Managing Components

Importing and Exporting Outside of WebDB

Oracle Replication and WebDB

✦ ✦ ✦ ✦

By now, you've had quite a bit of experience creating WebDB components. If you have been following along with the examples in this book, you have created reports, forms, charts, dynamic HTML pages, and menus to bind them all together.

You have also started to see how a WebDB system can encompass many different components, and you may have started to worry about how to manage all of them. This chapter focuses on the specific tools and utilities you can use to manage your WebDB components, from changing the name or copying a component to using the built-in version control for WebDB components to exporting and importing existing WebDB components.

Component Finder

We introduced you to the WebDB Component Finder in Chapter 3 of this book. The end of that chapter explained how to locate components using the main Component Finder page, as shown in Figure 19-1.

We will not go over this finder again, because you can refer to Chapter 3 for more details. Once you launch a search for a component using the Component Finder, the results are returned to you as a list of components that match your search criteria, as shown in Figure 19-2.

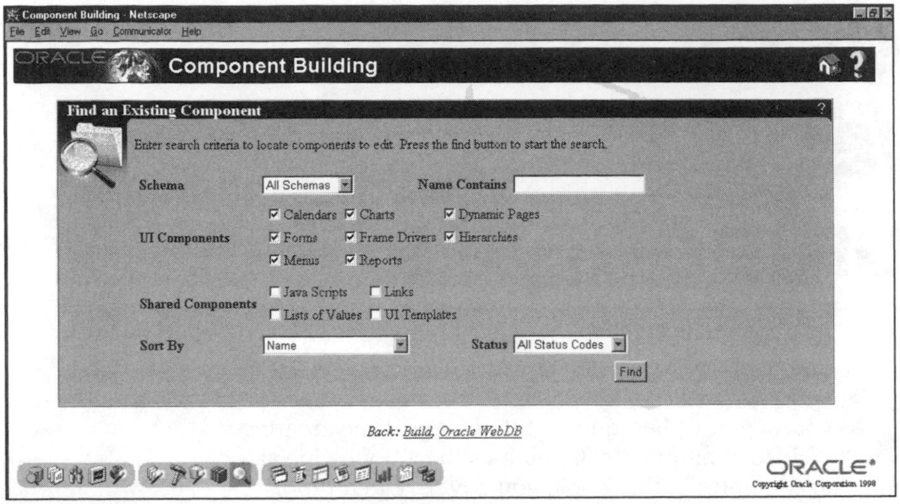

Figure 19-1: The main page of the Component Finder

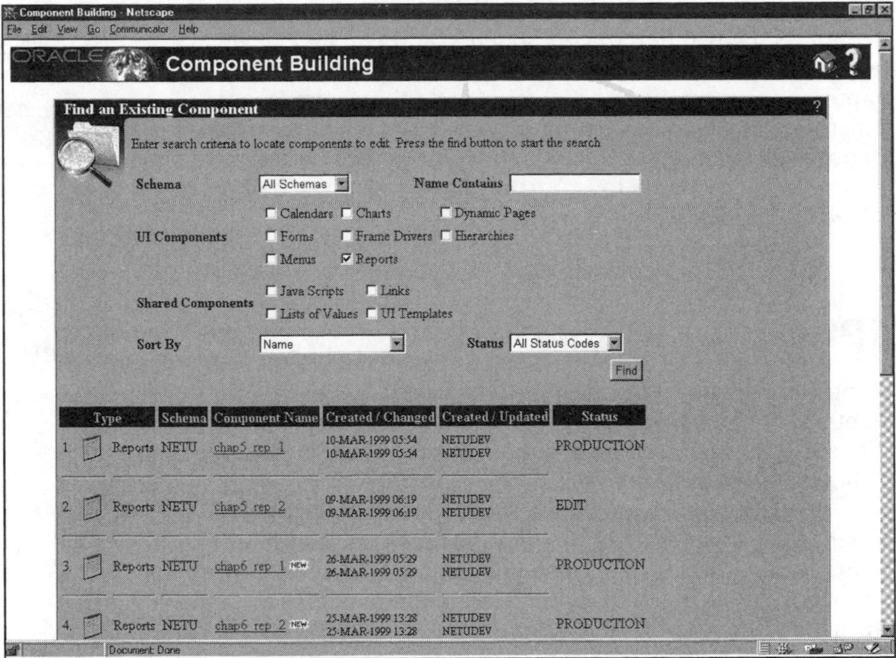

Figure 19-2: Component listing returned in the Component Finder

The list of components includes some basic information about each entry— the type of component, the schema the component is stored in, the name of the component, who and when created, and when it was last modified the component, and the current status of the most recent version of the component. The name of the component acts as a hotlink to the Manage Component page.

In order to demonstrate the administrative functions described throughout this chapter, you can use one of the components you created in an earlier chapter. You should log on to WebDB with the user name you used to create the other components earlier in the book.

1. Log on to WebDB as the NETUDEV user. Click on the Build Menu choice on the WebDB home page.
2. Click on the User Interface Components menu choice on the main Build page.
3. Click on the Find Components menu choice on the main User Interface Components page.
4. Uncheck all of the choices under UI components except for Reports. Click on the Find push button.

The page returned to you should look like the page shown in Figure 19-2.

You can see all the report components that you have created in earlier chapters, or that you imported from the files included on the CD-ROM that accompanies this book. In order to make this particular example clear, we have used a report that you should have built as a part of Chapter 5, the first chapter on reports. This report should have several versions, because you modified the report while you were building it. If you do not have a report with multiple versions, you can use any module with multiple versions to understand the topics in this section.

5. Click the report labeled "ch5_rep_1" in the list of components at the bottom of the page.

When you click a report with multiple versions, you bring up a version of the Manage Component page, as shown in Figure 19-3.

Most of what you will learn in this chapter revolves around choices you make from the Manage Component page. But before you can dive into the features of the menu choices on the page, you have to learn a little bit about the version control built into WebDB.

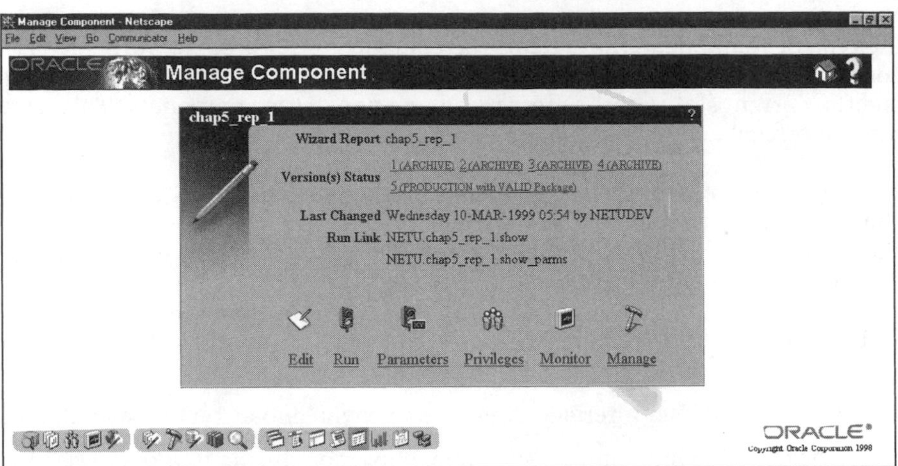

Figure 19-3: The Manage Component page for a report with multiple versions

Version Control

If you have created any WebDB components, and you have edited the components after you created them, you have already experienced the built-in version control feature of WebDB.

Every time you edit a component, WebDB stores the new parameters for the component in a new data row in the Oracle database. When you have finished your changes, WebDB assigns a status to the new version of the component. Typically, you generate your component when you finish changing its parameters and, typically, the component compiles successfully. These two actions result in a new version of the component being added to your WebDB system. The next time you bring up the Manage Component page for the component in WebDB, you see one more listing under the heading of Version(s). You would see the last listing having a higher version number and a status of PRODUCTION, while the previous version is now marked with a status of ARCHIVE. If you did not generate the component, or if the component was not generated successfully, you would still see a new version of the component, but it would have a different status associated with it.

This automatic versioning gives you an increased level of security when you are changing WebDB components. No matter how much you change a particular version of a component, the previous version is always available to you, safe and sound. The only problem is that the previous version is identified by a (somewhat) cryptic version number. At this time, you cannot add descriptive information to a version number, so you have to use your own methods to track which version number has which features.

Tip

It is so easy to restore previous versions that you can always restore a version of a component and see what it contained. If it was not the version you were looking for, you could either bring the previous version back or look for another version of the component. We suggest a method to track versions later in this chapter.

But all the earlier versions of a component are still there, waiting for you to bring them back to life. It is easy to restore a previous version of a component.

6. Click a previous version of the ch5_rep_1 component or whatever component you selected. You will see a page like Figure 19-4.

You are asked if you want to make a copy of the selected archive version of the component and make it into the current version of the component, which will be identified with the next highest version number. If you respond by clicking the Yes push button, you are immediately taken to the Edit page for the new version of the component.

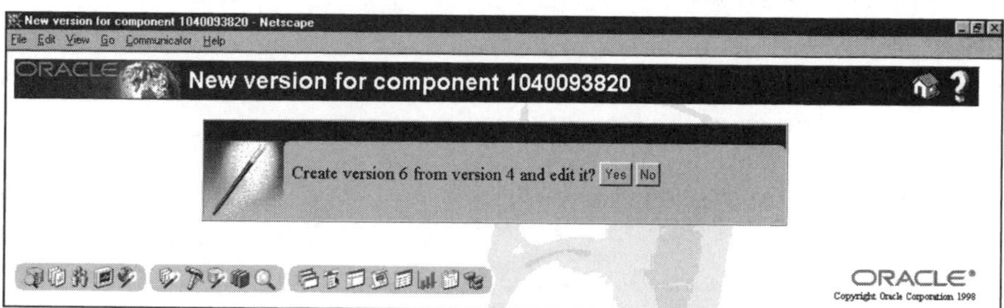

Figure 19-4: Restoring a previous version

7. Click the Yes push button in the New version . . . page.

The new version of the component is not created until you have clicked the Finish push button on the Edit page for the new component. If you leave the Edit page for the new component by clicking the Cancel push button, WebDB does not create a new version of the component. This makes sense. If you leave the Edit page by clicking the Cancel push button, no new version of the component is generated, so the existing version of the component is identical to the previous version and therefore serves no purpose.

8. Make a change to the header of the report in the Add Text panel of the Edit page.
9. Click the Finish push button.

The new version of the report should be listed on the Manage Component page when the generation of the new version is completed.

It is important to understand how versions work within WebDB, because most of the management functions you will learn about later in this chapter only work on the current version of a component. The next section introduces you to the basic management capabilities for WebDB components.

Managing Components

If you have been reading this book from the beginning, you are already quite familiar with some parts of the Component Manager. In fact, the Manage Component page is the final page delivered to you when you are creating user interface components.

You can change the parameters that control the generation of your WebDB components through the Edit menu choice and you can run your component directly or with parameters through the Run and Parameter menu choices, respectively. Because these choices have been extensively covered in earlier chapters, we will not go over them again in this chapter.

Instead, we will concentrate on the functions available to you once you select the Manage menu choice on the Manage Component page.

10. Click the Manage choice at the bottom of the initial Manage Component page for the ch5_rep_1 report component.

The new page looks like Figure 19-5, with six menu choices represented by icons in the middle of the page and four additional choices at the bottom of the page. The following sections describe the actions of five of these choices.

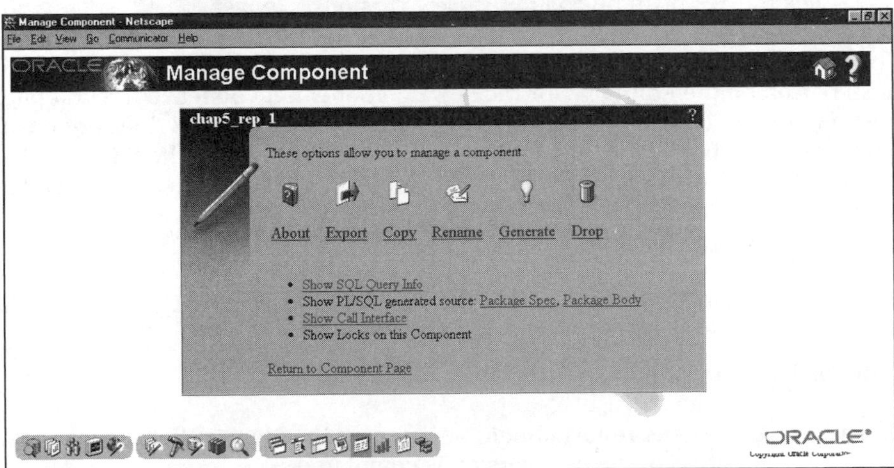

Figure 19-5: The Manage Component options page

 About

The About menu choice, as shown in Figure 19-6, gives you some basic information about the current versions of a component and a complete listing of the values of all the parameters that you have assigned for the creation of a component.

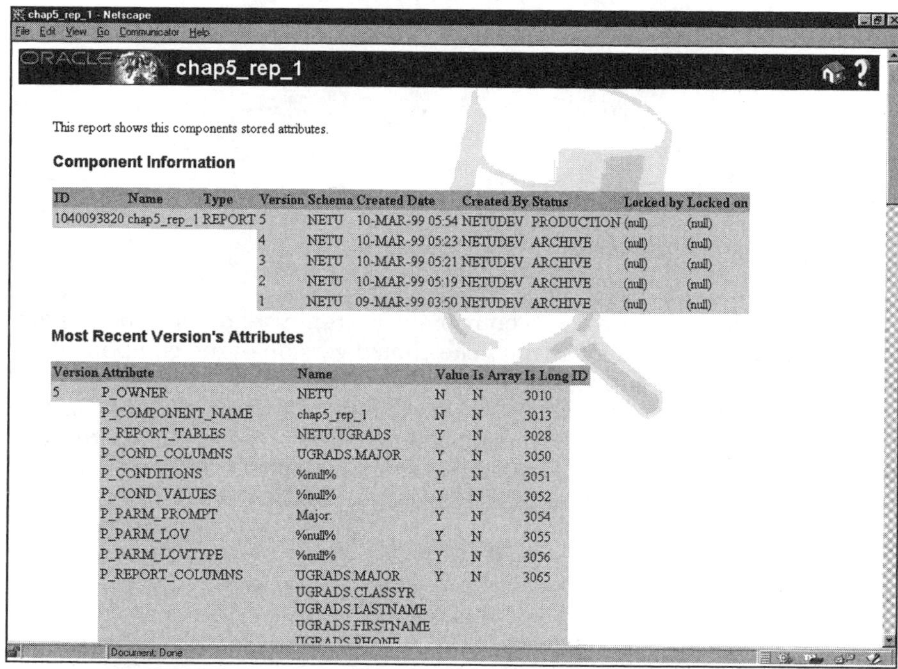

Figure 19-6: The About menu choice page

The information presented on the About page is essentially a recap of all the information stored in the WebDB data tables about the component. All of the values you entered through the pages of the creation wizard are listed, with the prefix P_ preceding a descriptive name.

When you look at the values returned on the About page, you are able to see inside WebDB. It's helpful to get to know the type of parameters used for a particular component, because many of them can be passed to your component if you are calling the PL/SQL package from a link, from another PL/SQL package, or directly from a browser. You will learn about these last two options later in this chapter.

When you click the Copy menu choice, WebDB delivers the Copy Component page, as shown in Figure 19-7.

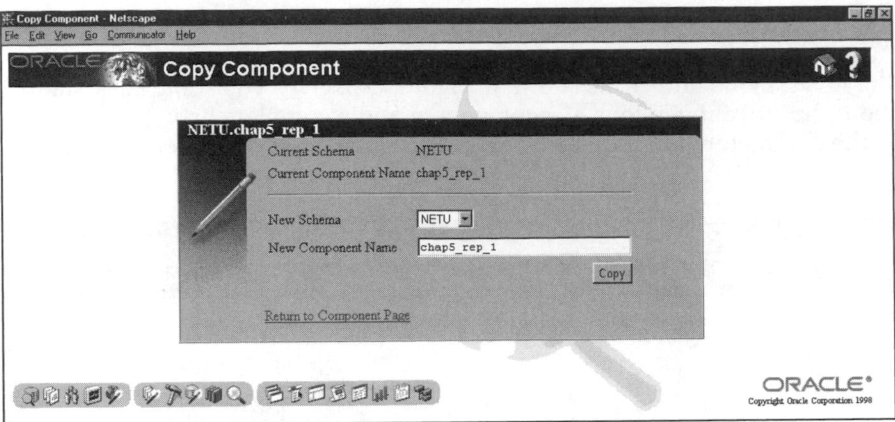

Figure 19-7: The Copy Component page

This page enables you to create a copy of the current version of a component under another name or in another schema. The copied version of the component is given a version number of 1, because it is a brand-new component. You can use this capability to create explicit versions of a component with meaningful names, as described in the sidebar titled "Version Maintenance." When you take this approach to versioning, every released version of a component has a version number of 1, so it's easy to identify if a component is actively part of the development process.

Rename

When you click the Rename menu choice, WebDB delivers the Rename Component page, as shown in Figure 19-8.

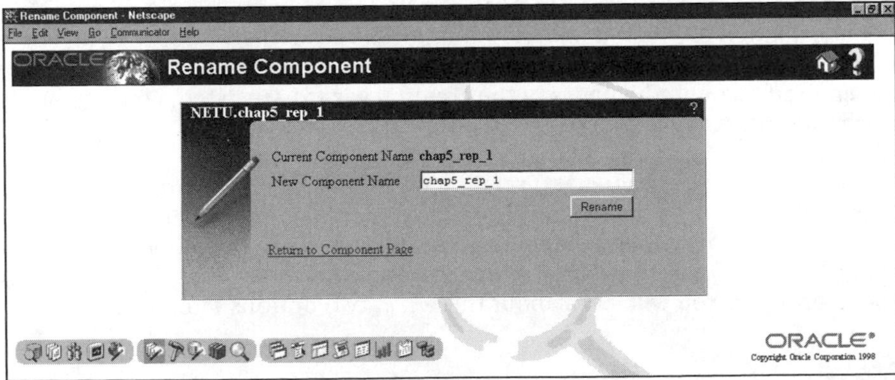

Figure 19-8: The Rename Component page

The Rename process is different from the Copy process in two ways. First, renaming a component renames all the existing versions of the component, not just the current one. Second, the new name for the component is applied directly to the component, so it has the effect of deleting the current name of the component by overwriting it.

 Generate

You should be familiar with the Generate process by now. You generate the PL/SQL package that is your run-time component when you click the OK push button at the end of a WebDB wizard process or when you click the Finish push button at the end of an editing session. Because these are typically the last things you do in your development process, why would you ever want to use the Generate choice?

Typically, you won't ever need to use it, but there may be occasions where you import the data in the WebDB tables, but not the packages created from that data. In this situation, it may be faster for you to use the Generate choice rather than entering Edit mode for a particular component.

When you use WebDB to export your components, the SQL script that is created includes a call to the Generate procedure, so the script automatically generates the component.

If you select the Generate choice for an existing component and return to the Manage Component page, you will see that there is no new version number for the component. Even though you may have heard the whirring of a disk drive which might have led you to believe that WebDB was creating a new package. WebDB did create a new PL/SQL package, but because it had the exact same characteristics of the current version, there was no need to increment the version number.

Keep in mind that a version is defined by a new set of parameters in the WebDB database, not a new copy of the resulting package.

 Drop

When you click the Drop menu choice, WebDB delivers the Drop Component page, as shown in Figure 19-9.

WebDB gives you the opportunity to drop each individual version of a component. By default, all the versions are selected for deletion by having the check box at the beginning of their name checked. Unless you want to delete a component completely, you should be careful to uncheck at least one of the boxes.

As you can probably guess at this point, dropping a version means that WebDB deletes the rows in the database that contain the parameters for that version of the component. Even if you drop all the versions of a component, any generated PL/SQL packages still exist. You have to delete them through SQL*Plus or some other maintenance tool if you want to get rid of the actual component.

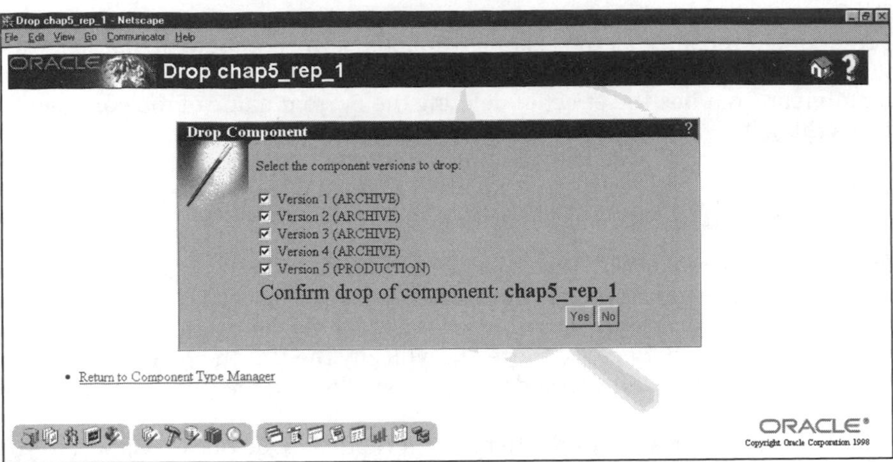

Figure 19-9: The Drop Component page

Version Maintenance

In an iterative development environment, it is very easy to end up with a lot of versions for a component. In fact, because it is so easy to change a WebDB component, it is almost inevitable that you end up with many versions of a given component. The built-in versioning feature of WebDB is great from the standpoint of always being able to cancel out changes by returning to a previous version, but it is less than ideal for identifying which version is which, because the only identifier is a version number.

You can avoid this type of version overload in one of two ways. The first is to be fairly ruthless about cleaning up versions during the development and release process. While your component is in developmental flux, you can just keep modifying the component and creating more versions. But as soon as you attain a steady state, you have to remember to go back to the Manage Component page and drop all the interim versions. This reduces the number of versions you have for a particular component, but you still have multiple versions of a component with "holes" in the version numbering scheme, as shown in Figure 19-10.

The second method is to make a fresh copy of each new version of a component that you want to keep. You can give each copy a more descriptive name, as shown in Figure 19-11, which can help to administer the different versions of a component.

In either case, it is also good practice to add some type of version indicator to your component, either in the header or footer of the component or, if your users object to seeing the version number on a page, as a hidden field. Having version numbers is not that useful if you have no way of knowing which version is being run at any particular time.

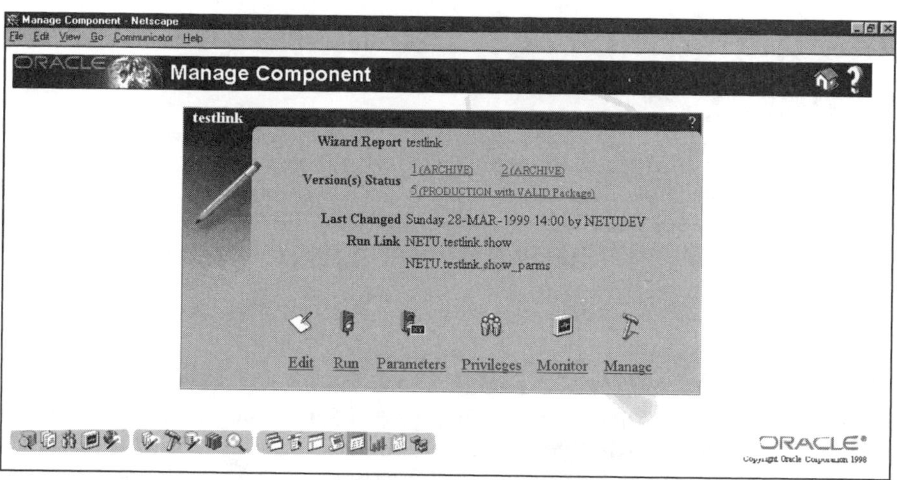

Figure 19-10: Version number holes

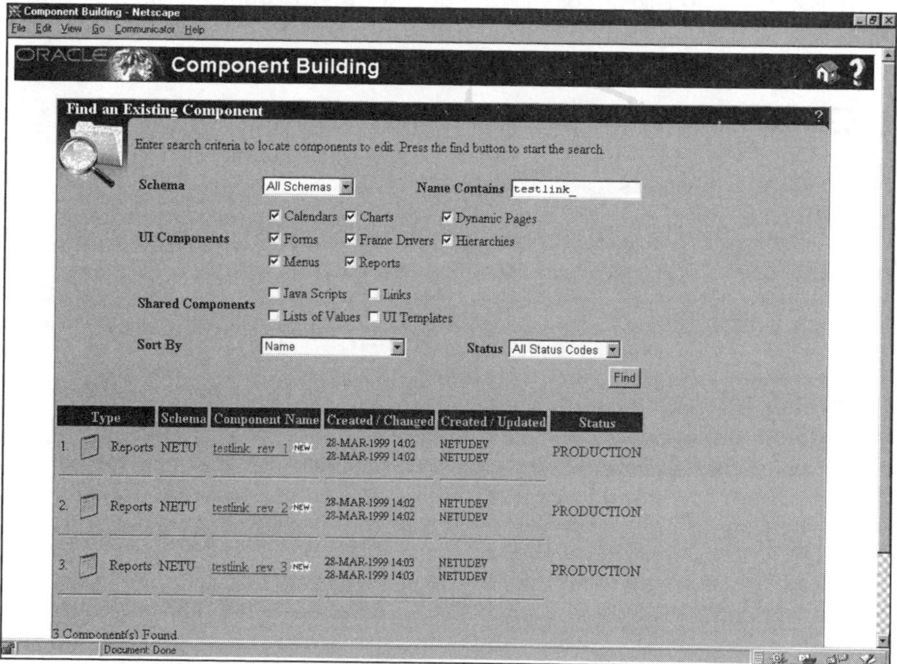

Figure 19-11: Different versions of a component as different components

The one management choice we have not covered yet is the Export choice. You actually have two different methods available to you if you want to export a WebDB component, so we cover this choice in its own later in this chapter.

Additional Choices on the Manage Component Page

Some menu choices are listed in text at the bottom of the Manage Component page. These menu choices are not as broadly useful as the ones covered previously. However, they are very useful in specific situations, such as understanding what is going on under the covers in your WebDB generated components and in the WebDB development environment.

Show/hide SQL query info

WebDB is built around data-driven HTML pages. Sometimes, a page returned from a component will not be what you expect. In this case, it may be helpful to be able to see the SQL that WebDB is using to build the page.

You can select the Show SQL Query Info link to have the actual SQL statements used for a page and the values that are bound with the bind variables shown at the top of the page, as illustrated in Figure 19-12 for the ch5_rep_1 report.

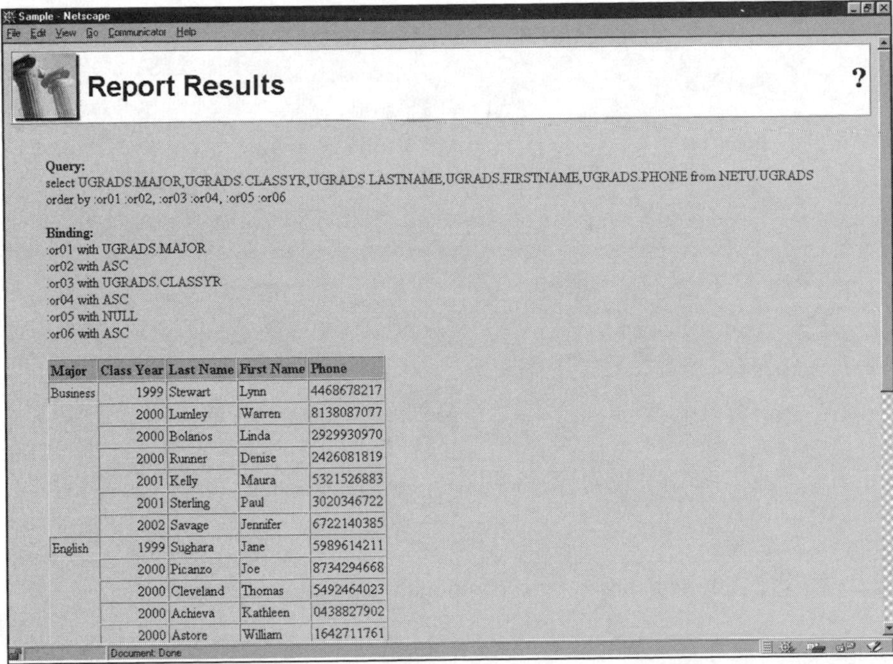

Major	Class Year	Last Name	First Name	Phone
Business	1999	Stewart	Lynn	4468678217
	2000	Lumley	Warren	8138087077
	2000	Bolanos	Linda	2929930970
	2000	Runner	Denise	2426081819
	2001	Kelly	Maura	5321526883
	2001	Sterling	Paul	3020346722
	2002	Savage	Jennifer	6722140385
English	1999	Sughara	Jane	5989614211
	2000	Picanzo	Joe	8734294668
	2000	Cleveland	Thomas	5492464023
	2000	Achieva	Kathleen	0438827902
	2000	Astore	William	1642711761

Figure 19-12: Showing SQL query info

Once you have selected this menu choice, you are returned to the Manage Component page. If this choice has been selected, the menu choice displays as Hide SQL Query Info, which turns off the display in the returned page.

PL/SQL code

The PL/SQL menu choice enables you to take a look at the actual code that WebDB generates for you. You can either view the Package Spec, which lists the procedures that are a part of the package and the parameters these procedures accept, or the Package Body, which includes all the PL/SQL code actually used to implement the procedures.

For the most part, we have found that looking at the package body is not really that helpful. There is a mass of code, much of which just calls other PL/SQL procedures. If you are very curious and have a good understanding of PL/SQL, the package body can give you some insight into how WebDB components actually work.

The package specification, or spec, is something you can use. Because you may have occasion to call the PL/SQL package from some other environment or PL/SQL package, you must know the details of the package spec if you want to use any of the procedures in the package correctly.

You can see that, for a report, the only procedure that has very many parameters is the SHOW procedure, and the parameters for that procedure look a lot like the parameters set from the Parameter form for the report.

There are two timestamps in the PL/SQL package specification for a component. The first is at the top of the code, which indicates when a package was initially created. The timestamp that comes below the `create or replace package` code is the time the current version was created. If you were to use the Generate choice for a component, even though the specifications for the component had not changed, you would still see a new timestamp in this part of the code, because the package was regenerated by the Generate choice.

Call interface

The Call Interface menu choice provides a list of the parameters called for a component, an illustration of calling the procedure for the component from another stored procedure, and a sample URL that describes how to call the procedure at run time. The default values are also shown for each of the parameters.

When you create links, you will find that you are given a list of parameters that can be passed values for a component. The information returned for the Call Interface choice, as shown in Figure 19-13, can help you to understand the best way to build your links.

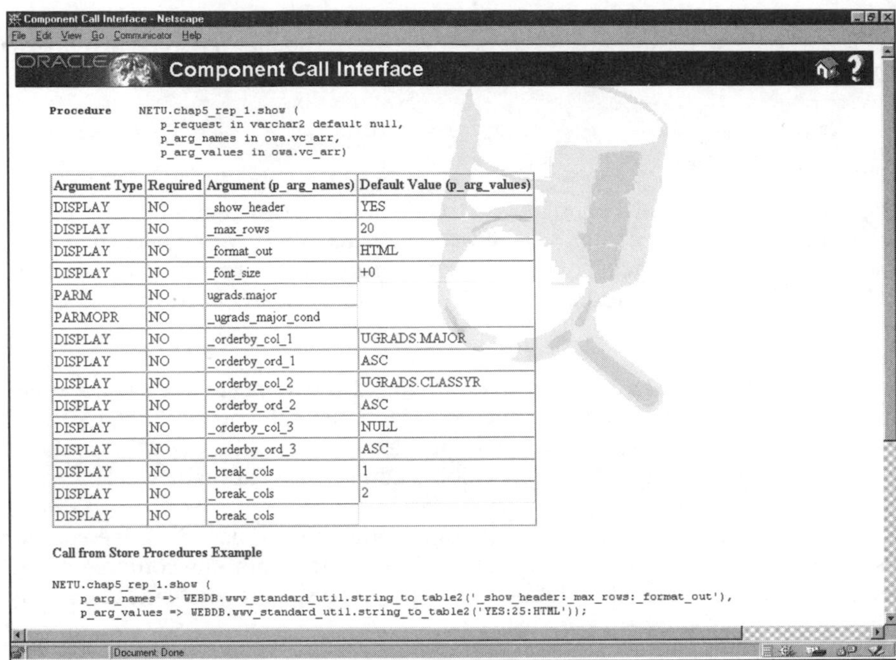
Component Call Interface

```
Procedure     NETU.chap5_rep_1.show (
                  p_request in varchar2 default null,
                  p_arg_names in owa.vc_arr,
                  p_arg_values in owa.vc_arr)
```

Argument Type	Required	Argument (p_arg_names)	Default Value (p_arg_values)
DISPLAY	NO	_show_header	YES
DISPLAY	NO	_max_rows	20
DISPLAY	NO	_format_out	HTML
DISPLAY	NO	_font_size	+0
PARM	NO	ugrads.major	
PARMOPR	NO	_ugrads_major_cond	
DISPLAY	NO	_orderby_col_1	UGRADS.MAJOR
DISPLAY	NO	_orderby_ord_1	ASC
DISPLAY	NO	_orderby_col_2	UGRADS.CLASSYR
DISPLAY	NO	_orderby_ord_2	ASC
DISPLAY	NO	_orderby_col_3	NULL
DISPLAY	NO	_orderby_ord_3	ASC
DISPLAY	NO	_break_cols	1
DISPLAY	NO	_break_cols	2
DISPLAY	NO	_break_cols	

Call from Store Procedures Example

```
NETU.chap5_rep_1.show (
    p_arg_names => WEBDB.wwv_standard_util.string_to_table2('_show_header:_max_rows:_format_out'),
    p_arg_values => WEBDB.wwv_standard_util.string_to_table2('YES:25:HTML'));
```

Figure 19-13: The returned Call Interface page

The syntax for the URL call can also help you understand how to integrate your WebDB components in with standard HTML pages in a site.

Show locks

Throughout this book, we have pretty much assumed that you will be the only user working on a particular component at a particular time. But because your Oracle database has the capability to have many users at the same time, WebDB also enables you to have many different developers simultaneously. However, just as no two users can write to the same row of data at the same time, no two WebDB developers can modify the same component at the same time. Although component locks are not actual locks on the underlying rows in the WebDB host database, the logical locking imposed by WebDB serves the same purpose as the database locks implemented by the Oracle database.

When one developer is working on a component, the component is locked. You may occasionally see a status description for a version in the Manage Component page such as "PRODUCTION locked by *username*," where the *username* identifies the database user who is actively modifying the parameters for a component.

When the component is locked, you are unable to edit or perform any administrative tasks on the component. You may, however, be able to run the package generated by the component, because this package is independent of the data rows that have been locked by another developer.

On occasion, you may find that a lock is held on a component in error. You can explicitly release the lock on a component through the Utilities menu in WebDB.

A WebDB developer has to have DBA privileges to release locks on components. If you are using the NETUDEV user to access the management options for a component, you are not able to choose this menu choice, because it does not have DBA privileges.

Import and Export Through WebDB

One of the great things about WebDB is that all the components you build are stored in an Oracle database. The parameters that control how a component is built are also stored within database tables and used to build the PL/SQL packages that are the actual components.

This architecture has several benefits. Your components are kept in a single, secure location. When you back up the Oracle database that hosts your WebDB application system, you are also backing up the components that make up the system. Finally, you can use the existing import and export capabilities of an Oracle database to move components from one Oracle database to another, which is described later in this chapter.

Exporting user interface components

It is very easy to export individual user interface components.

Click the Export choice on the Manage Component page for the report you have been working with.

WebDB returns a page that contains the text of an SQL script, as shown in Figure 19-14.

The generated export code is set up to do three things:

✦ Remove any existing copies of the component, which is identified by a unique number, by deleting any rows from the WWV_MODULES$ and the WWV_MODULE_DETAILS$ tables associated with that unique number. These two tables are the internal data tables used by WebDB to hold the parameters used to generate components.

✦ Add the rows into these same tables that define the most current version of the component.

✦ Generate the PL/SQL package for the component by calling the `build_procedure` for the component.

```
Netscape
File Edit View Go Communicator Help
---------------------------------------------------------
-- Export of Component: 1040093820
-- Owner: NETU
-- Name: chap5_rep_1
-- Version: 5
--
-- To import this component run this script in sqlplus as the Oracle user: WEBDB
--
-- Export Date: Monday    29 March    , 1999 05:13:31
-- Export Generated By: NETUDEV
--
set define off
prompt ...importing component: 1040093820

prompt ...removing existing component definition

delete from WWV_MODULE_DETAILS$ where module_id = 1040093820
/
delete from WWV_MODULES$ where id = 1040093820
/

prompt ...inserting component definition

insert into WWV_MODULES$ (
ID,
VERSION,
TYPE_ID,
NAME,
SCHEMA,
REQUIRED_ROLE,
STATUS_ID,
CREATED_ON,
CREATED_BY,
STATUS,
LOCKED_ON,
LOCKED_BY) values (
1040093820,
5,
3,
'chap5_rep_1',
'NETU',
null,
Document Done
```

Figure 19-14: SQL code for exporting a component

Are you the nervous type? Are you worrying that there may be two components with the same ID, which would mean that this script would delete an existing component when it is run against a different WebDB installation? Rest easy. WebDB uses a different seed number for different installations of WebDB to ensure that shared components from different installations have a unique ID.

In order to create an SQL script, you should select all the text in your browser and save it to a file, typically with an extension of .sql. You can run this script in SQL*Plus to load the component into an Oracle database and generate the PL/SQL package for the component by using the following command:

```
@filename
```

Notice that the comments at the top of the script instruct you to run the script as the WEBDB user, who is the owner of the WebDB system and data tables. This script loads the internal tables that hold the information about the component, so you must be the WEBDB owner.

The WebDB system user is normally the only user with access to the internal WebDB data tables, and this user always has access to the schema that holds the generated components.

You have to use the user account for the owner of the WebDB installation, which may or may not be the WEBDB user.

Exporting shared components

Shared components are different in a number of ways from standard user interface components. First, they do not belong to a particular schema in the Oracle database. They are stored in data tables that are part of the schema that owns WebDB, which is typically called WEBDB. Secondly, shared components are not generated at all. Generated user interface components simply include the shared components within the HTML pages that are generated by the component at run time.

Consequently, there is a different mechanism for exporting shared components. In order to use this utility, you have to log on as the owner of WebDB.

1. Log on to WebDB as the owner, or DBA, of WebDB.
2. Click the hammer icon in the middle section of the shortcuts toolbar, which takes you to the Utilities page. The Utilities page is also available as a choice off the main Build menu for users with DBA privileges. You will see a page that gives you two menu choices, as shown in Figure 19-15.

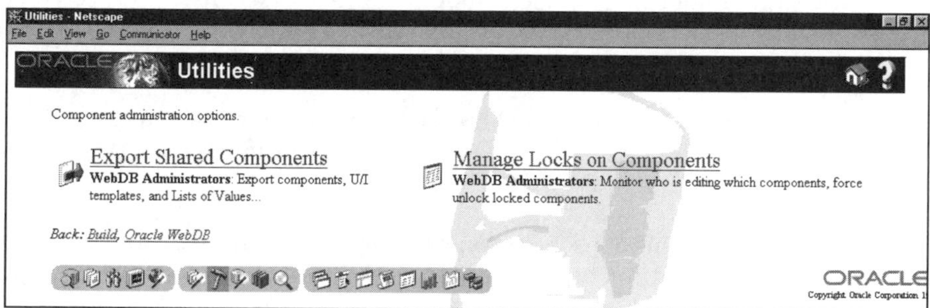

Figure 19-15: WebDB Utilities page

3. Click the Export Shared Components menu choice.

Note

You can use the other menu choice on the Utilities page to explicitly release the locks on a component, which were described in the previous section.

The next page that appears in your browser (shown in Figure 19-16) enables you to export any one of the types of shared components.

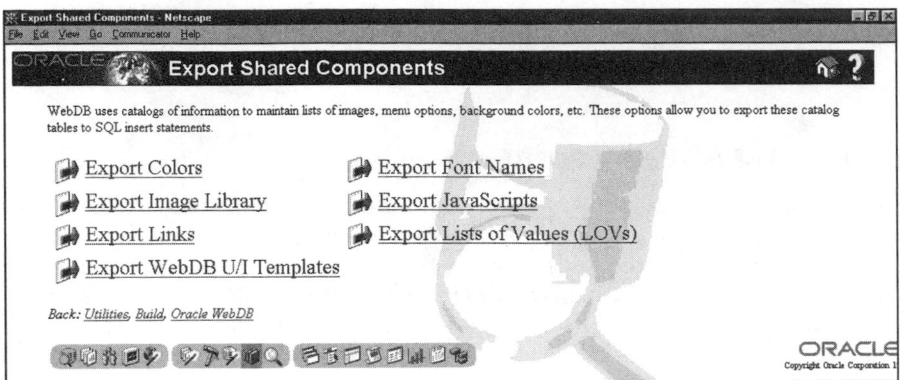

Figure 19-16: Exporting shared components

When you click any of the menu choices, you will get a page with an SQL script, just like you did when you exported an individual component. Once the script is displayed in your browser, you should copy and paste the script to a text file with a file extension of .sql, as you did with the scripts for the user interface components.

You may want to create a standard set of shared components that you will use across multiple WebDB development machines. Simply make sure a particular WebDB installation contains only the shared components you want to include in the library and then export those components to SQL scripts. When you install a new WebDB site, use SQL*Plus to load the scripts containing the standard shared components to reproduce them to the new server.

The Utilities menu is only available to DBA users, but you can export individual Link, Template, and Lists of Values components from the main page for each of these components, as shown in Figure 19-17.

Of course, with this approach, you can only export those shared components that reside in schemas you have access to, and the components must be exported one at a time.

Importing WebDB components

The end result of exporting either type of WebDB component is the same — a script file with the SQL statements needed to add the data back into the Oracle database that acts as the host for WebDB.

The easiest way to do this is to use SQL*Plus, an interactive SQL tool that comes with all Oracle databases.

To import a file, simply start SQL*Plus, making sure that you log on as the appropriate user — the owner of WebDB installation, who is typically called WEBDB.

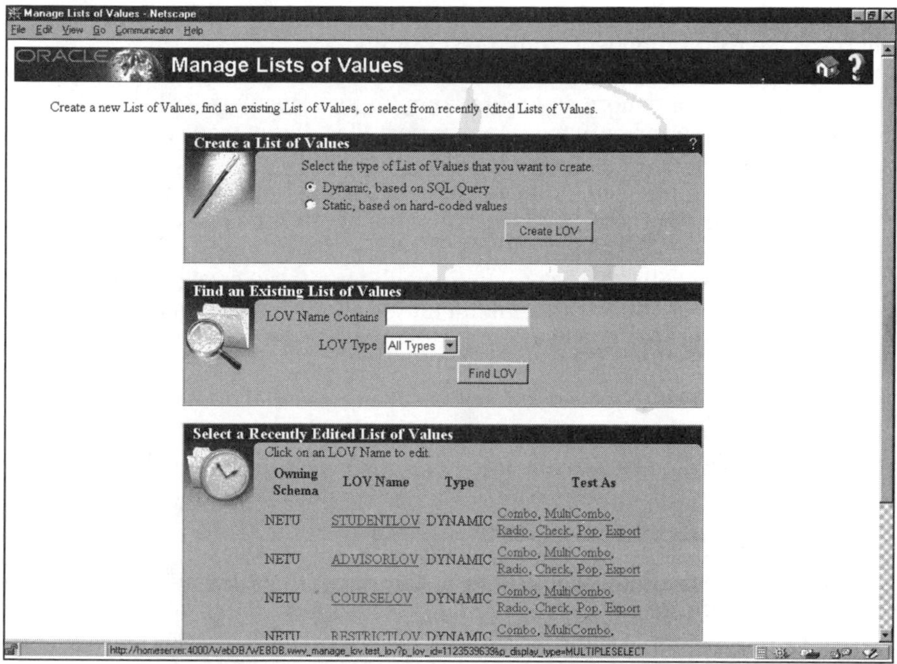

Figure 19-17: Manage Lists of Values main page with export option for each component

Once you start SQL*Plus, simply enter the at (@) sign (which indicates a script file), complete path and file name of the SQL file, and SQL*Plus runs the commands listed in the script file. If you set the directory list as the Start in directory on the shortcut icon for SQL*Plus for Windows to the directory that contains the script file, you do not need to indicate the path name.

If you want to run an SQL script with a name of REP1.SQL that exists in the c:\ directory, start SQL*Plus and log in as the owner of the WebDB environment. Then, enter the following line of code:

```
@c:\REP1.SQL
```

The script runs and the component loads.

Import and Export Through Oracle Utilities

The standard, recommended way to export and import components in WebDB is to export each individual user interface component to its own SQL script file and export each type of shared component into their own SQL script files.

There is a lot to be said for this practice. Once you have completed work on a component, exporting it to a script file ensures that it is safe. Even in the highly improbable event of an unrecoverable corruption of your Oracle database, you can still re-create the component from the script file.

However, as you build more and more complex systems with WebDB, you eventually end up with more and more export files. If you want to load an entire system, you will find yourself running a lot of scripts in SQL*Plus. Because each of the scripts is self-contained, you can combine all the individual export files into one larger file, or you can write some kind of batch file to run each of the scripts in turn.

But this seems like a lot of work to go through for a fairly straightforward task: to move an entire WebDB environment, including all the shared and user interface components, to another Oracle database. There is a more direct way to accomplish this task.

To accomplish this task, we turn to one of the Oracle database's standard utilities. There is a standard Oracle utility you can use to export all of the WebDB data: the `exp80` utility.

Note The `exp80` utility, as the name implies, is the export utility for Oracle8. If you are using an earlier version of Oracle, please consult your documentation for the appropriate program name. The export utility has remained stable for many years, so all the syntax discussed in this section also applies to earlier versions of the utility.

The `exp80` utility, hereafter referred to as the export utility, was designed to transfer data from one Oracle database to another through the use of a flat file. The export utility contains all the SQL statements necessary to create the data structures to hold data and the actual data itself. This information is written in a binary format to a standard disk file, normally called a dump file, which could be subsequently used with the corresponding import utility to load it into another database.

For the purposes of this book, you have installed the WebDB product in one schema, WEBDB, and the application system in another, NETU. Because all the data and procedures that make up a WebDB application system reside in two separate schemas, you can use the export utility to dump the contents of these schemas to a binary file, which can be used to re-create the environment on another machine.

You can use the export utility through a command-line interface or interactively. In order to understand the way the utility works, we will run the export utility interactively at first.

Note You should do this on a machine that has the export utility loaded on it and access to the server machine. Usually, this means you will run it from the server machine that contains the Oracle database for WebDB.

1. Start the export utility by entering the following line of code:

   ```
   exp80
   ```

2. Enter the user name and password for the owner of the database.

3. Accept the default value for the array fetch buffer size by hitting the Enter key.

Entering a larger buffer size usually results in better performance for the export utility, but because you are not exporting that much information, you can accept the default value of 4096.

4. Give the file a descriptive name, such as **webdb.dmp**, and hit the Enter key.
5. Enter **U** for an export of a particular user.

The E(ntire database) entry would export the entire database, while the T(ables) entry would simply prompt you for specific tables for export. Because you want everything from the WebDB owner's schema, the U(sers) choice is most appropriate.

6. Select the default entry for exporting grants by hitting the Enter key.
7. Accept the default of yes for exporting the table data (instead of just exporting the data structures for the tables) by hitting the Enter key.
8. Accept the default choice for the next choice about compressing extents by hitting the Enter key.
9. For the next prompt, enter the name of the owner of the WebDB environment and hit the Enter key. Hit the Enter key again to indicate that you have entered all the users you wish to export.

After you have completed entering this information, the export utility exports all the data structures and data contained in the schema for the owner of the WebDB environment. The sample WebDB environment we have used for this book created a dump file close to 9MB in size for the WEBDB schema.

Once you have exported the schema that contains the WebDB environment, you can go through the same process with the schema that contains the WebDB application system. For the examples in this book, you have probably been using the NETU schema.

You can accomplish the same task by calling the export utility directly from the command line. You only have to add parameters to the command line for the nondefault choices that you have made, so the code for calling the previous export job would be the following:

```
Exp80 netu/netu FILE=netu.dmp OWNER=(netu)
```

You have just learned another reason why it makes really good sense to have all of your components for a particular application system in a single schema. You will be able to export just that user schema to export all the PL/SQL packages for the components.

You can use the import utility to import the dump files you just created. Just as you can use a single command to export a dump file, you can use a corresponding single command to import the file using the `imp80` utility. To accomplish this for the WebDB environment file, the code is as follows:

```
imp80 webdb/webdb FILE=webdb.dmp OWNER=(webdb)
```

where the dump file is named webdb.dmp and it is in the current directory.

As with the export utility, the first parameter after the name of the import utility is the user name and password combination, the next parameter is the filename of the dump file, and the last parameter is the name of the owner of the schema in the target database.

You *must* import the dump files with the same user name that you used to export the files with. In this case, you have to import the WebDB dump file with the WEBDB user name, and you must import the NETU dump file with the NETU user name.

The dump files contain the SQL statements that create the data structures used by a schema. If the import utility encounters a data structure with the same name as a structure it is trying to create, it simply returns an error. Because of this, you should make sure you are loading your dump files into an empty, or nonexistent, schema. If a schema exists and contains a stored procedure with the same name as one you are trying to load, the import utility simply skips the creation of the entity when it gets a creation error. If you do not want to be informed of any of these type of creation errors, simply add the parameter `IGNORE=Y` to the end of the command line listed previously.

The end result of this approach is that loading a dump file into an existing schema does not replace any existing components with the newer versions in the dump file. Because the dump file is the complete schema, it makes sense to simply delete the target schema before loading the dump file. If you are unfamiliar with SQL commands, the syntax for dropping a user's schema and all the components in the schema is as follows:

```
DROP USER username CASCADE
```

where *username* is the name of the schema.

After you have dropped the user and its components, you have to re-create the user before loading the dump file.

Now that you know two ways to export and import WebDB components, which one should you use in which situation?

Choosing an Export Method

Which export method should you use? Before exploring this topic, it is worth spending just a little time explaining the differences between the two methods.

In the WebDB export process, each individual component is exported to an SQL script, which you can copy and save to a text file. The script is fully functional—from dropping any existing versions of a component to regenerating the component from the data files you have just loaded and easily readable. The WebDB process exports components and libraries as logical entities.

When you use the standard Oracle export utility, the entire schema for the WebDB development environment and the schema that owns the application are exported to binary files. These files are not readable by people and must be handled by the Oracle import utility. This type of export process is more like a physical process. The actual tables, the data they contain, and the stored procedures created from them are all exported to the dump files. When the files are reloaded, there is no recompilation of the components, and the stored procedures are simply reloaded back into the schema that owns them.

In most cases, the choice should be pretty clear. Using the standard Oracle export utility is what we call the *large mallet* approach—you dump and restore everything needed in the WebDB environment and as part of your development environment. If you are moving a complete WebDB site, using the export utility gives you what you want, all at one time.

But, heaven forbid you want to use any discretion in what you export and import. You cannot really exclude any components when you use this method. About all you can do is not load a particular application schema, or load more than one application schema that used the same shared components.

If you want to selectively load components as they are changed, you have to use the export scripts created for you with the WebDB export choice. The granularity for this type of export is a single component or library of shared components, which are much more flexible to work with.

In general, you will find that the choice of an export method is pretty easy. You will either copy an entire WebDB environment, which can be done with the Oracle export utility, or not, which requires you to use the standard WebDB export choices.

If we were to give a recommendation, we would suggest trying to use the standard WebDB export choice for each individual component and for the libraries of shared components. We know that making individual export files for each component may seem like a lot of work. However, the first time you try to recover an individual component from a dump file, any effort you put into making export files seems trivial when compared with the time you would spend trying to reload an entire dump file to its own schema and then exporting the component. Besides, if you have implemented a good programming scenario, you will find that the completion of a component calls for several actions, including cleaning up any earlier revisions. Adding the small task of exporting the component does not require much more time.

The bottom line is simple: Using the WebDB-provided export facility gives you the security and flexibility you may need, without much additional work in a good development environment. Not to mention that the export utility is not officially supported as a way of transferring WebDB components, so you may find yourself all alone if there is a problem.

Combining Multiple WebDB Sites

Right now, you are probably concentrating on a single WebDB application but, down the road, you may find that you want to create new WebDB sites using components that have already been created in a different WebDB development environment.

You can accomplish this by simply creating an export file or files from each site and loading them into the combined site. If you choose to use the export utility to move one of the sites to the new location, you have to use the standard WebDB export scripts to load the other set of components, because the export utility does not overwrite existing data structures in the target database.

A more likely scenario is when you want to load the shared components from multiple sites into a new WebDB site. You can accomplish this easily by creating a export file for the shared components and shared component libraries from each of the parent WebDB sites and then loading these .sql files using SQL*Plus.

WebDB uses a fairly sophisticated scheme to assign a unique ID to all components. There is very little chance that loading more than one shared component library or set of components could create a situation where one component could write over another component. Nonetheless, we recommend extensive testing whenever you combine multiple sites into a single WebDB environment.

Replication

Replication is one of the most powerful features of the Oracle database. Replication is a service that automatically creates and maintains duplicate copies of information stored in one copy of an Oracle database in another copy of an Oracle database.

Because all WebDB components are stored as PL/SQL packages in an Oracle database, you could use the built-in replication features of the Oracle database to create multiple copies of your WebDB system and the data that the system uses.

Initially, this might seem like a dandy idea. You can just instruct the Oracle database to replicate itself and voilá, you have multiple identical WebDB sites. In fact, it does work this way, although the process of planning and implementing replication strategies is certainly not trivial.

However, replication works best in certain situations, such as when a database is primarily used for read-only access. Although Oracle has sophisticated and powerful replication capabilities, some inevitable hurdles are imposed by the limits of physical geography.

Let's say you want to replicate all the data in a database that is consistently being updated. Each individual change in the data has to be replicated to other servers. Even more important, replicated data can be changed in more than one location at the same time. If a value for a specific row in a specific table in Site A is changed, it has to be replicated to Site B. The value in Site B could have been changed in the time that it took to replicate the value from Site A. Replication has to be intelligent enough to know how to handle this situation, which is as complex as any type of concurrency problem, with the added twist of a much longer time delay between a change by one user and the recognition of that change by another database.

Oracle's replication technology can handle this type of situation, but setting up Oracle replication can be a challenging task. Because there are a number of other good ways to replicate a WebDB site without using Oracle's built-in replication capabilities, it may not be worthwhile to use replication for duplicate WebDB sites.

And why would you want to replicate a system in the first place? After all, the Internet is a global phenomenon, and because WebDB is a tool for creating application systems that run over the Internet, why not just let everyone access a server on the Web?

Not every system you create with WebDB will necessarily be open for public use on the Web. Many of the systems you create will be deployed on self-contained intranets. And, you may very well have matching intranets in different physical locations.

If you had a WebDB application system in each location, a user in Location A would not have to hit the server in Location B, which would save network traffic over what could be a long distance and a slow line.

Of course, you will typically create a WebDB application in a single location before copying it to the rest of the sites in your organization. Because it is good practice to create all the components for an application under a single schema name, and because you can export and import schemas fairly easily, requiring replication to copy changes across multiple WebDB servers might be a bit of overkill.

Remember, the PL/SQL packages that make up the components of a WebDB system are probably not going to change that often after they have been created, tested, and deployed.

When a component changes, you should do the following to maintain the compatibility for replicated databases:

- ✦ Make sure the component works by itself.
- ✦ Make sure the component still supports the existing functionality or makes allowances for those features it no longer supports.

✦ Make sure the component still works properly in the context of the overall application.

✦ Explicitly deploy the new version of the component to your multiple WebDB sites. You will not be adding that much to your list of maintenance work.

Most importantly, remember the way that you create components in WebDB. You use the WebDB development environment to assign values to a number of parameters, and then you generate the component. With replication, you will replicate all of the changes to the parameter files that are a part of WebDB, and then replicate the new version of the generated PL/SQL package.

In the light of all this, automatic replication of changes is easier in one sense—you don't have to think about deploying newly modified versions of WebDB components. But overall, reducing the time spent copying your WebDB application system with replication does not significantly reduce the overall cost of implementing changes.

In some ways, in fact, we have found that automatic replication can lead to lax maintenance practices. You should be very conscious about the impact that changing any one component can have on your overall system, so you should always do fairly extensive testing before rolling out a new version of a component in an existing system. Automatic replication through the replication features of your Oracle database can sometimes result in having multiple copies of an incorrect component spread across your system before you know it.

Overall, we do not feel that the replication features of your Oracle database contribute that much to reducing the maintenance overhead for your WebDB application. If you already have replication set up for other purposes, you can hitch a ride by setting up replication for the schema that contains your WebDB application and the schema that contains the WebDB system itself, which is typically a user named WEBDB. If not, it is probably just as easy to use the standard Oracle import and export facilities to move the PL/SQL packages that make up your WebDB application system.

For more information about replication in an Oracle database, please refer to the Oracle documentation.

Wrapping Up

This chapter has given you an understanding of some of the basic administrative tools you can use to manage the components in your WebDB application. You have learned how to use the built-in version control in WebDB and how to import and export individual components and entire application systems.

The next chapter deals with one of the most important aspects of any production system: security.

✦ ✦ ✦

WebDB Security

✦ ✦ ✦ ✦

In This Chapter

✦ ✦ ✦ ✦

Web applications are no different from classic client/server or terminal-based applications when it comes to the need for security. Regardless of how you decide to deploy data to your users, you need to protect unauthorized access to the information in your databases. WebDB has been designed to build off your existing investment in Oracle database security by leveraging the security mechanisms provided by the Oracle database. The database offers a very comprehensive set of security features that enable you to protect your data right at the source. In addition to the standard Oracle security features, the designers of WebDB have provided some additional capabilities that help you deal with the stateless nature of the Internet. The resulting combination is a strong set of features that enable you to protect the data in your database from unauthorized access.

Oracle Security Concepts

Oracle's database security is based on the concept of *user names* and *passwords.* Every Oracle database user is required to provide a user name and password to connect to a database, just like they are required to provide a user name and password to connect to the network. An Oracle user is defined by the user name they are given for accessing the database. Each user name is given an associated password that must be provided whenever the user attempts to connect to the database. The user keeps their password confidential, while the user name is generally visible to other users of the database.

Oracle installations are organized around *instances,* which are equivalent to databases. Oracle uses instances to separate logical installations of the Oracle database. You will often find that development of an application occurs in one instance, but the production version of the application is run in a separate instance. This has the effect of protecting the production data from errors that occur during development. Later on in this book, you will see that the same strategy can be used with WebDB applications as well. User names are defined within Oracle instances and are specific to the instance under which they were created.

Oracle makes use of the user name both as a means of identifying the user to the system as well as organizing the content within the database. Database objects, such as tables, are considered owned by the user name that creates them. In this way, it is relatively easy to locate all of the objects associated with a particular user. For example, when you installed WebDB, you provided the installation program with a user name for WebDB. Oracle used that user name to store all of the tables and procedures for WebDB that were created as part of the installation. This technique makes it easy both to secure access to these objects and move them or back them up as a group.

Objects that one user creates are not normally accessible to other users unless specific access to these objects has been provided by use of the GRANT command. Specific permissions are authorized by *granting* access to a given object. You can GRANT users access to objects and you can GRANT privileges to users. For example, when a new user is created, Oracle grants the CONNECT privilege for the database by default within WebDB. This enables the user to connect to the database using the designated user name and password.

If you have lots of objects and lots of users it can become overly time-consuming to assign GRANTs. Oracle simplifies the process by providing support for *roles.* Oracle roles are abstract users, and you can GRANT privileges to roles just like you can GRANT privileges to users. For example, if you have a group of users that will all use the same set of applications, such as accounting, you can create an accounting role to service them. By granting privileges to the role and then granting the role to the users, you can simplify the process of setting up the accounting group. Any change to the role is cascaded to the users automatically.

Oracle has made the security system available to you directly through SQL, and you can use SQL*Plus to completely manage users and roles. To make the process easier, Oracle also provides the Enterprise Manager tool, which offers a graphical client/server interface for managing users and security.

The designers of WebDB have provided access to a subset of the security features that are available directly with SQL*Plus or Enterprise Manager. If you are familiar with all of the various Oracle security features, you will see that certain options are not provided within the WebDB interface. For example, although Oracle provides for the capability to expire passwords automatically after a certain amount of time, you cannot implement this feature directly within WebDB. However, WebDB provides access to all of the more common security features, and any account created with WebDB can also be managed with SQL*Plus or Enterprise Manager.

Creating Developer Accounts with WebDB

You can create users directly through the WebDB interface as well as grant access to database objects and defining roles. WebDB itself is built from packages and tables in the database and it comes with its own set of privileges and roles, which are used when you create new developers.

You will add two classes of users to the system: application developers and application users. Application developers are the programmers that will create the WebDB applications, which are then deployed to the end users. Application developers can also be identified as a part of subclasses, as you will see in the following sections. Application users are the end users that will use your WebDB applications. There are also likely to be at least several classes of end users. For example, within the Net University system there are Students, Faculty, and Alumni. You will give each of these different types of users access to different objects and allow them different groups of privileges. There is no need to give Students access to Alumni information, nor would you allow Students to have update access to TRANSCRIPT records. WebDB privileges give you the tools to limit access to your data to qualified users.

1. Select the Administer link from the WebDB home page to display the security menu shown in Figure 20-1.

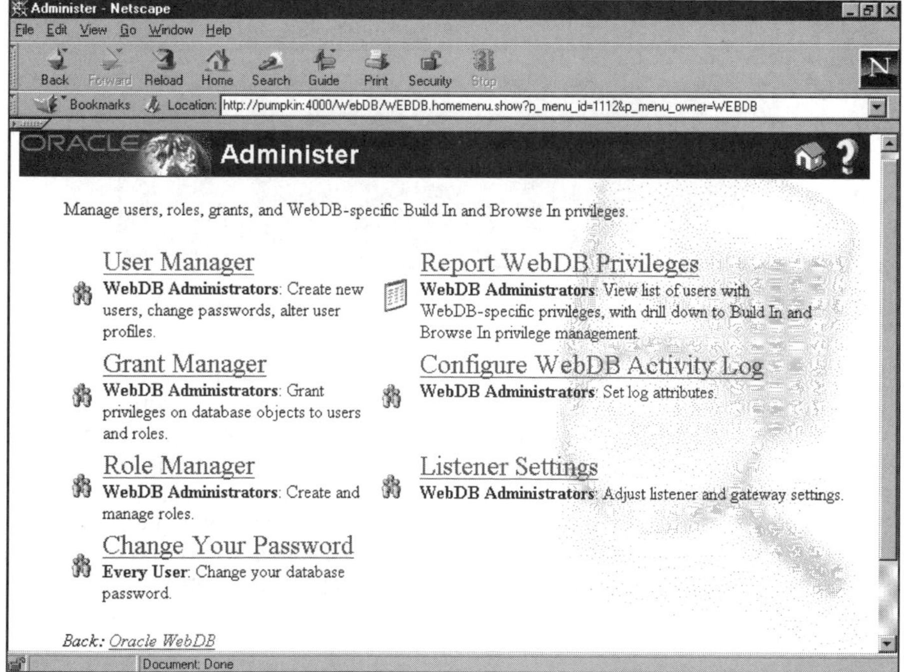

Figure 20-1: Main administration page

The WebDB security system is composed of the following five major functions:

- ✦ User Manager
- ✦ Grant Manager
- ✦ Role Manager
- ✦ Change Your Password
- ✦ Report WebDB Privileges

If you are logged on to WebDB as a nonprivileged user, you will not be able to see any menu choices other than Change Your Password. Be sure to connect to WebDB as the WebDB installation account in order to gain access to the security subsystem.

The first task in implementing a security plan is to define new users to the system using the User Manager. From the User Manager page, you can add new users to the system and provide them with access to the WebDB builders.

1. Select the User Manager link from the main administration page.

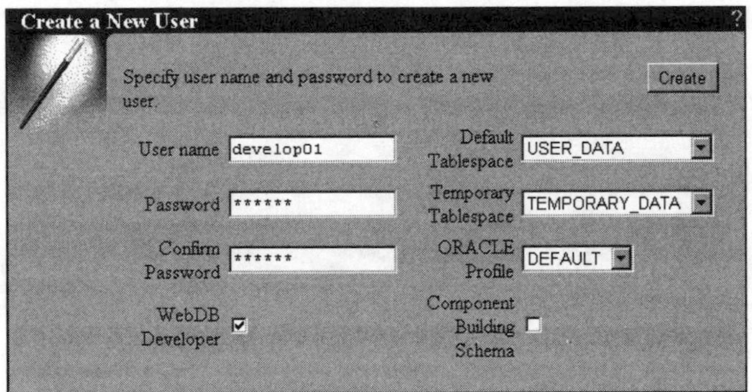

Figure 20-2: User Manager page

The critical panel on this page is the Create a New User panel, as shown in Figure 20-2, which enables you to define the information necessary to add a new user to the system. The key item is the User name field, which maps to a standard Oracle USERID. The User name field is restricted to 30 alphanumeric characters and it must begin with a letter. You are not allowed to use any embedded punctuation other than the underscore (_) character. The User name field permits you to enter both upper- and lowercase characters, but Oracle converts all USERIDs to uppercase when the value is used. Thus, the USERIDs "smith" and "SMITH" are considered identical.

Directly below the User name field is the Password field, which provides the password associated with the user name. The password is implemented as a password-style HTML form text field and the characters you enter into this field are masked by the asterisk character (*). Passwords follow the same length and character restrictions as user names, and you must re-enter the password into the Confirm Password field to ensure that you have entered the password correctly.

2. Enter the name **develop01** as the new user name, and set the password for this new account to **oracle**.

The right-hand side of the top panel is dedicated to determining the *quotas* for the new account. Quotas are limits or assignments to system resources such as disk space and CPU cycles. Oracle enables you to define a series of restrictions to accounts. The first two of these assignments, Default Tablespace and Temporary Tablespace, are typical of all Oracle accounts. Oracle divides the disk space that is allocated to a database instance into groups of logical storage areas called tablespaces. Each tablespace can further be implemented as a series of operating system disk files, making the database a collection of separate physical files. Internally, Oracle provides utilities that can work on tablespaces separately from the entire database. This can make certain operations such as database backup and tuning much simpler. When you create a new account, you must assign the account to several tablespaces. First, you assign a Default Tablespace, which is the disk area that Oracle uses to store any new objects created by the account.

Note

The tablespace assignment is only effective for the creation of new objects such as tables, views, and procedures. If the user enters new records into existing tables, that data will be stored in the tablespace (or tablespaces) in which the table itself was created.

The Default Tablespace field is implemented as a list box built from the system catalogs of the database in which you are running. It is possible that you do not have access to some tablespaces, and these are not displayed in the combo box. During query execution, the database sometimes needs to sort data temporarily in order to return results. Also, sometimes users want to create temporary tables that will be destroyed once they are finished with their current session. Oracle uses the Temporary Tablespace designation for this purpose. In most cases, the database will have a series of temporary tablespaces already defined, and they will be named in a way that indicates they are for temporary operations.

If you do not have tablespaces set up for your WebDB application, create them from outside WebDB using SQL*Plus or Enterprise Manager. WebDB does not provide facilities for creating or modifying tablespaces.

Users have to be assigned to a tablespace even if they are not going to create any objects. All Oracle database instances have at least one temporary tablespace along with the main SYSTEM tablespace, and by default users will be assigned to these two tablespaces, as shown in Figure 20-2.

3. Set the Default Tablespace and the Temporary Tablespace fields to the two tablespace values you created for WebDB during the installation process.

If you have performed a standard installation of an Oracle database, you have created default tablespaces. If the system you are using WebDB on is only a test system, you may want to use the default tablespaces as the values for the Default Tablespace and Temporary Tablespace fields. In any case, it is not a good idea to use the SYSTEM tablespace for any user accounts.

The ORACLE Profile field is a specialized quota setting that applies to other computing resources. Through the Enterprise Manager, you can create profiles that restrict such things as CPU usage, connect time, idle time, and the number of concurrent sessions. WebDB does not allow you to create new profiles, but you can select an Oracle profile for an account from the combo box.

You should assign profiles to WebDB accounts with care because using restrictive profile settings on accounts that work fine in a client/server environment can cause run-time problems for Web users. We recommend that you avoid using profiles until you are very experienced in deploying WebDB applications.

4. Accept the default ORACLE Profile value from the combo box.

The remaining two fields in the top panel are a pair of check boxes labeled WebDB Developer and Component Building Schema. Earlier in this chapter, we introduced you to the concept of roles, which provide a facility for assigning blocks of privileges to a group of users. During the installation process, WebDB creates several roles for working with WebDB. The main role is called WEBDB_DEVELOPER, which gives the user access to the various procedures and tables used within the WebDB development environment. You will learn about several other WebDB-related roles in the following sections, but WEBDB_DEVELOPER is the main role you will use. Normally, roles are added to a user from the Role Manager menu link on the main administration page. The Create a New User panel provides a shortcut for you in the form of the WebDB Developer check box. Selecting this option causes WebDB to add the WEBDB_DEVELOPER role to the new account when it is created.

Schemas used solely to store WebDB components for applications can be marked as such using the Component Building Schema check box. Oracle stored procedures, which form the backbone of WebDB, only inherit the privileges that have been explicitly granted to the account that owns them. This means that you have to grant explicit privileges (as opposed to roles) to any account that owns WebDB procedures. The developers of WebDB recommend that you store all of your WebDB components for a logical application into a single database schema to simplify the security process. You can tell WebDB that a particular account is being used for such a purpose by enabling the Component Building Schema check box.

5. Select the WebDB Developer check box.

There are two additional panels on the User Manager page: the Find panel and the Select panel. You can use the Find panel to search for a specified Oracle USERID using a pop-up panel. This panel searches the current Oracle instance for all user names, and it will even locate users that were not defined as part of WebDB. In fact, the users that you add to the system through WebDB act just like normal Oracle users that have been added through SQL*Plus or Enterprise Manager. Their only distinguishing characteristics are the WebDB-specific roles that may have been added to the USERID. The bottom panel lists the recently created users, and you can select names from this list to edit as needed. The data is sorted by the date the USERID was added to the system, and you may find that externally created accounts appear at the top of the list. This is especially true if you are adding information to an instance actively managed by other applications such as Enterprise Manager.

6. Click the Create button in the upper-right corner to store the new user.

Once you have saved the new user record, WebDB redisplays the account information along with a series of panels for modifying additional attributes of the new account, as shown in Figure 20-3. Because it is likely that you will want to modify certain aspects of the new account right away, WebDB's default behavior is to display the additional option tabs directly after you create an account. For the purposes of this example, however, it is easier to understand how these advanced privileges work by starting out with the default settings.

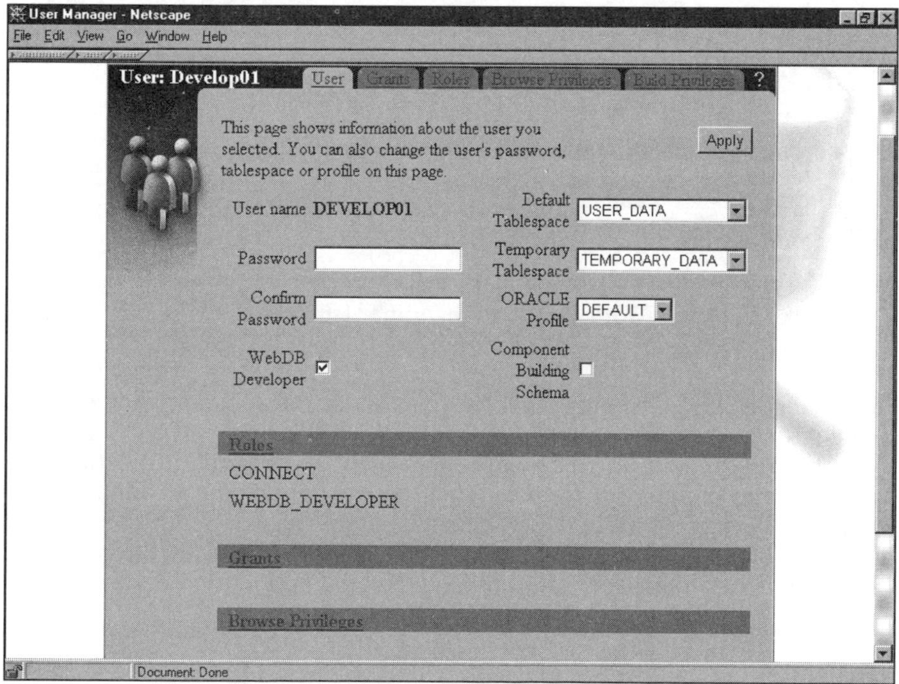

Figure 20-3: User Manager panel after creating a new account

Testing the default developer account settings

The default settings for a new account provide for the minimal amount of WebDB security authority. WebDB's strategy is to limit the capabilities of an account unless you *explicitly* request that additional privileges be assigned to the account.

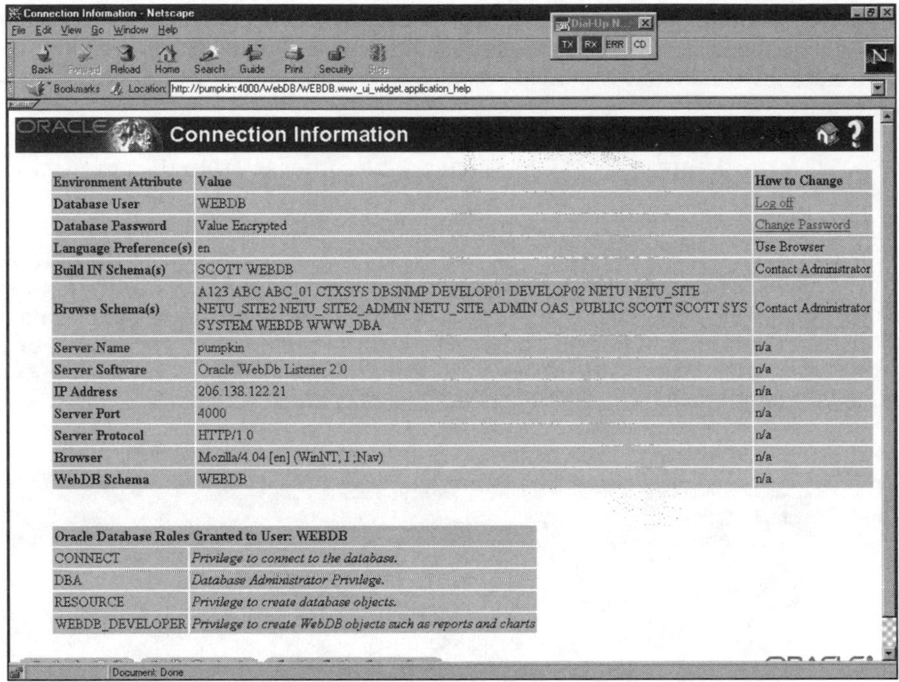

Figure 20-4: Connection Information page

1. Click the Oracle World image in the upper-left corner of the current page to display the Connection Information page shown in Figure 20-4.

This panel displays the connection information for the account you are using to connect to the database from within WebDB. Up until this point, you have been using the WebDB installation account exclusively. The default installation provides for a high level of authority for the WebDB account, including an additional set of Database Roles as shown in the lower table on this page. In order to see the effect of having limited development privileges, you need to disconnect from Oracle and then reconnect using the new account you created in the previous section.

2. Use the Log off link in the upper-right corner of the page to disconnect from Oracle.

3. Once the deauthentication page appears, use the Back button on your browser to navigate back to the Connection Information page.
4. Use the Application Home icon in the upper-right corner to return to the WebDB home page.
5. Use the OK button to respond to the Authorization Failed message and attempt to reconnect to Oracle. WebDB displays the panel shown in Figure 20-5.

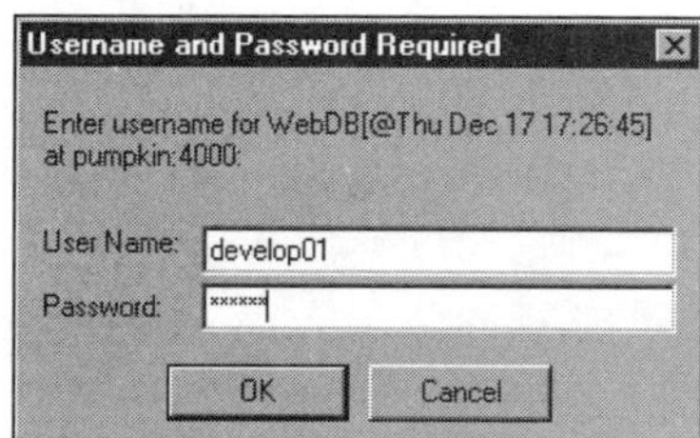

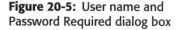

Figure 20-5: User name and Password Required dialog box

Because you have logged off the system, WebDB displays a dialog box that enables you reconnect to the database.

6. Enter the **develop01/oracle** user name and password to connect to the Oracle database.
7. Choose the Administer link on the main page to return to the administration page, as shown in Figure 20-6.

When you connect as the develop01 user, you will notice that the range of options at your disposal is limited. You are no longer able to create new accounts, assign roles, change listener settings, or grant access to database tables. WebDB reads the capabilities of the account that you used to log on to the database when it executes the procedure that builds the generated page for you. Because the account you created lacks certain privileges, WebDB removes these privileges from the display. You can add these additional authorizations to the develop01 account using the Roles and Grants tabs in the User Manager.

1. Use the Oracle World image to return to the Connection Information page and click the Log off link once again.
2. Navigate back to the User Manager page and reconnect using the webdb/webdb account.
3. Select the develop01 account from the Select Recently Created Users panel.

Once you have connected to Oracle with sufficient authority, you can add capabilities to the develop01 account.

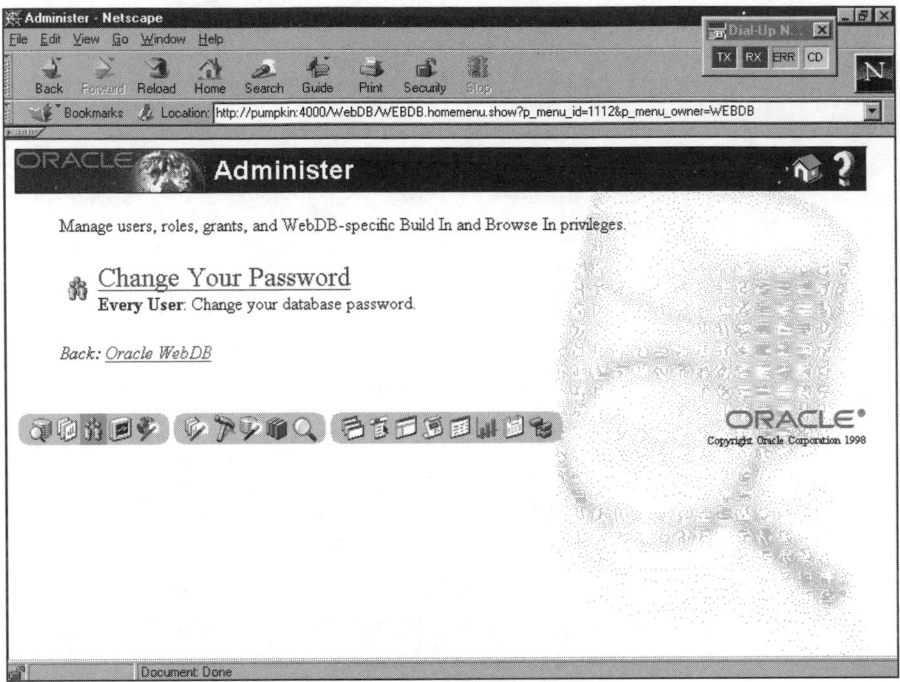

Figure 20-6: Modified administration page

Modifying account privilege settings

After you create a new account, or when you choose to modify an existing account, WebDB displays the additional information shown in the Figure 20-3.

This is the same panel that displays additional account information using a series of links and panels. The five classes of information you can change about a user are as follows:

- ✦ User Information
- ✦ Roles
- ✦ Grants
- ✦ Browse Privileges
- ✦ Build Privileges

The User Information consists of the basic USERID, password, and tablespace settings you used when the user account was created. You may have to change the default tablespace and temporary tablespace for an account using this panel. Users are provided with a separate panel for changing their passwords, but you are also allowed to modify their passwords for them from this panel.

The remaining four items on the current panel are cross-linked so that you can access them either by using the links on the body of the panel or the tabs at the top of the panel. The first item below User Information is Roles, which is associated with the user account. Roles are groups of security capabilities that are assigned to a user account and permit the user to have some additional authority within the database. Under the role section for DEVELOP01 there are two roles defined: CONNECT and WEBDB_DEVELOPER. The CONNECT role is an Oracle default role, and it defines the set of system privileges required to connect to the Oracle database and create basic objects within the assigned tablespace. The WEBDB_DEVELOPER role is created by the system when WebDB is installed. Unlike the CONNECT role, the WEBDB_DEVELOPER role does not provide access to any specific system privileges. This role is only used to control access to various object builders within WebDB. Each of the WebDB wizards checks to see that the defined user has access to the WEBDB_DEVELOPER role before proceeding. A user who lacks the WEBDB_DEVELOPER role can connect to the various builders within WebDB, but they cannot build or modify objects. In this example case, the role setting prevented the develop01 account from accessing the advanced administration objects. Specifically, the develop01 account requires the DBA role to be assigned to it in order for it to gain access to the advanced settings.

4. Use the Roles link on the body of the page or in the tab panel to navigate to the Roles page (shown in Figure 20-7).

WebDB provides the Roles tab to connect accounts to Oracle database roles and privileges. You can use the Search icon to the right of the Role field to search for defined roles and you can use the Add button to add the selected role to the specified account.

5. Use the Search icon to display a pop-up window of roles.

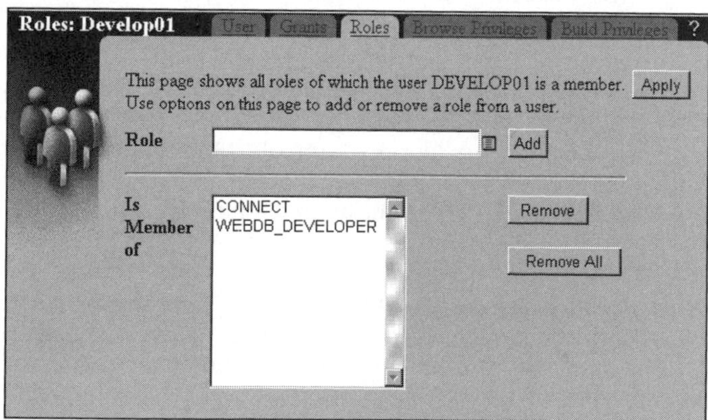

Figure 20-7: User Manager roles

Although Oracle describes the generic category as roles, you will find that the search window displays two types of items in the list: roles and privileges. Each item has the type listed in parentheses next to the name of the role, as shown in Figure 20-8.

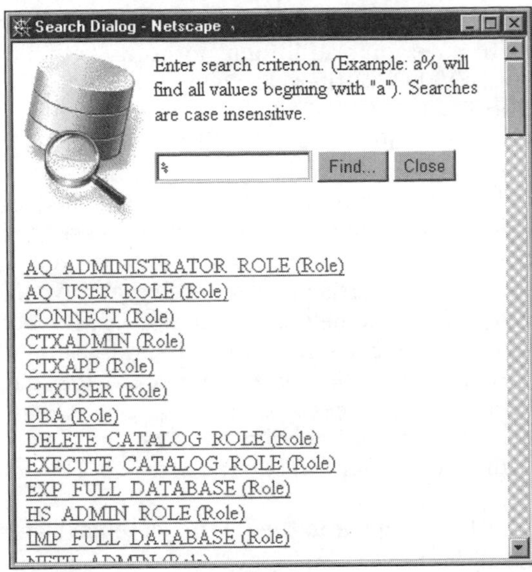

Figure 20-8: Roles and privileges

Certain logical functions within the Oracle database require multiple system privileges, so Oracle has grouped these privileges into a role. The DBA role, for example, has over 90 individual permissions associated with it. In order to simplify the assignment process, the DBA role has been defined, which includes all of the necessary privileges. Therefore, instead of having to assign all 90 privileges to each and every account acting as a DBA, you can simply assign the DBA role to those accounts.

You may need to assign an individual privilege to a user without giving that user access to any other privileges. Oracle offers over 90 different individual system privileges that provide access to specific features of the database instance. WebDB's role pop-up list shows both types of privileges, and you can choose either a particular individual privilege or role simply by clicking the associated link in the pop-up panel.

Providing a user with excessive privileges can have dire consequences for the security of your data. We strongly recommend against giving unnecessary authorizations to users, and also recommend against granting any privilege if you are unsure of its capabilities.

6. Select the DBA role from the pop-up list and return to the User Manager page.
7. Use the Add button to add the new role to this list of roles for develop01.

You can remove privileges by using the Remove and Remove All buttons in the body of the page. There are cases where you may need to temporarily add privileges to an account, such as assigning a temporary DBA, and you can remove these privileges when they are no longer needed through this panel. The Apply button saves the changes to the database, and WebDB refreshes the HTML page after the Apply operation completes.

8. Use the Apply button to save the changes for develop01.

You may find that you have the authority to view the list of roles and privileges, but you may lack the ability to grant them to other users. Oracle refers to the ability to grant authority by the term *Admin Option,* and not all authorizations carry this option by default. WebDB does not display privileges that you cannot grant in the pop-up window. The list of privileges is determined by the USERID that you are logged in under when you use the Roles page.

WebDB itself provides one specific role called WEBDB_DEVELOPER, which provides access to the various build wizards such as forms, reports, charts, calendars, and hierarchies. Any account used to develop WebDB objects needs this privilege. This is the only privilege that is specific to the component builders within WebDB. However, in order to gain access to the Site Builder Wizard, you must log on to WebDB using an account that has the Oracle DBA privilege.

Oracle has some default cross-referencing of privileges and roles that is not always intuitive to the user. Certain roles, such as the DBA role, automatically cause additional, unspecified roles and privileges to be assigned. In the case of the DBA role, for example, Oracle grants the associated UNLIMITED TABLESPACE privilege automatically. WebDB accounts for this in the display.

Object privileges

The authorities granted by using the Roles page are considered to be *system* privileges, because they apply to the Oracle system as a whole. It is also possible to define individual permissions that apply to complete schemas as well as to individual objects.

1. Use the Browse Privileges tab to navigate to the Browse Privileges panel shown in Figure 20-9.

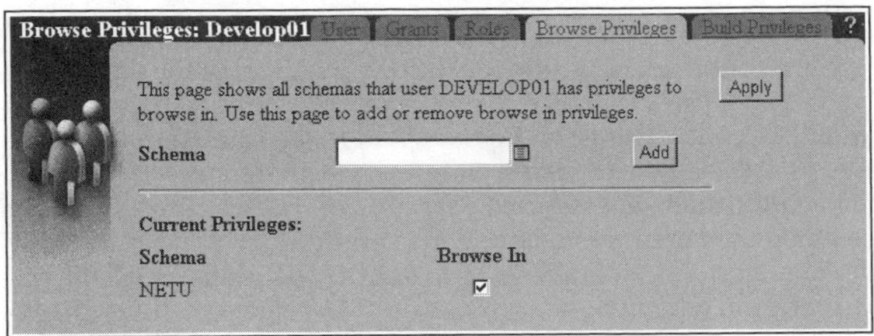

Figure 20-9: Browse Privileges panel

Oracle organizes database content according to USERIDs, and database objects created by a particular USERID are considered to be part of that USERID's schema. Many Oracle sites have taken advantage of this concept by creating applications inside of a single account without allowing individuals to log on to the account directly. For example, when you installed the Net University database, you were instructed to create a NETU USERID to hold the objects and the data. However, you have not specifically logged on to Oracle using the NETU account since the schema was created. This is a very common development strategy for Oracle installations. In any event, you would not want all of your users logging on to the database using the same USERID and password combination. This would make it almost impossible to track individual usage, and it would make it impossible to set individual permissions.

Conversely, if you provide every user with a unique logon, or groups of users with a specific logon, they will not be able by default to access the schema where the actual objects and data are stored. The solution to this problem is known in the Oracle world as *object* privileges. Object privileges are authorities granted for tables, views, procedures, and all other database objects. WebDB provides you with two mechanisms for assigning object privileges — one aimed at developers and one aimed at end users.

For developers, WebDB provides the Build Privileges page. There are two panels for granting privileges: the Browse panel and the Build panel. The Browse panel is shown in Figure 20-9. User accounts must be granted browse access to a schema in order view tables and objects in that schema. If the developer needs to create objects in a given schema, then they must be granted Build privileges, as shown in Figure 20-10. Developers are more likely to need access to the complete schema, and therefore it makes sense to provide access to all of the objects at once. You can use the Search icon to display a pop-up panel of USERIDs (schemas), and you can choose an individual schema by selecting the link on the pop-up panel. As with the Roles page, the Add button is used to add the selected schema to the Current Privileges list at the bottom of the panel. Once you have granted browse access to a particular account, then the account appears in the list box on the Build Privileges panel, as shown in Figure 20-10. In most cases, you will want to provide browse and build access to your developers in any schema in which they will be working.

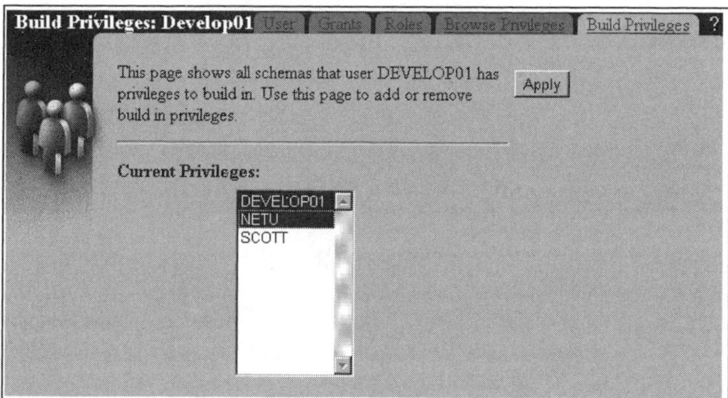

Figure 20-10: Build Privileges panel

2. Use the Search icon to find the NETU account and use the Add button to add it to the list of accounts that develop01 has access to.
3. Save the changes using the Apply button.
4. Navigate to the Build Privileges panel and highlight the DEVELOP01 USERID and the NETU USERID with your mouse. Use the Apply button to save this change. (This grants build access to the DEVELOP01 account.)

Although you will want to enable your WebDB developers to have read/write access to the entire schema in which they are developing, this will not be the default behavior for end users. You will typically want to assign very specific access to individual tables, views, and procedures to end users. Within WebDB, Oracle permits you to add *object* privileges to specified roles. For example, you could create an end-user role and assign specific table, column, and view permissions to that role. You will learn more about this in second part of this chapter on end-user security.

Although you can assign object privileges to roles, Oracle requires the USERID that owns the procedure to have direct object privileges to the underlying data. From WebDB's perspective, this means that you need to provide the USERID owner of your WebDB application with *specific* object privileges against the underlying database tables and views in the USERID, which owns these base tables. Stored procedures cannot use privileges that have been granted by ROLES. Therefore, you must grant explicit privileges to the USERID accessing the data. If you create all of your WebDB components for a given application within a single Component Building Schema, this makes the process of deploying privileges much simpler.

WebDB grants

WebDB defines individual object permissions as *grants*. These grants are accessible from the Grants tab on the User Manager menu.

1. Use the Grants tab to navigate to the Grants panel for the user `develop01`. WebDB uses Grants to authorize access to specific tables, views, and procedures, as shown in Figure 20-11.

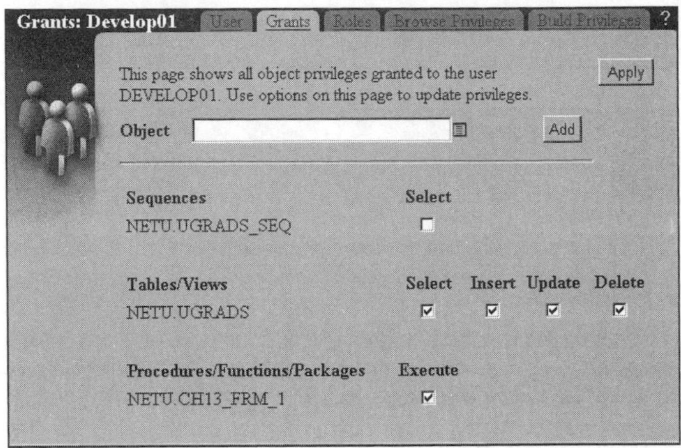

Figure 20-11: User grants

The Object field and the associated Search icon enable you to search for a list of objects on which you want to assign privileges. The list of objects that appears in the search list is based upon the objects that you have access to and the level of system privileges on your account. In general, you need to have access to an account with DBA privileges in order to use this panel to GRANT object access to other users. The functionality of this panel is duplicated on the Privileges link on the Manage Component panel, which you are more likely to use to set permissions on individual components. The Grants page within the User Manager is more suited to permitting access to multiple objects at one time for a single user.

As with the Roles panel, the Add button copies the selected object name from the Object field to the permissions panel. Once you have added the object, it appears in one of three different sections as a sequence, a table/view, or as a procedure. Tables and views are complicated. You can provide individual permission to use any of the four basic access methods for data: select, insert, update, and delete. Because WebDB browses the database through components, granting a user with a Browse privilege gives them read and write access to data. Keep this in mind when you grant the Browse privilege to end users. Once you have set permissions on the tables and views, you can safely permit access to them from within WebDB. You will learn more about deploying the browse functions directly to end users in Chapter 22. Figure 20-11 shows the Grants page as it would look had you selected several objects from the search window and used the Add button. It is not possible to select multiple objects at the same time with the search window, but you can use the Search and Add buttons repeatedly before saving your changes.

WebDB provides a simpler and faster interface for setting object grants from the main Administration menu.

2. The `develop01` account has DBA privileges and thus does not require any direct object settings. Use the Administer Users link on the menu panel to return to the main administration page.
3. Select the Grant Manager link to continue.

WebDB provides a search window that enables you to select objects by user, object type, and name. This search panel matches the main panel of the database object browse wizard, and it enables you to start assigning permissions by choosing objects, as shown in Figure 20-12.

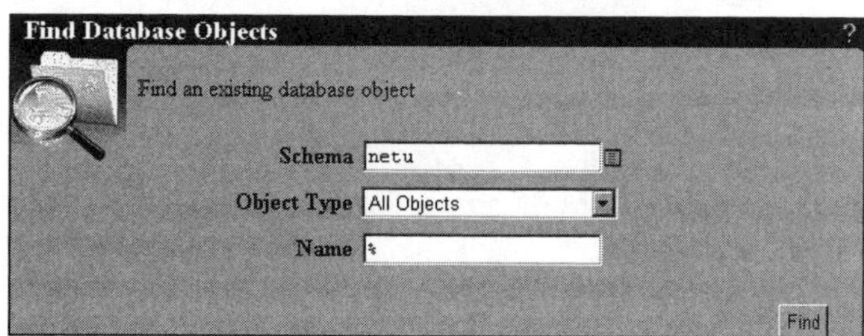

Figure 20-12: Find Database Objects page

Once you have entered some search criteria, WebDB creates pages of object names and object type icons that match the secondary browse windows, as shown in Figure 20-13.

You can choose an object to edit simply by selecting the name of the object, which is displayed as a link. Once you have selected an object, WebDB displays an alternate Grant panel, as shown in Figure 20-14.

This panel is slightly different from the Grant panel for individual users in that it enables you to select roles as well as individual users. If you have a large number of users that will all have a similar set of permissions, you can assign object privileges to a role rather than to an individual account. If you later need to add some additional object privileges, you can make the change at the role level rather than for each of the individual accounts.

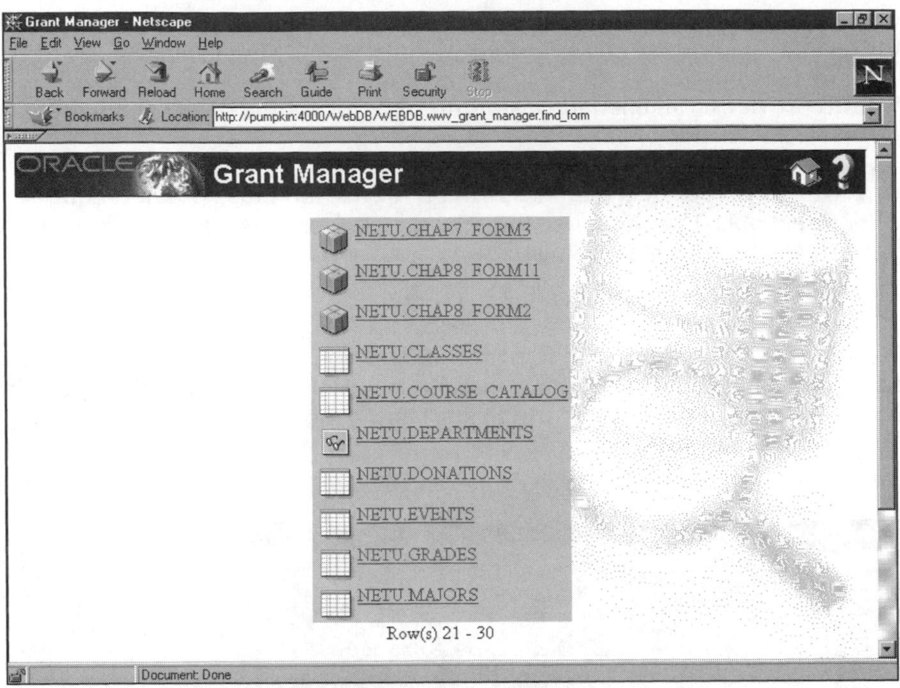

Figure 20-13: Browse list for NETU

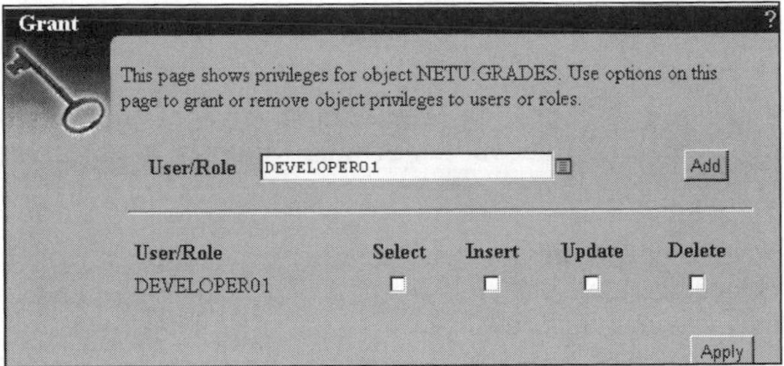

Figure 20-14: User and role Grant panel

In general, you will not need to set many individual permissions for development accounts, such as the develop01 user you created earlier. Developers are usually allowed a higher level of authority than end users. Although developers are generally given privileged accounts, it still makes sense for you to create separate accounts for each of your developers. WebDB automatically stores account information within its data dictionary whenever objects are created and modified. In addition, the performance tracking features of WebDB automatically track usage and performance statistics by user. If you require that each of your developers have their own unique Oracle account, you are better able to keep track of just what they are doing on a daily basis.

WebDB is a tool designed for power users as much as it is designed for professional developers. There may be times when you want to create pseudo-developer accounts and allow them access to the various tables and build wizards. However, these same accounts may lack the permission to add new accounts or to change system settings.

Creating Permissions for End-User Accounts

Security configurations for end-user accounts generally require more individualized settings, because you do not give them free reign to access all of the data in your database. WebDB makes the overall process easier because you can restrict access to the database completely and only allow users to view data using the components you build with the WebDB wizard.

End-user security is a combination of the following five separate components:

- User Account
- Role Assignments
- Procedure Permissions
- Table/View Permissions
- Data Access Descriptors

The basis of all the other security settings is the database's user accounts. Without a valid account, individual users are unable to connect to the database. (Another option here is to grant the components in your application to PUBLIC. This eliminates the need for individual user accounts altogether because you can set up a data access descriptor with a public user account.)

All WebDB users must have an account, even if you designate a single account for many users. You can assign each account in turn to any number of logical roles. WebDB comes equipped with one role for developers, but you are free to add your own roles for the applications you create. For example, in the Net University system, you would likely set up four different roles for UGRADS, ALUMNI, FACULTY, and ADMINISTRATION. As the application grows, you may need to add specialized roles for subgroups within each major role. The ADMINISTRATION department might be further broken down into ACCOUNTING, LEGAL, and MAINTENANCE, for example. A single user account can be part of multiple roles, and roles are a superior technique for assigning privileges to users. For example, the NETU system has 1,000 Alumni users. If you were to assign *object* privileges for each and every individual, you would have a full-time job just setting up security.

A better solution is to create a role and assign object privileges to the role. When new objects are created, you can then provide access to them by assigning permissions to the role rather than to the individual user accounts.

Object permissions for end users come in two basic flavors. Because all the WebDB components that you build are ultimately turned into database procedures, the main object permission you need to set is *procedure* security. Procedures have only a single security setting, namely, the EXECUTE privilege.

Let's say that you create a report called ALUMNI_RECORDS. Once the report has been built, WebDB generates a procedure called `ALUMNI_RECORDS.SHOW` for the report. If you want to enable end users to run the report, you must enable EXECUTE permission on the database procedure. You can assign this privilege in one of three ways. First, you can assign the EXECUTE privilege to an individual user account. Second, you can assign the privilege to a role you create and then assign users to that role. And last, but not least, you can make the report available to all users by assigning EXECUTE privilege to PUBLIC. By definition, all Oracle user accounts are assigned to PUBLIC.

The last item of concern in developing a security framework for end users is the Data Access Descriptors (DADs) used for connecting WebDB to the database. DADs are actually part of the deployment scheme for WebDB and Chapter 22 discusses them in detail. Thus far, you have used a single DAD to work with WebDB, but this will change as you begin to deploy applications. (In fact, you worked with multiple DADs within Site Builder in Chapter 18, although you were probably not aware of it.) DADs direct WebDB to request new logins to the database and you can mix and match DADs to enforce multiple levels of security within a single application.

Creating end-user accounts and defining roles

Within WebDB it is much more common for end users to be given GRANT access to procedures rather than explicit GRANTs to objects. After all, WebDB uses procedures to build components and the procedures inherit the explicit grants of the procedure owner. However, you can grant privileges directly to end-user accounts through WebDB. In fact, if you explicitly grant object privileges to your component building schemas, you will use the same process as you would for end-user accounts — or developer accounts, for that matter.

1. Navigate to the User Manager from the Administration menu and add two new users as follows:

   a. User name: `LAURENCE1`
      Password: `ORACLE`
      Default Tablespace: `WebDB`
      Temporary Tablespace: `Temporary`

b. User name: DEBORAH2
   Password: ORACLE
   Default Tablespace: WebDB
   Temporary Tablespace: Temporary

2. Return to the main administration menu shown in Figure 20-15.

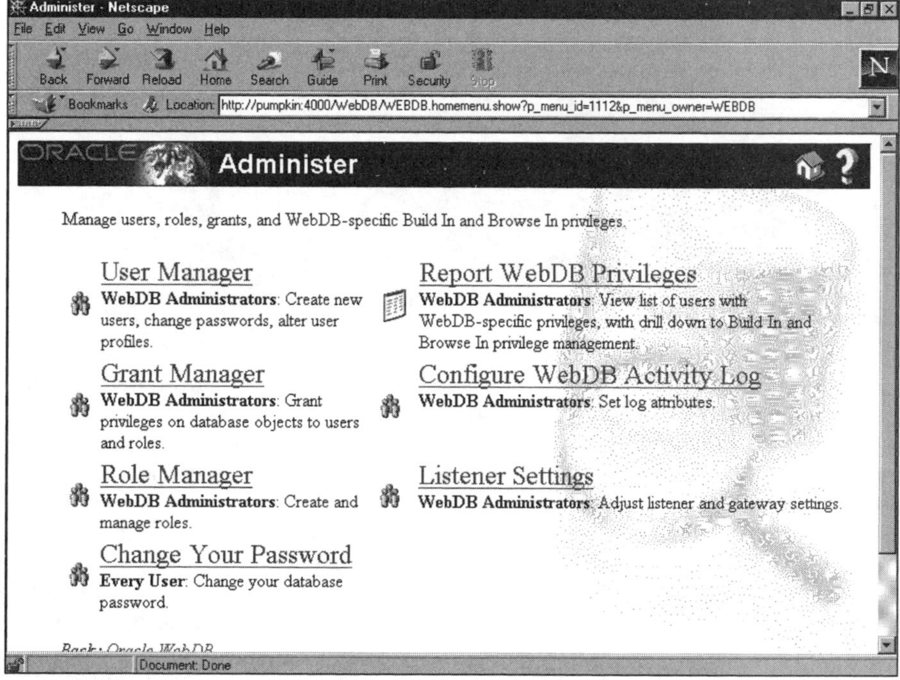

Figure 20-15: Main administration menu

Thus far, our concentration has been on the User Manager interface, which is used to add individual users to the system. Although you can add users to roles and provide GRANTs for users from this interface, it is faster and easier to use the Role Manager link and the Grant Manager link from the main administration panel to assign group security.

3. Use the Role Manager link to invoke the main Role Manager menu.

The main Role Manager menu is a simple three-panel page. The topmost panel provides a single role field that enables you to enter a role name. Roles follow the same rules for characters and lengths as individual user names and passwords. Once you have entered a role name, you can create the role using the Create button. The Find panel provides an interface for searching for existing roles within the current Oracle instance. Recently created roles are displayed in the bottom panel, and you can edit these roles by selecting their link name.

4. Enter the Role name **alumni** and click the Create button to proceed. WebDB displays a form similar to the one shown in Figure 20-16.

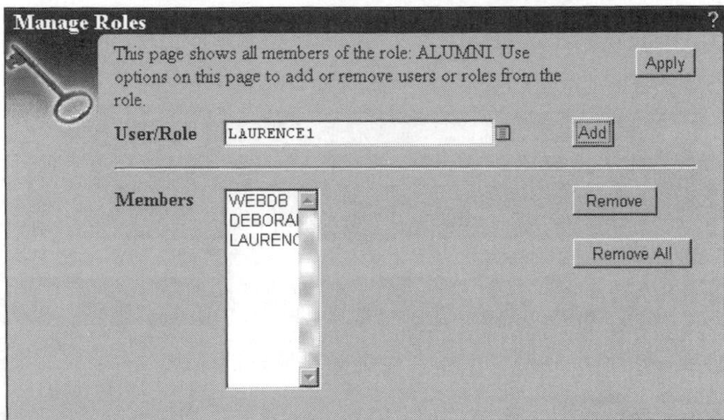

Figure 20-16: Role Manager member entry

Once you have created a role, the remaining task is to add user accounts to the role. Use the User/Role text field to enter account names, and the Search icon to the right of the field to find accounts using the familiar pop-up window. After you have selected an account record, you can use the Add button to insert the account name into the Members list box in the lower half of the panel. Conversely, you can select an entry in the Members list and use the Remove button to eliminate the account from the role. The Remove All button eliminates all of the accounts currently displayed in the Members list from the role. When you have completed your changes, use the Apply button to save the changes back to the database.

5. Use the Search icon to locate the DEBORAH2 user name and add it to the Members list.
6. Use the Search icon to locate the LAURENCE1 user name and add it to the Members list.
7. Save the changes by clicking the Apply button.
8. Return to the main administration panel.

Once you have attached a user name to a role, the only remaining requirements are to enable GRANTS on objects *directly* to the individual accounts, or *indirectly* through the role that you just created.

Granting users access to tables and views

When you attach users to a role, you are grouping users into categories that can then be managed as a group. In some cases, roles themselves confer privileges to users directly, such as when you assign the DBA role to a user. In other cases, the setting of the role merely creates the logical grouping, without enabling any privileges or access. For example, the ALUMNI role, which you created in the previous section, serves only to group users together and it does not in and of itself confer any privileges to individual users.

The next step in the grants process is to give base object access to individual accounts or roles using the Grant Manager. Base objects are the tables and views on which the various components are constructed. You can find the Grant Manager on the main administration menu, or on the Grants tab within the User Manager.

1. Select the Grant Manager link from the main administration menu. The main Grant Manager page is composed of two panels, as shown in Figure 20-17.

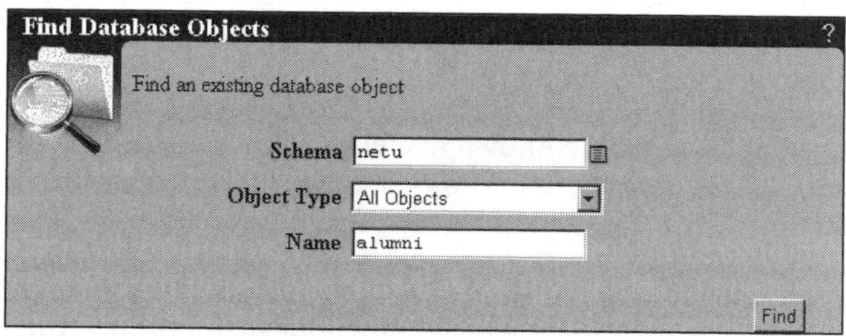

Figure 20-17: Grant Manager

The Grants tab on the User Manager is focused toward enabling grants for a specific user to a selected set of objects. In fact, the Grant Manager section of the User Manager is actually built from three separate tabs, the Browse Privileges tab, the Build Privileges tab, and the Grants tab. However, the focus of the main Grant Manager link on the administration menu is to drive permissions from objects down to users and roles. The lower panel lists recently created objects and the upper panel provides an object search window, much like you would find within the browse database wizard.

In Figure 20-17, you can see that the Find panel is composed of three fields: Schema, Object Type, and Name. The Schema field refers to the Oracle account that owns the object on which you wish to set permissions. During the installation of the Net University database, the NETU account was created, and it serves as the schema for the database objects. (It also serves as the component building schema for your WebDB application.) This is a very common deployment strategy for Oracle applications, and in many cases, you will find that a single schema owns the tables and views that comprise your applications. The Schema field offers a Search icon, so you can search for Oracle accounts from a pop-up list of values. In the example case, the NETU account owns all of the objects. It is possible that you will create WebDB applications in a separate schema from the schema in which your data is stored. In this case, you need to provide access to *both* schemas with object privileges. However, the standard strategy for WebDB applications is to grant object privileges to the component building schema and execute privileges on your procedures to your end-user accounts. For example, you might create a WebDB report in the NETU component building schema called netu_report. You could grant access to the tables used by the report to the NETU account and you could grant EXECUTE privilege on the procedure netu.netu_report to your end users.

Note WebDB will not display objects to which you do not have access when you conduct your search. You should use a DBA-enabled account when you build your permissions settings in order ensure access to the necessary database objects.

Just below the schema field is the Object Type field, which enables you to limit your search for objects to items of a specific type. This is a useful feature if you have schemas filled with objects. If you already know the name of the specific object you want to work with, you are free to enter the complete name or a partial name for the item in the Name text box. Once you have entered your criteria, it is a simple matter to use the Find button to search for objects that match your requirements.

2. Enter the search information shown in Figure 20-17, and use the Find button to continue. You are searching for objects that are owned by the netu account and whose object name is alumni (for the ALUMNI table).

Upon successfully entering search criteria, WebDB builds a results panel, as shown in Figure 20-18. WebDB uses its own internal procedures to produce the results as a series of HTML pages. The entries are displayed in alphabetical order by name, and the number of output pages depends upon the number of matching components that WebDB finds for the search criteria that you specified.

The GRANTs result pages make use of the same icons used by the browse database function. Although only the names of the matching objects are displayed in the results panel, you can determine the object type by looking at the icon to the left of the link name. Selecting a particular object is as simple as clicking the link name.

3. Click the NETU.ALUMNI link to display the details for the table object, as shown in Figure 20-19.

The Grant Manager page works almost identically to the Grants tab in the User Manager. The User/Role text field enables you to input user names or roles, and you can search for matching users and roles using the Search icon to the right of the text field. Although the text field does not provide any indicator variables to differentiate between a role and a user name, the search panel results page appends the word "role" in parentheses after every matching role.

Note Oracle treats role names as user names for the purpose of uniqueness, and it prevents you from creating a user name using the same name as a role and vice versa. Therefore, you cannot inadvertently use a role in place of a user name.

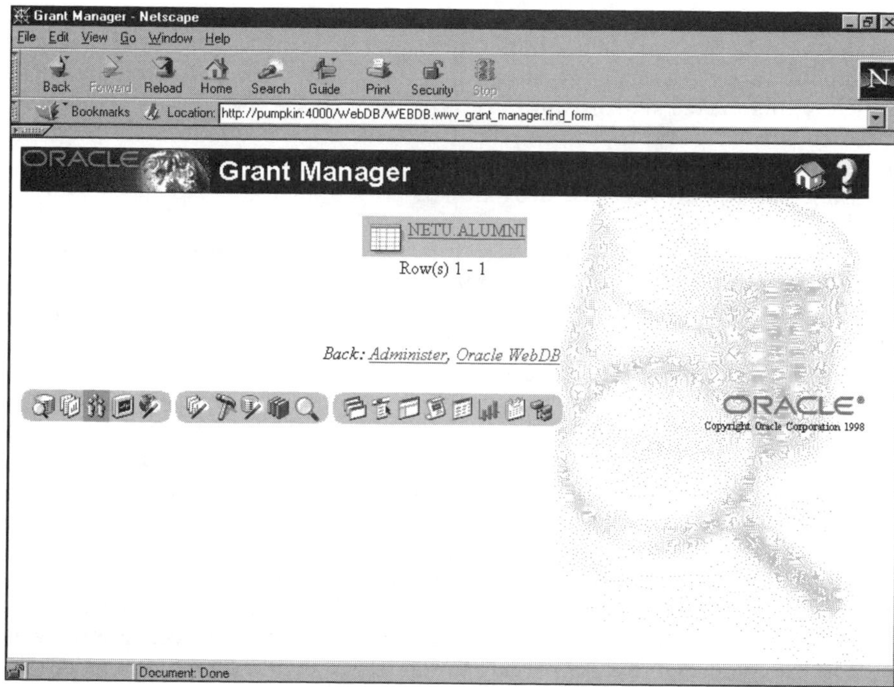

Figure 20-18: Grant search results

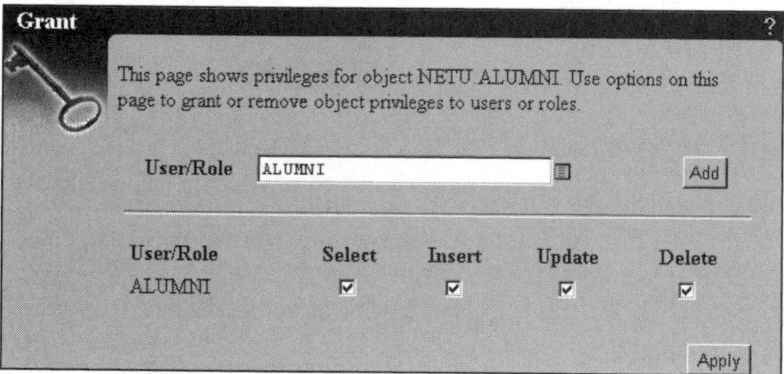

Figure 20-19: Grant Manager page

As with the other security panels, you can use the Add button to add the entry to the bottom half of the panel. Once you use the Add button, WebDB builds a set of security check boxes that match the object type you selected on the preceding panel. For stored procedures or WebDB components, the only setting is Execute, but tables and views have four possible values: Select, Insert, Update, and Delete. By enabling Execute on a procedure for a user or a role, you are permitting any operations that the procedure itself permits. Even if you explicitly prevent a user or role from updating a particular table, the user/role is still allowed to update the designated table through a procedure that they have been given execute access to. Logically this makes sense, especially if the table has some very explicit data integrity checking that is performed in the body of the procedure. Denying direct access to the table forces users to channel all updates through the procedure, thus ensuring that the proper rules are followed.

You may wish to build this type of security into your database if you have very sensitive data that is restricted on a record-by-record database. For example, you could build a procedure that returns the DONATIONS records for a given alumni record by the alumni ID number. You could then prevent direct read access on the DONATIONS table to ALUMNI users (or the ALUMNI role), thereby forcing read operations to use the procedure. This would ensure that the select rules embedded in the procedure would only return the proper records. It is possible to enforce a similar rule using views, as you will see in the next section. As with the other security panels, you are required to click the Apply button to save your changes to the database.

Oracle does not automatically use a procedure when a user lacks permission to access the table. You are still required to build the procedure and then build forms and reports that make use of the procedure. By eliminating direct access to the table or view, you are merely preventing any undesired ad-hoc access from occurring.

4. Use the Search icon to locate the ALUMNI role.
5. Using the Add button, add ALUMNI to the list of those accounts/roles that are permitted access to the ALUMNI table.
6. Check all four privileges: Select, Insert, Update, and Delete.
7. Save your changes using the Apply button.

If you are making several GRANT changes at once, you can use the BACK button on your browser to move back to the results list once you have saved your changes on the Grant Manager page. You are then free to select a new object and move directly to the Grant Manager page without having to requery the database.

Adding security settings to WebDB objects

Once you have created a set of user accounts and roles, you can begin adding them to the security list for objects.

1. Import the following components: ch20_qbe_ugrads, ch20_qbe_alumni, ch20_rep_alumni, and ch20_mnu_college.

You can set object level security through the administration menu as well as directly from the Manage Component panel within each of the builders. WebDB objects are nothing more than PL/SQL procedures, so the process of setting security on them is as simple as permitting or denying Execute permission on the procedure. The default behavior is to deny access to a given procedure. If you build an object and do not provide any security settings for it, then only accounts with the DBA role or the system privilege EXECUTE ANY PROCEDURE are able to run the component.

WebDB does not copy security settings along with the object when it is exported and imported. You need to rebuild any security settings if you import an object. The exception to this rule is menus, as WebDB will export and import security settings embedded *within* menu objects.

You can set security on any of the wizard-based components that you build with WebDB and on database objects, such as tables or views, but you cannot set individual security on shared components. The designers of WebDB created shared objects to allow code reuse within the other builders. If you wish to prevent access to these objects, you are expected to do so on a case-by-case basis inside the components in which they are deployed. For example, if you create a List-of-Values object that shows the list of RESTRICT codes for DONATIONS, you cannot provide a security setting for it. Rather, you would set security on the Form, Report, Calendar, Hierarchy, or Chart in which the LOV is used.

Although you can set security for an object from either the User Manager or the Grant Manager as discussed in the preceding sections, you may find that the easiest place to set permissions is from the Manage Component page. Each of the component builder wizards provides a Manage Component page, as you have seen in the various chapters on the build wizards themselves. On the Manage Component page, you will find a Privileges link that connects the component directly to the Grant Manager.

2. Navigate to the Manage Component page for the ch20_qbe_alumni form you recently imported and select the Privileges link to display the page, as shown in Figure 20-20.

The Grant panel from the Privileges link is automatically filled with the schema owner and the object name, as shown in Figure 20-20. The text for the schema owner and component are shown as text instead of as form fields because you are not permitted to change these settings on this panel. The User/Role text field matches the User/Role field on the Grant Manager page in the previous section. You can enter the name of the user or the role directly into the text box, or you can use the search function to find the user/role you wish to add. On this page, the Add button has been renamed Grant Execute Privilege to better reflect the functionality of the button. By definition, any component you access on this page will be a stored procedure, so the only setting you can make is to allow a user/role the ability to execute the procedure.

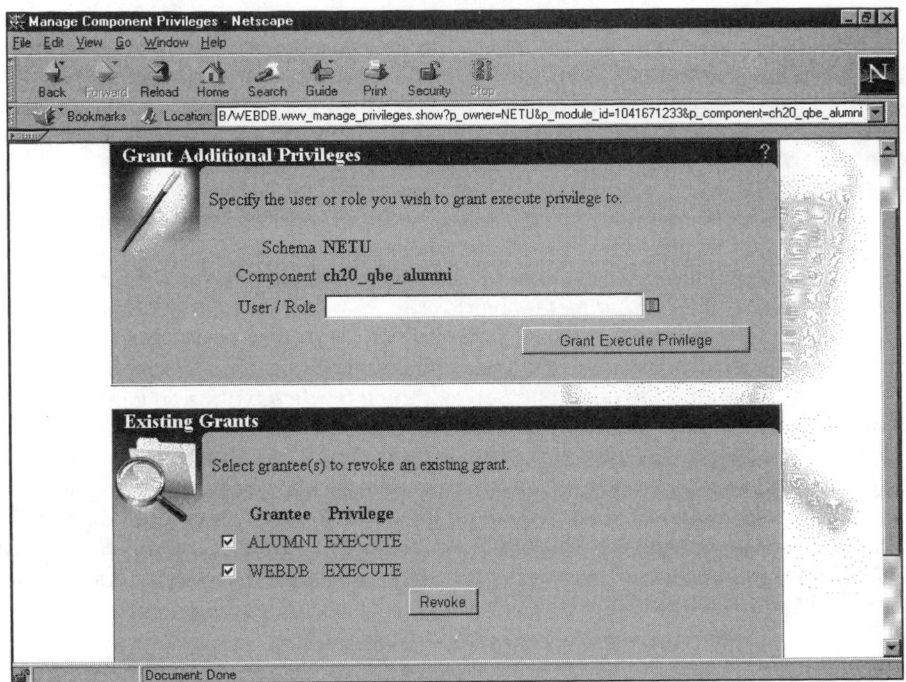

Figure 20-20: Grant Additional Privileges panel

Once you click the Grant Execute Privilege button, WebDB checks to make sure the user/role is a valid account and then it proceeds to add the permission to the database. The Grant Execute Privilege button stores the change, and WebDB refreshes the Existing Grants panel to reflect the additional permits by adding the user/role to the list and setting the check box to TRUE. The lower panel displays all of the permissions for the current object. If a particular user/role does not appear in this list, then it does not have access to the procedure.

The exceptions to this rule are those accounts with the DBA role or the system privilege EXECUTE ANY PROCEDURE.

In order to remove a permit using this panel, you must uncheck all the accounts that you *do not* wish to change and then click the Revoke button. Initially, this seems slightly counterintuitive, but it is not difficult to remember. You will notice that there is no facility for creating either users or roles from this page. The focus of this page is to set permits on the specified component, and the build wizard assumes that you have already created the user account or role with the administration menu.

3. Locate Alumni role using the search function.

4. Use the Grant Execute Privilege to save the permissions.

5. Return to the Manage Component page.

It is possible to mix both procedure security and record-level security within the same object by taking advantage of an Oracle database security feature. When WebDB connects to the database, it uses the connection information supplied by the user through the authentication dialog box. Chapter 22 discusses this technique in detail, but you need not be familiar with the details to see how this applies to WebDB security. Within the database realm, Oracle provides the USER SQL keyword that maps to the user account name the user entered to connect to the database. WebDB passes this information on through the listener to the database and you can make use of this feature when you build tables, views, or queries. The ch20_rep_alumni report you imported is built on a database view as shown in the following code:

```
create view alumni_individuals as select * from alumni where
password = user
```

In effect, the view contains all of the fields in the alumni table, along with a dynamic restriction. The restriction matches the value in the password field to the user name that Oracle maps to the USER keyword. Every time a user runs a query against this view, Oracle only returns records in which the password matches the user name used to log on to the database. If you give each record a different value for the password field and make each password a valid logon, you will have created record-level security. You might have been wondering why you added two ALUMNI records in the earlier section with the names LAURENCE1 and DEBORAH2. The reason was so the user name would match this view. Although this may be an extreme case, because we probably would not want to create 1,000 separate logons for each of the 1,000 alumni, the concept is a sound one. You will learn more about this in Chapter 22, but for now you can keep it in mind as a possible technique for implementing row-level security.

6. Navigate to the Manage Component page for the report ch20_rep_alumni, and modify the security privileges to permit the ALUMNI to run the report as you did with the form ch20_qbe_alumni.

Notice that almost all of the various components use the same basic form to enforce privileges. The only exceptions to this policy are shared components, which cannot be explicitly protected, and menus, which have security built directly into the body of the component.

Adding security to menus

At first glance, menus appear to have the same security settings as the other component objects, but this is only partially true. You must enable users to have access to the menu itself through the Privileges link on the Manage Component page as you do with the other builders. However, in addition to allowing access to the menu itself, you can also provide access to the submenus inside of the menu through the Menu Wizard.

As you might recall from Chapter 14, parent menus act as container objects for the child menus inside them. As such, it is not possible to manage child menus from the Manage Component page; rather, you must manage child menus from inside the parent menu.

The sample menu you imported for this chapter has three child menus: Alumni Biographical Information, Alumni Individual Biographical Information, and Ugrads Bio Information. WebDB permits you to set role security for each of these submenus as part of the menu building process.

1. Use the Menu Wizard to edit the menu ch20_mnu_collage, and then edit the Alumni Biographical Information submenu as shown in Figure 20-21.

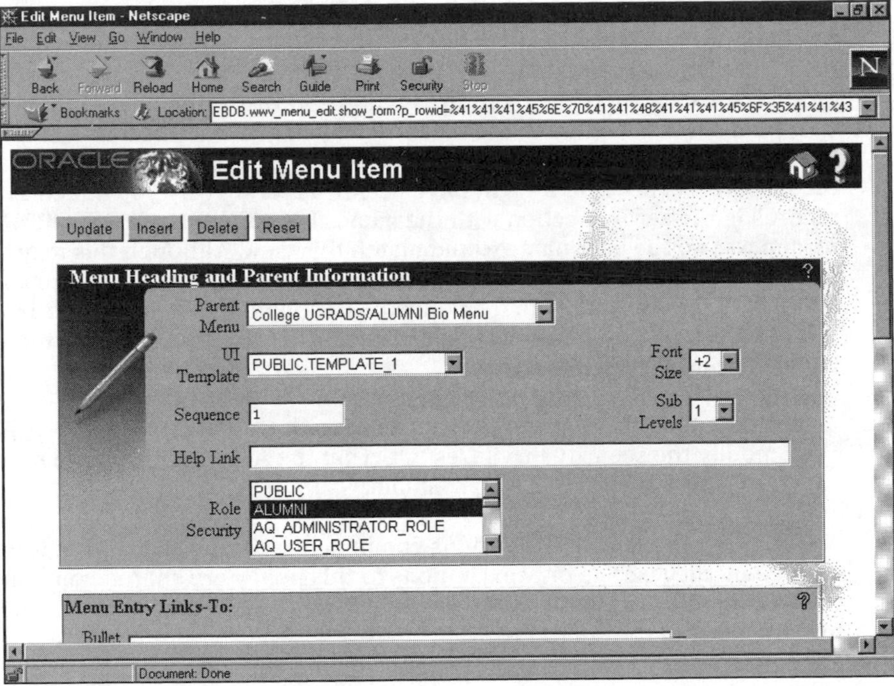

Figure 20-21: Edit menu security

The Menu Editor includes a multiselect list box that enables you to select Oracle roles that will have access to the specified submenu item. Notice that the ALUMNI role is already highlighted. This is one of the two differences that separate submenu security from the other component's security. When you import or export menus, WebDB imports and exports the attached submenu security along with the submenus themselves. This is different from all of the other build wizards, which do not export security settings along with the object. Second, the default behavior for submenus is to permit access to all users and roles that have access to the parent menu. Remember that the default behavior for WebDB components is to deny access. If you do not specifically select roles to permit access within the submenus, then WebDB allows all users to gain access to the submenu provided that they have access to the parent menu.

When you permit access to the submenu, you are not necessarily permitting access to the component object to which the submenu points. If the submenu points to another submenu, then you are in fact permitting access to that menu by enabling a role setting. However, if the menu item points to another component, such as a form or a report, you are only giving access to the menu item that points to the form or report. This means that the end user will see the menu choice, but they may not be able to run the component the menu points to. If you want the end user to be able to execute the actual component that the menu points to, you have to permit access to both the menu and to the component to which the menu points.

Because the submenu already permits the ALUMNI role to have access to the submenu items, you do not need to modify the menu. If you wish to add new roles to this item, all you need to do is to select them with your mouse.

2. Click the Update button to save the changes to the child menu.
3. Use the Return to Manage Component Page link to navigate back to the Manage Component panel for the current menu.

Within submenus, WebDB only saves the currently selected roles. If you want to add a new role permission to an existing submenu, you have to be sure that *all* of the desired roles are selected at the same time using Shift+mouse click or Ctrl+mouse click.

4. Use the Privileges link to add permission to access the menu to the LAURENCE1 account and the DEBORAH2 account.

Once you set the security for the menus and the components, and you create the Users, Grants, and Roles, all that remains is for you to test out the your security scheme.

Testing Security

You can test out your accounts by logging on to and out of WebDB as shown in the user management section of this chapter. Once you are familiar with how the security mechanisms work, you will most likely remain inside your browser to test out your logons. The first step in the process is to ensure that you have COOKIES enabled within your browser. You cannot log on to WebDB without setting a cookie — even to develop applications — but you must remember to keep this in mind when you deploy applications as well. Browser cookies are discussed in detail in Chapter 22, but for this chapter, you should remember that cookies must be enabled in order to run.

1. Exit your browser and restart it.
2. Enter the following URL into your browser:

   `http://pumpkin:4000/WebDB/netu.ch20_mnu_bio.show`
3. The first part of the URL `http://pumpkin:4000/WebDB/` varies based upon the settings that you used to configure WebDB. The second part of the URL is the user name for NETU followed by the menu you imported earlier in this chapter.

   Once you enter the link, WebDB prompts you for logon information using a dialog box.
4. Use the account LAURENCE1/ORACLE to log on to WebDB. The menu should display as shown in Figure 20-22.

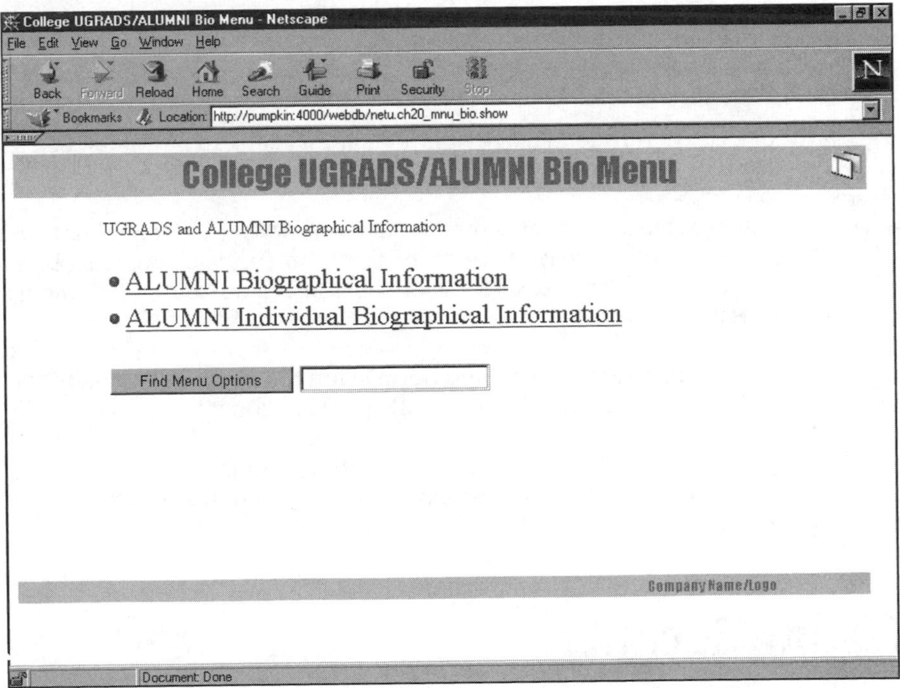

Figure 20-22: College biographical menu

WebDB displays the menu for the user under which you logged on. However, you may recall that the menu had three choices on it when you where editing it within WebDB. The third menu choice, the Ugrads Bio Information menu, is not available to the ALUMNI role and thus it does not appear in the body of the menu at run time.

The first link in the menu takes the user to a query-by-example form that enables the user to input query parameters and find matching ALUMNI records. The more interesting link in this case is the second link.

5. Select the Alumni Individual Biographical Information link to see the report shown in Figure 20-23.

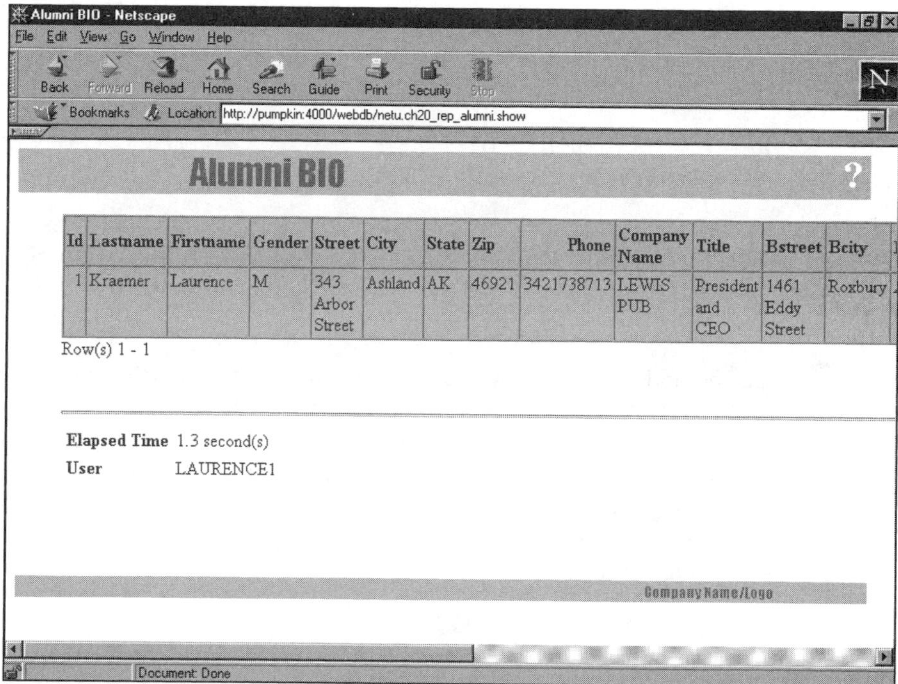

Figure 20-23: Alumni report with record-level security

This particular report is built on the ALUMNI_INDIVIDUALS view, which implicitly restricts the result set to all records where the logon matches the password field. The ALUMNI table is designed such that every record has a unique value for the password field, which is the FIRSTNAME of the alumni concatenated with the string representation of their ID number. As long as you assign the USERID to match the password field, each and every alumnus will only see his or her own record when this report is run. You could further add a link to this report that would enable the user to update the information using a form. In this manner, you would have the perfect self-service Web application, as each alumnus could update his or her biographical information as necessary.

Because you can assign a role to an account, it is not necessary for you to set permissions on the individual user accounts. However, you may find that the task of creating the 1,000 user accounts for the alumni to be a daunting process. You can automate this process by building scripts that you can execute within SQL*Plus. For example, the following SQL*Plus script creates a file you can then edit and run back through SQL*Plus to create the accounts:

```
spool alumni_accounts.sql
set heading off
set wrap off
select 'create user ' ||password ||
' identified by oracle default webdb temporary temporary;'
 from netu.alumni
/
select 'grant connect to ' ||password||';' from netu.alumni
/
select 'grant alumni to '||password||';' from netu.alumni
/
spool off
```

The resulting output file has three different statements for each alumni record: one to create the account, one to add the CONNECT role, and one to add the ALUMNI role.

Note You can add multiple roles to a user account inside a single GRANT statement by simply entering the role names separated by commas.

WebDB builds its list of grants and roles from the data within the Oracle data dictionary. If you add or modify accounts using SQL*Plus or Enterprise Manager, note that your changes appear in the WebDB pages just as if you entered the changes through WebDB.

Wrapping Up

WebDB's security mechanisms are built directly from the standards already in place within the Oracle database. If you are familiar with using Oracle USERIDs, passwords, grants, and roles at the database level, then you should have no problem applying that experience within WebDB. Novice developers will find that creating new accounts through the WebDB interface makes it easier to learn the idiosyncrasies of the Oracle security mechanisms.

With WebDB, user security is only half of the battle, because your database objects need to access through Database Access Descriptors and the WebDB listener. WebDB DADs determine when accounts need to be logged on to the database, and a single user can connect several times to a single site if necessary. We recommend that you work through Chapter 22 before you begin implementing a security scheme. Once you understand how WebDB applications are deployed, you will be better equipped to build your system security using the principles you learned within this chapter.

✦ ✦ ✦

CHAPTER 21

Monitoring WebDB Performance

✦ ✦ ✦ ✦

In This Chapter

Component Monitoring Utilities

Monitoring Concepts

Monitoring Database Objects

Component Monitors

Activity Log Settings

Site Builder Monitoring Tools

Site Builder Statistics

✦ ✦ ✦ ✦

One of the keys to a successful Web application is good performance. The biggest factor contributing to the slow performance of Web applications is typically the speed at which a user is connecting to your site.

If your applications make use of lots of large image files and users are typically connecting to your sites using 28.8 modems, they are likely to have a less successful experience using your applications. As higher-bandwidth Internet connections become available to users on a cost-effective basis, you can expect this to change. Intranet applications often do not suffer from this same problem, because these users are more likely to be connected to the Web server by a network backbone that offers much higher performance. However, despite the speedy connection, Web sites can often become slow if the server machine is straining under a heavy load of users.

There are many reasons for poor performance, including memory usage, lack of disk space, or even excessive use loads. Sometimes the problem is not with the entire Web infrastructure and server at all, but rather with poorly designed or enormously popular individual components. Even in cases where your applications are performing fast enough, you may find that your site is cluttered with unpopular items. Unpopular items are those objects that users are not choosing to access on your site. If you are spending time and resources to build components, it is important to know if the end users of your application are accessing them.

Although you may feel that your site is well designed and easy to use, your users may not feel the same way. Measuring usage patterns can help you to identify these conditions within your sites and to correct them. The key to avoiding performance problems is to understand exactly what is going on with your Web server and applications and take both corrective action and preventive action. WebDB provides a suite of reports, charts, and utilities to help you monitor and manage your WebDB components and WebDB sites.

Component Monitoring Utilities

There are two main tasks in monitoring a Web application. First, you need to keep track of the activity and identify bottlenecks and problem areas. Second, you need to be able to fix problems once you identify them.

Ideally, you want to be able to fix most problems directly through the browser interface, but this may not always be possible. WebDB supports both activities through a suite of four classes of monitoring tools for WebDB Web sites and components as part of the monitoring subsystem shown in Figure 21-1.

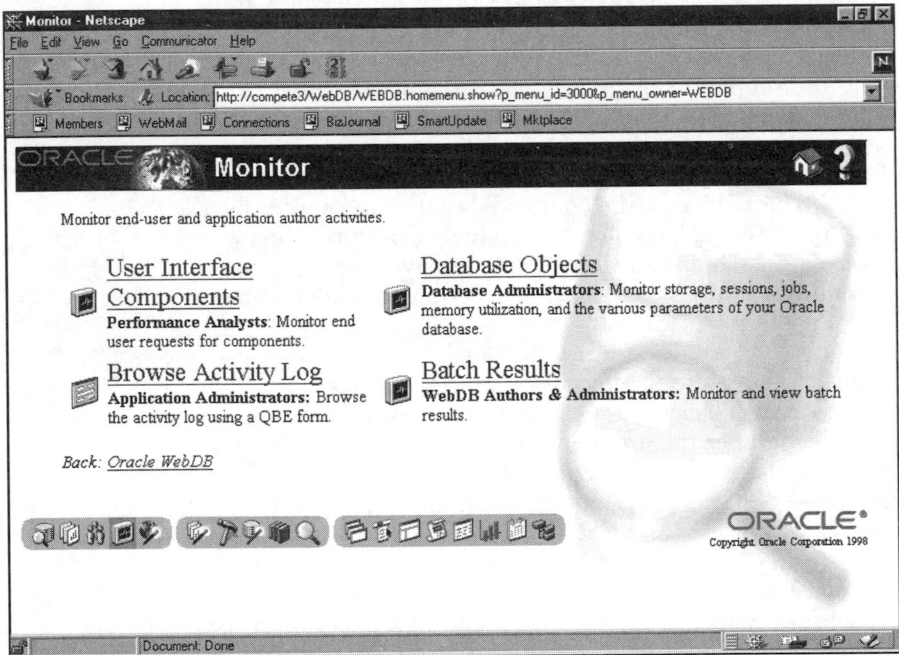

Figure 21-1: WebDB's Monitor menu

WebDB divides the component monitoring tools into four classes as follows:

✦ User Interface Components

✦ Database Objects

✦ Browse Activity Log

✦ Batch Results

User Interface Components are the actual components that make up the bulk of your Web site. They are typically the starting point for any analysis. The User Interface Components themselves are the database procedures used to create the HTML pages. As you no doubt recall from working with the component builders in the earlier sections of this book, each WebDB report, form, calendar, chart, hierarchy, dynamic pages, frame, and shared component is implemented as a database procedure. The User Interface Components Monitor is used to track the performance and activity of these individual components.

Underneath the database procedures are database objects such as tables and views. WebDB provides an interface for looking at the configuration and status of the underlying data through the Database Objects Monitor. While the User Interface Components Monitor is designed strictly for the WebDB environment, the Database Objects Monitor duplicates some of the functionality that you may be used to working with in the Oracle Enterprise Manager. This duplicate functionality is provided so that you can work entirely inside of the WebDB environment. Many Webmasters do not have experience in working with the database tools directly, and you will find that they are often more comfortable working with a browser-based tool for monitoring the underlying database.

The data for the run-time statistics is captured by the WebDB PL/SQL gateway. The actual performance data is stored in a series of database log files. You do not have to leave the WebDB environment to view these log files because WebDB provides the Browse Activity Log function that enables you to view the data directly. While the User Interface Components Monitor summarizes the data for you, the Browse Activity Log permits you to view the data directly.

When you deploy WebDB applications, you can enable users to run components interactively, as well as run tasks as background batch processes. The Batch Results Monitor is used to view the results of tasks that have been executed as background processes. This is the only panel that nonprivileged users have access to within the monitoring subsystem, and this is the only interface where they can find and view their batch results. Appendix B provides a complete discussion of the batch system.

User interface components monitors

All of the performance monitors within the WebDB environment are built using the WebDB component builders. The output and navigation of these reports should be familiar to you if you have worked with any of the component builders. The monitors are divided into two types of output: reports and charts. WebDB provides a visual clue for the output type by displaying the object type icon next to the link inside for every monitoring page.

WebDB enables monitoring for your components by default, but you are free to disable monitoring for an individual component through the Display Options panel within the wizards' interface. Each component wizard provides a Log Activity check box that you can use to disable component logging as desired.

Note Before you begin working through the examples in this chapter, load the following components into WebDB from the CD-ROM:

```
ch21_rep_donations.sql, ch21_cht_donations.sql,
ch21_dyn_state_gifts.sql, ch21_dyn_donations.sql
```

1. Navigate to the main monitor page by using the Monitor Activity menu choice.
2. Choose the User Interface Components link to display the page shown in Figure 21-2.

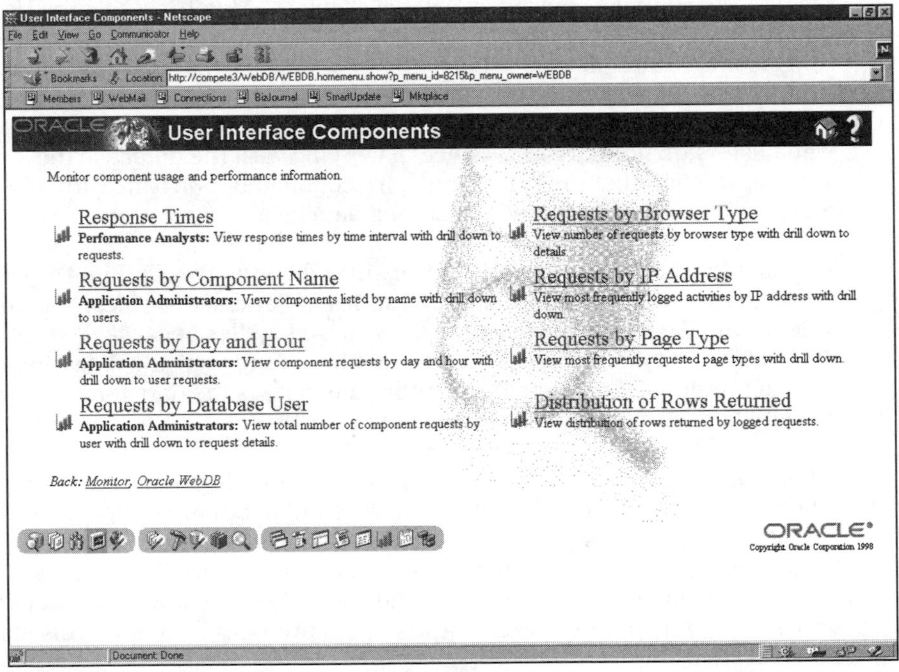

Figure 21-2: User Interface Components Monitor

The User Interface Components Monitor is entirely composed of charts, as you can see from Figure 21-2. The goal of this set of monitoring tools is to give you an overall picture of the performance of the site along two dimensions. You can use the charts in this section to get a feel for the speed of the overall site. The charts also provide you with demographics regarding the who, what, where, and when aspects of your site as shown in the Table 21-1.

Table 21-1
User Interface Chart Types

Chart Name	*Description*
Response Times	Charts the response times for components by time interval with drill-down to the log entries for each charting interval. This chart tells you how long it is taking WebDB to build and display your pages.
Requests by Component Name	Tracks the number of requests for each component and enables you to drill down and view the actual user counts by user for any single component. This chart tells you which of your components is the most popular.
Requests by Day and Hour	Charts the number of requests by day and the number of requests by hour, with drill-down to the details of any day or hour. This chart tells you when the peak times of user activity are occurring on your site.
Requests by Database User	Tracks the number of requests by Oracle USERID with drill-down into the detail logs for the USERID. This chart tells you which Oracle USERIDs are using your site and how often they are using it.
Requests by Browser Type	Charts the number of requests by each type of browser that is accessing WebDB. This chart tells you which browsers are being used to access your site and components.
Requests by IP Address	Tracks the number of requests by IP address with drill-down to the detailed log pages. This chart tells you where the users are connecting to your site from.
Requests by Page Type	Charts the number of requests by component type. This tells you which types of components (for example, menus, charts, reports, and forms) are being used by your users.
Distribution of Rows Returned	Tracks the number of records that are being returned by interval, including the number of times the user did not find any records. This tells you how much data is being sent to the browser on average.

These eight charts can be further grouped into three basic categories: the performance of your components, the usage patterns of your objects, and the demographics of your users.

Charting performance

The first item of concern in most production Web sites is the overall performance of the site. Web sites that serve up pages quickly are going to be popular and more successful than sites and components considered slow. Brisk performance is based on three factors: the speed of the user's connection, the amount of information packed onto each page, and the performance of the server. You will typically not have much control over the speed of a user's connection, but you do have control over the other two factors. Reports, charts, forms, calendars, hierarchies, and dynamic pages that are filled with large graphics are going to take a long time to load. Unfortunately, the WebDB monitors do not really measure how long it takes for the page to load into the user's browser. The only thing the listener can monitor is how quickly it serves pages up to the user. It cannot detect how long it takes the page to load completely into the user's browser.

If you need to include large graphic images into your application and if users are going to access your site with a low-bandwidth connection, you should be careful to test the performance of your pages by hand to ensure that they are performing briskly enough. WebDB cannot automatically help you with this task.

WebDB can help you determine how your server is performing using three of the charting objects — the Response Times chart, the Requests by Day and Hour chart, and the Distribution of Rows Returned chart.

1. Run the following components several times each, and be sure to step through multiple pages of output for the reports: ch21_rep_donations, ch21_cht_donations, ch21_dyn_donations, and ch21_dyn_state_gifts.
2. Navigate to the User Interface Components menu and choose the Response Times link to display the panel shown in Figure 21-3.

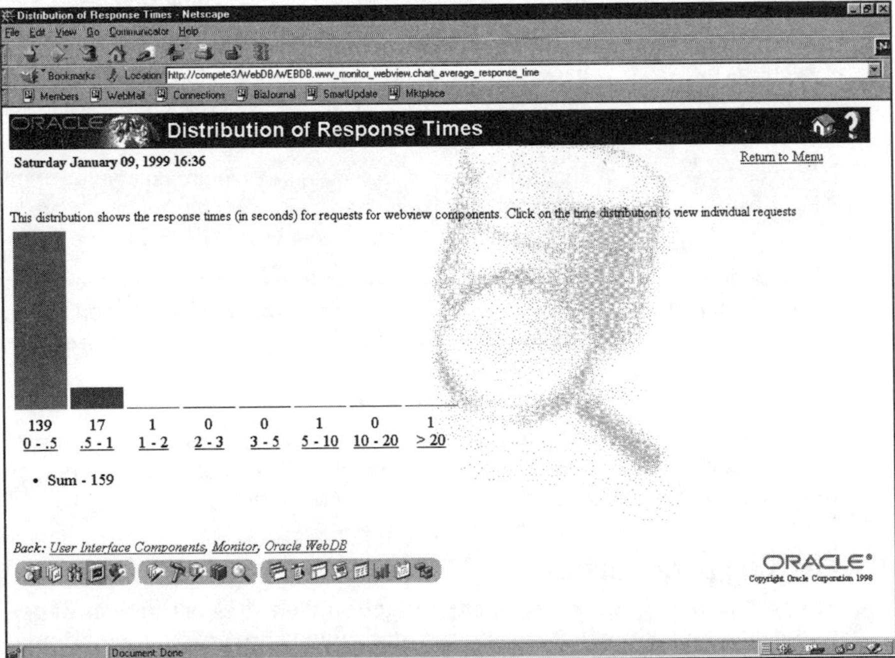

Figure 21-3: Distribution of Response Times page

The first step in the monitoring process is to review the overall performance of the site. The Distribution of Response Times chart shows a count of the number of requests for components plotted against the response time (in seconds) for those components. WebDB measures the response time as the amount of time it takes the listener to call the PL/SQL procedure and begin getting results back. The monitoring facility assumes that once the components have begun returning results, its job is done.

Charts that curve up to the left like the one shown in Figure 21-3 indicate reasonably good performance. In the example chart, the vast majority of requests are serviced within half of a second. From this chart, you can get a feel for the overall performance of your components. If you were to see charts heavily weighted to the right, this would indicate that the performance of your site is substandard. You cannot draw any hard and fast conclusions, however, because your components may be constructed using very sophisticated SQL statements. For example, if you are building reports using views that "roll up" lots of information from many data sources, these reports can take longer to run. The key is to be sure that each type of report is running as you expect it to.

WebDB makes it easy to delve into the details of the chart by providing automatic drill-down from each chart to the appropriate log details.

3. Click the time interval label link in the Response Times chart to display the detailed component requests, as shown in Figure 21-4.

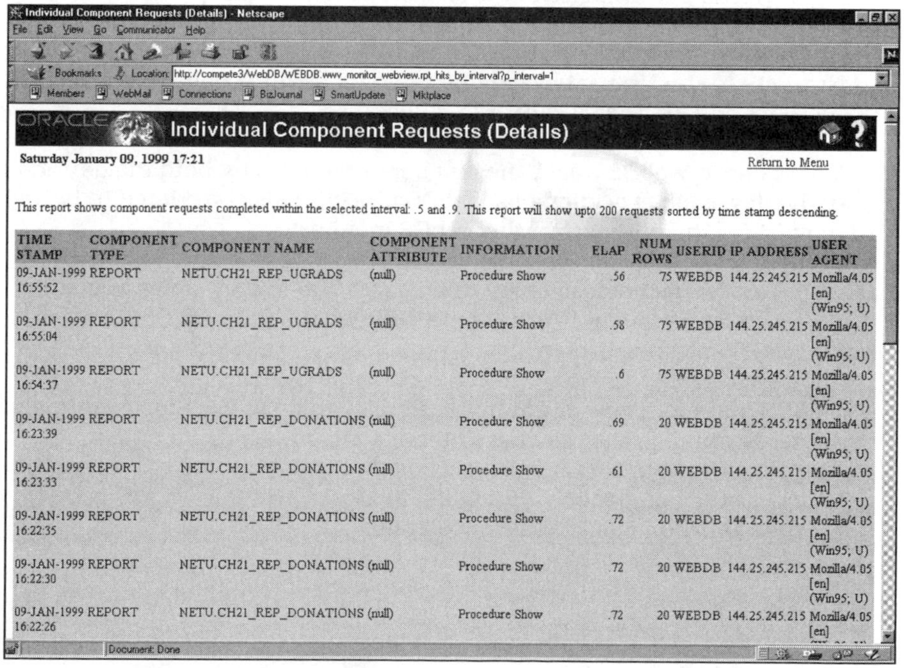

Individual Component Requests (Details) - Netscape

http://compete3/WebDB/WEBDB.wwv_monitor_webview.rpt_hits_by_interval?p_interval=1

Individual Component Requests (Details)

Saturday January 09, 1999 17:21

Return to Menu

This report shows component requests completed within the selected interval: .5 and .9. This report will show upto 200 requests sorted by time stamp descending.

TIME STAMP	COMPONENT TYPE	COMPONENT NAME	COMPONENT ATTRIBUTE	INFORMATION	ELAP	NUM ROWS	USERID	IP ADDRESS	USER AGENT
09-JAN-1999 16:55:52	REPORT	NETU.CH21_REP_UGRADS	(null)	Procedure Show	.56	75	WEBDB	144.25.245.215	Mozilla/4.05 [en] (Win95; U)
09-JAN-1999 16:55:04	REPORT	NETU.CH21_REP_UGRADS	(null)	Procedure Show	.58	75	WEBDB	144.25.245.215	Mozilla/4.05 [en] (Win95; U)
09-JAN-1999 16:54:37	REPORT	NETU.CH21_REP_UGRADS	(null)	Procedure Show	.6	75	WEBDB	144.25.245.215	Mozilla/4.05 [en] (Win95; U)
09-JAN-1999 16:23:39	REPORT	NETU.CH21_REP_DONATIONS	(null)	Procedure Show	.69	20	WEBDB	144.25.245.215	Mozilla/4.05 [en] (Win95; U)
09-JAN-1999 16:23:33	REPORT	NETU.CH21_REP_DONATIONS	(null)	Procedure Show	.61	20	WEBDB	144.25.245.215	Mozilla/4.05 [en] (Win95; U)
09-JAN-1999 16:22:35	REPORT	NETU.CH21_REP_DONATIONS	(null)	Procedure Show	.72	20	WEBDB	144.25.245.215	Mozilla/4.05 [en] (Win95; U)
09-JAN-1999 16:22:30	REPORT	NETU.CH21_REP_DONATIONS	(null)	Procedure Show	.72	20	WEBDB	144.25.245.215	Mozilla/4.05 [en] (Win95; U)
09-JAN-1999 16:22:26	REPORT	NETU.CH21_REP_DONATIONS	(null)	Procedure Show	.72	20	WEBDB	144.25.245.215	Mozilla/4.05 [en]

Document: Done

Figure 21-4: Response time details

WebDB displays the detailed log information for the time interval that you select and sorts the detailed data by the timestamp of the record. The log details show you all of the pertinent information about the component, the user, and the elapsed time for each component. From this detailed report, you can check for any components running slower than you expect.

Initially, you will probably not get much useful data until your users have had a chance to work with your WebDB application for a while. As the users access the components, you will begin to build a more useful set of data on which to draw some conclusions. For example, you might want to take snapshots of your overall response times by running and printing the Response Times chart every day when the system goes live and then once a week when you hit a steady state. By comparing the charts over a period of weeks, you can quickly spot both favorable and unfavorable trends.

If the overall performance of your application appears to be satisfactory, but several components appear to running slowly, you can review the log details shown in Figure 21-4 to identify components that are not performing up to speed.

Note

Poor performance of individual components is often a sign that users are accessing the data in way different from what you had planned. For example, if you are permitting query-by-example access to data in a large table, it is possible that the users are querying on nonindexed fields. Adding an index to the table for parameter fields can often solve this particular problem.

If the overall performance of the site shows a downward trend, you will want to review the overall usage patterns of your site.

Navigate to the User Interface Components Monitor page and select the Requests by Day and Hour chart shown in Figure 21-5.

In this chart, WebDB tracks the number of requests by both the day and each hour of the day. Each execution of a WebDB procedure is considered to be an individual request for the purposes of the WebDB monitor.

WebDB tracks requests for HTML pages and images stored within the database and fetched using a WebDB procedure. WebDB does not track fetches for *external* HTML pages and images.

WebDB initiates a new day at midnight, according to the time zone in which the server is running, and the chart intervals are broken down into hours and days. The date and hour text is built as a link that connects you to a list of USERIDs used to access the components during that period. From the USERID page, you can link down to the individual log file once again.

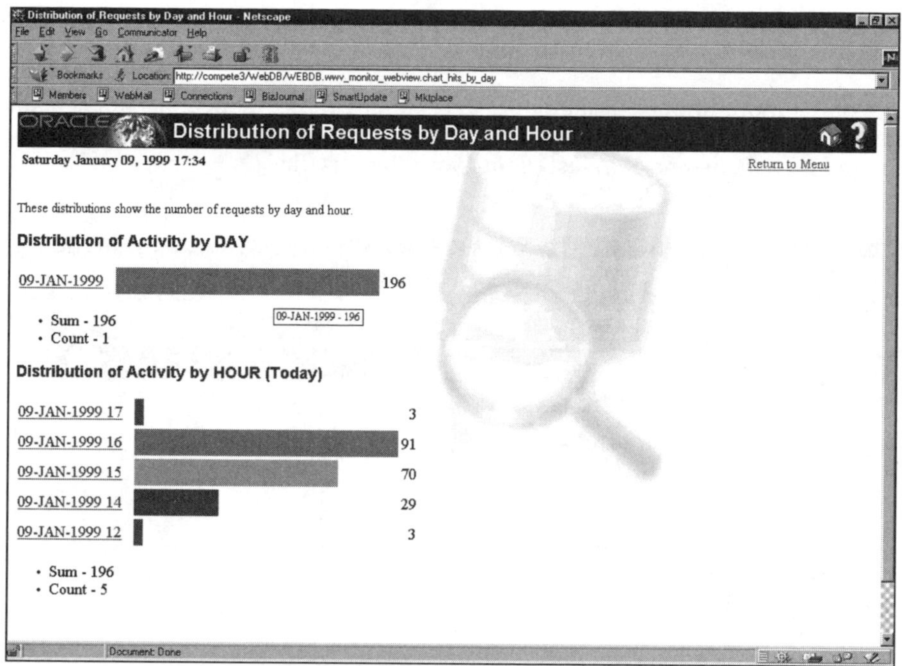

Figure 21-5: Requests by Day and Hour

You can use this chart to look for periods of heavy activity and then drill down to the individual USERIDs that are generating the activity in each time period. If you enable your users to log onto your site using a common Oracle USERID, then you are not likely to benefit very much from this chart. (Refer to Chapter 22 for details on deploying your components using separate Oracle USERIDs.) Most business sites show heavy usage during the normal business day, while hobby sites and consumer sites tend to show high levels of activity during the evening hours. Charts that show uneven access might indicate that the usage patterns do not match your expectations. If you cannot even out the usage of your site, then you may need to upgrade to a larger server in order to handle the load at peak times.

If you are using individual Oracle USERIDs for your users, you can use this chart to detect usage fraud on your site. In cases where a single USERID shows a lot of extra activity, it is possible that your users are "sharing" a single account.

In situations where the user load appears to be normal but performance is still running below desired levels, it is possible that the amount of data being returned to the browser is the culprit. To detect this situation, WebDB offers the Distribution of Rows Returned chart.

Navigate back to the main User Interface Components Monitor page and select the Distribution of Rows Returned link.

One of the more important factors in determining performance problems is the amount of data selected by users. WebDB offers the distribution graph shown in Figure 21-6 as a means of investigating your data traffic.

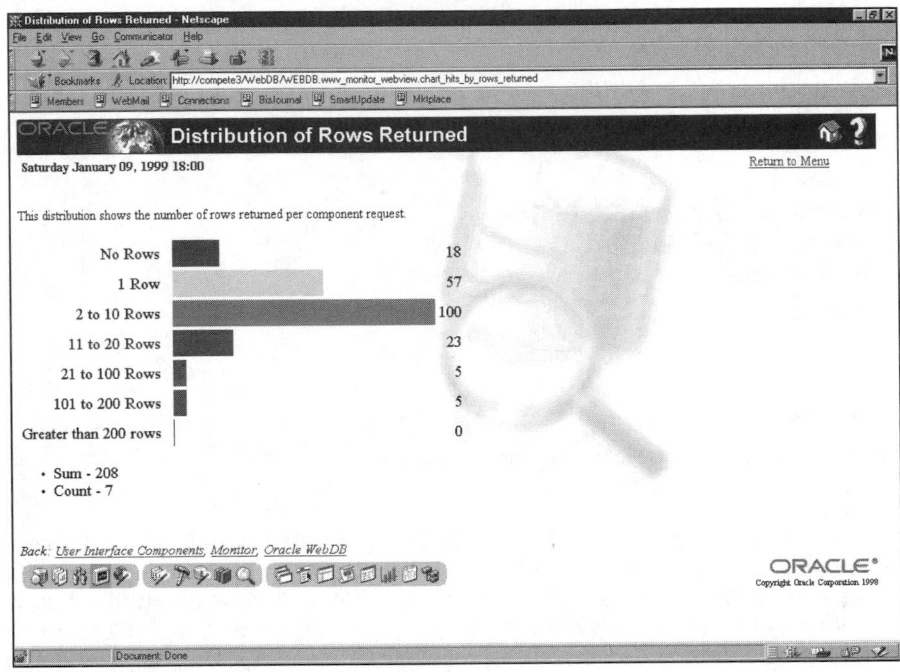

Figure 21-6: Distribution of Rows Returned chart

The chart shows the number of records returned by interval down the left-hand side of the chart and the number of components for each interval as a bar to the right. Two interesting statistics can be gleaned from this chart. First, you can determine the case in which your components are requesting excessive amounts of data. For example, if you find the majority of components are selecting over 200 records each time they execute, then you may have a problem. WebDB accumulates the counts by page and not by total record count. The chart measures the number of records displayed for *each* page as constructed by a component. If you build a report that displays 200 records with 20 records to a page, then this component is going to appear in the 11 to 20 category on the chart.

One of the features of the various build wizards is the capability of enabling the user to determine the maximum number of rows shown on a page. If you notice very high record counts, it is possible that your end users are electing to fetch too much data at one time. You can stop this behavior by eliminating the Maximum Rows parameter from the parameters form for your components.

WebDB does not measure the number of records for dynamic pages. This is due to the fact that WebDB does not construct the page breaks for this component, and therefore does not keep track of the data returned. If you have large numbers of dynamic pages objects, you may have a more difficult time isolating your performance bottlenecks.

WebDB does not provide links from the row distribution chart back to the individual components. The row distribution figures are accumulated by the run-time environment, so they are not mapped back to individual objects.

Charting popularity

In addition to tracking the performance of your overall site, you can also chart the popularity of individual components and component types. WebDB provides two chart objects for tracking the usage of individual components and component types: the Requests by Component Name chart, and the Requests by Page Type chart. The goal of these charts is to provide you with two key pieces of information. They give you insight into which of your components are popular. If you are having performance problems, you might want to separate your popular components onto separate servers to reduce your overall load. Also, you can determine which objects and object types are more useful to your users, which can assist you in the process of determining what types of objects to add to your site.

1. Navigate to the User Interface Components Monitor menu and choose the Requests by Component Name link to display the chart shown in Figure 21-7.

This particular chart is biased towards the internal WebDB components while you are in the development phase. The WebDB builders and run-time system are implemented as a series of PL/SQL objects, so they are subject to the same monitoring rules as any other WebDB component. As a developer, you are permitted to determine the logging and monitoring options for your components, but you do not have control over the WebDB components themselves. The designers of WebDB felt it was important for you to be able to monitor the performance of the run-time environment, so they chose to enable logging on portions of the WebDB system itself. Notably absent from this list are the component wizards, which behave somewhat differently from end-user components and are excluded from the monitoring process. Once your applications are deployed, you will see that your own run-time components bubble to the top of this chart.

The chart itself displays the component name to the left with a bar chart indicating the number of requests for the component as a colored bar to the right. The components are sorted by the most frequently requested component down to the least frequently requested components. You can drill down into the component by using the link attached to the component name in the chart.

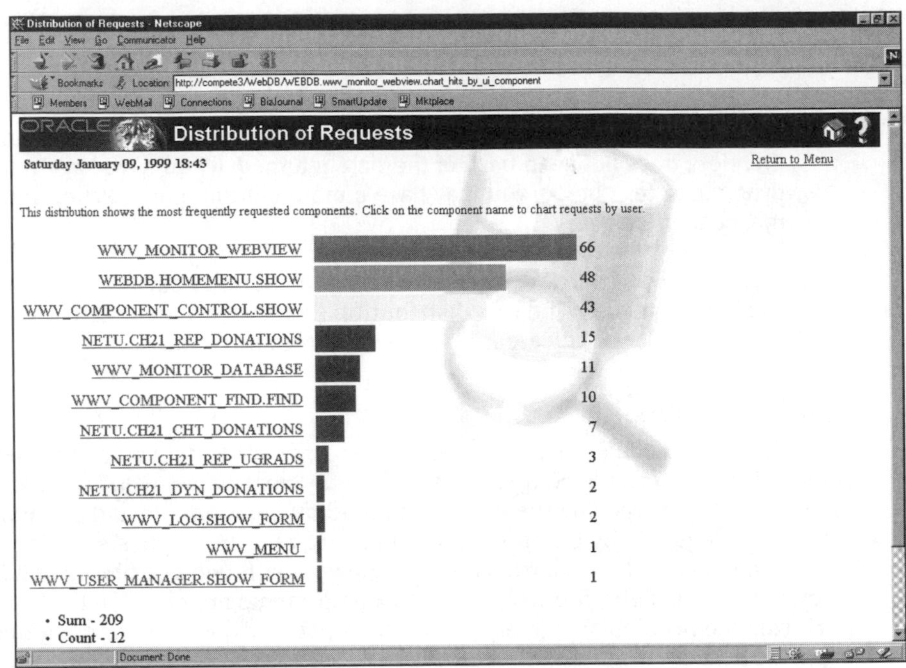

Figure 21-7: Distribution of Requests by component name

WebDB counts each page of a multipage report as a separate request for the object. If you have reports that display many pages of data, the component monitor records each request for a new page as a separate hit.

2. Click the link for any one of the objects you loaded for this chapter. Your screen should resemble Figure 21-8.

Figure 21-8 shows the ch21_cht_donations chart as being accessed by two different users — the WEBDB account and the DEVELOP01 account you created in Chapter 20. Unless you have used multiple accounts to access objects thus far in the book, you only see a single account in this chart. If you choose to deploy your WebDB applications using multiple USERIDs, you can use this drill-down chart to gauge the popularity of a given report by the individual user. This can help you determine whether a certain object is being used and who is using it. You can also use this data to investigate performance problems. If you notice that a single class of user is running a particular object repeatedly over a short period of time, it may make sense to break the object up into smaller pieces or to move it to an alternative server.

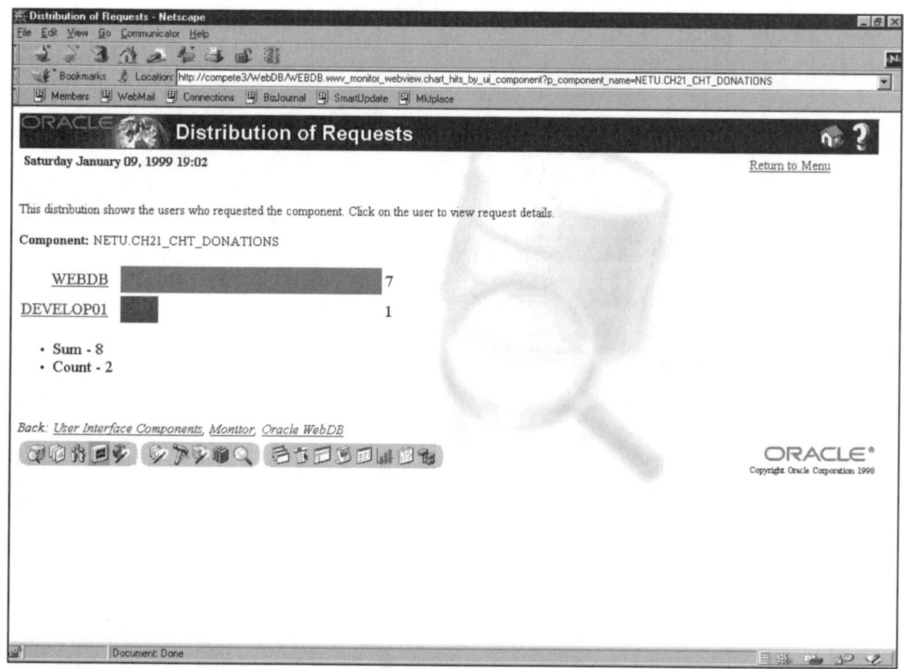

Figure 21-8: Distribution of Requests by user

If you are trying to determine if a particular object is being run repeatedly, you can drill down into the details by clicking the USERID in the Distribution of Requests chart to display the log file shown in Figure 21-8. The log itself, however, only shows the requests for the current object by the current user. In the example case, if you selected the ch21_cht_donations chart and clicked through to the WEBDB user, you would only see WEBDB's requests for the ch21_cht_donations chart in the log file. Repeat requests for a single object with similar timestamp entries probably indicate that the user is paginating through the report rather than requesting a new report execution.

In situations where you are experiencing poor performance, this may indicate that you need to add additional parameter fields for the user in order to cut down the need for pagination. WebDB provides a second chart for monitoring component usage that breaks the access down by category.

Navigate back to the main User Interface Components menu page and select the Requests by Page Type link to display the chart shown in Figure 21-9.

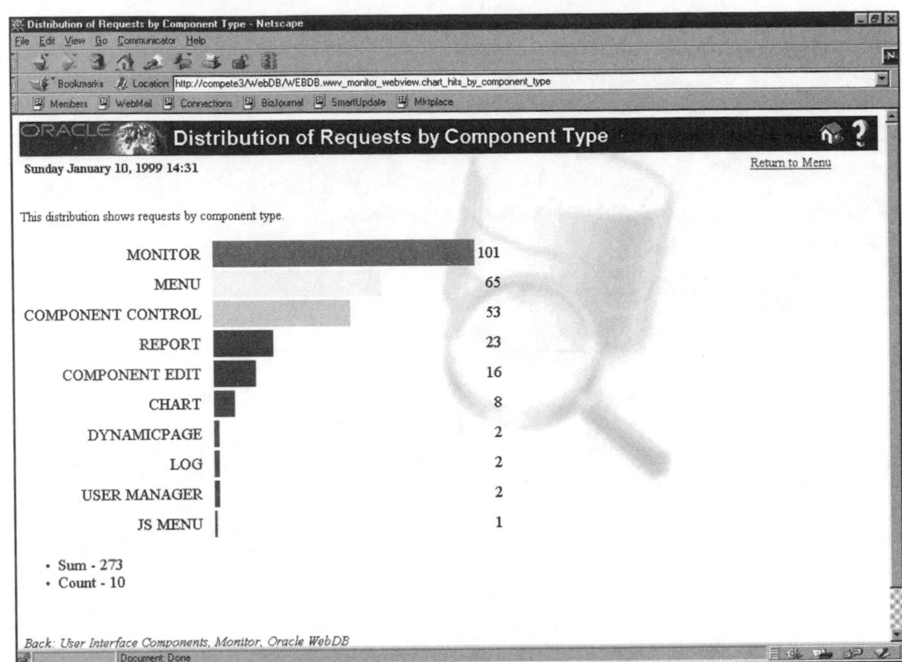

Figure 21-9: Distribution of Requests by Component Type

The items on this chart are organized by component type, and are displayed in a format similar to that used by the Component Name report. The difference is that the charting is performed by component type, enabling you to see usage of components by the component type. In Figure 21-9, you can see that the MONITOR object is the component type used most often, because you are currently doing the exercises in the chapter on monitoring. In most production situations, the monitor object does not display as the most widely used object.

From this particular chart, you can determine what types of objects your users prefer to work with — reports, forms, calendars, charts, hierarchies, or dynamic pages. WebDB uses the same calculation technique for this chart as it does for the component name chart, so requests for multiple pages within the same object count as multiple hits. The results of this chart are also affected by the record count for each object within your system. For example, if your WebDB application is comprised of ten reports and two graphs, you expect to see higher hit rates for the reports category. If you have a small number of a certain type of object, such as charts, yet the usage numbers are excessively high, then it is a good bet that your users would like more graphs.

Identifying users

The first two categories of charts and reports are designed to give you an overview of the performance of your application and which items are the more popular entries. In newsroom terminology, you have answered the "when" and the "what." Now all that is left to discover is the "who." The third and final group of reports in the User Interface Components monitoring menu helps you identify who is using your applications. From the WebDB perspective there are three aspects to identifying a user: the USERID, the IP Address, and the Browser Type.

Navigate to the User Interface Components Monitor page and select the Requests by Database User link to display the chart shown in Figure 21-10.

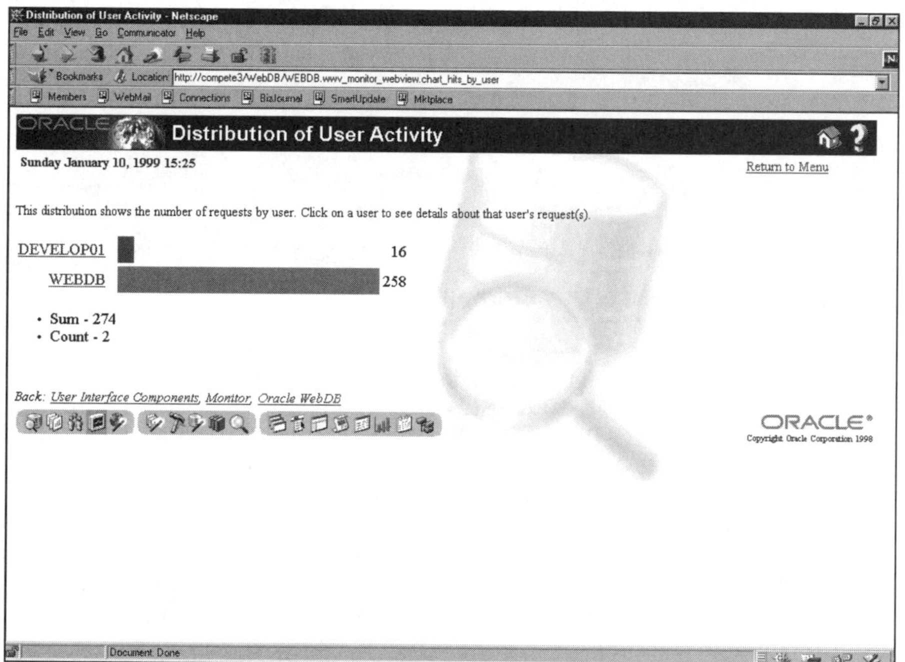

Figure 21-10: Distribution of User Activity chart

The chart shown in this figure matches the format of the chart shown in Figure 21-8. On the left-hand side you see the USERIDs, and on the right-hand side you see a bar chart and a numeric count for the number of requests by the specified USERID. As with the component name chart, each request for a new page of data is counted as a request. The difference with this chart is the capability to drill down into the USERID. Drilling down on the USERID link causes WebDB to show you all of the requests for the selected USERID, as shown in Figure 21-11.

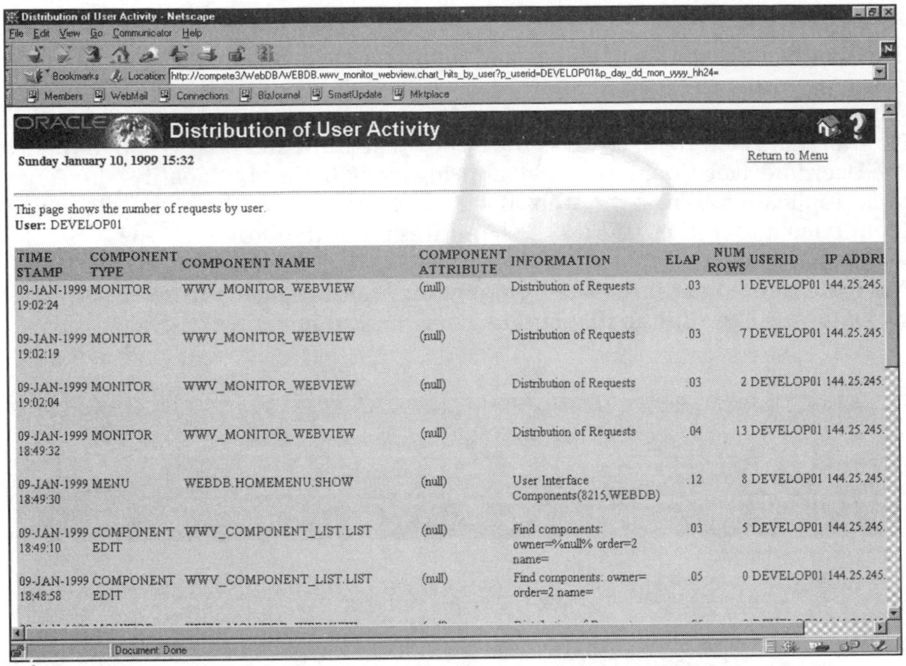

Figure 21-11: Distribution of User Activity page

This particular log view is very detailed, and it enables you to look at individual access records for each USERID. The log is sorted in descending order on the timestamp field, and all of the entries match the selected USERID. From this viewpoint, you can see all of the activity for a given user over the entire period of the log file. If you have divided your users into categories by assigning unique (or group) identifiers, then you are able to track the activity of your users down to the component level. One potential problem with this particular chart occurs when you enable multiple users to access the system using the same Oracle USERID. In this situation, there is no way to identify an individual user by USERID. The solution to this problem is to track the user by the user's IP address.

Navigate back to the User Interface Components menu and select the Requests by IP Address link to display the chart shown in Figure 21-12.

This alternative viewpoint shows you summary totals of access by individual IP addresses. If you have multiple users sharing the same Oracle USERID, they still have their own, individual IP address. This is not a perfect solution, because many dial-in users connect through dynamic IP addresses supplied by the dial-in server at system logon. However, it does provide a means for you to differentiate between users, especially for intranet applications where users are more likely to be given fixed IP addresses. You can drill down from this chart into the log details by clicking the IP address link. The log is organized by IP address and sorted by the timestamp field, with the most recent entries being shown first.

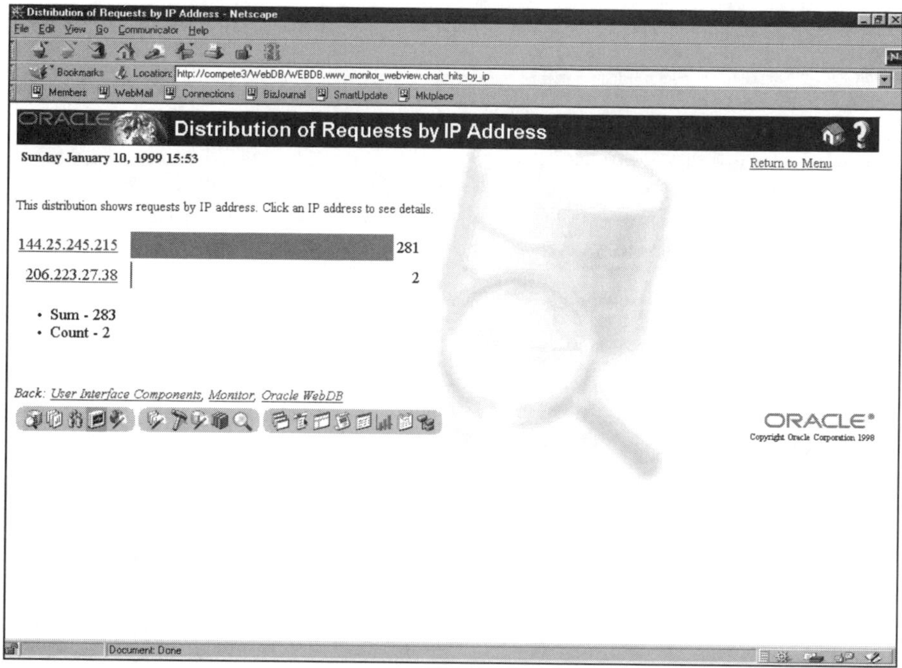

Figure 21-12: Distribution of Requests by IP Address chart

In addition to diving down into the details, WebDB also gives you a way to group users by one important, additional dimension.

Navigate to the User Interface Components Monitor menu and select the Requests by Browser Type link to display the chart shown in Figure 21-13.

This chart uses the familiar monitor format with the categories on the left-hand side and the values on the right-hand side. WebDB logs all activity by the internal browser identification field, including the version, the language setting, and the platform from which the user is browsing. From this chart, you can tell which browsers your users are working with and on which platforms they are working. This information can be vital when you are considering adding new features to the system. For example, you may decide to create some HTML pages with the Dynamic Pages Wizard that incorporate advanced HTML 4.0 code. Before you decide to proceed with this change, you can use the Browser Type chart to make sure your users are working with browsers that support the additional HTML 4.0 tags. Further, you may learn that the majority of your users are browsing from UNIX platforms, and this may lead you to certify your site for a multiplatform browser instead of a browser that is not popular in the UNIX world.

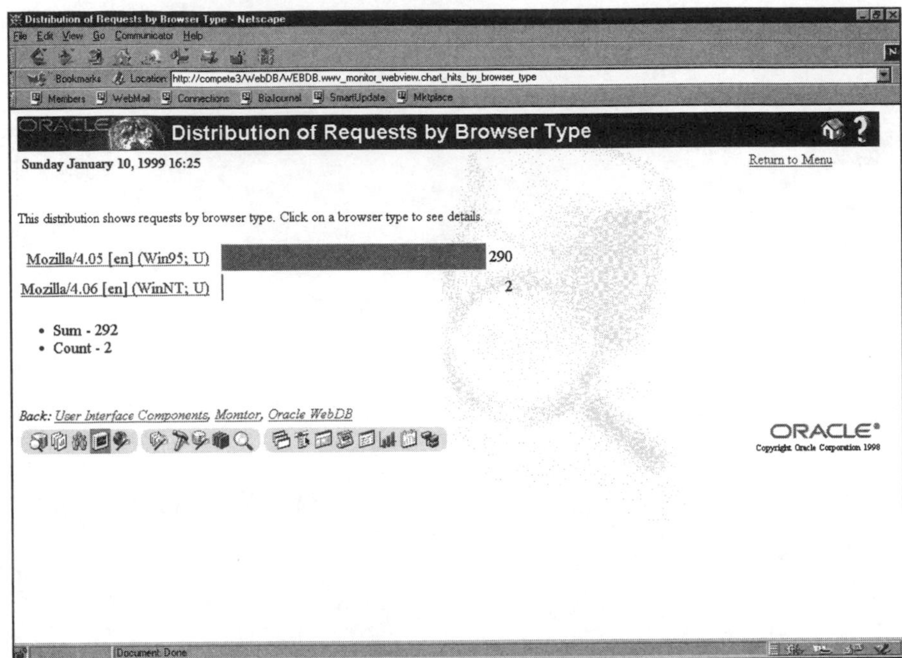

Figure 21-13: Distribution of Requests by Browser Type chart

Viewing the log file directly

The root of all of the available charts in the monitoring system is the log file. From many of the charts, you are able to drill down directly into the log file and view the relevant details of the particular chart with which you are working. WebDB provides an additional tool for viewing the log file directly through the Browse Activity Log report.

Navigate to the main Monitor menu and select the Browse Activity Log link to display the query panel shown in Figure 21-14.

WebDB provides a complete query-by-example report for the listener log file, as shown in Figure 21-14. You can enter search criteria for any of the individual columns that match display columns in the report, as shown in Table 21-2.

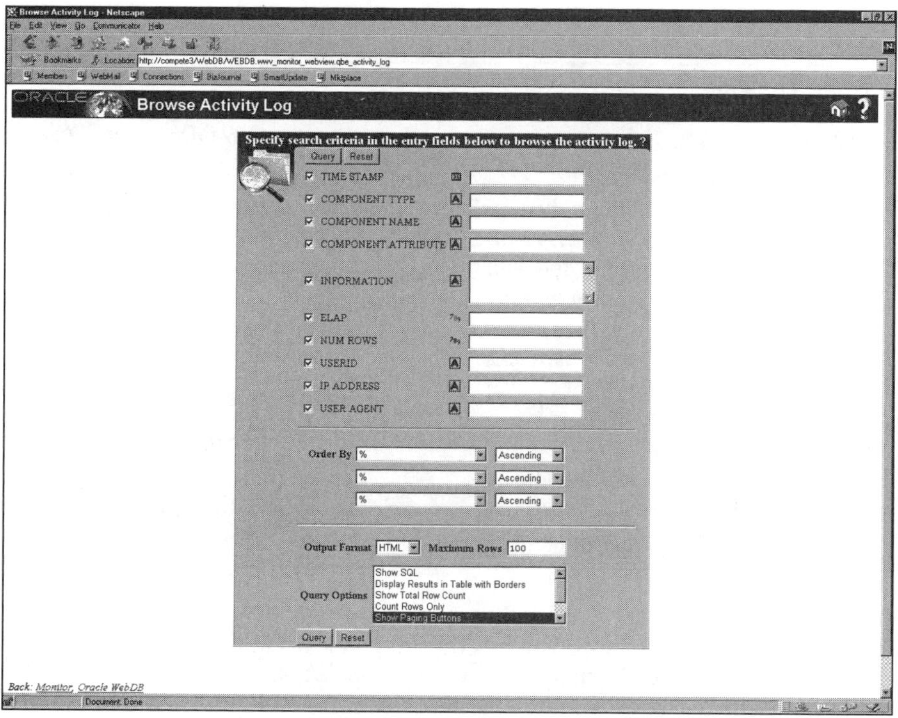

Figure 21-14: Browse Activity Log Query panel

Table 21-2
Log File Columns

Display Column	*Description*
Timestamp	Shows date and time down to the seconds interval for the record.
Component Type	Basic object type such as a report, a form, a chart, and so on.
Component Name	Name of the component, including the USERID, object name, and procedure call such as SHOW and SHOW_PARMS.
Component Attribute	Parameters that are passed to the procedures. If users run parameter forms, and values are passed to the underlying procedure, the parameter format is shown in this column.
Information	Description supplied by WebDB when the log record is written. This can contain extra information that can help you determine the exact series of events that caused the component to be run.

Continued

Table 21-2 (continued)

Display Column	*Description*
ELAP	Shows the elapsed time in seconds for WebDB to render the component.
NUM Rows	Shows the number of rows that the component returned to the browser. WebDB produces multiple records for each page generated, and the number supplied in this field matches the Maximum Rows parameter for each page. WebDB does not produce record counts for dynamic pages, and the number of rows are shown as zero for dynamic pages.
USERID	Oracle USERID used to run the component.
IP Address	Shows the IP Address of the workstation used to run the component.
User Agent	Shows the browser identification of the browser used to execute the component.

You are permitted to query on any of the fields shown in Figure 21-14 by supplying a value for the field and clicking the Query button. WebDB supplies icons next to each field to help you determine the datatype of the individual columns. WebDB also enables you to use the "%" wild card search character for any character-based data field.

Additional parameter fields enable you to sort the data by any of the columns, and you can set output parameters such as the format of the data and the maximum number of rows. If you are already using a Web log analysis tool, you can also output the data into ASCII format and then use your existing analysis tools to prepare reports against the raw log data.

Monitoring Database Objects

There are two aspects to monitoring the performance of your WebDB applications. In the preceding section, we introduced you to the various monitoring capabilities of the user objects through the User Interface Components monitoring tools. The run-time components are only half of the battle, however; you must also monitor activity at the database level in order to ensure that your site is performing up to expectations.

It is important to remember that part of the value proposition with WebDB comes from storing both your code and your data inside the Oracle database. While you are no doubt familiar with the increased reliability and scalability that comes from this strategy, it also means that you must be careful to monitor the performance of your database and the Oracle server.

Navigate to the main Monitor page and select the Database Objects link to display the panel shown in Figure 21-15.

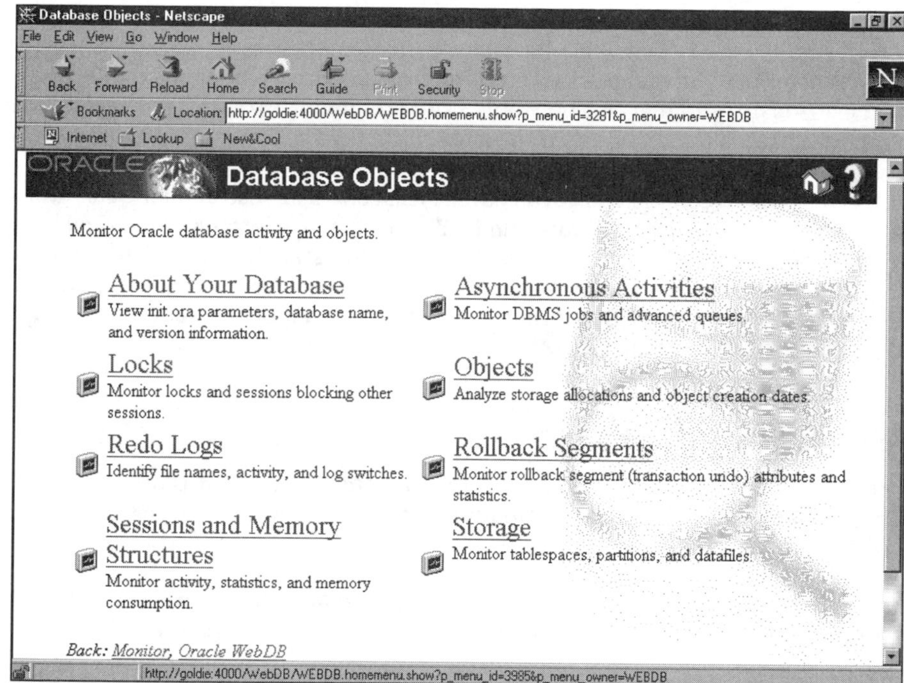

Figure 21-15: Database Objects Monitor menu

Following are the eight categories of database items to monitor:

- ✦ About Your Database
- ✦ Locks
- ✦ Redo Logs
- ✦ Sessions and Memory Structures
- ✦ Asynchronous Activities
- ✦ Objects
- ✦ Rollback Segments
- ✦ Storage

If you are familiar with the database administrator tasks for the Oracle database, then you will note that most of the preceding items are accessible through the Oracle Enterprise Manager. Ideally, you will have the services of a professional Oracle DBA at your disposal before you deploy your site into production. An experienced Oracle database administrator will likely have their own techniques and strategies for managing the database, and they are free to make use of these pre-existing tools and techniques. There is nothing exceptional about WebDB applications as far as the Oracle database is concerned. In fact, integration with the database is one of the strengths of the product.

WebDB provides the database-monitoring tools to supplement the facilities of the Oracle Enterprise Manager. The WebDB site administrator can use the database monitoring tools to complement the capabilities of the Enterprise Manager.

We would recommend that you have at least one database administrator available who is familiar with the care and feeding of the Oracle server before releasing a WebDB application into production. It is not necessary for you to have access to a full-time database administrator, but the Oracle server and database should be professionally installed and configured before you embark on any serious application deployment with WebDB.

About your database

The first item in the Database Objects menu is the About Your Database link. This link provides you with basic information about the Oracle server to which you are currently attached.

Navigate to the Database Objects menu from the Monitor menu and select the About Your Database link to display the page shown in Figure 21-16.

All of the items on this page refer to the basic settings of the Oracle server. The information is delivered as WebDB reports. None of these reports accept any parameters, because each link directly calls up a set of results. You cannot change any of the system parameters from these reports. The data these reports display gives you the basic configuration of the database. From this panel, you can determine the version of the Oracle server and all of the associated information about the Oracle instance in which WebDB is running. You are also permitted to view the initialization parameters set for the server from this interface.

Typically, you use the reports in this panel to verify that the server is properly configured. WebDB provides this set of reports so you do not have to leave the WebDB environment in order to verify these system settings.

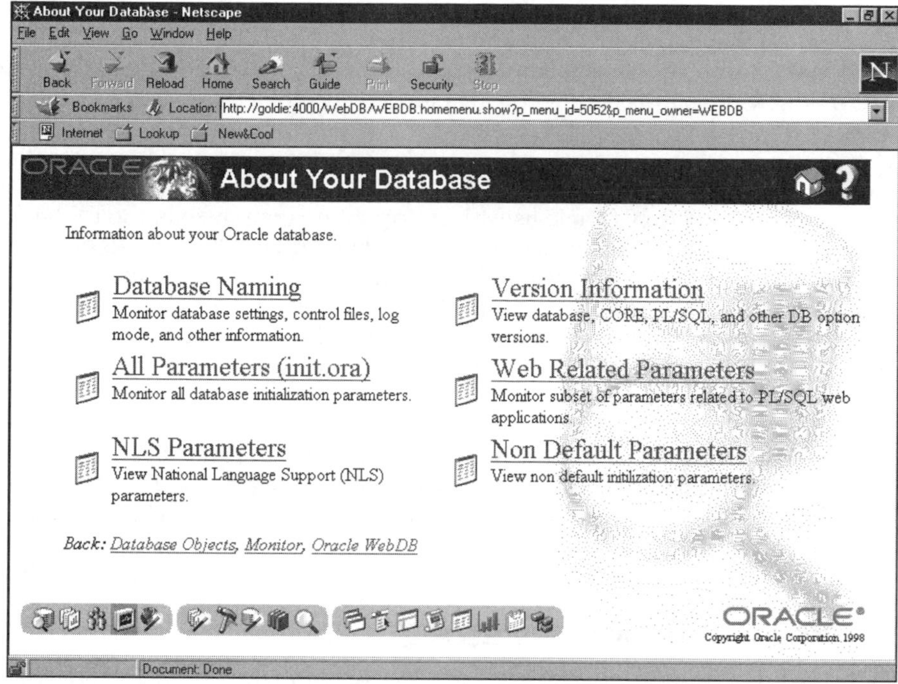

Figure 21-16: About Your Database page

Locks

The Oracle database controls multiuser access to objects by the use of database locks. Records are locked on an individual row-by-row basis in the database, which prevents multiple users from updating the same data at the same time. Because database updates within WebDB do not typically occur across multiple HTML pages, they do not typically lock multiple rows at the same time. Furthermore, WebDB defaults to optimistic locking, which only causes records to be locked at the exact moment they are updated. This limits the window of time in which updates from one user block updates from a second user. However, users accessing the same data from outside WebDB with other applications may open and hold locks on records that block WebDB users. You can use the lock reports within the Database Monitor to review the current status of locks within the current Oracle instance.

Within the development environment, WebDB manages locks on components using *logical* locks as opposed to *physical* locks. These logical locks can be managed through the Utilities menu choice, but they do not appear in the lock reports.

Redo logs and rollback segments

Oracle ensures that your data and transactions are reliable by the use of redo logs and rollback segments. Updates to the database are saved into redo logs, which can then be processed back against the database in the event of a system failure. The combination of database backups and redo logs ensures that your changes are not lost in the event of a system failure. WebDB provides the Redo Logs link to enable you to review the status of the redo logs for the current system.

When you write data to the database, Oracle copies the transaction information to a section of the database called a *rollback segment*. If an application needs to abort a particular transaction, Oracle uses the information contained in the rollback segments to restore the database to its original state. This is standard behavior for the database, and it is a requirement for supporting the transactional capabilities of SQL. In situations where you have lots of simultaneous updates to the database, the rollback segments can become a bottleneck. WebDB provides the Rollback Segments link on the Database Objects menu to enable you to check the status of the rollback segments.

You are not permitted to make any changes to either the redo logs or the rollback segments inside WebDB. If you detect a problem in this area of the database, you need to have access to the Enterprise Manager in order to make the necessary adjustments.

Sessions and memory structures

A large factor in determining the performance of your Oracle applications is the memory usage and allocation. The Oracle memory cache is called the System Global Area (SGA), and it contains the data cache and shared memory structures of the database. Through the Sessions and Memory Structures link on the Database Objects menu, you can monitor the status of the SGA from within WebDB. Much of the data shown in these reports and charts are of no interest unless you have experience working as an Oracle database administrator. However, you can run the reports and share the output with Oracle support or your local database administrator if you are having performance problems with your WebDB application. An Oracle DBA is able to determine that the SGA needs to be adjusted or tuned from the data in these reports.

Within the Sessions and Memory Structures section, there are two tools for monitoring individual user sessions inside the Oracle database. The Sessions link produces a report that shows the activity within the database on a user-by-user basis. The Sessions report contains a massive amount of detail about the users connected to Oracle, and it includes both WebDB users as well as users connected to Oracle using other tools and applications.

WebDB makes use of a feature known as *connection pooling,* which enables multiple end users to share the same connection to the database. WebDB makes at least one connection to the database for each DAD entry connected to Oracle. However, multiple end users may be accessing Oracle through the same connection within WebDB. The Sessions report provides no indication of when several users are connection-pooling through the same physical connection.

In extreme cases, you may find that you need to isolate a USERID and terminate its connection to Oracle. WebDB provides the Find and Kill Session(s) link to enable you to identify such processes.

1. Navigate to the Database Objects menu within the monitoring system and click the Sessions and Memory Structures link.
2. Choose the Find and Kill Session(s) link to display the panel shown in Figure 21-17 (use the Change to Form View link to show a single record per block).

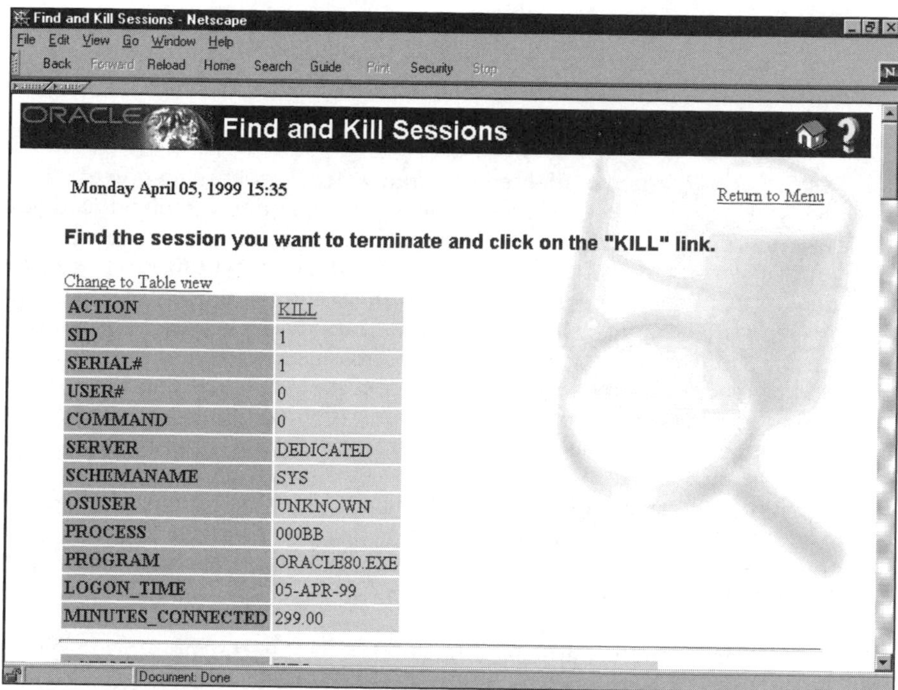

Figure 21-17: Find and Kill Sessions page

This panel can display in two formats: as a form view or as a table view. The form view shows a single session at a time and lists all of the sessions from top to bottom. The table view shows all of the sessions as a series of entries in an HTML table similar to the standard WebDB report format. WebDB displays less information on this panel than the in the Sessions report because the goal of this panel is to enable you to find sessions and terminate them. WebDB displays all of the sessions connected to Oracle both inside and outside WebDB. The Oracle database is composed of a number of system processes and all of them are connected to the database server and are listed in the report as shown in Figure 21-17. At the top of a report is a link next to the ACTION field called KILL. Clicking this link terminates the associated session. You do not have access to this option unless your WebDB account has the DBA role assigned to it.

Terminating user sessions should not be undertaken lightly. Killing a core Oracle session can cause the server to become unstable. We recommend that you get an Oracle DBA involved before you start terminating sessions. In situations where an end-user session is out of control, the ability to terminate the individual session is a powerful tool. However, if you are not familiar with the core Oracle server processes, you can inadvertently cause the server itself to shut down.

WebDB provides this facility to enable you to rid the system of stray processes directly from the browser interface. Because WebDB enables you to make use of any PL/SQL procedure, it is possible to create long-running update routines that may cause performance problems. You can use the Find and Kill Sessions report to identify the problem user session, and then terminate it with the KILL link.

Objects and storage

System performance is affected by three factors: processing power, memory, and disk storage. In the preceding sections of this chapter, we introduced you to the various tools WebDB provides for monitoring the performance of applications and your server in areas of processing speed and memory utilization. WebDB provides an additional set of reports and charts under the Database Objects menu for monitoring disk space allocation and utilization. These particular charts and reports are useful to you even if you are not an experienced Oracle DBA. They are easy to read and provide you with a simple mechanism for ensuring that you are keeping track of the amount of space your applications are using and how quickly your database tables and objects are growing.

Two different classes of reports and charts are in this category: Objects and Storage. The Objects menu is focused on analyzing storage space usage by USERID and object type, while the Storage menu is geared toward reviewing the total amount of disk space available to you.

1. Navigate to the Database Objects page within the monitoring system and choose the Storage link to display the menu shown in Figure 21-18.

Oracle stores all objects into allocation units called *tablespaces,* and each tablespace is itself mapped onto one or more operating system files. The Storage panel provides you with four reports and three charts that display the status of the various tablespaces within the WebDB database instance.

The starting point of your analysis will typically be the Chart of Tablespace Utilization link, which displays a set of charts showing the space utilization of the various tablespaces within your WebDB environment. From these charts you can determine whether or not you are running short of space in your tablespaces. Each of the charts has an associated report, and you can use the Report of Tablespace Utilization to review the status of your tablespaces in a report format.

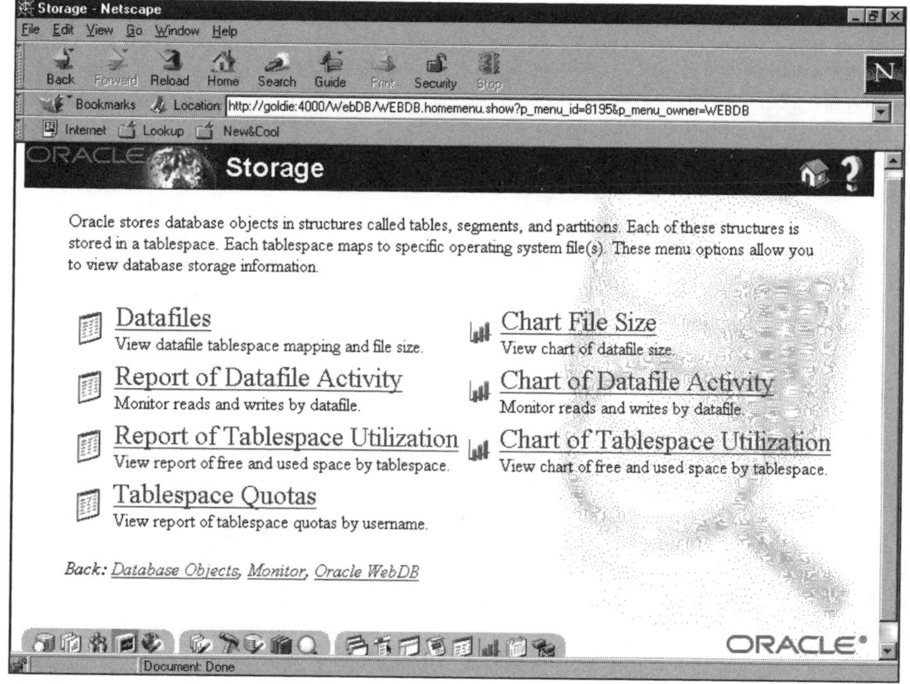

Figure 21-18: Storage page

Once you have taken a look at the status of your tablespaces, you can use the Datafiles and Chart File Size links to examine the physical operating system files to which your tablespaces are mapped. If necessary, you can even look at the physical reads and writes to the operating system files. At the very least, you can use the data in these reports to take a snapshot of your application's use of disk space and spot trends over a period of time. If you notice large jumps in the amount of space utilization over short periods of time, you may need to involve a professional Oracle DBA to help you determine the best course of action. Oracle provides the ability to limit database storage for users according to a quota system, and the final link on this page displays the quota limits for your users.

The owner of each Oracle object is charged for all storage consumed by that object. When end users insert records into tables, the owner of the table is charged for the disk space usage of the new record.

Once you notice that a particular tablespace is filling up, you can use the Objects link to review the details for the tablespace.

2. Navigate back to the Database Objects menu and select the Objects link to display the menu shown in Figure 21-19.

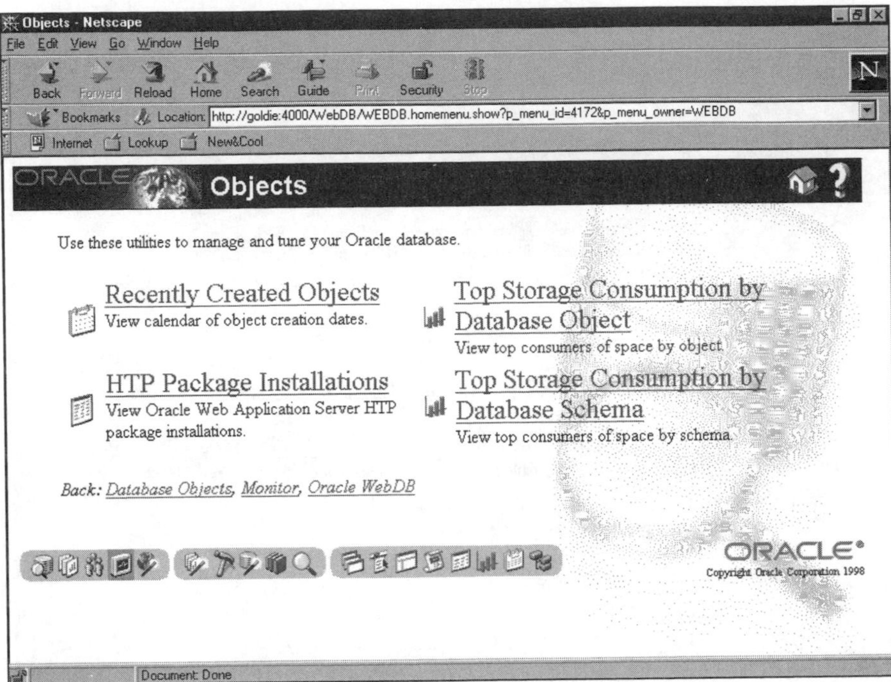

Figure 21-19: Monitor Objects menu

The Objects menu offers you four choices, as shown in Figure 21-19. There are two charts you can use to show you the Oracle objects that are consuming the most disk space, as well as the USERIDs using the most space. The best use of these charts is tracking the use of space and the size of objects over a period of time. By executing these charts on a weekly basis and comparing the results from week to week, you can spot trends in space utilization. Large changes in the size of objects over short periods of time are worth investigating. You can also use these trends as a tool for planning purposes. For example, if your largest tables are consuming 25 percent of your total space and they are growing at 10 percent per week, you can plan ahead and acquire additional disk space ahead of time.

This particular menu also provides a unique analysis tool in the form of the Recently Created Objects link. While all of the other links within the monitoring system are menus, reports, or charts, this particular menu choice points to a WebDB calendar object. The calendar itself is built dynamically by WebDB according to the dates on which all of the objects within your database were created. You can drill down on any individual date and view all of the objects that were created by any single Oracle USERID on that particular day. This can be a very powerful tool for investigating the history of the objects in your database. For example, you can determine the development patterns of your programmers by viewing the calendar across the development cycle for a particular application.

One additional report on this page displays the installation status of the Oracle HTP database packages. These packages are used by the database to render HTML pages, and they are used by WebDB and the Oracle Application Server as well. The report link on this page shows you the status of the installation of these packages.

Activity Log Settings

WebDB logs activity to a pair of database tables stored inside your WebDB installation. These activity logs are designed to roll back and forth much like the standard Oracle redo logs. WebDB continues to write information into the first activity log until it reaches the maximum number of days you have specified for that log. Once this saturation point is reached, WebDB begins writing to the second log and leaves the first log in a dormant state. When the second anniversary date is reached, WebDB stops writing to the second activity log. It also empties the first activity log before it begins writing to the first activity log once again. This enables you to copy the contents of the dormant log into a backup table for further analysis at a later date.

You can set the interval for the log switching within the administration subsystem.

Navigate to the main Administration page and select the Configure WebDB Activity Log link to display the page shown in Figure 21-20.

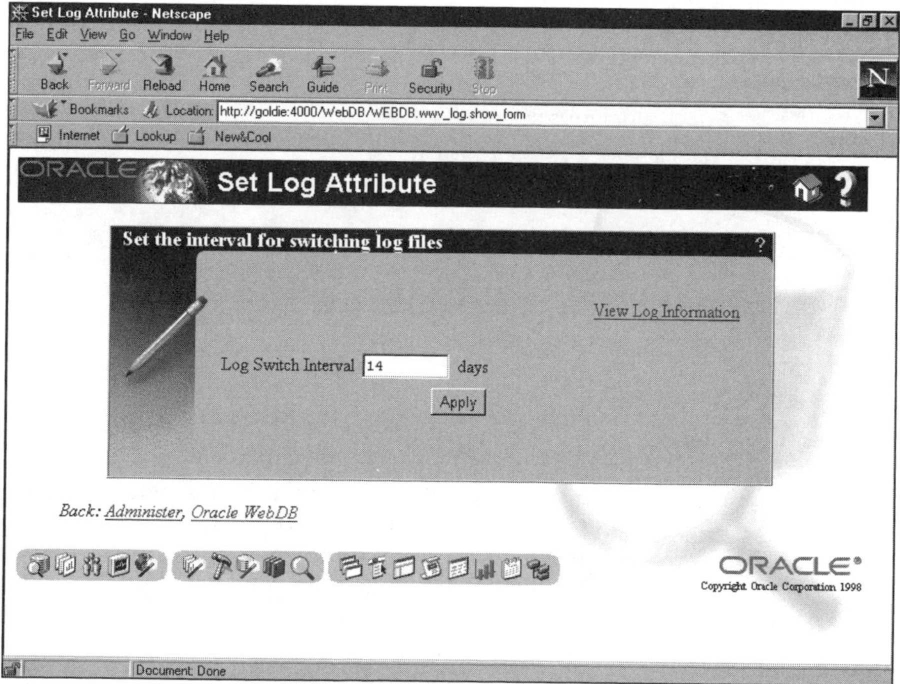

Figure 21-20: Set Log Attribute page

The only attribute you have control over for the activity logs is the number of days that WebDB waits between switching physical activity logs. The change is transparent to you, because WebDB monitoring reports work the same regardless of which log is currently being used for processing. The default behavior is to switch to a new log every two weeks, but you may wish to switch logs more frequently if your Web site generates a lot of activity.

Changing the interval is as simple as entering a new numeric interval value and saving the change using the Apply button. If you wish to view the details of the logging system, you can use the View Log Information link to display the log details, as shown in Figure 21-21.

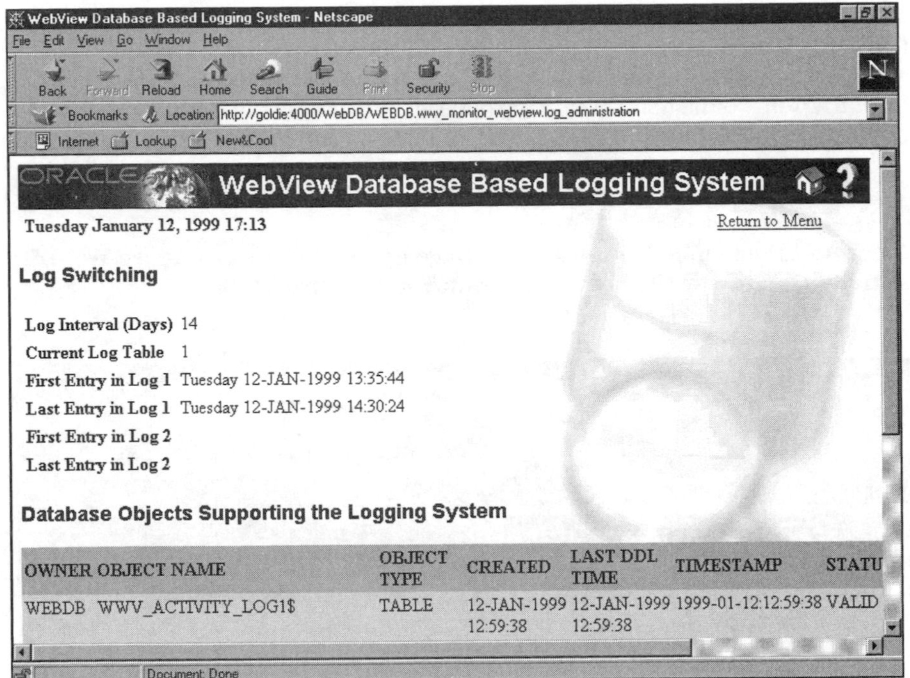

Figure 21-21: Database log details

The WebView Database Based Logging System panel shows two blocks of information. First, at the top of the panel, WebDB shows the log switching information. WebDB displays a value of either 1 or 2 for the Current Log Table field, and this is used to indicate that either WWV_ACTIVITY_LOG1$ or WWV_ACTIVITY_LOG2$ is the current log file. In either case, WebDB displays a date and timestamp that indicates the first and last entries for each of the two log files.

If you are interested in looking for long-term trends, you are free to export the data in the inactive log file to a backup table and create your own reports and charts against this backup table. This enables you to store and analyze the raw log data over a much longer period of time.

In the lower panel of the page is a summary block displaying the details for all of the objects that are part of the physical logging system. This panel does not contain a great deal of extra information, but you can see that the entire logging system is conceptually quite simple — it is composed entirely of two tables, two indexes, and an Oracle PL/SQL package.

Site Builder Monitoring Tools

The Site Builder tools within the WebDB environment have their own set of statistical reports, which are different than the component-monitoring tools you have worked with thus far. Site Builder acts as a hosting environment for complete Web sites and the statistical information it tracks is more concerned with Web site activity than with measuring the response times of individual components.

You are not necessarily able to track the speed and performance of your Web site with the Site Builder statistical tools, but you are able to judge the relative *popularity* of the various folders and objects within your WebDB site. The statistical reports inside of Site Builder are packaged in the toolbox section of the Administration menu.

We recommend that you complete Chapter 18 on Site Builder before you proceed with the following section.

1. Open the Net University site you created previously and navigate to the Site Administration menu within Site Builder. Choose the Site Statistics link in the Toolbox section to display the panel shown in Figure 21-22.

You will find that the Site Builder statistics are displayed at a higher level of abstraction than the component monitoring tools. The goal of the Site Builder statistical reports is to reveal the relative popularity of one component or another. The designers of Site Builder have broken the types of statistics into the following five categories:

- ✦ Hits
- ✦ Searches
- ✦ Folders
- ✦ Items
- ✦ Access

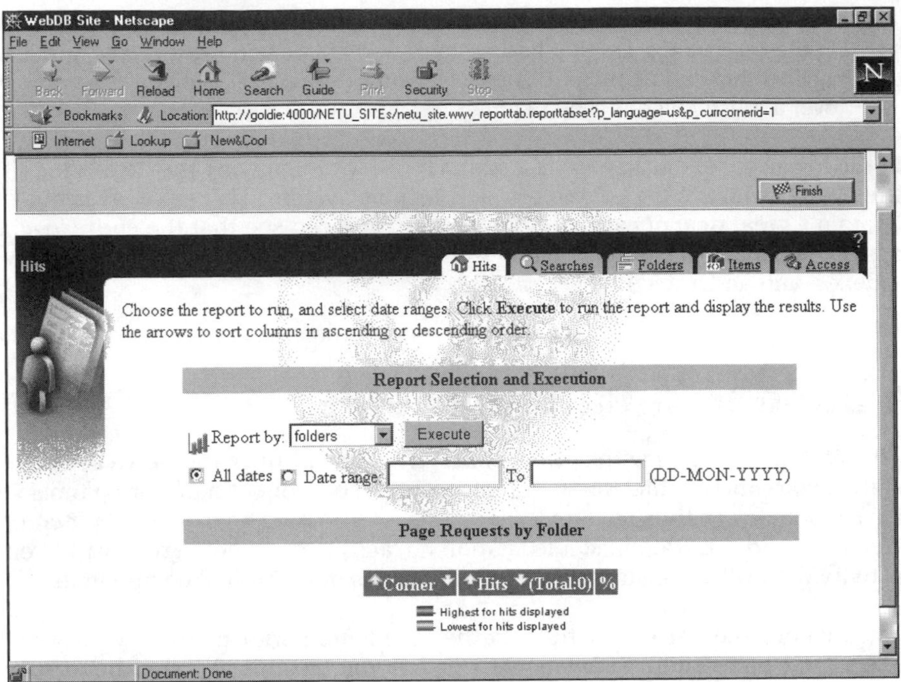

Figure 21-22: Site Builder statistics

Each of these reports is implemented as a series of interactive panels with a tab panel as the tool for navigating between reports.

The initial panel, Hits, displays a graph of the most popular hits within each corner and subcorner. WebDB counts every interaction within a corner as a hit and this chart gives you a quick view of which of your corners are the most popular. You can use the Report by list box to change the category of the report and select any of the subitems such as searches, folders, items, or access within the corner.

WebDB also provides a pair of date fields you can use to restrict the report to a range of selected dates. This is a particularly useful feature if you are trying to measure the impact of a new addition to a given corner. For example, you may have a consistently underutilized corner until you add some new components that spark some interest in that area of the site. In order to measure the short-term impact of your change, you may need to restrict the report to a smaller date range that provides you with the necessary level of granularity at which you can see the impact of the change. After all, you may not be able to accurately judge the impact of your change simply by looking at a report covering two weeks of data when your changes are only relevant for a single day within that time span.

The body of the chart changes as you select the various options using the Report by list box. The chart itself is an interactive page and you can use the gold arrows on the chart labels to expand and contract the data displayed.

2. Use the Execute button to view the hits by folder for your site.

Alternatively, you can use the remaining tab folders to view the statistical information by category directly. The Searches tab displays statistics on the most common, simple search phrases. You can use the results of this chart to help you make changes in the folders, categories, and perspectives that you create. For example, if you were to see a large number of searches for the phrase "Course Catalog" in the Net University site, you might decide to add a new subfolder within the site that provides Course Catalog reports.

The Folders tab displays statistics on the most popular folders and subfolders within each site. Popularity is measured by hits, so you may decide to drop unpopular folders or subdivide popular folders into smaller units based on the results of this chart. Once you have reviewed the activity at the folder level, you can use the Items tab to look at the details of each folder. You may find that a subset of items within a particular folder is causing the high degree of popularity of the folder. In cases where a single item is causing all of the activity within a folder, a realignment of folders and items may be required. Such a realignment might mean moving the popular item to another folder and subsequently removing the less popular folder itself.

Finally, you can review the list of users hitting your site by using the Access tab. As with the component builder monitoring reports, the Address reports include usage by account, IP address, and browser.

The default behavior within Site Builder is to limit statistical report access to site administrators. You can, however, permit the general public to have access to the site statistics through the main site administration panel.

3. Navigate to the Site link for the Net University site and select the main panel shown in Figure 21-23.

You can permit users to view the statistics for your site by using the Enable Public Users to View Site Statistics check box. The component monitoring tools provide you with the facilities for monitoring and measuring the performance of your site. Because this information is typically used by your systems administrator, it is unlikely that you will permit your public users to view the WebDB monitoring reports and charts. Within Site Builder, however, it is fairly common to give your end users access to such data. After all, your goal is to build a site that has the maximum impact for your organization, and there is no value in building items and folders that users ignore.

If you decide to phase out folders or categories, you can add news items to the main page of your site that point to the statistical reports. In the comments section you can announce your intention to eliminate links based upon the data in the statistical reports and enable your users to view the data themselves. Once you have the buy-in from your end-user community, you will find that the task of removing items is easy.

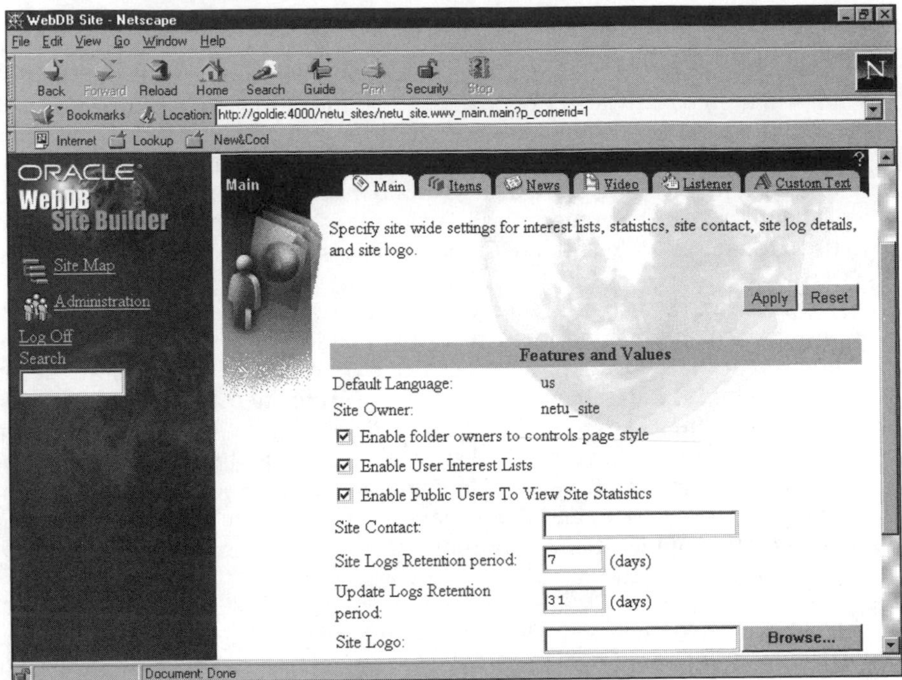

Figure 21-23: Permitting public users to view site statistics

Wrapping Up

Many things can have a positive or negative impact on your site, but two of the more important items are the performance of the site and the popularity of the items within the site. Sites that suffer from performance problems are rarely popular with users regardless of the cool items and applications contained within the site. It is hard for users to be productive and happy when their response times are poor.

In this chapter, you worked with a set of tools that can help you to judge the performance of your site and keep your applications moving along swiftly. Even in cases where the performance is solid, however, users complain if they are forced to navigate through reams of data just to find the items they are looking for. WebDB's monitoring tools enable you to determine just how popular each item in your site is as well as the profile of the users accessing these items.

By reviewing this data carefully, you can determine if users are having trouble finding the data they need, or if certain items are just not useful. You can use this information to realign your site and weed out the less popular items to make your site concise and easy to use.

✦ ✦ ✦

P A R T

V

Advanced WebDB Topics

✦ ✦ ✦ ✦

In This Part

✦ ✦ ✦ ✦

CHAPTER 22

Deploying WebDB Sites

✦ ✦ ✦ ✦

In This Chapter

WebDB Deployment Components and Architecture

Database Access Descriptors

Component Schemas

Deploying WebDB Applications

✦ ✦ ✦ ✦

Four major tasks are involved in the development of applications: design, development, testing, and deployment. The previous chapters in this book introduced you to the WebDB methodology for developing applications. Part of WebDB's value proposition is the reduced amount of design and development time it takes to deliver an application. Of course, this is partly due to the capabilities of the product itself. The individual wizards provide you with a very structured interface for building components, which reduces your testing requirements. The WebDB wizards also provide you with a fast methodology for developing the individual components, leaving you with only the deployment issue to deal with.

Application deployment is more art than science with WebDB, because the tool itself does not contain any specific deployment tools. Unlike some other application development environments, the components are in place and ready to go when you are finished designing them with the wizard interface. The designers of WebDB built the product to be easy to work with and highly productive, and no one would argue that this is not a good thing. However, the downside to this design is that WebDB lacks a layer of insulation between the design phase and the deployment phase. This places an additional burden on you as the developer to implement a deployment strategy that makes sense for your organization. In this chapter, we will introduce you to the various components of WebDB's deployment architecture, and you will learn how you can use these different components to implement a variety of run-time configurations.

WebDB Deployment Components and Architecture

The designers of WebDB concentrated on integrating the product tightly with the Oracle database and making the wizards easy to use. While we believe they have succeeded with both of these design goals, one questionable result of their efforts is the fact that no separate run-time environment exists for WebDB. You are probably familiar with other application development environments that provide you with separate sets of tools for developing and then deploying an application. Part of WebDB's elegance is the fact that there is no separate development environment outside of the browser. This makes it conceptually simple to install and use. However, the normal separation between development and deployment is not present in WebDB. Because of this, the process of deploying applications requires you to have a firm understanding of the components of the WebDB architecture. Once you understand the various parts of this architecture, you can then decide how to best deploy those parts to your users.

Logically, it is possible to divide the WebDB product into individual components and then consider how these pieces are used for development and deployment. The net result of this analysis is that the deployment process with WebDB is more an issue of strategy than it is a specific set of tools and utilities. Two basic categories of objects are part of your WebDB deployment. Following is a list of components that constitute the overall WebDB environment:

- ✦ Oracle database server
- ✦ HTP/HTF packages and OAS utilities
- ✦ WebDB procedures
- ✦ Database tables
- ✦ WebDB listener
- ✦ PL/SQL gateway
- ✦ External images
- ✦ Tables and data upon which the application is built

The starting point for any WebDB application is the Oracle database. WebDB is built with the services provided by the Oracle database, such as the PL/SQL language, and you cannot deploy a WebDB application without the database. WebDB applications are also designed to be data-driven, and the Oracle database is the foundation for both the development environment and for your deployed applications. If you are building Web sites that are nothing more than a series of static pages, WebDB is probably not the right solution. With WebDB, the root element for an application is the Oracle database server itself.

Layered within the database are sets of PL/SQL packages used by Oracle to render HTML output. These packages are commonly referred to as the PL/SQL Web Toolkit.

WebDB is built on top of these procedures, which were designed as part of the PL/SQL gateway for the Oracle Application Server. Oracle provides an additional set of procedures specific to the Application Server, which are called the OAS utility procedures. These utilities provide some additional services for managing Web objects such as cookies, and are part of the HTF/HTP installation. WebDB automatically installs all of these foundation packages during the WebDB installation process, and they appear as a set of PL/SQL packages in a separate schema.

WebDB itself requires an additional set of procedures built on top of the HTF/HTP packages. These packages are added to the WebDB account created when you install WebDB. From a development perspective, these packages implement the menu hierarchy and the various build wizards, and you are probably familiar with them from using the development environment. Additional packages and procedures, which you will normally work with directly, are used to implement many of the lower-level functionality of WebDB. For example, shared objects, such as lists-of-values, are not converted into a database procedure by the LOV Wizard. The LOV elements are written to a series of database tables, and an internal WebDB procedure handles all of the display of such elements at run time. Although there is a clear separation of these tasks internally, Oracle has not documented this separation for the first release of WebDB. As a result, you cannot know exactly which procedures are used by the wizards and which ones are used by WebDB internally.

In addition to these procedures, a number of database tables are used internally by WebDB. Some of these tables store the source definitions for the objects that you build, and some are used internally by WebDB. When you create an object with the component wizards, the source for the object is stored within these tables. However, the actual object is implemented as a PL/SQL package of its own. Shared components, on the other hand, are always stored as records within a table, and there is no one-to-one mapping with a stored procedure. As with the internal WebDB procedures, Oracle has not publicly documented the functionality of individual tables within the WebDB account, so there is no way for you to tell which tables you need for deployment. The safest and most accurate assumption for you to make is that all the WebDB procedures and tables are required for both development and deployment.

The listener is the next component of the architecture, and it is one of the most important pieces of the deployment puzzle. The listener is paired with the PL/SQL gateway. The listener itself is an HTTP server, which acts as a lightweight process for managing HTTP-style requests. The PL/SQL gateway is responsible for shuttling data to and from the database, and it works in conjunction with the listener. The PL/SQL gateway contains all of the necessary information for communicating with the SQL*NET and Net8 libraries. Physically, both the listener and gateway are delivered as several executable programs and DLL libraries.

There are three different options for choosing a listener. The default installation of WebDB uses a simple packaging with the HTTP listener and PL/SQL gateway combined into a single executable program called WDBLSNR. You also have the choice of using a third-party HTTP server as your primary Web server, in which case you only need the PL/SQL gateway program, WDBCGI. Finally, you can deploy WebDB components within the Oracle Application Server with the WebDB cartridge. WebDB actually requires some additional functionality not offered by the built-in OAS PL/SQL cartridge, and the developers of WebDB have built a special version of the PL/SQL cartridge for use with OAS that is called the WebDB cartridge.

The last component of the architecture is the images used by WebDB within the development interface. These images are stored in two formats: Graphic Interchange Format (GIF) files and Joint Photographic Expedition Graphics (JPEG) format files. Both formats are considered Web standards, and most browsers automatically handle images in these formats. WebDB stores these images outside the database, and the listener locates them and displays them within the development interface. However, the line between development and deployment is a gray area. For example, you may decide to enable your end users to browse the database using the Browse Wizard within WebDB. In this case, the browse functionality is part of the deployment of your application as well as the development. Because all of the WebDB pages use at least some of the external images, these image files are necessary for the deployment of your applications.

A WebDB application requires all seven of these base objects in order to function, and they are required whether you are building applications or deploying applications. This deployment architecture of WebDB is depicted in Figure 22-1.

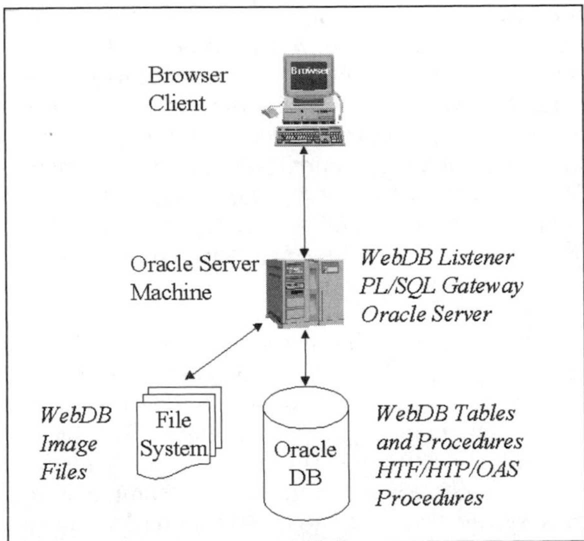

Figure 22-1: WebDB architecture components

The simplest possible deployment architecture from a system's perspective is within an intranet on a single server as shown in Figure 22-1. All of the components in this model are deployed on a single server machine, with the WebDB listener working directly with the database and acting as the HTTP server for the browser clients. From this viewpoint, it is not necessary to delve into the specifics of how the Oracle database itself is laid out. It does not matter how many USERIDs you have, nor does it matter where the data and procedures are stored within the database server. You may have several Oracle servers running on different machines and you can run a copy of WebDB on each of them, as shown in Figure 22-2.

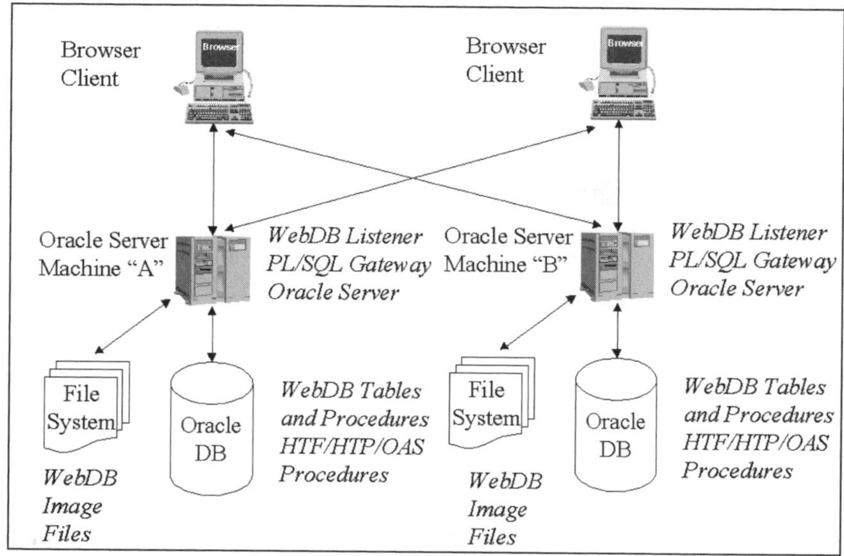

Figure 22-2: Deploying multiple copies of WebDB

The WebDB listener is associated with a particular server machine, Oracle instance, and port address. Users can navigate to either machine through the browser and gain access to a WebDB application on either machine provided they have the necessary permissions and logon information. Because WebDB itself does not mark individual components as being part of any particular application, you could have several logical applications stored within a single Oracle instance.

Note

The Site Builder component within WebDB does in fact provide a means to logically separate applications, but this capability does not translate down to the component object level. It is also possible to combine components into a logical application using component building schemas, which we discuss later on in this chapter.

The key element to understand is that an installation of the seven WebDB components constitutes both the *development* architecture as well as the *deployment* architecture. Furthermore, you cannot either build applications or deploy applications without including all seven components in some fashion.

Figure 22-3 shows the same seven components of the architecture layered as individual components.

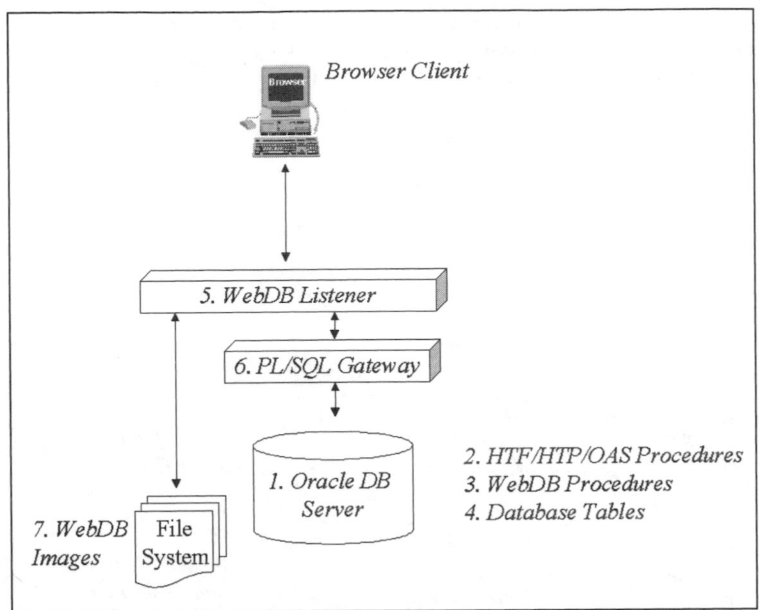

Figure 22-3: Deployment components

Any deployment strategy that you use for your WebDB applications must account for these seven components in one way or another. In particular, it is possible to substitute for the listener process and the PL/SQL gateway components, as well as relocating the database server and the database objects, which are covered in the following sections of this chapter. The default installation of WebDB uses the architecture as depicted in Figure 22-3.

Replacing the listener

One of the options available to you is to replace the listener with a third-party Web server. Chances are good that you already have some type of Web server in your organization, and you may want to integrate your WebDB applications with the existing Web server. You can easily link your existing Web server to the WebDB application simply by embedding a URL link that points to the WebDB listener within any page on your existing HTTP server application. The connection is not made from server to server, but rather from browser client to server.

For example, assume that you already have a Web server running on port 80 on machine A. Further, assume that you have a WebDB listener running on port 4000 on machine B. Adding a link such as the following in any page within Web server A connects the user to the WebDB application:

```
http://serverb:4000/DAD/component_name.show
```

In the previous code, *server* is the name of the server that contains the WebDB environment (machine B), the *DAD* is the name of the Data Access Descriptor, and the *component_name* is the name of the component created with WebDB.

Because it is so simple to connect the WebDB listener to your existing Web server by using links, you may simply choose to add links from your existing Web pages to the WebDB components. However, the WebDB listener suffers from some restrictions that may not be present in the Web server you are currently using. Specifically, the current version of the listener lacks the following capabilities:

- HTTP 1.1 support
- SSL
- CGI

The HyperText Transfer Protocol (HTTP) is the mechanism by which Web servers transfer content to Web browsers. The current version of the listener only supports the 1.0 version of the HTTP standard for transferring data between the two. There are two chief advantages of HTTP 1.1 over HTTP 1.0. First, the 1.1 version offers support for persistent TCP/IP connections to the server side of the equation. While HTTP itself is a stateless protocol, it is common for a single user to request subsequent pages over a short period of time. In fact, Web pages that have links to graphic images are a perfect example of this type of processing. The browser reads the HTML page and then immediately requests the additional graphics files from the Web server. Under the HTTP 1.0 specification, the Web server closes the TCP/IP connection after each page (or file) is delivered to the client. With the 1.1 enhancement, the Web server can keep the TCP/IP socket alive for a short period of time. This enables the Web server to improve efficiency by reusing the TCP/IP connection already open for subsequent data requests by a browser client. HTTP 1.1 also supports the capability to restart failed downloads without having to transfer the entire file all over again. The current version of the listener process does not support either of these capabilities.

For Internet-based applications, you may also need to support secure communications between the client browser and the Web server. This is especially true if you plan to build e-commerce-style applications. Most Web servers support a protocol called the Secure Sockets Layer (SSL) that you can use in conjunction with the HTTP protocol. The SSL protocol encrypts the data communications between the client and server and protects the integrity of the information sent between the two. The current version of the WebDB listener does not support the use of SSL.

Although the WebDB listener can serve static HTML files as well as PL/SQL data to the browser client, it does not have support for Common Gateway Interface (CGI) applications. Most Web servers provide a way to communicate between Web browsers and external programs on the server side by using the CGI protocol. The current version of the listener does not support a CGI interface, so it is not possible to call third-party programs from the WebDB listener. Please note that a CGI program using the WDBCGI.EXE program can call the WebDB PL/SQL gateway. This utility is supplied with the listener as shown in Figure 22-4.

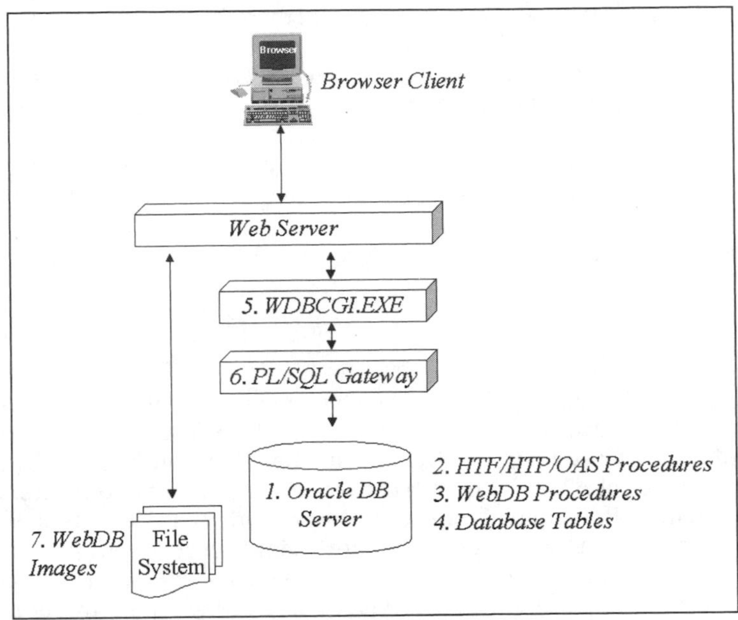

Figure 22-4: WebDB configured with a third-party Web server

WebDB provides the PL/SQL gateway portion of the listener as a separate program called the WebDB CGI Interface (WDBCGI). This program is linked with the Oracle SQL*NET and Net8 libraries, but it does not have the listener capabilities of the WDBLSNR program. Any third-party Web server must support CGI in order to be used with WebDB.

While it is possible to use a third-party Web server for developing applications with WebDB, we recommend that you use the WebDB listener during development. This simplifies the process of tracking errors and connecting to the image files the development interface uses.

Oracle has tested the third-party interface with Microsoft's Internet Information Server (IIS) Web server and the Apache Web server for UNIX. Theoretically, the WDBCGI program should work with any Web server that supports a CGI interface. In order to link WebDB to the Web server, you must copy the listener program WDBCGI.EXE to the cgi-bin directory. The Web server must have a copy of the

SQL*NET or Net8 client software installed and the Data Access Descriptors must point to the proper Oracle server. You will learn more about applying and using the data access descriptors in the next section of this chapter. It is not necessary to run the Oracle server on the same machine as the Web server, and both can be located behind a firewall on your network.

If you plan on using a third-party Web server, we recommend that you install SQL*Plus on the Web server as well as the SQL*NET or Net8 client libraries. You can use SQL*Plus interactively to test your connection to the Oracle database server before attempting to use the CGI interface. Doing so helps you isolate problems with the client libraries from configuration issues with the CGI interface and the Web server.

The only visible difference when using a third-party Web server is the format of the URLs passed between the browser and the Web server. For example, if you are using the integrated WebDB listener, the format of the URL string might look like the following:

```
http://pumpkin:4000/webdb
```

If you were to use a third-party Web server in place of the listener on the same host machine, the modified URL would be as follows:

```
http://pumpkin:80/cgi-bin/wdbcgi/webdb
```

The sole difference between the two is the addition of the CGI directory and the call to the WDBCGI program. The configuration behind the Web server would be irrelevant at this level of the interface, although the data access descriptors would have to be configured correctly in order to connect to the database properly.

The interfaces for third-party Web servers were the last part of the WebDB product to be built and tested. We recommend that you review the release notes and Oracle WebDB HTTP listener documentation carefully before you attempt to use WebDB with an external listener.

This type of configuration provides you with the ability to support both HTTP 1.1 and SSL by virtue of the fact that the listening component of the application is your Web server and not the WebDB listener. However, the downside to this configuration is likely to be the performance hit on the part of the CGI interface. While the built-in listener has facilities for maintaining connections to the database server, the CGI interface disconnects from the database after each command.

You have one additional choice for deploying the components of your application, and that is to use the Oracle application server as a host platform for WebDB.

Oracle Application Server and WebDB

The WebDB PL/SQL gateway is built around the same concepts as the PL/SQL cartridge shipped along with the Oracle Application Server. Both interfaces use the same concept of database access descriptors for capturing database connection information, and both make use of the PL/SQL Web Toolkit. However, the two interfaces are not identical, as the PL/SQL gateway for WebDB has some additional requirements that are not part of the PL/SQL cartridge interface. Most of these requirements are transparent to you from a usability perspective, but it is important to understand the differences. In general, existing PL/SQL cartridge applications should be able to run unchanged with the WebDB listener and PL/SQL gateway. However, WebDB applications should be deployed to OAS with the WebDB cartridge as shown in Figure 22-5.

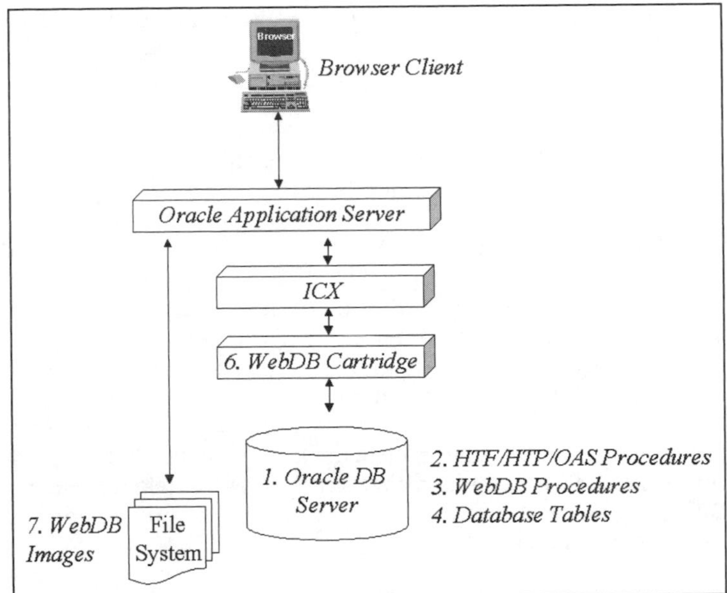

Figure 22-5: OAS and WebDB

The listener includes a library file called WDBCTX used as an interface between WebDB and the intercartridge exchange (ICX) interface of OAS. In order to connect the two interfaces, you must have administrative privileges on the OAS server. The WebDB cartridge is added as a new application with the name WebDB and the application type CWEB. The cartridge itself is called WDBCTX and you must provide OAS with the full path name of the library file. The entry point for this new shared object as required by OAS is wwwre_Entry, and the virtual path for the cartridge is /wdbctx.

For more information about these configuration options, please refer to the documentation for the Oracle Application Server.

In a similar fashion to the third-party Web server interface, the major visible change to the user is the modification of the URL string that connects to WebDB. The modified URL string in this case would look like this:

```
http://pumpkin:100/wdbctx/webdb
```

The server name and port number are those used by the Oracle application server and the virtual directory `/wdbctx` matches the address of the WebDB cartridge. The last parameter, as always, is the database access descriptor being used to connect to the database. By default, this starts the WebDB main menu, but you could replace the string `webdb` with an alternative DAD entry and append a procedure name to the string to call an individual WebDB component.

The Oracle Application Server provides an advanced set of load balancing and intercartridge features beyond the scope of this book. You may find the need to deploy your WebDB applications through the OAS engine if you want to combine these applications with preexisting OAS programs. Even if you are not currently using OAS, you may find that the load balancing capabilities of OAS are reason enough to deploy WebDB through the cartridge interface. OAS also features a number of prebuilt interfaces to support things such as electronic commerce and Web shopping carts, which you can access through the OAS ICX architecture.

Database Access Descriptors

One of the major innovations of both the PL/SQL cartridge and the WebDB PL/SQL gateway are the Database Access Descriptors (DADs). DADs are the mechanism by which users are authenticated and connected to the database by the PL/SQL gateway. While you are unlikely to alter your main listener settings or CGI interface once you have them installed and running, you may want to modify your DADs frequently. DADs can be used to provide a logical grouping of users and applications for your WebDB components.

The database access descriptor settings are found in the Administration menu under the Listener Settings option. The Change PL/SQL Gateway Settings link takes you to the main settings page, as shown in Figure 22-6. And each database access descriptor is composed of ten settings, which Table 22-1 describes.

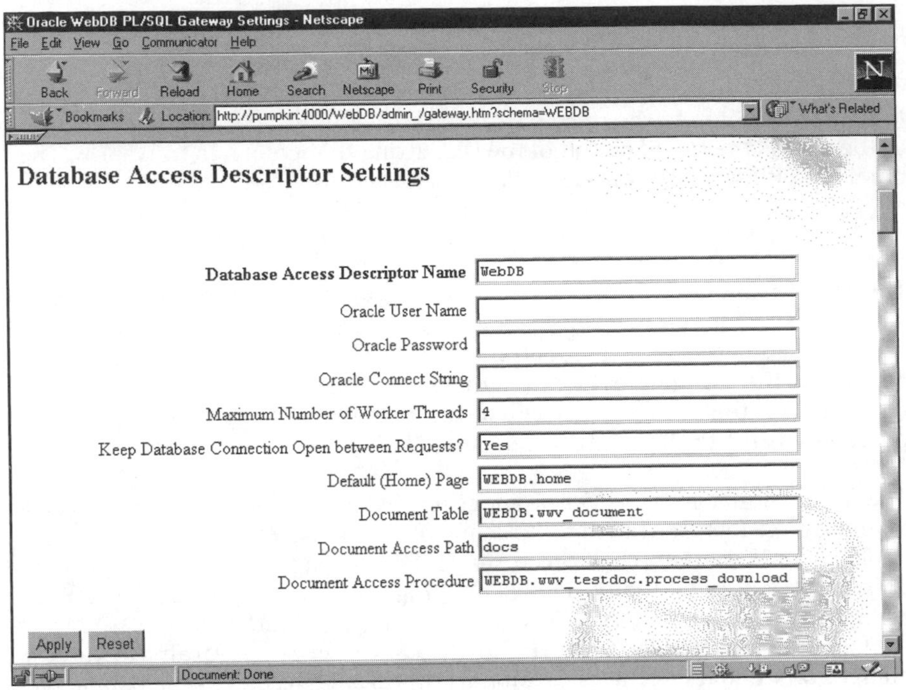

Figure 22-6: PL/SQL gateway settings

Table 22-1
Database Access Descriptor Fields

Field	*Description*
Database Access Descriptor Name	The Descriptor Name field identifies the entry in the DAD table and is used as part of the URL.
Oracle User Name	If a value is specified for this field, WebDB uses the value as the Oracle USERID to connect to the database. If this value is blank, WebDB prompts the user for this value at run time.
Oracle Password	If a value is specified for this field, WebDB uses the value as the Oracle password to connect to the database. If this value is blank, WebDB prompts the user for this value at run time. You cannot provide a value for the password field without providing one for the User Name field.

Field	*Description*
Oracle Connect String	The PL/SQL gateway links to the SQL*NET libraries, and this entry can be used to pass a SQL*NET alias for the connection. The string value entered into this field must match an existing SQL*NET host definition on the machine where the listener (or CGI program) is running. The actual database server can be located on a difference machine.
Maximum Number of Worker Threads	This entry is only meaningful when the listener and PL/SQL gateway are used together. The integer value entered into this field sets the number of threads that can be created on behalf of a given DAD entry. Typically, this value should be set at about 10 for an NT server. However, if you have many users connecting to the application using the same DAD with different USERIDs, then you may need to adjust this entry to a higher number.
Keep Database Connection Open between Requests?	This entry is only meaningful when the listener and PL/SQL gateway are used together. This entry should normally be filled in with the value Yes to indicate that WebDB should keep connections to the database open between URL requests. The connection to the database can be time-consuming when compared to the overall cost of processing a given URL, and keeping database connections open can improve performance.
Default (Home) Page	This entry determines the procedure that runs if no parameters are supplied for a given URL. In effect, this is the default home page for the DAD entry.
Document Table	Identifies the table that will be used to store uploaded files by Site Builder applications.
Document Access Path	Identifies the URL setting for files that have been uploaded into Site Builder.
Document Access Procedure	Identifies the PL/SQL procedure that will be used to complete the processing of a file download operation.

This group of ten settings provides you with the flexibility to tune your deployment strategy as necessary. Logically, these ten parameters can be divided into three distinct groups according to how they are used. The first group — made up of the Descriptor Name, Oracle User Name, Oracle Password, Oracle Connect String, and Default (Home) Page settings — controls the connection information. The second group controls settings used primarily for Site Builder, and includes the Document Table, the Document Access Path, and the Document Access Procedure. The final group is made up of two fields that control the performance settings for the gateway — the Maximum Number of Worker Threads and the Keep Database Connection Open between Requests? setting.

The connection field group is the main tool for logically linking a group of users together into a single application. The Descriptor Name becomes the physical name by which you refer to the group of users that are identified by the name. The Descriptor Name is used as part of the URL string that feeds the content to the browser. Within the development environment of WebDB, you have used a URL similar to the following string to connect to the WebDB build interface:

```
http://pumpkin:4000/webdb/webdb.home
```

The string `webdb` within the URL matches a Descriptor Name that has been defined as part of the PL/SQL gateway. When you installed WebDB, the default descriptor name webdb is automatically created. Even if you have allowed multiple developers to work with WebDB using separate Oracle USERIDs, you have most likely used the same DAD entry. After all, the Descriptor Name is nothing more than a logical connection. The physical connection is made using the secondary fields: Oracle User Name and Oracle Password. If these fields are left blank, WebDB displays a dialog box that prompts the user for logon information at run time. On the other hand, if these fields contain value strings, WebDB uses these values to log on to the database. Within the URL string, the information to the left of the Descriptor Name refers to the server (including the CGI information if it has been provided). The information to the right of the DAD name refers to the component being called. When a browser sends a URL to the PL/SQL gateway, the gateway checks its client-side cookies to determine if there is valid logon information for the DAD name from the individual TCP/IP client. If the gateway does not contain valid logon credentials for the session, it then uses the DAD entry information to either log the user on, or to prompt the user for logon information.

Consider the following two URL strings:

```
http://pumpkin:4000/webdb/webdb.home
http://pumpkin:4000/myapp/webdb.home
```

The two strings are identical except for the DAD names in the center of the strings. In order for WebDB to use these URLs, the strings `webdb` and `myapp` must match DAD entries in the PL/SQL gateway settings panel. If the string does not match an existing entry, then WebDB returns a "404 Page Not Found" error message to the browser. However, if DAD entry is valid, WebDB attempts to use the entry to connect to the database on your behalf.

In addition to the user name and password, you are free to specify a connection to a remote Oracle database server by entering a value in the Oracle connect string field. The value string you enter must match an existing SQL*NET or Net8 alias as set by the Oracle Nameserver or TNSNAMES.ORA file.

1. Click the Administer link from the main menu, and then select the Listener Settings link.

2. Navigate down to the first completely blank Database Access Descriptor section and add a new entry as follows:

```
Database Access Descriptor Name - netuprivate
Maximum Number of Worker Threads - 4
Keep Database Connection Open - Yes
Default Home Page - WEBDB.home
Document Table - WEBDB.wwv_document
Document Access Path - docs
Document Access Procedure- WEBDB.wwv_testdoc.process_download
```

3. Click the Apply button to save your changes.

4. Enter the following URL into your browser location field:

```
http://pumpkin:4000/netuprivate
```

Replace the server name and port number with values for your local server and port.

WebDB prompts you for logon information and then proceeds to display the WebDB builder interface. Although you have already logged on to the database in order to change the PL/SQL gateway settings, you logged on using the DAD entry webdb. By using the netuser DAD you are considered a different user by WebDB. From the development perspective, there is little value in using different DADs for your developers, because they are able to log on to the database using different USERIDs within the same DAD. The value is in using the DADs to separate logical groups of content during deployment.

From a security perspective, there are two types of application components within the WebDB environment: public and private. Public components are those objects to be made available to your entire user community, whether through an intranet or over the entire Internet. Although WebDB always requires a valid logon to the Oracle database, you are free to embed the user name and password directly into the DAD definition. Doing so causes WebDB to log on to the database automatically, and the connection is transparent to the user.

Private components are those objects restricted to the use of specific USERIDs. You will typically want to require an interactive logon for private components.

For example, in the Net University site, the events calendar and sports schedule are examples of public components. Although you store the source data for these objects in the database, you do not want to require the user community at large to have a user name and password in order to view this data. You want the public to be able to access these pages easily, and the public includes people that you may not be familiar with in advance.

One solution to this problem is to use static pages for public data, because the WebDB listener never requires logon information for static pages. However, the benefit to using WebDB is to drive your HTML pages from data in your database. As the Net University schedule changes, you do not want to manually update static schedule pages. If the pages are stored in the database, a WebDB component can automatically display the updated schedule as requested, without any manual intervention. The problem with this solution is that the PL/SQL gateway always requires logon information in order to connect you to the database. The solution is to create a public DAD that contains the logon information with preloaded values for the user name and password.

Conversely, you may want to require that your users have a valid, individual logon before they can access certain data items. For example, in the Net University application, there is place for NetU alumni to review their biographical information and keep track of one another. In the interest of privacy, you would not want members of the general public to have access to this information. You can protect this data by limiting access to these forms and reports to a specified DAD record that prompts for a valid user name and password. The connection between the DAD record and the component object is made at run time, which enables you to build components without having to worry about how they are later deployed. Any component can be serviced by any valid Database Access Descriptor, and any DAD can work with multiple components. For any DAD record, you are free to specify a home component through the Default Home Page entry. In the absence of a call to a specific component, WebDB uses the entry in this field to execute a specific PL/SQL procedure. You will learn how to use these entries to implement public and private components later in this section.

The second group of fields in the DAD record is made up of the Document Table, the Document Access Path, and the Document Access Procedure. These fields are used for accessing and storing files in both WebDB and Site Builder. Notice that for the new DAD record you entered, these values were simply copied from the WebDB DAD entry.

When you install WebDB, the entries for these fields are populated automatically by the installation program. The Document Table item is a concatenation of the schema owner and a table name (wwv_document). WebDB uses this entry to store information uploaded by an end user within a Site Builder application. WebDB normally creates a DAD record for you automatically when you create a site within Site Builder and this field will be filled in with the proper value during this process. You can change this value in order to accommodate the situation in which you wish to have multiple DAD records pointing to the same site. For the purposes of WebDB components, this item is not used, and you can copy the value for this field from the WEBDB DAD entry when you create a new DAD record. In the next section, you we will introduce you to the concept of component schemas, at which time you can consider replacing the value for this field.

The Document Access Path is a virtual directory WebDB uses to locate files that have been uploaded into Site Builder. The string entered into this field becomes a shorthand technique for extracting files directly. For example, assume that you have uploaded a file called sample.htm into a Site Builder site with the DAD of mysite and a document access path of docs. You can view the sample.htm file using a built-in link within Site Builder, or you can pass a URL such as the following directly through the browser interface:

```
http://pumpkin:4000/mysite/docs/sample.htm
```

The last field in this group is the Document Access Procedure, and contains the schema owner and procedure name for a procedure used to download a file to the browser. The default value for this field is the WebDB schema owner and the literal string wwv_testdoc.process_download. Normally, you take the default for this field as well, but there are cases where you may wish to change this value. The WebDB installation comes equipped with two scripts, docload.sql and testdoc.sql, that build the Document Access Table and the Document Access Procedure for a given schema. The WebDB installation program normally creates both of these objects.

1. If you are not already on the PL/SQL gateway settings page, use the Administer link from the main menu and then select the Listener Settings link.
2. Navigate down to the first completely blank Database Access Descriptor section and add a new entry as follows:

```
Database Access Descriptor Name - netupublic
Oracle UserName - netu
Oracle Password - netu
Maximum Number of Worker Threads - 4
Keep Database Connection Open - Yes
Default Home Page - WEBDB.home
Document Table - WEBDB.wwv_document
Document Access Path - docs
Document Access Procedure- WEBDB.wwv_testdoc.process_download
```

3. Click the Apply button to save your changes.

At this point, you should have two new DAD records entered into WebDB: netupublic and netuprivate. The two entries should differ only in a single respect: the netupublic account has the Oracle user name/password filled in and the private account has blank entries for those two fields.

4. Load the following scripts from the CD-ROM into the WebDB account using SQL*Plus:

```
ch22_dyn_alumni.sql
ch22_dyn_calendar.sql
ch22_mnu_sample.sql
```

The three items you loaded provide you with an example of using a public and private DAD. The ch22_dyn_alumni dynamic page object contains the graduation years, names, and majors for all of the alumni. This report should not be available to the public at large, and it should require a specific logon to the database. The ch22_dyn_calendar report, on the other hand, lists all of the events for Net University for the current academic year and it should be available to anyone who surfs to the Net University site. The ch22_mnu_sample menu contains two links — one for each report.

5. Exit your Web browser to close all connections, and make sure you close all of the open browser windows.
6. Restart your Web browser.

7. Enter the following URL, remembering to substitute your server name and port number:

```
http://pumpkin:4000/netupublic/netu.ch22_mnu_sample.show
```

WebDB displays the menu shown in Figure 22-7. WebDB does not prompt you for logon information because the DAD entry netupublic already had logon information included in the record.

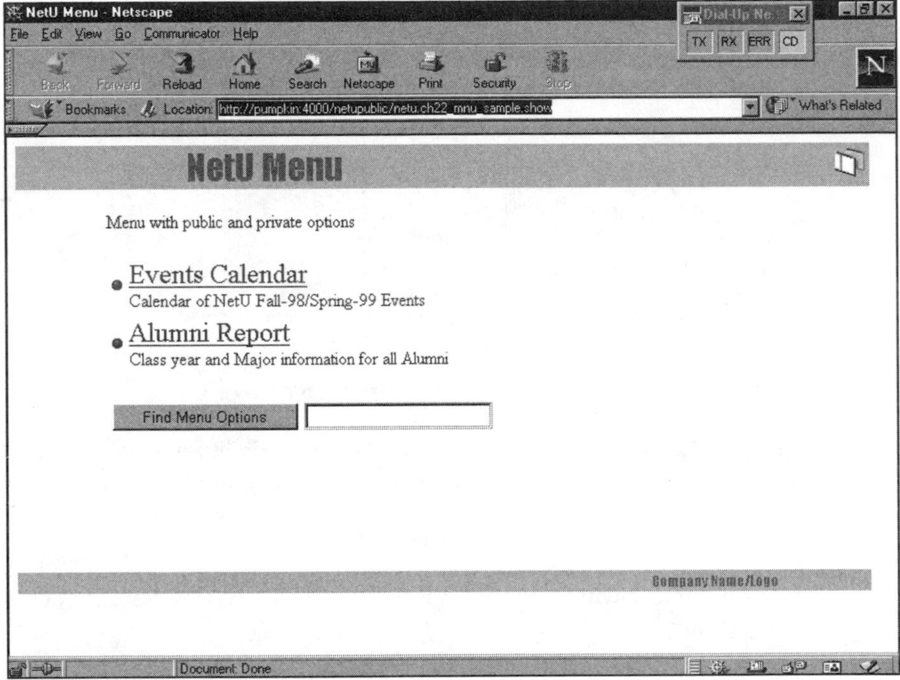

Figure 22-7: Sample menu with public access

8. Select the Events Calendar link.

The calendar link (as you will see shortly) has been deployed on this menu with the same public access, and selecting this link shows you the list of current events. As with the main menu, you are not required to supply any logon information because it has been included in the DAD.

9. Select the Alumni Report link.

When you select this second link, WebDB prompts you for a user name and password, and you can use either the WEBDB account or the NETU account to log on. If you fail to provide a proper logon, the page does not display. The alumni report is called using a different DAD record, one that requires the user to input a valid user name and password, which effectively secures the component from public access.

You must consider one additional item at this point. In both cases, the Oracle user name and password must have access to the component and the component must have access to the underlying data in order for the DAD record to work. In the case of the netupublic DAD record, the user name and password combination match the NETU account. Because all development thus far has been done in the netu account, the netupublic DAD has access to the calendar report. However, if the Oracle user name and password have not been granted access to the object through WebDB's standard security mechanisms, the DAD record is not able to connect to the object at run time.

The same is true for the netuprivate DAD record. The Oracle user name and password you supply must permit access to the selected object, or the connection will not be made. You will be successfully logged on to Oracle, but the selected object will not appear.

If you were to view the source for the individual menu choices, you would find that the two links look like the following lines of code:

```
/netupublic/netu.ch22_dyn_calendar.show
/netuprivate/netu.ch22_dyn_alumni.show
```

The link itself contains both the standard link text along with the DAD as a prefix to the link. The DAD is an elegant solution to the problem of deploying a WebDB Web site. You can create your components without regard to deploying them, and then use DAD records and menus to make these components available to users. Before you embark on creating DAD records and building components, however, it is important to consider one additional aspect of building components: the physical storage for component objects.

Component Schemas

Oracle organizes all database content by the USERID that owns the individual objects. Within a logical database, there are any number of USERIDs that own content along with a number of USERIDs used solely for connecting to the data in the storage schemas associated with the USERID. The Oracle database does not differentiate between a USERID created for the purpose of storing objects and a USERID created as a storage area for tables, views, and procedures. WebDB, however, notes that there is a logical difference between the two types of accounts.

1. Navigate to the Administer menu and select the User Manager.
2. Edit the NETU account as shown in Figure 22-8.

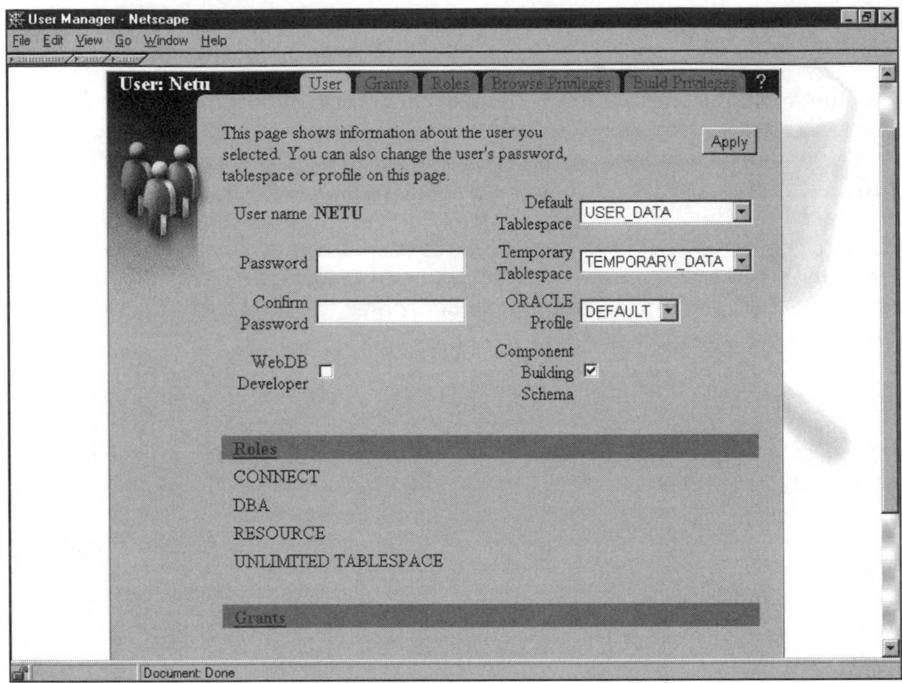

Figure 22-8: NETU component building schema

WebDB provides the Component Building Schema check box to indicate whether the Oracle USERID is used for connecting to the database. If the check box is selected, WebDB considers the account to be a component building schema. This means that WebDB assumes users will not be logging on to the account directly, but rather that the account is to be used as a container for tables, views, and procedures used by WebDB. Your application data need not be stored in the component building schema, but you should use this schema as the storage schema for all of your WebDB components for a logical application. When the check box is not selected, WebDB assumes that the USERID is a normal Oracle account used by end users for logging on to the database.

The Oracle database does not distinguish between the two. Only WebDB makes this distinction, but it is an important distinction from the application building perspective. WebDB applications should be stored within their own, unique USERID as a component building schema. There are several reasons for doing so. From an organizational standpoint, it is much easier to keep track of an application if all of the parts are kept in one place. This makes everything from import and export to backup and recovery much easier to manage. The second reason for doing so is to work around a problem in the security framework of the Oracle database. Users and roles can be given permission to use database procedures, but procedures themselves only see privileges that have been granted to the owner explicitly. Procedures take their privileges from the Oracle USERID that owns the procedure.

Keeping all the WebDB components (which are mostly procedures) in a single schema makes it much easier to manage from a security perspective.

For example, assume that Net University is a long-time Oracle database user and all of its existing data are stored inside an Oracle schema called NETU_DB. Net University decides to create a WebDB application called NETU_ALUMNI to provide access to interesting alumni data to the NetU alumni through the Web. The NETU_DB schema contains all of the tables, views, indexes, and custom stored procedures used by the existing applications. Because WebDB deploys all components as stored procedures, and stored procedures inherit the privileges of their owner (but not ROLE privileges), it makes sense to create all of the procedures within a single Oracle USERID. Doing so guarantees that table and view privileges only need to be granted to one account for the purposes of WebDB.

To continue the example, assume that the developers at Net University create a second WebDB application targeted at the undergraduates students called NETU_UGRADS. If the objects between the two applications do not have much in common, it makes sense to create this application in a third Oracle schema for this second application. The resulting design is shown in Figure 22-9.

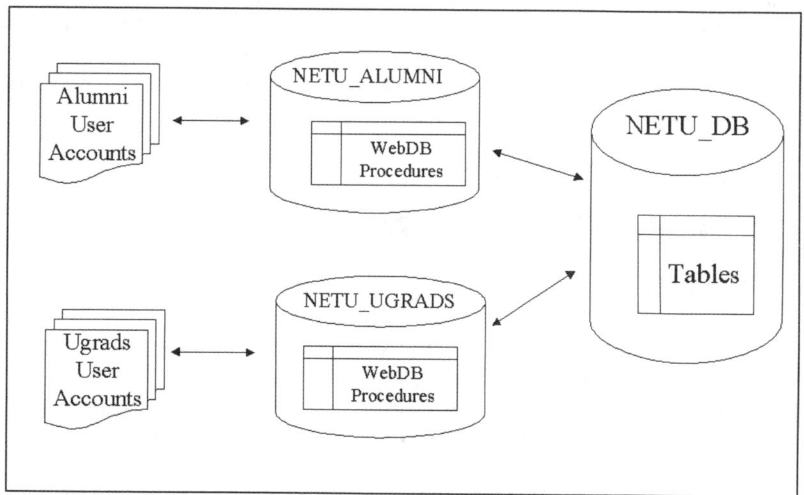

Figure 22-9: Component building schema diagram

In Figure 22-9, three Oracle USERIDs are used for storing content. The NETU_DB schema is the Oracle USERID that holds the tables and views for the application. The NETU_ALUMNI schema holds the WebDB stored procedures that access the alumni data in the NETU_DB, and the NETU_UGRADS schema holds the WebDB components that access the undergraduate data in the NETU_DB schema. Each developer that works on the NETU_ALUMNI application uses their own individual account to log on to the database, but all WebDB components are created in the user account NETU_ALUMNI. The NETU_ALUMNI account is given the necessary permissions to access the individual tables, views, and procedures in the NETU_DB account.

When it comes time to deploy this application, you can then provide access to the WebDB procedures in the NETU_ALUMNI schema to the individual end-user accounts, as shown in Figure 22-9. (The same rules apply to the NETU_UGRADS application.) This greatly simplifies your deployment task because you only have to assign table and view security to a single account for each application. Oracle automatically applies these privileges to the WebDB procedures at run time.

If you do not plan to allow your end users to browse the database, then this technique is even more powerful. You do not need to grant access to the NETU_DB objects to your end-user accounts at all. WebDB uses database procedures as the access mechanism for all of its objects, and the end users are only able to get to the underlying data through the WebDB procedures. If your users should be smart enough to use another method to connect to the NETU_DB schema with their own USERID, they will still not be able to access any of the data.

In its simplest incarnation, you can build the WebDB objects in the same schema as the database objects as we have done with the examples in this book. However, best practices dictate that you create separate WebDB component schemas for each of your WebDB applications. If you allow your developers to create WebDB components in their own USERIDs, you will be forced to give each developer account individual access to the underlying tables and you have no way to easily gather together all of the components for a single application.

Deploying WebDB Applications

Deploying WebDB applications requires you to consider two aspects of the application. First, you need to consider the application components themselves, such as the files, servers, and security. Then you need to consider how to package your applications logically and deliver them to your users. The previous sections of this chapter have covered the deployment components in detail, and this last section of the chapter concerns itself with the logical packaging of these applications.

One of the most important concepts to remember with WebDB is that there is no separate deployment model as you would find with other development tools. While we stated this repeatedly in the first portion of this chapter, it is worth repeating in the context of logical application deployment. In order to deploy applications built with WebDB, you must make the entire WebDB environment available to your users. This does not mean that you have to allow your users to have access to any of the component wizards directly.

WebDB applications are delivered as procedures, but certain objects, such as shared components, use database tables in the WebDB schema. Even if you build all of the components for your application inside a component building schema, you still need access to certain WebDB objects at run time. The designers of WebDB have not included a run-time environment with this release of the software, so there is no documentation as to exactly which WebDB components are required for supporting your applications. The end result is that you reach four points where you must make a decision before you deploy applications:

✦ Schema definition

✦ Development staging

✦ Server configuration

✦ Component deployment

The combination of each of these elements determines how you handle the process of developing and deploying WebDB applications within your organization.

Schema definition

WebDB schema definition is a combination of the component building schema technique and the use of database access descriptors. Although there are no specific tools for creating distinct logical applications within WebDB, you can effectively accomplish this task by using component building schemas. We recommend that you create a schema for each logical application you build and store all of the WebDB components for that application within this single schema. This makes the maintenance and deployment of your application much easier. You only need to assign object privileges to a single Oracle Account and you are able to use Oracle's Import and Export utilities to manage the compiled objects. Under this design scheme, a single target database schema can be accessed by multiple logical WebDB applications, as shown in Figure 22-10.

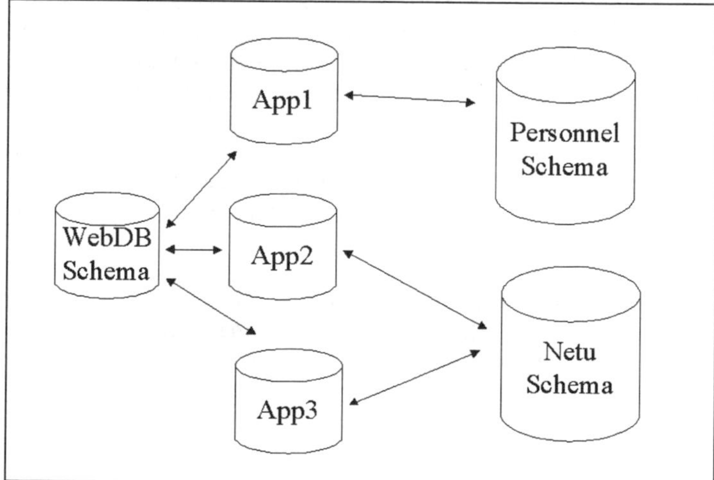

Figure 22-10: Schema deployment with WebDB

WebDB stores the source code for all of the procedures within a single schema as indicated by the WebDB database in Figure 22-10. The compiled PL/SQL procedures for each logical application are stored in their own Oracle component building schemas that are identified in the second tier of schemas. The data for these applications is stored in yet a third set of schemas at the far-right side of the diagram. Any single WebDB application can work with multiple databases and more than one logical WebDB application can work with a single data schema. The WebDB component building schemas become the holding areas for the application procedures deployed to the users.

Under this architecture, the WebDB schema itself is still used by the deployed application to handle such tasks as lists-of-values. If you have developers working in the WebDB schema at the same time as end users are running applications, there is the possibility the two colliding and causing problems. This is especially true if your developers are performing bulk loads and unloads of components. As long as your developers are not working on components that your end users are trying to execute, this should not be a major problem. However, if this is likely to be a problem, you may need to implement a staging area.

Development staging

Most professional application developers separate their development processes from the deployment area. This is normally true for both the data as well as the actual applications code. For example, if you were to design and build an Oracle developer application for Net University, you would probably make a copy of the core database and set up a separate instance for doing the development work. You would also create an area on the file system where the completed programs would be stored, and you would point end users to this finished program area for running the application.

It is possible to do the same thing with WebDB, although it takes a little more planning to do so. As shown in Figure 22-2, you can run multiple copies of both the Oracle server as well as the WebDB listener. As a result, you can create a development installation of WebDB and a deployment installation of WebDB. One problem that you will run into, however, is the fact that most WebDB components require you to include the owner of the table or view name in the procedure when you build the component. If you use a development schema and a deployment schema, you will still be forced to change the procedure to point to the correct object at run time.

The solution to this problem is to use two separate instances of Oracle, as shown in Figure 22-11. Both instances can use the same schema names and object names, and both instances can have WebDB installed.

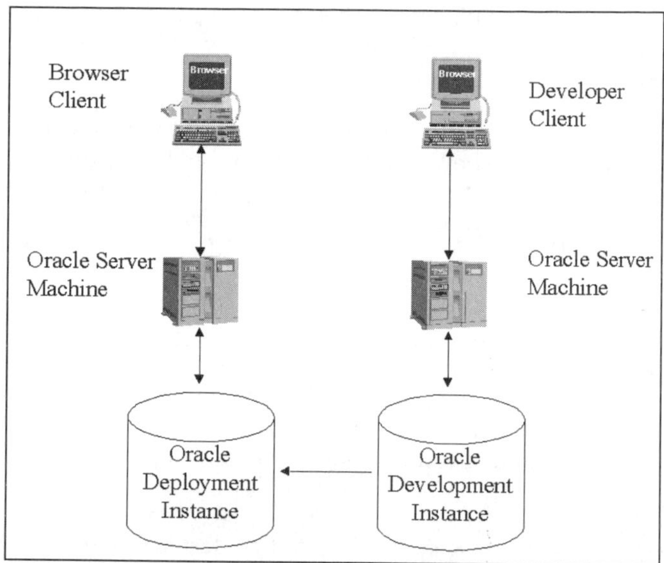

Figure 22-11: Running multiple Oracle instances

The secret to making this approach work is to use the same object names in both instances. When a developer has finished building a component (or an application), the various objects can be exported from the development instance and imported into the production instance. Keep in mind that a logical component might be composed of several physical components. For example, a WebDB report might have several shared components such as a list-of-values or template built into it. WebDB does not automatically export these referenced objects when you export the report; you need to export these other objects yourself. Furthermore, you still need to set security for the components in the production environment, and you may need to copy external image files to the proper directories on the production server. However, you will have successfully created a layer of insulation between your developers and your end users.

Server configuration

The server configuration is a relatively simple issue to resolve because only three options are available: use the WebDB listener, use a third-party Web server, or use the Oracle Application Server. The decision of which strategy to use is based upon the needs of your users and your Web architecture.

If you are deploying your WebDB application within an intranet or extranet where security is provided for you at the network layer, the WebDB listener is a good choice. The listener is lightweight, it can cache connections across user requests, and it is tightly integrated with the PL/SQL gateway. Furthermore, nothing prevents you from embedding links to another Web server if you want to connect your

WebDB applications to an existing application. This is a perfectly acceptable solution within an intranet environment, and the cross-server connections are transparent to your users.

If you need to deploy your application to the Internet, you may have to deploy your application using the CGI interface. The WebDB listener does not provide any load-balancing capabilities, which other listeners may handle, and it does not support SSL in its current incarnation. Chances are good that you already have a Web server in place, and you can use the CGI interface to connect WebDB to this existing server without difficulty.

The third option is to deploy your WebDB application as part of the Oracle Application Server. OAS supports advanced security features such as SSL and it supports load balancing and failover to make your WebDB applications more robust and scalable. Through the intercartridge exchange, you can blend your WebDB application with other OAS components, including Oracle developer applications, Perl, and C.

The Oracle Application Server is a highly sophisticated product in its own right. We advise you to consult the Oracle Web site for details on the many features of this award-winning product.

The server deployment of your applications is disconnected from the development process and nothing precludes you from deploying the same components using multiple strategies, as need dictates.

Component deployment

WebDB supports three different types of deployment interfaces: static HTML pages, WebDB menus, and WebDB sites. When you deploy your applications, you will likely find yourself using all of these options to get the structure you are looking for. Underneath the covers, you will almost always use WebDB components to display content to your users, but you can vary the manner in which the components are packaged.

The most common mechanism for deploying your components is to link to them from static HTML pages. This is particularly true if you already have an existing intranet or Internet application in place. You may be replacing some of your static pages with dynamic content built with WebDB. In such cases, you may replace links in your static pages with new links to WebDB components as these components become available. Static WebDB pages permit you more freedom in handcrafting the HTML code, which may be necessary to create the particular look and feel you are trying to achieve with your company's home page. In fact, many corporate sites use lots of images and image maps on their master pages for just this reason. The pages in your WebDB application can use templates that emulate or complement the look of these static HTML pages.

WebDB supports a Menu Wizard, and you can deploy your applications using these menus. Once again, you may want to embed the link to your menu into an existing static HTML page. For example, the main Net University home page might feature an animated GIF that invites users to click through to see a list of upcoming campus events. Behind the GIF, a WebDB menu might list various categories such as sports, lectures, and parties.

WebDB components can also be delivered through the Site Builder interface. In Chapter 18 you were introduced to the basic concepts of Site Builder, including how to create a site. Site Builder offers a formal structure for deploying interactive Web sites, and WebDB components can be plugged directly into this structure.

Wrapping Up

WebDB applications are easy to build, but they lack some of the formal processes for delivery you may be used to in more structured development environments. This is partly due to the youth of WebDB, but there is also a conscious aspect to this design. Web applications by their very nature are more dynamic than their client/server brethren. Web applications are often designed and implemented quickly to leverage a window of opportunity. The designers of WebDB built the product in such as way as to enable you to deploy your applications quickly and easily.

Despite this fact, you can still apply a more formal framework for deploying your WebDB applications. You also have the flexibility to deploy these applications using your existing Web infrastructure. In the next chapter, you will see how you can use the Site Builder tools as a framework for delivering your WebDB content.

✦ ✦ ✦

Site Builder — Part II

In This Chapter

Chapter 18 introduced you to the Site Builder capabilities of WebDB, and you created and customized your site with Site Builder. The Site Builder Wizard and the Site Builder administration tools are only half of the solution, however, as most of the power of Site Builder lies in the hands of the users. Through Site Builder you can create a framework for your site, but the real value comes from the content loaded into the site.

Typical collaborative Web sites suffer from several problems. The information is often disorganized and hard to find, which causes users to stop working with the site. Even when the site is organized, the information may appear to be disorganized if individual users have made use of their own styles and techniques for building the content. If you try to provide a universal framework that contributors must use to build content, the information is often stale by the time it actually gets posted to the site.

Site Builder — Part I: Review

Site Builder is the answer to all of these problems. It provides the framework for organizing and searching for content as well as a built-in template for making content appear in a uniform fashion. Contributors do not have to format the information in any way in order to take advantage of the display templates, and this helps them submit content in a more timely fashion.

Web sites built with Site Builder are ideal if the site is going to be a collaboration of efforts. You can divide Web applications into categories such as e-commerce, online catalog, and stock trading. Almost any Web site that needs to access the Oracle database can use WebDB components. However, sites that involve collaboration amongst a community of users are appropriate applications for Site Builder.

Site Builder provides a framework for organizing your content, searching for items, and displaying information using a consistent format. The basic framework of Site Builder requires that all sites have a certain look and feel. The left-hand side of an application serves as the navigation panel, and the body of the page on the right-hand side contains content organized into categories. But if you are building a merchandising site, you might not want to use this format as the look and feel for your site. Instead, you might create a series of flashy static Web pages for the top part of your site and then link these pages to WebDB components for displaying and ordering items.

For instance, suppose you are selling a fairly sophisticated piece of equipment such as a computer or a camera. Once you have sold the product to a consumer, you might want to point that consumer to a section of your Web site where they can exchange information with other users. This type of collaboration is exactly where Site Builder is most effective, because it already comes equipped with all the pieces you need to build a collaboration framework.

In order to understand how you can use Site Builder for Web applications, think of the example of a store. First, you decide what type of things you want to sell—shoes, clothes, food, furniture, and so on. Next, you find a location and build the store. Then, you decide on a color scheme, the layout for your store, and the store logo. Finally, you have to fill the store with merchandise so your customers have something to purchase. The merchandise serves two purposes: it draws people into your store and it provides your profit.

Within WebDB, Site Builder is your store and the layout, color scheme, and images are the brand for your store. The folders, categories, and perspectives define the type of merchandise you have in the store, and the items uploaded into the site become the merchandise. A store is a type of framework—it is ideal for displaying merchandise and enabling people to select items and buy them. Stores are very flexible objects; they can be laid out in many different ways, they can be used to sell a variety of goods, and they can be built with a wide range of color schemes. You can use a store to sell many things, yet all stores share the same basic characteristics. Web sites built with Site Builder are much like the store: They can be used for a wide variety of tasks, but they all share the same basic format. Site Builder is ideal for building Web applications that consist of information organized for the purpose of collaboration. In this chapter, you will go through the process of releasing your Site Builder site to your users.

Site Builder Applications and Security

Several factors can affect the design of your Site Builder site, but the most basic issue you will deal with is whether or not to make your site an anonymous Web site. Anonymous Web applications do not require that the user supply an individual user name and password in order to connect to the site. Anonymous sites need not be made available to the general public, and they can be hidden behind a firewall or within an intranet. The alternative is to make your Site Builder application an authenticated Web application in which the users must log on to the application before they are allowed to view content. This is not necessarily an either/or decision. You might choose to make the overall Site Builder site an anonymous Web application, but you can still require logons for accessing certain components of the site. When the Site Builder Wizard generates your Web site, it creates it as an authenticated site for the purpose of adding content and administration. However, public users are able to connect to the site itself.

Creating user accounts for Site Builder

Site Builder accounts are Oracle database USERIDs — they are no different than the user accounts that you worked with in Chapter 22. Accounts you create with any of the Oracle interfaces such as SQL*Plus and Enterprise Manager appear within both Site Builder and WebDB. Site Builder groups all of its security functions inside the administration panels under the Access Managers category.

The examples in this chapter assume that you have completed Chapter 18 and built the Net University Web site.

1. Connect to the Net University Web site using the following URL string, substituting the name of your machine and port number for the string `server`:

   `http://server:4000/nu_site/`

The default connection to the Web site is an unauthenticated connection and you need to use the LogOn to NetU link in order to gain access to the Administration menu.

2. Select the LogOn to NetU link and supply the nu_site_admin user name and password to connect as the default administrative user.
3. Select the Administration link to display the Administration page and navigate down to the Access Managers section, as shown in Figure 23-1.

There are four tools in the Access Managers panel. The Personal Information link is the first link you are likely to access. It enables you input biographical information for the current account. The User link creates and manages accounts, and the Group link enables you to connect these accounts into logical groups of users. The final link in this group is the Privilege link, which permits you to assign permissions to the users and groups that you create with the User and Group links.

4. Start by selecting the Personal Information link to display the page shown in Figure 23-2.

Figure 23-1: Administration menu – Access Managers panel

The Personal Information page is available to both privileged accounts and nonprivileged accounts. When you enter a content item into your site, Site Builder automatically associates this item with your USERID. You can use the Personal Information page to provide additional details about your account, such as your real name and phone number. When you log on as the administrator, this page is connected to the site administrator account. When your end users log on to your site, this page connects each user to their own Personal Information page. To avoid confusion, the top banner of the page always displays the user name of the currently connected user. This page enables you to enter personal background information such as your full name, address, e-mail address, and other contact information. Users can also change their password by entering and confirming a new password in the Features and Values section.

If your users have employee photographs, they can upload them to the site using the Photograph field.

5. Change the password of the nu_site_admin account to **admin**.
6. Enter biographical information for the various personal information fields as shown in Figure 23-2.
7. Upload the photograph file admin_photo.jpg as the picture for the administrative account.
8. Save your changes using the Apply button and click the Finish button to return to the administration panel.

Adding user accounts

The User link on the administration panel connects you to panels that enable you to create end-user accounts for your site. These are standard Oracle accounts that enable your users to access the Oracle database from outside WebDB and Site Builder as well as within these applications.

Chapter 20 provides a more detailed reference to Oracle security and we recommend that you review this chapter in detail before developing your security scheme for Site Builder.

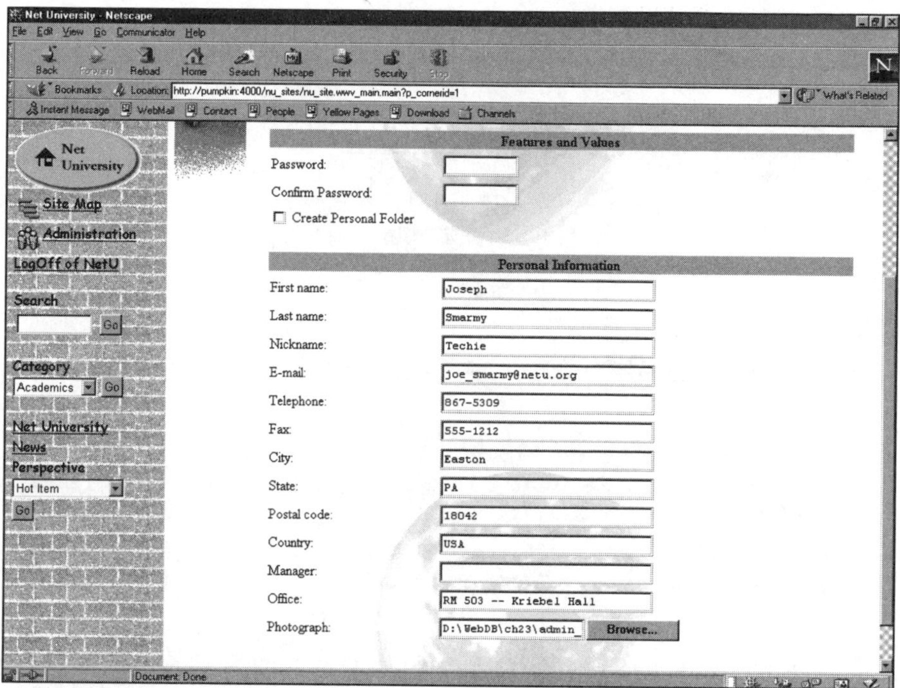

Figure 23-2: Access Managers – Personal Information page

WebDB provides a similar set of security panels in both the WebDB development interface and the Site Builder panels. This duplication is necessary in order to make both WebDB and Site Builder self-sufficient. It is possible to deploy Web sites with Site Builder that do not contain any WebDB-built components and vice versa. By providing security panels inside Site Builder, you can maintain all aspects of your site completely inside the Site Builder environment. The account information you enter into either set of panels is cross-referenced with the other panels for you automatically.

1. Select the Users link to display the panel shown in Figure 23-3.

The Create User panel inside Site Builder is almost identical to the equivalent panel inside WebDB with two notable exceptions. The Create User panel inside of Site Builder does not offer either the WebDB Developer check box or the Component Building Schema check box that you find on the same panel in WebDB. The developers of Site Builder removed these two options from the Site Builder version of the panel because they do not apply specifically to Site Builder. However, if you create a new user in Site Builder and subsequently review the account inside the WebDB security subsystem, you will see these two settings for the account. You will not usually set any user account to the Component Building Schema status, because this setting is intended solely for those accounts that serve as data stores for an application's components. There may be cases, however, when you want to allow a Site Builder user to have access to the WebDB build capabilities, and you need to add the WebDB developer permission to this account in such cases.

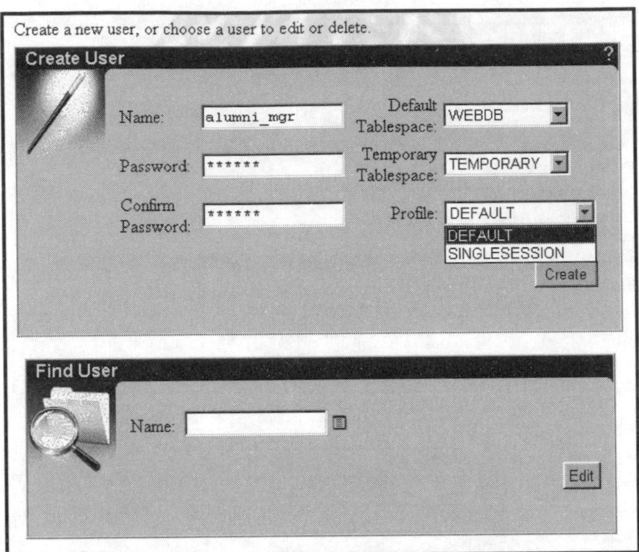

Figure 23-3: Access Managers – Create User panel

In all other respects, the Create User panel in Site Builder works the same as its equivalent panel in WebDB. To create a new account, all you need to do is enter the information for the account into the fields at the top of the panel and then click the Create button to store the changes.

You might need to use one particular setting on this panel more often inside of Site Builder. Oracle enables you to define profiles for accounts that control parameters beyond simple permissions related to the account. For example, you could create a profile called "9-to-5" and set options that only allow the user to log on from 9 a.m. to 5 p.m. on weekdays. You cannot create profiles inside either WebDB or Site Builder — you must use an external tool such as SQL*Plus or Enterprise Manager to create and manage profiles. However, both Site Builder and WebDB display profiles in the Profile combo box shown in Figure 23-3. As part of the installation process, Oracle creates a profile called SingleSession that prevents any single account from logging on to the database multiple times. Should you decide to provide your users with individual logon accounts, you can set the profile on these accounts to SingleSession and prevent multiple users from sharing the same account. This is a particularly powerful feature in cases when your users are required to pay for access to your Web site.

WebDB tracks the logon information using cookies, and the same user can open multiple browser sessions from a single machine regardless of the SingleSession setting. This is due to the fact that WebDB does not need to complete the logon process for subsequent browser sessions.

Site Builder user accounts are divided into three basic categories: administrators, folder managers, and users. These designations are added to the account during the privilege granting process, rather than during the account creation process. The starting point for any account is to create the account.

There is one exception to this rule. If you are adding an existing Oracle user to a Site Builder application, you do not need to add a new account for them within Site Builder. The find panel locates all of the current Oracle accounts in the instance in which Site Builder is running. You can locate the existing account and modify it within Site Builder.

2. Create a new account called alumni_mgr with the password "alumni" as shown in Figure 23-3, and select a tablespace and temporary tablespace for this new account.
3. Click the Create button to store the new account.
4. Scroll down to the Find panel and use the icon to locate your account.
5. Click the Edit button to modify the account information, as shown in Figure 23-4.

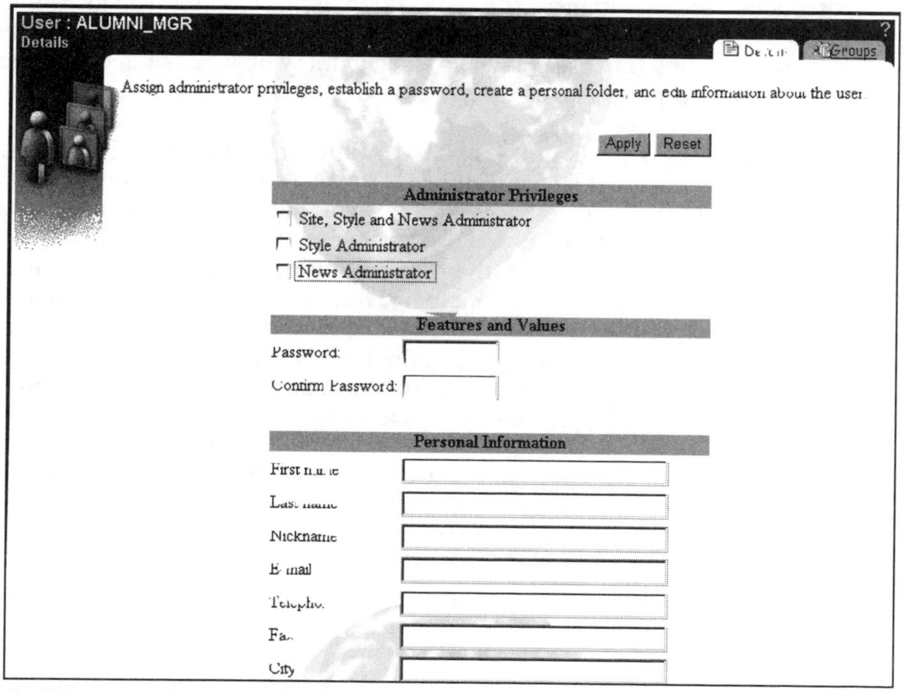

Figure 23-4: Edit user accounts panel

The edit account panel within Site Builder is significantly different from the edit account panel within WebDB. For the most part, you are creating end-user accounts within Site Builder and the edit panel is geared toward adding biographical information for accounts rather than providing security information. The main edit page is almost identical to the page you used to modify the site administrator account for your site, with the exception of the Administrator Privileges panel.

Site Builder treats the site administrator account as a special case, and this account automatically has full privileges for the site in which it was built. You can give new accounts specialized privileges as well, but they are not given these privileges by default. In the following sections, we show you how to add individual privileges to accounts and groups within a site. The three choices on this panel are special privileges as follows:

- ✦ Site, Style and News Administrator
- ✦ Style Administrator
- ✦ News Administrator

If you enable your users to contribute content to your site, you can restrict them to submitting news items only. News items are time-sensitive content items that are often considered to be less formal than other types of content. You will be introduced to news items in the last section of this chapter. The lowest level of site privilege you can grant to an account is the ability to manage news items for the site. By selecting this check box for an account, you give that account access items such as the expiration dates for news.

The next level of permission is the Style Administrator setting. This setting controls the look and feel of folders and content. You can enable an account to access the style settings and create and modify styles such as the look and feel of the Navigation Bar. By default, however, the account does not have the capability to set the style for a folder. You have to grant explicit permissions against the folder itself in order to enable the account to change folder information. If you grant an account the privilege to edit styles but you do not give them specific folder privileges, they are only able to create new styles, but not apply them to folders. You may have graphic artists on staff to create styles for you, but you may not want to give the artists the ability to apply these styles to folders.

The last setting is the equivalent of the super-user setting, and it gives the account site administrator status. Many large sites have multiple administrators, and it is a good idea to give each administrator his or her own account. In fact, a single administrator may manage several sites and it is easier for that individual to have a single account with privileges in multiple sites rather than forcing them to memorize multiple user names and passwords.

The second tab panel on the edit user panel enables you to add the current user to a group. Groups inside Site Builder provide a similar service to roles inside the WebDB AppBuilder environment. You can designate permissions to a group and then attach users to that group. This makes the whole process of distributing permissions much, much easier. For the moment, you can ignore the group panel, because you do not yet have any groups to which you can assign users.

1. Add some biographical information for your alumni_mgr account and enable the News Administrator check box for that account.
2. Click the Apply button to save your changes.
3. Click the Finish button to exit the alumni_mgr account.
4. Add a new user called ugrads_mgr with the password ugrads and then modify this account to be a news administrator as you did with the alumni_mgr account.

The Chapter 23 directory on the companion CD-ROM includes a script called UGRADS_ACCOUNTS.SQL that creates user accounts for all of the UGRADS records in the NetU database (75 records in all). You need to modify the script to use a proper default tablespace and temporary tablespace if you did not use the default WEBDB and TEMPORARY tablespaces when you installed WebDB. You can run this script through SQL*Plus as user SYSTEM to quickly install accounts for all of the UGRADS students.

5. Run the UGRADS_ACCOUNTS.SQL script to create accounts for all of your students, or repeat the process you followed for the alumni_mgr account and ugrads_mgr account to create new accounts for at least two ugrads records (Achieva and Baker). Use the last name of the student as the USERID. Do not set the News Administrator permission for your student accounts.
6. Return to the main administration panel.

If you plan to make your site available to the general public, you do not need to add any accounts for these users. You still need to create manager and administration accounts to maintain the site, but you do not need accounts for the public users.

If you build your site with anonymous logons, you will not be able to permit your users to create Personal folders or interest lists (which are described later in this chapter), because Site Builder will have no way of identifying individual users.

Adding groups

Site Builder uses the same *conceptual* grouping techniques that WebDB uses to combine users into logical teams with similar privileges and access. If you are building an authenticated site, you will want to make use of groups to simplify the process of deploying security settings and permissions.

1. Use the Group link in the Administration menu to display the panel shown in Figure 23-5.

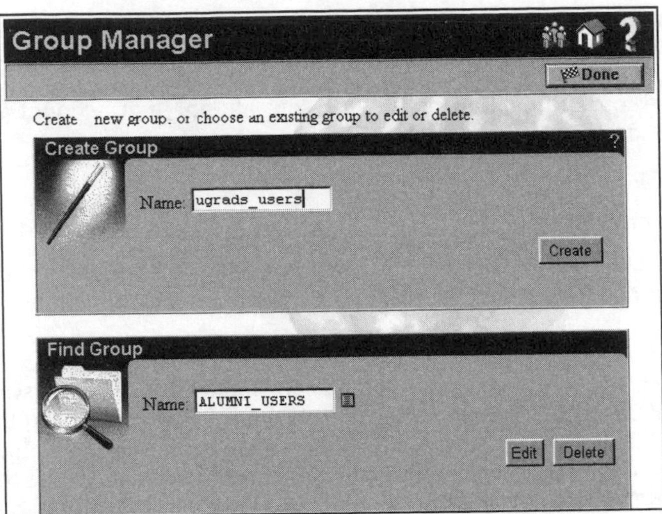

Figure 23-5: Creating groups within Site Builder

The Create Group panel is simple in structure because the only function it supports is the creation of a new group record. Site Builder groups are not equivalent to WebDB roles, which are standard Oracle ROLE objects. Site Builder groups are simply records that are entered into a series of security tables inside the Site Builder schema. The group permissions you create are only valid within Site Builder, and they are only valid for the current site in which you are working. Because Site Builder groups are only valid inside Site Builder, you can create groups that have the same name as individual users, if you wish.

If your users are members of several sites you can reuse the Oracle USERID, but you have to reimplement groups within each and every site. Normally your users have different levels of permissions in different sites, and keeping group information specific to a site makes sense in light of this fact.

1. Create the group alumni_users by entering this string in the name field and clicking the Create button.
2. Create a second group called ugrads_users in the same fashion.
3. Scroll down to the Find panel and locate the group UGRADS_USERS.
4. Click the Edit button to edit the settings for this group.

The main panel for the group editing function is the Details panel. The only setting you can change on the Details panel is the owner of the group. By default, the site administrator is the owner of all groups created in each site. However, if you create additional administrative users, you may wish to designate these accounts as owners of the group.

5. Click the Users tab to display the panel shown in Figure 23-6.

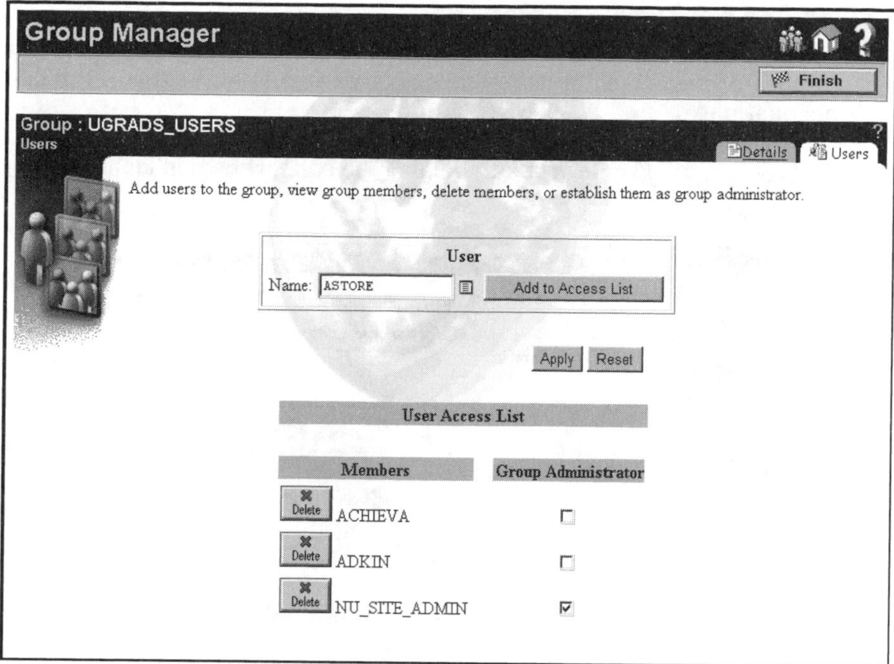

Figure 23-6: Adding users to a group

The Users panel works very similar to the security panels inside the WebDB development interface. You can locate an account by using the Find icon, and then use the Add to Access List button to add the account to the group. You must save all changes to the database by using the Apply button.

You can only perform three functions with the Users panel: you can add users to a group, you can delete users from a group, and you can designate a user account as a certified administrator for the current group. Only group administrators have the authority to add and delete users from the group. There may be cases where you allow certain users to manage the membership of their group without giving them any other authority, such as the ability to manage folders or content.

1. Select the first user in the UGRADS table, ACHIEVA, and add it to the group UGRADS_USERS.
2. Select the user UGRADS_MGR, add it to the Members list, and set this account as the group administrator.
3. Click the Apply button to save your changes.
4. Add a new group called UGRADS_VIEW.
5. Add the USERID BAKER to this new group.
6. Navigate back to the main administration panel.

Adding privileges to accounts

The final panel in the Access Managers group is the Privileges panel. This panel duplicates the three check box settings that appear at the top of the Edit User account page.

1. Select the Privilege link to display the panel shown in Figure 23-7.

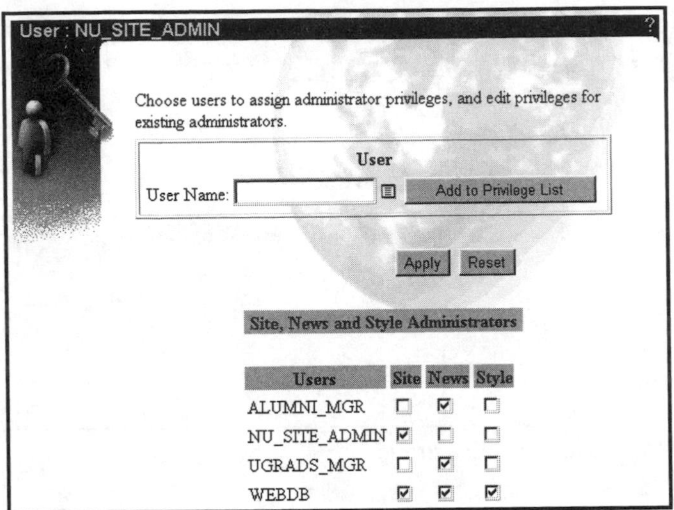

Figure 23-7: Privileges panel

You can only grant three privileges to Site Builder users within a site, as described previously. A user account can administer news, edit and maintain styles, or serve as an alternative site administrator. The default behavior for this panel is to display all of the users that have been granted any of these privileges. You can add users to this list and grant them any of the three privileges through this panel, or you can grant the same authority from inside the Users link.

By default, Site Builder grants the WebDB user and the site administrator accounts all three privileges. If you decide to designate some additional user accounts as administrators, you can do so from this panel.

Although these are the only privileges you can grant to an account, they are not the only permissions. In the next section of this chapter, you will see that user accounts can be granted some folder-specific permissions in addition to these base system privileges.

2. Use the Finish button to exit the Privileges panel without making any changes.

Adding users and groups to folders

Once you have created users and groups, you can deploy these accounts to the folders that make up your Site Builder site. Folder permissions are stored inside the folder object itself and you can set security options from the Folder Editor.

1. Scroll to the Content Managers section of the Administration panel and select the Folder link.
2. Select the Edit icon for the STUDENTS folder to display the panel in Figure 23-8.

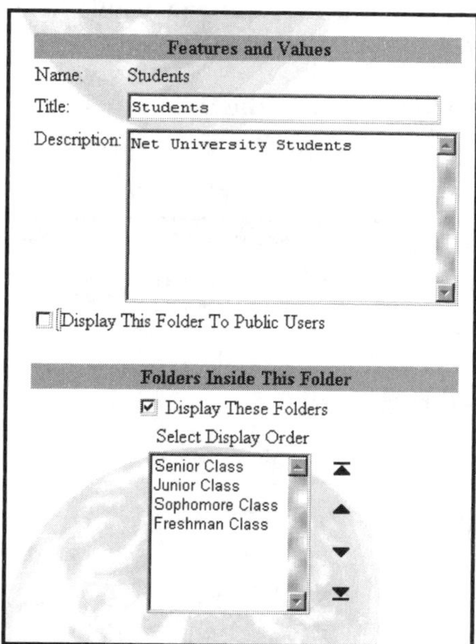

Figure 23-8: Folder Manager – Students folder

In Chapter 18, you created the basic hierarchy of folders that comprise the Net University site. Once you have created your users and groups, you can assign permissions for these users within the folders and subfolders.

The first section of the folder panel, as depicted in Figure 23-8, should be familiar to you from Chapter 18. This panel controls the overall display of the folder and the base permissions. The critical item from a security standpoint is the Display This Folder To Public Users check box. By default, your folders are not made available to the public. If you enable this check box, the general public is able to view the items loaded into the folder. *This would make the folder into an anonymous folder, as opposed to an authenticated folder.* There will be cases where you might have some folders in your application set as public (anonymous) folders, while others require that the user log on to the site in order to view the contents.

The lowest level of detail from Site Builder's perspective is the folder object. Site Builder does not provide any tools for setting security on individual items, only on folders.

In the example Net University site, there is a mix of both anonymous and authenticated folders. For example, if the Net University Site Builder application serves as the primary Web site for Net University, then the main folder must be a public folder. You would not want to require that visitors to the NetU site have an account simply to view the Web site. Within the root folder, you could create several folders that would be open to public access, but you would leave the other folders, such as the Students folder, as private folders.

3. Leave the Student folder as is and navigate to the User panel, as shown in Figure 23-9.

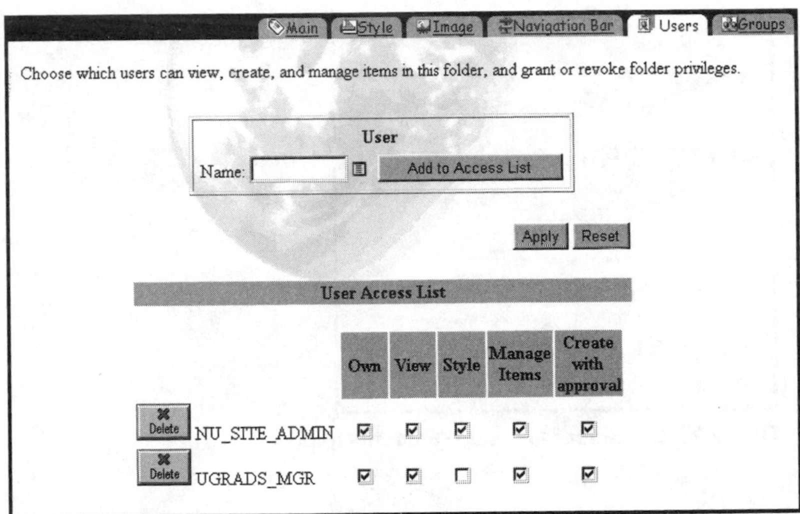

Figure 23-9: Setting user security for a folder

Each folder and subfolder inside Site Builder has five possible permissions you can set for user accounts that access the site, as shown in the following list:

- ✦ Own
- ✦ View
- ✦ Style
- ✦ Manage Items
- ✦ Create with approval

The most powerful permission that you can grant to any user account or group is the *Own* permission. When you create a site with Site Builder, the administration account owns all the folders that you create by default. At first glance, you might assume that ownership of a folder is limited to a single user account. In fact, multiple users and/or groups can be granted ownership of a folder. The own privilege grants the holder the ability to manage the folder completely, including the ability to add, delete, and update any items that might be contained within the site. Granting the Own privilege to a user account effectively makes that user a system administrator for that folder.

The second privilege in the list is the *View* privilege, which is the least powerful of all the permissions on this panel. A user account must have the View privilege set in order to view both the folder and any items contained within that folder. The user cannot add content to the site, however, unless he or she has been granted the Create with approval privilege.

Once the user has been granted the *Create with approval* privilege, he or she is able to add new content to the specified folder in any of the supported content formats. When a user adds a new item to a folder, Site Builder marks the item as "pending." The only users who are able to see the pending item are the users who input the new item and any user who has the Own privilege for that folder. The only exception to this two-phase policy is news items, which are automatically approved when they are posted to the site.

Users can be granted the authority to edit items and move them around within folders without having the authority to approve pending changes through the *Manage* privilege. The ability to approve content items is considered more powerful than the ability to merely manage the folder itself from Site Builder's perspective.

The final permission you can grant is the ability to change the *Style* of the folder. Once a style has been set for a folder, all the content within that folder appears in a consistent manner. You might grant a user the authority to approve content without allowing that user the ability to change the look and feel of the folder itself.

The permissions on this panel are independent of one another, which gives you the flexibility to tailor the capabilities for any given user. Functionally, the panel works like any of the other add panels. You select a user account with the Find icon and then you add the user to the access list by using the Add to Access List button. Once the user has been added to the list, you can enable permissions by selecting the appropriate check boxes and using the Apply button.

1. Find the UGRADS_MGR account and add it to the access list.
2. Grant the following permissions to the UGRADS_MGR account: Own, View, Manage Items, Create with approval.
3. Save these changes using the Apply button.
4. Select the Groups link to display the Groups permissions panel shown in Figure 23-10.

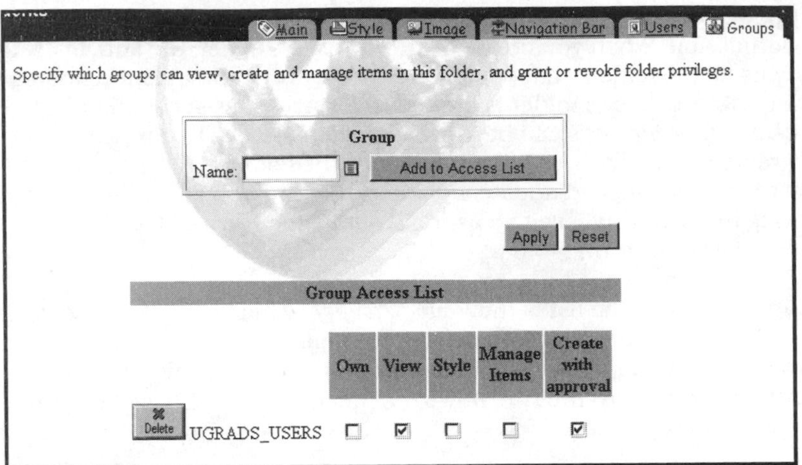

Figure 23-10: Group permissions for a folder

You can apply the same permissions to a group of users that you can apply to individual accounts. Normally you will assign user permissions to the managers of a folder and group permissions to the end users of a folder. However, there are exceptions to this rule. For example, you may decide that none of your end users should have the ability to add items to your site, and you want to keep the add capability solely in the hands of your folder managers. Over time you might find the need to delegate the Create with approval privilege to some of your more responsible users. You can still keep these users as part of the end-user group, but you can also add them to the individual user list for a folder and give them Create with approval privileges.

In the case of the Net University site, you might want to allow all of the students to have the ability to add content to the site.

1. Locate the UGRADS_USERS group and add it to the access list.
2. Grant the View and Create with approval privileges to this group.
3. Locate the UGRADS_VIEW group and add it to the access list.
4. Add the View privilege for this group.
5. Save your changes.

Earlier on in this chapter, you may have only added the ACHIEVA undergraduate record to the UGRADS_USER group, and the BAKER record to the UGRADS_VIEW group. Remember this when you test out the security scheme later on.

6. Click the Finish button to exit the Folder edit panel.
7. Click the Done button to save your changes to the folder hierarchy.

One final piece of information is critical to managing the security of your folders. Any folder-specific security settings you make to a folder are not applied to the subfolders contained with that folder. If you want users to have access to specific subfolders, you must explicitly provide them with subfolder privilege settings.

Adding Content to Your Site

Chapter 18 introduced you to the basic components of a Site Builder application: the Navigation Bar, the banner area, the content area, folders, categories, and perspectives. These objects form the building blocks for all Site Builder applications.

Your site will typically start off with a theme, which is the basic purpose of the site. For the fictional Net University site, the Site Builder application is an information center for the University. The folders in this application form the basic categories for the items contained on the site. Within Net University are three main constituents — Alumni, Students, and Faculty. The Students group is further subdivided into Freshmen, Sophomores, Juniors, and Seniors. Each folder has a number of categories that correspond to an area of interest within the folder: events, academics, and athletics.

Although this is an oversimplification of what you might need for a real university, it does provide a basic organization that you can use as an example. In the real world, each of these categories could be a Web site or Site Builder application of its own. Many large colleges and universities have entire Web sites just for their sports teams. There is no reason why you could not use this same technique with Site Builder. You could just as easily create a Site Builder application dedicated entirely to Net University's sports teams and then build a folder for each team: Men's Basketball, Women's Basketball, Men's Football, and so on. The folders might then consist of the schedule, players, game results, and press coverage.

There is no hard and fast rule about what level you should use to organize your Site Builder application — it depends upon the level of detail your content is likely to take. The entity that drives the level of detail for your site is the content. The items stored or referenced within your Site Builder site are your content. Content items can take a variety of formats, as shown in the following list:

- Text Items
- Files
- Multiple Files
- Imagemap
- URLs
- WebDB Component

✦ PL/SQL Call

✦ Folder Link

Every content item loaded into a Site Builder application has a number of common attributes. Each item can be stored within a folder as part of a given category and each item has a title and a description. In addition, you can assign each item to a number of perspectives and index it by designated keywords. You will see these attributes in action later on in this section.

The most basic of all content items is the *Text Item,* which is nothing more than a block of HTML text. Text is the perfect choice for short messages where the content is nothing more than a message. WebDB permits you to embed HTML tags in the text itself, so the item can display with fancy HTML rendering if you wish.

The next in the list is the *File* content item, which is a binary file added as content to the site. You still provide a title and a description for the item, but the link itself points to a binary file downloaded to the browser. The file is stored inside the Oracle database as a LONG RAW column. When the link is accessed at run time, Site Builder passes the file to the browser with the appropriate file extension and MIME type. For example, if you store an Adobe Portable Display Format (PDF) file in your site, Site Builder sends the file back to the site as PDF MIME type when the file is accessed. The browser deals with the file according to the current settings for that MIME type. Site Builder does not attempt to manage the MIME settings for the file, and it does not alter the attributes of the file when it is stored in the database.

If you have a single content object composed of several items, you can use the *Multiple Files* content type. It is identical to the FILE format in all aspects with the exception of one. While you can only upload one file content item with the File type, you can upload multiple files with the Multiple File type. For example, if you have a Microsoft Word document and a separate spreadsheet as a single logical content item, you can use the Multiple File content type to display this object.

The *Imagemap* format is used to upload a graphic image with an associated client-side image map file. For example, you could upload a map of the Net University campus along with an image map of URLs to activate when a user clicks a given location.

If you need to reference another Web site from within your Site Builder application, you can use the *URL* content item to provide the link. With the URL content item, you can specify a complete URL string as the link for the content item. When the user activates the link in the content item, he or she is transferred to the location specified by the URL.

You can also use this format to connect to *WebDB Component* objects. The WebDB content item type is intended to be the means by which you link to WebDB components from within Site Builder. However, the WebDB content item type suffers from one critical problem. All WebDB components that you plan to call using the WebDB component type must be public components. If you wish to call a

WebDB component controlled by a specific DAD record, then you must call it using a URL string and not as a WebDB component.

If you have created your own PL/SQL procedures, you can add these items as content objects. Chapter 24 provides details on building your own PL/SQL procedures, which are most often used as part of the Oracle Application Server. These procedures can be called directly from Site Builder folders as content items. PL/SQL procedures represent the ultimate in flexibility because they can output their own streams of HTML code.

The last type of content item is a *Folder Link*, which is used to link an item in one folder with a related item in another folder. Typically, you use the Folder Link to make note of a major content item in one folder in a secondary folder. For example, say the Net University football team wins a game against their biggest rival. You might post a content item in the Students folder that describes this victory. By using a Folder Link, you could also cross-reference this entry in the Alumni folder as well. This saves you from having to duplicate the entire article in multiple folders.

1. Connect to the main site for Net University and log on as the nu_site_admin site administrator, as shown in Figure 23-11.
2. Select the edit button in the upper-right corner of the page.

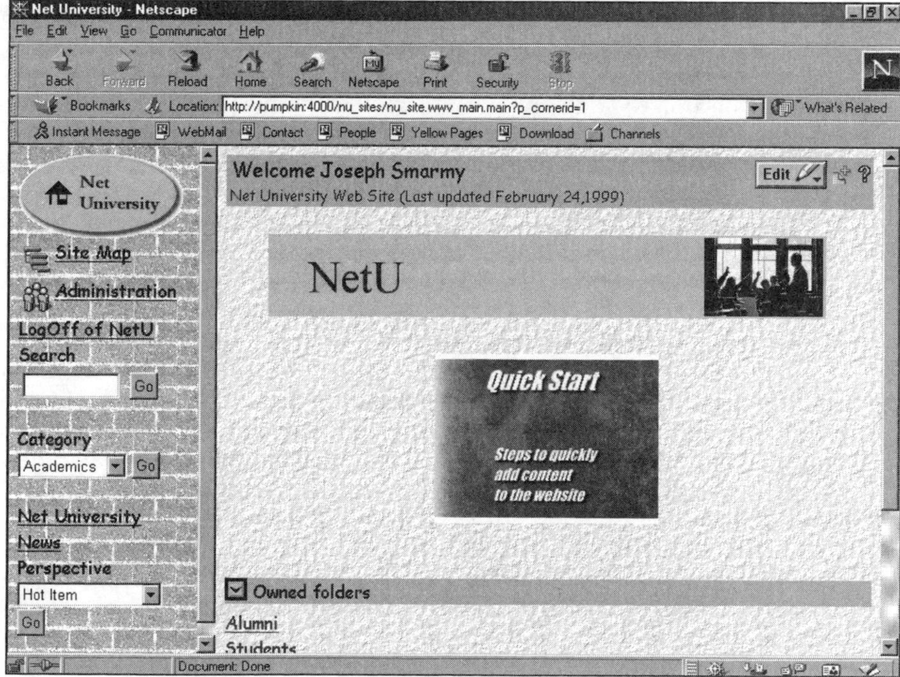

Figure 23-11: Main Net University home page

3. Delete the Quick Start item in the root folder by using the Delete icon next to the image.
4. Confirm the delete operation.
5. Click the Add item button to display the panel shown in Figure 23-12.

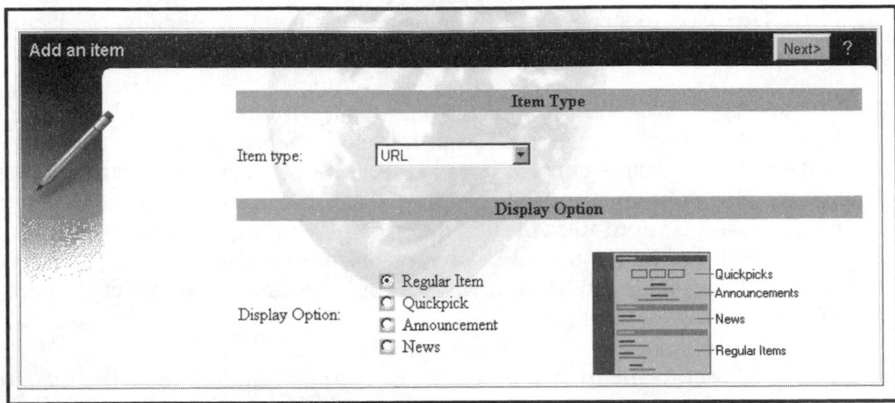

Figure 23-12: Adding an item to the NetU site

Adding an item to a folder is accomplished by using a wizard interface that guides you through the process. Normally you start the process by navigating to the folder that you wish to add the content to, and then selecting the Edit button. If the Edit button does not appear in the upper-right corner of the folder page, you do not have permission to add content to this folder. In this particular case, you are positioned in the root folder for the site. You are going to start by adding the Net University mascot as the first entry into the root folder.

The first selection you must make in the wizard is the item type, using the drop-down list box. The list of items matches the content types discussed at the beginning of this section. Select the URL item type from the combo box.

There are four possible display options for any one content item that are detailed in the lower panel on the first page of the wizard. *Regular Items* are the most common, and they appear inside folders and categories. *Quickpick* items are intended to be links to common functions or other sites and they appear at the top of your pages. You will most often create a Quickpick item as a hotlink to a popular menu choice or external URL site. For example, a Quickpick item for the Net University site might be a link to NCAA athletics site, or to the eFollett college textbook site.

Announcements are positioned just below the Quickpick items, and they are intended to serve as special content items with a limited life span. They share the same format as the Regular Item type, but they are displayed at the top of the page within each folder.

News items are the last type of content, and they are handled differently than other content items. Generally speaking, News items have a limited life span and appear in a special category within each folder. For example, suppose that a limited number of tickets to the sold-out Net University football game have suddenly become available. You can use a News item to announce the availability of these tickets in the Events category of the Students folder and include a link to a page where the user can purchase the tickets.

The Net University mascot will be an announcement item inside of the root folder, so choose the Announcement item format and click the Next button to continue.

The next panel in the wizard varies by the type of item that you select, and once you select an item type and display option for an item and complete the wizard you cannot change these options. Within the wizard, however, you can move back and forth between panels as you see fit. A number of fields appear in every panel regardless of the item type, as shown in Table 23-1.

Table 23-1
Common Required Settings and Values

Item	*Description*
Title	The title of the item is the string of text that displays as the first part of the item. It also serves as the link to the item itself. You can enter simple text, or you can include HTML formatting tags inside of the title string, such as <B> or <I>. Imagemaps are the only item type that do not support titles, because the image itself is the title and the description.
Description	The description field is the extended text that appears below the item to fully explain the associated content item. Site Builder automatically wraps the text for you, but as with the title string, you can embed HTML tags within the text to control the formatting yourself. Imagemaps do not have descriptions because the image itself serves as the description.
Category	Categories match the category settings that are created as part of the site. Categories are only available for Regular items, and Quickpicks, Announcements, and News items all appear in their own separate display areas as described previously.
Expiration	The Expiration combo box contains a range of days an item remains valid. The dates range from 1 day to 120 days in various increments, or you can set an item to be permanent, in which case it never expires. Expired items are not physically deleted until the system administrator executes the purge function.

The remaining items on the Required Settings and Values panel vary according to the item type that you select. Table 23-2 lists the remaining fields that can be displayed on the second panel and the items to which they are connected.

Table 23-2
Extended Item Type Fields

Item	*Description*	*Item Associated*
URL	Fully qualified URL string that points to a Web address. Any valid URL string is allowed, including URLs with parameters. You can also call WebDB components as URL strings.	URL
Filename	Filenames are the operating system files with extensions, which are subsequently loaded into the database within the site. Site Builder maintains the file extension along with the file so that the MIME type can be passed along to the browser when the file is downloaded to the client.	File, Multiple File
Text	Block of text and HTML tags that are similar in format to the description string described previously.	Text Item
Image	Image file in GIF or JPEG format that displays as the content item. The image is uploaded into the database when the content item is created.	Imagemap
Image Map	Block of image map HTML text associated with the image file. The image map code must follow the format for a client-side image map file.	Imagemap
Image Map Name	Logical name for the image map associated with the image map code and displayed as the title.	Imagemap
Folder	A folder is an internal link to another folder in the Site Builder site. You cannot explicitly enter a folder link, but Site Builder displays a panel that enables you to select a folder.	Folder
WebDB Component	Combo box of WebDB components that have been made accessible to the public role from inside WebDB. This list only contains the SHOW procedures inside any package. If you want to connect an item to a parameter-based component, you have to connect to it through the URL item type.	WebDB Component
PL/SQL Code	Custom PL/SQL code that includes calls to HTF/HTP procedures and functions. Chapter 24 contains a detailed discussion of these procedures.	PL/SQL call

The item you are entering is a URL item type, as shown in Figure 23-13.

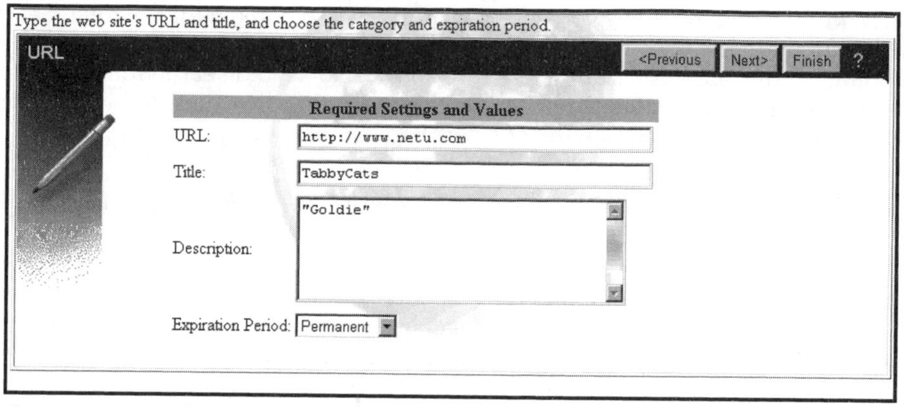

Figure 23-13: Add URL item type

1. Enter an address for the URL string that will be connected to the item. This address can be any valid URL address string.
2. Enter a title and description and set the expiration date for the item to Permanent.
3. Click the Next button to display the panel shown in Figure 23-14.

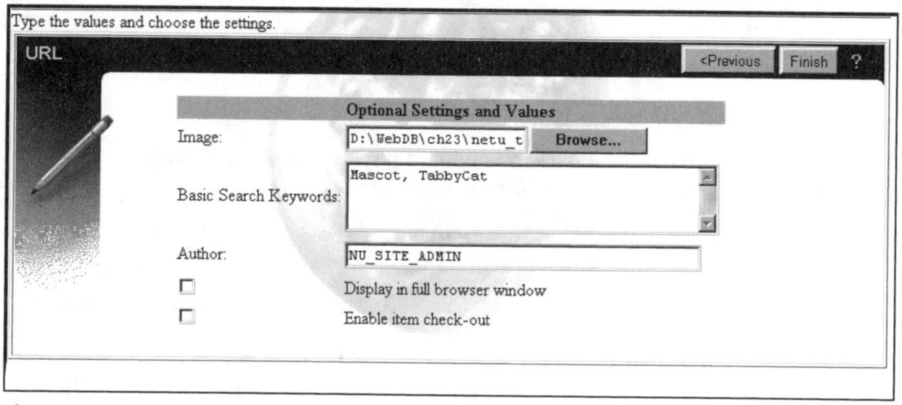

Figure 23-14: Optional Settings and Values panel

Three items appear on the Optional Settings and Values panel regardless of the type of item you create. The first item is the name of an image file that will be used as the image icon associated with the item when it is displayed in the site. This image file can be either a GIF or JPEG format file and serves the same purpose as an icon does on your desktop. The next item on the panel is the Basic Search Keywords text box, which stores keywords you want to be associated with the item. Search fields are not case sensitive and you can enter multiple keywords separated by commas. Both the basic search function and the advanced search function use these strings. The third field on the panel is the author text field and it will be filled in with the USERID used to enter the new item.

Refer back to Chapter 18 for a more detailed discussion of perspectives and categories.

If you have created perspectives for your site, a list of perspectives appears in a multiselect list box on this panel. You can use your mouse to select multiple perspective records for any item. Once you associate perspective records with an item, your end users are able to select records by their associated perspective values. The next block of fields are check boxes that control how the item displays when it is run, and the number of options varies with the item type, as shown in Table 23-3.

Table 23-3
Display Option Check Boxes

Check Box Item	*Description*	*Applies to*
Display in full browser	Causes the item to display in its own browser window.	URL, FILE, TEXT, FOLDER, WEBDB, PL/SQL
Display in frame	Causes the item to display in a separate frame window created by Site Builder.	TEXT, WEBDB, PL/SQL
Display in place	Causes the item to display directly below the text description on the same page as the title and description.	TEXT, WEBDB, PL/SQL

The final item on the panel is a check box that indicates whether this item can be checked out by a user with the Create or the Manage privilege for the current folder. The site itself must have the Enable Item Checkout setting enabled for this check box to have any meaning. You can find this setting within the Site link on the main administration panel. You will typically use this setting to enable users to edit text items or download files and edit them while still keeping a placeholder for the item.

4. Select the NETU_TABBYCAT.GIF image for the image field and enter any keywords that you like.
5. Click the Finish button to save your new entry.

6. Click the View icon in the upper-right corner to complete your editing session and the TabbyCat mascot logo appears as shown in Figure 23-15.

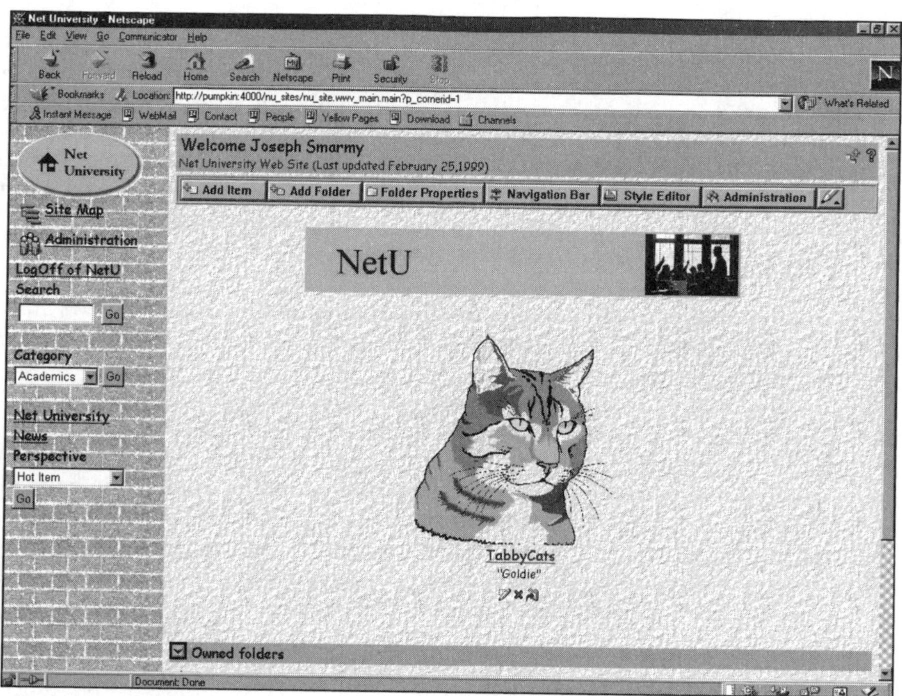

Figure 23-15: TabbyCat logo in the Net University site

Adding WebDB Components to the Site

Site Builder treats WebDB components as a special type of content and the Add-Item Wizard provides a specific entry solely for WebDB components. When you choose the WebDB item type, the wizard displays a list box of available components you can select from to use as the content item. You need to be aware of several critical restrictions with this interface, however.

Site Builder only displays components that have been granted public access. This effectively eliminates any security that surrounds the item. For example, assume that you are using an authenticated Site Builder site and every user has his or her own USERID. You can protect the WebDB component from unauthorized access by placing it in a folder accessible only to authorized users. This protects the item inside Site Builder, but it does not protect the item outside the Site Builder interface, because it is now marked as a public access item.

Chapter 22 provides a detailed description of URL-based component deployment, and we recommend that you review this chapter for more details on building URLs for WebDB components.

The Add-Item Wizard only displays the SHOW procedure for your components — it does not provide access to either the SHOW_PARMS procedure or shared component objects such as links. This prevents you from displaying query-by-example panels to your users as well as eliminating any parameter-based procedures from being used as content items. The solution to this problem is to use the URL item type to display WebDB components. For example, assume that you have created a WebDB component that is a report listing all the students for a particular class year with the class year as a parameter.

1. Use SQL*Plus to load the WebDB component ch23_rep_ugrads.sql script in the Chapter 23 directory of the Examples on the accompanying CD-ROM to create this example report.

Ideally, you would put a link to this report in each of the Student subfolders for each class year. For each link, you would pass the class year parameter so that this report would show the names and photos of all of the students in each class. Unfortunately, Site Builder does not allow you to do this, because it cannot accept parameters or call the SHOW_PARMS procedure that would prompt the user for the parameter value at run time. The solution to this problem is to use the URL item type and call the component directly. The following string shows the format of the URL:

```
http://pumpkin:4000/WebDB/netu.ch23_rep_ugrads.show?p_arg_names
=classyr&p_arg_values=1999
```

You need to replace the server name and port number, and you probably need to create your own DAD entry to replace the `WebDB` entry to put this command into production. If you do not want your users to have to log on a second time, you can use the public DAD entry built automatically by the Site Builder Wizard when the site was created. The parameter name and parameter values are passed to the procedure on the command line as arguments to the procedure.

One option to hide such details would be to create your own HTML page with push buttons for each of the class years. Each push button could in turn connect to the WebDB report with the correct parameters. You could then upload the HTML page as content to the site and ignore the URL format type altogether for WebDB components.

Using Other Accounts to Add Content

You created some additional managerial accounts and end-user accounts in the first part of this chapter, and you can use these accounts to add content to your site (provided that they have the proper permission).

1. Start by logging off the NetU site and then logging back on using the UGRADS_MGR account.

The first thing you notice when you log back on to the account is that you only see the root file folder and the Students folder. The UGRADS_MGR account only has access to these folders and Site Builder hides any folders and subfolders that have not been explicitly granted to the current logon record.

2. Open the Students folder.
3. Choose the Edit button and add the following three new items to the Students folder:

```
URL
Quickpick
URL Link : http://www.ncaa.com
Title: NCAA College Sports
Image: netu_icon1.gif

URL
Quickpick
URL Link: http://www.efollett.com
Title: eFollett Used College Books
Image: netu_icon2.gif

File
Regular Item
File: netu_courses.pdf
Title: NetU Course Catalog
Category: Academics
```

4. Set your own description for each item. The net result of adding these three items will be the page shown in Figure 23-16.

The UGRADS_MGR account has permission to manage elements in the student folder, and items that are added to the folder are immediately made available to the site. The remaining undergraduate student accounts do not have this same level of permission.

1. Log off the site and then log back on using one of the Students accounts assigned to the UGRADS_USR group, such as ACHIEVA or BAKER.
2. Add another Regular Item to the site, make it a text item in the Academic folder, and use any data that you wish as the title and description. Choose the Hot Item perspective for this entry.
3. Return to view mode for your site and then log off the site.
4. Log on using the BAKER account.

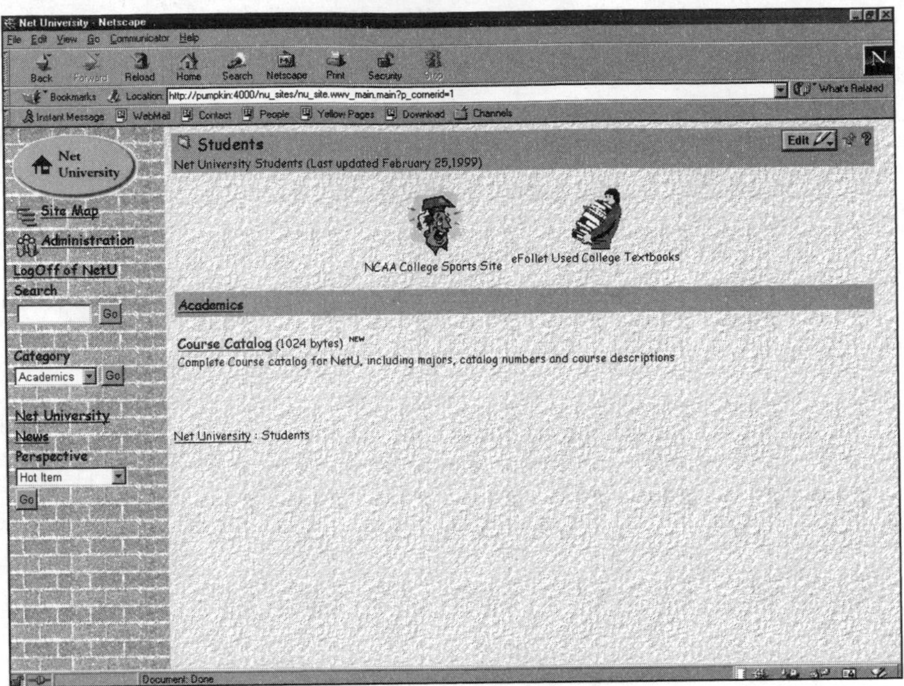

Figure 23-16: NetU site with Quickpick and Regular items

When you log back on to the NetU site, you do not see the item that was just added by the ACHIEVA USERID because that item has not been approved by the folder administrator, as shown in Figure 23-17. The item you added while logged on to the site as ACHIEVA has been entered into the system, but it has been marked as a pending change. The ACHIEVA account sees the item, and any account marked with the OWN or MANAGE privilege also sees the new item. These privileged accounts also have the opportunity to approve the pending item.

5. Log off the site.
6. Log on as the UGRADS_MGR account.

Once you connect to the site as a privileged user, you only see the item when you actually open up the Students folder. Site Builder automatically creates a special internal category inside each folder that serves as the Approval folder. When you open any folder using a privileged account, you see this folder appear as shown in Figure 23-18.

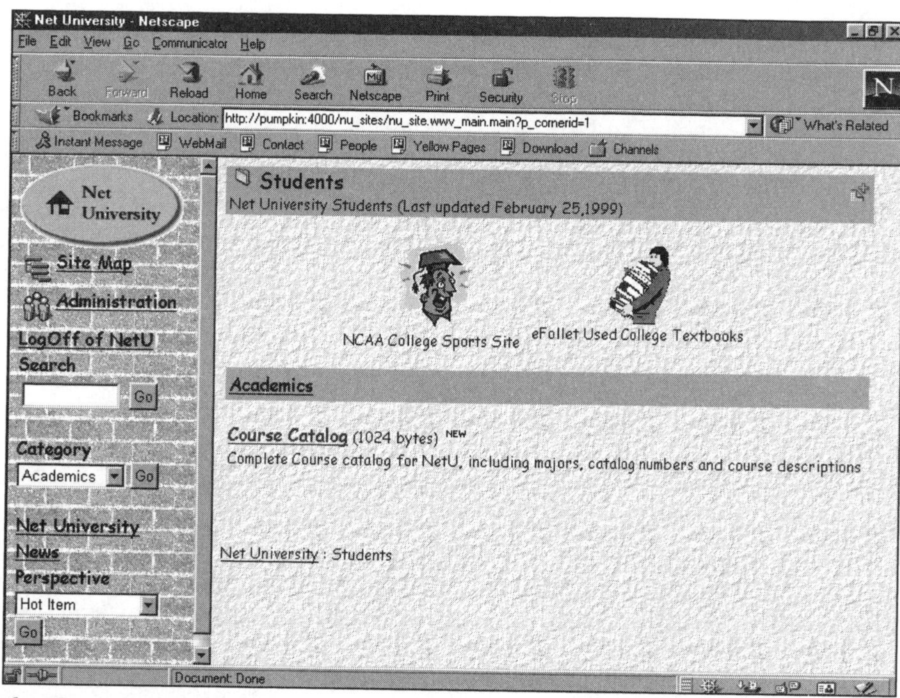

Figure 23-17: NetU site with a view-only account

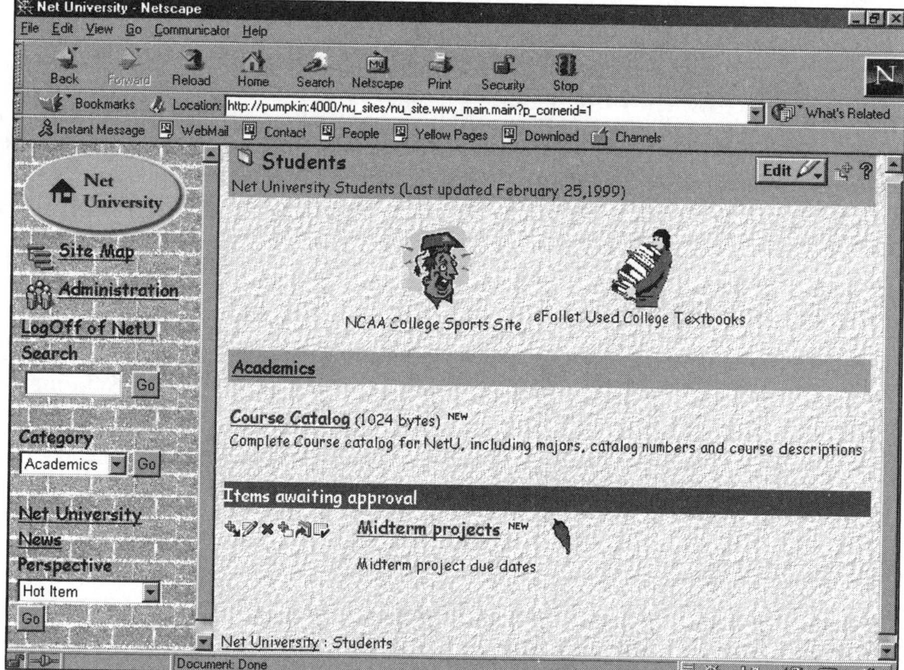

Figure 23-18: Approval folder

Site Builder displays a New icon next to the pending item called the Approve function. This function does not display a dialog panel, but rather serves as a one-button menu for marking the pending item as approved. You do not have a chance to confirm your choice, and the entry becomes final as soon as you use the Approve function. If you accidentally approve an item and want to revoke the approval, you have a limited number of choices.

Site Builder enables you to build sites with item checkout capabilities and revision control. If you have enabled this option, as described in Chapter 18, you can check the item out and not check it back in. The item would remain online but not visible to users until it is checked back in. Your only other alternative would be to edit the item directly, or to delete the item.

7. Use the Approve icon to approve the new item.
8. Use the View icon to display the site.

Notice that the Hot Item perspective icon displays to the right of this new item. Users can use the combo boxes for the perspectives and categories in the Navigation Bar to search for content. Site Builder only allows you to search for content items by either a single perspective or category setting. However, users can perform multikeyword searches using the advanced searching capabilities of Site Builder, which we discuss in detail in the next section.

Although the subfolders for the class years are stored inside the Students folder, notice that you are not allowed to view these folders with any account other than the site administrator account. Site Builder does not cascade permissions to subfolders automatically. In the case of the Net University example, you might create a group for each class year and enable all members of the class year to add items for their class year. You might also enable classes to view each other's folders, but only enable students to add items to their own class years. Within each class, you can assign a folder administrator who is able to approve pending items and serve as the folder "moderator."

Advanced Topics

The best way to gain experience with your Site Builder site is to add items to the site and connect as a different class of user to test out your security scheme. You will find that Site Builder is easy to work with and does not require a steep learning curve from the user perspective. However, certain aspects of your Site Builder site require a little bit more explanation.

News items

In the previous section, we described the four types of display formats available for your items: Regular Items, Quickpicks, Announcements, and News items. In order to enable your users to contribute content in any of the first three formats, you must use authenticated logons and provide specific modification privileges. The exception to this rule is the News item display type.

News items are provided as a means of relaying information amongst the users of a site or a folder. News items appear inside of a particular folder just like any other type of content, but they are stored inside their own special category. Most of the content for your site is likely to be composed of three main item types: Files, URLs, and WebDB Components. You can deploy these objects to your users inside Site Builder as content items. For the most part, you will find that these items are either Quickpick items or Regular Items inside categories within a folder. For example, you might publish the current course list as a report inside the Student folder in the Academic category. The athletic calendar might be published inside the Events category, along with the social calendar.

These items represent official publications from the University, and you may want to ensure that they are of a certain standard. It is likely that only a few people within the organization have the authority to create such items. Contrast this against a large constituency of possible users. With the undergraduate classes, this is not really a problem, because you have only 75 students. However, if you wanted to provide logons for all of the NetU alumni, you are talking about 1000 accounts. Do you really want to create and administer that many accounts? However, all of these alumni represent a valuable group of users that have good information to contribute. One of the ways to capture information from this public group is to enable your site to accept news items from public users.

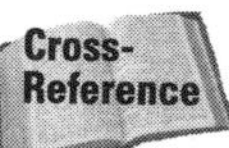

Chapter 18 explains how to enable this setting within the overall site. We recommend that you read Chapter 18 carefully before you enable public news contributions on your site.

News items can be input into any folder that allows public access. In the case of Net University, you might create a public folder for Alumni called Class News. Alumni can freely add news items, which appear in the news section of the page. News items can be in any of the eight item type formats, so users are not restricted as to what types of content they can load. The difference is that the entries are marked as news and therefore do not need to be as formal as other types of content.

While items are displayed in a "last-in, first-out" order in categories, new items are displayed randomly in each folder.

Enabling public news contributions does have its risks. Because the items do not go through an approval process the content appears directly on the site. Users can anonymously post offensive material to your Web site using this mechanism, so you must weigh the risks against the return.

Advanced searching

Site Builder provides the Basic Search capability on the Navigation Bar by default. A user can enter a string into the Search text box on the Navigation Bar and Site

Builder searches the title, description, and keywords of all items for matching values. Users can surround words with the "%" wildcard character to search for substrings. As your site grows, this can make the task of searching more difficult as more and more items match the same set of keywords and phrases.

Site Builder provides a second search panel called the Advanced Search panel, which you can enable for a folder on the Navigation Bar Editor.

Chapter 18 discusses the process for modifying the Navigation Bar on a folder-by-folder basis.

The Advanced Search panel shown in Figure 23-19 enables users to perform Boolean searches using a combination of "and" and "or."

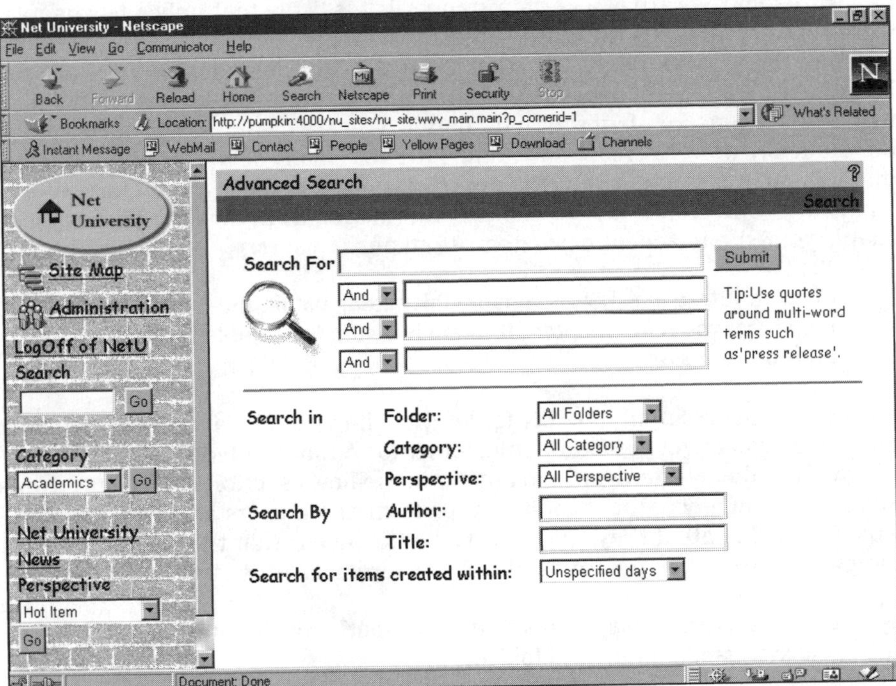

Figure 23-19: Advanced Search panel

Although you can add links to perspectives and categories on the Navigation panel, you can save space on the Navigation Bar by deploying them on the Advanced Search panel instead. The top portion of the panel enables the user to enter a combination of phrases and keywords. The bottom portion of the panel enables the user to search in specified folders, categories, and perspectives. You can even search for items that have been entered by a certain individual, or within a certain period of time.

Wrapping Up

Adding content to Site Builder sites is an evolutionary process, and each site you build will evolve differently. The layout of your folders and the mix of items and formats that you implement are driven largely by the users of the site. Site Builder solves one part of the problem by providing a consistent framework. However, the larger problem with most sites is one of content.

No matter how visually stimulating your site is, you will fail to keep users coming back if you cannot deliver the content they want in a timely fashion. By eliminating the complexity of formatting content for the Web using Site Builder, you make it easier for users to contribute content, and this helps keep your Web site fresh and interesting.

In the next chapter, we will take you through the process of adding advanced PL/SQL procedures to your site. Through these advanced procedures, you can add features such as e-commerce functionality that Site Builder can deliver.

✦ ✦ ✦

CHAPTER 24

Integrating PL/SQL Logic

✦ ✦ ✦ ✦

In This Chapter

Oracle HTML Packages

Oracle's PL/SQL Web Toolkit

Oracle Application Server's OWA Packages

Integrating HTP/OWA Procedures with WebDB

Debugging and Advanced Concepts

✦ ✦ ✦ ✦

The precursor to Oracle's WebDB product was a set of PL/SQL packages that enabled you to output Oracle data in HTML format. These packages were combined with the PL/SQL cartridge within the Oracle Application Server to provide a solution for building dynamic HTML applications from Oracle data. The original PL/SQL packages were known as the HTF/HTP packages, and they offered a very low-level interface to both the database and HTML. Coding the creation of HTML pages at this level is not as productive as working with WebDB, but the packages do enable you to control the data in a fashion that is not possible with WebDB alone.

You can take advantage of the power of these packages, as well as the more generalized ability of PL/SQL to implement logic, when you build components in the WebDB environment. In this chapter, we take a look at building some of these advanced features, as well as investigating techniques for handling errors within procedures and debugging custom PL/SQL procedures.

Oracle HTML Packages

As part of the Oracle Application Server PL/SQL cartridge, Oracle created a series of procedures that enable you to embed HTML code within PL/SQL procedures. There are two types of procedures, which in turn are organized into two separate Oracle packages — the *HTP* (or *hypertext procedure)* package and the *HTF* (or *hypertext function)* package.

The HTF and HTP packages are almost identical in functionality and design. Each of the major HTML tags is represented by a procedure within the HTP package. The various procedures within the HTP package output HTML tags along with custom data and send the results back to the current output stream. The HTF procedures shadow the HTP procedures and are used solely for nesting functions. In most cases, you will use the HTP procedures, because HTF calls are not passed back to the PL/SQL gateway. They are only used to format results within a call to an HTP procedure. For example, to print a string of bold text into the standard output stream, you could use the following fragment of code:

```
htp.bold('Hello World!');
```

However, if you wish to print this string with strong emphasis, you need to wrap the bold command within the strong command as follows:

```
htp.bold((htf.strong('Hello World!'));
```

The HTF package is designed solely for handling this type of contingency, and you will find that every HTP procedure has an associated HTF procedure. Unless you are nesting functions frequently, however, you will almost always use the HTP version of each procedure.

Each HTP/HTF procedure is designed to support one of the HTML tags, and Oracle continues to add new procedures to these two packages. The Oracle Application Server comes equipped with these packages by default, but WebDB automatically installs them if they are not already in place. In addition to inserting HTML tags, you may have the need to handle some specialized Web processing such as reading and writing cookies. Oracle provides the Oracle Web Agent (OWA) packages to address this requirement. The OWA packages are built on the same HTF/HTP foundation as WebDB. We introduce the nine separate OWA packages in the next section of this chapter.

The HTML procedures in the HTF and HTP packages can be grouped into the following logical units:

- ✦ Printing and Formatting
- ✦ Document Structure
- ✦ Document Body
- ✦ Frames
- ✦ Lists
- ✦ Tables
- ✦ Form Objects

Because these procedures are used as you add PL/SQL code to expand the reach of the HTML pages created for you by WebDB, you should understand what they do for you, which is covered in the next section.

Printing and formatting

The Printing and Formatting procedures send a string of text into the standard output stream. They are the main mechanism for creating and formatting text output. You will find most of these procedures familiar if you are experienced in the use of the basic HTML tags. Table 24-1 lists the major printing and formatting procedures, and most of these tags support both the HTF and HTP versions.

We have only included those procedures that are normally used within WebDB. The actual list of procedures is quite extensive, but many of these additional procedures will either be ignored by WebDB or will interfere with the processing of WebDB if explicitly used.

Table 24-1
Printing and Formatting Procedures

Procedure	*Description*
htp.print (string)	Sends a standard string of text to the output stream of the PL/SQL gateway
htp.emphasis (string)	Formats the enclosed string with emphasis tags
htp.keyboard (string)	Formats the output-string in monospace formatting – suitable for showing code or user input instructions
htp.teletype (string)	Formats the text in typewriter style – similar to the keyboard procedure
htp.strong (string)	Formats the enclosed string with strong HTML tags
htp.bold (string)	Formats the string in boldface text
htp.italic (string)	Formats the string in italics text
htp.br	Inserts a new line into the output stream
htp.line	Inserts a horizontal line in the output stream

Document structure

WebDB automatically creates document objects for you in the process of building your dynamic pages. However, Oracle Application Server developers are responsible for building the complete HTML page from start to finish. To address this requirement, the HTF/HTP packages come equipped with procedures that you can use to design the required HTML document structures in addition to the HTML data. Using these particular tags within WebDB components typically has little or no effect, because WebDB has already specified them. You may make use of them, however, if you are creating your own complete components.

Table 24-2
Document Structure Procedures

Procedure	*Description*
htp.htmlOpen	Creates the required <HTML> tag within a document. Using this procedure can cause problems within WebDB, as WebDB normally opens and closes pages for you.
htp.htmlClose	Generates the closing tag </HTML> used with htmlOpen.
htp.headOpen	Defines the HTML document head by inserting the <HEAD> tag.
htp.headClose	Generates the closing tag for the document head </HEAD>.
htp.bodyOpen	Inserts the <BODY> tag into the HTML document.
htp.bodyClose	Generates the closing tag for the document body.
htp.title (string)	Inserts a title into your document that is bracketed by the <TITLE> and </TITLE> tags.
htp.meta (description string, name, content)	Generates document information for use by the browser. Typically, you would use the meta tag to provide information for search engines. This does not apply when working with WebDB, because the pages are dynamically generated. However, you can also use this tag to refresh or redirect Web pages. For example, using the following line of code causes the page to refresh every five seconds:

```
htp.meta('Refresh',NULL,5);
```

The meta procedure is powerful enough that it warrants some extra discussion. Within the HTML world, you are probably familiar with using the <META> tag for providing search indexes with page information. For example, using the following code as the standard META tag of your page enables Web search programs to index this page as being related to information about WebDB:

```
<META NAME="description", CONTENT="webdb, oracle, html,
programming">
```

However, with WebDB, the pages are generated dynamically for you from the database and Web search engines do not have access to these pages to begin with, which invalidates the use of the <META> tag for this particular purpose.

You can use the <META> tag to set other attributes that WebDB will not override. For example, you can use the <META> tag to cause a page to refresh according to a set interval as shown in the following fragment:

```
<META HTTP-EQUIV="Refresh" CONTENT="5">
```

In this example case, the browser automatically refreshes the page every five seconds. You could also add additional parameters to the CONTENT parameter to redirect users to a new page, or ensure that the browser fetches a new copy and not a cached copy of the page. The htp.meta procedure can be used to send this type of information into the WebDB HTTP streams as shown in the following line of code:

```
htp.meta('Refresh',NULL,'5;http://pumpkin/someotherpage.htm');
```

The first parameter is the meta type and the second parameter is the name or description of the tag. The second parameter is generally left as null for refreshes and redirects. The final parameter is a string value that gets mapped to the CONTENT parameter and you are free to supply any valid content values to this string.

Advanced document structure procedures

Oracle does not differentiate between the capabilities of various HTF/HTP procedures within their documentation, but from an ease-of-use perspective it helps to break the more complicated routines into their own category. So far, you have looked at routines that are mostly simple procedural calls. The procedures in this section require some additional explanation because they each accept a number of run-time parameters that can have a dramatic effect on the output. Each of these procedures maps to a standard HTML tag, but you need to work with them carefully to understand how the tags are generated from the values you load into the procedures. Oracle supports a long list of these objects, but WebDB-compatible routines are as follows:

- ✦ Anchor
- ✦ Comments
- ✦ FontOpen/FontClose
- ✦ Header
- ✦ Img
- ✦ Mailto
- ✦ PreOpen/PreClose

Anchor

The htp.anchor procedure is one of the most powerful procedures in that it enables you to build links to other objects from within PL/SQL procedures. Within the WebDB environment, you can explicitly embed anchors in your documents within any of the text blocks. The htp.anchor procedure gives you the tools to build dynamic links inside WebDB components. Calls to the htp.anchor procedure take the following format:

```
htp.anchor( URL string, Text/image string, Name, Attributes)
```

The first parameter is the URL link that is called when the user attempts to access the link at run time, and the second parameter is the string of text or image that connects to the link. You can also name the link by using the Name parameter and pass along any additional HTML attributes supported by the ANCHOR tag in the attributes parameter position. For example, to link a string of text to another page you might use the following code:

```
htp.anchor('http://pumpkin/mypage.html', htf.bold('Link to this
page'),null,null);
```

In the preceding snippet of code, notice the use of the HTF version of the bold procedure. This was necessary in order to nest the bolding of the text within the call to the anchor procedure. If you wish, you can add some parameters to the ANCHOR tag, such as TARGET=new_window, to cause the link to open into a new browser. Within static HTML pages, you are likely to use anchors with NAME values to enable users to jump from one section of the page to another. This is less common within WebDB, because WebDB automatically paginates output for you.

Comments

The htp.comment procedure is used to embed developer comments into the source for a Web page. By default, your users do not see these comments displayed on the page, but they become visible if users look at the source for the page. You can use the comments procedure to embed system documentation into your output files that can be effective in debugging problems at run time. The comments procedure accepts a single string of text as shown in the following example:

```
htp.comment('PAGE=ALUMNI1, AUTH=JFM, VERSION=1.8');
```

You can use PL/SQL code to dynamically build the comment string and pass it to the comments procedure or you can hard-code the string. In the preceding code block, the comment string includes some author information along with a version indicator. Should a user experience some difficulty with the application, your support desk could instruct them to view the source and search for this string. You would then be able to track the version of the component that caused the problem.

fontOpen and fontClose

The htp.fontOpen and htp.fontClose procedures are always used in pairs to set the font characteristics for a given block of text. The htp.fontOpen procedure accepts four parameters as follows:

```
htp.fontOpen(color, fontface, size, attributes)
```

The color parameter is passed as a string using the hex color format (#C0C0C0), and the `fontface` is a string that matches a font known to the browser. The `size` parameter is an integer value and refers to the relative size of the text. Positive integers are used to increase the size, and negative values can be passed to shrink the associated text. The call to this procedure should preface the generation of your text and a call to htp.fontClose is required to end the font setting as shown in the following code:

```
htp.fontOpen('#C0C0C0',null, -2,null);
htp.print('Hello World!');
htp.fontClose;
```

Most HTML tags support a number of custom extensions commonly referred to as *attributes*. You can pass values for these attributes by using the attributes parameter for any HTP procedure that supports them.

Header

The htp.header procedure is used to input document headings and levels within your HTML pages. Although WebDB automatically includes such information in the pages that it builds on your behalf, you can combine the htp.header procedure with dynamic database data to provide an additional layer of customization. The htp.header procedure accepts three parameters as shown in the following code segment:

```
htp.header(level number, text string, alignment, wrap-
indicator);
```

The level number is an integer value that sets the heading level for the associated string and the text string is the value displayed as the header. The last two parameters are optional and are used to set the alignment (with the values of left, right, and center) and whether or not the text string should wrap around (with the values of wrap and nowrap). The following block of code shows the htp.header procedure in action:

```
htp.header(1, 'This is a level one heading',null,null);
```

Img

The htp.img or image procedure is used to load a graphic image onto a page. Oracle enables you to load simple images as well as images along with image maps. Dynamic images are particularly useful if you are planning to add your own menu bar to the body of a form. The format of the htp.img procedure is as follows:

```
htp.img(url, alignment, alternate, ismap, attributes);
```

The only required parameter for this procedure is the URL, which is a string that points to the location of the image. You are free to pass a string value for the alignment parameter to justify the image, and you can pass an alternate value to be displayed in the event that the browser does not support images. Oracle provides an additional set of procedures to create image maps and the fourth parameter passes the name of the associated map file. As with any of the other extended HTML tags you are free to pass strings of other attributes, such as horizontal and vertical positioning, using the attributes parameter. The following block of code loads the logo image from a virtual directory into a fixed size on a page:

```
htp.img('/netu/netu_logo.gif',null,null,null,'HEIGHT=20,
WIDTH=30');
```

Calls to the htp.img procedure can include references to WebDB virtual directories as shown in the preceding example. Oracle provides a second version of this procedure, htp.img2, that is used for handling images with client-side image maps.

Mailto

The htp.mailto procedure creates an HTML HREF tag that points to the text and electronic mail address specified in the call to the procedure. The format of the htp.mailto procedure accepts four parameters as follows:

```
htp.mailto(emaddr, text, name, attributes);
```

The `emaddr` and `text` fields are associated with the e-mail address string and text description that displays on the page. You can provide a link name for mailto link as well as passing the usual string of extended attributes as shown in the following example:

```
htp.mailto('joe_smith@net.com', 'webmaster@Netu',null,null);
```

preOpen and preClose

There are cases in which you do not want the browser to format your text, but rather to display the text directly as it was entered into the source file. Oracle provides a pair of procedures that initiate a preformatted section and then terminate a preformatted section with the htp.preOpen and htp.preClose routines. Although htp.preOpen accepts some parameters, it is usually executed without parameters. While your browser normally ignores things such as tabs, spaces, and carriage returns, it displays all text between the <PRE> and </PRE> tags exactly as entered. As the following example shows, you can use these two procedures to output text in a specific format:

```
htp.preOpen;
htp.print('                              Alumni Donations Report');
htp.print('                                       Summary Data');
htp.preClose;
```

Additional procedures

Oracle provides additional procedures that enable you to create objects such as HTML Lists, Tables, and Frames. Because WebDB creates most of these objects for you, it is not likely that you need to use these procedures directly within WebDB. Each new release of Oracle Application Server and WebDB includes new procedures provided to support enhancements to the HTML standard. You can review the procedures in the OAS_PUBLIC USERID using the browse database capability of WebDB to look for new procedures and additional procedures such as list, table, and frames utilities that this chapter has not discussed.

Forms

Additional sets of procedures that have some relevance to your work with WebDB are the form-building procedures. WebDB, of course, provides an advanced form-generation capability all on its own, but you may find the need to create some additional subforms in order to support specialized processing within one of your component objects. For example, you may wish to add some additional buttons to a form to add new functionality not provided through the WebDB run options. (Separate FORMS require separate submit buttons, however, which can lead to unintended results.) By embedding a form object into the page, you can add your own navigational and data entry fields. Table 24-3 lists the various form procedures and their example usage.

Oracle provides HTP procedure calls for all of the common form objects, and you are free to use them within WebDB components. Because WebDB uses form objects, you might be tempted to use the individual form items by themselves without using the surrounding htp.formOpen and htp.formClose routines. We advise against doing so, because the structure of the output does not always guarantee that your fields are embedded between valid form tags.

It is safer to create your form objects inside explicitly created form tags as shown in the following example:

```
htp.formOpen('/netu/mycgi');
htp.print('Username ');
htp.formText('v_username',10,20);
htp.br;
htp.print('Password');
htp.formPassword('v_password',10,20);
htp.br;
htp.formClose;
```

This example code segment creates a simple form that displays a user name and password field for the user. The use of specialized form items within a page can provide you with additional flexibility you can use to supplement your WebDB components. In the third section of this chapter, we show you how to apply these routines to the PL/SQL code entry points within the various wizards. However, before you begin experimenting with the HTF and HTP procedures, it is important to look at one additional set of functionality.

Table 24-3
Sample Form Procedures

Procedure	*Description*	*Example*
htp.formOpen (url, method, target, encryption type, attributes)	Creates a form object to hold subform items such as push buttons or hidden text fields	`htp.formOpen('Netu.myproc.show','POST');`
htp.formClose	Closes a previously opened form by embedding a </FORM> tag into the output stream	`htp.formClose;`
htp.formSubmit (name, value, attributes)	Creates a submit push button within a form area	`htp.formSubmit(NULL,'Push Me!');`
htp.formText (name, size, maxlength, value, attributes)	Creates a text field of a specified length that accepts a fixed number of characters	`htp.formText('lname', 20, 30);`
htp.formPassword (name, size, maxlength, value, attributes)	Creates a text field that does not echo the characters entered	`htp.formPassword ('Password',10,20);`
htp.formHidden(name, value, attributes)	Creates a text field that is not displayed in the form – useful for storing local information within the Web page	`htp.formHidden('myfield');`
htp.formCheckbox (name, value, checked, attributes)	Generates a check box field within a form	`htp.formCheckbox('yesno', 'Yes_No');`

Oracle Application Server's OWA Packages

In order to improve the interaction between the database and the Web browser, Oracle provides an additional set of procedures called the Oracle Web Agent (OWA) packages, which were created for the original Oracle Web Application Server. Oracle has since renamed the Oracle Web Application Server to the Oracle Application Server, but the utilities themselves still carry the legacy of the OWA name.

The OWA packages provide some functionality above and beyond the basic HTF/HTP utilities, and you may need some of this functionality within WebDB. WebDB itself uses the OWA packages, so they are part of the WebDB installation, even if you are not using the Oracle Application Server. Table 24-4 lists the various OWA packages along with a basic description of their capabilities.

Table 24-4
OWA Utility Packages

Package	*Description*
OWA_COOKIE	This package sends cookies to and from your client browser to the server. Cookies are helpful in storing information across sessions, and the OWA_COOKIE package simplifies the process of working with cookies. WebDB itself uses this package to maintain login information between the client browser and the listener.
OWA_IMAGE	This package enables you handle image maps by providing a set of procedures to determine the X and Y coordinates of a mouse click within an image map.
OWA_INIT	The OWA_INIT package provides a series of constant values used to help you convert cookie settings between time zone variations when the client and server are located within different time zones.
OWA_PATTERN	This package contains a set of procedures used for the purposes of string manipulation and search mapping. The three functions within this procedure offer you three different techniques for performing pattern matching between strings of data.
OWA_OPT_LOCK	This procedure implements a general-purpose optimistic locking scheme used by WebDB to verify modified records before they are written back to the database.
OWA_PARMS	The parameters procedure fetches and sets data in PL/SQL arrays, and it is used by WebDB to perform updates against tables.
OWA_TEXT	The text utility package provides a high-level interface for manipulating strings of data and formatting the resulting output on HTML pages.

Continued

Table 24-4 (continued)

Package	*Description*
OWA_SEC	This package implements a security mechanism for users and procedures used by both OAS and WebDB.
OWA_UTIL	This package provides a set of information utilities that report on the status of the PL/SQL environment. WebDB uses this package internally to display the listener settings and path configuration.

Each of these packages provides a number of features that warrant a detailed discussion outside the WebDB environment. Programmers that are building applications for the Oracle Application Server using the PL/SQL cartridge work with each of these procedures extensively. However, within the WebDB environment, there is less need to work with these procedures directly because the wizards handle most of the complex coding for you. The OWA_COOKIE package is worth investigating in more detail, though, because you may need to work with cookies directly.

Working with OWA_COOKIE

If you wish to carry information over from one session of your browser to subsequent sessions, you need to store the information in some format. The commonly used Web slang for this information is *cookies* and they are generally stored somewhere on your desktop by the browser. Cookies enable your Web applications to store useful information about you and use that information in subsequent sessions. For example, if you wish to acknowledge the return of an existing user to an application, you might record their previous visit within a cookie file. When the user returns to your application, the system can search for a matching cookie and respond accordingly.

Cookies can be defined as being transient, which enables them to expire after a certain date. Browser users do not have to accept cookies and most browsers allow the user to turn off cookies or at least to receive a message when a cookie is sent to them.

WebDB applications require browser cookies to maintain connection and state information even if you do not explicitly plan to make use of cookies.

The OWA_COOKIE package contains four procedures:

- ✦ OWA_COOKIE.GET
- ✦ OWA_COOKIE.GET_ALL
- ✦ OWA_COOKIE.REMOVE
- ✦ OWA_COOKIE.SEND

Oracle PL/SQL packages can handle complex datatypes and the OWA utilities have been designed to leverage this capability. Within the OWA_COOKIE utility, Oracle has created a compound datatype called COOKIE to describe the format of a cookie record. This compound object takes the following format:

```
type cookie is RECORD
{
  name varchar2(4096),
  vals vc_arr,
  num_vals integer
}
```

When you attempt to get the value for a given cookie or set of cookies, Oracle returns the data to you in the cookie record format. To obtain the value for a specified cookie, use the OWA_COOKIE.GET procedure as shown in the following example fragment:

```
owa_cookie.get('ITEM1');
```

The OWA_COOKIE.GET utility searches your cookie file for the item called `ITEM1` and returns the compound datatype cookie to the calling program. Within the cookie record are three fields: name, vals, and num_vals. The Name field is the item name, which you passed in as a parameter; the vals field holds the value for the item; and num_vals field returns an integer that displays the number of values. In the case of the OWA_COOKIE.GET procedure, the num_vals variable always returns 1 or 0. If you wanted to get all of the currently defined cookies, you would use the OWA_COOKIE.GET_ALL procedure, which takes no input parameters but returns an array of type cookie with name and value pairs. In this case, the num_vals variable contains the number of name/value pairs that were found. Within a block of PL/SQL code, you can select all the cookies and then loop through the result set to find the name/value pairs you are interested in.

You can remove any cookie entries you find by using the OWA_COOKIE.REMOVE procedure, which takes the following format:

```
owa_cookie.remove(name, value, path)
```

The `name` and `value` parameters are varchar2 strings, and they must match a name/value pair. The path of the cookie can be used to remove a name/value pair that is not unique to a single application, and it defaults to null. The OWA_COOKIE.REMOVE procedure must be called within the header of the HTTP stream before the document is opened. WebDB provides an entry field that matches this requirement, and you will see this in the next section.

Oracle also permits you to create cookie file entries by using the OWA_COOKIE.SEND procedure, which generates a cookie file entry within the user's browser environment. This procedure is the most complicated, and it takes six parameters as shown in the following code fragment:

```
owa_cookie.send(name, value, expires, path, domain, secure);
```

The only required values are the first two, which are the name and value pair for the cookie. The third parameter is a date field used to hold an expiration date for a cookie. The path, domain, and secure settings allow for a lower level of control over the cookie and are unlikely to be used directly within the WebDB environment. All three of these parameters default to null. Setting the cookie can be as simple as setting the name value pair as follows:

```
owa_cookie.send('COLOR','Blue');
```

Both the remove and send procedures output a string of text to the output stream that acknowledges the completion of the action.

Integrating HTP/OWA Procedures with WebDB

Using the HTP and OWA packages requires you to have a working knowledge of PL/SQL procedural syntax. WebDB is built entirely on PL/SQL packages, but so far you have been completely insulated from the lower-level PL/CODE. The HTP and OWA procedure calls can only be called in the context of a PL/SQL procedural block. Appendix B contains a complete guide to the specifics of PL/SQL syntax, but you can work with PL/SQL within WebDB without having a detailed knowledge of the syntax.

1. Import the report file ch24_rep_classes.sql

Most of the WebDB wizards provide a panel you can use for entering specialized PL/SQL code. The entry point for this code is the Add advanced PL/SQL code page, and it is provided as the final page within the following wizards:

- ✦ Forms
- ✦ Reports
- ✦ Calendars
- ✦ Charts
- ✦ Hierarchies

WebDB provides four entry points for entering PL/SQL procedures, and they are all contained on the single panel. Despite the simplicity of this mechanism, it provides you with a great deal of power for customizing the generated HTML pages.

2. Open the ch24_rep_classes report and navigate to the Add advanced PL/SQL code page, as shown in Figure 24-1.

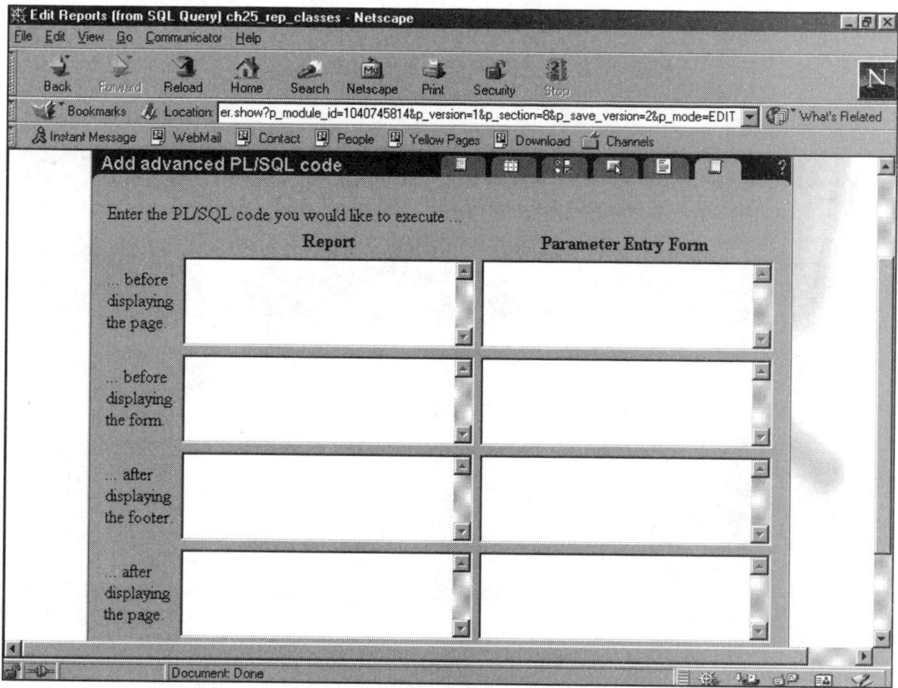

Figure 24-1: Add advanced PL/SQL code page

The four entry points appear in pairs of two. The four text boxes on the left-hand side of the page apply to the resulting component object and the four text boxes on the right apply to the parameter form for the object if one exists. Each of the four entry points applies to a certain area of the HTML output page, and this is easier to understand by entering sample code into each window.

3. Enter the following PL/SQL commands into the four text boxes in the left-hand panel from top to bottom. Be sure to enter the semicolon to end each line as shown in the code.

```
htp.print('Before page');
```

Enter this code into the . . . before displaying the page box.

```
htp.print('Before form');
```

Enter this code into the . . . before displaying the form box.

```
htp.print('After footer');
```

Enter this code into the . . . after displaying the footer box.

```
htp.print('After page');
```

Enter this code into the . . . after displaying the page box.

4. The Add advanced PL/SQL code page should look like the page shown in Figure 24-2. Once you have entered the procedures as shown, use the Finish button to save the changes and then run the report.

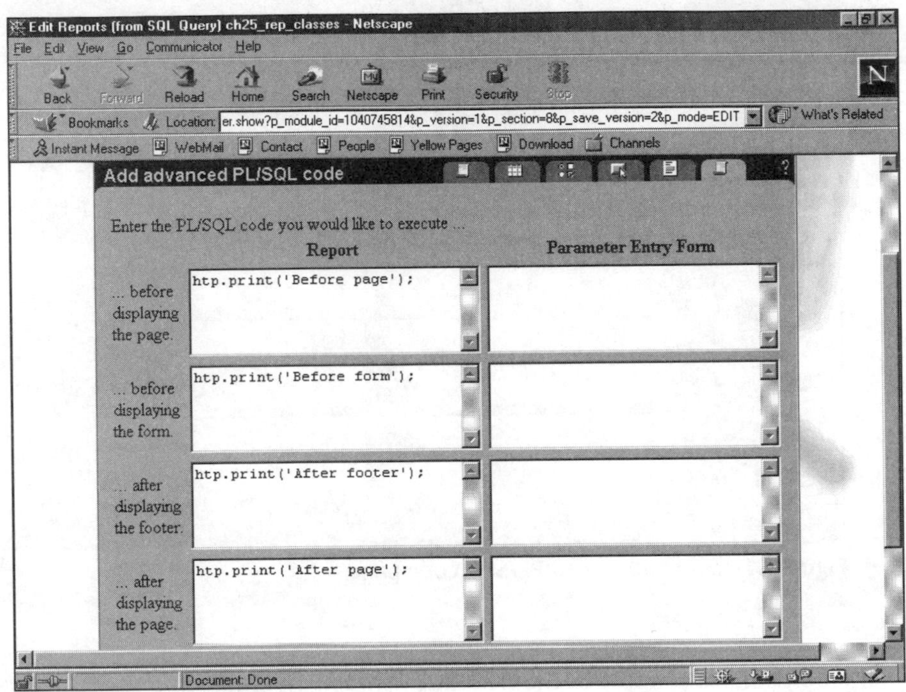

Figure 24-2: PL/SQL entries

Notice that the calls to the HTP procedures cause a block of text to be written to each segment of the HTML output, as shown in Figure 24-3. The first text item shows the string Before page and it appears before any other output in the page. WebDB invokes the procedure as part of the HTTP header that follows the data in the output stream. If you were to view the source code for this page, you would find that the Before page string appears ahead of the <HTML> tag in the output.

Under most conditions, there is little value in having any code appear before the start of the HTML document. The exception to this rule is the OWA_COOKIE.REMOVE and OWA_COOKIE.SEND procedures, which *must* be called within the header. By invoking the code in this procedure block within the header, you are free to make use of these two routines to set cookie and remove cookie values. Remember that on the Display Options panel, which precedes the Add additional PL/SQL code panel, you have the ability to add straight HTML text as header and footer text. The entry fields on the PL/SQL code panel provide you with the opportunity to mix HTML and code using the HTP and OWA procedures.

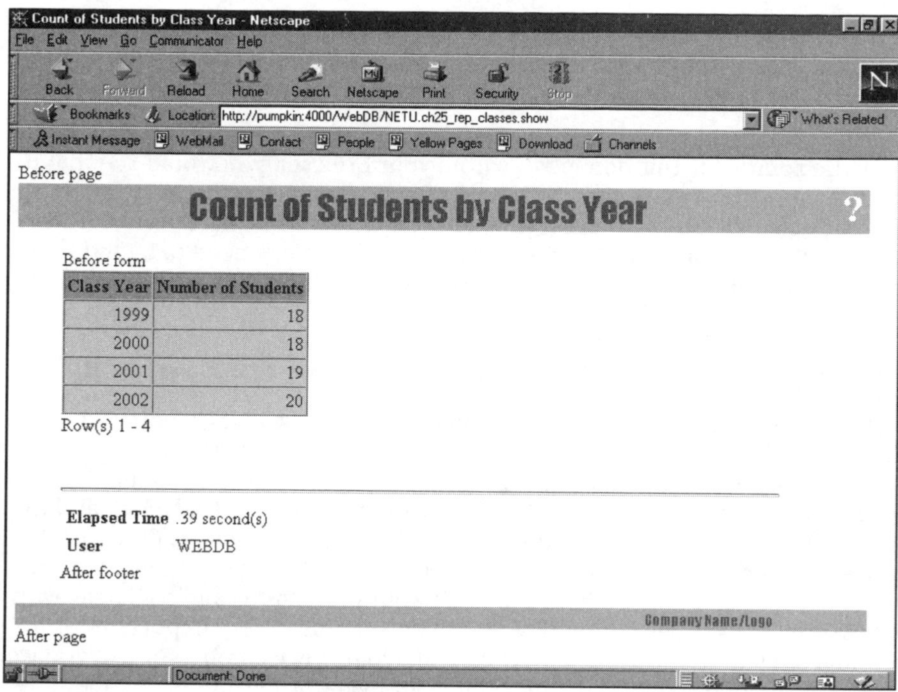

Figure 24-3: Output of HTP procedures

The second block of custom code that appears is the string Before form and it is executed before WebDB inserts the <FORM> tag into the document. WebDB keeps track of the current state of most output pages by using hidden fields within the document and this requires that <FORM> and </FORM> tags be inserted into the resulting document. WebDB invokes the second PL/SQL code window just ahead of creating the FORM tags in the output. In our example case, the executed code is a simple print statement, but you are free to use any of the HTF/HTP and OWA procedures within this code block. In fact, if you wish to add your own form field items, you are free to create your own form elements by using the htp.formOpen and htp.formClose procedures within this code block.

Form tags must be completely enclosed and we recommend that you create separate form objects if you wish to add form items to multiple sections of the HTML page. This ensures that your custom inserts do not interfere with the form tags generated by WebDB. For example, if you want to add form objects within each of the PL/SQL entry points, make sure that you wrap each section in its own set of <FORM> and </FORM> tags. Be advised, however, that the use of multiple forms requires multiple submit buttons, and this can lead to problems with the user's interaction on your pages.

The third block of text appears after the WebDB footer. The footer contains any of the display options settings selected, such as timing information and USERID. You can see the text string After footer as it appears in Figure 24-3. If you plan to display information within the footer it is a good idea to use the Display Options panel to remove any of the information that WebDB loads into the footer in order to save valuable screen space.

The final text string appears at the very bottom of the document and, if you were to view the source for this document within your browser, you would see that it actually appears outside the <HTML> and </HTML> tags. Although the text appears on the page, the browser does not consider this text to be part of the HTML document itself. As the HTML standard evolves, you may need to include information outside the scope of the document itself that the browser can use.

Adding database access code to PL/SQL blocks

WebDB surrounds the code that you enter into the four PL/SQL entry windows with the required begin/end delimiters. Although you do not see them in the code window, they are inserted into the generated PL/SQL code for you automatically. Oracle calls these unnamed blocks of code *anonymous PL/SQL blocks,* and they are one of the main structural components for the PL/SQL language. (Technically, these procedures are not anonymous blocks because WebDB embeds them within a named procedure.) Normally you provide your procedures and packages with a name, but Oracle does not require you to do so. This is very important for a product such as WebDB, because it could become very cumbersome if you were forced to provide a specific, unique name for every little snippet of code. The entries you make into the four PL/SQL code windows on the Add additional PL/SQL code panel are implemented as anonymous blocks of code that are then inserted in the named procedure when it is created.

In the example you worked with in the preceding section, the entire procedure was a simple call to one of the HTP print routines. However, you can input any valid block of PL/SQL code into these windows, and that is the real power of the PL/SQL entry windows. The output shown in Figure 24-3 could just as easily have been created with the Add Text panel used for inputting title text for the form. The power of the PL/SQL code windows is their ability to add additional SQL code into these panels and have this code processed as part of the procedure.

Note We recommend that you carefully review the specifics of PL/SQL if you are not familiar with PL/SQL programming before you attempt any complicated programming with the code windows. The WebDB interface assumes that you are familiar with the particulars of PL/SQL and it does not provide you with any assistance or meaningful error messages for PL/SQL problems within the wizard interface.

1. Edit the ch24_rep_classes report and navigate to the Add additional PL/SQL code panel.
2. Replace the text in the . . . before displaying the page PL/SQL window with the code in Listing 24-1.

Listing 24-1: PL/SQL code block to select date

```
declare
v_curdate varchar2(40);
begin
select to_char(sysdate, ' Day, Month DD YYYY HH:MI')
into v_curdate from dual;
htp.bold('Page displayed on: '||v_curdate);
end;
```

WebDB enables you to add any valid block of PL/SQL code as part of the form, but you must follow some careful formatting rules. Notice that in Listing 24-1 the code includes a pair of begin/end identifiers, even though WebDB is required to enter them for you automatically. The need for the additional begin/end keywords is a result of using local variables within the scope of the procedure. PL/SQL requires you to indicate your plans to use local variables through the DECLARE keyword, which itself requires a set of begin/end braces. These are provided for you automatically by WebDB, but you must then add your own set of begin and end tags for any procedural PL/SQL code inserted after the DECLARE keyword.

3. The code in Listing 24-1 is quite simple — the routine declares a local variable, selects the current date and time into the variable, and finally prints the value into the HTML document. Notice how each line of PL/SQL code is terminated by the use of the semicolon character as required by PL/SQL. Save this change to the procedure using the Finish button and rerun the report to produce the screen shown in Figure 24-4.

Notice the formatting of the date and time string at the top of the page. Because this block of code is included as part of the page header, it is refreshed for each page if the report were to output multiple pages of data. Although this particular example is quite simple, you can see the potential power of this interface. The PL/SQL blocks can be used to implement a complete read/write interface, as you will see in the next section.

Advanced PL/SQL code

The code windows for entering PL/SQL statements on the Add additional PL/SQL code panels are relatively small. If you have any experience in working with PL/SQL code, you have no doubt reached the conclusion that these panels are not sufficient for working with long or complicated procedures. However, because the entry panels are themselves PL/SQL code windows, you are free to call out to any existing PL/SQL procedure. If you plan to build large or complicated procedures, it is simpler and easier to build your code outside WebDB. A more comprehensive example can show you the full power of the PL/SQL code windows.

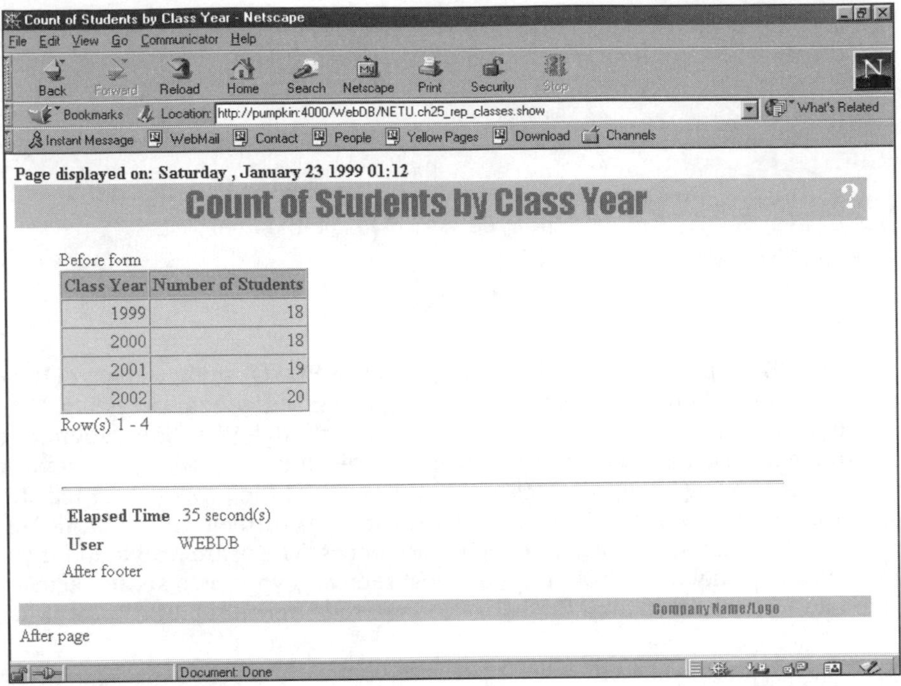

Figure 24-4: PL/SQL code with SQL

1. Load the report file ch24_rep_events.sql into the WebDB schema by using SQL*Plus with the user name and password for WebDB.
2. Load the following two PL/SQL scripts into the Net University account using SQL*Plus with the user name and password for the NETU user.

```
ch24_plsql_buy_tickets.sql
ch24_plsql_show_ticket_form.sql
```

Normally, you use the WebDB account to load in your components. However, the two PL/SQL scripts shown previously must be loaded into the NETU account, just as you installed the original sample database tables.

Listing 24-2: **Buy_tickets PL/SQL procedure**

```
–
– Listing 24-2
–
– Buy_tickets procedure
–
create or replace procedure buy_tickets (p_id number,
p_eventid number, p_no_of_tickets number,p_cc_type varchar2,
p_cc_number number)
```

```
as
  v_ticket_price number(5,2);
  v_extended_price number(8,2);
begin
—
— Select the ticket price for the event
—
select ticket_price into v_ticket_price from events
where eventid=p_eventid;
—
— If the ticket_price is blank, print default
— message
—
if v_ticket_price is null then
  htp.htmlOpen;
        htp.headOpen;
        htp.header(1,'Tickets are not required for this
event');
        htp.headClose;
        htp.bodyOpen;
        htp.print('EventID not found for selection');
        htp.bodyClose;
        htp.htmlClose;
        return;
end if;
—
— Found valid event, insert ticket purchase into
— tickets table
—
insert into tickets (id, eventid, no_of_tickets, cc_type,
cc_number, trans_date) values (p_id, p_eventid,
p_no_of_tickets, p_cc_type, p_cc_number, sysdate);
—
— Update events availability to record the
— number of tickets purchased
—
update events set availability = availability - p_no_of_tickets
where eventid = p_eventid;
v_extended_price := v_ticket_price * p_no_of_tickets;
—
— Output a result message
—
htp.htmlOpen;
htp.headOpen;
htp.header(1, 'Ticket Sale Completed');
htp.headClose;
htp.bodyOpen;
htp.print('$'||to_char(v_extended_price)||
'was charged to your card number:'||to_char(p_cc_number));
htp.bodyClose;
htp.htmlClose;
end buy_tickets;
```

The listing shown in the preceding panel, although a bit complex, is a PL/SQL procedure that accepts a number of parameters and inserts a record into the tickets database table. The procedure outputs status messages in HTML format by using the HTF/HTP packages.

This procedure has been simplified for the example, and you will notice that it does not include any PL/SQL error-handling code. Furthermore, the procedure outputs all messages in HTML format, which forces the procedure to be used only within a Web environment. Ideally, you would separate the output routines into a second procedure to provide an extra level of insulation. The code as shown ignores these conventions in order to make the listing easier to read and understand.

The first part of the procedure accepts a number of parameters and then validates the EVENTID field by selecting the TICKET_PRICE from the EVENTS table. If the TICKET_PRICE is null, a message is printed informing the user of this fact, and the procedure terminates. If the TICKET_PRICE is valid, the routine inserts a record into the TICKETS table that records the necessary information. Once a record has been inserted into the TICKETS table, the procedure updates the EVENTS table to reduce the availability field by the number of tickets that were sold. Finally, the procedure prints the completion of the process as an HTML message.

Note We have made this procedure overly simple so as to keep the focus on HTML processing. In a production environment, you would want to take additional precautions in the procedure, such as error handling for each insert and update statement. All of the parameter values should be validated for correctness against database columns, including those parameters that do not join to other tables.

3. Run the report ch24_rep_events to display the form shown in Figure 24-5.

The Events report shown in Figure 24-5 displays a single record from the EVENTS table on each page. You can use the NEXT and PREVIOUS buttons to navigate your way through the data in this report. For our sample application, it would be useful if students could buy tickets for these events directly from this Web page. It is certainly possible to build a link into this report that would call a WebDB form object to perform this task. However, you can also use the HTP procedures and the BUY_TICKETS stored procedure to provide this service directly from the existing report page. Consider the following code listing.

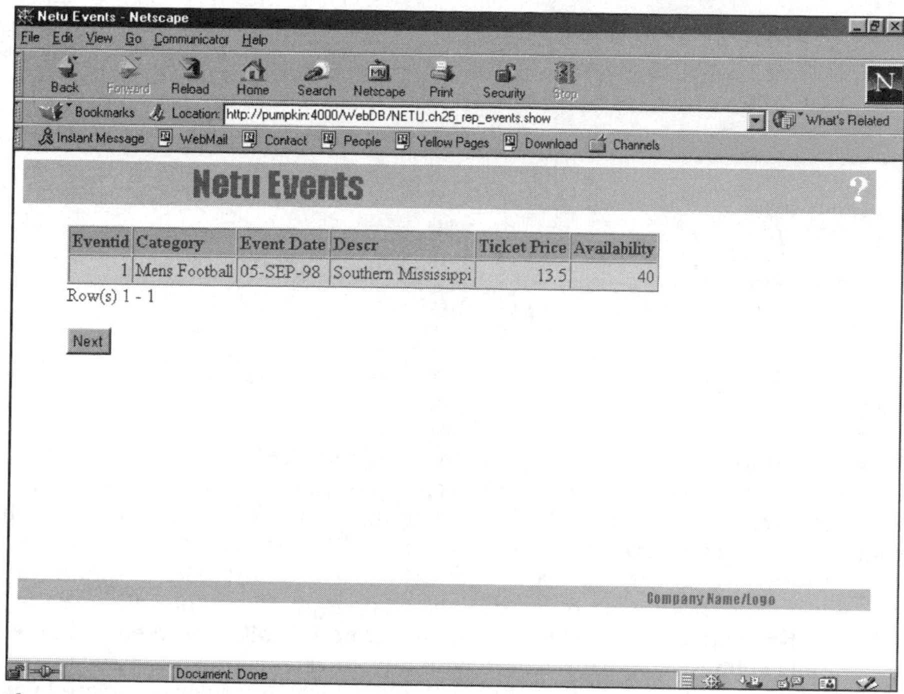

Figure 24-5: Events report

Listing 24-3: **Creating a form with HTP procedural code**

```
--
-- Listing 24-3
--
-- Display ticket form in HTML
--
create or replace procedure show_ticket_form as
begin
  htp.print(htf.bold('Fill in field values and use the push
button to buy ticket'));
  htp.br;
  htp.formOpen('netu.buy_tickets');
  htp.teletype('Student Id___:');
  htp.formText('p_id',5,5);
  htp.br;
  htp.teletype('Event Id_____:');
  htp.formText('p_eventid',5,5);
  htp.br;
  htp.teletype('# of Tickets_:');
  htp.formText('p_no_of_tickets',5,5);
  htp.br;
  htp.teletype('Credit Card');
```

Continued

Listing 24-3: *(continued)*

```
    htp.br;
    htp.teletype('AMEX,MC,VISA_:');
    htp.formText('p_cc_type',5,5);
    htp.br;
    htp.teletype('Card #_______:');
    htp.formText('p_cc_number',10,10);
    htp.br;
    htp.formSubmit(NULL,'Buy Ticket');
    htp.formClose;
  end;
```

This procedure creates an HTML form by using the HTF/HTP procedures to build the required components. Two special aspects to this code may not be immediately obvious, even to an advanced PL/SQL programmer. The htp.formOpen procedure is called with a single parameter value of netu.buy_tickets, which is the name of the insert procedure you created earlier concatenated with the USERID that owns the procedure. The formOpen procedure uses this parameter as the value for the ACTION item with the <FORM> tag of the generated HTML. This means that when the form is submitted, the procedure netu.buy_tickets will be called. WebDB automatically binds each of the fields within the form and their associated values and passes them along as part of the FORM GET process.

If you look carefully, you will notice that the names of the HTML FORM fields match the names of the parameters in the BUY_TICKETS procedure. The exception to this is the SUBMIT button, which is not given a name value, but is left NULL instead. This is one of the very powerful features of WebDB and HTML, as any form fields not explicitly named are not passed as part of the FORM submission process. This enables you to add any number of extra fields to the form that can be used for informational purposes.

Note We recommend that you do not enter long PL/SQL scripts directly into the PL/SQL code windows within WebDB. A better solution is to create your code as a series of named procedures (as in Listing 24-3) that can then be called from the code windows. You need to store these procedures in the same USERID as the component in order to keep the two objects together, but this should not be difficult to remember. As you can see from the preceding instructions, this makes the PL/SQL entry window within WebDB easier to read. You will also find that the process of creating large PL/SQL procedures is much easier to manage if you use the Oracle Procedure Builder.

1. Edit the report ch24_rep_events and add the following snippet of code to the . . . after displaying the footer code window:

   ```
   netu.show_ticket_form;
   ```

2. Save the changes and run the report to produce the page shown in Figure 24-6.

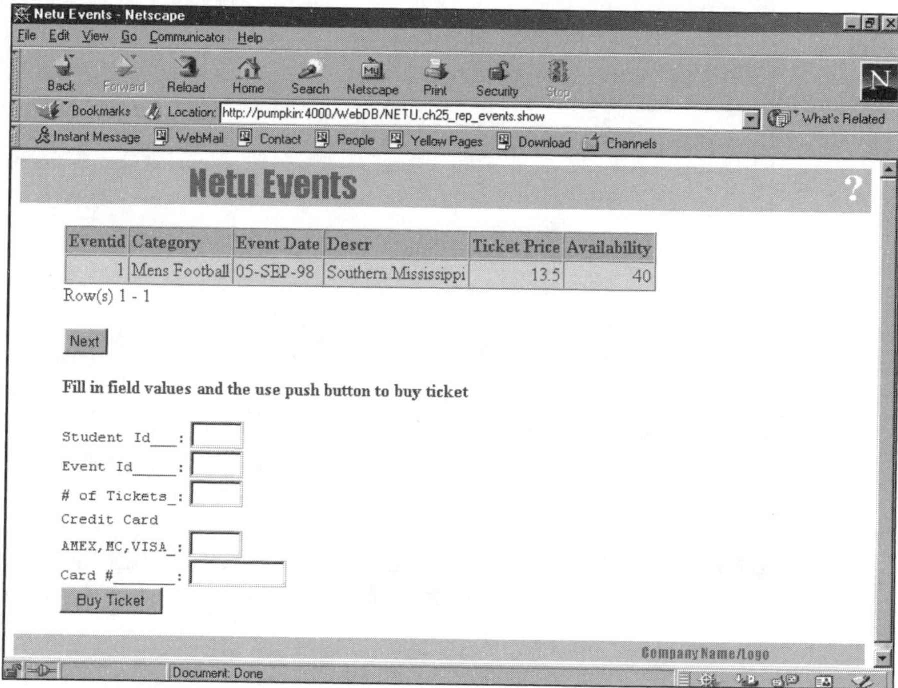

Figure 24-6: Events report with ticketing HTML code

WebDB calls the SHOW_TICKET_FORM procedure after the footer display as instructed to produce an HTML form as shown in Figure 24-6. The form itself is quite simple, but it would be a small matter to add colors, fonts, and images to give the routine a more professional look.

3. Enter the following values into the form fields and click the Buy Ticket button to update the database:

```
Student Id: 1001
Event Id: 1
# of Tickets: 3
Credit Card: AMEX
Card #: 123456789
```

As you can see from Figure 24-7, the procedure executes and outputs an HTML status message informing you that the data was entered successfully. This is not exactly true, because there is no error-handling code in the program. However, it would be a simple matter to modify the procedure to add error handling for the INSERT statement as shown in the following code fragment.

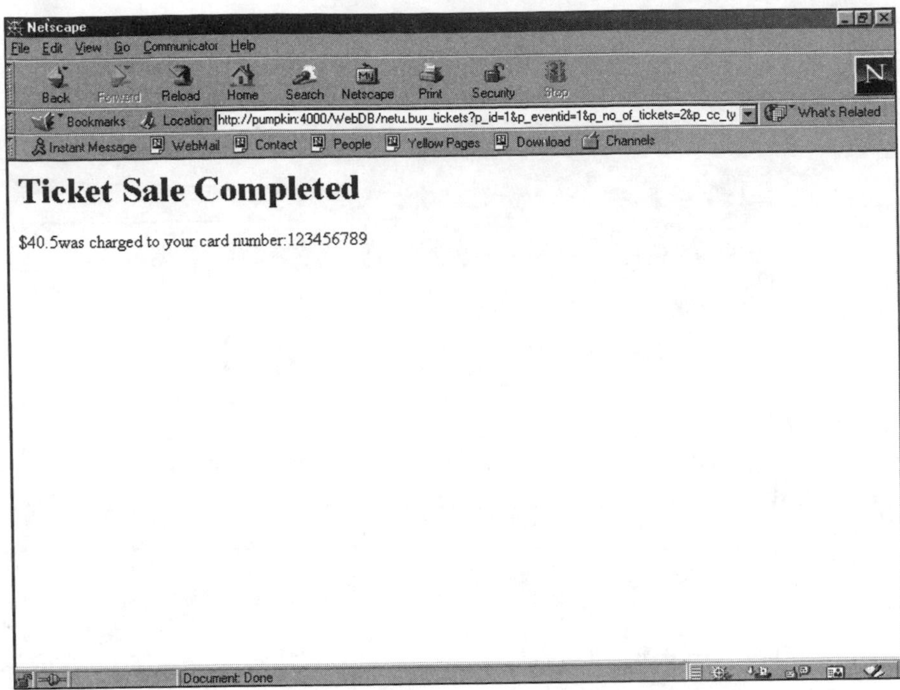

Figure 24-7: Return status message from procedure

```
–
– Found valid event, insert ticket purchase into
– tickets table
–
begin
       insert into tickets (id, eventid, no_of_tickets,
cc_type,
       cc_number, trans_date) values (p_id, p_eventid,
       p_no_of_tickets, p_cc_type, p_cc_number, sysdate);
exception
       when others then
              htp.print('SQL Error Message:'||substr(SQLERRM,
1, 200));
end;
```

You can surround your individual PL/SQL statements with their own begin/end blocks and use the EXCEPTION statement to trap errors. In the previous sample code, the error message is displayed to the browser using the htp.print procedure along with the first 200 characters of the error message text.

4. Navigate back with your browser and use the Reload button in the browser menu to refresh the page, as shown in Figure 24-8.

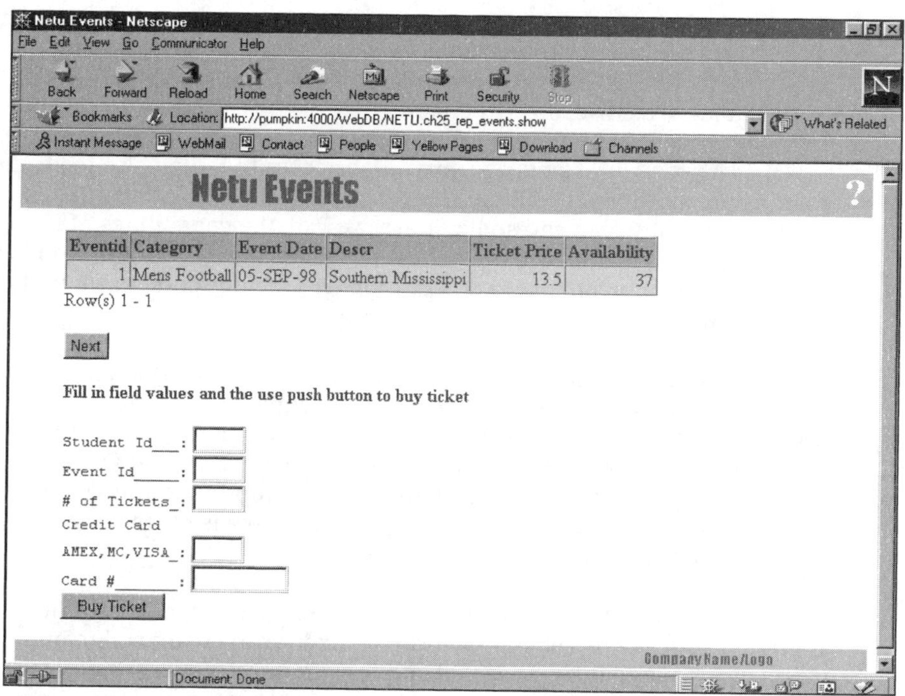

Figure 24-8: Updated Events table

In a production application, you could easily add a link to the report that would call the custom procedure directly. This enables you to create a shopping cart–style application using the standard WebDB components. The difference with a WebDB application is that the data is securely written to the database (not to a local cookie file), so if the user is disconnected from the network, the data is safely stored in the database. It would be a simple matter to set a status value in the TICKETS table and enable a user to return to the system at a later point (with a valid USERID and PASSWORD) to make changes to the stored data before completing the purchasing process.

WebDB performs a database fetch to load the data into the page. You can see that the AVAILABILITY field drops to 37 from 40 once the first block of tickets has been ordered.

Debugging and Advanced Concepts

The link between PL/SQL procedures and WebDB is very powerful. Once you have mastered the basic techniques, you can build some powerful applications by integrating PL/SQL code with your applications. Although WebDB only provides a single panel for each wizard in which to enter PL/SQL code, you are free to call procedures directly as links anywhere WebDB links are used. Even existing static HTML pages can insert records into the database simply by mapping the ACTION parameter to a PL/SQL procedural call. (You can also embed PL/SQL code in Dynamic Pages, as discussed in Chapter 12.)

PL/SQL is a procedural language, providing access to if-then-else logic and looping functions in additional to simple database-manipulation statements. We recommend that you spend some time reviewing the capabilities of PL/SQL in order to maximize your investment in WebDB. If you are new to PL/SQL, you have probably found it is difficult to detect problems in your code through the WebDB environment.

Although WebDB provides the Show/Hide SQL Query Info function in the Manage Component menu, there is really no way to adequately search for PL/SQL errors within WebDB. The designers of WebDB are responsible for making sure that the generated WebDB procedures work correctly, so it is rare that you need to view PL/SQL debug information within WebDB. The exception to this rule is those PL/SQL procedures that you build yourself, and there is no easy way to debug these procedures or edit them within WebDB.

There are two solutions for building external PL/SQL procedures. The simplest solution is to make use of your favorite text editor to create and manipulate your code. Once you are ready to install and test the code, you can simply use SQL*Plus as the host environment. Through SQL*Plus, you can cut and paste your code into the edit window, or you can use the at (@) command to load a script file into the workspace. Within SQL*Plus, you can show the errors in any procedure by creating the procedure and using the Show Errors command, as shown in Figure 24-9.

The `show errors` command displays a table that shows each line of code along with the associated error message from the PL/SQL compiler. This is not a perfect solution, because a simple error such as forgotten semicolon can sometimes result in pages of errors. However, it is light years ahead of the WebDB environment, which does not even show you an error message.

The second and better solution is to use Oracle's Procedure Builder, which is packaged in with the Oracle Developer tools. Procedure Builder is a custom edit and run-time environment for developing PL/SQL code, and it features an advanced debugger as well as code editing utilities. Figure 24-10 shows the Procedure Builder with the source for the SHOW_TICKET_FORM procedure open in the debug and edit windows.

```
Oracle SQL*Plus
File Edit Search Options Help
end;
--
-- Update events availability to record the
-- number of tickets purchased
--
update events set availability = availability - p_no_of_tickets
where eventid = p_eventid;
v_extended_price := v_ticket_price * p_no_of_tickets;
--
-- Output a result message
--
htp.htmlOpen;
htp.headOpen;
htp.header(1, 'Ticket Sale Completed');
htp.headClose;
htp.bodyOpen;
htp.print('$'||to_char(v_extended_price)||
'was charged to your card number:'||to_char(p_cc_number));
htp.bodyClose;
htp.htmlClose;
end buy_tickets;
/

Warning: Procedure created with compilation errors.

SQL> show errors
Errors for PROCEDURE BUY_TICKETS:

LINE/COL ERROR
-------- -----------------------------------------------------------------
25/9     PLS-00103: Encountered the symbol "HTP" when expecting one of the
         following:
         := . ( @ % ;
         The symbol ":=" was substituted for "HTP" to continue.

SQL> |
```

Figure 24-9: SQL*Plus with Show Errors command

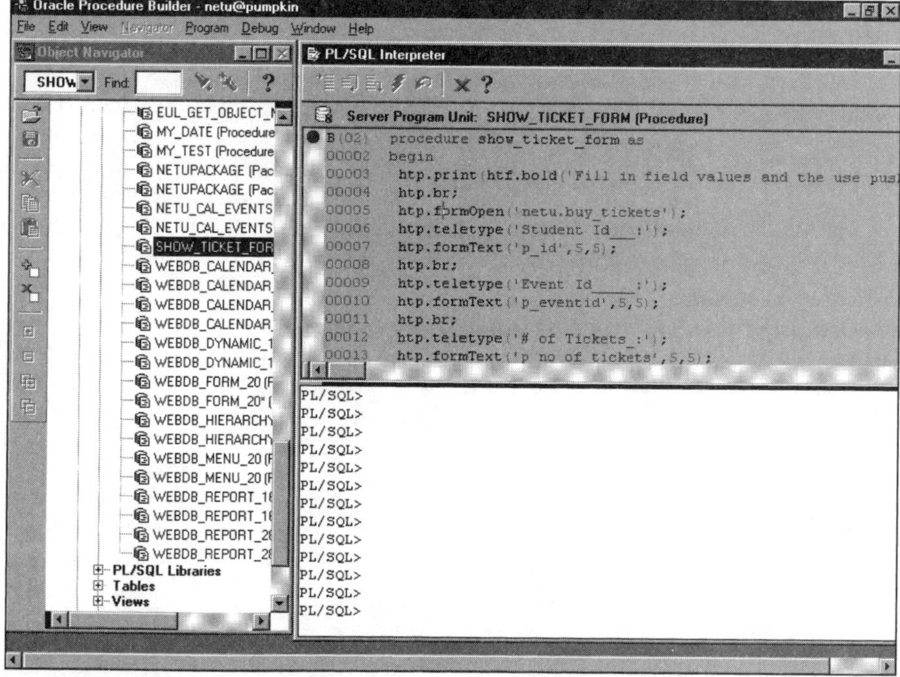

Figure 24-10: Procedure Builder

A detailed examination of the many features of the Procedure Builder are beyond the scope of this book, but we encourage you to locate a copy of this utility if you plan to undertake any serious custom PL/SQL development.

Wrapping Up

The PL/SQL language has long been a cornerstone of the Oracle database and development environments. WebDB itself is built with PL/SQL, and Oracle has taken great pains to provide access to HTML directly from PL/SQL procedures. The designers of WebDB built the product with productivity in mind, and this sometimes causes a lack of flexibility. In this chapter, you have seen how you can overcome these limitations by building your own custom PL/SQL procedures and combining them with WebDB.

Despite this power, you should resist the temptation to drop down into PL/SQL coding until you have exhausted the native capabilities of WebDB. Relying too heavily on PL/SQL code can make your applications difficult to maintain for subsequent developers who may not be familiar with the specifics of PL/SQL coding.

✦ ✦ ✦

Appendixes

PART

VI

✦ ✦ ✦ ✦

In This Part

✦ ✦ ✦ ✦

On the CD-ROM

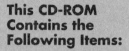

✦ ✦ ✦ ✦

This CD-ROM Contains the Following Items:

The Net University Sample Database Packaged as a Self-Extracting ZIP File

A Directory of Scripts and Files for Each Chapter

✦ ✦ ✦ ✦

Net University Sample Database

The CD-ROM contains a self-extracting ZIP file of the Net University sample database. The sample database is composed of a series of PL/SQL scripts and image (GIF) files that are used to install and load the Net University model. Chapter 2 provides a tutorial on installing this database.

Directory of Sample Scripts

The CD-ROM contains a directory hierarchy labeled "exercises" that contains subdirectories for each chapter in which you are required to create or modify a component object. The files in these directories are stored in one of the following formats:

- PL/SQL Script
- GIF Image
- JPEG Image
- HTML
- Adobe PDF

The PL/SQL Script format is the most common format, as this is the format WebDB uses for importing and exporting component objects. Each component (form, chart, report, and so on) is packaged into a single PL/SQL script file that can be loaded into the database through SQL*Plus. In addition, we have created a single script file in each chapter folder that you can use to load all of the examples for that chapter into the system at once. Furthermore, the root "exercises" folder provides a single script file that you can use to load in all of the examples at once.

Graphic images that are used within the exercises are stored in either GIF or JPEG format, with the vast majority being stored in the lower resolution GIF format. The same image file is often used for exercises in multiple chapters, but a copy of the image is stored in each chapter folder to make them easier to work with.

Certain advanced examples make use of extended HTML code, and these examples are stored in HTML format on the CD-ROM. There is also a single file in Adobe PDF format that is used to simulate the loading of a large report file into Site Builder.

Table A-1
Sample Exercise Files

Chapter	*File Name*	*Description*
	examples.sql	Master script that calls each of the chapter script files
5	ch5_rep_1.sql	List of students by class year, with major and telephone number
5	ch5_rep_2.sql	Modified student list with breaks for majors and class years
5	ch_5.sql	Master install script for Chapter 5
6	ch6_rep_1.sql	List of students with major and class year that uses a parameter prompt for Major
6	ch6_rep_2.sql	Students and transcripts report
6	ch6_rep_3.sql	Students and transcripts report with a parameter for student ID number
6	ch6_rep_4.sql	Summary report for majors with counts of students
6	ch6_rep_5.sql	Student grade point averages organized by Major
6	ch6_sql1.sql	SQL query text
6	ch6_sql2.sql	SQL query text
6	ch6_sql3.sql	SQL query text
6	ch6_link_script.sql	Special script that loads in mirror copies of three of the reports built in Chapter 6 along with the required link objects
6	ch_6.sql	Master install script for Chapter 6
7	degreelov.sql	List-of-values for degrees
7	ch7_frm_1.sql	Query-by-Example form for Majors
7	ch7_frm_2.sql	Query-by-Example form for course catalog

Chapter	File Name	Description
7	ch7_frm_3.sql	Form for inserting new majors
7	ch_7.sql	Master install script for Chapter 7
8	alumnilov.sql	Alumni
8	courselov.sql	Course list-of-values
8	fundlov.sql	Fund list-of-values
8	restrictlov.sql	Restrict list-of-values
8	chap8_frm_1.sql	Form for inserting records into Donations table using a stored procedure
8	chap8_frm_2.sql	Master-detail form for Majors and Courses
8	chap8_rep_1.sql	Majors report
8	chap8_lnk_1.sql	Link to chap7_frm_3 form
8	ch_8.sql	Master install script for Chapter 8
9	chap9_cht_1.sql	Chart of donations by fund code
9	chap9_cht_2.sql	Chart displays contributions made to all funds by fund restriction
9	chap9_cht_3.sql	Chart summing all gifts by restriction
9	chap9_cht_4.sql	Chart of largest donors
9	chap9_sql1.sql	SQL query text
9	chap9_sql2.sql	SQL query text
9	ch_9.sql	Master install script for Chapter 9
10	ch10_rep_events.sql	Details of NetU events (sports, social, and so on)
10	ch10_rep_schedule.sql	Schedule report of NetU events
10	netu_cal_events.sql	Completed calendar
10	map_*.gif	Image files for each location on campus
10	ch_10.sql	Master install script for Chapter 10
11	advisorlov.sql	List-of-values for student advisors
11	studentlov.sql	List-of-values for students
11	chap11_hie_1.sql	Hierarchy of student advisors and students
11	ch_11.sql	Master install script for Chapter 11
12	ch12_dynamic1.htm	HTML code for formatting dynamic page
12	netu_banner.gif	Banner image of NetU logo

Continued

Table A-1 *(continued)*

Chapter	*File Name*	*Description*
12	ch12_dyn_example1.sql	Completed Dynamic Pages object
12	ch12_rep_ugrads.sql	Report of students with a parameter value for ID
12	ch12_fdr_example1.sql	Completed Frame Driver object
12	ch_12.sql	Master install script for Chapter 12
13	netu_lov_gender.sql	Completed List-of-Values object for Gender
13	ch13_rep_1.sql	Example report of Students with a parameter for Gender
13	netu_lov_majors.sql	Completed List-of-Values object for majors
13	ch13_frm_1.sql	Sample form to insert new student records (uses netu_lov_gender object)
13	ch13_rep_2.sql	Student report with parameter for Majors
13	ch_13.sql	Master install script for Chapter 13
14	netu_home.htm	Default HTML home page for NetU
14	netu_about.htm	Linked About page for NetU home page
14	netu_logo.gif	Net University banner logo
14	netu_tabbycat.gif	Logo for the NetU mascot, the TabbyCat
14	ch14_mnu_example1.sql	Starting menu for hands-on examples
14	ch14_cht_departments.sql	Chart of the number of courses in each academic department
14	ch14_mnu_example2.sql	Completed menu from hands-on section
14	ch_14.sql	Master install script for Chapter 14
15	ch15_tohex.htm	HTML page for converting color values to HEX codes
15	ch15_listing1.sql	PL/SQL procedure to convert short numbers to hexadecimals
15	ch15_listing2.sql	PL/SQL procedure to convert from hexadecimal to integer values
15	netu_bg.gif	Stucco background for use as a backdrop for report pages
15	netu_campus.gif	GIF image of the NetU campus buildings
15	netu_heading.gif	University image for upper-left corner of page
15	netu_help.gif	Graphic image of a question mark for use with templates

Chapter	File Name	Description
15	netu_home.gif	Home image for navigation back to the NetU home page within templates
15	netu_internal_use.gif	Small background image using light gray text for use as a backdrop on sensitive report pages
15	netu_ivy.gif	Ivy image suitable for use as a border
15	netu_logo.gif	Net University corporate logo
15	netu_notes.gif	Large background with the ivy image displayed to the right large enough to fill the entire background (it will not be tiled when displayed)
15	netu_tabbycat	Picture of the NetU mascot, the TabbyCat
15	ch15_images.sql	Script that loads all of the images for the examples in Chapter 15
15	netu_tmp_standard.sql	Standard NetU display template
15	netu_tmp_unstructured.sql	Unstructured display template
15	ch15_rep_catalog.sql	Sample report file for the course catalog table
15	netu_home.htm	Home page for NetU (copied from earlier chapter)
15	netu_about.htm	About page for NetU (copied from earlier chapter)
15	ch_15.sql	Master install script for Chapter 15
16	netu_js_showvalue.js	JavaScript source file – tests numeric strings for values greater than 5
16	netu_js_alert.js	JavaScript source file – Hello World
16	ch16_lov.sql	List-of-Values objects for alumni, funds, and restrictions
16	ch16_frm_donations.sql	Form for adding donations records to database
16	netu_js_makenull.js	JavaScript source file – replaces null values with NULL string
16	netu_js_range_1_to_50000.js	JavaScript source file – checks for number in range 1 to 50,000
16	netu_js_currentyear.js	JavaScript source file – checks date entered against current year
16	netu_js_donation.js	JavaScript source file – compares donation amount with check number
16	ch_16.sql	Master install script for Chapter 16
17	netu_class_totals.sql	SQL script to create a view of donations totals by class year

Continued

Table A-1 *(continued)*

Chapter	*File Name*	*Description*
17	ch17_rep_students.sql	Report of students with class years and majors
17	ch17_rep_classes.sql	Report showing the number of students in each class year
17	lnk_netu_classes.sql	Completed link as built during hands-on example
17	ch17_cht_gender.sql	Chart of gender distribution with a parameter for class year
17	ch17_frm_students.sql	Form to update student records
17	lnk_frm_ugrads.sql	Completed link as built during hands-on example
17	lnk_cht_gender.sql	Completed link as built during hands-on example
17	ch_17.sql	Master install script for Chapter 17
18	netu_logo.gif	Net University logo for Site Builder site
18	netu_bg.gif	Background image for use as wallpaper in the Net University Site Builder site
18	netu_content.gif	Wallpaper for use with the content area within Net University Site Builder site
18	netu_banner.jpg	High-resolution image for use as the header banner in the Net University site
18	netu_hot.gif	Icon image for use with perspectives
18	netu_cost.gif	Icon image for use with perspectives
18	netu_tabbycat.gif	Alternative background image
18	ch_18.sql	Master install script for Chapter 18
20	ch20_qbe_ugrads.sql	Query-by-Example form for student records
20	ch20_qbe_alumni.sql	Query-by-Example form for alumni records
20	ch20_rep_alumni.sql	Report of alumni records on a view which matches the logon id with the password field in the alumni record
20	ch20_mnu_college.sql	Sample menu for use with security examples
20	create_passwords.sql	SQL*Plus script to create a file of accounts for all UGRADS records
20	ch_20.sql	Master install script for Chapter 20
21	ch21_cht_donations.sql	Chart of donations records by restriction codes
21	ch21_dyn_donations.sql	Dynamic HTML report of donation records
21	ch21_dyn_state_gifts.sql	Dynamic HTML report showing the summary of donation records by state

Chapter	File Name	Description
21	ch21_rep_donations.sql	Report of donation records sorted by year and gift amount
21	ch_21.sql	Master install script for Chapter 21
22	ch22_dyn_alumni.sql	Dynamic HTML report showing NetU alumni records
22	ch22_dyn_calendar.sql	Dynamic HTML report that lists all of the events for the NetU academic year
22	ch22_mnu_sample.sql	Sample menu that shows the effects of using WebDB security
22	ch_22.sql	Master install script for Chapter 22
23	admin_photo.jpg	Photo image to be used for the site administrator
23	ugrads_accounts.sql	SQL*Plus script that creates default accounts for all UGRADS records
23	netu_tabbycat.gif	Image file of the Net University mascot
23	ch23_rep_ugrads.sql	Report showing student names and class pictures with a parameter prompt for class years
23	netu_icon1.gif	Icon image for use with content items
23	netu_icon2.gif	Icon image for use with content items
23	netu_courses.pdf	Adobe PDF file report of the NetU course catalog
23	ch_23.sql	Master install script for Chapter 23
24	ch24_rep_classes.sql	Report showing the total students for each class year
24	listing_24_1.sql	Source code listing that selects date and time from Oracle database
24	ch24_rep_events.sql	Report that shows each NetU event on a separate page
24	ch24_plsql_buy_tickets.sql	PL/SQL procedure that enables a user to buy tickets to NetU events.
24	ch24_plsql_show_ticket_form.sql	PL/SQL procedure that creates a form for use with the Events report
24	ch_24.sql	Master install script for Chapter 24

Image files are either copied to a file system directory or loaded into Site Builder. They cannot be installed with a single install script, but the relevant chapters show you how to move them to the proper locations.

Loading Examples into the System

You should install the PL/SQL script files using SQL*Plus, which is WebDB's standard import/export utility as well. The first step for any installation is to set SQL*Plus' working directory to the directory where the source files are located.

The source files themselves take up less than 1MB of disk space, and we recommend that you copy the entire exercises directory tree to a local hard drive before you attempt to install any of the components.

Set your working directory

The process of setting the working directory for SQL*Plus varies by platform. For most graphical user interface platforms, you can set the working directory from the properties sheet, as shown in the Figure A-1.

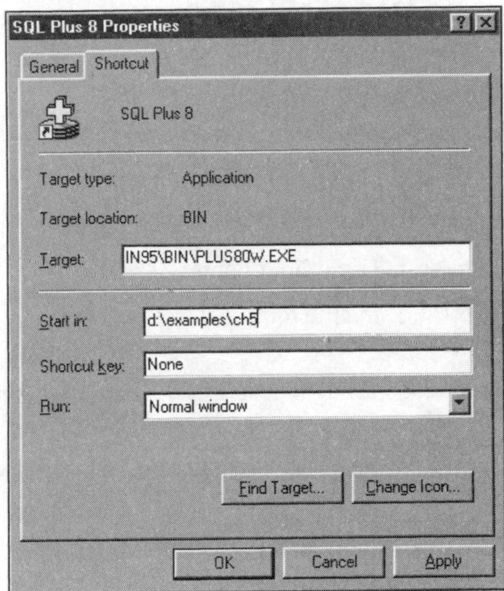

Figure A-1: Properties sheet for SQL*Plus

The critical setting is the Start in setting (or working directory). You need to point this setting to the directory where the script files are located. For example, assume that you have copied the exercises directory to your local hard drive C:\. The result is a series of subdirectories much like the following list:

```
c:\exercises\ch5
c:\exercises\ch6
...
c:\exercises\ch24
```

In order to load an individual component into the database, set your working directory (the Start in settings under Windows) to the full directory path where the component is stored on your hard drive. For example, to load the first component for Chapter 5, ch5_rep_1.sql, set your working directory to the example path c:\exercises\ch5.

Experienced SQL*Plus users will note that you can specify a complete path for SQL scripts inside SQL*Plus, making it unnecessary to set the working directory as described in the previous section. However, this technique will not work for the scripts that load groups of components, as these scripts make use of relative directory paths. We recommend that you set the working directory for SQL*Plus in order to avoid this problem.

Connect to SQL*Plus and load a single component

You must load WebDB components into the system using the WebDB account, even if the components were created using a different USERID. The WebDB import utility makes use of certain tables not made public to other Oracle accounts, forcing you to use the WebDB account in order to load components into the system. Because the WebDB account is equipped with DBA privileges, you may not be permitted access to this account. In such cases, you need to involve your systems administrator in order to gain access to the WebDB account (or to load the components in for you). Once you have connected to SQL*Plus, as shown in Figure A-2, the process of loading in a component is quick and easy.

Certain chapters contain instances where scripts need to be run inside the Net University account. In such cases, the hands-on instructions explicitly list this requirement.

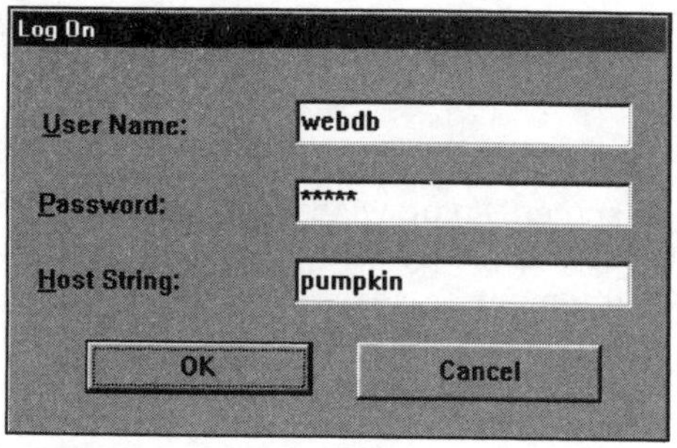

Figure A-2: Connecting to SQL*Plus

Components are loaded by entering a command string into SQL*Plus. The command string is nothing more than the name of the SQL script proceeded by the @ command character. For example, to load in the first report in Chapter 5, enter the following command:

```
@ch5_rep_1.sql
```

Once you enter the command string, SQL*Plus reads the script and begins loading the component into the system. As the script is processed you will see a series of messages appear on the screen confirming that each step of the process has completed. SQL*Plus displays a final message at the end of the script to let you know that the component has been loaded and the resulting procedure has been generated, as shown in Figure A-3.

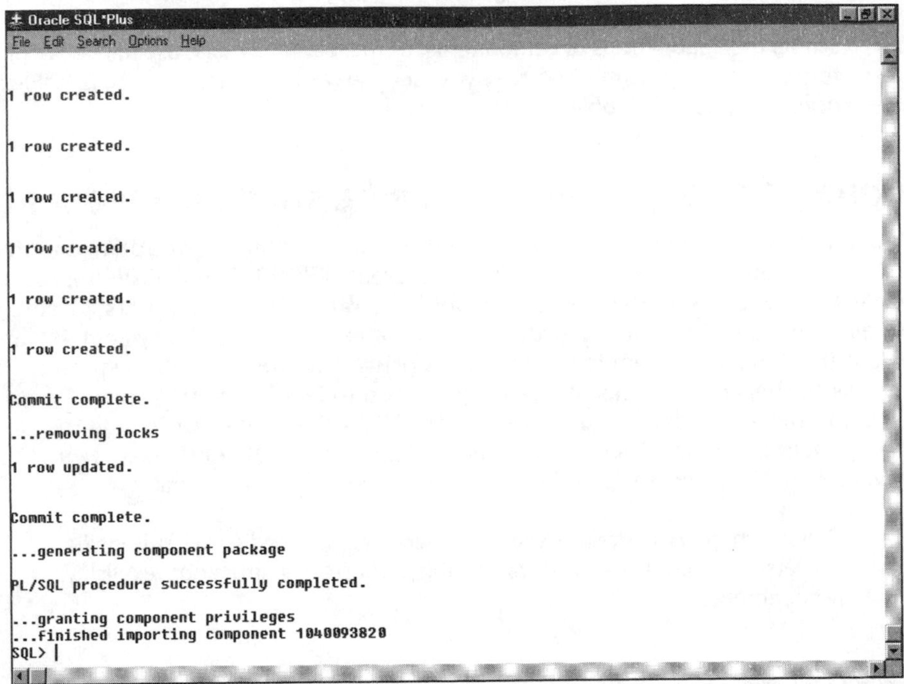
Oracle SQL*Plus
File Edit Search Options Help
1 row created.
1 row created.
1 row created.
1 row created.
1 row created.
1 row created.
Commit complete.
...removing locks
1 row updated.
Commit complete.
...generating component package
PL/SQL procedure successfully completed.
...granting component privileges
...finished importing component 1040093820
SQL> |

Figure A-3: Output from loading a procedure

The length of the output varies by the type of component that has been loaded, and in most cases, the top part scrolls off the screen. If you wish to keep a record of the input process, you can echo the log records to a file by using the spool feature of SQL*Plus as shown in the following code fragment:

```
spool filename
@c:\exercises\ch5\ch5_rep_1.sql
spool off
```

The spool command echoes the output to the filename that you specify as a parameter to the spool command. Although this feature causes the output messages to be echoed to the specified filename, it does not allow you to see the actual commands being executed. You can display the actual SQL code interactively by entering the following command into SQL*Plus before executing your load script:

```
set echo on
```

The echo command causes SQL*Plus to display the actual SQL code that is being executed to load the pieces of your component. If you are having problems loading a component into your system, the echo command can give you some insight into which commands are causing the problem.

Loading multiple components

You have the option of loading in all of the components for a single chapter by using the master script for each chapter stored in the subdirectory for the chapter (ch_5.sql, ch_6.sql...ch_24.sql).

These scripts are loaded using the exact same instructions as with the individual components. The main exercises directory contains a master script called exercises.sql that you can use to load all of the chapter exercises at once. In order to use this script, you must change the working directory for SQL*Plus to point to the main exercises directory path. The exercise script automatically locates the subdirectories by using relative path settings embedded within the script itself.

WebDB

Oracle's WebDB Trial software can be downloaded from Oracle at:

http://technet.oracle.com/software/download.htm

On the Web

Check the site http://www.webdb-bible.com for updates, new samples, and more information on WebDB.

✦ ✦ ✦

Using a Batch Interface to WebDB

✦ ✦ ✦ ✦

In This Appendix

Configuring the Batch Queues

Submitting Objects to the Batch Queues

Managing Batch Queues

✦ ✦ ✦ ✦

The Oracle database provides a job queue system built directly into the server. This job queue system works very much like the batch job systems provided by most operating systems. The chief difference is that the Oracle processing queues are implemented directly inside the database, which makes these queues particularly powerful for managing data-intensive tasks. For example, if you add large volumes of new data to a table each day, you could schedule an index rebuild on the table to run inside the database each evening. The index rebuild could be scheduled and run by the processing queues inside the database itself.

WebDB provides an interface to the Oracle database queues that enables you to schedule component execution to run inside the server. At first glance, you probably do not have much use for this interface in light of how WebDB itself works. Most of the queries you run inside WebDB are designed to return data in small increments to a user through the browser interface. By their very nature, these queries are designed to run quickly and operate against a small subset of data. However, it is not a requirement that they do so. For example, you might build a report object that summarizes data from several large tables and then sorts the results. This type of query might take several minutes to complete, or it might even take hours to complete if the system is very busy or you are working with a particularly large amount of data.

As a user, you may not want to wait around for this type of query to complete. The solution is to run your report as a batch task in the database and come back to view the results at a later point in time. You can use WebDB's batch interface to run your report as a batch job in the background. This frees up your browser to pursue other tasks without forcing you to wait until the report processing has completed. In effect, this enables the report to work asynchronously.

Configuring the Batch Queues

In order to run tasks in the background, the Oracle database must have background processing enabled. You cannot enable background processing from inside WebDB, but you can check the status of the batch queue settings.

1. Connect to WebDB using a DBA account and invoke the Monitor menu.
2. Choose the Batch Results link to display the Batch Results panel shown in Figure B-1.

There are two main links on the Batch Results panel: the Batch Results Manager link and the DBMS Job Configuration link. The Batch Results Manager page is available to all users of WebDB, but the DBMS Job Configuration page only displays for users that log on with a DBA account to WebDB.

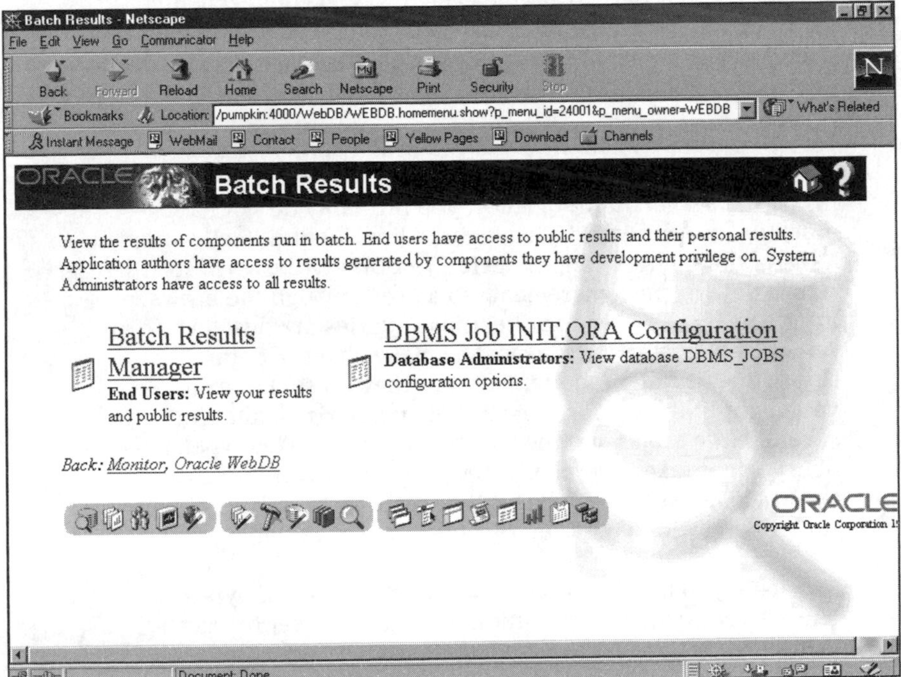

Figure B-1: Batch Results menu

3. Select the DBMS Job INIT.ORA Configuration link to display the page shown in Figure B-2.

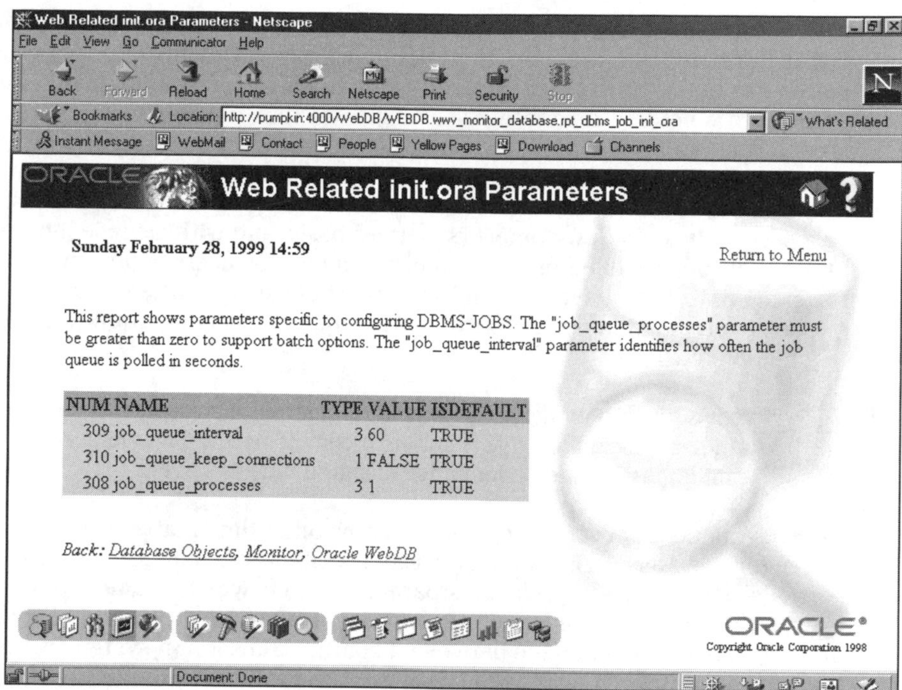

Figure B-2: Web Related INIT.ORA Parameters page

A series of parameters set in the INIT.ORA file determines the database queue configuration. The Oracle database server is configured through a series of operating system files managed outside the database. Many server settings, such as the maximum number of open cursors and the allocation of memory, are controlled by entries in the configuration files. You can create any number of these configuration files, but the default installation of Oracle creates the INIT.ORA file for these parameters. These configuration files can have literally hundreds of parameter entries in them, but only three of the entries are relevant to the batch queues. The three parameters shown in Figure B-2 are as follows:

✦ job_queue_processes

✦ job_queue_interval

✦ job_queue_keep_connections

Changing any of the settings in the INIT.ORA file can have dire consequences for your database server. These settings should only be changed by a qualified DBA who has experience with managing the Oracle server.

Oracle sorts its parameters by parameter name. The last parameter shown in Figure B-2 is actually the most important parameter. The job_queue_processes parameter determines the number of batch queues that exist in the server. If this parameter is not set to an integer value greater than 0 (the default), you are not able to run batch jobs in the server. If this value is set to a nonzero value, then Oracle uses the value entered as the number of job processes to run. Normally, you only need to set this value to 1, which creates a single job queue process. WebDB processes jobs on a first-come, first-served basis, and with a single job queue, process orders are filled one at a time. If you have 50 users submitting jobs all at the same time, your users will find that they have to wait when there is a single job queue. If you plan to service lots of batch requests, you may want to set this value to a higher setting.

We advise you to work with your DBA to determine the appropriate value for this parameter. Processing large numbers of simultaneous batch jobs can have a significant impact on the performance of your database server.

The job_queue_interval setting controls how often the database server checks the queue for new tasks. The parameter value is an integer number with a value of seconds. The default value for this parameter is 60, which means that the server checks the queue once every 60 seconds for work to be processed. If you were building a real-time interface between disparate transaction systems with Oracle as the middleware, you might need to set this interval to a lower setting. However, the default value of 60 is probably sufficient for WebDB applications. The job_queue_keep_connections parameter is displayed on this panel because it is part of the DBMS queue subsystem, but it is not relevant for WebDB applications. It is a performance setting for middleware applications as well, and you do not need to change this setting for WebDB.

Although you can view the INIT.ORA settings from the panel shown in Figure B-2, you cannot change the values inside WebDB. To make a change, either edit the configuration file for Oracle manually and then restart the database, or use the Enterprise Manager (as shown in Figure B-3) to change the job_queue_processes setting.

The job_queue_processes setting is a dynamic parameter and you do not need to shut down the database for your change to take effect (provided you are making the change with the Enterprise Manager). All you need to do is locate the job_queue_processes parameter, change the value to a nonzero integer, and save the change with the Apply button.

If the job_queue_processes parameter is set to 0, change the value with the Enterprise Manager, or have a DBA change this setting for you.

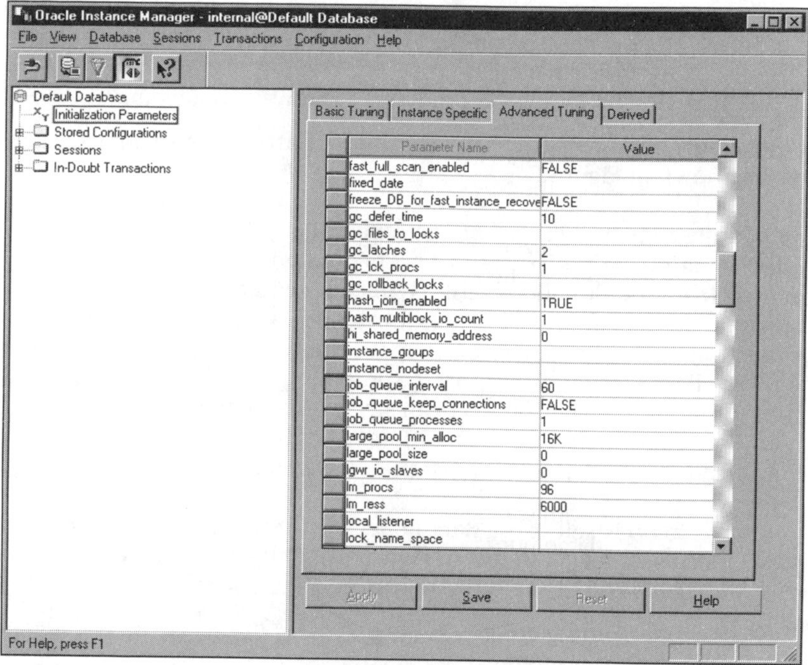

Figure B-3: Enterprise Manager – advanced tuning

The default value for this parameter is 0. You need to have this value set to 1 or greater in order to complete the remaining examples in this appendix.

The remaining link on the Batch Results page in Figure B-1 enables you to view the results of jobs that have been submitted to the job queue. Before you work with this particular page, it helps to have an object you can submit to the batch system.

Submitting Objects to the Batch Queues

WebDB provides batch queue support for its core component objects. Component support objects such as shared components and menus cannot be processed with batch queues. The following WebDB objects support the batch queue interface:

✦ Forms (QBE and Stored Procedures only)

✦ Reports

✦ Charts

✦ Calendars

In order for components to work with the batch subsystem, it must be modified to provide the Batch Interface button on the Parameters menu.

1. Load the APB_REP_DONATIONS report into the WebDB account.
2. Edit the report and navigate to the Parameter Entry Form Display Options panel, as shown in Figure B-4.

The apb_dep_donations report is a sample report that joins data from the Alumni table and the Donations table. The report sorts data on several fields, and selects all 5000 records from the Donations table. While you could certainly run this report interactively, you might also want to make it available as a batch report. As you will see in next section, WebDB enables you to make the results of a batch job available as public output. If this Donations report is something that multiple users are likely to run within the same time period, you can save processing cycles by submitting it as a batch job once and then enabling multiple users to view the results. There is nothing complicated about setting the batch function for an object.

3. All you have to do is select the Batch check box on the Parameter Entry Form Display Options panel, as shown in Figure B-4. Once you select this option, WebDB adds a Batch button to the report on the Report Parameter Entry Form.

Specify buttons that will be used on the Report Parameter Entry Form.

Show Button	Name	Location	Alignment
☑ Run	Run Report	Top	Left
☐ Save	Save	Top	Left
☑ Batch	Batch	Top	Left
☑ Reset	Reset	Top	Left

Figure B-4: Enabling batch options for a report

4. Exit the edit session for this report by clicking the Finish button, and then navigate to the parameter link, as shown in Figure B-5.

You are free to add any additional parameters for your object, just as you would when running the report interactively. However, instead of using the Run button, you click the Batch button to execute the report.

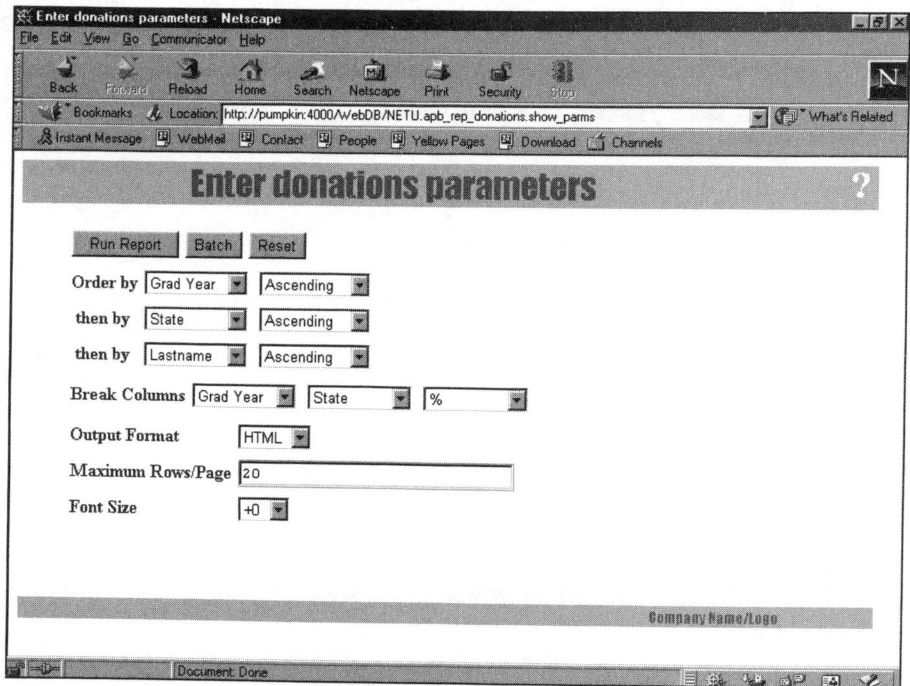

Figure B-5: Using the Batch button

5. Click the Batch push button to run the report.

WebDB displays a simple page (shown in Figure B-6) that contains the title of the report, the job number, and a link to view the results of the report. The title displayed matches the name and layout of the title as it was entered into the report, just as if you were running the report interactively. If you use a template for your component object, WebDB uses this same template to display the title on this batch queue panel. Once you have submitted a job to the batch queue system, WebDB gives it a job number and displays this job number back to you on the status panel. You can use the job number to search for your job in any one of the status screens, but you can also use the report name to locate your job if you lose the job number.

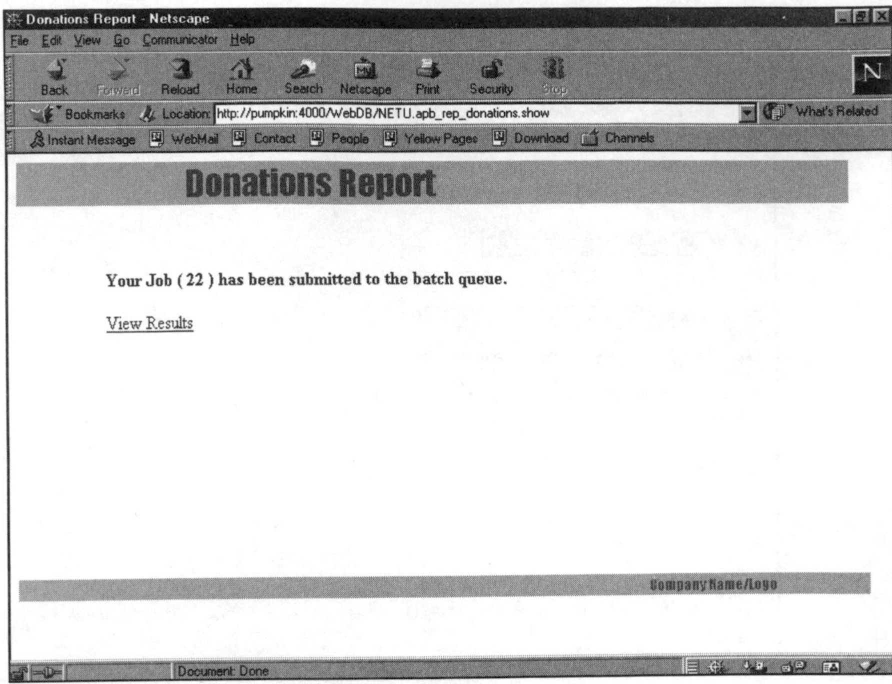

Figure B-6: Batch queue submit status page

The View Results link does not actually connect you to your output; rather, it connects you to a status panel from which you can view the results.

1. Use the View Results link to display the Stored Results Manager page, as shown in Figure B-7.

The Stored Results Manager page consists of three sections: the Queued Results panel, the Find Stored Results panel, and the Recently Submitted Results panel. The Queued Results panel lists the jobs currently in the queue sorted by the ascending job number. Each job has either a "queued" status, which indicates that it has been scheduled to run, or a "running" status, which indicates that the job is currently being processed. WebDB also displays a Remove link you can use to delete the job from the queue, either before it runs or while it is running. However, only users that have DBA privileges are able to use this link. If you are waiting for your job to finish processing, you can use the Requery button to refresh the queue and results panels.

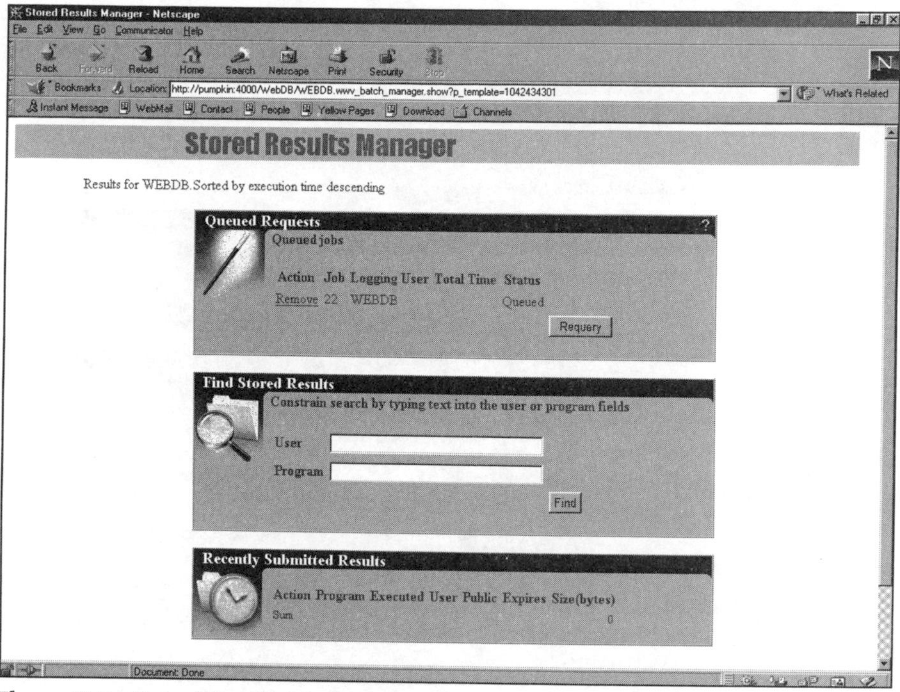

Figure B-7: Stored Results Manager panel

2. Click the Requery button until your report job appears in the bottom panel, as shown in Figure B-8.

The middle panel enables you to search for results using either a USERID string or a report name. The result of using the Find option is a page just like the panel shown at the bottom of the page in Figure B-8.

The Recently Submitted Results panel has the following seven columns:

- ✦ Action
- ✦ Program
- ✦ Executed
- ✦ User
- ✦ Public
- ✦ Expires
- ✦ Size (bytes)

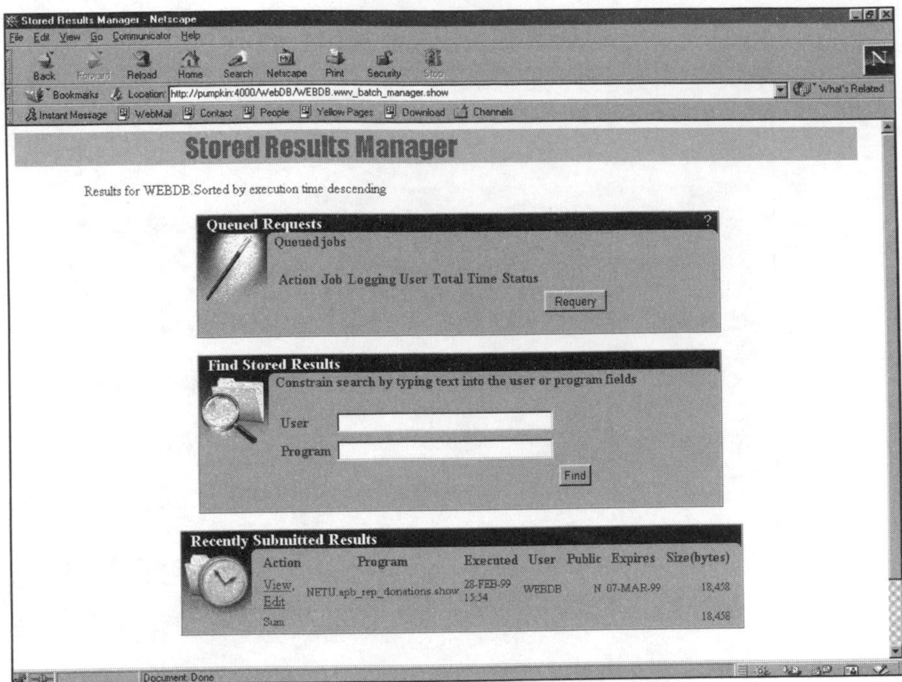

Figure B-8: Completed batch job display panel

The Action column contains two links: one to view the output and one to edit the output options. Users can view their own batch output or they can view any output that has been marked as public. The Edit link displays a panel that enables a DBA or batch owner to set the results of a batch job as public. The Program column displays the owner and procedure name of the report, and the Executed column displays a date and time stamp recording when the batch job began execution. The User field contains the Oracle USERID that submitted the job to the batch queue. If the user or a DBA set the output to be accessible by the general public, the Public column displays a "Y" value, indicating that the report is available to any user. By default, WebDB keeps the results of the batch job stored for seven days, and the expiration date appears in the Expires column. You can change the expiration period and the public access indicator using the Edit link.

Batch jobs are handled differently than interactive jobs, and WebDB executes the entire report and stores the results inside of a table in the database. The Size column displays the total number of bytes of storage used by the output of the object. In the example, the Donations report uses about 18,000 bytes of disk space in the database.

1. Use the Edit link to display the panel shown in Figure B-9.

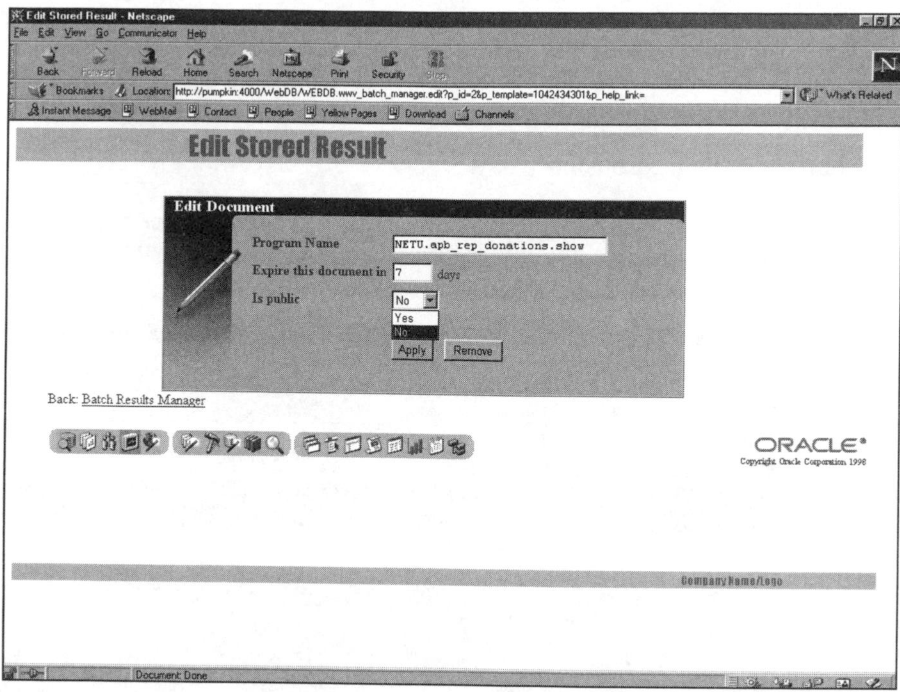

Figure B-9: Edit Stored Result page

The batch job owner or DBA account is permitted to edit the results of the batch job. Specifically, you can set the expiration date, make the results public, or delete the results from the database. The default value for the expiration date is seven days, which means that WebDB keeps the batch results stored and available for viewing for seven days from the date of execution. This is not always the best setting. For example, the Donations report includes the donation records for alumni sorted by their year of graduation and the state in which they live. In the example case, assume that donation records are posted once a day to the Donations table, and that the entire accounting department for Net University is likely to want to see the results. Instead of having each user run the report for themselves, you could run this report as a batch job at the end of every day. However, because new gifts are posted at the end of every day, it is probably a good idea to mark the results as being valid for only one day. You can use the Expire this document setting to ensure that the report is removed after one day. WebDB automatically ages the report for you and keeps the Expire this document field synchronized with the date of execution. For example, if you edit the batch results on the day the report is run, the default value for the Expire this document field is seven days. However, if you return to this panel on the following day, WebDB sets this field to six days automatically as part of the aging process.

The default behavior for a batch job is to make the results private. Only the batch job owner and accounts with DBA privileges are able to view the results. You can use the Is public combo box to modify this setting and make the results available to the public at large. For the example Donations report, you can use a DBA account to run the report at the close of each day and then make the results available to the public on the next business day.

2. Change the Is public combo box setting to Yes and click the Apply button to save the change and display the panel, as shown in Figure B-10.

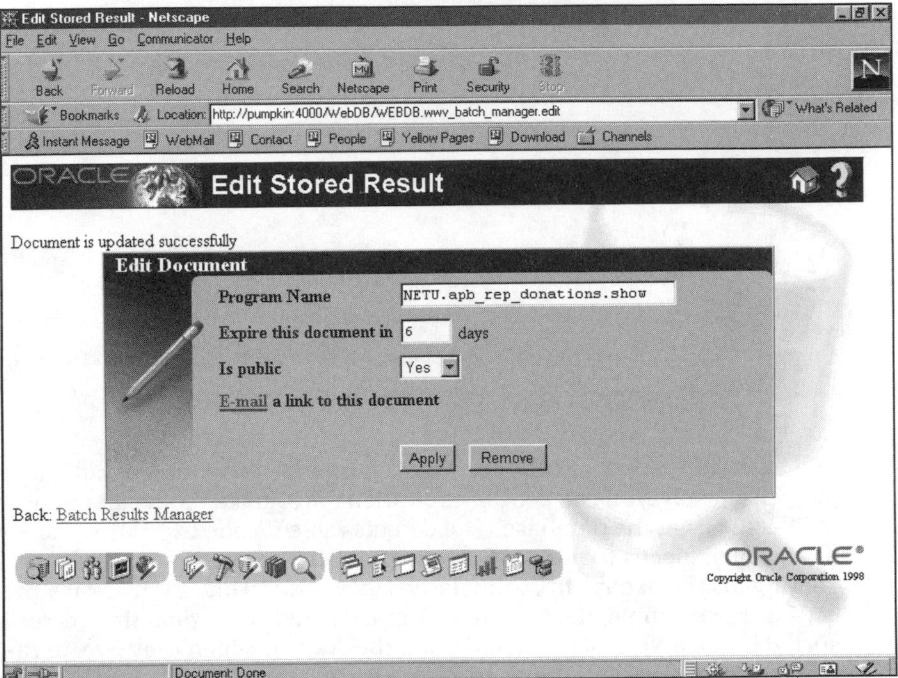

Figure B-10: Updated document link

Once you make the report public, WebDB adds a link on the panel that enables you to e-mail a link to the report to another user. The link includes the current DAD record, so the user must have a valid logon to Oracle, but they need not have access to the report itself because the output has been made available to the public. The WebDB component program itself does not inherit the public security setting — only the current output of batch results is accessible to the public. You do not have to use the e-mail link to publish the results. You can also view the URL string and publish it elsewhere on your site.

1. Click the Batch Results Manager link to return to the Stored Results Manager page.
2. Use the View link to display the batch output, as shown in Figure B-11.

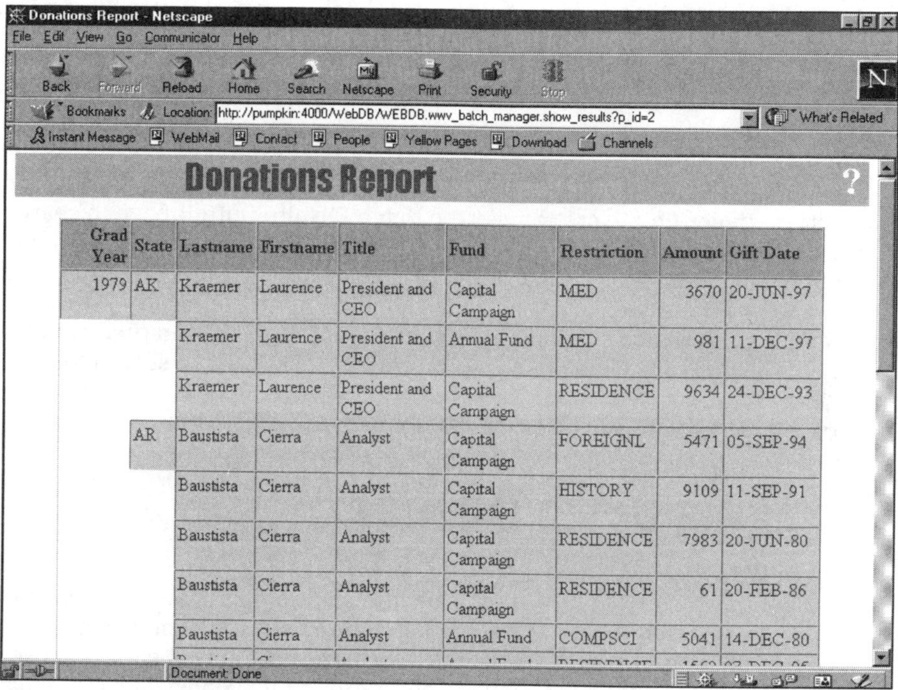

Grad Year	State	Lastname	Firstname	Title	Fund	Restriction	Amount	Gift Date
1979	AK	Kraemer	Laurence	President and CEO	Capital Campaign	MED	3670	20-JUN-97
		Kraemer	Laurence	President and CEO	Annual Fund	MED	981	11-DEC-97
		Kraemer	Laurence	President and CEO	Capital Campaign	RESIDENCE	9634	24-DEC-93
	AR	Baustista	Cierra	Analyst	Capital Campaign	FOREIGNL	5471	05-SEP-94
		Baustista	Cierra	Analyst	Capital Campaign	HISTORY	9109	11-SEP-91
		Baustista	Cierra	Analyst	Capital Campaign	RESIDENCE	7983	20-JUN-80
		Baustista	Cierra	Analyst	Capital Campaign	RESIDENCE	61	20-FEB-86
		Baustista	Cierra	Analyst	Annual Fund	COMPSCI	5041	14-DEC-80

Figure B-11: Viewing batch results

The batch results appear just like any other component output page, and you cannot tell that the object is not "live" from viewing the page. If the source data for the report involves complicated joins and sorts, however, you may notice the difference in performance, because WebDB is displaying precalculated results. The data initially appears much quicker to the browser because the processing work has already been done. The output is displayed with a call to the Batch Results Manager using a URL much like the following string:

```
http://pumpkin:4000/WebDB/WEBDB.wwv_batch_manager.show_results?
p_id=2
```

The key to the string is the job parameter, which points to the job submission ID. WebDB writes the results of a batch operation into a table called WWV_BATCH_RESULTS$. The results from the report or form are written as a series of HTML records using a sequence number and the submission ID. You can use the format of the previous URL string along with the submission number of your batch job as a link on any other object or menu. When you submit a job to the batch queue, WebDB makes an entry in the WWV_BATCH_SUBMISSIONS$ table. The job number echoed back to you when you submit a job matches an entry in this table. You can use this job number to display the results with a URL string. For example, a DBA could run the Donations report as a batch job each night after the day's donations have been posted. Before the job has even executed, the DBA can obtain the job number and edit a menu link to point to the updated results. Once the job has completed, the DBA can set the output to be publicly accessible. When users log on in the morning, they can navigate to a familiar link in the menu system to view the current results.

Alternatively, end users can use the Batch Results Output page to search for results. The Batch Results Manager link in Figure B-1 links users to the same panel shown in Figure B-8. If end users wish to view their results directly after submitting the job to the system, they can navigate directly to the results page. Typically, they do not go directly to this page, but perform other tasks and then navigate to the Batch Results page inside the monitoring menu system to search for and view result files.

Managing Batch Queues

From WebDB's perspective, the DBA doesn't have to do much to maintain the batch processing facility. For the most part, the system takes care of itself. However, if many users submit batch jobs, the batch processing system can get backed up. The Oracle database server itself can be blazing along under these conditions because the problem is not one of capacity, but rather one of constraints. When a large number of users submit batch jobs and only a single job process queue is in operation, batch jobs will get backed up. It's exactly like having only one line open at the supermarket. No matter how fast the cashier is working, there are always people waiting in line. The solution is to create some additional job processes using the job_queue_processes parameter.

An experienced Oracle DBA can monitor the batch processing operations closely using the Asynchronous Activities menu inside the monitoring system.

1. Select the Database Objects link from the Monitor panel.
2. Select the Asynchronous Activities link to display the panel shown in Figure B-12.

WebDB provides three functions for monitoring the DBMS job queues in the database. A DBA can use this panel to view the configuration of the DBMS queues, look at the details of defined jobs, or monitor the processing of running jobs. The WebDB batch process interface makes use of the standard DBMS job queues, but there are other server tasks that work with these queues as well. An experienced DBA can monitor the overall DBMS queue system from these panels, but the average WebDB administrator does not need to work with these functions directly.

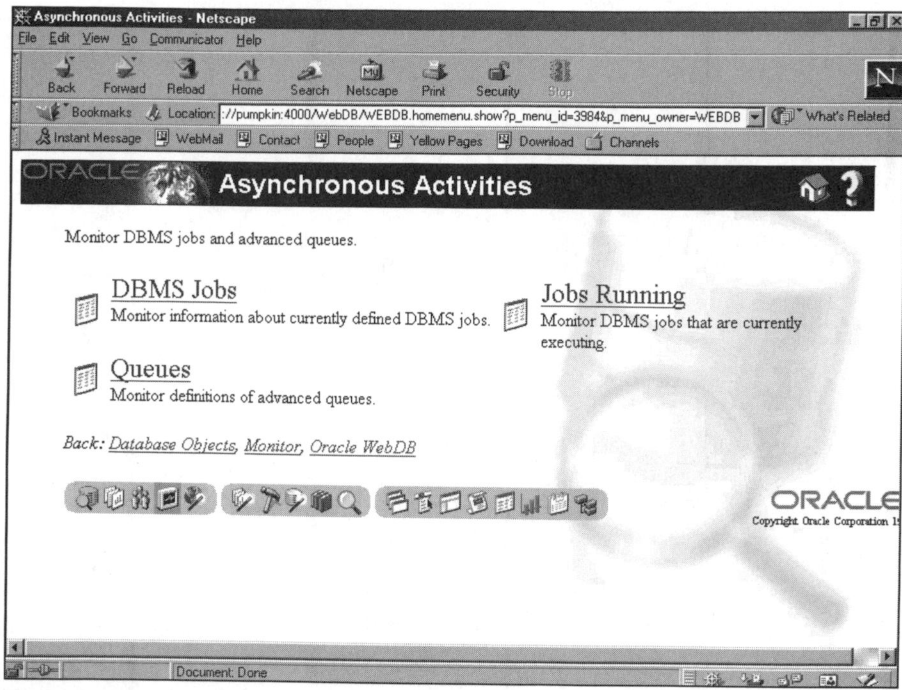

Figure B-12: Asynchronous Activities menu

Wrapping Up

WebDB's batch processing system can improve the overall efficiency of your system by enabling you to save output for reuse. Data that remains static for certain periods of time can be made available as batch reports. This saves processing time and it can improve the user's response time experience because the data is prefetched and formatted by the batch processing system. Data that is highly dynamic or requires lots of interaction with individual records is probably not a good candidate for batch processing. WebDB gives you the flexibility, however, to make use of batch operations in cases where it does make sense from a business perspective.

✦ ✦ ✦

APPENDIX C

Adding Security to the WebDB Environment

✦ ✦ ✦ ✦

In This Appendix

✦ ✦ ✦ ✦

WebDB uses the standard Oracle USERID and ROLE schemes to implement security. By using the database security mechanisms, WebDB makes it easier for you to build applications that dovetail with the security procedures you already have in place within your database. When you build your own components with the WebDB development tools, you are permitted to assign security permissions to those objects as the needs of your environment dictate. The one exception to this rule is the panels and menus that are part of the WebDB environment itself.

Once you have granted a user the WebDB developer role, you are effectively giving that user the ability to use all of the WebDB tools and utilities. The user is still governed by object security, and the user will not have access to schemas and objects to which he or she has not been granted access. Furthermore, certain operations, such as terminating a user process, require access to DBA capabilities, which are not provided by the WebDB developer role.

The WebDB Security Table

The developers of WebDB included a structure underneath the covers of the development environment to address this issue for their own needs. Although they have not published this interface, you can take advantage of its structure to customize the security to your own needs.

Within the WebDB schema is a table called WWV_SYS_PRIVS$. It stores all the security information used internally by

WebDB. The structure of the security table is simple, and it is composed of the following fields:

- Type_name
- Owner
- Name
- Grantee
- Privilege
- Created_By
- Created_On

The *type_name* field is the primary mechanism for grouping blocks of functionality within the WebDB system. Table C-1 lists the ten different categories of type_name.

Table C-1
Type_name Definitions

Type_name	*Description*
ADMIN	Controls administrative tasks, such as modifying users or adding roles. Although developers are not able to add new accounts without the DBA privilege, you can remove any of the individual links from the admin panels through the ADMIN type.
BATCH	Controls access to the Batch button on any parameter form. By default, this capability is granted to the general public. If you remove this capability, batch processing is disabled even if you have enabled the button on component objects.
BROWSE	Controls access to the browse database panels. This is granted to WebDB developers by default.
BUILD	Controls access to the build user interface panels. This is granted to WebDB developers by default.
EXPORT	Controls access to the export panels. By default, developers are granted access to the ability to export components. Removing this privilege prevents developers from exporting any components.
LOV	Each combo box within the WebDB development environment has an underlying LOV object that populates the combo box at run time. Many of these LOV objects are granted public access, and LOV records are the second most numerous entry in the WWV_SYS_PRIVS$ table.
MENU	All the panels that contain links to other panels are implemented as menus. Menu records are the most common entry found in the WWV_SYS_PRIVS$ table. Each menu record in this table has a matching record in the WWV_MENU$ table.

Type_name	*Description*
MONITOR	Controls access to the Monitor system and database functionality within WebDB.
SCHEMA	Each time you enable a USERID to have access to a component building schema (or data schema), the WebDB system writes a record confirming this fact as a SCHEMA record.
SITE	Controls access to the SITE wizard and panels from the main menu. By default, you must be granted both the DBA and WebDB developer role in order to gain access to the SITE tools.

The *owner* column stores the owner *name* of all objects. WebDB enters a security record for all menus and links on menus. You can find records in the WWV_SYS_PRIVS$ table for every menu in your system that has permissions associated with it. Permission for individual objects is managed with Oracle ROLE grants, but access to menus is controlled by the security table. Initially, the user accounts WEBDB and SCOTT own most of the records in the WWV_SYS_PRIVS$ table. As you create menus in your component building schemas, this changes.

The *grantee* column contains the name of the USERID or ROLE to which the security record applies. Oracle requires that USERIDs and ROLEs are unique values, so you will not run into a conflict between a USERID and a ROLE. When WebDB attempts to display a panel or menu to a user, it checks the USERID and all ROLEs that have been granted to the USERID against the records in this table using the grantee column. If there is a match, WebDB displays the panel or link.

The *privilege* column contains one of three values: BROWSE IN, BUILD IN, or EXECUTE. If the record is a menu record or link record, the value for the privilege field is always EXECUTE. If the record is of the type_name SCHEMA, it may have either the BROWSE IN or BUILD IN values. This indicates whether or not a given user account has the authority to build in or browse in the named component building schema.

WebDB inserts the *CREATED_BY* and *CREATED_ON* fields automatically for each record as a record stamp. WebDB automatically inputs the USERID of the record creator and the time stamp into the record.

Using the Security Table to Revoke Privileges

You can modify security records to either enable or disable access to the various functions within the WebDB environment.

Chapter 20 provides complete instructions on creating and managing developer accounts. The examples in this appendix assume you have read through Chapter 20.

1. Connect to WebDB using a privileged account and create a new WebDB developer account called DEVELOP01 with a password of ORACLE.
2. Mark the account as a WebDB developer.

Assume, for example, that you do not want your developers to have access to Site Builder. By default, all developers that have been granted the WebDB developer role have access to the Site Builder Tools.

3. Navigate to the Browse Database menu hierarchy and select the WWV_SYS_PRIVS$ table object using the WebDB account.
4. Enter **BROWSE** as the Type Name query parameter as shown in Figure C-1.
5. Click the Query & Update button.

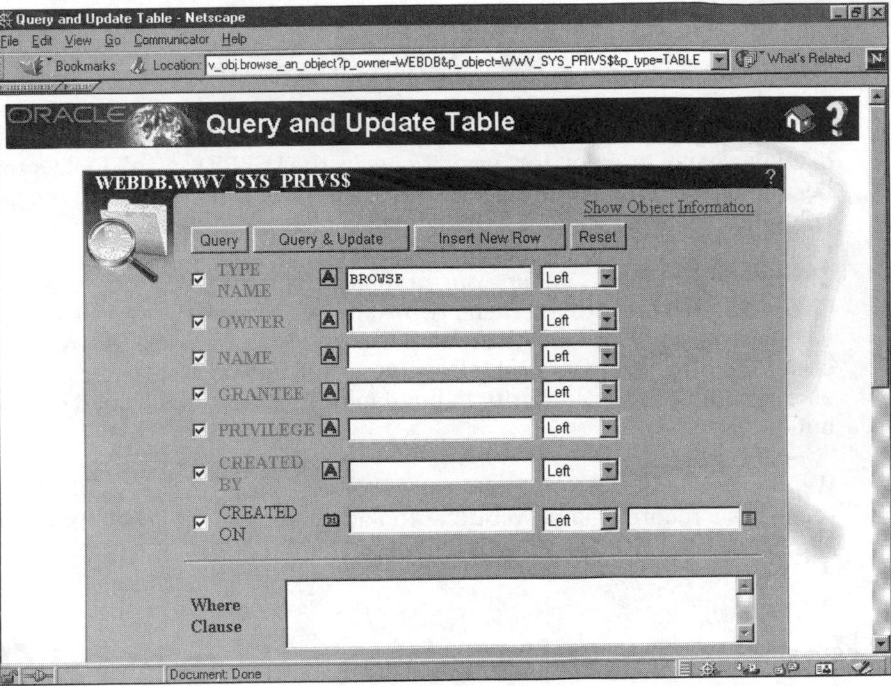

Figure C-1: Querying the WWV_SYS_PRIVS$ table

The result of your query should be one record, as shown in Figure C-2.

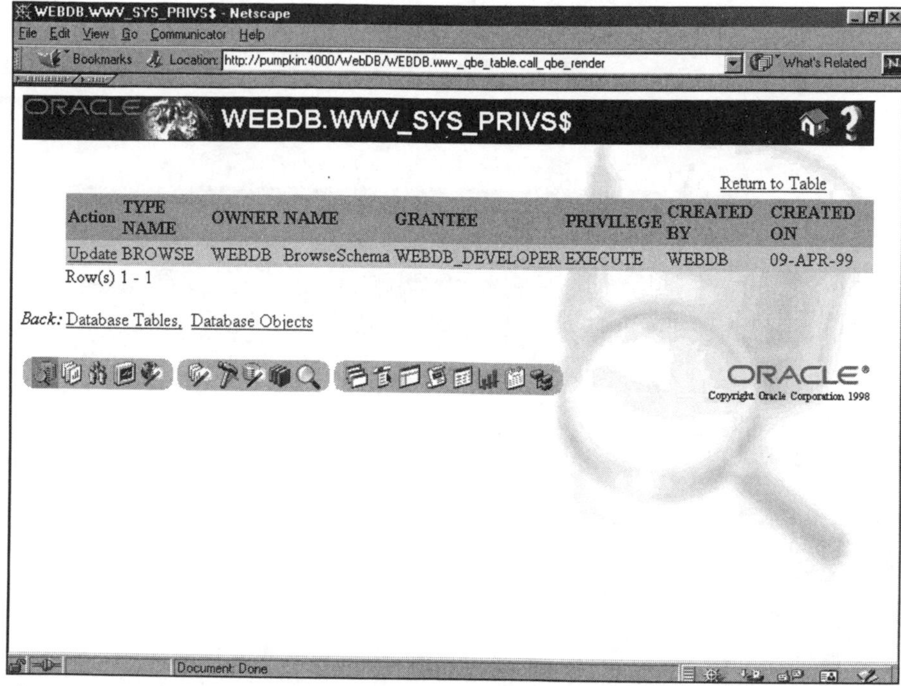

Figure C-2: Site record in the WWV_SYS_PRIVS$ table

When WebDB is installed, it assigns the BROWSE capability to the WebDB developer role. As long as a user connects with this role, they are given access to the BROWSE capabilities within WebDB.

1. Use the Update link to edit the WEBDB_DEVELOPER record.
2. Change the GRANTEE field value to **XYZ** and update the record.
3. Log off WebDB and then reconnect using the WebDB account.
4. Click the Browse link to display the panel shown in Figure C-3.
5. When you reconnect as a WebDB user, notice that you can no longer browse the database. The only user/role that has access to Site Builder is the fictional XYZ account. Log on to SQL*Plus as WEBDB and reinstate the browse privilege using the following SQL statement:

```
update wwv_sys_privs$ set grantee='WEBDB_DEVELOPER' where
type_name='BROWSE'
```

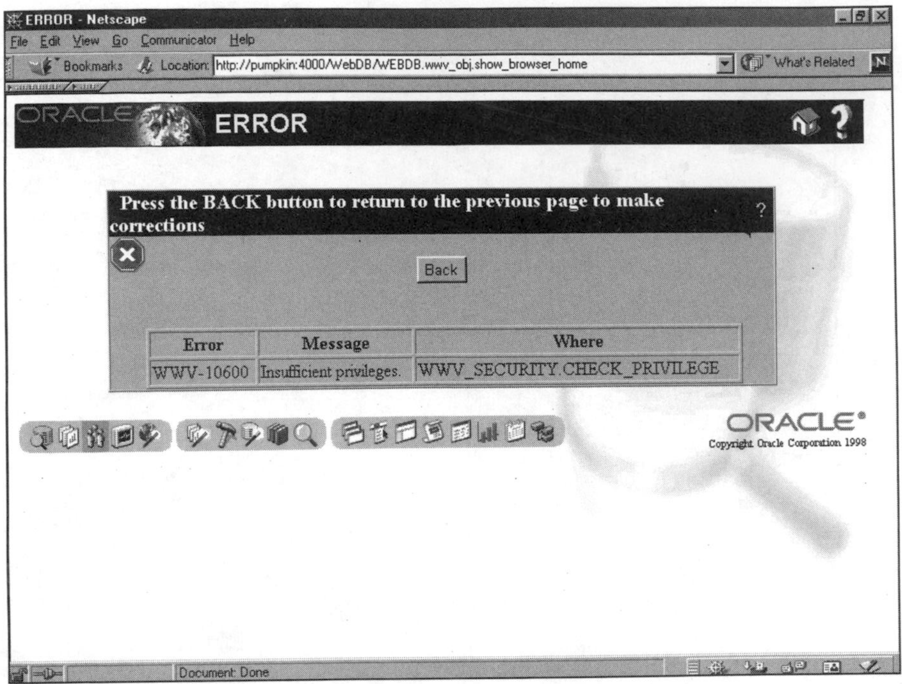

Figure C-3: Browse error message

Using the Security Table to Add Privileges

In addition to removing privileges, you can also use the WWV_SYS_PRIVS$ table to add new privileges for a user account. For example, by default, only accounts with the WEBDB_DEVELOPER role can use WebDB to browse the database. However, you can add a public record to the WWV_SYS_PRIVS$ table that gives all users access to the browse menus.

Authorizing a USERID with BROWSE functionality and access to a designated schema gives that user *complete* access to all the database objects in the specified schema.

1. Navigate to the Browse Database panel and select the WWV_SYS_PRIVS$ table in the WEBDB schema.
2. Enter **BROWSE** as the type_name, and click the Query & Update button.
3. Use the Update link to edit the record as shown in Figure C-4, and change the grantee from **WEBDB_DEVELOPER** to **PUBLIC**.

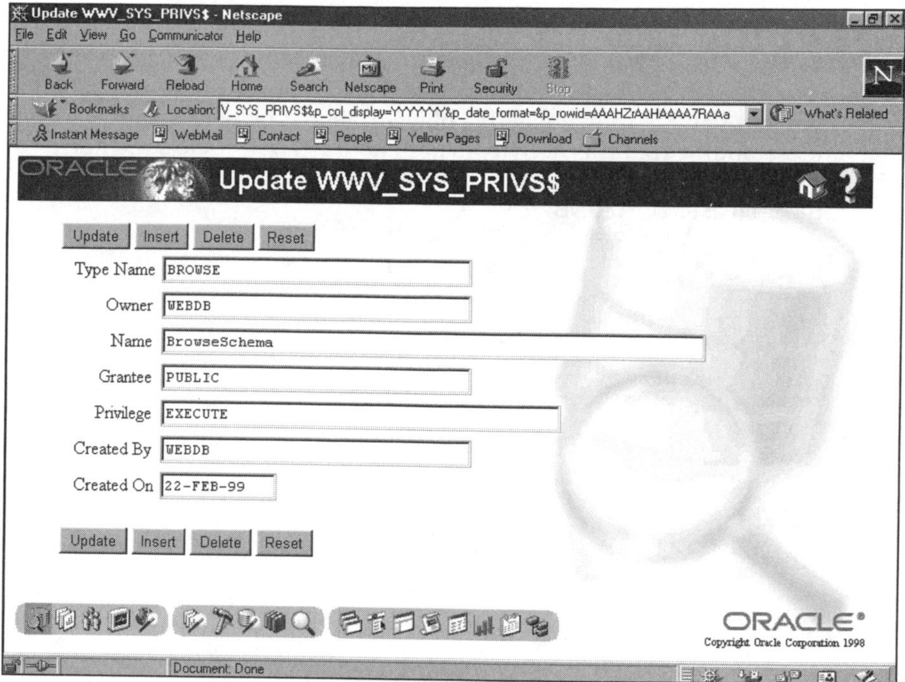

Figure C-4: Changing grantee to PUBLIC

This change enables all accounts to have access to the BROWSE functionality within WebDB. The public user is not automatically granted access to database objects, but they are allowed to see the browse screens.

There is one additional piece of functionality hidden inside the security table within WebDB. Records that have the type_name field with a value of MENU are menu panels. Normally, such records have a number in the NAME field. This number matches a value in the MENU_ID field in the WWV_MENU$ table. If you wish either to allow access to a particular WebDB menu, or to prevent access to a menu, you can edit the associated WWV_SYS_PRIVS$ record to make this change.

For example, menu 3281 in the WebDB system shows the Database Objects Monitor Panel. By default, this page is displayed for all DBA accounts and WEBDB_DEVELOPER accounts. Suppose you wanted to prevent this individual menu from being accessible to your developers, but not your DBAs. You would remove the WWV_SYS_PRIVS$ record with the name value of 3281 and grantee value of WEBDB_DEVELOPER. Database administrators would still see this panel, but all other users and developers would be prevented from viewing the entire Database Objects subsystem. This does not actually remove the aforementioned functionality, as the user can still enter the URL string to gain access to the menu item directly.

Wrapping Up

Oracle does not officially support direct modification of the WWV_SYS_PRIVS$ table, but you are free to use this object to fine-tune your security with the understanding that this activity is not endorsed by Oracle's technical support organization. Oracle has plans to provide a support interface to this facility in future releases of WebDB.

✦ ✦ ✦

Index

SYMBOLS

A

B

continued

C

continued

continued

D

E

continued

continued

G

H

continued

I

continued

L

continued

M

continued

N

O

P

continued

Q

R

continued

S

continued

continued

U

V

IDG BOOKS WORLDWIDE, INC.
END-USER LICENSE AGREEMENT

READ THIS. You should carefully read these terms and conditions before opening the software packet(s) included with this book ("Book"). This is a license agreement ("Agreement") between you and IDG Books Worldwide, Inc. ("IDGB"). By opening the accompanying software packet(s), you acknowledge that you have read and accept the following terms and conditions. If you do not agree and do not want to be bound by such terms and conditions, promptly return the Book and the unopened software packet(s) to the place you obtained them for a full refund.

1. **License Grant.** IDGB grants to you (either an individual or entity) a nonexclusive license to use one copy of the enclosed software program(s) (collectively, the "Software") solely for your own personal or business purposes on a single computer (whether a standard computer or a workstation component of a multiuser network). The Software is in use on a computer when it is loaded into temporary memory (RAM) or installed into permanent memory (hard disk, CD-ROM, or other storage device). IDGB reserves all rights not expressly granted herein.

2. **Ownership.** IDGB is the owner of all right, title, and interest, including copyright, in and to the compilation of the Software recorded on the disk(s) or CD-ROM ("Software Media"). Copyright to the individual programs recorded on the Software Media is owned by the author or other authorized copyright owner of each program. Ownership of the Software and all proprietary rights relating thereto remain with IDGB and its licensers.

3. **Restrictions On Use and Transfer.**

   (a) You may only (i) make one copy of the Software for backup or archival purposes, or (ii) transfer the Software to a single hard disk, provided that you keep the original for backup or archival purposes. You may not (i) rent or lease the Software, (ii) copy or reproduce the Software through a LAN or other network system or through any computer subscriber system or bulletin-board system, or (iii) modify, adapt, or create derivative works based on the Software.

   (b) You may not reverse engineer, decompile, or disassemble the Software. You may transfer the Software and user documentation on a permanent basis, provided that the transferee agrees to accept the terms and conditions of this Agreement and you retain no copies. If the Software is an update or has been updated, any transfer must include the most recent update and all prior versions.

4. **Restrictions On Use of Individual Programs.** You must follow the individual requirements and restrictions detailed for each individual program in Appendix A of this Book. These limitations are also contained in the individual license agreements recorded on the Software Media. These limitations may include a requirement that after using the program for a specified period of time, the user must pay a registration fee or discontinue use. By opening the

Software packet(s), you will be agreeing to abide by the licenses and restrictions for these individual programs that are detailed in Appendix A and on the Software Media. None of the material on this Software Media or listed in this Book may ever be redistributed, in original or modified form, for commercial purposes.

5. Limited Warranty.

(a) IDGB warrants that the Software and Software Media are free from defects in materials and workmanship under normal use for a period of sixty (60) days from the date of purchase of this Book. If IDGB receives notification within the warranty period of defects in materials or workmanship, IDGB will replace the defective Software Media.

(b) IDGB AND THE AUTHOR OF THE BOOK DISCLAIM ALL OTHER WARRANTIES, EXPRESS OR IMPLIED, INCLUDING WITHOUT LIMITATION IMPLIED WARRANTIES OF MERCHANTABILITY AND FITNESS FOR A PARTICULAR PURPOSE, WITH RESPECT TO THE SOFTWARE, THE PROGRAMS, THE SOURCE CODE CONTAINED THEREIN, AND/OR THE TECHNIQUES DESCRIBED IN THIS BOOK. IDGB DOES NOT WARRANT THAT THE FUNCTIONS CONTAINED IN THE SOFTWARE WILL MEET YOUR REQUIREMENTS OR THAT THE OPERATION OF THE SOFTWARE WILL BE ERROR FREE.

(c) This limited warranty gives you specific legal rights, and you may have other rights that vary from jurisdiction to jurisdiction.

6. Remedies.

(a) IDGB's entire liability and your exclusive remedy for defects in materials and workmanship shall be limited to replacement of the Software Media, which may be returned to IDGB with a copy of your receipt at the following address: Software Media Fulfillment Department, Attn.: *Oracle® WebDB Bible*, IDG Books Worldwide, Inc., 7260 Shadeland Station, Ste. 100, Indianapolis, IN 46256, or call 1-800-762-2974. Please allow three to four weeks for delivery. This Limited Warranty is void if failure of the Software Media has resulted from accident, abuse, or misapplication. Any replacement Software Media will be warranted for the remainder of the original warranty period or thirty (30) days, whichever is longer.

(b) In no event shall IDGB or the author be liable for any damages whatsoever (including without limitation damages for loss of business profits, business interruption, loss of business information, or any other pecuniary loss) arising from the use of or inability to use the Book or the Software, even if IDGB has been advised of the possibility of such damages.

(c) Because some jurisdictions do not allow the exclusion or limitation of liability for consequential or incidental damages, the above limitation or exclusion may not apply to you.

7. **U.S. Government Restricted Rights.** Use, duplication, or disclosure of the Software by the U.S. Government is subject to restrictions stated in paragraph (c)(1)(ii) of the Rights in Technical Data and Computer Software clause of DFARS 252.227-7013, and in subparagraphs (a) through (d) of the Commercial Computer—Restricted Rights clause at FAR 52.227-19, and in similar clauses in the NASA FAR supplement, when applicable.

8. **General.** This Agreement constitutes the entire understanding of the parties and revokes and supersedes all prior agreements, oral or written, between them and may not be modified or amended except in a writing signed by both parties hereto that specifically refers to this Agreement. This Agreement shall take precedence over any other documents that may be in conflict herewith. If any one or more provisions contained in this Agreement are held by any court or tribunal to be invalid, illegal, or otherwise unenforceable, each and every other provision shall remain in full force and effect.